WRITING
Self-Expression and Communication

JULIA DIETRICH AND MARJORIE M. KAISER

University of Louisville

HARCOURT BRACE JOVANOVICH, PUBLISHERS

San Diego   New York   Chicago   Atlanta   Washington, D.C.
London   Sydney   Toronto

To John Dietrich and Gregory Acker

ISBN: 0-15-598250-8

Library of Congress Catalog Card Number: 85-80874

Printed in the United States of America

Cover photograph courtesy of Armando Salas Portugal.

PREFACE

Writing is a powerful instrument of thought. In the act of composing, writers learn about themselves and their world and communicate their insights to others—writing confers the power to grow personally and to effect change in the world.

—National Council of Teachers of English,
Commission on Composition Position Statement

We believe that Freshman English is the most important course a college student takes. No other course is as empowering. Writing is both an examination of one's own experience and a medium through which to communicate. Purely personal expressions are typically limited and idiosyncratic, but public statements not grounded in personal experience and conviction rarely ring true. The integration of these two functions is the key to powerful writing.

Writing: Self-Expression and Communication has been structured to encourage such a view of writing. All major writing assignments in the book develop from expressive journal entries, responses to readings, and discussions. It is our hope that those who use the book will enjoy the process of developing a position in this way and will become more adept at both the intellectual and technical skills that produce effective writing.

Our writing of the text itself followed this process. It was based on our combined forty-four years of teaching experience, and we are grateful to all the students who have taught *us*. It was also enriched by much reading and discussion with our colleagues. We owe much to the many researchers and theorists who have developed the discipline of rhetoric out of which this book has grown. We are grateful to Frank Nuessel of the University of Louisville, Mary Kirtz of the University of Akron, and Millard Dunn of Indiana University Southeast, all of whom led us to readings we have used in the text. Special thanks to Ann Carter and Lynn Van Dyke of Lafayette College, Robert Small of Virginia Polytechnic Institute and State University, and Fred Carpenter of Norman, Oklahoma, for their reflections on writing and the context in which it is taught. To David Alexander of Singer-Link Corporation, we owe thanks for his expertise on the special conventions of technical writing.

Furthermore, we are happy to acknowledge the criticism of reviewers who helped us rethink and revise parts of the text. We very much appreciate the thoughtful and encouraging responses of Professors William Covino of San Diego State University, Eileen Meagher of the University of Tennessee at Chattanooga, Maureen Potts of the University of Texas at El Paso, and Diane Quantic of Wichita State University. Above all, we owe much to our friends and colleagues who discussed this project with us and shared our enthusiasm, never letting on that they might be growing tired of hearing about "the book."

We gladly give our thanks to Bill McLane for his faith in the project as well as his professional skill; also to Sarah Smith, Eleanor Garner, Merilyn Britt, and Melanie Rawn, whose cheerful work at HBJ made completion of the book as smooth as possible for us; to Giovanna Burks, the graduate assistant who managed the permissions file for us and did not have the heart to walk out and leave us with a table full of uncollated manuscript, even if it was Friday afternoon; to Mark Zorn, who not only typed the manuscript beautifully but paid us the compliment of wanting to talk about its content; to the Department of English and the School of Education at the University of Louisville for their consistent support of our efforts.

Although we have chosen here to define basic terms of the writing process for those students who may never have heard them before, we recognize that many students have had the benefit of first-rate instruction in writing before they come to college. There are wonderful teachers of writing from kindergarten through senior high school, and as a result of our work with teachers (particularly through the Louisville Writing Project) we have had the opportunity to know many of them and their work. Their insights and practices, too, have helped to shape this text.

Finally, we thank each other for being conscientious and tolerant and for having a sense of humor. Collaborating on a textbook is certainly not the easiest thing one can do; we have both grown through this experience in ways we are only beginning to know.

Julia Dietrich
Marjorie M. Kaiser

TO THE STUDENT

This book should help you understand how writing is affected by its audience and purpose. It should also help you gain control of your writing process as well as the conventions through which writers communicate with their readers.

Part I, "Learning the Process of Writing," asks you to do a series of writing tasks and to reflect on what you discover. It then surveys the writing process from prewriting to editing. Each chapter in Part II asks you to engage in several short, informal writings in your journal that will help prepare you for the more formal writing project at the conclusion of the chapter. These informal writings may be responses to the readings, personal observations, or expressions of feelings, opinions, or attitudes. Each chapter gives you the opportunity to experience all phases of the writing process and emphasizes the importance of a meaningful context for writing (a specific writing occasion, a specific audience, and purpose). Each chapter focuses on a particular theme and offers readings that provide related ideas for your consideration.

CONTENTS

Part I

LEARNING THE PROCESS OF WRITING

A textbook, however fine, cannot teach you to write more effectively. You must *interact* with a text, with a class, and with an instructor to improve your writing skills. To make sure that you derive the greatest benefit from Part I of this text, you will need to supplement it in three important ways. First, you will need a journal. You will be asked to record in it your responses to readings, research, visuals, discussions, and other group experiences. Consider your journal as important as the text itself. Second, you will need to value or learn to value the ideas, opinions, and responses of your classmates and others. You will frequently be asked to consider others' contributions and to share your own so you can retain perspective on the issue at hand.

Third, as you approach Part I, you will need an attitude of openness. "Learning the Process of Writing" asks you to engage in reading, thinking, responding, and writing without telling you why each activity is useful, logical, or helpful. As you proceed through the various activities, you will learn for yourself the value of much of what you have done. Ultimately, at the conclusion of Part I, your discoveries will be confirmed by a full discussion of the processes you engaged in. If you feel rudderless at any point and want to skip ahead to read that discussion, there will be no harm done. The discussion will be much more meaningful for you, however, if you approach the activities with a spirit of discovery and with faith in yourself and the text.

CHAPTER 1

Experiencing the Process

The human race, in its poverty, has unquestionably one really effective weapon—laughter. Power, money, persuasion, supplication, persecution—these can lift at a colossal humbug—push it a little, weaken it a little, century by century; but only laughter can blow it to rags and atoms at a blast. Against the assault of laughter nothing can stand.

—Mark Twain
"The Mysterious Stranger"

For years now theorists have been working to define humor. Physiologists have described what happens physically when a human being laughs: a laugh, they say, is " '. . . an abrupt strong expiration' followed by 'a series of expiratory-inspiratory microcycles superimposed upon the larger expiratory movements.' "* Psychologists have offered various hypotheses of what people find funny and why. Some things seem to be funny to all humans (e.g., pratfalls); other events or subjects are amusing in only some cultures. Some topics that could once have been counted on to get a laugh may no longer seem like laughing matters: woman driver jokes come to mind here. Age, too, seems to affect our response. Do you remember this joke from your childhood?

Q. What did one wall say to the other wall?
A. I'll meet you at the corner.

*From W. F. Fry, Jr., "Humor in a Physiological Vein," *Beckman Instruments Newsletter* (1969), quoted in *The Psychology of Humor,* ed. by Jeffrey H. Goldstein and Paul E. McGhee (New York: Academic Press, 1972) 51.

Terrible. At least, most adults think so. But most six-year-olds think it is a howler.

There will always be individuals who just are not amused by something that almost everyone else finds funny. Conversely, most of us have had the experience of laughing until we could hardly breathe at something that got only polite chuckles from everyone else in the room. It is an experience one remembers.

The research done on humor has given us some interesting insights into why it might be that we find certain things funny, but the subject is far from closed. We do know, however, that there is no "correct" response to a joke, cartoon, or anything else that may have been intended to amuse us. Whether any one of us will be amused by something depends on who we are, what the something is, how we feel when we encounter it, and many other factors that will come to light later.

Humor is the topic that you will be asked to think, read, and write about in this chapter as you practice the writing process. The goal is not for you to become an expert on humor—and indeed this text does not provide enough material for that—but for you to learn enough about the topic to do the final writing assignment of the chapter. You do not have to write anything funny. As you work through this section of the text, you will be asked to draw on your own experience and judgment, on the experience and judgment of others, and on the theories you read about.

RECORDING YOUR RESPONSES

In your journal, write a paragraph about each of the following cartoons, jokes, and humorous essays. Consider the following in each response:

1. If you find any of these funny or amusing, explore what is in each that creates the humor for you.
2. If you do not find any of these funny or amusing, try to explain why it lacks humor for you. Why might others see humor in it?
3. What in your own experience might lead you to respond as you do to a sample here, a set of samples, or any part of one?
4. What kinds of people are the probable intended audience of each sample or set of samples?

When you have completed this task, you will have seven response paragraphs in your journal. You might want to share the samples with some friends outside the class to compare their responses with your own.

1. *Q.*   How many ——— does it take to change a light bulb?
   A.   Three. One to hold the bulb and two to turn the ladder.

One variation:

Q.   How many psychiatrists does it take to change a light bulb?
A.   Only one. But the light bulb has to really want to change.

2.

3. The Early Essays

Woody Allen

Following are a few of the early essays of Woody Allen. There are no late essays, because he ran out of observations. Perhaps as Allen grows older he will understand more of life and will set it down, and then retire to his bedroom and remain there indefinitely. Like the essays of Bacon, Allen's are brief and full of practical wisdom, although space does not permit the inclusion of his most profound statement, "Looking at the Bright Side."

On Seeing a Tree in Summer

Of all the wonders of nature, a tree in summer is perhaps the most remarkable, with the possible exception of a moose singing "Embraceable You" in spats. Consider the leaves, so green and leafy (if not, something is wrong). Behold how the branches reach up to heaven as if to say, "Though I am only a branch, still I would love to collect Social Security." And the varieties! Is this tree a spruce or poplar? Or a giant redwood? No, I'm afraid it's a stately elm, and once again you've made an ass of yourself. Of course, you'd know all the trees in a minute if you were nature's creature the woodpecker, but then it would be too late and you'd never get your car started.

But why is a tree so much more delightful than, say, a babbling brook? Or anything that babbles, for that matter? Because its glorious presence is mute testimony to an intelligence far greater than any on earth, certainly in the present Administration. As the poet said, "Only God can make a tree"—probably because it's so hard to figure out how to get the bark on.

Once a lumberjack was about to chop down a tree, when he noticed a heart carved on it, with two names inside. Putting away his axe, he sawed down the tree instead. The point of that story escapes me, although six months later the lumberjack was fined for teaching a dwarf Roman numerals.

On Youth and Age

The true test of maturity is not how old a person is but how he reacts to awakening in the midtown area in his shorts. What do years matter, particularly if your apartment is rent-controlled? The thing to remember is that each time of life has its appropriate rewards, whereas when you're dead it's hard to find the light switch. The chief problem about death, incidentally, is the fear that there may be no afterlife—a depressing thought, particularly for those who have bothered to shave. Also, there is the fear that there is an afterlife but no one will know where it's being held. On the plus side, death is one of the few things that can be done as easily lying down.

Consider, then: Is old age really so terrible? Not if you've brushed your teeth faithfully! And why is there no buffer to the onslaught of the years? Or a good hotel in downtown Indianapolis? Oh, well.

In short, the best thing to do is behave in a manner befitting one's age. If you are sixteen or under, try not to go bald. On the other hand, if you are over eighty, it is extremely good form to shuffle down the street clutching a brown paper bag and muttering, "The Kaiser will steal my string." Remember, everything is relative—or should be. If it's not, we must begin again.

On Frugality

As one goes through life, it is extremely important to conserve funds, and one should never spend money on anything foolish, like pear nectar or a solid-gold hat. Money is not everything, but it is better than having one's health. After all, one cannot go into a butcher shop and tell the butcher, "Look at my great suntan, and besides I never catch colds," and expect him to hand over any merchandise. (Unless, of course, the butcher is an idiot.) Money is better than poverty, if only for financial reasons. Not that it can buy happiness. Take the case of the ant and the grasshopper: The grasshopper played all summer, while the ant worked and saved. When winter came, the grasshopper had nothing, but the ant complained of chest pains. Life is hard for insects. And don't think mice are having any fun, either. The point is, we all need a nest egg to fall back on, but not while wearing a good suit.

Finally, let us bear in mind that it is easier to spend two dollars than to save one. And for God's sake don't invest money in any brokerage firm in which one of the partners is named Frenchy.

On Love

Is it better to be the lover or the loved one? Neither, if your cholesterol is over six hundred. By love, of course, I refer to romantic love—the love between man and woman, rather than between mother and child, or a boy and his dog, or two head-waiters.

The marvelous thing is that when one is in love there is an impulse to sing. This must be resisted at all costs, and care must also be taken to see that the ardent male doesn't "talk" the lyrics of songs. To be loved, certainly, is different from being admired, as one can be admired from afar but to really love someone it is essential to be in the same room with the person, crouching behind the drapes.

To be a really good lover, then, one must be strong and yet tender. How strong? I suppose being able to lift fifty pounds should do it. Bear in mind also that to the lover the loved one is always the most beautiful thing imaginable, even though to a stranger she may be indistinguishable from an order of smelts. Beauty is in the eye of the beholder. Should the beholder have poor eyesight, he can ask the nearest person which girls look good. (Actually, the prettiest ones are almost always the most boring, and that is why some people feel there is no God.)

"The joys of love are but a moment long," sang the troubadour, "but the pain of love endures forever." This was almost a hit song, but the melody was too close to "I'm a Yankee Doodle Dandy."

On Tripping Through a Copse and Picking Violets

This is no fun at all, and I would recommend almost any other activity. Try visiting a sick friend. If this is impossible, see a show or get into a nice warm tub and read. Anything is better than turning up in a copse with one of those vacuous smiles and accumulating flowers in a basket. Next thing you know, you'll be skipping to and fro. What are you going to do with the violets once you get them, anyhow? "Why, put them in a vase," you say. What a stupid answer. Nowadays you call the florist and order by phone. Let *him* trip through the copse, he's getting paid for it. That way, if an electrical storm comes up or a beehive is chanced upon, it will be the florist who is rushed to Mount Sinai.

Do not conclude from this, incidentally, that I am insensitive to the joys of nature, although I have come to the conclusion that for sheer fun it is hard to beat forty-eight hours at Foam Rubber City during the high holidays. But that is another story.

4. **Census**

Langston Hughes

"I have had so many hardships in this life," said Simple, "that it is a wonder I'll live until I die. I was born young, black, voteless, poor, and hungry, in a state where white folks did not even put Negroes on the census. My daddy said he were never counted in his life by the United States government. And nobody could find a birth certificate for me nowhere. It were not until I come to Harlem that one day a census taker dropped around to my house and asked me where were I born and why, also my age and if I was still living. I said, 'Yes, I am here, in spite of all.'

" 'All of what?' asked the census taker. 'Give me the data.'

" 'All my corns and bunions, for one,' I said. 'I were borned with corns. Most colored peoples get corns so young, they must be inherited. As for bunions, they seem to come natural, we stands on our feet so much. These feet of mine have stood in everything from soup lines to the draft board. They have supported everything from a packing trunk to a hungry woman. My feet have walked ten thousand miles running errands for white folks and another ten thousand trying to keep up with colored. My feet have stood before altars, at crap tables, bars, graves, kitchen doors, welfare windows, and social security railings. Be sure and include my feet on that census you are taking,' I told that man.

"Then I went on to tell him how my feet have helped to keep the American shoe industry going, due to the money I have spent on my feet. 'I have wore out seven hundred pairs of shoes, eighty-nine tennis shoes, forty-four summer sandals, and two hundred and two loafers. The socks my feet have bought could build a knitting mill. The razor blades I have used cutting away my corns could pay for a razor plant. Oh, my feet have helped to make America rich, and I am still standing on them.

" 'I stepped on a rusty nail once, and mighty near had lockjaw. And from my feet up, so many other things have happened to me, since, it is a wonder I made it through this world. In my time, I have been cut, stabbed, run over, hit by a car, tromped by a horse, robbed, fooled, deceived, double-crossed, dealt seconds, and mighty near blackmailed—but I am still here! I have been laid off, fired and not rehired, Jim Crowed, segregated, insulted, eliminated, locked in, locked out, locked up, left holding the bag, and denied relief. I have been caught in the rain, caught in jails, caught short with my rent, and caught with the wrong woman—but I am still here!

" 'My mama should have named me Job instead of Jesse B. Semple. I have been underfed, underpaid, undernourished, and everything but undertaken—yet I am still here. The only thing I am afraid of now—is that I will die before my time. So man, put me on your census now this year, because I may not be here when the next census comes around.'

"The census man said, 'What do you expect to die of—complaining?'

" 'No,' I said, 'I expect to ugly away.' At which I thought the man would laugh. Instead you know he nodded his head, and wrote it down. He were white and did not know I was making a joke. Do you reckon that man really thought I am homely?"

5.   (Untitled)

Mark Twain

Well, then there was just one other case; it was a testimonial 'bout a poor fellow who went to visit a dentist, a certain Doctor Tushmaker, to have his tooth out.

Well, the dentist pulled, and the tooth wouldn't come, but the patient's right leg came up.

The dentist said, "Whaddaya doin' that for?"

The patient said, "Because I can't help it!"

The dentist said, "You come back at the end of the week—I'll take care of you."

Well, during the week, the dentist invented an instrument combining the properties of the screw, the lever, the wedge, the hammer, and the incline plane.

The patient came back and sat in the chair; one turn of the crank and out came the tooth. Its roots were hooked under the patient's right big toe. . . . Then his whole skeleton was extracted. . . .

They had to send him home in a pillow case.

6.

From *Black Maria* (Simon & Schuster). Copyright © 1960 by Charles Addams.

7. Desiderata

Max Ehrmann

Go placidly amid the noise and the haste, and remember what peace there may be in silence. As far as possible, without surrender, be on good terms with all persons. Speak your truth quietly and clearly; and listen to others, even to the dull and the ignorant; they too have their story. Avoid loud and aggressive persons; they are vexatious to the spirit. If you compare yourself with others, you may become vain or bitter, for always there will be greater and lesser persons than yourself. Enjoy your achievements as well as your plans. Keep interested in your own career, however humble; it is a real possession in the changing fortunes of time. Exercise caution in your business affairs, for the world is full of trickery. But let this not blind you to what virtue there is; many persons strive for high ideals, and everywhere life is full of heroism. Be yourself. Especially do not feign affection. Neither be cynical about love; for in the face of all aridity and disenchantment, it is as perennial as the grass. Take kindly the counsel of the years, gracefully surrendering the things of youth. Nurture strength of spirit to shield you in sudden misfortune. But do not distress yourself with dark imaginings. Many fears are born of fatigue and loneliness. Beyond a wholesome discipline, be gentle with yourself. You are a child of the universe no less than the trees and the stars; you have a right to be here. And whether or not it is clear to you, no doubt the universe is unfolding as it should. Therefore be at peace with God, whatever you conceive Him to be. And whatever your labors and aspirations, in the noisy confusion of life, keep peace in your soul. With all its sham, drudgery and broken dreams, it is still a beautiful world. Be cheerful. Strive to be happy.

Deteriorata

National Lampoon

You are a fluke of the universe. You have no right to be here. Deteriorata, Deteriorata. Go placidly amid the noise and waste. And remember what comfort there may be in owning a piece thereof. Avoid quiet and passive persons unless you are in need of sleep. Rotate your tires. Speak glowingly of those greater than yourself and heed well their advice, even though they be turkeys. Know what to kiss and when. Consider that two wrongs never make a right, but that three do. Whenever possible, put people on hold. Be comforted that in the face of aridity and all disillusionment and despite the changing fortunes of time, there is always a big future in computer maintenance. You are a fluke of the universe. You have no right to be here. Whether you can hear it or not, the universe is laughing behind your back. Remember the Pueblo. Know yourself. If you need help, call the FBI. Exercise caution in your daily affairs, especially with those persons closest to you—that lemon on your left, for instance. Be assured that a walk through the ocean of most souls would scarcely get your feet wet. Fall not in love, therefore. It will stick to your face. Gracefully surrender the things of youth: birds, clean

From *National Lampoon Radio Dinner* (record album), © 1972, Blue Thumb Records.

air, tuna, Taiwan. And let not the sands of time get in your lunch. Hire people with hooks. For a good time call 606–4311 and ask for Candy. Take heart that amid the deepening gloom, your dog is finally getting enough cheese. And reflect that whatever misfortune is your lot, it could only be worse in Milwaukee. You are a fluke of the universe. You have no right to be here. Whether you can hear it or not, the universe is laughing behind your back. Therefore, make peace with your God whatever you conceive Him to be: hairy thunderer or cosmic muffin. With all its hopes, dreams, promises, and urban renewal, the universe continues to deteriorate. Give up. You are a fluke of the universe. . . .

Generalizing about Your Responses

Now review your paragraph responses to the items and write a new entry in your journal in which you try to generalize about the thoughts you set down. What kinds of items did you find humorous? What do they have in common: theme, purpose, style? Were you equally amused by visual and verbal attempts at humor? How important are your own experiences in determining your responses? For example, could a true cat lover find the cartoons funny? Would one's recent experience with a psychiatrist have any effect on the way a person might respond to the lightbulb joke?

IDENTIFYING SOURCES OF HUMOR

Share these generalizations in class discussion, keeping in mind your specific responses to individual examples and using those to illustrate your contributions to the discussion. The aim of this sharing is for you to identify the various sources of humor represented in these samples and to see the range of responses possible on any given item. During the sharing, make a list in your journal of all the sources of humor identified.

Now that you have some generalizations, based on the class's experience, about why some things are funny, you may find it interesting to consider the major theories that others have offered.

Superiority

This theory holds that we laugh because we are pleased to see that others are less fortunate, less beautiful, less intelligent, less graceful than we are. By laughing, we make fun of the inferior others and revel in our own superiority. This sounds like nasty business, and indeed it can be. But the superiority can also be playful, as when we tease friends about mistakes they really are not embarrassed about. And certainly we mean no harm when we tell about something silly we ourselves have done and invite our friends to laugh with us. In this last case, we are enjoying the pleasure of feeling superior as we tell the story about the silly self who did the deed.

Incongruity

The incongruity theory holds that we laugh when we see or hear something that does not fit the view of the world we have composed for ourselves. If the incongruity makes us feel some strong emotion like fear or pity or guilt, the strong emotion will block the laughter. But something ridiculous or improbable that does not incite any strong emotion in us is very apt to make us laugh in surprise.

Relief

According to this theory, we laugh in relief at having escaped some threat. A joke may describe a situation in which it is likely that someone will get hurt. This raises the anxiety of the listeners, and the punch line then diffuses this anxiety by making it clear that the victim is someone different from the listeners—less smart, less sophisticated. Just by understanding the joke, the listeners are able to distance themselves from the victim and feel safe from the threat. Sigmund Freud is often associated with the relief theory of humor because he believed that most jokes present a threat of aggression or sexual embarrassment and give pleasure by allowing the listener to confront and then escape these threats.

As you have probably discovered, these theories are not mutually exclusive. The relief theory, for example, assumes that we feel superior to the victim. The theories are included here not because you will be asked to judge among them but because each adds to our understanding of why we laugh at certain things. The following excerpt from John Morreall's *Taking Laughter Seriously* may refine that understanding.

ABOUT HUMOR

As you read the selection, here are some considerations to think about and some guidelines to follow:

1. Morreall generalizes about the sources of adult humor and presents the reader with two different kinds of incongruity as the basis of humor: incongruity in things and incongruity in presentation. As you are reading, make lists in your journal of the subcategories Morreall proposes under each kind of incongruity.
2. If in your reading you come across names that are unfamiliar to you, jot them down and ask a friend or relative for help in identifying the individuals.
3. Also as you read, compare the generalizations from your class about sources of humor with Morreall's ideas about incongruity. To what extent are the two sets of generalizations compatible?

The Variety of Humor

John Morreall

. . . Most adult humor . . . is based on incongruity and not on simple surprise. Perhaps the most important thing to note about incongruity is that a thing or event is not incongruous *simpliciter,* but only relative to someone's conceptual scheme. Incongruity is a violation of a pattern in someone's picture of how things should be. What any individual finds incongruous will depend on what his experience has been and what his expectations are. If an intelligent being from another galaxy visited Earth and were confronted with a situation which we consider funny (incongruous), he would not find it incongruous unless he had had experience with similar situations before and so had some expectations for what situations of this type are supposed to be like. Without such expectations, at most, the visitor would find our comic situation "funny" only in the more basic way that he finds Earth situations in general funny—they are new to him and so evoke simple surprise.

We do not need to imagine visitors from other planets to understand how an appreciation of humor of incongruity depends on an appropriate conceptual background. (Since the humor of incongruity is the only kind I will be talking about from now on, I will use the term "humor" to mean the humor of incongruity.) Our own children often fail to get certain kinds of adult humor because they lack the requisite conceptual patterns. This applies not just to sophisticated verbal play and to sexual humor, but even to many instances of humor based on adult social conventions, sarcasm, etc. The disparity between the child's naive picture of the world and the adult's sophisticated picture also explains why adults often find children's speech and behavior so amusing, even when the children are not trying to be funny.

Adults from different cultures often fail to appreciate each other's humor, because they don't have the same picture of the world and so do not find the same things incongruous. This is why a joke is often not funny when it is translated into another language. What Wittgenstein said about language-games—that to share a language-game is to share a form of life—applies nicely to humor. To share humor with someone we need to share a form of life with him.

Not only do we not appreciate the humor of very different cultures, but we often find humorous their *ordinary* customs. Many raised in traditional Western culture have found the customs of so-called primitive peoples amusing, but we should remember that it works the other way as well. This ethnocentrism of what we find incongruous is captured nicely in a story told by Margaret Mead. A Plains Indian had just placed food on a new grave, when a white man looking on jocularly asked, "Do you expect the dead man to come up and eat that food?" To which the Indian responded, "As soon as your dead come up to smell the flowers you place on their graves."[1]

What different people find funny also varies between different stages in the history of a single culture. It may be hard for us to imagine today, but when the use of the fork was introduced into England a few hundred years ago, people found this new eating instrument extremely funny. Even the technique of vaccination against smallpox was greeted with a great deal of ridicule. In looking back at the dress and customs of previous generations, too, of course, we are often amused because they differ from our own. . . .

Reprinted from *Taking Laughter Seriously* by John Morreall by permission of the State University of New York Press. Copyright © 1983 by State University of New York.

There are variations, also, in what individual adults in a single culture at any given time find humorous; one's educational level, social class, profession, sex, etc., can all make a difference here. As any after-dinner speaker knows, the jokes that would go over big at a meeting of academics might not go over at all at a meeting of a labor union. And there is a noticeable difference between the cartoons in, say, the *New Yorker* and the *National Enquirer*. There are even differences in what individuals find funny based on their unique personalities and perspectives. To explore all the different factors that influence the individual's sense of humor, however, would require much more space, and much more empirical data, than we have available. The few details we have given here will have to suffice as illustrating our main point—that what a person finds incongruous depends on what he finds congruous, and that the latter is based on the conceptual patterns which have been built up in his experience.

We can turn now to investigate some of the different ways in which laughter stimuli may involve incongruity. Perhaps the most basic distinction to be made here is between incongruity in some object or situation, and incongruity in the way a person represents a situation. For convenience we can call these two "incongruity in things" and "incongruity in presentation." One way to see this distinction is to contrast two kinds of comic entertainment. A comedian, it has been said, is someone who says funny things—essentially a teller of jokes—while a comic is someone who says things funny. Red Skelton is a good example of the former, George Carlin of the latter. Sometimes this distinction is expressed as the distinction between "humor" and "wit": humor, one writer says, "consists primarily in what is observed, whereas wit originates in the observer."[2] Because I am using the term "humor" to cover both these phenomena, however, I will not put the distinction in this way.

Using the general categories of "incongruity in things" and "incongruity in presentation," we can explore some different kinds of humor. Let's begin with incongruity in things. . . .

Perhaps the simplest kind of incongruity in things, and the one that most often makes us laugh, is some deficiency in an object or person, which renders it or him inferior as the kind of thing it is supposed to be. A scrawny dog, for example, or a dilapidated car, can be funny in this way. The humorous deficiencies of persons are more numerous than the deficiencies of things, and can be divided roughly into four categories: physical deformity, ignorance or stupidity, moral shortcomings, and actions that fail. A word can be said about each of these, particularly the last.

Physical deformity, underdevelopment, or weakness is probably the oldest human deficiency to be found humorous. As far back as the *Iliad* (Book II) we find humorous descriptions of deformity. There Thersites is spoken of as "the ugliest man that had come to Ilium. He had a game foot and was bandy-legged. His round shoulders almost met across his chest; and above them rose an egg-shaped head, which sprouted a few short hairs." A good deal of the Greek gods' laughter was at deformity—the crippled Hephaistos was the laughingstock of Olympus. Today our moral sensitivity may prevent us from laughing at deformity in real life, but we still laugh at it in the theater, films, cartoons, and jokes. The fat person, the person with the huge nose, the very ugly person, are all stock laugh getters. Indeed, if we look at the costumes of clowns, they are based almost exclusively on deformity.

Closely allied to our laughter at physical deformity is our laughter at ignorance and stupidity. We laugh at children's naiveté partly because it is a type of ignorance. We laugh at the yokel and the village idiot. Whole genres of jokes, such as the now-waning Polish joke, are based on stupidity. We also laugh at the absentminded professor, who is intelligent in theoretical matters, but who is forgetful or doesn't have practical intelligence. A stock way of getting a laugh in a play is to have some character speak or act in ignorance of some fact that we in the audience are aware of. And even a poor joke can provide a laugh if someone listening to it fails to get it—we'll laugh not at the joke, but at his lack of understanding.

Moral shortcomings, too, have been a standard object of laughter throughout history. The miser, the liar, the drunkard, the lazy person, the lecher, the gossip, the coward, the hypocrite—these are all stock comedic characters. Plato even went so far as to say that moral shortcomings were the *only* object of laughter. Though this is an exaggeration, a good deal of our laughter is directed at people's vices. Indeed, in conversation we often get a laugh simply by suggesting that a person is stingier than everyone knows he is, or that he lies more, drinks more, etc.

Our fourth category of humorous deficiencies with persons—actions that fail— often overlaps with the other three categories, for deformity, stupidity, and vice are often manifested in what people do. But there are humorous possibilities, too, in actions that fail not because of any shortcoming in the person, but because of a defect in someone or something else (e.g., a defective tool), or because of a chance event (e.g., a sudden thunderstorm). Whenever someone is trying to achieve some goal, that is, it can be funny if he fails.

Even when an action does not fail, it can be incongruous, and so humorous, when it is not carried out relatively smoothly. The awkward action, the interrupted action, the action performed by someone who is disorganized or distracted, are all stock devices in comedy. Superfluous gestures in an action can also be funny, because they do not contribute to the goal at hand. A classic example would be the lavish arm movements of the character Ed Norton (Art Carney), on the television series "The Honeymooners," whenever he was about to write a letter, make a pool shot, etc. The humor in these pointless gestures was always heightened by the angry reaction they got from Norton's impatient friend Ralph (Jackie Gleason).

The humor in practical jokes, too, is in large part based on incongruity in actions, only here someone is deliberately causing the failure of the action. In the typical practical joke someone engineers the situation so that another person who is trying to achieve a certain goal will fail or meet with some misfortune. The classic practical joke of removing a person's chair as he attempts to sit down is a paradigm case. "Candid Camera," a popular television show of the 1960s, consisted almost exclusively of practical jokes. In one of their best, a conventional car was fitted with an extra large fuel tank in the trunk and under the rear seat. A woman from "Candid Camera" drove the car into gas stations and asked the attendant to "fill it up." As the gauge on the pump passed the 25-gallon mark, and then the 30- and 40-gallon marks, the attendant would begin to look very concerned—perhaps this car *couldn't* be filled up! A similar stunt involved the driver coasting into a gas station with the engine removed from her car, and asking the attendant to see what was wrong under the hood.

There is another kind of incongruity in actions, which is the reverse of failure. We sometimes laugh when someone *succeeds* in doing something by exerting only a small amount of effort, much less than we would judge necessary to achieve the goal at hand. The plucky hero of the silent film, for example, often got laughs by escaping a very dangerous situation with some simple maneuver that would never work in real life. It is the incongruity of disproportion between effort and result, too, I think, that at least partially explains our laughing when a character like W. C. Fields gets out of a tight spot with a clever lie.

Related to this laughter at serendipity and cleverness is our laughter at situations in which an action fails, but it does not matter to the people involved because they do not even notice. A good example is the joke about the two Englishmen riding on a noisy train. The first says, "I say, is this Wembley?" The other responds, "No, Thursday." To which the first says, "I am too." These two have completely misunderstood each other, but no matter—they *thought* they were communicating.

Deficiencies of various sorts, then, constitute one major kind of incongruity in things. A second kind of incongruity is one thing seeming to be another. When we experience one thing or action A that bears a strong resemblance to another thing or action B, we tend to see A as B. In some instances, as where we have been fooled by a rubber snake and then laugh on discovering that it is only rubber, we may actually have misidentified A as B, and then suddenly seen our mistake. But even where we are not deceived by the B-ness of A into a mistaken judgment that A is B, there is a shift between seeing A as what is is, and seeing it as illuminated by the image of B.

A common form of the incongruity of one thing seeming to be another is the humor of mimicry. The professional comedian doing very realistic impressions of celebrities is only a sophisticated version of what countless peoples all over the world have done for centuries—talking and acting with the intonation, facial expression, and gestures of another person in order to get a laugh.

We also enjoy seeing or hearing about the successful impostor, as long as we are aware, of course, that he is an impostor. The character of the flim-flam man, portrayed so well in the movies by W. C. Fields, is a rich source of comic possibilities. We laugh, too, at the occasional newspaper story about the person who has successfully impersonated a physician, especially if the impostor actually performed a bit of surgery.

The person who pretends to be something other than he is need not be doing so for anyone's amusement; he need not even be consciously aware of his own pretense. We often find people funny who "put on airs," who act as if they are richer or more important than they really are, and in doing so take themselves completely seriously. Indeed, their inflated opinion of themselves makes their pretense all the more humorous, because the incongruity is not just between what they are and what they seem to be, but also between what they are and what they think of themselves as being. . . .

A third kind of incongruity in things is coincidence. If we happened to run into a friend who told us that he just had his appendix out, for example, this by itself would not be humorous. But if the next two people we talked to told us that they just had the same operation, we might well find this funny. Appendicitis, we assume, is a random occurrence, and the odds against any three particular individuals experiencing it at the same time are very great. And so it is incongruous that we should run into three recent appendectomy patients in a row. Comedies often use the unexpected repetition of events and even lines to get a humorous effect, as when in Molière's *Le Tartuffe* the maid Dorine confronts first one and then the other of a pair of lovers, and each expresses a grievance against the other in virtually the same words (act 2, scene 4). Unimaginative people often try to get a laugh in a similar way, by repeating some current catch phrase all day long in each successive situation. Our amusement at unexpected repetition, too, I think, provides an answer to Pascal's question: Why do we find identical twins funny? We expect people, especially adults, to be unique, and so when we find two that look alike—especially if they are dressed alike—we are surprised. As Bergson says, identical twins look as if they were manufactured; and human beings are the last thing we expect to look this way.

In the humor of coincidence or unexpected repetition, then, there need be nothing funny about the individual things or events; what is incongruous, and therefore funny, is their juxtaposition. The same is true with a fourth kind of incongruity—the juxtaposition of opposites. By itself, a St. Bernard dog is not funny. Nor is a Mexican chihuahua. But when two such dogs are seen together, as in the hackneyed *National Enquirer* photos, they are funny. Similarly, there need be nothing funny about people from the upper class or people from the lower class, but countless comedies have made use of the humorous possibilities in juxtaposing them. A long line of comedy teams, including Laurel and Hardy and Burns and Allen, have exaggerated their physical and psychological differences precisely to get this effect of incongruity.

To get an incongruous juxtaposition, we need not join opposites; in the case of [a] bowling ball in the refrigerator, for example, what [is] funny [is] simply that two things [are] put together that [have] no connection with each other. The bowling ball, which fits perfectly well into certain settings, [has] been placed into a setting where it [doesn't] belong at all. We could count the presence of things in inappropriate situations as a fifth kind of humorous incongruity, but this category would surely be very wide and would partially overlap our other categories. Perhaps it is best to stop our cataloguing here and treat the kinds of incongruity we have cited so far not as an exhaustive list, but simply as illustrations from a potentially infinite list. To be sure, there are kinds of incongruity we have not discussed—the violation of physical laws in cartoons comes to mind here. But once we understand that wherever there is a regularity or pattern in a person's picture of things [and that] there is room for incongruity when that pattern is violated, we can continue the list for ourselves.

Earlier in this chapter we distinguished between incongruity in things and incongruity in presentation. Having explored several examples of the first, we can turn to the second. Incongruity in presentation, as mentioned earlier, is not so much found as created; it lies not so much in the matter at hand as in the way a person presents the matter.

There are several levels at which incongruity can be found in any medium of communication. However, since spoken and written language is by far the most common medium, we will limit our discussion pretty much to them. The lowest level of incongruity in language involves merely the sounds of the spoken word or the shape of the written word, apart from the word's meaning. Excessive alliteration, for example, is incongruous and so potentially humorous, as are multiple rhymes and the weak internal rhymes used by humorists like Ogden Nash. Deliberate or accidental mistakes in pronunciation, spelling, grammar, or other nonsemantic aspects of language, can also be funny. Verbal slips and spoonerisms, for instance, are humorous even when they don't result in new, unintended words. And dialect jokes usually rely for a good deal of their effect on being told with mispronounced words and broken grammar.

We also enjoy playing with syllables, as in speaking Pig Latin, "Op-talk," and other play languages. We can abuse morphemic patterns to get sentences like "If it's feasible, let's fease it," and P. G. Wodehouse's "He may not have been actually disgruntled, but he was certainly far from gruntled."

Like other linguistic patterns, rules of syntax can be violated; but because such violations tend to destroy sense, there are not many pieces of humor based on violations of syntax. (We can play with syntax without violating it, as in jokes whose syntax makes them ambiguous, or as in the following joke, which was popular in Eastern Europe in the 1960s: "Under capitalism, man exploits man. Under communism it is vice versa.")

At the next higher level we have humor which involves the meanings of the words to some extent, but which still depends heavily on the phonological and typographical mechanics of language. Jokes that turn on the use of homonyms fall into this category, as do pronunciation and spelling errors that result in unintended words. But perhaps the most common form of this kind of humor is the simple pun in which a person uses a certain word in a conversation because it has a secondary meaning that is also somehow connected to the topic at hand (or has a homonym so connected). If we are talking about football, for example, someone might say, usually with emphasis on the punning word, "Let's *pass* on to talk about something else." Because such puns involve little cleverness or insight, and because the punster often has to strain the conversation to make his pun, many people have a strong dislike for puns; hence their reputation as "the lowest form of humor." Especially tiresome can be the punning contest, in which everyone gets in on the act by racking his brains for words related to the topic, or homonyms of such words, and then building essentially meaningless comments around them. And for every person who detests puns and tries to quash such games, it seems that there are many more lovers of puns to keep the game going. Some people, indeed, have a mania for punning. King James I was so fond of puns that he required them of his courtiers.

Puns need not be as simple as the example just cited. Though I am a staunch opponent of puns in general, I can appreciate the occasional one that shows cleverness, especially if it is used to actually say something, and not just to keep the punning game going. Perhaps my favorite was a short dramatic review of the play *I Am a Camera,* which read simply: "No Leica."

Somewhat cleverer than the simple pun is the double entendre. As in the simple pun, a word or phrase is used that has two meanings. But here both of the meanings fit into the sentence to make grammatical sense. The sense of "pass" in which we pass a football cannot be given to the word in "Let's pass on to talk about something else." But in a double entendre there is true semantic ambiguity to the sentence as a whole. Consider the story about the English bishop who received the following communication from one of the vicars in his diocese: "My Lord, I regret to inform you of my wife's death. Can you possibly send me a substitute for the weekend."[3] Not only are there two meanings for "substitute," but each gives us a different way of interpreting the sentence.

As this example shows, the humorous double entendre plays on meanings that are not just *different,* but in some way *opposed* to each other. Often the opposition is between a nonsexual meaning and a sexual meaning, particularly when the sexual meaning is taboo. Ambiguous sentences that have different, but not opposed, meanings are not likely to be humorous. When we hear a sentence like "I saw the bank from the bridge," for example, we may be sensitive to the fact that, out of context, "bank" here could refer to a river bank or to a financial institution, but this ambiguity is not likely to amuse us.

Similar in effect to the double entendre are the mispronunciation, the spoonerism, the verbal slip, and the typographical error that result in a second meaning for the sentence. Here again it is opposed, and not simply different, meanings that we find most humorous; though of course we may simply laugh because a mistake has been made. Perhaps we find such errors funniest when we think of them as "Freudian slips," as revelations of what the person would really like to say, but feels constrained not to.

Like the verbal errors above, mistranslations can be humorous simply as errors, but are more humorous when they yield a new meaning that is somehow opposed to the original. For example, the Biblical phrase "The spirit is willing but the flesh is weak" was once translated into the Russian equivalent of "The liquor is good but the food is bad." A good deal of the humor here comes from the contrast between the religious profundity of the original and the secular triviality of the translation.

The kinds of humor in language we have been considering thus far have been based on incongruities in the simpler aspects of language, such as pronunciation, spelling, and the assignment of meaning to words. But, as we move up to higher forms of what we have called humor of presentation, we find incongruities not so much in the "mechanics" of language as in what is being said, the message that the language is being used to convey. While puns and lower forms of humor are basically playing with words, the higher forms of humor, or "wit" as it has traditionally been called, is basically playing with ideas. William Hazlitt described wit as "an arbitrary juxtaposition of dissonant ideas, for some lively purpose of assimilation or contrast, generally of both." The witty comment will often consist of an amusing comparison of two things that normally would not be thought of as similar. When Aristophanes describes a certain statesman as having a voice like a pig on fire, for example, we experience a kind of pleasurable surprise at thinking of the man in these unfamiliar terms.

The resemblance appealed to in the witty comment cannot be too close, or it will tend to be obvious and so not surprising. Nor can it be too distant. After all, everything is similar to everything else in some respect or other. If we pick out only a nonessential or a very general feature that two things have in common, this is not likely to have much effect on our listener. A witty comparison will pick out a feature that is somehow essential in or characteristic of the things being compared, [and] will, as Locke says, find striking and unexpected resemblances.

Though wit is often based on similarities between things, it can take other forms as well. Sometimes the witty comment achieves its effect by looking at a situation from an incongruous point of view. To understand the comment we have to shift to that point of view from our ordinary one; doing so amuses us and we express our amusement in laughter. A character in a comedy of Labiche, for instance, shouts up to his neighbor, who has dirtied his balcony, "What do you mean by emptying your pipe on my terrace?" The man responds, "What do you mean by putting your terrace under my pipe?" The new perspective the pipe smoker has playfully adopted here is absurd, of course, but as long as we can understand what that perspective is, we can be amused by his comment. More often the shift in perspective in humor is not to an absurd point of view, but only to one which we do not ordinarily adopt, as in Oscar Wilde's turn-around of an old saying: "Work is the curse of the drinking classes." Comics have created many very funny routines simply by taking ordinary situations and asking us to view them from the perspective of, say, an animal or a visitor from space.

Another humorous device related to the shift in perspective is play with categories, describing something in one category as if it were in another. There is a scene in Woody Allen's *Annie Hall* in which Allen goes into a room to kill a spider and comes out with a very troubled look on his face. "You've got a spider in there the size of a Buick," he says, "definitely a *major* spider." What's funny here is not just the comparison of the spider to something very large—a car—but Allen's use of a specific brand name of car. "A spider the size of a car" would not have been nearly as funny as the line used, because it would have involved merely exaggeration. But by using the expression "the size of a Buick," Allen has shifted categories from talk of physical objects of different sizes to talk of cars. For something to be "the size of a Buick" it has to be a motor vehicle or something of the sort. But, of course, spiders are not in this category at all. A similar category shift makes Allen's use of the phrase "*major* spider" funny, too. In taxonomy, spiders categorized as major would be larger than other spiders; but Allen's pronunciation of the word "major" indicates that he means more than that. Allen's meaning is that this spider is of great *importance,* as, say, a major fire or a major earthquake would be. And ordinary spiders simply aren't in this category.

. . . We find another rich source of incongruity in the violation of logical principles. What seems to work best here is not a complete lack of logic in a piece of reasoning, but rather a violation of some logical principle in a piece of reasoning that is just logical enough to sound somewhat plausible. In Mark Twain's *Innocents Abroad,* the author offers his homage at the Tomb of Adam: "The tomb of Adam! How touching it was here in a land of strangers, far from home . . . to discover the grave of a blood relation. . . . I leaned upon a pillar and burst into tears. . . . Noble old man—he did not live to see me." The incongruity here is in the illogic of Twain's reasoning; far from being "a blood relation," Adam is his *most distant* relative. But what makes Twain's tribute especially funny is the ring of plausibility it has. Indeed, in some pieces of humor based on logical incongruities, it may take some logical expertise to figure out just where the reasoning goes wrong. Almost everyone would agree that the following graffiti is invalid as a syllogism, but few are able to put their finger on the mistake involved.

> **A stale pretzel is better than nothing.**
> **Nothing is better than God.**
> **Therefore, a stale pretzel is better than God.**

Some pieces of humor even work a logical incongruity into an interchange between two characters so that not only is the incongruity accepted as if it made sense, but the person responding to the incongruous line actually builds on the incongruity. In the Marx Brothers' *Animal Crackers,* for instance, Chico says to Groucho, "He thinks I look alike," to which Groucho responds, "Well, if you do, it's a tough break for both of you."

An interesting genre of humor based on the violation of logical principles is the Irish bull. Sometimes these are close to things people actually say, and what is at fault is not the person's reasoning so much as the way he expresses himself, as in the following:

> **Policeman: "Say you! If you're going to smoke here, you'll have to either put out your pipe, or go somewhere else."**

The logical mistake here is certainly no worse than that made by an Omaha woman who, when asked by an interviewer about her television-watching habits, said, "Oh, I never watch TV. I turn it off more than I turn it on."

Yet often in Irish bulls it is not just the wording but the reasoning that is incorrect, as in:

> **Irishman: "Be gorra I wisht I knew the place where I am goin' to die, and sure and I'd niver go there!"**

Another kind of humor is based, not on the violation of logic, but on a spurious appeal to logical or quasilogical principles. In one of Myron Cohen's best jokes, a man is in bed in the afternoon with his neighbor's wife, when suddenly they hear her husband coming through the front door. The man jumps out of bed and scrambles into the closet, where he buries himself under some clothes, shoes, and other closet odds and ends. The suspicious husband bursts in through the bedroom door and shouts, "Okay, where is he?" He looks under the bed, behind the draperies, in the bathroom, and then finally in the closet. When he at last pulls away the paraphernalia covering the man, he triumphantly asks, "And what are *you* doing here?" To which the man replies, "Everybody's got to be *some*place."

Statements can be humorous, too, when they sound informative, but are actually just tautologies. Here are two examples:

Everything tastes more or less like chicken.

You can get anywhere in 10 minutes if you go fast enough.

Conversely, a statement can be amusing when it sounds tautologous, and perhaps even is, but is somehow illuminating nonetheless. The maxim "A rich man is just a poor man with money" is like that, as are many pieces of folk wisdom.

Paradoxes are often amusing in a similar way: at first they appear to be necessarily false, because self-contradictory; but then we see that the contradiction is only apparent and that the statement actually reveals something true. According to a story told about Picasso, an art dealer bought a canvas signed "Picasso" and travelled to Cannes to see if it was genuine. Picasso took one look and said, "It's a fake." A few months later the man bought another canvas signed "Picasso" and returned to Cannes. Again Picasso said, "It's a fake." "But *cher maître,*" the man protested, "it so happens that I saw you with my own eyes working on this very painting several years ago." Picasso simply shrugged his shoulders and replied, "I often paint fakes."

The last kind of linguistic humor we will consider is based on the breaking of pragmatic rules, the rules governing the use of language in particular communication situations. Pragmatic incongruity may come into our use of language, first of all, in the connection between an assertion and the state of affairs it purports to refer to. When someone makes a statement that we know is a gross exaggeration or an outright lie, we may be amused by the "lack of fit" between the statement and reality. Tall tales in fiction can be funny in a similar way. When we hear about the amazing feats of someone like Paul Bunyan, we may laugh because we know that no human could perform such feats. Exaggeration of what is possible sometimes combines with logical incongruity, as in Carl Sandburg's yarn about the man who was so tall that he had to climb a ladder to shave himself.

A related kind of incongruity exists between the semantic content of someone's utterance and the tone, gestures, or facial expression with which he speaks it. We find it funny to listen to someone read a serious speech, for example, with an insufficiently serious tone, or with an overly grave one, or with inappropriate gestures or facial expressions. Sarcasm is often funny because it is clear from the way the person is saying what he says that he doesn't mean it. Sometimes too, as in humorous understatement and overstatement, it can be obvious simply from the situation that the person is being ironic. On a Monday morning a condemned man was being led to the scaffold, the story goes, when he said, "What a lousy way to start the week!"

Written language can be funny when there is an incongruity between the message and the way it is expressed. Gag signs such as "THIMK" and "ESCHEW OBFUSCATION" work by violating the very maxim they express. And signs such as "Want to learn to read? Call 458-1000" are funny because they could not serve as a message to their intended audience. A real life example of this second kind of incongruity is the sign on the doors of post offices, "No dogs allowed, except seeing-eye dogs."

Another area of pragmatics that is a rich source of humor is presupposition. Linguists and philosophers have discussed presupposition a great deal in recent years, and have used the word in different ways. For our purposes, we can say that when utterance U presupposes proposition P, then P has to be true in order for U to be used successfully. The command "Close the door," for instance, presupposes such propositions as "There is a door to which I am referring" and "The door is open." Unless there is a door and it is open, "Close the door" cannot be used as a command—if these words are uttered, as Austin says, they will "misfire."

One way to get incongruity from an utterance that has presuppositions is simply to use it when we know that it will "misfire," that is, when it is obvious that the presupposed propositions are false. For instance, on arriving home after a busy day a woman might say to her husband, "I'm exhausted—let's call the White House and tell them we can't make it." A sophisticated joke of this type is Martin Mull's "Do you realize that man is the only animal that chews the ice in its drink?" For this to serve as a real piece of information, there would have to be several species that had iced drinks. There aren't, of course, and so this is just a piece of silliness.

Another way to play with presupposition is to use an utterance, usually a question, which presupposes something that is false, but not obviously so, and which is nonetheless embarrassing to the person to whom it is addressed. Asking someone, "Do you still pick your nose all the time?" presupposes that at least in the past the person did frequently pick his nose. By uttering this question we give the impression that it is common knowledge that he had, and still might have, this nasty habit. Lots of hostile and mock hostile humor works in this way by putting the hostile content not in the utterance, but in what the utterance presupposes. Johnny Carson, on the "Tonight Show," once said to Ed McMahon, after McMahon had corrected him on his pronunciation of some word, "Well, I'm sure that Durwood Kirby won't be like that when he's sitting there." If Carson had put the playfully hostile content into what his utterance *said,* if his statement had been "I'm going to replace you with Durwood Kirby," then his utterance wouldn't have been very funny. But by making a statement that *presupposed* that McMahon was being replaced, Carson made it sound as though everyone could just assume that he was firing McMahon, which in the situation was quite funny.

Though there are many more aspects to the pragmatics of language, and thus many more places where humorous incongruity can be worked into our use of language, we cannot hope to examine them all here. I have been trying merely to touch on a few of the major kinds of pragmatic incongruity.

Notes

[1] Quoted in Jacob Levine, Ed., *Motivation in Humor* (New York: Atherton Press, 1969), p. 177.

[2] Richard Boston, *An Anatomy of Laughter* (London: Collins, 1974), pp. 60–61.

[3] I owe this joke to Victor Raskin, who presented it in a paper, "The Linguistic Relativity of Humor," at the Second International Conference on Humor, Los Angeles, August 1979.

Comparing Generalizations

Share with your classmates your journal responses to the reading. To what extent do the class members see agreement or parallels between their generalizations about the sources of humor and those of Morreall? You need not force parallels nor discard class generalizations in favor of Morreall's. Your reading and your class-generated ideas both add to your general understanding of humor and how to explain it.

"Well, I put on the cruise control. Let's play cards."

"I like it. It's Humphrey Bogart without the arrogance."

Comparing Two Cartoons

On page 14, Morreall states, "As any after-dinner speaker knows, the jokes that would go over big at a meeting of academics might not go over at all at a meeting of a labor union. And there is a difference between the cartoons in, say, *The New Yorker* and *The National Enquirer.*" Examine the two cartoons above and discuss with your class the differences between them.

Discuss also why it is that certain jokes would be successful at a meeting of academics but would not be appreciated at all at a labor union meeting. Can you think of specific jokes that would be funny in certain settings but not in others?

Considering Audience Response

Below are some jokes, cartoons, and anecdotes and some audiences with whom they might be shared. Think about each example and how it would affect the proposed possible audiences. Record in your journal how you think each audience would respond to the material.

Sample
An explorer was describing some of his adventures in Africa to an audience of women.

"Suddenly I came upon a tribe of wild women," he said, "who, strangely enough, had no tongues."

"Heavens! No tongues?" exclaimed one of the women. "How could they talk?"

"They couldn't," said the explorer. "That's what made them wild."

Possible Audiences
1. a gathering of the local chapter of the National Organization for Women
2. a group of Girl Scouts
3. female college students
4. female native Africans
5. a stag party

"I'm not ready for another relationship yet, Eddie. The last one was too painful."

Copyright © 1984 by Baloo. Reprinted courtesy of Playgirl Magazine.

1. regular readers of *Jack and Jill*
2. regular readers of *Family Circle*
3. regular readers of *Playboy*
4. regular readers of *Watch Tower* (a religious newspaper)

Q: Why don't more elephants go to college?
A: Very few ever finish high school.

1. second and third graders
2. guests at a high school commencement
3. males and females your age
4. high school dropouts

Doctor to overweight patient: "And this medication should be taken on an empty stomach, Mr. Howard— if such an opportunity ever presents itself."

1. Weight Watchers meeting
2. Mr. Howard
3. first-year medical students
4. regular readers of *Reader's Digest*

GREAT ART OF OUR TIME
Kennedy Contemplating The Bust Of McCormack

1. Republicans and Democrats
2. today's teenagers
3. artists and art students
4. politically-in-the-know folks in their forties

One evening as I was walking through the woods behind my house, I came upon a pup tent where some small boys were camping out. I overheard them talking: "There's a rock right under my sleeping bag," said one voice. Another moaned, "That's nothing— I'm trying to sleep on a root. I wish I was home in my nice soft bed." "Yeah, me too," cried another. "I'm cold and thirsty. Let's go home!" "Are you crazy?" said the obvious leader of the group. "If we go home now, they'll never let us do this again!"

1. six- and seven-year-olds
2. PTA gathering
3. Effective Parenting Group
4. teenagers

In her review of Katharine Hepburn's performance in the play, *The Lake,* Dorothy Parker wrote: "Katharine Hepburn runs the gamut of emotions from A to B."

1. Katharine Hepburn's family
2. theater goers
3. producer and backers of the play
4. grade school children

1. senior citizens
2. students in a macramé class
3. people who have had a suicide in the family
4. children under six

"Oh, Lester! Not my macramé!"

Drawing by Booth. Copyright © 1973 by The New Yorker Magazine, Inc.

"Funky Winkerbean" by Tom Batiuk. Copyright by and permission of News America Syndicate.

1. American teenagers
2. foreign students
3. mothers of American teenagers
4. members of the Daughters of the American Revolution

Characterizing an Audience

When you decided how you thought each audience would respond to the items, you probably had in mind certain factors that a person might consider in selecting a humorous item for a particular audience. No doubt, you thought about factors such as age and sex. Make a list with your class of all the other factors you can think of that affected your opinion on whether an audience would be apt to find a piece of humor funny.

Listing the Purposes of Humor

When individuals choose to use humor in their interactions with others, they do it for a reason; consciously or unconsciously, the person has a goal in mind in addition to making others laugh. When a teacher tells a joke just before distributing a final examination, he probably is trying to help his tense, nervous students relax a bit. When a politician intersperses her speech with jokes or anecdotes that ridicule the opposition, no doubt her objective is to establish a oneness, a sense of identification, in her audience. Using your own thoughts and discussions on the subject of humor, create with the class a list of all the purposes you can think of for using humor.

Some of the purposes you listed may be very practical, as encouraging relaxation and creating a sense of identification are. You may also have identified purposes that are essentially moral—constructive, edifying. In other words, humor, spoken or in print, can cause individuals or groups to think about their own behavior—their "foibles and follies," as the eighteenth-century satirists might have said—or to reexamine the values, beliefs, and mores of their class, their society, or their culture.

Erma Bombeck makes many women laugh at their own inadequacies as mothers and housewives. She also reminds readers of all ages of their contrariness, irresponsibility, and laziness when they were children and teenagers. Humorous works by James Thurber, Mark Twain, or Art Buchwald may give readers cause to reflect on the prejudice, hypocrisy, or injustice in society.

Thinking about Purpose, Audience, and Effect

The advertisement that follows appeared in a little book entitled *Meet Mr. Bomb: A Practical Guide to Nuclear Extinction* edited by Tony Hendra, independently published in the early 1980s in New Hampshire and labeled as an "Official U.S. Government Parody." The book contains a special message from the president and has four major parts: an introduction to Mr. Bomb and a section each on what to do before Mr. Bomb's arrival, during a nuclear holocaust, and after.

With your class, consider the ad and decide what you think its purpose is. Discuss also your responses to the following questions:

1. Who is the intended audience?
2. What responses do you think the writers hoped for in their readers?
3. How effective could this item be if it were made less offensive?

An Advertisement for Preparation H-Bomb

Tony Hendra

"WITH HALF MY FAMILY MELTED, NO FOOD, NO WATER, AND NO MEDICAL ASSISTANCE, THE LAST THING I NEED IS HEMORRHOIDS!"

Studies show that radiation from a nuclear blast could significantly alter the size of many common inflammations, including hemorrhoids. In recent tests, irradiated subjects developed hemorrhoids two to three times their own body size. In some cases these hemorrhoids themselves developed hemorrhoids. Clearly in a nuclear situation you're going to need an ointment far more powerful than any available today. Preparation H-Bomb contains Strontium 90 to literally blast away the torture and itch of radioactive inflammations. With all the other possible discomforts of shelter life, you won't need the added burden of two- to three-hundred pound hemorrhoids. Stock up now for a pain-free future.

Analyzing the Comics as Social Comment

One of the most popular vehicles for humor is the comic strip. The "funnies" appeal to readers of all ages, life styles, and subgroups of a culture. It is generally believed that our comic strips tend to reflect American culture, politics, and family life. Think about the extent to which the strips you read encourage reflection on individual or social issues. Select two humorous comic strips that you read regularly, and in your journal write your analysis of each. Tell what individual or social issues are presented and what potential you see in the strips for prompting social or moral reform.

THE MECHANICS OF WRITING

Preparing a Draft

Now that you have reflected on your own and your classmates' experiences and understandings of humor and have done some reading on the subject, you are well prepared to deal with the following hypothetical problem. Review your journal before you begin to write.

From Tony Hendra's *Meet Mr. Bomb: A Practical Guide to Nuclear Extinction* (New London, NH: High Meadow, n.d.).

Assignment

You are a member of the editorial staff of the campus newspaper. The next issue will carry a feature story on the revised program for Freshman Composition that has recently been instituted on campus. The article will spell out the higher standards for admission into regular Freshman Composition and will explain that the high failure rate in Freshman Composition in the past has been due to the poor preparation many students have had before enrolling in college. The article will also elaborate on how unprepared students will be able to work their way through preparatory courses, which in turn will help them succeed when they *do* qualify to enroll in the composition class. The feature-page editor wants to run the following cartoon along with the article and has obtained permission to reprint it.

One member of the editorial board strongly argues against using the cartoon. He says that it is "in bad taste and counterproductive—not funny." The feature-page editor defends its use as "an appropriate and effective use of humor." The editor must make the final decision, and she wants the opinions of the other members of the editorial board. Whether she runs the cartoon or

Cartoon by Glen Dines, courtesy of *Phi Delta Kappan.*

pulls it, she will be in for a fight and will have to defend her decision. What she needs from the staff is more than a vote for or against; she needs well-reasoned arguments that will help her decide and that she can use in defending her choice. Write a memo of no more than 500 words giving her your views on the issue. Make it clear what you think she should do and why. To give her some confidence in your opinion, demonstrate your understanding of the cartoon's potential for humor and discuss why this potential would or would not be realized for readers of your campus newspaper. Organize your memo so that it is easy to read and persuasive.

When you have reviewed your journal and readings, made whatever notes are necessary, and decided on your position on the issue, draft your memo, selecting what seems to be the most appropriate organization for the presentation of your ideas and their support.

Getting Audience Response: A Revising Workshop

Bring your draft to class for a Revising Workshop. In small groups, share your papers with your classmates and assist each other by responding to the questions below in relation to each paper. At least two other students should respond to each paper.

1. What is the writer's position on the issue? Where in the memo is the position first stated? Is this an appropriate placement for the reader? How does the writer back up his or her position? (Logic? Examples? Definitions? Anecdotes? Statistics?) Mark any support that seems questionable or needs expanding.
2. Which opposing arguments does the writer acknowledge? How does he or she dispose of these arguments? Mark any passages that seem questionable or need expanding.
3. What tone does the writer express in the memo? (Serious? Humorous? Satiric? Officious? Pompous?) How will the audience respond to this tone? Mark any passages or words that you think might offend the intended reader.
4. What seems to be the purpose of each paragraph? Why do the paragraphs seem to be in this order? Comment on any paragraph that seems to be out of order.

Before you write the second draft of your memo, take into consideration the responses your classmates offered during the Revising Workshop. You are not compelled to agree with their ideas and to rewrite your paper accordingly, but you do have an obligation to think about their ideas and to treat them seriously.

Redrafting

Now, write the second draft of your memo, making whatever revisions you have decided are necessary—for clarity, to improve the support of your position, to keep your tone appropriate and consistent, to improve the order of your paragraphs.

Polishing Your Work: An Editing Workshop

Return to your small group with your second draft for an Editing Workshop. In this group session, your aim is to assist each other in reviewing the memos for mechanical flaws and problems with form. In this workshop, as in the previous one, each person's paper should be reviewed by at least two students using the following questions:

1. How closely does the paper follow the memo format as shown in Appendix B?
2. Are there any sentences or parts of sentences in the memo that confuse you or cause you to reread to grasp the meaning? If so, bracket these as needing repair.
3. Place a mark (X) in the margin of the paper on any line in which you see what you perceive as an error in spelling or punctuation. Use as many marks as there are errors in each line.

Examine the responses of your classmates to your paper. If sentences are bracketed, try to decide what the problems are with such sentences. If you find marks indicating spelling or punctuation errors, try to understand what those errors are and how they should be corrected. For help, consult the Editing Guide (Chapter 12). Make notes in your journal as to the kinds of sentence and mechanical errors you are making.

Preparing Your Final Version

Now you can make the revisions you feel are necessary for a persuasive and polished memo. Bring your final copy to class to submit to your instructor and possibly to share with your class.

CHAPTER 2

Understanding the Process

A REVIEW OF YOUR COMPOSING PROCESS

In Chapter 1 you were taken through a series of activities which led up to a formal writing task. You were asked to respond to various humorous cartoons, jokes, and stories and to consider why each seemed funny or not to you and the effect they might have on others. To broaden your understanding of humor, you read about the subject and shared responses to your reading, working with your classmates to arrive at some generalizations about the sources and purposes of humor and the critical role of audience factors in its success. Through your study of samples of humor, your reading, your written responses, and your class discussions, you gained a broader perspective on the subject and composed a memo about a controversial cartoon for a hypothetical situation.

By reviewing your reading and your journal you were able to decide on your position on printing the cartoon under question and to begin drafting your memo. You found support for your position and selected a pattern of organization. In workshop groups your classmates responded to your draft on the clarity of your ideas, the accuracy of your explanations, your tone, and your organization. These responses afforded the opportunity to consider other readers' genuine reactions to your work and to rethink your memo in light of those reactions. After redrafting your memo you returned to your group for help in editing. Your classmates assisted you in polishing your memo, checking for mechanical flaws and sentence problems. Armed with these suggestions, you wrote your final draft.

As a result of this entire process, you probably moved from a limited personal view of humor to an expanded understanding of its sources, purposes, and effects on a variety of audiences. Your writing reflected this movement from personal reactions and thoughts toward more generalized ideas about humor. Also, your writing of the memo progressed from early drafting for discovery to polishing for a final version.

STAGES IN THE WRITING PROCESS

Do you think your memo to the editor would have been different if you had not done the prior thinking, discussing, and reading? Perhaps you would have given the same advice, perhaps not. Even if your advice would have been the same, you probably could not have given so many good reasons to back it up. And your memo would probably not be as well developed and clear in its analysis if you had not done some thinking and writing about the subject before you wrote the first full draft of it.

How was the memo you finally turned in different from the first draft you took to your Revising Workshop? Did it have different ideas and more reasons to support your advice? Were there more arguments against the opposing view? Was it clearer and easier to read? It would not be surprising if you answered yes to all of these questions.

Only with the simplest and most casual kinds of writing, like personal letters and notes, can we know exactly what we want to say and write it out the first time. Most writing tasks require us to plan and gather data and reflect on our own and others' experience, then to draft and think it all through again as we are working. When we have a draft (second, third, fourth, and on up) that really embodies all of our thoughts on the subject and says what we want to say, then it is time to improve it for the reader. Writing is a process that includes several different activities. Although these are usually called "stages," they are not as separate or as linear as that term might suggest. Learning to write is a matter of learning about the stages and about efficient methods of working through each stage and combining them into an efficient process. In the rest of this section we will investigate the stages in the writing process: prewriting, drafting, revising, and editing.

Prewriting

Prewriting is the term given to all of the activities that prepare us to write a first draft. These generally include defining the writing task, gathering material, and planning the first draft. *Defining the writing task* means clarifying for ourselves why we are writing (i.e., what we have to accomplish in this particular letter or essay or memo) and what our particular audience requires. (See below the section "Audience and Purpose" for more extended discussion of audience and purpose.)

Gathering material may be as simple as recalling information or impressions we already have in our heads or as complex as reading everything in print on our subject or interviewing everyone involved in an event. For example, when you wrote in your journal your responses to the cartoons, jokes, and humorous anecdotes, you gathered information simply by putting your own feelings into words and recording your thoughts about the reasons for your response. But the memo to the editor required you to review your journal and your reading notes to get needed information. If the writing task had been even more complex, you may have needed to do library or other research in order to have enough data to support a generalization.

Composing a generalization that the data supports is a prewriting activity that usually begins as we gather information and continues as we plan the first draft. As soon as you read the assignment to write the memo, did you immediately take a position and find that some reasons for your position were coming into your head? This seems to be what most of us do. As soon as we have a writing task and some background information, we begin to generalize. Then we look for more data, which either supports our original generalization or prompts us to change or refine it. Thus, while we gather the facts we are beginning to *plan the first draft.* We are deciding what we will say and probably making notes about the order in which we will present various ideas and their support. Armed with these notes—which are often no more than a rough list—we are ready to try a first draft. Actually, there is no single point at which we should move from prewriting to drafting. Some people begin drafting as soon as they have gathered most of their material. They explain that drafting helps them see more clearly how their ideas fit together. Other people draw up elaborate and detailed plans before they begin drafting. Neither system is better than the other. Each of us just has to discover what works best for us. The early drafter, however, has to be willing to write many drafts, starting over until he or she comes to the right generalization and an effective organization. This might be called the trial-and-error method.

Obviously, we prewrite differently for different tasks. The technique that helps us gather information for one task may be no help at all with another. The strategy of recalling family stories of our grandparents could be very helpful in giving us a plot for a short story, but it would not help us write a petition to enter a closed class. Conversely, consulting our printed schedules and the college bulletin should give us information we need for the petition, but it is not a very relevant way to develop material for fiction. And when we are faced with an exam essay, we have to marshal our material and plan very quickly— a direct contrast to the elaborate research and planning we do for a term paper. In the rest of the chapters in this text, therefore, we will examine various prewriting strategies in relation to specific writing tasks.

Drafting

First drafts are made to be thrown out or at least buried beneath revisions, but they are an important part of the writing process. Drafts serve two purposes: (1) they allow us to put all of our material on paper, and thus to see it all at once as we never could in our heads; (2) by putting all of our material before us, they enable us to evaluate it. As we draft, we put our thoughts and our supporting data into words, sentences, and paragraphs, and we can see and hear it all together for the first time. If our writing task is a relatively simple one, the first draft may be close to what we want and may need only some fine-tuning. But with more complicated writing tasks, the first draft often brings to light some real or apparent contradictions or leaps in logic, or suggests to us that material should be added or rearranged. We may then be able to go right to a second draft in which we make the needed adjustments, or we may have to gather some more data or go back and think the subject through again. First drafts are never wasted, even if they end up in the trash. They serve to help us clarify our ideas and our means of presenting them. A later chapter of this text will give you some strategies for evaluating your drafts and deciding what remains to be done.

Some people write their first drafts very quickly. Others work more slowly, improving each sentence before going on to the next and looking for exactly the right word before they go on. Both methods have been known to work well for the simpler, shorter writing tasks. For longer papers, however, it is impossible to envision the work as a whole; more than one draft is necessary. There is no point in slowing down to polish each sentence to perfection if you may decide in the next draft that your statement no longer fits or that you no longer believe what it says. We urge you, therefore, to practice writing at a fairly quick pace and expect to do several drafts. Remember, though, that there is no point in going so quickly that you lose track of your purpose or the point you are making.

Revising

To revise is to *reenvision,* to see again. When our ideas have been shaped into a draft, warts and all, they are before us, and we can evaluate them. Of course, we have been reconsidering and making changes as far back as the prewriting stage, and our ideas and the way we present them have been getting clearer. But once we have a draft, we can put more of our energy into clarifying and improving. Even if we realize that most of the first draft just will not do, it gives us a clearer idea of what needs to be done in the second draft. If our writing task is complex and fairly lengthy, it is not unusual to go through three or more drafts, each improving substantially on the previous one. A willingness to write several drafts is a characteristic shared by most successful writers.

In each writing task, no matter how difficult, there comes a blessed moment when we realize that we are in control of our ideas. We have seen the work from all angles, considered all of its implications, questioned and confirmed our own assumptions and assertions, countered all of the points the opposition may raise, answered any questions the reader may have, and told the story accurately. Of course, we may think of additional examples or details, but we are confident that we have not overlooked anything that would cause us to change our generalization. In short, we have it right. Do you remember reaching this point in your writing of the memo about the cartoon? It is very satisfying to realize that we have truly come to understand our subject and have the reasoning to support our position. It makes any amount of drafting worthwhile.

From this point on, we can concentrate on the effectiveness with which we present our writing. Here we are focusing entirely on our readers. Will they be able to follow the train of thought? Is there any chance they could fail to see how a sentence or paragraph follows from the one before it? Will they understand all the words? Is there anything they might object to?

Developing this ability to imagine an audience's reaction is *essential* to learning to write effectively. Think back to the Revising Workshop you took part in earlier. Did group members indicate that they found a part of your memo unclear? Did they convince you? Or do you still think it was understandable? Of course, you were all trying to imagine whether your memos would have been logical and convincing to the hypothetical editor, so there is no way to know for sure. If there is even a chance that something is unclear, however, that statement or paragraph in doubt should be revised. Naturally, what we write sounds clear to us because we know what the constructions mean. Sometimes we find it hard to believe that a passage is not clear. But the work in revision groups this term should heighten your sensitivity to the parts of your writing that readers find difficult. Soon you will be able to spot more of the potential problems in your papers without the help of the group. We all need someone else's opinion on some of the things we write, even after we have become quite good at revising on our own. "Let me read this to you, and you can tell me how it sounds" or "Read this and tell me what you think"—these are the words of someone who knows how hard *and how important* it is to anticipate the reader's response.

Editing

It is both demanding and rewarding to think through a subject and to work out strategies that will present it most effectively to a reader. Compared to these activities, making sure that the words are correctly spelled and that the sentences are correctly constructed and punctuated may seem to be minor considerations. It does make sense not to worry about these things until the last draft. There is no point in going to the dictionary for the spelling of "egregious" if there is a chance that the word will not be used in the final draft.

Although sentence construction, spelling, and punctuation are the last details writers tend to, these "surface features" are what the readers encounter first. The words as they appear on the page are all the writers have to communicate their ideas to the readers. Generally, readers suspect that writers who are careless or uninformed about small things are likely to be careless and uninformed about big things—like their ideas and opinions.

When readers notice misspelled words or when they have to read a sentence twice to figure it out, they are distracted from the writer's train of thought. Thus, each of these surface errors decreases the power of writing to inform or entertain or persuade. After several Editing Workshops in which the group members point out sections of your paper in which they find distracting surface errors, you should become more aware of the kind of errors you are likely to make. With practice and some help from your instructor, and perhaps with some guidance from Part III in this text, you will become more skilled at recognizing and correcting surface errors.

Prewriting, drafting, revising, editing are each essential to successful writing. While it is convenient to discuss these stages individually and to focus on one stage at a time for certain exercises while you are learning to be a better writer, your own experience has shown you that the stages are not easily separable. Even as we draft, we may decide to return to the prewriting stage, and we may do some revising even as we are working on the first draft.

THE VALUE OF EXPRESSIVE WRITING

When you recorded in your journal your own response to the humorous items in Chapter 1, you were gathering information from your own experience. If the final assignment had asked you not for a reasoned argument but for your preference (i.e., Do you want to run the cartoon or not?), it would have been enough for you to consult only your own experience and feelings. But because you also heard your classmates' responses and read others' ideas about humor and how it works, you were able to offer more than just a preference.

If we ignore our own experience, we are likely to come to a generalization that we do not feel much identification with or belief in. For example, if we are just slightly embarrassed by the cartoon, we should not ignore that when we decide to recommend printing it or not printing it. But neither should we base our recommendations on our reactions alone. This process of coming to a conclusion or taking a position on an issue is a process of comparing our own experiences with those of others, until we have enough information to support a generalization or opinion, and then of comparing our generalizations with others' until we are confident that we have looked at the problem from all angles.

To reflect the process of building from personal experience to a generalization, this text will always ask you to do some *expressive* writing to prepare for each formal writing assignment. Expressive writing is the form of writing that expresses and discovers our own thoughts and feelings. Most often we write in this manner only for ourselves, as when we record in a journal how we feel about the things that happen to us. Many people keep such a journal so they have an outlet for their feelings, a record of their thoughts as they grow older, and a place to write down reminiscences. For you as student writers, we will give specific topics on which to write so that you will be sure to have a record of your experiences to draw on for the formal writing assignments.

WRITING TO LEARN

In Chapter 1 you wrote numerous thoughts in your journal which helped clarify your own and others' responses to humor. You also explored, analyzed, and categorized the notion of humor and its sources, purposes, and impact.

Until the final writing task, your memo to the feature-page editor, you wrote only for yourself. No one else read your journal though you used it as a source for discussion. In other words, you wrote to record and to learn.

It is not only in a composition class that we write to learn. In other college classes, you may be called upon to do two kinds of writing: writing to *learn* and writing to *demonstrate* your learning. You will probably be called upon to write essays and papers. A professor may also ask you to summarize material, analyze a chart, or describe an experiment so he or she can gauge your comprehension of the subject.

Equally important is the writing you do on your own to help you understand a subject. Most students keep a notebook for each course they are enrolled in and take notes from lectures, films, and readings. In addition, students who write to learn regularly think about the subject on their own—summarizing, analyzing, interpreting, and evaluating the course content. Such students also take time to study graphic material—charts, graphs, tables—and to verbalize the concepts represented in them. When review time arrives, they are far ahead of others who have simply amassed facts, principles, and information of all kinds.

In the business, social, and political communities, individuals are called upon to study a proposal, a report, or detailed information and to comprehend a topic before it is used in decision making or before it is presented to others. Writing about such material helps individuals to understand it and to demonstrate that they know it.

The skills of gathering, summarizing, and generalizing aid us in writing to learn just as they do in more formal methods of writing. Naturally, because this writing is done for ourselves and not for other audiences, we need not be concerned with correctness of form, appropriateness of style, or mechanical accuracy. We *are* concerned, however, with pulling material together and organizing it in such a way that it makes sense to us as learners. Chapters 8 and 9 may provide you with useful approaches as you begin writing to learn.

AUDIENCE AND PURPOSE

Audience

Whereas the audience for most expressive writing and writing to learn is yourself, other kinds of writing are generally addressed to other readers: a single individual, as in the memo you wrote to the feature-page editor; a group of readers, such as a committee, members of an organization, or of a particular age; or the general public, such as readers of a letter to the editor or of an essay or poem published in a magazine or book. In any composition task, writers need to be aware of who their readers will be. Naturally, in a composition class, the instructor is always a secondary audience but one who can also determine how effectively a given paper addresses its particular primary audience.

What difference does audience make in the substance and style of our writing? And how do we tailor writing to suit that audience? You discovered through your analysis in Chapter 1 that certain kinds of humor were probably inappropriate for certain audiences because of characteristics such as their age, sex, race, religious or political affiliation, moral code, and so on. Just as we would consider one or more of these characteristics and other factors, such as setting, when we decide to use humor, so would we consider them in addressing a piece of writing to a specific individual or group. Even when we address our writing to a general but unknown audience, such as the readership of a particular magazine, we consider what that readership might be like, what their expectations and needs might be. Considering our audience in the prewriting stage and generally throughout the writing process helps us to make decisions about what ideas and supporting detail we will include, how we will organize our ideas, what our sentence structure will be like, and what our tone will be.

Think about how two letters requesting a loan would be different if one were addressed to your mother and one to a wealthy but distant relative. No doubt your style and tone would be warm and informal with your mother, more formal and reasoned with a distant relative. In the latter you might pay more attention to effective organization and a variety of sentence patterns than you would feel were necessary for your mother.

Or consider a writing task in which you are to explain the processes by which stalagmites and stalactites are formed. How would this explanation vary if you were submitting it both to your geology professor and to children in a fourth grade class? Probably your sentence structure and vocabulary would vary as would your tone. You would probably be more informal in addressing the young audience and your organization might be different, too. The professor might expect technical terms while those same terms would likely confuse fourth graders. In addition, the amount of information and detail you would include for the children might be much less, and you might supplement the writing with pictures or drawings that you would not provide for your professor.

In both these writing tasks you would want to edit your work carefully, checking spelling, punctuation, and so on. In other kinds of writing this effort to assure correctness may not be relevant. When you write in your journal to help you learn about a topic, to clarify your thinking, or to express your feelings, you are your own audience, and superficial correctness is not a high priority. Likewise, informal communications with friends and loved ones—notes, cards, and postcards—may not demand the attention to correctness that formal writing does.

Purpose

Just as audience considerations help us make decisions about the nature of our writing, so does the purpose of a writing task. When we write for audiences other than ourselves, we generally have one of the following purposes in mind:

Sharing Feelings and Thoughts

We write to share our personal feelings and thoughts with close friends and loved ones but also, on certain occasions, with our colleagues or associates. These include letters of all kinds—from Valentine notes to formal expressions of congratulation. We also express our feelings and sense of the world when we create some poetry and fiction.

Providing Information

In our example about explaining the processes by which stalagmites and stalactites are formed, our audience varied but our purpose remained the same: to provide information. We are often called upon to explain a process or subject to a particular audience. On an essay examination we might want to inform a professor of what we know about the reign of Queen Elizabeth I. Or we might need to prepare a letter that lists and describes for a high school student the requirements of a college composition course. In writing to give information, we try to organize and present as much explanation and detail as are necessary to leave our particular audience with few questions on the subject.

Moving Others to Thought, Feeling, and Action

Though we might occasionally say that any effective writing is persuasive in the sense that it is vivid, credible, or refreshing, writing termed *persuasive* generally is that in which we try to get an audience (one person or many) to see our side of an issue or to take action in a way we propose. In the writing task you just completed, your memo to the feature-page editor was meant to convince her that your decision was the right and logical one. You wanted her to behave in a certain way.

When we write persuasively, we are trying to sell something to someone. Whether the writing is advertising copy designed to motivate readers to buy the latest model Buick, a detailed legal brief with the intent to convince a jury of the innocence of a defendant, or a formal letter of recommendation for a college applicant, the writer seeks to move the audience to some kind of action. In other arguments, we may not be directly recommending specific action but rather trying to help an audience understand an issue, see the complexities of a proposal, or think in a certain way about an idea. Consideration of the needs, interests, and predispositions of our audience becomes very important if we hope to be successful in achieving our goal in persuasive writing.

Although writing may be intended primarily for one of these three purposes, more often than not we find a blend of purposes. A writer giving information may often include expressions of feeling as a means of developing a point or drawing in the reader. Similarly, much persuasive writing may contain passages of information and expressions of the writer's personal feelings which may help support an argument in a manner judged to be the most effective for a particular audience.

When we write only for ourselves, our purposes may include all the ones discussed above. We may write to communicate our feelings or simply record our experiences and what we think about them; we may write to convince ourselves about a particular issue or to explore our thoughts on a subject; we may summarize material in order to learn it or compile all the information we know on some topic. In other words, we may write for ourselves for any and all purposes.

Finally, what difference does it make to us as writers whether we are consciously aware of our audience and purpose? Particularly in writing for others, knowing our audience and purpose will help us make decisions about what material to include or reject, which strategies to use to develop the material, the most effective organization of the material, the appropriate style and tone, and finally about correctness. The most successful writing for others makes its basic purpose clear and appeals most effectively to its readers.

STRATEGIES FOR ACHIEVING PURPOSE

Once you know your purpose and your audience for a paragraph, an essay, or a memo, you are ready to choose the most appropriate strategies for developing your writing. Some methods that writers have traditionally found useful are explained here. These strategies are natural and satisfying for readers because they reflect the way humans think; meeting the expectations of a thinking reader can help you achieve your purpose.

Narration

A narration recounts a sequence of events in order to convey information or experience to a reader. Narration can be seen as a response to the question, "What happened?" or "What happens?" You might think of it as a method of development used exclusively by the writer of the short story, the novel, or the ballad, but writers use narration in a variety of writing forms. You use narration extensively in both personal and business letters or in such documents as accident reports. When you include anecdotes or accounts of your own experience to introduce or conclude a piece of writing or to illustrate a point, you are clearly narrating.

An exam question that asks you to trace the events of such and such is expecting a narrative from you. The directive to discuss what led up to the Constitutional Convention of 1787 likewise demands that you provide a sequential account of what happened. Certain process questions, despite the terms *describe* or *explain,* really ask you to narrate a series of steps or stages:

> Describe the psychomotor development
> of infants from birth to age four.
> or
> Explain the proper method of CPR.

While you may not think of narration as the predominant mode for most of your academic writing, it can be a useful strategy to incorporate with others.

Notice in the following passage from an article in *Consumer Reports* how the writer includes narration in a discussion designed to inform consumers:

Fish 'n' Chips

Almost any food tastes best when it's really fresh. Think ahead a few months to garden-fresh tomatoes and corn, to apples right off the tree. Fish fresh from the water is delicious, too. But fresh fish isn't readily available everywhere. In some areas, it's frozen fish or no fish at all. . . .

Attempts have been made to translate fish and chips to America as a fast-food specialty, most notably through the "Arthur Treacher's" chain. Other fast-food restaurants have also added fried fish to their menus to go with their french fries. But fish-and-chips-to-go doesn't seem to be a threat to the All-American hamburger. Most people who fancy the combination probably buy their fish and french fries in the supermarket in frozen form and reheat them at home. (Indeed, even in England, some nonpurist fish-and-chip places are resorting to using frozen fish.)

CU [Consumers Union] decided to see how well fish and french fries from the frozen-food bin rivaled their fresh competitors from the fish store and the vegetable market. We looked at 38 frozen-fish products in batter, breading, or sauce. We evaluated a broad range of frozen french fries in various styles. We developed recipes for fish and fries. And, for good measure, we checked the fish and chips available from "Arthur Treacher's" and the fries to be bought at other American fast-food places. Our fundamental consideration in the tests was taste, but we looked at nutrition, wholesomeness, and general quality as well. . . .

Using narration can enhance your reader's interest in what you have written. The language in narration is concrete, and the details of a "story" motivate personal involvement on the part of an audience. Interspersed appropriately within an argument, an informative report, or a petition, narration can help bring to life what might otherwise be dull, abstract prose.

Quite often, narration is the strategy that occurs to you first. It just seems natural to "start at the beginning." But for many audiences and purposes, it is better to use something other than straight narration. Imagine that you are on a committee that reviews student petitions. You have hundreds of petitions to read each semester. What question is in your mind as you begin reading each one? How would you react to one that began "My grandfather came to this country in 1899. He settled in Detroit, where he and my grandmother had seven children"? You would probably be asking yourself, "Why is the writer telling me this?" and you would be very impatient until you found out in the last of many paragraphs that the writer is petitioning to take an exam early so she can attend a family reunion. Your frustration may make you less likely to support the petition. The writer would have done better to let you know at the very outset what she is petitioning for. Keep in mind that readers always want to know *why* you are giving them information. Before you begin a narrative, ask whether your readers are informed enough and motivated enough to stick with you. You may decide to integrate narration with other development strategies or to use another strategy altogether.

Description

Though you may immediately think of poetry and fiction with their verbal portraits of people and scenes as typical forms that rely on description, you use description in nearly everything you write. A journal entry may be simply a description of your surroundings or of a person you admire. In letters you tell about a new friend—the person's appearance and personality—or you describe your latest clothing purchase or the new car you want. In reports, essays, or memos, writers rely on description to create images in words. Advertisements offer verbal pictures of products to accompany photographs or drawings of them. Describing vividly a person, an object, or a feeling, sound, taste, or smell can contribute immensely to the effect of nearly anything you write.

Of course there is writing that makes little or no use of description. Some business correspondence, for example, seems skeletal and indeed achieves its purpose without elaboration:

"Please send 9 cartons of 3709Y cotton batting @ $13.11. Bill us for $117.99. Thank you."

And a set of instructions accompanying a machine similarly achieves its purpose without description:

Remove battery compartment door by depressing the door latch located on the cabinet bottom. Insert 4 "C" size carbon zinc or alkaline type batteries into battery compartment. Make sure the positive (+) end of each battery is installed as illustrated inside the battery compartment.

Aside from these types of writing and some extremely technical articles, most writing does utilize description. On the other hand, it is rare to find writing that is purely descriptive.

In using description in your writing for an audience other than yourself, you want to select the most vivid and precise details you can to help your reader see or sense each part of what you are describing. You also want the details to hang together to create an overall impression. Notice in the following excerpt from a restaurant review how the critic uses description to support her judgment:

The shellfish are the way to start, preferably in an assortment on a platter, giving three or four (or a ravenous twosome) a taste of everything. There are piquant mussels on the half shell with minced sweet red peppers and Apalachicola oysters with a fresh, briny taste. The crayfish—from Louisiana in winter and the Sacramento Delta the rest of the year—also come with instructions on how to eat them, courtesy of the waiter. Just snap off the tail, slit the underside with a thumbnail or the point of a knife, and out comes a sweet and tender tail morsel. With a squeeze of lemon or a drop of Tabasco (huge bottles of the pepper sauce are provided for every table), steamed cray-fish are about as good as eating gets. Shrimp in the shell come with shredded lettuce and a spicy *rémoulade* sauce with a horseradish tang that starts the nose twitching and the eyes tearing. For a really good cry, proceed to the fiery house gumbo, chock-full of chicken, shrimp, and just about anything one can think of with a topping of rice to cool things down. Forget both the house salad—a motley and sloppy mixture of greens with mediocre tomatoes and artichokes when I had it—and the smoked chicken salad with apples and pecans—an updated Waldorf. The latter isn't found in traditional Creole kitchens as far as I know, but it is a regular offering at DuVall's other San Francisco restaurant, Cafe Royale, where it is done much better.

While the writer's aim here is to inform her readers and persuade them that her judgment is sound, she accomplishes these purposes primarily through her use of description. We see, smell, and taste the seafood, and our mouths water; we see, smell, and taste the "sloppy mixture of greens with mediocre tomatoes," and our appetites wane. Our overall impression of the Ritz Cafe after reading this paragraph, however, is positive.

Describing is not simply listing details; it includes selecting an order for those details that will create the most effective total picture or dominant impression you want your reader to have. In what order are the details given in the following descriptions of where to run?

Where to Run

James F. Fixx

At last you're ready to run in earnest. The important thing is to go outside and *do* it. Many people feel they have to have a special place, but actually any place that's relatively smooth and safe from traffic will do. For what they're worth, a few thoughts on where to run:

I'd be inclined to stay away from tracks, because I find a quarter-mile track one of the world's dreariest places. The chief problem is the treadmill effect. To run a mile you've got to pass the same point four times, and this makes even a short run seem endless.

It's more fun to run in parks or on country roads. Not far from my house is a pretty little park with broad grassy areas, a stream and a pond, two gazebos, and a year-

Review by Caroline Bates, "Specialités de la Maison—California," *Gourmet,* January 1985, 32.

From *The Complete Book of Running* by James F. Fixx. Copyright © 1977 by James F. Fixx. Reprinted by permission of Random House, Inc.

round flock of Canada geese. If I'm just coasting, it takes me about eight minutes to run around the circumference; I call it a mile. I never run for long in the park—the treadmill effect again—but occasionally I'll do a couple of turns there for variety's sake.

Or I go out on the roads, heading either north into hills and undeveloped country or south toward Long Island Sound with its shoreline of woods and beaches. It depends on what I feel like looking at. If you're not fully familiar with the roads and trails in your area, a U.S. Geological Survey map will help.

You'll find that every course has its own peculiar character. Not far from my house is a mile-long stretch of pavement—it's called Laddins Rock Road—that does to me what the poppy field did to the Cowardly Lion. Every time I run there I feel sluggish, but as soon as I'm through it I feel fine again. There's another stretch of road that always makes me feel good. Even though part of it is uphill, I can count on feeling fine there. I can't explain either case.

What about simply staying at home and running in place? If for some reason that's what you want to do, fine. So long as you make your heart beat fast enough . . . you'll be getting a measurable training effect whether or not you go anywhere while you're doing it. But you'll be missing most of the fun of running—the variations of scenery and seasons, the sun and wind, the pleasure of running with friends. You may find running in place an ideal form of exercise, but you couldn't pay me to do it.

Illustration or Exemplification

When you provide examples to achieve your purpose, you are *illustrating* or *exemplifying*. This is perhaps the most common method or strategy used in developing writing. Whether you are arguing a point to change a reader's mind or explaining information, examples support your generalizations and add concreteness to your writing. Illustration is often used in concert with other strategies of development, but on occasion an entire piece may be developed by an extended example. For further discussion of this strategy, see Chapter 9.

Comparison and Contrast

Another method of development is to compare two or more ideas, events, concepts, or items. Comparisons usually focus on similarities as well as differences while contrasts may focus strictly on the differences. A comparison may help your readers understand something by comparing it with something familiar to them. You may demonstrate that two or more things, which are seemingly different, are in reality quite similar. Or you might want to show that things thought to be the same are really very different. Finally, you might want to argue that though two things are similar, one is clearly preferable to the other.

Ways of organizing the development of a comparison include the point-by-point approach and the subject-by-subject approach. (See Chapter 9, p. 318, for discussion and illustration of these two approaches.) Before deciding which pattern you will use in a paper or on an examination essay, you will need to consider what you want to emphasize in your comparison and what effect you want to have on your reader. On occasion, a writer takes neither approach in a comparison and discusses only one item or subject, counting on the reader to know the comparable points about the other. Notice the way the writer of the following paragraph concentrates on only one side of his comparison and assumes that the reader knows the characteristics of the other:

> Roger Davidson, one candidate for student government president, has demonstrated in his previous administrative roles a tendency to reign like the Wizard of Oz. His style is autocratic, as he demonstrated when he introduced numerous resolutions without consulting his constituency. When challenged, he relied upon intimidation. It's high time student voters took a peek behind the curtain to discover the real Roger Davidson.

Classification

Classification is a method of organizing material into categories. Advertisements in your daily newspaper are classified, for example, by *Items For Sale, Help Wanted, Services, Houses for Sale or Rent,* and so forth. This method of organizing makes reading the ads much simpler and faster than it would be if the items were arranged simply in, say, alphabetical order. Similarly, when you break down your discussion according to categories or classifications, you are helping your reader *see* and understand the relationships between your individual points rather than as a mass of separate items. While writers may use classification as a method to develop an entire report or essay, more often than not classification is found in connection with other methods, such as comparison and contrast and definition.

Breaking a subject down into classes reflects the way our minds work; we classify our friends, restaurants we have been to, instructors we have had, and so on. When you do this in your writing, you are helping your readers understand information or your view of the topic in a manner similar to the way the human mind works. Your job in developing through classifying is (1) to define your subject and to delineate your categories, each of which shares something in common, and (2) to provide details about and examples of each category. Your categories should not overlap; that is, no item should be able to fit into more than one category, and your categories should cover your entire subject. See Chapter 4 for exercises in classifying.

Definition

In much of the writing you do it may be necessary to tell your reader the meanings of terms or concepts. Often a definition is simply a phrase or a sentence:

"The Vapors," Victorian women's classic sickness, was more social than medical.

A terrine, a dish of meat or fish cooked in earthenware, is a poor relation of the pâté.

On other occasions a definition of a more complex term or concept may require a paragraph or more:

> Group dynamics examines how people behave in group situations and aims at understanding the factors that make a group effective. It focuses on different leadership styles and how leaders influence others. In addition, it looks at how decisions are made within a group and at what are considered appropriate and inappropriate behaviors in a group. Finally, it is concerned with patterns of communication within a group as well as factors such as cohesiveness and openness. Research done in this field of inquiry can provide useful information to people functioning in groups in all kinds of settings.

Your purpose in writing and your audience will always determine the length and complexity of the definitions you compose.

Extended definitions are essentially essays that allow a writer to explain his or her view of a complex subject. Such an essay may include a standard or generally agreed upon definition and then go far beyond that to elaborate and illustrate a new form of reference, a new way of looking at or making sense of a subject. In elaborating on the subject, writers may select a variety of other methods of development: they may compare or contrast one meaning with others, they may define the term or concept and show what the subclasses are, they may give examples, they may deal with the subject as a process and take the reader through the steps of that process. Extended definitions often take advantage of a variety of strategies. Notice the variety of methods in the following paragraphs:

Career Education and Vocational Education: Points of Clarification

Curtis R. Finch and N. Alan Sheppard

> As can be seen, career education has been implicitly defined in many ways. To some, it has been only a new term for vocational education, and to others it has described all of education. For many it has meant a new emphasis on existing programs, while some have seen it as completely new programs or courses to be added on or to replace traditional content. Of course, others view it as synonymous with vocational education; however, this is not the case. Although vocational education is a necessary component of career education, career education is not vocational education. All vocational education is a part of career education; however, career education goes beyond vocational education, since it links learning activities with jobs along the entire range of skills—from the subtechnical to the professional career (requiring a baccalaureate

degree). In addition, career education emphasizes self-awareness, career awareness, and decision-making skills to improve individual choices concerning work and education or training.

Career education then is more than vocational education. A key difference is between preparing for a single job or occupation and a concern for how education affects the sum total of one's lifework. The concern of career education is more than that of developing mere economic producers. Rather, its focus is on people who are workers as well as consumers, members of family groups, citizens of the community and the world, and individuals striving to fulfill the best that is in them or becoming all that they are capable of becoming.

Career education, then, is rather inclusive in that it encompasses all of vocational education and much of general education, plus career exploration, career selection, career entry, and career progression. By way of contrast, vocational education has a unique but more limited mission of skill development or specific occupational preparation.

At the same time, career education is not synonymous with all of education. Career education involves that portion of the educational process which relates to the preparation for work and/or that which relates to career development. Education, on the other hand, relates to all of the roles, settings, and events of a person's life. Career education is not seen as synonymous in meaning with education. Education is more concerned with the cultivation of those artistic and moral sensibilities and qualities of intellect that mean success in living in the larger context. This includes transmission of diverse cultural heritages and full participation of individuals in their society as consumers, members of family groups, and citizens of the community and the world.

For additional examples of extended definitions, see Phyllis Schlafly's "Understanding the Difference" (Chapter 3, p. 74), John Molloy's "The Success Suit" (Chapter 4, p. 113), and William Kaufman's "Some Emotional Uses of Money" (Chapter 7, p. 219).

Keeping your purpose and your audience in mind can help you decide which methods of development, or strategies, and which patterns within those strategies are the most appropriate for your project. As we have seen, much effective writing does not follow a formula but blends one strategy with another or modifies a strategy or a pattern in light of purpose and audience. Following a particular method of development or pattern throughout an essay can be extremely useful in an exam when your time for writing is limited. See Chapter 9 for using formulas and patterns in composing examination essays. For help on how to utilize these methods of development and patterns as prewriting techniques, see Chapter 4.

Part II

PRACTICING THE PROCESS OF WRITING

In Part II of this text, you will have the opportunity to practice the writing process, learn to use it efficiently, and adapt it to different writing tasks. Each chapter emphasizes a particular dimension of the process and describes strategies you can use to manage it more effectively. The chapters invite you to consider particular themes and to write expressively on your own experiences and your responses to the readings before you begin the major writing tasks. These expressive writings prepare you to write final drafts that are true to your own experience and values and reflective of what you believe.

CHAPTER 3

Using Personal Experience

THEME _Male and Female in the 1980s_

SKILL FOCUS _Considering Audience and Purpose_

As you discovered in Chapter 1, audience is a critical factor when we use humor. We want to select the appropriate piece of humor to help us achieve our purpose with a particular person or group. Likewise, knowing the audience for our writing helps us make decisions about content, style, and tone. Similarly, defining the purpose of our writing at once restricts and simplifies our writing task. These two considerations provide us with basic limitations within which to begin writing, help keep us on track as we write, and give us a framework for reviewing what we have written.

The theme in this chapter, "Male and Female in the 1980s," asks you to think about the ways in which men and women view themselves in our society and how they are viewed by others. How do individuals as children develop a sense of their maleness or femaleness? How does the culture establish different expectations for males and females? What part does the media play in establishing these expectations? Has the women's movement had the impact its members have hoped for? What are some stories of male or female discrimination, in your own experience, and how have those experiences shaped the image you have of yourself, your goals and hopes? Reading, reflecting on, and responding to the issues in this chapter will help you understand yourself as male or female, will help you clarify your thinking about others, and will give you practice in expressing yourself for a variety of purposes and to a variety of audiences.

The final project of this chapter includes four different but related composition tasks: you will write about a personal experience and you will compose a friendly letter, a personal but formal self-report, and a persuasive response to a speaker.

Before Reading

In a journal entry *not* to be shared, explore your expectations for your future. What do you expect you will be doing 10 years from now? Consider your career and your personal goals: marriage or not, family or not, leisure activities, role in the community, and so on. Or, if you have been married or have already pursued a career for some time, reflect on your earlier expectations and how realistic or unrealistic they were.

Ellen Goodman, a popular syndicated columnist, reports on a 1983 survey of 8,000 students, male and female, of eastern colleges whose high expectations seem remarkable alike. As you read her column, consider Goodman's questions about the practicality of such high expectations for life.

The "Unrealistic" Certainty of the Young May Offer Hope

Ellen Goodman

BOSTON—Diana Zuckerman doesn't look at her recent computer printout sheets with the entirely objective eye of a research psychologist. Something has emerged out of the Seven College Study she's directing at Radcliffe that is unexpected and intriguing.

The figures she lays out on her desk suggest that the women and men at these elite Eastern schools are beginning to express almost identical hopes, values, expectations and life plans.

The career plans of women look almost exactly like those of men. Law, medicine, business and communications attract the sexes equally. Only 10 of the 8,000 women studied at what used to be called the Seven Sister Colleges—Barnard, Bryn Mawr, Mt.

Holyoke, Radcliffe, Smith, Vassar and Wellesley—chose homemaking as her future career.

The personal goals of men, in turn, look a great deal like those of the women. About a third of the 1,000 men at the two fully coed schools in this study—Harvard and Vassar—said they would prefer to stay home or work part-time with their pre-school children. The sexes ranked both "time to spend with spouse" and "career" as high priorities.

There in her figures, among the duly designated "best and brightest," are both men and women with great expectations. Men and women who plan to be tops in their field without sacrificing their personal, family lives. Men and women who expect to have it all.

In many ways, the goals they set reflect the women's movement ideal. Yet, looking at those life plans and thinking about the world as it is, Ms. Zuckerman can't help expressing a reservation: "Maybe they are unrealistic."

Such a thought is not unique to this woman or this study or this Cambridge campus.

Last week in Atlanta, a faculty member at Emory University talked to me about her women students. The younger generation doesn't foresee any special problem getting ahead because they are women, she said. Nor do they predict any trouble balancing family and career. Their certainty, their calm, seem to her, well, unrealistic.

In Florida last month, another woman satirized the expectations of a favorite niece from that generation: corporate officer by 29, full-time mother from 30 to 35 and back on the track to vice president. No problem, smiled this doubtful woman, whose own life was a testimony to the troubles of getting derailed. "They're so unrealistic," she sighed in frustration.

It is no coincidence that all of my reality-testers are in mid-life, people in their 30s and 40s who have done time in the real world. Their concerns for the young people they know are genuine, yet colored by their own experiences and compromises.

They worry whether men and women are going out into the world as unprepared for its pitfalls as pre-schoolers crossing a highway. They worry whether they, as the older generation, are doing enough to point out the dangers—over here is sex discrimination, over there are inflexible working conditions—so the young won't get wiped out by the first truck.

On the other hand, some wonder whether this ignorance is an asset. Perhaps it's only the unrealistic young who accomplish great things, even great changes.

Diana Zuckerman looks at her findings and asks herself, "Are the students out of their minds and, therefore, must be helped to be realistic? Or is being so sure of their goals going to give them the boost they need to make it happen?"

It's a series of questions that seem familiar to most of us. Surely parents ask it about their children. The young musicians, artists, reformers at home tell us of their dreams and we face a conflict. We want to encourage and protect them.

Should we tell them the odds against making a pro basketball team, warn them about the annual income of a ballerina, teach them about the struggle of a political life? Will we have made them safe or just killed their dreams? Are we wiser than the young or just wearier?

There is probably some good reason why younger people reject the cautions of their elders. Ms. Zuckerman, who is only 32, notes that, "The younger women who are really sure of their goals say that what was true for me and my generation is not true for them. They are saying that we just don't know."

Maybe the great expectations of these young men and women will breed disappointment. But maybe they'll fuel change. How many of us, after all, are leading lives that were once terribly, terribly unrealistic?

After Reading

Respond in your journal to the following:

1. Is it unrealistic for young men and women to imagine that they can "have it all"? Is it more unrealistic for women than men?
2. To what extent have your own expectations been shaped by your parents, other family members, others older than you?
3. Who is Ellen Goodman's audience generally? What does the columnist hope her audience will do or think?

Before Reading

In your journal, do a focused free writing (i.e., writing whatever comes to mind)* on what aging means to you. Write two or three pages without pausing to think what you are going to say next. You may want to consider the following questions:

1. At what point do you think you may not welcome getting older?
2. To what extent do you think people's attitudes toward you may change as you age?
3. If you could choose an age to be forever, which would you choose? Why?
4. What rewards and what problems do you associate with getting older?

In the following article, which first appeared in 1972, Susan Sontag invites her audience to think about how the "ordeal" of aging affects women more than men, why it does so, and what women can do about it.

As you read, keep the following questions in mind and jot down some responses to them in your journal.

1. Why, according to Sontag, do men not panic about aging as women seem to?
2. The author claims that women are "brought up to be never fully adult," that only one standard of female beauty exists: the *girl*. To what extent are these claims still true today? Has contemporary society begun to discover beauty in older women as it does in older men? What part has the media played in shaping your perceptions of beauty and age?
3. How does Sontag contrast the way men and women regard their physical appearances? In your experience and from what you see around you, are the author's comments still valid?
4. According to the author, why do men prefer that women be "docile," "not fully grown up," "childish, immature, weak"?
5. Though Sontag reproaches males for their need to see women as childlike, dependent, and irresponsible, she also assigns blame to women for letting

---

*Free writing and focused free writing are discussed at length in Chapter 4.

themselves fall into the trap. What advice does she offer to women as an option? How many women do you know or see today who are acting on her advice? What are their lives like?

The Double Standard of Aging

Susan Sontag

"How old are you?" The person asking the question is anybody. The respondent is a woman, a woman "of a certain age," as the French say discreetly. That age might be anywhere from her early twenties to her late fifties. If the question is impersonal— routine information requested when she applies for a driver's license, a credit card, a passport—she will probably force herself to answer truthfully. Filling out a marriage license application, if her future husband is even slightly her junior, she may long to subtract a few years; probably she won't. Competing for a job, her chances often partly depend on being the "right age," and if hers isn't right, she will lie if she thinks she can get away with it. Making her first visit to a new doctor, perhaps feeling particularly vulnerable at the moment she's asked, she will probably hurry through the correct answer. But if the question is only what people call personal—if she's asked by a new friend, a casual acquaintance, a neighbor's child, a coworker in an office, store, factory—her response is harder to predict. She may side-step the question with a joke or refuse it with playful indignation. "Don't you know you're not supposed to ask a woman her age?" Or, hesitating a moment, embarrassed but defiant, she may tell the truth. Or she may lie. But neither truth, evasion, nor lie relieves the unpleasantness of that question. For a woman to be obliged to state her age, after "a certain age," is always a miniature ordeal.

If the question comes from a woman, she will feel less threatened than if it comes from a man. Other women are, after all, comrades in sharing the same potential for humiliation. She will be less arch, less coy. But she probably still dislikes answering and may not tell the truth. Bureaucratic formalities excepted, whoever asks a woman this question—after "a certain age"—is ignoring a taboo and possibly being impolite or downright hostile. Almost everyone acknowledges that once she passes an age that is, actually, quite young, a woman's exact age ceases to be a legitimate target of curiosity. After childhood the year of a woman's birth becomes her secret, her private property. It is something of a dirty secret. To answer truthfully is always indiscreet.

The discomfort a woman feels each time she tells her age is quite independent of the anxious awareness of human mortality that everyone has, from time to time. There is a normal sense in which nobody, men and women alike, relishes growing older. After thirty-five any mention of one's age carries with it the reminder that one is probably closer to the end of one's life than to the beginning. There is nothing unreasonable in that anxiety. Nor is there any abnormality in the anguish and anger that people who are really old, in their seventies and eighties, feel about the implacable waning of their powers, physical and mental. Advanced age is undeniably a trial, however stoically it may be endured. It is a shipwreck, no matter with what courage elderly people insist on continuing the voyage. But the objective, sacred pain of old age is of another order than the subjective, profane pain of aging. Old age is a genuine ordeal, one that men and women undergo in a similar way. Growing older is mainly an ordeal of the imagination—a moral disease, a social pathology—intrinsic to which is the fact that it afflicts women much more than men. It is particularly women who experience growing older (everything that comes *before* one is actually old) with such distaste and even shame.

The emotional privileges this society confers upon youth stir up some anxiety about getting older in everybody. All modern urbanized societies—unlike tribal, rural societies—condescend to the values of maturity and heap honors on the joys of youth. This revaluation of the life cycle in favor of the young brilliantly serves a secular society whose idols are ever-increasing industrial productivity and the unlimited cannibalization of nature. Such a society must create a new sense of the rhythms of life in order to incite people to buy more, to consume and throw away faster. People let the direct awareness they have of their needs, of what really gives them pleasure, be overruled by commercialized *images* of happiness and personal well-being; and, in this imagery designed to stimulate ever more avid levels of consumption, the most popular metaphor for happiness is "youth." (I would insist that it is a metaphor, not a literal description. Youth is a metaphor for energy, restless mobility, appetite: for the state of "wanting.") This equating of well-being with youth makes everyone naggingly aware of exact age—one's own and that of other people. In primitive and premodern societies people attach much less importance to dates. When lives are divided into long periods with stable responsibilities and steady ideals (and hypocrisies), the exact number of years someone has lived becomes a trivial fact; there is hardly any reason to mention, even to know, the year in which one was born. Most people in nonindustrial societies are not sure exactly how old they are. People in industrial societies are haunted by numbers. They take an almost obsessional interest in keeping the score card of aging, convinced that anything above a low total is some kind of bad news. In an era in which people actually live longer and longer, what now amounts to the latter *two-thirds* of everyone's life is shadowed by a poignant apprehension of unremitting loss.

The prestige of youth afflicts everyone in this society to some degree. Men, too, are prone to periodic bouts of depression about aging—for instance, when feeling insecure or unfulfilled or insufficiently rewarded in their jobs. But men rarely panic about aging in the way women often do. Getting older is less profoundly wounding for a man, for in addition to the propaganda for youth that puts both men and women on the defensive as they age, there is a double standard about aging that denounces women with special severity: Society is much more permissive about aging in men, as it is more tolerant of the sexual infidelities of husbands. Men are "allowed" to age, without penalty, in several ways that women are not. . . .

Middle-class men feel diminished by aging, even while still young, if they have not yet shown distinction in their careers or made a lot of money. (And any tendencies they have toward hypochondria will get worse in middle age, focusing with particular nervousness on the specter of heart attacks and the loss of virility.) Their aging crisis is linked to that terrible pressure on men to be "successful" that precisely defines their membership in the middle class. Women rarely feel anxious about their age because they haven't succeeded at something. The work that women do outside the home rarely counts as a form of achievement, only as a way of earning money; most employment available to women mainly exploits the training they have been receiving since early childhood to be servile, to be both supportive and parasitical, to be unadventurous. They can have menial, low-skilled jobs in light industries, which offer as feeble a criterion of success as housekeeping. They can be secretaries, clerks, sales personnel, maids, research assistants, waitresses, social workers, prostitutes, nurses, teachers, telephone operators—public transcriptions of the servicing and nurturing roles that women have in family life. Women fill very few executive posts, are rarely found suitable for large corporate or political responsibilities, and form only a tiny contingent in the liberal professions (apart from teaching). They are virtually barred from jobs that involve an expert, intimate relation with machines or an aggressive use of the body, or that carry any physical risk or sense of adventure. The jobs this society deems appropriate to women are auxiliary, "calm" activities that do not compete with, but aid, what men do. Besides being less well paid, most work women do has a lower ceiling of advancement and gives meager outlet to normal wishes to be powerful. All outstanding work by women in this society is voluntary; most women are too inhibited by the social disapproval attached to their being ambitious and aggressive. Inevitably, women are exempted from the dreary panic of middle-aged men whose "achievements" seem paltry, who feel stuck on the job ladder or fear being pushed off it by someone younger. But they are also denied most of the real satisfactions that men derive from work—satisfactions that often do increase with age.

The double standard about aging shows up most brutally in the conventions of sexual feeling, which presuppose a disparity between men and women that operates permanently to women's disadvantage. In the accepted course of events a woman anywhere from her late teens through her middle twenties can expect to attract a man more or less her own age. (Ideally, he should be at least slightly older.) They marry and raise a family. But if her husband starts an affair after some years of marriage, he customarily does so with a woman much younger than his wife. Suppose, when both husband and wife are already in their late forties or early fifties, they divorce. The husband has an excellent chance of getting married again, probably to a younger woman. His ex-wife finds it difficult to remarry. Attracting a second husband younger than herself is improbable; even to find someone her own age she has to be lucky, and she will probably have to settle for a man considerably older than herself, in his sixties or seventies. Women become sexually ineligible much earlier than men do. A man, even an ugly man, can remain eligible well into old age. He is an acceptable mate for a young, attractive woman. Women, even good-looking women, become ineligible (except as partners of very old men) at a much younger age.

Thus, for most women, aging means a humiliating process of gradual sexual disqualification. Since women are considered maximally eligible in early youth, after which their sexual value drops steadily, even young women feel themselves in a desperate race against the calendar. They are old as soon as they are no longer very young. In late adolescense some girls are already worrying about getting married. Boys and young men have little reason to anticipate trouble because of aging. What makes men desirable to women is by no means tied to youth. On the contrary, getting older tends (for several decades) to operate in men's favor, since their value as lovers and husbands is set more by what they do than how they look. Many men have more success romantically at forty than they did at twenty or twenty-five; fame, money, and above all, power are sexually enhancing. (A woman who has won power in a competitive profession or business career is considered less, rather than more, desirable. Most men confess themselves intimidated or turned off sexually by such a woman, obviously because she is harder to treat as just a sexual "object.") As they age, men may start feeling anxious about actual sexual performance, worrying about a loss of sexual vigor or even impotence, but their sexual eligibility is not abridged simply by getting older. Men stay sexually possible as long as they can make love. Women are at a disadvantage because their sexual candidacy depends on meeting certain much stricter "conditions" related to looks and age. . . .

Poor people look old much earlier in their lives than do rich people. But anxiety about aging is certainly more common, and more acute, among middle-class and rich women than among working-class women. Economically disadvantaged women in this society are more fatalistic about aging; they can't afford to fight the cosmetic battle as long or as tenaciously. Indeed, nothing so clearly indicates the fictional nature of this crisis than the fact that women who keep their youthful appearance the longest—women who lead unstrenuous, physically sheltered lives, who eat balanced meals, who can afford good medical care, who have few or no children—are those who feel the defeat of age most keenly. Aging is much more a social judgment than a biological eventuality. Far more extensive than the hard sense of loss suffered during menopause (which, with increased longevity, tends to arrive later and later) is the depression about aging, which may not be set off by any real event in a woman's life, but is a recurrent state of "possession" of her imagination, ordained by society—that is, ordained by the way this society limits how women feel free to imagine themselves. . . .

Aging is a movable doom. It is a crisis that never exhausts itself, because the anxiety is never really used up. Being a crisis of the imagination rather than of "real life," it has the habit of repeating itself again and again. The territory of aging (as opposed to actual old age) has no fixed boundaries. Up to a point it can be defined as one wants. Entering each decade—after the initial shock is absorbed—an endearing, desperate impulse of survival helps many women to stretch the boundaries to the decade following. In late adolescence thirty seems the end of life. At thirty, one pushes the sentence forward to forty. At forty, one still gives oneself ten more years.

I remember my closest friend in college sobbing on the day she turned twenty-one. "The best part of my life is over. I'm not young any more." She was a senior, nearing graduation. I was a precocious freshman, just sixteen. Mystified, I tried lamely to comfort her, saying that I didn't think twenty-one was *so* old. Actually, I didn't understand at all what could be demoralizing about turning twenty-one. To me, it meant only something good: being in charge of oneself, being free. At sixteen, I was too young to have noticed, and become confused by, the peculiarly loose, ambivalent way in which this society demands that one stop thinking of oneself as a girl and start thinking of oneself as a woman. (In America that demand can now be put off to the age of thirty, even beyond.) But even if I thought her distress was absurd, I must have been aware that it would not simply be absurd but quite unthinkable in a *boy* turning twenty-one. Only women worry about age with that degree of inanity and pathos. And, of course, as with all crises that are inauthentic and therefore repeat themselves compulsively (because the danger is largely fictive, a poison in the imagination), this friend of mine went on having the same crisis over and over, each time as if for the first time.

I also came to her thirtieth birthday party. A veteran of many love affairs, she had spent most of her twenties living abroad and had just returned to the United States. She had been good-looking when I first knew her; now she was beautiful. I teased her about the tears she had shed over being twenty-one. She laughed and claimed not to remember. But thirty, she said ruefully, that really is the end. Soon after, she married. My friend is now forty-four. While no longer what people call beautiful, she is striking-looking, charming, and vital. She teaches elementary school; her husband, who is twenty years older than she, is a part-time merchant seaman. They have one child, now nine years old. Sometimes, when her husband is away, she takes a lover. She told me recently that forty was the most upsetting birthday of all (I wasn't at that one), and although she has only a few years left, she means to enjoy them while they last. She has become one of those women who seize every excuse offered in any conversation for mentioning how old they really are, in a spirit of bravado compounded with self-pity that is not too different from the mood of women who regularly lie about their age. But she is actually fretting much less about aging than she was two decades ago. Having a child, and having one rather late, past the age of thirty, has certainly helped to reconcile her to her age. At fifty, I suspect, she will be ever more valiantly postponing the age of resignation.

My friend is one of the more fortunate, sturdier casualties of the aging crisis. Most women are not as spirited, nor as innocently comic in their suffering. But almost all women endure some version of this suffering: A recurrent seizure of the imagination that usually begins quite young, in which they project themselves into a calculation of loss. The rules of this society are cruel to women. Brought up to be never fully adult, women are deemed obsolete earlier than men. In fact, most women don't become relatively free and expressive sexually until their thirties. (Women mature sexually this late, certainly much later than men, not for innate biological reasons but because this culture retards women. Denied most outlets for sexual energy permitted to men, it takes many women *that* long to wear out some of their inhibitions.) The time at which they start being disqualified as sexually attractive persons is just when they have grown up sexually. The double standard about aging cheats women of those years, between thirty-five and fifty, likely to be the best of their sexual life.

That women expect to be flattered often by men, and the extent to which their self-confidence depends on this flattery, reflects how deeply women are psychologically weakened by this double standard. Added on to the pressure felt by everybody in this society to look young as long as possible are the values of "femininity," which specifically identify sexual attractiveness in women with youth. The desire to be the "right age" has a special urgency for a woman it never has for a man. A much greater part of her self-esteem and pleasure in life is threatened when she ceases to be young. Most men experience getting older with regret, apprehension. But most women experience it even more painfully: with shame. Aging is a man's destiny, something that must happen because he is a human being. For a woman, aging is not only her destiny. Because she is that more *narrowly* defined kind of human being, a woman, it is also her vulnerability.

To be a woman is to be an actress. Being feminine is a kind of theater, with its appropriate costumes, *décor,* lighting, and stylized gestures. From early childhood on, girls are trained to care in a pathologically exaggerated way about their appearance and are profoundly mutilated (to the extent of being unfitted for first-class adulthood) by the extent of the stress put on presenting themselves as physically attractive objects. Women look in the mirror more frequently than men do. It is, virtually, their duty to look at themselves—to look often. Indeed, a woman who is not narcissistic is considered unfeminine. And a woman who spends literally *most* of her time caring for, and making purchases to flatter, her physical appearance is not regarded in this society as what she is: a kind of moral idiot. She is thought to be quite normal and is envied by other women whose time is mostly used up at jobs or caring for large families. The display of narcissism goes on all the time. It is expected that women will disappear several times in an evening—at a restaurant, at a party, during a theater intermission, in the course of a social visit—simply to check their appearance, to see that nothing has gone wrong with their make-up and hairstyling, to make sure that their clothes are not spotted or too wrinkled or not hanging properly. It is even acceptable to perform this activity in public. At the table in a restaurant, over coffee, a woman opens a compact mirror and touches up her make-up and hair without embarrassment in front of her husband or her friends.

All this behavior, which is written off as normal "vanity" in women, would seem ludicrous in a man. Women are more vain than men because of the relentless pressure on women to maintain their appearance at a certain high standard. What makes the pressure even more burdensome is that there are actually several standards. Men present themselves as face-and-body, a physical whole. Women are split, as men are not, into a body and a face—each judged by somewhat different standards. What is important for a face is that it be beautiful. What is important for a body is two things, which may even be (depending of fashion and taste) somewhat incompatible: first, that it be desirable and, second, that it be beautiful. Men usually feel sexually attracted to women much more because of their bodies than their faces. The traits that arouse desire—such as fleshiness—don't always match those that fashion decrees as beautiful. (For instance, the ideal woman's body promoted in advertising in recent years is extremely thin: the kind of body that looks more desirable clothed than naked.) But women's concern with their appearance is not simply geared to arousing desire in men. It also aims at fabricating a certain image by which, as a more indirect way of arousing desire, women state their value. A woman's value lies in the way she *represents* herself, which is much more by her face than her body. In defiance of the laws of simple sexual attraction, women do not devote most of their attention to their bodies. The well-known "normal" narcissism that women display—the amount of time they spend before the mirror—is used primarily in caring for the face and hair.

Women do not simply have faces, as men do; they are identified with their faces. Men have a naturalistic relation to their faces. Certainly they care whether they are good-looking or not. They suffer over acne, protruding ears, tiny eyes; they hate getting bald. But there is a much wider latitude in what is esthetically acceptable in a man's face than what is in a woman's. A man's face is defined as something he basically doesn't need to tamper with; all he has to do is keep it clean. He can avail himself of the options for ornament supplied by nature: a beard, a mustache, longer or shorter hair. But he is not supposed to disguise himself. What he is "really" like is supposed to show. A man lives through his face; it records the progressive stages of his life. And since he doesn't tamper with his face, it is not separate from but is completed by his body—which is judged attractive by the impression it gives of virility and energy. By contrast, a woman's face is potentially separate from her body. She does not treat it naturalistically. A woman's face is the canvas upon which she paints a revised, corrected portrait of herself. One of the rules of this creation is that the face *not* show what she doesn't want it to show. Her face is an emblem, an icon, a flag. How she arranges her hair, the type of make-up she uses, the quality of her complexion—all these are signs, not of what she is "really" like, but of how she asks to be treated by others, especially men. They establish her status as an "object."

For the normal changes that age inscribes on every human face, women are much more heavily penalized than men. Even in early adolscence, girls are cautioned to protect their faces against wear and tear. Mothers tell their daughters (but never their sons): You look ugly when you cry. Stop worrying. Don't read too much. Crying, frowning, squinting, even laughing—all these human activities make "lines." The same usage of the face in men is judged quite positively. In a man's face lines are taken to be signs of "character." They indicate emotional strength, maturity—qualities far more esteemed in men than in women. (They show he has "lived.") Even scars are often not felt to be unattractive; they too can add "character" to a man's face. But lines of aging, any scar, even a small birthmark on a woman's face, are always regarded as unfortunate blemishes. In effect, people take character in men to be different from what constitutes character in women. A woman's character is thought to be innate, static—not the product of her experience, her years, her actions. A woman's face is prized so far as it remains unchanged by (or conceals the traces of) her emotions, her physical risk-taking. Ideally, it is supposed to be a mask—immutable, unmarked. The model woman's face is Garbo's. Because women are identified with their faces much more than men are, and the ideal woman's face is one that is "perfect," it seems a calamity when a woman has a disfiguring accident. A broken nose or a scar or a burn mark, no more than regrettable for a man, is a terrible psychological wound to a woman; objectively, it diminishes her value. (As is well known, most clients for plastic surgery are women.) . . .

Women have a more intimate relation to aging than men do, simply because one of the accepted "women's" occupations is taking pains to keep one's face and body from showing the signs of growing older. Women's sexual validity depends, up to a certain point, on how well they stand off these natural changes. After late adolescence women become the caretakers of their bodies and faces, pursuing an essentially defensive strategy, a holding operation. A vast array of products in jars and tubes, a branch of surgery, and armies of hairdressers, masseuses, diet counselors, and other professionals exist to stave off, or mask, developments that are entirely normal biologically. Large amounts of women's energies are diverted into this passionate, corrupting effort to defeat nature: to maintain an ideal, static appearance against the progress of age. The collapse of the project is only a matter of time. Inevitably, a woman's physical appearance develops beyond its youthful form. No matter how exotic the creams or how strict the diets, one cannot indefinitely keep the face unlined, the waist slim. Bearing children takes its toll: the torso becomes thicker; the skin is stretched. There is no way to keep certain lines from appearing, in one's mid-twenties, around the eyes and mouth. From about thirty on, the skin gradually loses its tonus. In women this perfectly natural process is regarded as a humiliating defeat, while nobody finds anything remarkably unattractive in the equivalent physical changes in men. Men are "allowed" to look older without sexual penalty.

Thus, the reason that women experience aging with more pain than men is not simply that they care more than men about how they look. Men also care about their looks and want to be attractive, but since the business of men is mainly being and doing, rather than appearing, the standards for appearance are much less exacting. The standards for what is attractive in a man are permissive; they conform to what is possible or "natural" to most men throughout most of their lives. The standards for women's appearance go against nature, and to come anywhere near approximating them takes considerable effort and time. Women must try to be beautiful. At the least, they are under heavy social pressure not to be ugly. A woman's fortunes depend, far more than a man's, on being at least "acceptable" looking. Men are not subject to this pressure. Good looks in a man is a bonus, not a psychological necessity for maintaining normal self-esteem. . . .

Beauty, women's business in this society, is the theater of their enslavement. Only one standard of female beauty is sanctioned: the *girl*. The great advantage men have is that our culture allows two standards of male beauty: the *boy* and the *man*. The beauty of a boy resembles the beauty of a girl. In both sexes it is a fragile kind of beauty and flourishes naturally only in the early part of the life-cycle. Happily, men are able to accept themselves under another standard of good looks—heavier, rougher, more thickly built. A man does not grieve when he loses the smooth, unlined, hairless skin of a boy. For he has only exchanged one form of attractiveness for another: the darker skin of a man's face, roughened by daily shaving, showing the marks of emotion and the normal lines of age. There is no equivalent of this second standard for women. The single standard of beauty for women dictates that they must go on having clear skin. Every wrinkle, every line, every grey hair, is a defeat. No wonder that no boy minds becoming a man, while even the passage from girlhood to early womanhood is experienced by many women as their downfall, for all women are trained to want to continue looking like girls.

. . . Society allows no place in our imagination for a beautiful old woman who does look like an old woman—a woman who might be like Picasso at the age of ninety, being photographed outdoors on his estate in the south of France, wearing only shorts and sandals. No one imagines such a woman exists. Even the special exceptions—Mae West & Co.—are always photographed indoors, cleverly lit, from the most flattering angle and fully, artfully clothed. The implication is they would not stand a closer scrutiny. The idea of an old woman in a bathing suit being attractive, or even just acceptable looking, is inconceivable. An older woman is, by definition, sexually repulsive—unless, in fact, she doesn't look old at all. The body of an old woman, unlike that of an old man, is always understood as a body that can no longer be shown, offered, unveiled. At best, it may appear in costume. People still feel uneasy, thinking about what they might see if her mask dropped, if she took off her clothes.

Thus, the point for women of dressing up, applying make-up, dyeing their hair, going on crash diets, and getting face-lifts is not just to be attractive. They are ways of defending themselves against a profound level of disapproval directed toward women, a disapproval that can take the form of aversion. The double standard about aging converts the life of women into an inexorable march toward a condition in which they are not just unattractive, but disgusting. The profoundest terror of a woman's life is the moment represented in a statue by Rodin called *Old Age:* a naked old woman, seated, pathetically contemplates her flat, pendulous, ruined body. Aging in women is a process of becoming obscene sexually, for the flabby bosom, wrinkled neck, spotted hands, thinning white hair, waistless torso, and veined legs of an old woman are felt to be obscene. In our direst moments of the imagination, this transformation can take place with dismaying speed—as in the end of *Lost Horizon,* when the beautiful young girl is carried by her lover out of Shangri-La and, within minutes, turns into a withered, repulsive crone. There is no equivalent nightmare about men. This is why, however much a man may care about his appearance, that caring can never acquire the same desperateness it often does for women. When men dress according to fashion or now even use cosmetics, they do not expect from clothes and make-up what women do. A face-lotion or perfume or deodorant or hairspray, used by a man, is not part of a disguise. Men, as men, do not feel the need to disguise themselves to fend off morally disapproved signs of aging, to outwit premature sexual obsolescence, to cover up aging as obscenity. Men are not subject to the barely concealed revulsion expressed in this culture against the female body—except in its smooth, youthful, firm, odorless, blemish-free form.

One of the attitudes that punish women most severely is the visceral horror felt at aging female flesh. It reveals a radical fear of women installed deep in this culture, a demonology of women that has crystallized in such mythic caricatures as the vixen, the virago, the vamp, and the witch. Several centuries of witch-phobia, during which one of the cruelest extermination programs in Western history was carried out, suggest something of the extremity of this fear. That old women are repulsive is one of the most profound esthetic and erotic feelings in our culture. Women share it as much as men do. (Oppressors, as a rule, deny oppressed people their own "native" standards of beauty. And the oppressed end up being convinced that they *are* ugly.) How women are psychologically damaged by this misogynistic idea of what is beautiful parallels the way in which blacks have been deformed in a society that has up to now defined beautiful as white. Psychological tests made on young black children in the United States some years ago showed how early and how thoroughly they incorporate the white standard of good looks. Virtually all the children expressed fantasies that indicated they considered black people to be ugly, funny looking, dirty, brutish. A similar kind of self-hatred infects most women. Like men, they find old age in women "uglier" than old age in men. . . .

The convention that wives should be younger than their husbands powerfully enforces the "minority" status of women, since being senior in age always carries with it, in any relationship, a certain amount of power and authority. There are no laws on the matter, of course. The convention is obeyed because to do otherwise makes one feel as if one is doing something ugly or in bad taste. Everyone feels intuitively the esthetic rightness of a marriage in which the man is older than the woman, which means that any marriage in which the woman is older creates a dubious or less gratifying mental picture. Everyone is addicted to the visual pleasure that women give by meeting certain esthetic requirements from which men are exempted, which keeps women working at staying youthful-looking while men are left free to age. On a deeper level everyone finds the signs of old age in women esthetically offensive, which conditions one to feel automatically repelled by the prospect of an elderly woman marrying a much younger man. The situation in which women are kept minors for life is largely organized by such conformist, unreflective preferences. But taste is not free, and its judgments are never merely "natural." Rules of taste enforce structures of power. The revulsion against aging in women is the cutting edge of a whole set of oppressive structures (often masked as gallantries) that keep women in their place.

The ideal state proposed for women is docility, which means not being fully grown up. Most of what is cherished as typically "feminine" is simply behavior that is childish, immature, weak. To offer so low and demeaning a standard of fulfillment in itself constitutes oppression in an acute form—a sort of moral neo-colonialism. But women are not simply condescended to by the values that secure the dominance of men. They are repudiated. Perhaps because of having been their oppressors for so long, few men really *like* women (though they love individual women), and few men ever feel really comfortable or at ease in women's company. This malaise arises because relations between the two sexes are rife with hypocrisy, as men manage to love those they dominate and therefore don't respect. Oppressors always try to justify their privileges and brutalities by imagining that those they oppress belong to a lower order of civilization or are less than fully "human." Deprived of part of their ordinary human dignity, the oppressed take on certain "demonic" traits. The oppressions of large groups have to be anchored deep in the psyche, continually renewed by partly unconscious fears and taboos, by a sense of the obscene. Thus, women arouse not only desire and affection in men but aversion as well. Women are thoroughly domesticated familiars. But, at certain times and in certain situations, they become alien, untouchable. The aversion men feel, so much of which is covered over, is felt most frankly, with least inhibition, toward the type of woman who is most taboo "esthetically," a woman who has become—with the natural changes brought about by aging—obscene.

Nothing more clearly demonstrates the vulnerability of women than the special pain, confusion, and bad faith with which they experience getting older. And in the struggle that some women are waging on behalf of all women to be treated (and treat themselves) as full human beings—not "only" as women—one of the earliest results to be hoped for is that women become aware, indignantly aware, of the double standard about aging from which they suffer so harshly.

It is understandable that women often succumb to the temptation to lie about their age. Given society's double standard, to question a woman about her age is indeed often an aggressive act, a trap. Lying is an elementary means of self-defense, a way of scrambling out of the trap, at least temporarily. To expect a woman, after "a certain age," to tell exactly how old she is—when she has a chance, either through the generosity of nature or the cleverness of art, to pass for being somewhat younger than she actually is—is like expecting a landowner to admit that the estate he has put up for sale is actually worth less than the buyer is prepared to pay. The double standard about aging sets women up as property, as objects whose value depreciates rapidly with the march of the calendar.

The prejudices that mount against women as they grow older are an important arm of male privilege. It is the present unequal distribution of adult roles between the two sexes that gives men a freedom to age denied to women. Men actively administer the double standard about aging because the "masculine" role awards them the initiative in courtship. Men choose; women are chosen. So men choose younger women. But although this system of inequality is operated by men, it could not work if women themselves did not acquiesce in it. Women reinforce it powerfully with their complacency, with their anguish, with their lies.

Not only do women lie more than men do about their age but men forgive them for it, thereby confirming their own superiority. A man who lies about his age is thought to be weak, "unmanly." A woman who lies about her age is behaving in a quite acceptable, "feminine" way. Petty lying is viewed by men with indulgence, one of a number of patronizing allowances made for women. It has the same moral unimportance as the fact that women are often late for appointments. Women are not expected to be truthful, or punctual, or expert in handling and repairing machines, or frugal, or physically brave. They are expected to be second-class adults, whose natural state is that of a grateful dependence on men. And so they often are, since that is what they are brought up to be. So far as women heed the stereotypes of "feminine" behavior, they *cannot* behave as fully responsible, independent adults.

Most women share the contempt for women expressed in the double standard about aging—to such a degree that they take their lack of self-respect for granted. Women have been accustomed so long to the protection of their masks, their smiles, their endearing lies. Without this protection, they know, they would be more vulnerable. But in protecting themselves as women, they betray themselves as adults. The model corruption in a woman's life is denying her age. She symbolically accedes to all those myths that furnish women with their imprisoning securities and privileges, that create their genuine oppression, that inspire their real discontent. Each time a woman lies about her age she becomes an accomplice in her own underdevelopment as a human being.

Women have another option. They can aspire to be wise, not merely nice; to be competent, not merely helpful; to be strong, not merely graceful; to be ambitious for themselves, not merely for themselves in relation to men and children. They can let themselves age naturally and without embarrassment, actively protesting and disobeying the conventions that stem from this society's double standard about aging. Instead of being girls, girls as long as possible, who then age humiliatingly into middle-aged women and then obscenely into old women, they can become women much earlier—and remain active adults, enjoying the long, erotic career of which women are capable, far longer. Women should allow their faces to show the lives they have lived. Women should tell the truth.

After Reading

In your journal, write a response to this article about how it made you feel and what it made you think. Were you shocked, angry, sympathetic, disgusted, overjoyed, smug, guilty? Just try to record your feelings about Sontag's ideas and her expression of them. Try to include, too, what the article made you think. Did you think of yourself? Your friends? Your family? And how you or these others fit the images Sontag draws of men and women? Did you think about how things have changed or should change? Or should not change?

Before Reading

Did you or any of your classmates think that, in attempting to generalize about males and females in our society and their relationships, Susan Sontag creates stereotypes? Whenever we try to generalize about humans by sex, race, religion, or nationality, we run the risk of being accused of stereotyping. Patrick Canavan and John Haskell in the next article analyze what they see as the "great American male stereotype," its characteristics and costs. They also propose alternative behaviors.

As you read this essay, keep the following questions in mind:

1. What is the GAMS? What are the costs and benefits of pursuing GAMS?
2. What are the five elements of the GAMS and what do they result in for men?
3. Contrast the authors' terms: task-orientation and maintenance oriented.
4. How is androgyny defined in the article?
5. The authors contend that each individual has five centers. What are these centers, and how does this schema provide a way of looking at alternate behaviors?
6. What audience are Canavan and Haskell addressing? What is their purpose in writing for that audience?

The Great American Male Stereotype

Patrick Canavan and John Haskell

Stating the Case

In American society, men must deal with the conflict that is generated between the realities of their lives and the stereotype of the Great American Male—the male who is:

1. Successful in business—has a high corporate position with a great deal of responsibility, power, etc.
2. Financially productive—owns a house, has a car for himself and wife, has good clothes.

3. Sexually attractive—physically in good condition and attractive so that women other than his wife find him physically desirable.
4. Physically productive—can build things, repair cars, etc., as well as be capable of producing physically attractive offspring.
5. Knowledgeable—about the business world, the state of the economy, the political situation, and his own personal and professional goals and directions.

Few American males can say that they fit the Great American Male Stereotype (GAMS). Some say they have no interest in achieving such a goal and that to try to do so is a waste of time and energy and a denial of the constraints of reality. However, so much time, concern, and energy (consciously or unconsciously) goes into achieving GAMS that the different aspects of it and the resulting messages delivered to American males of all ages need to be analyzed and discussed.

American men need to consciously decide which elements of the GAMS they desire and why; American children need to be exposed to both the *costs* and *benefits* of pursuing GAMS. To date the cost has not been thoroughly exposed and discussed in the same way the benefits have.

The cost of pursuing GAMS can be physical disability or early death, heart disease, fatigue, heart failure, overweight, ulcers, high blood pressure, frustration, anger, hostility, alcoholism, drug dependency, cigarette smoking, few intimate relationships, failure, and few collaborative relationships.

The benefits of achieving GAMS are clearly pointed out by the advertising media: popularity, happiness, satisfaction, access to quality goods, attractive surroundings (including people), feeling of security, power, and sexual pleasure.

Behind the stereotype are achievement; competition; power; success; and conflict—each with its own relevance and role to males.

Achievement   The need for achievement is high in American males because achievement means status and acceptability. Achievement is defined by society as successful performance in the work world. Status is awarded to men who are professionally and/or financially successful. Academic achievement is considered important because it is perceived as the major path to professional and financial success.

Competition   Beating someone else is considered to be the way to obtain success. Beginning in early childhood play with neighborhood children through the work years into retirement, score cards are kept—first by the parents and, once learned, by the men themselves. The question is always "How am I doing compared with others?" The score card gets carried into school (grades), sports (best athlete), sex (how many, how often, performance), work (advancement, salary, title), home (house, cars, family), and retirement (travel, time demands). As a consequence of this competition, a sharp sense of analysis is developed. Others' strength, vulnerability, and potential are quickly assessed. The defensive nature of this process makes it extremely difficult to develop collaboration and intimate relationships.

Power and Success   The stereotype overemphasizes power and success. If a man has influence over others and decision-making powers within an organization, then he is considered to be successful. The emphasis on power and success means that a male is usually striving toward a goal somewhere in the future. Consequently, his energies are put into achieving that goal and rarely if ever into the reality of the present. The unhappiness of not being something or not achieving anything takes precedence over the reality of now. Today seems unimportant, the experience of today is denied, and the relationships and tasks of today are forgotten.

Conflict   Because of the competitive element to the male stereotype, the combative technique of problem solving is much easier for men to use than the collaborative technique. The male world is filled with conflict, but males generally do not distinguish between productive and dysfunctional conflict but use conflict as a vehicle for advancing themselves by eliminating or badly damaging the competition. The dependence on conflict as a prime method of problem solving often limits the long-term growth and development of the individual male.

The elements of GAMS—conflict, success and power, competition, and achievement—result in male behavior that values work as the number one priority in life. Only through work can the male achieve GAMS, and consequently the other elements of life (family relationship, friends, recreation, growth, and development) take second or, more frequently, lower priority.

To the male, *task orientation* is essential if he is to be successful at work, where tasks need to be defined, delegated, pursued, and accomplished in an orderly, rational manner. Additionally, task orientation is so strong that many males must deal with immediate, concrete problems and have difficulty or no ability when dealing with the intangible, more amorphous processes of such items as long-range planning, either for an organization or for their own personal and professional development.

Task orientation also requires a perceived ability to make fast, concrete, perfect, and irrevocable decisions. Any male who can do this is perceived as being extremely capable, talented, and having the potential for achieving GAMS. Because of the competitive position accepted by men, the need to be defensive of one's position and abilities is paramount, and therefore the brittleness of these processes and the individual is well hidden and rarely, if ever, is perceived by others. The "capable male" never shows how afraid or fragile he is while operating in this mode.

Task orientation of males means that men are not very conscious of or skilled at the maintenance functions of life. From childhood into the work world, men have had the maintenance functions delegated to women (mother, lover, wife, secretary). Because women have performed the maintenance functions, men have been allowed (or forced) to concentrate primarily on the task at hand. Mother helped to develop dialogue between two quarreling children or between a child and the father. The lover/wife takes on the cooking, recreation planning, or household chores, and the secretary makes coffee, sharpens pencils, or soothes feelings to make her boss's job easier.

Men are comfortable in dealing with women on a sexual level or in a maintenance role. Today's resistance to women (much of it covert) in middle and top level management positions is due to women no longer being in an easily identifiable role (sexual object or maintenance) and demanding to compete on an equal level. This demand is not easily accepted by the male in pursuit of GAMS because it moves a woman from being primarily maintenance oriented into the predominately male category of task orientation and asks that a woman be treated like a male.

The denial of past roles by women challenges men to assess their own behavior and their attitudes toward their own roles at work and at home. However, the optimal resolution of this problem is not to have women adopt male attitudes and behavior. Much is wrong with the male stereotype and little has been done to effectively explore other alternatives or to encourage experimentation. The choices seem to be as follows:

1. To adopt GAMS and become task oriented;
2. To adopt the traditional female role and become maintenance oriented;
3. To take the desirable characteristics of each role and let each person select that which suits him/her best (the androgynous option).

The latter refers to a changing definition of what is appropriate behavior for men and women at home, at work, or in their social lives. To become androgynous is to have a wide behavioral spectrum—behaviors that have been traditionally labeled as "male" as well as behaviors that have been traditionally labeled as "female."

For most men, becoming androgynous means acquiring maintenance behavior in addition to the more familiar task-oriented behavior. Thus, a man who is androgynous is able to support other men and women when support is needed, collaborate or take a secondary role when the situation warrants it, listen to and counsel subordinates and peers about personal problems—i.e., to let emotions show, to do things that support, help, and develop themselves and others. For most women, becoming androgynous means developing the task-oriented, problem-solving, and rational thinking aspects of their behavior.

Of course, these examples are based on stereotypes. To become androgynous, each of us must assess the characteristics, skills, and behaviors that he/she currently uses and ascertain where development is necessary. Androgyny as a goal requires that each of us has available those characteristics, skills, and behaviors that have been traditionally seen as male as well as those characteristics, skills, and behaviors that have been traditionally seen as female. For some men and women, this means concentrating on the development of the task-oriented side; for other men and women, this means concentrating on the development of the maintenance-oriented skills.

Historically, behavioral choices have been narrowed by our sex. It is now time to increase the choices and educate everyone in the processes of choice and selection, not in the behavior and attitudes of a specific sex role. The Women's Movement has begun this process and many men have quietly made their own decisions and choices. New individual decisions still need to be made.

Finding a Way Out

Alternative Behaviors

A simple model of being human is that each individual has five *centers*, each of which provides the person's major focus in a certain way at any given time. Each has a *place* which, if recognized and utilized as a source of important data, allows an individual to "check in" and read himself or herself.

Intellect   The mind and its consequent focus on rational thought, problem solving, and task analysis—deliberate, logical, and controlled. The intellectual center operates through the *mind* and communicates through a person's thoughts. The other centers can and do interface with the flow of this "computer" (e.g., strong feelings), but the intent of the mind is to process information, subjective as well as objective, without distortion.

Emotions   Feelings and the emphasis on comfort or discomfort with ourselves, others, and our situations—spontaneous, irrational, autonomous, and uncontrollable. A person's emotional center operates through the central nervous system, the "gut," and the heart. The direct emotional flow of person with environment is influenced by past learnings and norms (typified by children who respond directly and overtly to fear, concern, excitement, and joy).

Physical Body energies and the focus on pleasurable and painful sensations. Our physical center "speaks" to us through the flow of blood, breathing, and the muscular system and skeleton. Illness and good health are the sensed opposites in this center.

Sexual Our genital responses and the awareness of tension and release—powerful, private, and highly socialized. Our sexual center "speaks" to us through our genitals and erogenous areas. Sexual fantasy, a product of the intellectual center, is an example of how this center can be influenced.

Spiritual Growing and transcending, with its emphasis on aliveness and stasis, ephemeral, transpersonal, and holy. The spiritual center is experienced through an awareness that we are no longer simply "I" and separate, bounded by time and the immediate. The spiritual center, when primary in our lives, takes us beyond ourselves, closer to more ultimate concerns, calls purposes into question, and exposes us to the cosmic.

Life is a flowing through situations wherein these centers "share the spotlight." At times we choose where to be centered (e.g., when we choose to learn computer programming [intellectual center] and apply ourselves until we have the thought processes necessary for developing this skill). At other times our center of operation is determined by an event in our environment (e.g., a loved one questions his or her commitment to a primary relationship, and strong feelings of vulnerability and rejection become the focus of our lives [emotional center]). The ebb and flow of these centers within each of us is occurring in a social milieu where others are also ebbing, flowing, changing, and operating with varying degrees of awareness of which center is "onstage." The more attuned a person is to the tones, shifts, and cues of the varying centers, the more conscious that person can be of "life." Conversely, the more out of touch, blocked, or denied the person is in relation to his or her own centers, the less able to transact effectively with the environment the person will be in having needs met and in growing as a person.

Interpersonal transactions occur through these centers. Growthful, life-enhancing relationships result from *resonance,* the accurate "picking up on" where the other is centered. This requires a developed sensitivity (innate and/or learned) to the self and a willingness to allow the other to pass into the self. This difficult skill is the basis of interpersonal relationships.

Centers and Androgyny

If movement toward androgyny is valued intellectually, speaks to emotional comfort, holds out pleasure to the senses, is sexually releasing, and/or enlivens the humanness of the person, *then* facilitating changes in all of the centers is called for. The following is a discussion of actions for all centers which, in concert, can help a *male* experience various aspects of androgyny and the potential it has for developing him as a human being.

Intellect The concept of androgyny has some immediate appeal—a broader range of behaviors, liberation from unrewarding patterns, a hope for healthier relationships. There are, however, years of entrenched patterns and programs that speak to being male—those GAMS outlooks and behaviors that account to a great extent for how we see ourselves today. Letting go of the GAMS personality, values, thoughts, plans, and predicted rewards is no easy matter. The mind tapes cannot be "erased." They can, however, be altered by application and practice. Information can be introduced that counterbalances existing thought structures, accentuates the GAMS-androgyny dilemmas, and adds a vocabulary to our "inner conversation" that can result in new learnings.

Some suggestions for working with the intellectual center are as follows:

- Join a men's group.
- Read articles and books on men's liberation, androgyny, women's liberation.
- Read reactionary male literature, anti-liberation literature, radical, and anti-male feminist literature (to get to know the extremes).
- Do a cost-benefit analysis for yourself of GAMS and androgyny.
- Change one relationship consciously toward a more androgynous definition and study the consequences.
- Write a one-page statement on androgyny and you.
- Fantasize your answer to the question "If I were more androgynous in a world that supported this, I would find myself. . . ."
- Fantasize your answer to "By becoming more androgynous I would give up . . . and I would gain. . . ."

Emotions   As males, we live under the shadow of a stereotype that labels us as cold, distant, critical, and *emotionally unexpressive*. Note: the stereotype does not label us as unemotional, but as inhibited in expression of feeling. Also, the stereotype pins on us the inability or reluctance to take in, allow, accept, and encourage the expression of feelings by others.

In men who accept GAMS, emotionality is "managed" through the mind. Childhood experiences, peer group pressure, and the norms of the working world have conspired to limit the male to a range of acceptable feelings running from "I'm fine" to "I'm feeling lousy." The rich vocabulary of emotions, the experiential depth of feelings, and the much feared sense of being "out of control" (i.e., out of one's mind and genuinely into the emotional center) are suppressed, avoided, denied, and, when too powerful to be kept down, allowed to explode onto the surface in unmanageable, violent, and destructive ways or to implode with those same consequences incurred by the person himself.

Some suggestions for working on the emotional center to bring it beyond the atrophied GAMS state are as follows:

- Encounter groups set up with this goal in mind.
- Reading.
- Taking risks with allowing glimmers of feelings. (Typical cues are sweaty palms, preoccupation, lump in the throat.)
- *Not* changing any current behavior, but allowing the feelings about it (e.g., work, primary relationship, etc.) to occur and giving these feelings time and space to be, to work themselves out, and to evolve as they do when accepted.

Physical   Health, pleasure, tone, agility, and grace are the values of most cultures, primitive or civilized. Neglecting the body or overpurchasing services to avoid doing physical activity is debilitating, speeds the aging process, lessens the availability of energy, and destroys the "mood" and projection of the self.

Sadly, too many males abandon their bodies through devotion to the job. Sitting, driving, drinking, and overeating, as well as lack of exercise, nervousness, tension, cigarettes, and other contributors to ill health are too often combated with drugs rather than intelligent cultivating of the body. If no effort is made to stop the entropic processes, the body is prone to illness.

Some ways to counter cellular death and to create a healthy physical center are as follows:

- **Meditation.**
- **Fast days.**
- **Isometrics.**
- **Acceptance of the body (using a mirror and some caring).**
- **Adequate sleep.**
- **Massage.**
- **Stretching, exercising, jogging.**
- **Dancing.**
- **Sensory awareness exercises.**

Sexual   The sexual center is problematic to manage because it involves the ego and has its own cycles and rhythms. Sex is as basic as breathing and other biological needs. As a symbol and an act of intimacy, openness, and connectivity, it can be a fragmented portion of the self, a life and measure of its own that acts as a barometer of our attractiveness and "loveworthiness."

When inappropriately managed, the sexual center invades the process of living through doubt, guilt, compulsion, and, most sadly, as a filter through which personal relationships are seen. Male-female relationships in our culture are "polluted" by the silent, covert, desperate underworld of disowned but strongly felt sexual intentions. Going beyond this is a necessary step in dechauvinizing the culture.

Some activities that contribute to better management of the sexual center are as follows:

- **Reading (especially Reich, Horney, and May).**
- **Honest dialogue with primary partners.**
- **Human sexuality programs.**
- **Systematic self-analysis of intentions in relationships.**
- **Observation of responses to new people—awareness.**
- **Owning needs for intimacy and closeness and distinguishing them from the need for sex.**
- **Experimentation with sexual rhythms.**
- **Awareness of fantasies and critique of content and frequency.**

Spiritual   The spirit is experienced via *transcendence* in the secular sense of the word. The awareness of larger order purposes, the "high" experiences of nature—childbirth, discovery, orgasm, accomplishment—are the indicators of our higher order human nature, the tastes and glimpses of our own evolution. We are rarely involved in our own transcendence and growth; too frequently we are rooted in the humdrum and routine. We feel that our spiritual center, the level of our purpose and meaning manifested in experience, is outside of ourselves, a product of "twists of fate." But within each of us is a *readiness* for new experience that we can impact, and it is toward this that we can focus our energies.

Some methods of developing the spiritual center are as follows:

- Prayer.
- Focus and clarity during religious services.
- Regular meditation.
- Chanting.
- Rhythmic dancing.
- Reading.
- Study with a spiritual leader.
- Great endeavor in search of the miraculous.
- Fasting extensively.
- Being "high."

With some effort, each of the named centers can receive our attention, energy, and care so that we can grow beyond the male stereotype and into our whole selves—into our androgynous conditions.

After Reading

Write a journal entry in which you respond to the following statement from the article: "Androgyny as a goal requires that each of us has available those characteristics, skills, and behaviors that have been traditionally seen as female." Try to write for two to three pages. Agree or disagree and think of traditionally male and female characteristics, skills, and behaviors that illustrate the authors' generalities. Consider your own characteristics, skills, and behaviors and label which of these are traditionally male and which are traditionally female.

Before Reading

In this excerpt from *The Power of the Positive Woman,* Phyllis Schlafly contrasts believers in women's liberation with the female she identifies as "the positive woman." As you read, be aware of the following questions:

1. What is dogma? What does the author specify are the three basic dogmas of the women's liberation movement?
2. What are the five principles that Schlafly believes underlie women liberationists' goals? According to the author, how does the "positive woman" react to each of these principles?
3. What seems to be the purpose of the Schlafly selection? For whom is Schlafly writing? Do you feel that you are part of her intended readership?

Understanding the Difference

Phyllis Schlafly

The first requirement for the acquisition of power by the Positive Woman is to understand the differences between men and women. Your outlook on life, your faith, your behavior, your potential for fulfillment, all are determined by the parameters of your original premise. The Positive Woman starts with the assumption that the world is her oyster. She rejoices in the creative capability within her body and the power potential of her mind and spirit. She understands that men and women are different, and that those very differences provide the key to her success as a person and fulfillment as a woman.

The women's liberationist, on the other hand, is imprisoned by her own negative view of herself and of her place in the world around her. This view of women was most succinctly expressed in an advertisement designed by the principal women's liberationist organization, the National Organization for Women (NOW), and run in many magazines and newspapers and as spot announcements on many television stations. The advertisement showed a darling curlyheaded girl with the caption: "This healthy, normal baby has a handicap. She was born female."

This is the self-articulated dog-in-the-manger, chip-on-the-shoulder, fundamental dogma of the women's liberation movement. Someone—it is not clear who, perhaps God, perhaps the "Establishment," perhaps a conspiracy of male chauvinist pigs—dealt women a foul blow by making them female. It becomes necessary, therefore, for women to agitate and demonstrate and hurl demands on society in order to wrest from an oppressive male-dominated social structure the status that has been wrongfully denied to women through the centuries.

By its very nature, therefore, the women's liberation movement precipitates a series of conflict situations—in the legislatures, in the courts, in the schools, in industry—with man targeted as the enemy. Confrontation replaces cooperation as the watchword of all relationships. Women and men become adversaries instead of partners.

The second dogma of the women's liberationists is that, of all the injustices perpetrated upon women through the centuries, the most oppressive is the cruel fact that women have babies and men do not. Within the confines of the women's liberationist ideology, therefore, the abolition of this overriding inequality of women becomes the primary goal. This goal must be achieved at any and all costs—to the woman herself, to the baby, to the family, and to society. Women must be made equal to men in their ability *not* to become pregnant and *not* to be expected to care for babies they may bring into the world.

This is why women's liberationists are compulsively involved in the drive to make abortion and child-care centers for all women, regardless of religion or income, both socially acceptable and government-financed. Former Congresswoman Bella Abzug has defined the goal: "to enforce the constitutional right of females to terminate pregnancies that they do not wish to continue."

If man is targeted as the enemy, and the ultimate goal of women's liberation is independence from men and the avoidance of pregnancy and its consequences, then lesbianism is logically the highest form in the ritual of women's liberation. Many, such as Kate Millet, come to this conclusion, although many others do not.

The Positive Woman will never travel the dead-end road. It is self-evident to the Positive Woman that the female body with its baby-producing organs was not designed by a conspiracy of men but by the Divine Architect of the human race. Those who think it is unfair that women have babies, whereas men cannot, will have to take up their complaint with God because no other power is capable of changing that fundamental fact. On some college campuses, I have been assured that other methods of reproduction will be developed. But most of us must deal with the real world rather than with the imagination of dreamers.

Another feature of the woman's natural role is the obvious fact that women can breast-feed babies and men cannot. This functional role was not imposed by conspiratorial males seeking to burden women with confining chores, but must be recognized as part of the plan of the Divine Architect for the survival of the human race through the centuries and in the countries that know no pasteurization of milk or sterilization of bottles.

The Positive Woman looks upon her femaleness and her fertility as part of her purpose, her potential, and her power. She rejoices that she has a capability for creativity that men can never have.

The third basic dogma of the women's liberation movement is that there is no difference between male and female except the sex organs, and that all those physical, cognitive, and emotional differences you *think* are there, are merely the result of centuries of restraints imposed by a male-dominated society and sex-stereotyped schooling. The role imposed on women is, by definition, inferior, according to the women's liberationists.

The Positive Woman knows that, while there are some physical competitions in which women are better (and can command more money) than men, including those that put a premium on grace and beauty, such as figure skating, the superior physical strength of males over females in competitions of strength, speed, and short-term endurance is beyond rational dispute.

In the Olympic Games, women not only cannot win any medals in competition with men, the gulf between them is so great that they cannot even qualify for the contests with men. No amount of training from infancy can enable women to throw the discus as far as men, or to match men in push-ups or in lifting weights. In track and field events, individual male records surpass those of women by 10 to 20 percent.

Female swimmers today are beating Johnny Weissmuller's records, but today's male swimmers are better still. Chris Evert can never win a tennis match against Jimmy Connors. If we removed lady's tees from golf courses, women would be out of the game. Putting women in football or wrestling matches can only be an exercise in laughs.

The Olympic Games, whose rules require strict verification to ascertain that no male enters a female contest and, with his masculine advantage, unfairly captures a woman's medal, formerly insisted on a visual inspection of the contestants' bodies. Science, however, has discovered that men and women are so innately different physically that their maleness/femaleness can be conclusively established by means of a simple skin test of fully clothed persons. . . .

Another silliness of the women's liberationists is their frenetic desire to force all women to accept the title *Ms* in place of *Miss* or *Mrs.* If Gloria Steinem and Betty Friedan want to call themselves *Ms* in order to conceal their marital status, their wishes should be respected.

But that doesn't satisfy the women's liberationists. They want all women to be compelled to use *Ms* whether they like it or not. The women's liberation movement has been waging a persistent compaign to browbeat the media into using *Ms* as the standard title for all women. The women's liberationists have already succeeded in getting the Department of Health, Education and Welfare to forbid schools and colleges from identifying women students as *Miss* or *Mrs.*[1]

All polls show that the majority of women do not care to be called *Ms.* A Roper poll indicated that 81 percent of the women questioned said they prefer *Miss* or *Mrs.* to *Ms.* Most married women feel they worked hard for the *r* in their names, and they don't care to be gratuitously deprived of it. Most single women don't care to have their name changed to an unfamiliar title that at best conveys overtones of feminist ideology and is polemical in meaning, and at worst connotes misery instead of joy. Thus, Kate Smith, a very Positive Woman, proudly proclaimed on television that she is "Miss Kate Smith, not Ms." Like other Positive Women, she has been succeeding while negative women have been complaining. . . .

The Five Principles

When the women's liberationists enter the political arena to promote legislation and litigation in pursuit of their goals, their specific demands are based on five principles.

(1) They demand that a "gender-free" rule be applied to every federal and state law, bureaucratic regulation, educational institution, and expenditure of public funds. Based on their dogma that there is no real difference between men and women (except in sex organs), they demand that males and females have identical treatment always. Thus, if fathers are not expected to stay home and care for their infant children, then neither should mothers be expected to do so; and, therefore, it becomes the duty of the government to provide kiddy-care centers to relieve mothers of that unfair and unequal burden.

The women's lib dogma demands that the courts treat sex as a "suspect" classification—just as race is now treated—so that no difference of treatment or separation between the sexes will ever be permitted, no matter how reasonable or how much it is desired by reasonable people.

The nonsense of these militant demands was illustrated by the Department of Health, Education and Welfare (HEW) ruling in July, 1976, that all public school "functions such as father-son or mother-daughter breakfasts" would be prohibited because this "would be subjecting students to separate treatment." It was announced that violations would lead to a cutoff of federal assistance or court action by the Justice Department.

When President Gerald Ford read this in the newspaper, he was described by his press secretary as being "quite irritated" and as saying that he could not believe that this was the intent of Congress in passing a law against sex discrimination in education. He telephoned HEW Secretary David Mathews and told him to suspend the ruling.

The National Organization for Women, however, immediately announced opposition to President Ford's action, claiming that such events (fashion shows, softball games, banquets, and breakfasts) are sex-discriminatory and must be eliminated. It is clear that a prohibition against your right to make any difference or separation between the sexes anytime anywhere is a primary goal of the women's liberation movement.

No sooner had the father-son, mother-daughter flap blown over than HEW embroiled itself in another controversy by a ruling that an after-school choir of fifth and sixth grade boys violates the HEW regulaton that bars single-sex choruses. The choir in Wethersfield, Connecticut, that precipitated the ruling had been established for boys whose "voices haven't changed yet," and the purpose was "to get boys interested in singing" at an early age so they would be willing to join coed choruses later. Nevertheless, HEW found that such a boy's chorus is by definition sex discriminatory.

The Positive Woman rejects the "gender-free" approach. She knows that there are many differences between male and female and that we are entitled to have our laws, regulations, schools, and courts reflect these differences and allow for reasonable differences in treatment and separations of activities that reasonable men and women want.

The Positive Woman also rejects the argument that sex discrimination should be treated the same as race discrimination. There is vastly more difference between a man and a woman than there is between a black and a white, and it is nonsense to adopt a legal and bureaucratic attitude that pretends that those differences do not exist. Even the United States Supreme Court has, in recent and relevant cases, upheld "reasonable" sex-based differences of treatment by legislatures and by the military.[2]

(2) The women's lib legislative goals seek an irrational mandate of "equality" at the expense of justice. The fact is that equality cannot always be equated with justice, and may sometimes even be highly unjust. If we had absolutely equal treatment in regard to taxes, then everyone would pay the same income tax, or perhaps the same rate of income tax, regardless of the size of the income.

If we had absolutely equal treatment in regard to federal spending programs, we would have to eliminate welfare, low-income housing benefits, food stamps, government scholarships, and many other programs designed to benefit low-income citizens. If we had absolutely equal treatment in regard to age, then seventeen-year-olds, or even ten-year-olds, would be permitted to vote, and we would have to eliminate Social Security unless all persons received the same benefits that only those over sixty-two receive now.

Our legislatures, our administrative departments, and our courts have always had and still retain the discretion to make reasonable differences in treatment based on age, income, or economic situation. The Positive Woman believes that it makes no sense to deprive us of the ability to make reasonable distinctions based on sex that reasonable men and women want.

(3) The women's liberation movement demands that women be given the benefit of "reverse discrimination." The Positive Woman recognizes that this is mutually exclusive with the principle of equal opportunity for all. Reverse discrimination is based on the theory that "group rights" take precedence over individual rights, and that "reverse discrimination" (variously called "preferential treatment," "remedial action," or "affirmative action") should be imposed in order to compensate some women today for alleged past discriminations against other women. The word "quotas" is usually avoided, but it amounts to the same thing.

The fallacy of reverse discrimination has been aptly exposed by Professor Sidney Hook. No one would argue, he wrote, that because many years ago blacks and women were denied the right to vote, we should now compensate by giving them an extra vote or two, or by barring white men from voting at all.

But that is substantially what the women's liberationists are demanding—and getting by federal court orders—in education, employment, and politics when they ask for "affirmative action" to remedy past discrimination.[3]

The Positive Woman supports equal opportunity for individuals of both sexes, as well as of all faiths and races. She rejects the theories of reverse discrimination and "group rights." It does no good for the woman who may have been discriminated against twenty-five years ago to know that an unqualified woman today receives preferential treatment at the expense of a qualified man. Only the vindictive radical would support such a policy of revenge.

(4) The women's liberation movement is based on the unproven theory that uniformity should replace diversity—or, in simpler language, the federalization of all remaining aspects of our life. The militant women demand that *all* educational institutions conform to federally determined rules about sex discrimination.

There is absolutely no evidence that HEW bureaucrats can do a better or fairer job of regulating our schools and colleges than local officials. Nor is there any evidence that individuals, or women, or society as a whole, would be better off under a uniform system enforced by the full power of the federal government than they would be under a free and competitive system, under local control, using diverse methods and regulations. It is hard to see why anyone would want to put more power into the hands of federal bureaucrats who cannot cope with the problems they already have.

The militant women demand the HEW regulations enforce a strict gender-free uniformity on all schools and colleges. Everything from sports to glee clubs must be coed, regardless of local customs or wishes. The militants deplore the differences from state to state in the laws governing marriage and divorce. Yet does anyone think our nation would be improved if we were made subject to a national divorce law devised by HEW?

The Positive Woman rejects the theory that Washington, D.C., is the fountainhead of all wisdom and professional skill. She supports the principle of leaving all possible control and discretion in the hands of local school and college officials and their elected boards.

(5) The women's liberation movement pushes its proposals on the premise that everything must be neutral as between morality and immorality, and as between the institution of the family and alternate lifestyles: for example, that homosexuals and lesbians should have just as much right to teach in the schools and to adopt children as anyone else; and that illegitimate babies and abortions by married or single mothers should be accepted as normal behavior for teachers—and funded by public money.

A good example of the rabid determination of the militant radicals to push every law and regulation to the far-out limit of moral neutrality is the HEW regulation on sex discrimination that implements the Education Amendments of 1972. Although the federal statute simply prohibits sex discrimination, the HEW regulation (1) requires that any medical benefit program administered by a school or college pay for abortions for married and unmarried students, (2) prohibits any school or college from refusing to employ or from firing an unmarried pregnant teacher or a woman who has had, or plans to have, an abortion, and (3) prohibits any school or college from refusing admission to any student who has had, or plans to have, an abortion. Abortion is referred to by the code words "termination of pregnancy."[4]

This HEW regulation is illogical, immoral and unauthorized by any reasonable reading of the 1972 Education Act. But the HEW regulation became federal law on July 18, 1975, after being signed by the president and accepted by Congress.

The Positive Woman believes that our educational institutions have not only the right, but the obligation, to set minimum standards of moral conduct at the local level. She believes that schools and colleges have no right to use our public money to promote conduct that is offensive to the religious and moral values of parents and taxpayers. . . .

Notes

[1] HEW Regulation on Sex Discrimination in Schools and Colleges, effective July 18, 1975, #86.21(c) (4).

[2] *Kahn* v. *Shevin,* 416 U.S. 351 (1974) upheld Florida's property tax exemption for widows only. *Schlesinger* v. *Ballard,* 419 U.S. 498 (1975) upheld a United States Navy rule that permitted female officers to remain four years longer than male officers in a given rank before being subject to mandatory discharge.

[3] The largest antidiscrimination settlement in history (*Equal Employment Opportunity Commission* v. *American Telephone and Telegraph Company,* 365 F. Supp. 1105, E.D. Pa. 1973) required back pay of $38 million (mostly to women) and the signing of a consent decree that mandates the telephone companies to give preferential treatment (reverse discrimination) to females over better-qualified males in order to achieve "goals,"

"intermediate targets," and "timeframes" for the "full utilization" of women "at a pace beyond that which would occur normally." 1 CCH Emp. Prac. #1869 at 1553.

[4]*Federal Register,* vol. 40, no. 108, pp. 24137–145, sections 86.40, 86.57, and 86.21.

After Reading

In your journal record your responses to the following:

1. How do you feel after reading the selection? How many of Schlafly's ideas do you agree with? Disagree with? What does your own experience contribute to your response to Schlafly?
2. What action does the author want her audience to take? What does she want them to think and/or feel?
3. To what extent does Schlafly generalize about women liberationists and about "Positive Women"? Does she create stereotypes? How does she support her characterizations of these two kinds of females?
4. What are some of the assumptions that lie beneath Schlafly's words?

Before Reading

In "The Rising of the Women Means the Rising of the Race," Annie Laurie Gaylor argues that women's equality is critical to world advancement. Consider the following questions as you read this article:

1. How does Gaylor utilize Webster's definition of civilization in her argument?
2. What kinds of support does Gaylor use in arguing that we can see ourselves as neither civilized nor humanistic until women are treated as the equals of men?
3. What is a patriarchal family? Why, according to the author, does patriarchy create problems?
4. For whom do you think Gaylor intended her article? Who reads *The Humanist?*

The Rising of the Women Means the Rising of the Race

Annie Laurie Gaylor

We easily perceive that the people furthest from civilization are the ones where equality between man and woman are furthest apart—and we consider this one of the signs of savagery. But we are so stupid that we can't see that we thus plainly admit that no civilization can be perfect until exact equality between man and woman is included.

—Mark Twain, November 6, 1895

This article first appeared in *The Humanist* issue of January–February 1983 and is reprinted by permission.

Mark Twain is not alone in observing this phenomenon. It does indeed seem to be peculiarly true that "one can judge a civilization by the way it treats its women," as the less well-known author, Helen Foster Snow, has written.

The status of women in any given culture or time can serve as the litmus test for judging whether that culture upholds humanist values. Moreover, women's equality means, as Twain pointed out, the advancement not only of women but of civilization itself. James Oppenheim put it succinctly when, in 1912, he penned a song commemorating a strike by women mill workers in Massachusetts. The lyrics to "Bread and Roses" include the line: "The rising of the women means the rising of the race." It should come as no shock that the people who have led and lead the battle for women's rights have been humanists—those reformers, thinkers, and activists devoted to "the rising of the race," that is, devoted to human welfare.

But being devoted to human welfare is only part of *Webster's* definition of a humanist: "humanism: devotion to human welfare, interest in or concern for *man;* a philosophy that rejects supernaturalism, regards *man* as a natural object, and asserts the essential dignity and worth of *man* and *his* capacity to achieve self-realization through the use of reason and scientific method."

Webster's Dictionary describes a noble and uplifting philosophy of reason and compassion, but it obviously is a description which could have profited from a feminist-minded editor! The exclusion of women from such revealing symbols of our culture as dictionary definitions is unfortunately but one of the ways half of the human race has been denied its dignity, worth, and self-realization—those values central to humanism. Rectifying the monumental discrimination faced by women at all levels will surely become the greatest humanist revolution ever witnessed, the effects of which will be felt in every avenue of our existence, and which will ultimately redefine every institution and human relationship. The emancipation of women is the "short cut" toward humanizing the world; feminism is the necessary ingredient without which humanity cannot progress.

If the words *progress* and *civilization* are to be used interchangeably, it is instructive to note the meaning of civilization. *Webster's* (this time offering a nonsexist definition) defines civilization as: "An ideal state of human culture characterized by complete absence of barbarism and nonrational behavior, optimum utilization of physical, cultural, spiritual, and human resources, and perfect adjustment of the individual within the social framework."

Keeping this kind of definition in mind, it becomes even easier to understand why women's equality is pivotal to world advancement, especially when one considers the many barbarisms which have been directed at women, including physical cruelties such as widespread rape, foot-binding, and genital mutilation.

The nonrational behavior by those who resist women's movement for equality has been ably demonstrated, starting with Aristotle. Aristotle was the first Western philosopher to postulate that "man is rational," yet, as Bertrand Russell noted, he was so irrational himself in his attitude toward women that he insisted that they have fewer teeth than men. From Aristotle onward, nonrational convictions about women have been given credence, all evidence to the contrary. Physicians in the nineteenth century, alarmed at women's determination to be educated, warned that terrible fates awaited educated women, whose blood from the uterus would rise to the brain and cause, of course, "hysteria." Today, women's enemies have warned that working women will be rewarded with everything from hirsutism (after all, they are masculinizing themselves) to juvenile delinquent offspring. Female anti-feminists have uttered their share of nonrational pronouncements, epitomized by Eagle Forum president Phyllis Schlafly, whose infamous "virtuous woman" statement, "When a woman walks across a room, she speaks with a universal body language that most men intuitively understand. . . . Virtuous women are seldom accosted by unwelcome sexual propositions or familiarities, obscene talk, or profane language," rivals Proverbs 31:10, "Who can find a virtuous woman? For her price is far above rubies," for sexism.

There can never be optimal use of human resources when one half of humankind has traditionally been consigned to second-class citizenship and told that their creative, scientific, and intellectual impulses are "likely to induce a distempered state of mind." This was a poet laureate's advice to Charlotte Bronte, who subsequently wrote him a reply in which she apologized for thinking. "In the evenings," she wrote, "I confess, I do think, but I never trouble anyone else with my thoughts. . . ."

The last of *Webster's* requirements for civilization is "perfect adjustment of the individual within the social framework." While it can be argued that such a development would be as unattainable as a utopia and that even men can scarcely lay claim to "perfect adjustment," it is certain that individuals can never truly adjust to second-class citizenship without serious consequences to their self-worth. Who has ever heard a prospective father voice a wish for a girl "because girls are more apt to make a difference in the world"? Yet various opinion polls continue to reveal that a majority of prospective parents continue to hope that their first child will be male. Who can truly "adjust" if adjustment means they are denied opportunity or self-realization merely because their interests do not fall within the traditional sex-role categories? Far too much "adjustment" is asked of persons in a society in which gender becomes more important than individuality or interest.

In John Stuart Mill's essay, *The Subjection of Women,* Mill remarked not only upon the degradation of women but upon the ill effects injustice has upon men who benefit:

> **Think what it is to be a boy, to grow up to manhood in the belief that without any merit or any exertion of his own, though he may be the most frivolous and empty or the most ignorant and stolid of mankind, by mere fact of being born a male he is by right the superior of all and every one of an entire half of the human race: including probably some whose real superiority to himself he has daily or hourly occasion to feel. . . . What must be the effect on his character of this lesson?**

What, indeed?

The easy acceptance of beliefs which glorify master-slave relationships is one probable outcome, particularly in nations in which Christians, through their religious teachings, are primed for such hierarchical arrangements. Once a society has accepted such a relationship between the sexes, it may with little adjustment impose such domination upon another class of people and likewise justify it because of differing physical characteristics. The enslavement of African people at the dawn of the United States is the obvious example. It seems hardly coincidental that in both the nineteenth and the twentieth centuries American black people and women as a whole have enjoyed parallel liberation movements.

Neuropsychologist James W. Prescott has advanced a theory based on a cross-cultural study linking violence, sexism, and racism to the effects of repression of physical affection toward infants and sexual repression imposed on adolescents. It is possible to view his findings from another perspective. If misogyny, racism, violence, slavery, and religiosity are all linked, the element they may have in common is the repression of women. Patriarchies, which operate under a code that treats women, children, and defeated enemies as property, will be unlikely to foster nurturing attitudes. At those times when child care is devalued as "women's work," when children are proof of virility as well as property, and when physical affection is discouraged except for procreation (alternatively, for male privilege alone), offspring will not feel highly cherished. Patriarchal values encourage negative, anti-social behavior and conquest. The violence Prescott correlated with lack of physical affection is actually *male* violence: war, torture, punitive laws, and aggressive crime.

Feminist theorist Gloria Steinem believes that the traditional patriarchal family is the model upon which authoritarian governments are built: "The patriarchal family is the model and microcosm of other authoritarian structures. The root of any authoritarian system, its bottom line, is possession by men of women as a means of production."

Modern history's most extreme example of patriarchy-run-amok is "the Fatherland" imposed by Adolf Hitler. Hitler, in *Mein Kampf,* openly vowed to treat women's fertility as a state-run resource. One of his first actions upon being elected into power was to padlock abortion clinics. He also opposed contraception. *Kinder, kirche, kuche* became part of Hitler's war-cry. He looked upon "Aryan" women as breeding machines, their children as fodder, Jews and political dissidents as slaves to be "exterminated," and the world as a place to conquer through violence.

If it is true that the world cannot advance if half its human occupants are degraded or denied opportunity, so it follows that, when social movements retreat to barbarism or nonrational codes of behavior, women's subjugation is necessary. Decisions by a class of men to dominate women go hand in hand with decisions to dominate nature, other races, or other nations.

The United States is currently enduring a return to patriarchal values as a backlash to the new freedoms women have claimed in the past decade. In a pre-election cartoon lampooning President Ronald Reagan, Reagan was pictured in a cowboy hat vowing: "A pregnant woman in every home! A gun in every holster! Make America a man again!" True to form, Reagan is mustering an unparalleled military buildup at the expense of social programs, especially those affecting women and children, an estimated 70 percent of which target the poor. The Census Bureau estimates that, of nearly thirty million persons in the United States living at or below the poverty level, 68 percent are *women.* While a policy of cutting aid to "women and children first" is being practiced, the war machine is being cranked up in accord with patriarchal tradition. . . .

Despite the stumbling blocks faced by women, the strides made in a century's time are remarkable.

In examining the impact of women's rights in one sphere alone—that of reproduction—it is possible to envision just how revolutionary sexual equality could be.

If women bear only those children they truly desire and for which they can care, the global impact of the "rising of the women" will be quite awe-inspiring. Newly acquired technology gives women this opportunity. Choice and control over motherhood directly affect the quality of life at every level. Reproduction bears a symbiotic relationship to so many of our planet's problems. In some cases, it causes them, as with overpopulation and dwindling resources; in other cases, it exacerbates them, as with human aggression, both personal and national, and the ever-present tragedies of famine and disease.

Women's second-class citizenship means that poverty, illiteracy, and victimization by crimes disproportionately affect them. It may take years—hopefully not centuries—before women's freedom will begin to have a significant impact on such global crises as war, poverty, and overpopulation. Meanwhile, those working for women's rights can take comfort in knowing that the freeing of women will truly be "the rising of the race"—the world's ultimate step forward toward human liberty.

After Reading

In this article, perhaps you noticed that Gaylor identifies Phyllis Schlafly as a female antifeminist and quotes in paragraph seven a part of Schlafly's now famous statement about virtuous women: "Virtuous women are seldom accosted by unwelcome sexual propositions or familiarities, obscene talk, or profane language." Write a response to the Schlafly statement, basing it on your own experience, that of others, and on your reading.

It is often enlightening to put ourselves in the place of another, to try to imagine how that person might respond to an issue or situation. This kind of role playing can enable us to see more clearly a point of view that is different from our own and thus to clarify our own and perhaps develop ways of supporting it when we present our opinion to others. Try this role-playing idea by composing a dialogue between Gaylor, author of "The Rising of the Women Means the Rising of the Race," and Patrick Canavan or John Haskell, authors of "The Great American Male Stereotype." The dialogue might begin in the following way:

> *Canavan:*   With new opportunities made possible with the help of the women's movement, it seems to me, Annie, that many women today are pursuing the same goals that have led men to aspire to the GAMS. That's just moving out of one kind of trap and into another.
>
> *Gaylor:*
> (Continue the dialogue for four or five speeches for each author.)

In this dialogue you have created, you were well aware of the importance of audience because as you wrote each speech you were addressing another individual directly. You knew some things about both individuals' ideas and attitudes and, as a result, what they might say in response to each other. In much of the writing that you do, you may know your audience well; in other writing, you may know much less. In any case, audience is a vital consideration in the writing process.

AUDIENCE

Writing for Ourselves

Usually when we keep a diary or a journal we are writing expressively and only for ourselves. We may simply want a record of our activities, feelings, hopes, and disappointments. Or we may choose to explore our feelings, experiences, and relationships, to clarify what we feel and think about ourselves and others, about new ideas or changes in our lives.

We may also use a journal—as you are using one in your writing course to respond to your reading—to reflect on your experience, to react to others' ideas, and perhaps to learn new material. In all of these writing situations, though we may occasionally share our thoughts, we write primarily for ourselves; and our writing generally reveals more about us than it does about any subject, event, or material. It is always our perception of our world. Of course, journal entries may serve as sources for other kinds of writing: you might pull out an incident you recorded in your journal and turn it into a letter, story, or poem; responses to an article or essay might be reworked into a book review; study notes can prove useful for composing a class paper. In these cases, a writer transforms material written for self into material for others.

WRITING FOR OTHERS

The audiences we address beyond ourselves may range from our dearest friend or closest family member to a wide and completely unknown group of readers. In our daily lives we may write letters to loved ones, send directions to a friend on how to reach our home, invite friends or family to gatherings, or express our thanks for hospitality. At the other end of the spectrum, we may write poems or stories for publication or letters to the editor of a newspaper, in which cases we know little or nothing specific about our audience. In between these extremes falls much of the writing that we do.

We often write letters, memos, or reports for individuals or groups that we know less well than our friends or families. But we may know how these audiences feel about an idea or plan or sometimes what their values and assumptions are. And we may know how best to appeal to them or provide them with information. Often, though, we may know no more than a name, position, or group membership. Whatever we can ascertain about an audience can be useful in knowing how to approach or address it. Questions we can ask ourselves about a given audience might include the following:

1. What is the age of my audience? Range of ages?
2. What is the general educational level of my audience?
3. What is the sex (or race) of my audience?
4. Does the audience clearly represent a single religious, philosophical, or political orientation?

5. Are there basic values shared by the members of my audience?
6. How much does my audience know about the subject of my writing?
7. What predispositions or attitudes does the audience have in relation to my subject?

Figuring out as much as we can about an audience for whom we are writing can help us know how much information to include, what language and usage are appropriate, what tone is best, what sentence length and overall length should be. It can help us know how to appeal logically and emotionally in a persuasive piece and which details, examples, or anecdotes will communicate our point the best.

One very special audience all students address in their academic course work is the instructor. Generally, in writing examination essays or papers, the student realizes that the professor is an expert in a certain field: he or she knows the subject well and is in a position to evaluate the work of students in the course. In writing to be graded by an instructor, your purpose ordinarily is to demonstrate that you have mastered a body of knowledge or a skill. Beyond the classroom, the purposes of writing vary, and generally the writer is not simply writing to demonstrate mastery.

To illustrate how your writing changes depending on your audience, write the first few sentences of the following situations:

1. A journal entry in which you express how you felt about a dinner experience in a restaurant where the food was poorly prepared and overpriced and the service was inadequate.
2. A letter to the manager of the same restaurant letting him know your feelings about your experience.
3. A review of the restaurant which will appear in the local newspaper.

As you wrote each of these and reread them, you probably noticed that they sounded different. In the journal entry you might have found yourself using a very informal style—perhaps sentence fragments, personally picturesque expressions of disgust or anger. You probably did not write a formal introductory sentence or worry about transitions or support for your feelings. Your audience was yourself: *you* had the experience and did not need to include details to make a point.

When you addressed the restaurant manager in the second assignment, you probably were more careful about identifying the specific evening of your dinner, your waiter or waitress, the particular problems with the food, the service, and the cost. Your audience made it necessary for you to provide more information. You likely wrote in complete sentences and chose your language more carefully to express your disappointment in a more formal way than you did in the first piece.

Finally, the third task, the restaurant review, is based on the same bad experience. Your writing probably became even more formal in tone, perhaps more detailed, and better organized than the first and second pieces. For example, in your journal entry for yourself, you might have written something like the following:

> Salad dressing yuk! Sickeningly sweet, flabby, gritty spinach.

In the piece to the restaurant manager, your comment on the poor quality of the salad might have been expressed in the following way:

> Unfortunately, the spinach salad was both flabby and gritty, and the dressing was far too sweet.

In writing for the newspaper, you might have expressed your distaste for the salad as follows:

> A good spinach salad is not hard to find in this city; aside from obtaining fresh clean spinach and tossing it with a delicate dressing that doesn't overpower, there is little one need do to provide a first-rate salad. Sadly, *Stella's Steak House* fails to do even that.

PURPOSE

When we write for ourselves, as in the journal entry on the bad restaurant experience, our purpose may be therapeutic—simply *to express our feeling* on paper. The act of writing down feelings truly helps some people feel better. We may also want *to explore the meanings* of those feelings or experiences or *to clarify them* or *to discover what we think* about an issue or idea or our own goals or hopes. As noted earlier, individuals may also write for themselves to organize, digest, and *learn material.* In general, when we write for ourselves we write *to express ourselves and to discover meaning.*

When we write for others, we may want *to share our feelings and thoughts, to give information,* or *to move someone else to thought, feeling, or action.*

Sharing Feelings and Thoughts

Some examples of writing specifically to share feelings and thoughts include thank-you notes and notes or letters of sympathy or congratulation, but it is also common to express feelings of love, nostalgia, depression, elation, and even outrage and hatred in writing to friends, family, or even a business concern, school official, or community or political leader.

Giving Information

We write to give information to many different audiences. Often we need to provide instructions, to explain data or policies, as in an office memo to co-workers or in an assignment sheet a teacher might distribute. We may be called on to present facts, descriptions of events, or statistics for a report to colleagues or superiors or for a news release. In writing to give information we may need to be totally inclusive or we may be expected to summarize material. (For specific information and assistance on summarizing, see Chapter 8.) We may also give information about ourselves in letters of application or about others in letters of nomination or recommendation. And, of course, even such seemingly insignificant items as telephone messages and notes on the refrigerator are generally meant to give information. Examples of informational writing abound on the shelves of libraries and bookstores and on magazine racks.

Moving Others to Thought, Feeling, or Action

Some of the most important writing done in the world is intended to bring about change in the reader. Writing home to convince a parent that you need extra money, trying to persuade a friend to visit for the weekend, or creating a petition to get a course requirement waived are everyday examples in all of our lives of writing to influence others. We try with written language to change another's attitude or feeling or to convince him or her to behave in a certain way. Position papers, letters to the editor, editorials, letters of complaint, political statements, advertising material, persuasive articles and columns, argumentative essays, and letters of recommendation are just some of the forms writing takes when we try to influence the thought, feelings, or action of readers.

Fiction, poetry, and drama, are also examples of efforts to move others to feeling, thought, and action. Typically, we think of these art forms as attempts to express feelings. But they may certainly provide information at the same time, and surely their ultimate purpose is to move readers. Some literature, such as the work of John Steinbeck or Charles Dickens, clearly sought social change and action or at least social awareness on the part of readers. Some other novelists have been more subtle or have chosen to bring readers' attention to personal rather than social problems. But all literature that is intended to be shared aims to elicit a response from the reader even if it is nothing more than mild amusement.

Much everyday writing may have *multiple* purposes or intentions. The following examples, however, rather clearly suggest a *single* purpose. Can you identify the intention of each?

A really well-equipped kitchen can make the preparation of meals more effective and more effortless. Basic appliances you will need include a reliable stove with a regular and a microwave oven, a double sink with garbage disposal, a refrigerator-freezer including an ice maker, and a dishwasher. In addition to these large appliances, several smaller pieces of equipment are extremely useful and time saving: a food mixer, a blender or food processor, and an electric can opener and knife sharpener. Other small appliances that might be desirable depending on your particular interests would include a waffle iron/sandwich grill, an electric wok, a crockpot, a pasta machine, and so on. . . .

I've often wondered if you remember those summer days we spent in my backyard when we were in grade school. They were such carefree yet intense days. We did so many crazy and wonderful things together. I recall the time we played circus, and I had to roar like a lion under the old overturned baby bed while you pretended to be a lion tamer. Do you ever think about those times? I guess we were closer then than we've ever been since. . . .

Citizens of Plainview, it's time to open your eyes to the flagrant abuse of political power in your city government. The mayor of your city and the members of the City Council have long since ceased to be concerned about your welfare. They got themselves elected by promising improvements in city streets, police services, and sanitation, and by vowing to increase recreational facilities for our young people and programs for the elderly. Minimal progress has been made in any of these areas in the last three and a half years. Instead of working for improvement in services for you, these elected officials have focused their attention on more showy pursuits such as attracting industry and more commercialism to our community. You don't need to sit and hope that things will change in the next four years. You can make a difference by supporting new candidates for the office of mayor and City Council membership. You do not have to take what you get in Plainview. You can make the changes happen by joining the local chapter of the Democrats for Public Action and by voting in the next election. Voting is a right. Use it or lose it.

Few Pure Purposes

Much of the writing we read as well as that which we produce ourselves blends the three purposes or aims that we have discussed. A writer with the intent of moving a reader to action might certainly share his or her own feelings in the process. In providing information about how to do something, a writer might present the reader with several alternatives but also recommend a particular one over the others. In writing to share even feelings of sympathy we probably try to convince the reader that we stand ready to help in any way we can. In expressing our anger to another person by writing an irate note, we may be trying simultaneously to convince that person (and perhaps ourselves) that we are justified in feeling the anger. Observe in the following letter what the various purposes seem to be. What is the main intention? How effective is the letter?

```
Mr. Edward Sauers, Personnel Director
Elk Valley Toy Manufacturing Company
Elk Valley, West Virginia
```

```
Dear Mr. Sauers:

    I am writing this letter in response to your listing of
a vacancy in the Accounting Department of Elk Valley Toy Man-
ufacturing Company. I graduated last June with my bachelor's
degree in accounting and have since been seeking employment
```

in my field. I was an outstanding student in my graduating
class, fourth out of 211 students in my program, and I believe I have the necessary qualifications to do excellent
work in the kind of job you describe in your listing.

In this letter I have included my resume with a list of
local references that you may feel free to contact. I would
be more than happy to come to your office for an interview at
your convenience. I feel confident that if you gave me the
opportunity I could demonstrate my capabilities, my willingness to work hard, and my cooperative and congenial manner.
Thank you.

Sincerely,

Becky Groveton

Despite the typical overlapping of aims, it is wise to keep in mind your basic
purpose as you plan and write any kind of piece. This will give you a focus
and may keep you from roaming too far from what you really intend to do.

Now examine a second letter Mr. Sauers received. What purposes does it
seem to be addressing? How effective is it?

Mr. Edward Sauers, Personnel Director
Elk Valley Toy Manufacturing Company
Elk Valley, West Virginia

Dear Mr. Sauers:

I have recently moved to Elk Valley from Pittsburgh
where I lived all of my life until this past month. I moved
here because my mother and father divorced, and I wanted to
be near my father who moved here. It was a difficult decision
to make, but I like the town all right and am looking for a
job now. I saw in the newspaper that you had a vacancy in
your accounting department, and I'd like to apply for the
job. I do have training in accounting from a small college in
Pittsburgh, so I know I could do the work, but more important
I just love toys and, of course, the children they are intended for. I feel I have a real love for children and am extremely sensitive to the kinds of toys boys and girls really
enjoy. It would be such a joy to work around things that make
little ones happy. Toys can do so much to brighten the spirits of children when they're feeling depressed or lonely. I
know the doll collection I had when I was little meant a lot
to me. (Incidentally, I still have most of them, which I intend to pass on to my own children one day.) I'm sure you can
appreciate my attachment to dolls.

```
     I would be thrilled for a chance to talk with you more
about toys and the job opening whenever you are free.
```

```
                                        With best regards,

                                        Robin Hensley
```

Both letters clearly address more than one purpose; yet as you can tell, one more than the other keeps its basic purpose foremost for the reader.

Keeping your basic purpose in the forefront as you write can help you decide whether chunks of material or individual details are appropriate, useful, and necessary. If your main purpose, for example, is to inform another student of how to go through the registration process at the college, it will probably obscure the information if you include many expressions of your hostility, confusion, or dismay based on your own experiences with the process. Similarly, if you are assigned to write a critical review of a novel, your main purpose no doubt is to move others to thought, feeling, or action (i.e., influence them to read and appreciate the book or not), but in composing the review it may be important to provide information about the story along the way so that your criticism makes sense. Students sometimes include too much information about the story, so their reviews amount to little more than plot summary.

Your classmates can be very helpful when they review your drafts in Revising Workshop. It often takes a reader other than yourself to notice when you seem to be straying too far from your basic purpose.

Assignment

You have read and responded in your journal to several articles and essays and have reflected on your own experiences and attitudes in relation to the theme "Male and Female in the 1980s." The project for this chapter has four parts in which you will write on this theme for different audiences and purposes.

As you read the four assignments, notice that in each you are asked to deal with essentially the same subject matter. What varies for you as writer is your specified audience and purpose. As you write the parts of the assignment, observe how your style, language choices, tone, and structure vary depending on these changes of audience and purpose.

1. You are to compose a journal entry in which you recall from your childhood and adolescent years when you understood that you were a male or female and thus were supposed to act accordingly. What incidents can you remember that told you that you were to behave, look, or feel or express yourself in a certain way, depending on your sex? Explore this idea by retelling the incidents that you can remember—they might have taken place at home, at school, church, in the neighborhood, and so on, and they might have been with family, friends, teachers, or books. Write without regard for correctness for three to four pages in your journal.

THE FAMILY CIRCUS ®   By Bil Keane

"How old do babies hafta get to start bein'
boys and girls?"

Your audience here is yourself. But, although you are exploring your past experience and feelings for the purpose of recording and clarifying your identity as a unique individual, you will probably share this entry with others.

2. Review your journal entry and think about what the narrative says to you. Is your experience the kind you would like other young people to have as they are growing up? If so, why? If not, why not? To what extent have your feelings now changed from those feelings of the past which you recorded? What accounts for the changes?

Building on your recollections, your thoughtful consideration of the current meaning of that past experience, and your responses to the reading of this chapter, your next writing task is to compose a friendly letter. A close friend about to become a parent has written to you asking for your ideas about this male-female concept. "I don't really care whether we have a boy or girl," your friend writes, "but I'm really confused these days—what with the women's movement and all the talk about stereotyping and androgyny. You seem all together to me. Please tell me how you were treated as a male (or female) as you were growing up, how you felt about it, and how it's affected you."

Select any specific prewriting strategy to help you get started here (see Chapter 4 for various techniques), and write a two- to three-page letter to this close friend. Your purpose is to share information and feelings. Your friend is *not* asking for advice.

3. (Review what you have read and written for the entire chapter in preparation for this next part of the assignment.)

A team from the psychology department of a local university is conducting a survey of how embedded sex role stereotyping is among college students in the 1980s. You have been asked to participate in this study by submitting a two- to three-page report of your own childhood and adolescent experience as a male or a female and the extent to which you were influenced by stereotyping and might still be. You may be asked to go in for an interview for more in-depth exploration of your experience.

(Remember, you are giving information to a group of psychologists whom you do not know personally. Employ any additional prewriting strategies here that you feel are necessary for getting started.)

4. (The fourth part of this writing project builds on the material you have written here as well as all your readings and responses throughout the chapter.)

In one of a series of special presentations, you recently heard a talk by a guest lecturer in social psychology, Dr. Bryson. The topic was "Children of the 1960s: A New Generation," and the speaker asserted that students in college now are extremely fortunate in being freed of the sex role stereotypes that plagued students until recent years. "No longer do young men and women suffer," she said, "the debilitating effects of the male or female label which has carried with it certain proscribed modes of behavior and expression as well as definite career and life expectations."

The lecture caused considerable discussion among students in the lecture hall. On the following day one of your professors sensed the strong interest and feeling that the speech had aroused and assigned each member of the class to write a two- to three-page response to the lecture. He said he would sort through them and select the best ones to submit to Dr. Jones, the professor who invited the guest speaker. Using your own personal experiences and what you know of your classmates' and others' experiences, write your response. Your aim is either to agree or disagree with Dr. Bryson's generalizations and to support your opinion with experiences you have had or know of. Utilize any additional prewriting strategies that you feel would be useful at this stage.

Revising Workshop

When you have completed drafting all four parts of the writing assignment, bring them to the Revising Workshop. In small groups, share your papers with your classmates, assisting each other by responding to the following questions in relation to each of the four projects. Each person's papers should be responded to by at least two other students. *Do not* be concerned with editing problems at this stage.

1. How clear is the basic purpose of each part of the assignment?
2. To what extent is the designated audience appropriately addressed in each part? Mark any places where the writer seems to lose track of his or her audience. If you were the intended audience for the second, third, and fourth parts, what questions would you raise in response to the paper? Is there any statement you would object to? Is there any section of the paper where you would like more information?
3. To what extent do the language, style, tone, and structure seem suitable for the designated audience and purpose of each part of the set of papers?
4. Comment on the sentence structure. Are any sentences choppy? Any too long? Any weakened by excess words?
5. In reviewing all four parts together, what changes do you note in style, language choice, tone, sentence structure, and overall organization? Do the changes seem sufficient given designated audiences and purposes? Mark places in the second, third, or fourth parts where you think additional changes might be considered.

Before you write the second drafts of the last three parts (it is rarely appropriate to redraft journal entries), consider carefully the responses your classmates have made to your papers and revise to clarify your purposes and to address more effectively your various audiences. Make the changes that will keep each paper consistent in the tone and the style appropriate for each audience and purpose.

Editing Workshop

Return to your small group with the second drafts. In this group session, the Editing Workshop, your goal is to help each other review your three papers for mechanical flaws and any problems with form. In this workshop, as in the first one, each person's paper should be reviewed by at least two other students. Use the following questions in responding to each of the second drafts:

1. Are there any sentences or parts of sentences that confuse you or cause you to have to reread them to grasp the meaning? If so, bracket these as needing additional consideration.
2. Place an *X* in the margins of the papers on any line where you notice what you perceive as an error in spelling or punctuation. Use as many marks as there are errors.
3. Put a *C* in the margin of any line where you find a trite expression or cliché.
4. Put a *G* in the margin of any line where you see what you perceive as an error in grammar or usage.

Examine the responses of your classmates to your papers. If sentences are bracketed, try to decide what the problems are with those sentences. If you find marks indicating grammar, spelling, punctuation errors, or clichés, try to understand what those errors are and how they should be corrected. For help, consult the Editing Guide (Chapter 12). Make notes in your journal about the kinds of errors you seem to be making. Finally, edit again to correct any errors and then submit your papers.

CHAPTER 4

Explaining an Issue

THEME *Clothing Choices*

SKILL FOCUS *Generating Ideas*

Like other chapters, Chapter 4 will provide experience in all phases of the writing process. The particular skill stressed here is *generating ideas*. You are offered various strategies for coming up with ideas or discovering what you want to say.

The theme of this chapter is *clothing choices,* a subject all people share an interest in whether they are fashion conscious or simply view clothing as a practical necessity. You may never have thought about what your apparel might say about you, or you may be keenly aware of how your clothes reflect your personality and values. Reading about, responding to, and writing about this theme may give you more insight into yourself and will add to your understanding of others. Related more directly to this course, these assignments will help you realize the interdependence of the skills of reading, thinking, and writing.

The final writing project of this chapter will ask you to use the ideas in the readings and your responses to them. Your own cumulative perceptions of the theme will help you explain to an ill-informed audience the complexity of this subject and what clothing means to humans.

Before Reading

The following short selection is from Alice Walker's novel *The Color Purple*. Celie, the main character, has left her husband and moved in with Shug Avery, a woman who sings in a nightclub. The excerpt is from a letter Celie writes to her sister Nettie, a missionary in Africa, who has commented on the foolishness of wearing heavy western clothing in the African heat. A country girl with little knowledge of sophisticated ways, Celie has made a pair of pants as a present for Shug at a time when it was customary for women to wear skirts. As you read the selection, ask yourself the following questions:

1. What does Celie consider when she designs a pair of pants?
2. How will her process of designing change when she makes pants for people she does not know?

The Color Purple

Alice Walker

Dear Nettie,

. . . I sit in the dining room making pants after pants. I got pants now in every color and size under the sun. Since us started making pants down home, I ain't been able to stop. I change the cloth, I change the print, I change the waist, I change the pocket. I change the hem, I change the fullness of the leg. I make so many pants Shug tease me. I didn't know what I was starting, she say, laughing. Pants all over her chairs, hanging all in front of the china closet. Newspaper patterns and cloth all over the table and the floor. She come home, kiss me, step over all the mess. Say, before she leave again, How much money you think you need *this* week?

Then finally one day I made the perfect pair of pants. For my sugar, naturally. They soft dark blue jersey with teeny patches of red. But what make them so good is, they totally comfortable. Cause Shug eat a lot of junk on the road, and drink, her stomach bloat. So the pants can be let out without messing up the shape. Because she have to pack her stuff and fight wrinkles, these pants are soft, hardly wrinkle at all, and the little figures in the cloth always look perky and bright. And they full round the ankle so if she want to sing in 'em and wear 'em sort of like a long dress, she can. Plus, once Shug put them on, she knock your eyes out.

Miss Celie, she say. You is a wonder to behold.

I duck my head. She run round the house looking at herself in mirrors. No matter how she look, she look good.

You know how it is when you don't have nothing to do, I say, when she brag to

Grady and Squeak bout her pants. I sit here thinking bout how to make a living and before I know it I'm off on another pair pants.

By now Squeak see a pair *she* like. Oh, Miss Celie, she say. Can I try on those?

She put on a pair the color of sunset. Orangish with a little grayish fleck. She come back out looking just fine. Grady look at her like he could eat her up.

Shug finger the pieces of cloth I got hanging on everything. It all soft, flowing, rich and catch the light. This is a far cry from that stiff army shit us started with, she say. You ought to make up a special pair to thank and show Jack.

What she say that for. The next week I'm in and out of stores spending more of Shug's money. I sit looking out cross the yard trying to see in my mind what a pair of pants for Jack would look like. Jack is tall and kind and don't hardly say anything. Love children. Respect his wife, Odessa, and all Odessa amazon sisters. Anything she want to take on, he right there. Never talking much, though. That's the main thing. And then I remember one time he touch me. And it felt like his fingers had eyes. Felt like he knew me all over, but he just touch my arm up near the shoulder.

I start to make pants for Jack. They have to be camel. And soft and strong. And they have to have big pockets so he can keep a lot of children's things. Marbles and string and pennies and rocks. And they have to be washable and they have to fit closer round the leg than Shug's so he can run if he need to snatch a child out the way of something. And they have to be something he can lay back in when he hold Odessa in front of the fire. And . . .

I dream and dream and dream over Jack's pants. And cut and sew. And finish them. And send them off.

Next thing I hear, Odessa want a pair.

Then Shug want two more pair just like the first. Then everybody in her band want some. Then orders start to come in from everywhere Shug sing. Pretty soon I'm swamp.

One day when Shug come home, I say, You know, I love doing this, but I got to get out and make a living pretty soon. Look like this just holding me back.

She laugh. Let's us put a few advertisements in the paper, she say. And let's us raise your prices a hefty notch. And let's us just go ahead and give you this diningroom for your factory and git you some more women in here to cut and sew, while you sit back and design. You making your living, Celie, she say. Girl, you on your way.

Nettie, I am making some pants for you to beat the heat in Africa. Soft, white, thin. Drawstring waist. You won't ever have to feel too hot and overdress again. I plan to make them by hand. Every stitch I sew will be a kiss.

Amen,

Your Sister, Celie
Folkspants, Unlimited.
Sugar Avery Drive
Memphis, Tennessee

After Reading

Record in your journal your reactions to the reading. Even though this response is one you will write just for yourself and it calls only for your reaction (about which you cannot be wrong), you may ask yourself, "How do I begin?" or "What will I say?" Our advice is write and find out. There is a great advantage in just recording your thoughts and feelings as they occur to you and looking for patterns and generalizations afterward. If you try to sum things up too soon, you are likely to shut out some of your response. And writing your response is better than just thinking it because writing preserves the thought and allows you to look it over in its entirety. The following are some methods for recording your response.

STRATEGIES FOR GENERATING IDEAS

Free Writing

Many writers have found *free writing* a useful way to start themselves thinking and to put down their thoughts on paper. When you do free writing, you decide to write whatever occurs to you for a specified period of time or number of pages. You never stop writing. You record whatever you are thinking, no matter how repetitive or unimportant it may seem. Some people keep a journal using free writing: every day they do free writing for so many minutes or so many pages. They say it is a good way to discover what is really on their minds.

When free writing, do not stop to worry about spelling or punctuation. You can even write in sentence fragments as long as you will be able to tell what you meant when you go back later to read it. This is writing you do for yourself, and the purpose is to record your thoughts and feelings so they will be accessible to your conscious mind. Here is an example of an unfocused three-minute free writing:

> Why aren't hardware stores open at night? Who needs a gasket or epoxy in the morning? Guess there's an answer to that––people who work with those things, not just those of us who play with them. And it used to be play. Watch Dad change the washer, build a dry stone wall. More fun for us. He was always tired, resentful. It is easy to think things are out to trip you up. Why do I care about things? Never used to. Never minded that the shower leaked in the apartment on Ludlow Ave. Steve's problem. Not mine. Where is Steve? Who lives there now? Is it still such a charged place or would it be drab with no familiar people, no sense of what we all have in common. How good is Skyline chili if you're not likely to run into Ted and Dottie there on a Sun. morning?

Free association is what holds this piece together. The writer just began writing and followed wherever his mind led. Much of what he wrote is mysterious to us: Who is Steve? What does he have to do with the leaky shower on Ludlow Avenue? But the writer was writing for himself, and it makes perfect sense to him. Looking over what he wrote, he could see that there were two topics on his mind that day: a complaint about house repairs and nostalgia for an earlier, carefree time in his life. Once he identified these two ideas, he realized that they were very much related. If he continued to do free writing every day or so over weeks or months he would see how his attitudes toward responsibility for a home did or did not change, and he would find out what else was important to him. It is always healthy and gratifying to understand ourselves a bit better. And, if this writer had been assigned to write a paper on a topic of his choice, his free writing would be very helpful in giving him a topic. He could write about the burden that comes with owning things and having to keep them repaired or about what makes us nostalgic.

Focused Free Writing

It is rare, of course, to be assigned to write on a subject of your choice. Most assignments in school specify the subject. Often, you will be asked to choose a topic that examines a small segment of the subject under study. In a sociology class called Group Dynamics, for example, you may be assigned to write a paper on some aspect of the research on groups. It is up to you to decide on an issue that interests you and that you can cover well within the assigned length of the paper.

To generate ideas on a particular subject, *focused free writing* can be very helpful. This is free writing in which you stay within the bounds of one subject. If no new thought occurs to you while you are writing about the subject, you simply keep writing the name of your subject until a new thought does come or until the time limit you had set is up. Here is an example of a *focused free writing* on group dynamics:

> What makes the right size group for different pur-
> poses? A question I'd like to know the answer to. Pairs
> of people work well if the two people are compatible—if
> the purpose is sharing work for a joint report or prod-
> uct of some kind, two might be best. For discussion, you
> really need, it seems to me, three or four, so there's
> really an exchange of ideas and opinions. Or what about
> the way people behave in groups—who assumes leadership?
> How much control over a project are people willing to
> give up? How much would I give up? Depends on how much I
> care about it or care about the other people. Or whether
> it's graded. When I worked on the student directory, I
> fought for. . . .

Notice how this student sorted through some general thoughts on the subject and then some possible topics and finally seems to have focused on the question, "How much control over a project are people willing to give up?" She then begins to answer that question from her own experience. This is a very good way to search for a topic and to begin to consider possibilities.

Because she considers her own experience from the start, the topic she chooses will probably be more meaningful to her than one someone else suggests. Of course, not every focused free writing delivers a topic, but each one should help you get a bit closer.

Focused free writing has uses beyond generating a topic for an assignment. Like unfocused free writing, it can be a journal entry that helps you understand yourself better. Also, if you respond to your reading by free writing, you will probably find that you are much better prepared to use what you have read because you will remember it better. You will also have better recall and understanding of the subject because you have reacted to it and have considered it in light of your own experience.

Now, in your journal, write your response to the selection from *The Color Purple*. Do this focused free writing until you have filled three pages. Remember, keep writing and do not lift your pen from the paper.

Before Reading

The following excerpts from Alison Lurie's *The Language of Clothes* are from her chapter titled "Fashion and Status." Lurie uses concepts in this chapter from Thorstein Veblen's 1912 book, *The Theory of the Leisure Class*, to suggest that changing fashions in clothing are influenced by people's desires for high status.

Before you read the selection, do the following:

1. Name as many as you can of the prominently displayed labels on clothing (e.g., Pierre Cardin ties signed in large letters).
2. Name some clothing styles that are no longer fashionable.

As you read the selection, try to answer the following questions:

1. What constitutes "high status" as Lurie uses the term? (As you will see, a 4.0 grade point average or the ability to play the guitar are not very important in this value system. What is the criterion for measuring a person's status in the system Lurie describes?)
2. How do Conspicuous Consumption, Conspicuous Waste, and Conspicuous Leisure differ from each other?

Fashion and Status

Alison Lurie

Man from the earliest times has worn clothes to overcome his feelings of inferiority and to achieve a conviction of his superiority to the rest of creation, including members of his own family and tribe, and to win admiration and to assure himself that he "belongs."

—Lawrence Langner

Clothing designed to show the social position of its wearer has a long history. Just as the oldest languages are full of elaborate titles and forms of address, so for thousands of years certain modes have indicated high or royal rank. Many societies passed decrees known as *sumptuary laws* to prescribe or forbid the wearing of specific styles by specific classes of persons. In ancient Egypt only those in high position could wear sandals; the Greeks and Romans controlled the type, color and number of garments worn and the sorts of embroidery with which they could be trimmed. During the Middle Ages almost every aspect of dress was regulated at some place or time—though not always with much success. The common features of all sumptuary laws—like that of edicts against the use of certain words—seem to be that they are difficult to enforce for very long.

Laws about what could be worn by whom continued to be passed in Europe until about 1700. But as class barriers weakened and wealth could be more easily and rapidly converted into gentility, the system by which color and shape indicated social status began to break down. What came to designate high rank instead was the evident cost of a costume: rich materials, superfluous trimmings and difficult-to-care-for styles; or, as Thorstein Veblen later put it, Conspicuous Consumption, Conspicuous Waste and Conspicuous Leisure. As a result, it was assumed that the people you met would be dressed as lavishly as their income permitted. In Fielding's *Tom Jones,* for instance, everyone judges strangers by their clothing and treats them accordingly; this is presented as natural. It is a world in which rank is very exactly indicated by costume, from the rags of Molly the gamekeeper's daughter to Sophia Western's riding habit "which was so very richly laced" that "Partridge and the post-boy instantly started from their chairs, and my landlady fell to her curtsies, and her ladyships, with great eagerness." The elaborate wigs characteristic of this period conferred status partly because they were both expensive to buy and expensive to maintain.

By the early eighteenth century the social advantages of conspicuous dress were such that even those who could not afford it often spent their money on finery. This development was naturally deplored by supporters of the status quo. In Colonial America the Massachusetts General Court declared its "utter detestation and dislike, that men or women of mean condition, should take upon them the garb of Gentlemen, by wearing Gold or Silver lace, or Buttons, or Points at their knees, or to walk in great Boots; or Women of the same rank to wear Silk or Tiffiny hoods, or Scarfes. . . ." What "men or women of mean condition"—farmers or artisans—were supposed to wear were coarse linen or wool, leather aprons, deerskin jackets, flannel petticoats and the like.

To dress above one's station was considered not only foolishly extravagant, but deliberately deceptive. In 1878 an American etiquette book complained,

> It is . . . unfortunately the fact that, in the United States, but too much attention is paid to dress by those who have neither the excuse of ample means nor of social claims. . . . We Americans are lavish, generous, and ostentatious. The wives of our wealthy men are glorious in garb as are princesses and queens. They have a right so to be. But when those who can ill afford to wear alpaca persist in arraying themselves in silk . . . the matter is a sad one.

Contemporary Status: Fine Feathers and Tattered Souls

Today simple ostentation in dress, like gold or silver lace, is less common than it used to be; but clothes are as much a sign of status as ever. The wives of our wealthy men are no longer praised for being glorious in garb; indeed, they constantly declare in interviews that they choose their clothes for ease, comfort, convenience and practicality. But, as Tom Wolfe has remarked, these comfortable, practical clothes always turn out to have been bought very recently from the most expensive shops; moreover, they always follow the current rules of Conspicuous Consumption, Waste and Leisure.

At the same time, as high-status clothes have become superficially less gorgeous they have increasingly tended to take on an aura of moral virtue. A 1924 guide to good manners clearly suggests this:

> An honest heart may beat beneath the ragged coat, a brilliant intellect may rise above the bright checked suit and the yellow tie, the man in the shabby suit may be a famous writer, the girl in the untidy blouse may be an artist of great promise, but as a general rule, the chances are against it and such people are dull, flat, stale, and unprofitable both to themselves and to other people.

The implication is that an ill-dressed person is also probably dishonest, stupid and without talent. Today this idea is so well established that one of our foremost historians of costume, Anne Hollander, has refused to admit that true virtue can shine through ugly or ragged clothes, as in the tale of Cinderella:

> In real life . . . rags obviously cannot be "seen through" to something lovely underneath because they themselves express and also create a tattered condition of soul. The habit of fine clothes, however, can actually produce a true personal grace.

In a society that believes this, it is no wonder that many of those who can ill afford to wear alpaca—or its modern equivalent, polyester—are doing their best to array themselves in silk. Popular writers no longer complain that those of modest means wear clothes above their rank; instead they explain how best to do so: how to, as the title of one such book puts it, *Dress for Success.* At the moment there are so many such guidebooks it may seem surprising that their advice is not followed by more people. However, as my friend the lady executive remarks, "wardrobe engineering won't do much for you if your work is lousy . . . or if you're one of an army of aspirants in impeccable skirted suits all competing for the same spot. As with investment advice, once everyone agrees that it's the thing to do, it's time to look for value somewhere else."

There are other problems with dressing to advance your status professionally. First and most obviously, it is very expensive. The young executive who buys a high-priced suit instead of a stereo system or a week's vacation in Portugal or the Caribbean is giving up certain present pleasure for possible future success in a society that regards hedonistic self-fulfillment as a right. Second, there are one's colleagues to consider. For many people, agreeable working conditions and well-disposed birds are worth more than a possible promotion in the bush. The clerk who dresses like his boss is apt to be regarded by other clerks as a cold fish or an ass-kisser; the secretary in her severe skirted suit is seen as snotty and pretentious: Who does she think she is, in that getup? Moreover, somebody who is distrusted and disliked by his or her equals is very unlikely ever to become their superior. It is also a rare boss who wants to have employees who dress exactly as he or she does—especially since they are usually younger and may already have the edge in appearance. Fortunately for the manufacturers, however, there are more ways than one of advertising high status. Today, "simple," "easy-care," and "active" may be the bywords of fashion copy; but fashionable luxury, waste and inconvenience continue to flourish in new forms. . . . .

Conspicuous Multiplication

Wearing a great many clothes at once is a burdensome and often unpleasantly hot form of Conspicuous Consumption; changing into different outfits for different activities is a nuisance. An alternative or supplementary way of demonstrating high status is to own many similar garments, so that you almost never wear exactly the same costume. The extreme case of this is the person who—like Marie Antoinette—never wears the same thing twice. Today such extravagance is rare and felt to be excessive, but the possession of a very large wardrobe is still considered charming by those who follow what Veblen called "pecuniary canons of taste." F. Scott Fitzgerald, in a famous scene, describes the effect of Jay Gatsby's extensive collection of shirts on Daisy Buchanan:

> He took out a pile of shirts and began throwing them, one by one, before us, shirts of sheer linen and thick silk and fine flannel, which lost their folds as they fell and covered the table in many-colored disarray. While we admired, he brought more and the soft rich heap mounted higher—shirts with stripes and scrolls and plaids in coral and apple-green and lavender and faint orange, with monograms of Indian blue. Suddenly, with a strained sound, Daisy bent her head into the shirts and began to cry stormily. "They're such beautiful shirts," she sobbed, her voice muffled in the thick folds. "It makes me sad because I've never seen such—such beautiful shirts before."

The particular type of Conspicuous Consumption that consists in the multiplication of similar garments is most common among women. In men it is more rare, and usually associated either with dandyism or with great and rapidly acquired wealth, as in the case of the bootlegger Gatsby. A man who gets a raise or a windfall usually buys better clothes rather than more of them, and he has no need to wear a different outfit each day. Indeed, if he were seen to vary his costume as often as his female colleagues do he would be thought vain and capricious—perhaps even unstable. Monotony of dress is only a minor fault, though a man who wore the same tie to the office every day for a week would probably be considered a dull fellow.

For a woman, on the other hand, variety in dress is essential, and the demand for it starts very early. In America many girls in secondary school or even younger feel acute embarrassment about wearing the same outfit twice in the same week—let alone on consecutive days. Even if they own relatively few garments they will go to great lengths to combine them differently and to alter the total effect with accessories. So strong is this compulsion that quantity is usually preferred to quality, and shoddy new garments to well-made old ones. In terms of the struggle for status, this may be the right decision: young girls may not be able to recognize good clothes, but they can certainly count.

This female sense of the shamefulness of repetition persists into adult life. One of the most double-edged compliments one woman can give another is "Oh, you're wearing that pretty dress *again!*" (Men, who know no better, are forgiven such remarks.) Often the compulsion continues into old age: my mother, when nearly ninety, still liked to appear in a different outfit each day "so as not to be boring." But it seems to be strongest among women in offices, for whom the fact that a colleague arrives at work on Tuesday in the same costume she was wearing on Monday is positive proof that she spent the intervening night unexpectedly at somebody else's apartment.

The constant wearing of new and different garments is most effective when those you wish to impress see you constantly—ideally, every day. It is also more effective if these people are relative strangers. If you live and work in an isolated country village, most of the people you meet will already have a pretty good idea of your rank and income, and they will not be much impressed if you keep changing your clothes. If you live in or near a city and work in a large organization, however, you will be seen often by the same people, but most of them will know little about you. Having a large and up-to-date sartorial vocabulary then becomes a matter of the first importance, especially if you have not yet established yourself socially or professionally. For this reason, it is not surprising that the most active supporters of the fashion industry today are young women in places like London and New York.

What is surprising, though, is the lengths to which this support can go. Many young working women now seem to take it for granted that they will spend most of their income on dress. "It's awfully important to look right," a secretary in a London advertising agency explained to me. "If a girl lives at home it'll be her main expense. If she's living in town, even sharing a flat, it's much harder. I'm always in debt for clothes; when I want something I just put it on my credit card. I know things cost more that way. But, well, take these boots. They were eighty-nine pounds, but they were so beautiful, I just had to have them, and they make me feel fantastic, like a deb or a film star. All my friends are the same." . . .

Conspicuous Labeling

Not long ago, expensive materials could be identified on sight, and fashionable men and women recognized Savile Row tailoring or a Paris designer dress at a glance. In the twentieth century, however, synthetics began to counterfeit wool, silk, linen, leather, fur, gold and precious stones more and more successfully. At the same time, manufacturing processes became more efficient, so that a new and fashionable style could be copied in a few months and sold at a fraction of its original price. Meanwhile, the economic ability to consume conspicuously had been extended to millions of people who were ignorant of the subtleties of dress, who could not tell wool from Orlon or Schiaparelli from Sears Roebuck. As a result there was a world crisis in Conspicuous Consumption. For a while it seemed as if it might actually become impossible for most of us to distinguish the very rich from the moderately rich or the merely well-off by looking at what they were wearing.

This awful possibility was averted by a bold and ingenious move. It was realized that a high-status garment need not be recognizably of better quality or more difficult to produce than other garments; it need only be recognizably more expensive. What was necessary was somehow to incorporate the price of each garment into the design. This was accomplished very simply: by moving the maker's name from its former modest inward retirement to a place of outward prominence. Ordinary shoes, shirts, dresses, pants and scarves were clearly and indelibly marked with the names, monograms or insignia of their manufacturers. The names or trademarks were then exhaustively publicized—a sort of saturation bombing technique was used—so that they might become household words and serve as an instant guide to the price of the clothes they adorned. These prices were very high, not because the clothes were made of superior materials or constructed more carefully, but because advertising budgets were so immense.

When this system was first tried, certain critics scoffed, averring that nobody in their right mind would pay sixty dollars for a pair of jeans labeled Gloria Vanderbilt when a more or less identical pair labeled Montgomery Ward could be purchased for twelve. Others claimed that consumers who wanted a monogram on their shirts and bags would want it to be their own monogram and not that of some industrialist they had never met. As everyone now knows, they were wrong. Indeed, it soon became apparent that even obviously inferior merchandise, if clearly labeled and known to be extravagantly priced, would be enthusiastically purchased. There was, for instance, a great boom in the sale of very ugly brown plastic handbags, which, because they were boldly stamped with the letters "LV," were known to cost far more than similar but less ugly brown leather handbags. Cotton T-shirts that faded or shrank out of shape after a few washings but had the word Dior printed on them were preferred to better-behaved but anonymous T-shirts. Those who wore them said (or were claimed in advertisements to say) that they felt "secure." After all, even if the shirt was blotchy and tight, everyone knew it had cost a lot of money, and if it got too bad you could always buy another of the same kind. Thus Conspicuous Consumption, as it so often does, merged into Veblen's second type of sartorial status.

Conspicuous Waste: Superfluous Drapery

Historically speaking, Conspicuous Waste has most often involved the use of obviously unnecessary material and trimmings in the construction of clothing. The classical toga portrayed in Greek and Roman sculpture, for instance, used much more fabric than was really needed to cover the body, the excess being artistically if inconveniently draped over one arm.

Anne Hollander has written most perceptively about the use of superfluous draped cloth in medieval, Renaissance and Baroque art. In preindustrial Europe, as she points out, cloth was the most important manufactured commodity, "the primary worldly good." Beautiful material was as admirable as gold or blown glass, and occupied far more space. The ownership of elaborate and expensive clothing was an important proof of social dominance. A single aristocrat sitting for his portrait, however, could only wear one luxurious outfit at a time. The display of many yards of velvet or satin behind him would suggest that he owned more such stuff and was able, in modern terms, to fling it around. Even after immensely full and trailing garments ceased to be worn, at least by men, excess drapery survived in art: it is notable for example in the paintings of Hals and Van Dyck and the sculptures of Bernini. The Frick Collection portrait of the Earl of Derby and his family "shows the family out of doors, standing on bare earth with shrubbery in the foreground and trees behind. But on the right side of the painting, behind the earl, next to a column that might conceivably be part of a house, fifty yards of dark red stuff cascade to the ground from nowhere. So skillfully does Van Dyck fling down these folds that their ludicrous inconsequence is unnoticeable. . . ."

Traditionally, as Ms. Hollander remarks, superfluous drapery has been a sign not only of wealth and high rank but of moral worth: angels, saints, martyrs and Biblical characters in medieval and Renaissance art often wear yards and yards of extra silk and velvet. Drapery derived additional prestige from its association with classical art, and thus with nobility, dignity and the ideal. Marble columns and togalike folds (occasionally, actual togas) were felt to transform the political hack into a national statesman and the grabby businessman into a Captain of Industry. As Ms. Hollander notes, Westminster Abbey and the Capitol in Washington, D.C., are full of such attempted metamorphoses, frozen into soapy marble.

Excess drapery survives today in middlebrow portrait painting, causing over-the-hill industrialists, mayors and society women to appear against stage backgrounds of draped velvet or brocade, the moral and economic prestige of which is somehow felt to transfer itself to them. Successful academics, I have noticed, are often painted in this manner: posed before velvet curtains, with their gowns and hoods and mortarboards treated in a way that recalls the idealized drapery and stiffened halos of Renaissance saints. (Appropriately, the halos of professors and college presidents are square rather than round.)

The use of superfluous fabric in costume never died out completely. During most of the period between 1600 and 1900, for instance, respectable middle-class and upperclass women wore a minimum of three petticoats; fewer than this was thought pathetic, and indicated negligence or poverty. Skirts were inflated with hoops or bustles to provide a framework on which to display great quantities of cloth, while overskirts, panniers, flounces and trains demanded additional superfluous fabric. A fashionable dress might easily require twenty or thirty yards of material. Elaborate trimmings of bows, ribbons, lace, braid, and artificial flowers permitted yet more prestigious waste of goods. Men's clothing during the same period used relatively little excess fabric except in outerwear, where long, full coats and heavy capes employed yards of unnecessary cloth, adding greatly to their cost and to the apparent bulk of their wearers.

A glance through any current fashion magazine will show that the use of superfluous fabric today, though on a much more modest scale, is by no means outmoded. Expensive clothes are often cut more generously, and fashion photography tends to make the most of whatever extra material the designer provides, spreading it over prop sofas or blowing it about in the air. Even the most miserly excess of cloth may now be touted as a sign of prestige: a recent advertisement in *The New York Times* boasts of an extra inch in the back yoke of Hathaway shirts which, the manufacturer sobs, costs them $52,000 a year.

Wastage of material in the form of trimming, though less striking than it was in the past, still persists. Today, however, it is often thinly distinguished as practical. A prestigious shirt, for instance, has a breast pocket into which nothing must ever be put; the habit of filling it with pens and pencils is a lower-middle-class indicator, and also suggests a fussy personality. A related ploy, especially popular between the two World Wars, was the custom of embroidering everything with the owner's initials. This may in some cases have had a practical function, as in the separation of laundry, but—and more importantly—it also added conspicuously to the cost of the garment.

Superfluous Personalities

Changing styles, of course, are another and very effective form of Conspicuous Waste. Although I do not believe that fashions alter at the whim of designers and manufacturers—otherwise they would do so far more often—it is certainly true that when social and cultural changes prompt a shift in the way we look the fashion industry is quick to take advantage of it, and to hint in advertising copy that last year's dress will do our reputation no good. When new styles do not catch on other ploys are tried. A recent one is to announce with disingenuous enthusiasm that fashion is dead; that instead of the tyranny of "this year's look" we now have a range of "individual" looks— which are given such names as Classic, Feminine, Sporty, Sophisticate and Ingénue. The task of the well-dressed liberated woman, the ads suggest, is to choose the look—or, much better and more liberated, *looks*—that suit her "life style." She is encouraged, for instance, to be sleek and refined on the job, glowingly energetic on holiday, sweetly domestic at home with her children and irresistibly sexy in the presence of what one department at my university has taken to calling her "spouse-equivalent." Thus, most ingeniously, life itself has been turned into a series of fashionable games, each of which, like jogging or scuba-diving or tennis, demands a different costume—or, in this case, a different set of costumes (winter/summer, day/night, formal/informal). The more different looks a woman can assume, the more fascinating she is supposed to be: personality itself has become an adjunct of Conspicuous Waste.

Men traditionally are not supposed to have more than one personality, one real self. Lately, however, they have been encouraged by self-styled "wardrobe engineers" to diversify their outward appearance for practical reasons. According to these experts, the successful businessman needs different sets of clothes in order to "inspire confidence in" (or deceive) other businessmen who inhabit different regions of the United States. This idea is not new, nor has it been limited to the mercantile professions. A former journalist has reported that as a young man he consciously varied his costume to suit his assignment. When sent to interview rich and powerful Easterners, he wore clothes to suggest that he was one of them: a dark-grey flannel Savile Row suit, a shirt from André Oliver or Turnbull & Asser, a Cartier watch of a sort never available at Bloomingdale's and John Lobb shoes. "What you have to convey to rich people any-where," he explained, "is that you don't have to try; so what you're wearing shouldn't ever be brand-new." New clothes, on the other hand, were appropriate when interview-ing the *nouveau riche;* and since they might not recognize understated wealth, he (somewhat reluctantly, but a job is a job) would also put on a monogrammed shirt and Italian shoes with tassels.

When assigned to official Washington, this particular journalist took care to be three or four years behind current New York modes. "Washington hates fashion, espe-cially New York fashion. The message should be, I am not attempting style; I am a man of the people, a regular fellow." He would therefore wear a somewhat rumpled pin-striped suit, a white shirt and a nondescript tie. Before leaving Manhattan he would get his hair cut shorter than usual. On the other hand, if he were sent to California, or were interviewing a writer, artist or musician anywhere in the country, he would try to let his hair grow or rumple it up a bit. He would wear slacks and a good tweed jacket over a turtleneck shirt; if the interviewee were financially successful he would add an expensive watch or pair of shoes to this costume. Still other getups were appropriate— and available—for the Midwest, Texas, the South, Continental Europe and Britain.

When this system works it is no longer Waste; nor, since the clothes are delib-erately chosen to blend into their surroundings, can they be called Conspicuous. But as the journalist himself remarked, clothes alone cannot disguise anyone, and the trav-eling salesman or saleswoman who engineers his or her wardrobe but not his or her voice, vocabulary or manners may simply be practicing Conspicuous Waste without its usual reward of enhanced status—let alone a rise in sales figures.

Conspicuous Leisure: Discomfort and Helplessness

Once upon a time leisure was far more conspicuous than it usually is today. The history of European costume is rich in styles in which it was literally impossible to perform any useful activity: sleeves that trailed on the floor, curled and powdered wigs the size, color and texture of a large white poodle, skirts six feet in diameter or with six-foot dragging trains, clanking ceremonial swords, starched wimples and ruffs and cravats that prevented their wearers from turning their heads or looking at anything below waist level, high-heeled pointed shoes that made walking agony and corsets so tight that it was impossible to bend at the waist or take a normal breath. Such clothes proclaimed, indeed demanded, an unproductive life and the constant assistance of ser-vants.

These conspicuously uncomfortable and leisurely styles reached an extreme in the late eighteenth century at the court of Versailles. The political and sartorial revolu-tion that followed freed both sexes temporarily, and men permanently, from the need to advertise their aristocratic helplessness. Men's clothes became, and have remained ever since, at least moderately comfortable. Women's fashions on the other hand, after barely ten years of ease and simplicity, rapidly became burdensome again and contin-ued so for the next hundred years.

Urban middle-class clothing today, though it does not usually cause pain, makes anything more than limited activity awkward. It is hard to run or climb in a business suit and slick-soled shoes; and the easily soiled white or pale-colored shirt that signifies freedom from manual labor is in constant danger of embarrassing its wearer with grimy cuffs or ring-around-the-collar. Urban women's dress is equally inconvenient. It should be pointed out, however, that inconvenience may be an advantage in some situations.

A friend who often does historical research in libraries tells me that she always gets dressed up for it. If she is obviously handicapped by high heels, a pale, elegant suit and a ruffled white blouse, the librarians will search the stacks for the heavy volumes of documents and old newspapers she needs and carry them to her, dusting them on the way. If she wears a sweater, casual slacks and sensible shoes, they will let her do it herself. The same ploy would probably work for a man if he were middle-aged or older.

The Rise and Fall of the Sack Suit

It is now almost two hundred years since the more extreme manifestations of Conspicuous Leisure in male clothing, but this principle, in a modified form, continues to separate white-collar from blue-collar men. Though the shirt may now be light blue, tan or striped, "white-collar" status is still signaled by the sack suit, which became standard in the mid-nineteenth century when the middle class had become largely urban and its occupations largely sedentary. . . . The sack suit is a kind of camouflage costume; it echoes the colors and shapes of the urban landscape. When well-tailored, the loose, square-cut jacket and tubular trousers also have a personal camouflage function: they conceal the soft belly and spindly legs characteristic of inactive persons who are no longer young.

The sack suit, as John Berger has recently pointed out, not only flatters the inactive, it deforms the laborious. It was designed for men who did little or no physical work and were therefore tall in relation to their breadth; it accommodated and emphasized the gestures of walking, sitting, speaking and pointing, but not those of running, lifting, carrying, hauling and digging. In addition, since it rumpled and soiled easily, it demanded to be worn indoors or on city streets. When physically active men with broad shoulders, deep chests and well-developed muscles put on cheap versions of the sack suit they looked misshapen, even deformed: as Berger puts it, they seemed "uncoordinated, bandy-legged, barrel-chested, low-arsed . . . coarse, clumsy, brutelike." Today backbreaking physical labor and the physique that goes with it are less common; but the same brutish effect is produced whenever a professional football player or wrestler appears in a suit off the peg.

The triumph of the sack suit meant that the blue-collar man in his best clothes was at his worst in any formal confrontation with his "betters." This strategic disadvantage can still be seen in operation at local union-management confrontations, in the offices of banks and loan companies, and whenever a working-class man visits a government bureau. Also, since the suit deforms the athlete and disguises the weakling, it may give the latter an undeserved edge in sexual competition. Not all social situations favor the sack suit, however: imagine, for instance, a bureaucrat climbing up out of his flooded cellar in a muddy, bedraggled helpless condition, followed by a plumber in rubber boots and sturdy, good-looking work clothes that show no sign of damage.

Recently the sack suit seems to be losing ground, especially outside large cities and in professions such as teaching, journalism and architecture. This change may be related to the recent shift in fashion from ambulatory sports such as golf and shooting to more vigorous pastimes like jogging and tennis. New styles have appeared to suit the man who has jogged himself into muscularity and no longer needs to conceal a pot. The unathletic white-collar male who affects such styles, however, is taking a risk: presently he may find himself looking remarkably feeble and podgy in his tight designer jeans and sport shirt while he (and if he is really unlucky, his girl friend) wait for some trim, well-built auto mechanic to diagnose his engine trouble. . . .

Conspicuous Outrage

Quentin Bell, whose fascinating study *On Human Finery* follows Veblen in designating economic competition as the principal force behind the vicissitudes of fashion, has suggested that to the categories of Conspicuous Consumption, Waste and Leisure should be added conspicuous Outrage, or the deliberate wearing of clothes that do not conform to the standards of "good taste." It is effective because of the rule that the more important any occasion is to the participants, the more careful and formal will be their dress. At job interviews, for example, the prospective employer may if he or she wishes appear in slacks and sweater; the candidates, even if of higher status, must wear suits or dresses. Sometimes the relative importance of an occasion to its different participants is ritual rather than economic, as for example at a wedding, where costumes range from the elaborate outfits of the wedding party to the less formal ones of distant relatives and acquaintances. The friend who, disapproving of the match or of marriage in general, comes to the ceremony in faded jeans and an old flannel shirt is practicing Conspicuous Outrage. The same rule causes us to attend parties given by those to whom we feel superior in relatively casual clothes; when this casualness is carried to a point where our contempt for the event is obvious we become Conspicuously Outrageous. A similar ploy is also frequently, and perhaps more forgivably, adopted by artists when visiting patrons whose wardrobes are far better equipped for the display of consumption, waste and leisure. Here it is not a direct insult that is intended, but merely an evasion of "pecuniary canons of taste."

People who decide to practice Conspicuous Outrage, of course, must be sure they will be instantly recognizable at the event in question. If they are not, they run the risk of being roughly escorted out by those who assume they have crashed the party to get free drinks. I once saw this almost happen to a rock star in a two-day beard and stained T-shirt who, through motives of boyhood friendship—mixed, it must be admitted, with scorn of the whole affair—came to an elaborate publisher's party. His error was to assume that his face would be as well known in the literary world as it was in the music industry.

The wearing of outrageous clothes primarily in order to attract negative attention—to annoy and offend—may also in a sense be a claim for status. The teenage punk in the torn, filthy T-shirt, and his or her formal equivalent, the Punk Rocker in the artificially torn T-shirt silk-screened with a symbolic representation of filth in the form of four-letter words, may be admired by their peers if not by us. Moreover, the wearers of such garments are often persons of low status and power, for whom to be noticed at all is a step up.

After Reading

In your journal, record your response to the selection from *The Language of Clothes*. How did you feel while you were reading the selection? What do you think of Lurie's ideas? Your response need not deal with the prereading questions, but you may use those if you like. Your response may be a focused free writing if you choose.

ASKING PROBING QUESTIONS

When you have written your entry, look back over it. Did you compare the selection to the excerpt from *The Color Purple?* Did you compare the motives of the fashion industry as Lurie describes them with Celie's motives in making pants? Did you use the categories of Conspicuous Consumption, Conspicuous Waste, and Conspicuous Leisure to help you sort out your response? Did you think about the kinds of clothes you buy and try to identify the things you consider when you shop? Did you think of styles that are examples of Lurie's generalizations? Or examples that seem to contradict her generalizations? Did you ask yourself, "What is fashion?" Or status? Or style? Did you ask why you reacted as you did to the readings or why people are motivated to buy fashionable clothes?

It is likely—though not inevitable—that you did one or more of these things, which demonstrate common strategies in our thinking: comparison and contrast, classification, exemplification, definition, and analysis of cause and effect. These strategies reflect the ways in which the mind comes to understand something. When we are confronted with a problem—say, a car that will not start—we solve it by asking, "What was wrong the last time the car wouldn't start?" [comparison]; "Does the same thing happen every time I turn the key?"; "What kinds of responses does the car give when I try to start it?" [classification]; "What are some things that can go wrong with the ignition system?" [exemplification]; "What has to happen under the hood for the car to start?"; "Why is this happening to me?"; "Why this morning?" [cause and effect]. Even an experienced mechanic who knows the answers to many of these questions will still run through the answers as a way of solving the problem.

These same mental operations are likely to be apparent in much of our writing just because they are common strategies of our thoughts. They may appear on the surface as when someone writes "The fashion industry's values are very different from Celie's" [comparison], or they may not appear in the writing itself but give rise to other statements. For example, in the sentence "As a reason for choosing particular clothes, status seems a poor choice," the comparison is implicit. The writer must have compared status with other reasons in order to have judged it poor.

Because these strategies are so common in our thinking and writing about any subject, they can be used for generating material when given an open assignment. Below are some questions you might ask to spur your thinking about X when you are asked to write a paper about X:

1. What is X like? How is it different from similar things? [comparison and contrast]
2. What divisions or classes exist with X? [classification]
3. What are some examples of X? [exemplification]
4. What is X? When does X cease to be X? [definition]
5. What are the causes of X? What are the effects of X? [cause and effect]

Share your responses to the Lurie reading in class discussion and record in your journal the reactions that differ from yours. Your purpose is just to ensure that you will have this information to use in a later assignment.

Before Reading

A *New York Times* best-seller for five months in 1978, John Molloy's *The Women's Dress for Success Book* proposes a business uniform for women. Until women adopt a uniform and thus gain a collective image, according to Molloy, they will never achieve equality with men in the business world.

Before you read, recall an experience you have had in which your clothing seemed inappropriate or made you feel uncomfortable in a specific situation. Try to remember your feelings on that occasion and what accounted for them.

As you read the Molloy excerpt, consider the following questions:

1. What is the "success suit"? What are the specifications for cut, material, pattern, and color?
2. Why, according to Molloy, should women not wear their uniform on social occasions?
3. Why does Molloy think women need to wear the uniform to succeed in business?

The Woman's Dress for Success Book

John T. Molloy

Instant Clothing Power for the Businesswoman

Every woman in the United States has, at one time or another, been given second-class treatment simply because she is a woman. The list of people who give women short shrift is long. It includes hotel employees, store clerks, receptionists, telephone operators, doctors, and bureaucrats. Business people of both sexes are prime offenders. They simply do not take women as seriously as they take men. To the woman who does not work, all of this is annoying. To the business or professional woman, it is devastating.

The women's movement has given women more professional clout, but they still have a long, long way to go before they are on an equal footing with men. Legislation, governmental guidelines, and government pressure have made it a lot easier for women to get jobs. In fact, in many areas reverse discrimination has taken over, and women have a decided edge.

But as far as success on the job and opportunity for advancement go, the old prejudices are still enormous obstacles for women.

The Business Uniform

There is one firm and dramatic step women can take toward professional equality with men. *They can adopt a business uniform.*

That is not a suggestion I casually put forth on the basis of a spur-of-the-moment notion. This suggestion is the product of years of laborious research involving thousands of men and women. That research led not only to the conclusion that businesswomen should adopt a uniform, but it also gave me more than ample information to spell out exactly what that uniform should be. A detailed explanation of the research for this project follows later in this chapter.

Like many of my research projects, this one came about almost accidentally. I had a luncheon appointment with three executives of a major corporation at a New York restaurant. I didn't know them or what their first names were. I only had the last name of one of them.

The appointment was for 12:30 P.M. I arrived five minutes early, looked around, and decided that since these executives obviously had not shown up yet, I'd have a drink at the bar. When I had them paged fifteen minutes later, I discovered to my embarrassment that they were sitting less than ten feet away. They were three of the best and most conservatively dressed women I had ever met, yet I had never considered the possibility that they might be my executives. I had been looking for three men.

When I apologized, they told me my reaction was normal. They said they always had trouble when they were away from the office. One said she was tempted to carry her desk plaque around with her. It said "VP SALES." They all agreed that their problem was especially acute when they traveled. At hotels and motels they felt particularly put upon. Desk clerks and porters seemed monumentally disinterested in accommodating them. One woman was particularly steamed up over the fact that when she traveled with her assistant, a man in his early thirties, he got preferential treatment every time.

It immediately occurred to me that her assistant had a sign that everyone could read. He undoubtedly wore a suit and tie, and that suit and tie said "Businessman." It occurred to me that the woman who made the facetious suggestion about carrying her VP SALES sign around with her had really hit on something. I came to the conclusion that there was a real need to develop a sign for business*women* to wear that is just as effective as the sign worn by business*men*.

I decided to explore that situation. My organization conducted a nationwide survey. The response showed that, indeed, there was no outfit that was widely regarded to be anything approaching a uniform for the business or professional woman.

Further research . . . showed the following:

- There should be a uniform.
- Beyond any doubt the uniform should be a *skirted suit and blouse.* In most cases the suit should be dark and the blouse should contrast with the skirt and jacket.

This outfit will give businesswomen a look of authority, which is precisely what they need.

If women are to enjoy widespread success in all industries, they must adopt this uniform. It is their best hope.

One indication that the skirted suit will be widely adopted is the fact that in some industries it already has been adopted. In banking and finance—particularly in the Wall Street area, which is the center of American business—few successful women would consider regularly wearing anything but the skirted suit.

When this uniform is accepted by large numbers of businesswomen, as I am confident it will be, it will be attacked ferociously by the enemies of women, many of whom are themselves women. The uniform issue will become an acid test to see which women are going to support other women in their executive ambitions.

The entire fashion industry is going to be alarmed at the prospect of women adopting a business uniform. They will see it as a threat to their domination over women.

And they will be right. If women adopt the uniform, and if they ignore the absurd, profit-motivated pronouncements of the fashion industry when they select their uniform, they will no longer be malleable. They will automatically and irrevocably break the hold that the male-dominated fashion industry has had over them.

If the work uniform is adopted, it will cut dramatically into the fashion industry's sales of both high-priced and low-priced garbage. So the industry should indeed feel threatened.

The fashion industry might use one of two methods to combat this threat.

First, they can use the industry's favorite ploy—the disappearing act. Whenever they don't want something on the market, they simply take it off. Poof! It's gone. That's what the industry does to any alternative to anything they are pushing at any given time. If they decide to do this with the skirted suit, they probably will leave unacceptable token elements of it on the market. That means suits selling for more than $350 and less than $60. But they can't do this without the cooperation of the retail establishment. If the fashion industry tries to take the skirted suit off the market, women should let out a loud, collective howl. And they should close their pocketbooks.

The other method the fashion industry might use to fight back is to start creating nothing but suits for women to wear on social occasions, in hopes that fashion groupies—and subsequently great numbers of other women—will start wearing suits to parties. Their objective would be to undermine the effect of the skirted suit as the business uniform.

If you are a businesswoman, you should *not* wear your skirted suit uniform for nonbusiness occasions. There are two reasons.

First, it really will undermine the effectiveness of your skirted suits as business uniforms. Men can get away with wearing their "uniform" on social occasions because everyone recognizes the suit and tie as primarily a business uniform. But the skirted suit has not yet been established as a women's business uniform. When the world has been preconditioned to think of it as such, women will have more leeway to wear it socially.

Secondly, my research shows that the skirted suit is not effective for social occasions. The suit gives you authority and a sense of presence in business. But that's not what most women want on social occasions. They want to be attractive and to have fun. Research shows that they are most likely to accomplish both wearing a dress.

The skirted suit, however, should become the uniform for almost all business and political situations. Women appearing on television should wear it. Leaders of the feminist movement should wear it, because in order for the women's movement to win, women must achieve equal status in their jobs. And they cannot have equal status and equal pay without a collective image equal to that of men. Without a uniform there is no equality of image. . . .

The Success Suit

If I had let my research stop with the conclusion that the skirted suit is the best outfit for a woman's business uniform, I could not have given businesswomen the specific information that my client corporations required—or that you require when you go out to buy a skirted suit.

The Right Skirted Suit

In researching the particulars of the skirted suit and blouse ensemble, we used many of the same techniques described earlier in this book. We found the indirect question, computer-controlled, large-number survey particularly useful. The "indirect question" part of it means that we didn't come right out and ask subjects such questions as "What do you think of the suit the woman in this picture is wearing?" Instead, we would do such things as show them two pictures of the same woman with one variable—the suit, or the blouse, or whatever—and ask them such questions as "Which woman has the better job?"

In our testing of skirted suit ensembles, we surveyed more people than we did in the first seven years of our research on men's clothing.

This chapter, therefore, is the "postgraduate course" in the skirted suit as the woman's business uniform.

As I'm sure you realize, you don't want to rush out and buy the first skirted suit you see. Some cuts, colors, and patterns work; others don't. Some materials are better than others. And you must wear the right blouses with the right suits.

Cut   Our research indicates that the man-tailored blazer suit works best. Specifically, that means a jacket with a blazer cut and matching skirt.

The jacket should be cut fully enough to cover the contours of the bust. It should not be pinched in at the waist to exaggerate the bust.

The sleeves must be long.

This suit should be worn *without* a vest. Vests make women more sexually attractive and, therefore, less authoritative.

Although scarves are not an essential part of the uniform as a man's tie is to his uniform, they can be effective attention-getting devices. . . .

Suits with skirts that fall just below the knee test best. Minis and midis come and go, but the most efficient business suits have not varied in length more than two inches in the last seven years. So if you buy one that's slightly below the knee, you should have a garment that will serve you for years. (This is one reason why if businesswomen adopt the skirted suit as a uniform, they will be taking a major step toward liberation from the fashion industry.)

Material   The materials that test best are wool and linen. Synthetics that accurately capture the feel and look of wool and linen work as well. I recommend them, although not as strongly as real wool and linen.

The synthetics and combinations of natural fabrics and synthetics travel very well. If you prefer natural fabrics even while you travel, I suggest tweeds. They look good even after three hours on a plane. For traveling in the South, I would recommend combinations of cotton and polyester that look like linen. Linen takes a beating when you travel.

Pattern   Only three patterns tested well.

1. Solids
2. Tweeds—or what I call the bushy British pattern (It's an indefinite pattern that virtually acts as a solid.)
3. Plaids

The plaids that work are not the exaggerated ice cream seller's plaid, but they are one or two degrees stronger than those in a man's business suit.

Women are not tied into as drab a look in suits as men. In fact, drabness is usually not as effective for women. The pinstripe, which is the high status symbol for men, is a strong negative in women's suits. It gives off the "imitation man" effect, particularly in pantsuits, and that look destroys a woman's authority with men.

Colors That Test Best   Please note. The color suggestions are based on thousands and thousands of hours of research. If they are not taken *exactly* as written, they will not have the desired effect.

The two colors that tested best in a solid-colored wool or linen suit are

Gray that is two or three shades lighter than charcoal. (It's the average gray of a man's suit.)
Medium-range blue (the average blue in a man's suit).

The other colors that tested very well are*

navy	steel gray	black
charcoal gray	dark brown	deep maroon
medium-range gray	beige	deep rust
camel		

Tweed suits are multicolored. But the only tweed suits we were able to test were those with a dominant color. Tweed works well with these dominant colors:

rust	medium-range gray
brown	blue (ranging from medium to navy)

Tweed suits often have accent threads throughout the suit.

• If the dominant color is rust, the best accent thread is blue or deep brown.
• If gray is dominant, the best accent thread is blue.
• If brown is dominant, the best accent threads are beige or blue.
• If blue is dominant, the best accent threads are white or beige.

Those accent threads work well because by picking them up in the blouse, you form a psychologically more effective ensemble.

Plaids also are multicolored. They have three sets of colors in them:

1. A dominant color. (Sometimes there are two dominant colors, such as blue and gray.)
2. Accent colors.
3. Accent threads.

*The colors in this and other lists are not ranked in order of preference.

The following dominant colors test best in plaids.

navy	medium-range gray	charcoal gray
gray (two shades lighter than charcoal)	blue-gray deep maroon	rust

The following accent colors test best in plaids.

white	charcoal gray	beige
black	navy	dark brown
rust	medium-range blue	tan

We were not able to test all combinations under all circumstances; therefore, I do not have information on accent threads in plaid.

Colors to Avoid Avoid these colors for suits:

most pastels, particularly pink and pale yellow
most shades of green
mustard (Mustard tested so poorly that if someone gives you a mustard suit, I suggest you burn it.)
bright red, bright orange, bright anything else
any shade that would be considered exotic.

If you show up at the office with an exotic color, you will be the envy of the fashion fans you work with, but male executives will not trust you. In general, stay away from colors with names like sea mint green or salmon pink. At the same time be aware that most advertising for women's clothes is written to sell, not to describe the item. Sometimes they give an exotic name to a standard color, so you might have to see the item before rejecting it.

Blouses

Our research on blouses was as heavy as our research on the suits themselves.

Your decisions on which blouses to wear with which suits should not be emotional or aesthetic decisions, since the blouse you put with the suit will make a measurable difference in the psychological impact of the suit.

The blouses I am going to discuss will all be in solid colors, not only because it would have been impossible to test all the variations of patterns but because solids tested best. (Plaid blouses also tested well for businesswomen's suits.)

The solid blouses we tested worked best when they were cotton or silk; however, you can go with any synthetic or any combination of natural fiber and synthetic that looks like cotton or silk.

The blouse should be simply cut, with no frills or lace.

The best neckline is the equivalent of having a man-tailored shirt with one button open; the blouse collar may be worn either inside or outside the coat.

How well blouse colors tested depended on several variables. Overall the best were the following:

white	medium blue
white on white	navy
pale yellow (not bright yellow)	cocoa
	dark brown

straw or pale beige	black
ecru	light gray
beige	pink (dark, bright, pale,
khaki	or end-on-end)
tan	orange
denim blue	Chinese red
light blue	maroon
end-on-end blue (this	rust
means there is a	pale green
certain texture in the	kelly green
material to add to the	gold
color)	salmon

Effective Combinations

To drive home the point that you must take care when you combine suits and blouses, I will show the different effects of the first suit on the list (the gray) when combined with different blouses.

With the gray suit . . .

- a white blouse gives you very high authority, a high status rating, and a business executive image without offending even 1 percent of the male executive population.
- a black blouse increases your authority so much that you offend 15 percent to 20 percent of the executive population, particularly men over forty-five.
- a pale yellow blouse weakens your authority but increases your image of likability, credibility, and trust-worthiness.
- a maroon blouse gives you a high sense of presence.
- a light blue blouse softens you almost to the point where you have trouble being authoritative. A medium blue or an end-on-end blue softens you even further.
- a gray blouse destroys your authority, credibility, and upper middle class image. I don't know why, but it just works that way.
- a pale pink blouse will destroy your authority in some companies and enhance it in others. Pink and gray is a fine aesthetic combination, and it can give you authority if the people in the company are used to seeing men in authority with pink shirts. If they're not used to that, the pink blouse will lessen your authority.

There are hundreds of variations possible with each suit, and, therefore, I'm not going to list each of them separately. The three major areas in which the businesswoman should make her clothes count—authority, presence, and trust—are given in the following lists. Some of the suit and blouse combinations appear on more than one list. That simply means that that particular combination tested as being effective in more than one area; therefore, the categories are not mutually exclusive.

Authority Outfits These combinations create a high authority image for a woman:

1. A solid gray suit . . . with a white blouse
    or with a white-on-white blouse
       with a pink man-tailored blouse in corporations where the men generally wear pink shirts.

2. A medium-range blue suit with a white blouse.

3. A navy blue suit . . . with a white blouse

      or with a white-on-white blouse

      with a gray blouse

      with a maroon blouse.

4. A charcoal gray suit with a white blouse

      or with a pink blouse in companies where pink shirts are worn regularly by the men.

5. A medium-range gray suit with a black blouse

      or with a white blouse.

6. A camel suit only with a deep blue blouse and only in the South.

7. A dark brown suit only with a white blouse and only in the Midwest.

8. A beige suit only with a deep blue blouse and only in the Sun Belt or in the summer.

9. A deep maroon suit with a white blouse

      or with a black blouse.

10. A deep rust suit . . . with a black blouse

      or with a white blouse.

11. A black suit with a white blouse.

12. A steel gray suit . . . with a white blouse

      or with a rust blouse.

None of the plaid suits rate as highly authoritative, so on any day that you have to bull your way through a difficult situation, you should stick with one of the suits on the above list.

Presence Outfits   Researchers have learned that if two six-footers and one person five feet six or shorter are in a closed environment and the discussion becomes heated, the two six-footers will start talking to each other and will ignore the shorter person, unless that person has a strong sense of presence. The sex of the short person is inconsequential unless it is a woman using sex as an attention-getting device. This is a problem for most businesswomen, who cannot be overtly sexy but must hold their own in heated discussions. Our studies indicate that the best nonsexual attention-getting device is color. Certain color combinations can give a woman this needed sense of presence.

The following suit and blouse ensembles tested best for a sense of presence:

1. A gray suit .... with a white blouse

      or with a rust blouse

      with a pink blouse

      with a maroon blouse

      with a black blouse.

2. A medium-range blue suit with a white blouse

      or with a dark blue blouse

      with a camel blouse

      with a beige blouse

      with a maroon blouse

      with a dark brown blouse

      with a deep rust blouse.

3. A navy blue suit .... with a white blouse

>   *or* with a rust blouse
>   with a medium-range gray blouse
>   with a pale yellow blouse
>   with a tan blouse
>   with an orange blouse
>   with a red blouse
>   with a gold blouse.

4. A charcoal gray suit ..... with a white blouse
>   *or* with a pink blouse.

5. A medium-range gray suit with a pink blouse.

6. A dark brown suit .... with a white blouse
>   *or* with a navy blouse
>   with a light blue blouse
>   with a rust blouse
>   with a maroon blouse.

7. A beige suit with a navy blue blouse.

8. A black suit .... with a white blouse
>   *or* with a black blouse.

9. A camel suit with a blue blouse (those shades of blue generally found in men's clothing).

10. A steel gray suit .... with a rust blouse
>   *or* with a maroon blouse.

Believability Outfits   You have to be believed to be trusted. Women have a greater difficulty making other women believe them than they do men.

Therefore, our research in this area concentrated more heavily on women subjects than did the research in many other areas.

The ensembles in which you are most likely to be believed (by both men and women) are these:

1. **A medium-range blue suit with a white blouse.**
2. **A navy blue suit with a white blouse**
   or **with a pale yellow blouse.**
3. **A medium-range gray suit with a medium-range blue blouse.**
4. **A deep maroon suit with a white blouse.**
5. **A deep rust suit with a white blouse.**
6. **A tan suit with a medium-range blue blouse.**
7. **A beige suit with a medium-range blue blouse.**
8. **A camel suit with a medium-range blue blouse.**

Popularity Outfits   Everybody in corporate America knows that it can help you to find someone higher up in the corporation who will help you up—a sponsor. This can be tricky for a woman because if she attaches herself to a man with a higher corporate rank, the attachment often appears sexual. There is another unfortunate fact: Women complain frequently that other women do not help them. And women have to overcome those two obstacles.

To get a sponsor, you first have to be liked by that person. You will be liked or disliked more on your mannerisms and your attitude than on the way you dress. But your clothes can help. Our research shows that if you wear certain colors, you will appear to be in a bright, cheery mood, and if you appear to be in a bright, cheery mood most of the time, you are much more likely to be liked by both men and women.

The colors are simple: a blue and pale yellow combination, or a beige (or tan or camel) and blue combination. Any time you wear a blue suit with a pale yellow blouse or a beige suit with medium or light blue blouse, you can sit at your desk and beam at everyone, and they'll think you're blissfully happy—while you're planning to take over the company.

After Reading

Respond in your journal to the following:

1. Implicit in this reading is a definition of *success*. In a sentence, summarize Molloy's idea of success. To what extent does this notion of success differ from your own? What part, if any, does clothing play in your notion of success?
2. Read the following section on making lists and then write a list of all the different kinds of clothes or "uniforms" you wear for different occasions or purposes (e.g., attending class, working, doing yard work).

MAKING LISTS

Making lists is a useful strategy for simply jogging your memory. Most folks make a list before a trip to the grocery, and many of us make lists as reminders of chores that we need to do. In learning to write, list making is another way to begin generating ideas. It may require little more than remembering what we already know from our own past experience, such as the ingredients necessary for oatmeal cookies, or what we have previously learned about a subject, say, the major events of the Civil War.

Writing other kinds of lists may require more than just remembering. For example, if we were preparing to write a feature story on urban versus rural living, we might want to jot down all the reasons that we can think of that people might choose to live in the city or in the country. Or, as a first step toward writing an exam essay calling for an interpretation of the symbolism in a piece of literature, a student would likely list all the symbols she could think of and what they seemed to represent. When you are using a list to generate thoughts about a particular subject, be sure to include everything you can think of on the topic; do not eliminate anything at the list-making stage. The idea is to get everything down and then think about the list.

Now, make your list in response to the second item (above) and share it and your thoughts on the first item with your classmates.

Before Reading

In 1980, Lisa Birnbach made a considerable amount of money with her satiric *The Official Preppy Handbook,* which included sections on all aspects of the preppy life style. A hefty portion of the book is devoted to preppy clothing—what it is like, where to buy it, and so forth. In the following excerpts, Ms. Birnbach sets down the basic principles of preppy fashion and explains the importance of monogramming, the pink/green color combination, and madras.

Fashion Fundamentals

Lisa Birnbach

The Ten Underlying Principles for Men and Women

Amateur historians have speculated that Preppies all dress alike because they got in the habit from wearing school uniforms. Not so. Preppies dress alike because their wardrobes are formed according to fundamental principles that they absorb from their parents and their peers. And although the Preppy Look can be imitated, non-Preps are sometimes exposed by their misunderstanding or ignorance of these unspoken rules.

1. Conservatism

Preppies wear clothes for twenty-five years and no one can tell the difference. The fabrics, the cuts, the colors are the same, year after year after year. A kilt from 1958, a ten-year-old tweed overcoat, a three-button suit bought in 1940 can all be worn until they fall apart.

2. Neatness

(Except for a brief period of rebellion during secondary school.) Preppies' shirts stay tucked in, through all kinds of strenuous exercise. Shoes are polished. Socks stay up. Sweaters are patched the moment holes appear in the elbows.

3. Attention to Detail

Subtleties of cut, weave, or color distinguish the merely good from the Prep. A small percentage of polyester in an oxford cloth shirt or a lapel that's a quarter of an inch too wide can make all the difference. Cuff buttons on a suit jacket that can actually be unbuttoned are the hallmark of the natty dresser. Everything matches—some Preppies go so far as to change their watchbands every day.

4. Practicality

Prep clothes are sensible: rain clothes keep you dry; winter clothes keep you warm; collars are buttoned down so they don't flap in your face when you're playing polo. Layering is a natural response to varying weather conditions.

5. Quality

Everything in the wardrobe should be well made. Fine fabrics and sound construction are taken for granted, hand tailoring is not unusual. Preppy clothes are built to last, since they certainly won't go out of style.

6. *Natural Fibers*

Wool, cotton, and the odd bits of silk and cashmere are the only acceptable materials for Prep clothes. They look better. They require professional maintenance. They are more expensive. They are key.

7. *Anglophilia*

The British have a lot to answer for: Shetland sweaters, Harris tweeds, Burberrys, tartans, regimental ties.

8. *Specific Color Blindness*

Primary colors and brilliant pastels are worn indiscriminately by men and women alike, in preposterous combinations. In some subcultures, hot pink on men might be considered a little peculiar; Preppies take it for granted.

9. *The Sporting Look*

Even if they've never been near a duck blind or gone beagling, Preppies are dressed for it. Rugged outerwear (snakeproof boots, jackets that will keep you warm at 60 degrees below zero) and hearty innerwear (fishermen's sweaters and flannel-lined khakis) are *de rigueur* in even the most sophisticated suburbs.

10. *Androgyny*

Men and women dress as much alike as possible and clothes for either sex should deny specifics of gender. The success of the Lanz nightgown is based on its ability to disguise secondary sexual characteristics, while the traditional fit for men's khakis is one size too big.

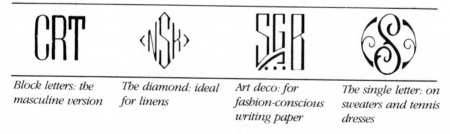

Block letters: the masculine version	*The diamond: ideal for linens*	*Art deco: for fashion-conscious writing paper*	*The single letter: on sweaters and tennis dresses*

By Oliver Williams, from *The Official Preppy Handbook,* copyright © 1980 by Lisa Birnbach. Reprinted with permission of the publisher, Workman Publishing, New York.

The Politics of Monogramming: When Your Own Initials Will Do

Preppies have known it for years: who needs LV or YSL when you can lay claim to a discreet EBW III? In fact, most Preppies are so proud of their monograms that they put them on virtually everything in sight.

The monogram itself must be tasteful. Women may occasionally choose a rather loopy script, but its use should be confined to writing paper and—at the outside— sheets and guests towels. Linens, silver, and cocktail glasses are conventionally monogrammed by Preps and non-Preps alike. But Preppies also put monograms on wastebaskets. A classic Prep present is a monogrammed needlepoint tennis racquet cover.

Clothing, of course, is a natural for monograms, though the conventions of monogramming are very strict. Men's shirts, for example: they must be monogrammed right, or not at all.

Although men's monograms are usually rather small and discreet, women's tend to be more elaborate. Sweaters, turtlenecks, jewelry, and tennis clothes are all fair game. Women's monograms are usually larger, with the last initial centered. They tend to hover about the collarbone, and navy blue is the color of choice, regardless of background shade.

One of the most trying sartorial problems for Preppies is that of too many initials. What if you have four names? Or more? And what if one of your names has a complicated initial, like DeW? Sadly, no compromise will do. If it isn't possible (because of space limitations or uncooperative tradespeople) to use the correct complete monogram, the Preppy does without. If your own initials are enough, it's probably enough that only you know what they are.

The Virtues of Pink and Green

The wearing of the pink and the green is the surest and quickest way to group identification within the Prep set. There is little room for doubt or confusion when you see these colors together—no one else in his right mind would sport such a chromatically improbable juxtaposition.

By Oliver Williams, from *The Official Preppy Handbook,* copyright © 1980 by Lisa Birnbach. Reprinted with permission of the publisher, Workman Publishing, New York.

Not just any shade of pink and green will do. Seafoam green and girl-baby pink would be as unthinkable as a wide tie or Famolare wedgies. No, this is unashamed, outrageous go-for-broke hot-hot pink and hubba-hubba electric wild lime green.

To help in understanding the full potential of this color combination, we have prepared a little exercise. You will need a pink and a green crayon (Crayola yellow-green and carnation pink) or, better yet, felt-tip markers (Flair pink and green are acceptable, or Pentell numbers 111 and 109). Study the figures above carefully. When you have fully absorbed all the details, color them in. Color the areas numbered 1 pink. Color the areas numbered 2 green. Then color your friend's copy of *The Official Preppy Handbook* differently. The possibilities are endless.

Madras

If there is one fabric that is quintessentially Preppy, it is madras. True madras, of course. The real thing is one of the oldest fabrics in the cotton trade, a fine, hand-loomed cotton that is imported from Madras, India. What sets true madras apart from imitations is that it "bleeds": the murky colors—navy blue, maroon, mustard yellow—of its distinctive plaids are imparted by vegetable dyes that are guaranteed to run.

Since the colors are so unstable, madras has to be treated very carefully. Shirts, shorts, and items that are not going to be dry-cleaned must be soaked in cold salt water for at least twenty-four hours before they are washed the first time. This sets the dyes. Then they really should be washed separately for months thereafter, because the colors will still run. Old madras takes on a lovely soft look and feel with many washings (the crux of the fabric's appeal to Preps), though jackets, which are dry-cleaned, of course, maintain that sharp plaid.

After Reading

Respond in your journal to the following:

1. To what extent do you agree with the 10 principles of preppy fashion? Explain the principles on which you base your clothing purchases. (Think about the last few items of clothing you purchased.)

2. Brainstorm as many different subgroups in your culture you can think of that can be identified by their style or type of clothing or "uniform." With each subgroup include the items of clothing that are part of the look of that group as well as your own ideas about how these groups are perceived by your society. Here are some strategies for brainstorming and clustering.

BRAINSTORMING AND CLUSTERING

Brainstorming is another strategy for helping you set down on paper all the thoughts and feelings you may have on a subject. Like free writing and making lists, brainstorming is a spontaneous strategy rather than a systematic, logical one. A writer simply thinks about a subject or question and writes down what-ever comes to mind related to the subject. The writing might be in sentences or fragments and may have no particular order or pattern.

Sometimes small groups or even a whole class will brainstorm, thereby providing additional stimulation for the individual writer. When your class-mates offer ideas, they remind you of facts, interpretations, or thoughts that you had not previously considered. But even individual brainstorming can be very productive if you try not to censor yourself. Let the ideas flow; you can always eliminate irrelevant ideas later in the process.

A typical example might be as follows. When students were preparing to write a personal narrative about their experience with food during their child-hood, one student began her work with the following brainstorming:

```
          cookies--no one knew about preservatives then
     ice cream treat (Dad liked it--never noticed I didn't)
   moon pies and Dr. Pepper at Beresford's a real sugar hit
          good food at dinner (breakfast and lunch were
                         do-it-yourself)
                         fried chicken
                         wilted lettuce
                    cucumbers in vinegar
                          baked ham
                          pot roast
                     mashed potatoes always
                       no meat on Friday
        that cake for my birthday with turquoise icing
```

Notice that the "brainstorm" is not exhaustive. Nor is it a simple list of foods; some items have thoughts and feelings attached to them. The writer is dredg-ing up material that can be useful as she proceeds to think about her narrative.

More structured than brainstorming, another strategy that can help you generate ideas on a subject, particularly a personal experience, feeling, or at-titude, is called *clustering*. Clustering includes free association as a way of dredging up what may have become blurred in your memory. Suppose you are asked to write a paper telling about a meaningful childhood experience and you do not know where to begin. You need to choose a technique that will help you recall a number of experiences, then to select one that stands out for some reason or another, and finally to begin analyzing and discovering the meanings of the experience.

A first step in clustering is to write the key word or words for explora-tion—in this case "childhood"—in the center of a blank page:

*my
Childhood*

Then simply write (as rapidly as you can) words that come to you about your childhood. As words come to you that seem related, let them follow one another in a line out from the center of the page as this student did:

In this example, a student recalled some key aspects or parts of four different childhood experiences that he remembered. These were not related to each other. Now he can pull out the two or three of these that seem most appealing and do further clustering on these experiences to determine how much he can really remember. Then he can decide which one has the most meaning for him. This student remembered more about his amateur hour experience than his broken leg experience, as you can see by his two clustering pages (opposite).

In addition, the student discovered through this process what the amateur hour experience had meant to him. He recalled how he and his sister Pat worked out detailed skits with costumes and memorized lines and really acted things out in the hope of winning Daddy's prize for the amateur show, while little brother David won for his inane horse imitation which took no preparation whatsoever. The writer realized that while he resented this unfairness he also remembered fondly the joyous aspects of the experience: the fun and laughter, mother's delight at all the acts, the wonderful refreshments, and the

no talent
cute and little
always the winner
horse sounds
David - 4

cape
fake mustache
10 years old
melodrama
nervous
sis

amateur hour

daddy's pride
showmanship
my interest in acting
resentment

Daddy
top hat
fake microphone
booming voice
partiality

Saturday night
popcorn
living room stage
mother applauds
big bottles of soda

Mom's chocolate cake

Welcome home

my broken leg

2 miles away
new red bike
fishing hole
sunny

hospital
pain
attention
shame

Rob
12 to my 9
speed biker
double dog darer

general gaiety of the occasion. His clustering began the process of the discovery of meaning that would continue as he began the first draft of his paper.

This technique, also called *mapping,* can help you see what you know and can organize your memories, ideas, or information. The technique is useful in generating material for any kind of writing from personal anecdotes to research reports.

Having read, discussed, and thought about the various statements clothes can make about us and what clothes can do for us and having considered your own clothing and its meaning and your guidelines for purchasing clothing, you are ready to respond to the following writing situation.

Assignment

A 1948 alumnus of your institution has recently visited the campus and experienced great distress at the various changes he observed in the school and in the student body. When he returned home, he wrote the following letter which was published in your school newspaper.

```
To the Editor:
     My recent visit to the campus was a grave disap-
pointment. Of course, we all expect some things to
change in 36 years--new buildings, more students, new
courses, and so on. The change that shocked me most, as
it would any mature educated person, was the appearance
of the students. Frankly, I was offended. When I was a
student at _____, male students wore coats and ties, and
females wore skirts and blouses or dresses and looked
nice. This attire showed that we took education seri-
ously and that we wanted to be the best we could be.
What I saw when I visited made it clear to me that stu-
dents have simply decided to indulge themselves--to wear
whatever pleases them regardless of what is appropriate
for an academic life. I fail to understand the outra-
geous variety of apparel I saw. Perhaps I'm way behind
the times, but I fail to see why students at _____ can't
dress the way they used to--to show respect for their
school and for themselves.
                    Sincerely,
                    A Disappointed Member of the Class of '48
```

In the newspaper the following week appeared this response from a student:

```
Dear "Class of '48":
     All of us here at _____ are very sorry that you were
so outraged by the clothing you saw when you visited the
campus. You ought to know, though, that people have a
right to wear whatever pleases them on this or any cam-
pus, and it's nobody's business but their own. Maybe
```

```
when you were a student everyone looked alike, but today
students are more concerned with individuality. Clothing
has nothing to do with taking education seriously; in
fact, I can't imagine a person in a coat and tie doing
any really creative thinking. Today students attend col-
lege to work and learn, not to dress up to make a good
impression on somebody.
                        A Student
```

Having read both letters, your task is to prepare a feature article for the school news-paper in response to the issue raised by "Class of '48" and the student. Your article will be read by all the readers of the newspaper and, you hope, by "Class of '48" and the respondent as well. You understand that what seems to be needed is an explanation of the variety of clothing that people wear today on campus. Readers need to be informed of the complexity of this issue and to be helped toward an understanding of how people use clothing.

HOW TO BEGIN

The following discussion will help you begin by identifying the writer's as-sumptions and categorizing your ideas.

Identifying Assumptions

Whenever you set out to explain something to someone, you have to begin by asking what he or she knows or believes already. The writer from "Class of '48" knows what he saw, and he tells us what he thinks about it. It is a bit more difficult to say what his *assumptions* are. An assumption is a belief that the writer takes for granted and therefore does not feel the need to support or defend. Sometimes assumptions are stated, as when the alumnus says, "The change that shocked me most, as it would any mature educated person, was the appearance of the students." The writer *assumes* that any mature, educated person would react as he did. Usually, however, assumptions are not stated; rather, they lurk below the surface of the written word. For example, consider the sentence ". . . male students wore coats and ties, and females wore skirts and blouses or dresses and looked nice." The writer assumes that coats and ties or skirts and blouses or dresses are what look nice and the current dress on campus does not look nice. He does not support or defend these judg-ments; he assumes that his readers will accept them.

The student's response to "Class of '48" likewise is based on certain be-liefs or assumptions. The student assumes that the other students share his regret ("All of us here at _____ are very sorry . . .") and that today's students are motivated by individualism. To enable readers to understand the issue of campus clothing more fully, you will need to understand both the conclusions and assumptions of both writers. Begin by identifying the assumptions in the alumnus' letter and those in the student's response. How many can you add to the ones already pointed out?

A consideration of the assumptions and conclusions of the writers will help you know how best to explain what readers need to know. You have also accumulated in your journal a number of entries related to your readings in this chapter which can provide you with material for composing your article. Through reading, writing, and discussing, you have considered the part that clothing plays in your own life and in the lives of others. You have thought about what our clothing can say about us to others.

Review your readings and journal entries and make a list of particular reasons why people wear the clothing they do. There is no set number of reasons that you should have on your list. Just put down as many specific reasons as you can come up with on the basis of your readings, discussion, and journal entries. Try to make the reasons as concrete and specific as you can. Include your own personal reasons as well as reasons that others—individuals as well as groups—have for choosing the clothing they do.

Categorizing

Now, examine your list carefully to see if there are some broad categories that the reasons fall into. *Categorizing* a list—looking for general ideas or concepts to encompass the individual items—is a crucial skill for anyone who tries to make sense out of isolated specifics. Not only does this process help us understand the concept or idea better, but it may also help us articulate the material for another person. Having first generated a variety of specific reasons why people wear what they do, we are in a position to find the categories inherent in the material. Thus, this method is an inductive rather than a deductive one and is a basic strategy for beginning to organize our thoughts.

Below are examples of a student's listing and categorizing process:

```
              Contents of My Handbag

        wallet          note pad
        comb            checkbook
        lipstick        Lifesavers
        Tums            Kleenex
        white-out       ticket stub
        rabbit's foot   blush-on
        pens, pencils   extra screws for glasses
        address book    loose change
        glasses case    pizza coupon
        apple           aspirin
```

Derived Categories

Stationery Supplies	Grooming Items	Financial Items
address book	comb	wallet
note pad	lipstick	checkbook
pens, pencils	blush-on	loose change
white-out	Kleenex	pizza coupon

Medicinal Items	Edible Items	Eye Care Wear	Souvenir Items
Tums	apple	glasses case	rabbit's foot
aspirin	Lifesavers	extra screws	ticket stub

The student was able to form categories that took into account *all* her items. Notice that her categories do not overlap; no item could fit into more than one grouping. Seeing such relations is a process of trial and error. We sort and shuffle items until we have found the categories most appropriate to our purpose, which include all our specifics and do not overlap. The groupings will help us think about and articulate a subject, concept, or idea. Once we have the categories, we also have the specifics that illustrate the category.

Try categorizing the following list of specifics about a city.

statues	department stores
taxes	twice weekly garbage collection
pollution	trains
hotels	theater
parks	cabs
bars	the zoo
noise	slums
buses	museums
concerts	traffic
movies	crowds
crime	fountains
shops	fashion
government	dying
a variety of good restaurants	change

Share your categories with your classmates, and note how individuals will have arrived at different ways of grouping the items.

The categories we see may depend on our purpose for categorizing. As with simple specifics—items or concepts—we can use the process to help us deal with lists of more complex items such as causes, reasons, developments, or phrases. When asked to think about how popular music has changed in the last 10 years, a student generated the following list of specific changes he could think of:

the Michael Jackson phenomenon
Boy George (of Culture Club)
Punk/New Wave

```
        Bruce Springsteen's down-and-out lyrics
                    Annie Lennox
                     New Grass
                    Pat Benatar
                    Anne Murray
              Joni Mitchell doing jazz
        takeover by Moog (synthesized music)
                death of John Lennon
```

Using this list of changes that the student has generated, sort and shuffle the items until you have a set of categories that will not overlap and which will contain all of the items. With the new categories, you will have clarified the subject for yourself and will be in a position to explain to others how popular music has changed in the last decade without simply listing for them all the isolated, specific signs of change. In other words, you will have *organized* that which was disorganized before. *And* you will have your specifics to use for illustrations of the categories of change.

Return to your list of reasons why people wear the clothes they do. The sorting and shuffling process might be easier if you put each specific reason on an index card and then move the cards around on a table in front of you to see what seems to go with what (much as in a Scrabble game, in which you might move the letter tiles about with the hope of seeing a new combination of letters that makes a word). When you have arrived at satisfactory categories—(probably three or four)—for your list of reasons, double-check to see that the categories allow you to include *all* your reasons and that they are not overlapping.

Using your categories along with their subordinate reasons as your major divisions, write the first draft of the body of your article for the newspaper. Keep your audience in mind as you write, but pay most attention at this stage to getting the ideas down. Remember, your aim is essentially to inform readers of the complexity of this business of clothing.

When you have a draft of the body of your explanation that satisfies you in terms of its content, write your lead-in by referring to the letters in the school newspaper and your intent in the article.

Revising Workshop

Bring your draft to class for a Revising Workshop. In small groups, share your papers with each other, assisting each other by responding to each in relation to the questions below. Each draft should be commented on by at least two other students. Try not to worry about mechanical problems at this stage.

1. What seems to be the purpose of the draft (implied or stated)? If the purpose is stated, is the statement in an appropriate place? If implied, is it nevertheless clear for the reader?
2. What are the categories within the writer's explanation? Where are these named? Is there sufficient discussion of each category and illustration? Are the sec-

tions of the explanation in an effective order? Mark any section or example that seems questionable or needs expanding.

3. How effective is the lead-in to the article?

4. What tone does the writer express in the article (serious, humorous, sarcastic, pompous)? How will the audience respond to this tone? Mark any passages that you think might offend the audience. Be prepared to explain why.

5. As part of the intended audience, what questions would you raise in response to the article? Is there any statement you would object to? Any section of the article where you would like more information?

6. Comment on the sentence structure in the article. Are any sentences choppy? Any too long? Any weakened by excess words?

Before writing your second draft, take into account your classmates' responses during the Revising Workshop. You need not agree with all their ideas, but you do have an obligation to consider them. You may need to rethink your categories or even your list of reasons if there are problems there. If there are problems with tone you may need to analyze the needs and predispositions of your audience again.

Now, write the second draft of your article, making whatever revisions you have decided are necessary to create the most effective article in light of your purpose and your audience.

Editing Workshop

Return to your small group with your second draft for an Editing Workshop. In this session you will review each other's drafts for mechanical flaws or problems with form. Again, at least two students should respond to each draft, using the following questions:

1. Are there sentences or parts of sentences in the article that confuse you or cause you to have to reread to grasp their meaning? If so, bracket these.

2. Place an X in the margin of the draft on any line in which you see what you perceive as an error in spelling or punctuation. Use one mark for each error you perceive.

3. Put a C in the margin of any line in which you find a trite expression or cliché.

4. Place a G in the margin of any line in which you perceive an error in grammar or usage. Use one mark for each error you perceive.

Examine the responses of your classmates to your draft. If sentences are bracketed, try to decide what their problems are. Ask for help if you cannot remedy them. If you find marks indicating spelling, punctuation, grammar or usage mistakes, try to identify the problems. For help, consult the Editing Guide (Chapter 12). Make notes in your journal about the kinds of sentence and mechanical errors you tend to make.

Now, make the final revisions that you deem necessary for a finished copy and submit the polished article to your instructor.

CHAPTER 5

Expressing Your Opinion

THEME *Purposes of Education*

SKILL FOCUS *Supporting Generalizations*

In our interactions with each other, we frequently express our opinions about what we see, hear, and experience. Often our opinions are little more than, "Yes, I think it was a great movie!" or "No, the lecture just didn't make any sense." We always have the privilege of speaking our judgments whether we can back them up or not. We exercise this privilege each time we vote, particpate in an opinion poll, or simply choose a restaurant for a dinner out. Often, though, in academic, community, and work situations, we need to back up our opinions. In this chapter, you will be presented with some strategies that will help you know how to support your opinions. You will see what kinds of support are available and how to express your opinions so you can influence others.

The readings and the activities in this chapter invite you to consider the ideas of others, to reflect on your own experience, and to formulate your stance on the purpose of education. Why is education of value to you? To your children? To the children of the community in which you pay (or will pay) taxes to support schools and colleges? What should that education be? How large a part of your education are your years of formal schooling? What should be the purposes of education? While the readings are merely a sampling on this theme, your full participation in this chapter can help you clarify your own understanding of this important subject and help you express your opinion on an educational issue.

The final writing project of this chapter is a position paper. In preparing for that paper you will read and respond, recall your own education thus far, consider your own goals for education, and develop a defensible position for an audience that needs your thoughtful opinion.

Before Reading

In "Engaging Students in the Great Conversation," Neil Postman contrasts what individuals generally learn from television with what they learn in school and proposes that, rather than compete with television, schools need to develop a very different curriculum for the future. As you read, consider the following questions:

1. How does Postman define the TDs and the TSs?
2. How is television a curriculum, and what are the five characteristics of the TV curriculum that Postman defines?
3. What forms the center of Postman's proposed school curriculum? Why does the author find history so important to the curriculum?

Engaging Students in the Great Conversation

Neil Postman

In prophesying about the effects of technology on schools by the year 2000, we must consider at the outset the two most prevalent positions on the matter. The first is that of the technological determinist. The TD, as we may call him or her, believes that there is nothing much we can do about the future except to surrender ourselves to the new technologies. The school of the future, the TD says, will derive its agenda from the demands of television, the computer, satellites, and other technologies. The role of the educator is to develop philosophies that will rationalize the uses society makes of these technologies and that will prepare us to accept the ways in which the technologies use us. Above all, the educator must not stand in the way of the future, whose direction is determined by the shape of technology.

An apt illustration of the views of the TD is the following quotation, which was part of the commencement address at Emerson College in June 1981. Its author is Leonard H. Goldenson, chairman of the board of the ABC television network:

> [W]e can no longer rely on our mastery of traditional skills. As communicators, as performers, as creators—and as citizens—[the electronic revolution] requires a new kind of literacy. It will be a visual literacy, an electronic literacy, and it will be as much of an advance over the literacy of the written word we know today as that was over the purely oral tradition of man's early history.

Putting aside Goldenson's demonstration of his own lack of mastery over the traditional skills to which he refers, we may say that here is the technological determinist's position, pure and serene. The future has arrived in the form of electronic media; the skills of the past may be declared obsolete: there is nothing to do but accommodate ourselves to the new order.

At the opposite extreme is the position of the technological somnambulist. The TS believes that the new technologies raise no important challenges, that the effects of such technologies are vastly overrated, and that the future of the school is secure. Because of the strong influence of the TS mentality, there are still education conferences that take as their themes such topics as the nongraded curriculum, phonics versus word recognition, or new methods of evaluation—in other words, topics that deal with the technical aspects of teaching. Armed with expertise about pedagogy, the TS heads toward the future relatively untroubled about the possibility that when he or she arrives there, the classroom may be empty or, if not, that this expertise may be irrelevant. The analogy that comes to mind is that of a blacksmith in the year 1905. He is entirely occupied with perfecting his techniques, attends conferences on such topics as new methods of shoeing mares, and is content to believe that the horseless carriage is a fad.

In ridiculing these two positions by stating them in their extreme forms, I do not mean to say that each is completely devoid of merit. The technological determinist is well aware of the fact that the modern idea of the school arose in the 16th century as a response to the invention of the printing press. The TD assumes, therefore, that the idea of the school will be re-created in the 21st century as a response to the electronic media. The TD may well turn out to be right.

The technological somnambulist, on the other hand, knows that the central, and therefore most enduring, function of the school has been to promote the skills and values of literacy. The TS believes this function to be unassailable—remembering, with a wry smile, the millions of dollars wasted by school administrators on closed-circuit TV systems only a few years ago. The TS also remembers how teaching machines and 8mm films were supposed to replace textbooks, and he feels that the past (and therefore the future) is on his side. He may have a point.

Nonetheless, both of these positions are wrong, and dangerously so. They have in common their reification of the future. Both the TD and the TS conceive of the future as something that *happens,* not something that is *made.* They believe with Omar that the Moving Finger is writing a future over which humans have no control. Neither piety, wit, nor tears will change a line of it. The TD and the TS are, to use Karl Popper's word, historicists: History moves inevitably forward, independent of human intentions and efforts. And that is why either of them can comfortably address such a question as, What will schools be like in the year 2000? Like Marx, they need only to uncover what the future has in store for us. A sense of history and some imagination are all that is required to guess.

Meaning no offense to the spirit of my assignment, I reject the form of the question. I am no historicist. I do not believe that the "future" will bring anything, or that "it" is moving inexorably anywhere—least of all that "it" will take care of itself. I believe only that the "future" will be a consequence of what we do now as a response to our understanding of the problems we face. I believe with Marshall McLuhan that "the future of the future is the present." In other words, the Moving Finger belongs to us, and it is in these terms that I must approach my assignment.

By my reckoning, only twice before in western culture have educators had to face the kind of problem our new symbolic environment poses. The first time was in the fifth century B.C., when Athens was undergoing a rapid change from an oral culture to an alphabetic-writing culture. The second was in the 16th century, when Europe underwent a radical transformation as a result of the printing press. What we are facing now is the rapid changeover from a culture organized around typography to a culture based on the electronic image.

As a consequence, it is obvious that the major educational enterprise now being undertaken in the U.S. is not happening in the classroom but in the home, in front of the television set—not under the jurisdiction of school administrators and teachers but of network TV executives. I do not mean to imply that this situation is the result of a conspiracy or even that those who control TV want this responsibility. I mean only to say that—like the alphabet in the fifth century B.C. or the printing press in the 16th century—television has, by its power to control the time, attention, and cognitive habits of our youths, inevitably gained the power to control their minds and character as well. This is why I call television a curriculum. As I understand the word, a curriculum is a specially constructed information system whose purpose is to influence, teach, train, or cultivate the mind and character of the young. Well, television does exactly that, and it does it relentlessly; in so doing, it competes successfully with the school curriculum. In fact, it damn near obliterates it.

I believe it will help us to keep in mind the difference between written language and television if we remember that letters on a page must be psychologically transparent if one is to read fluently. To the extent that a reader attends to the form or shape of letters, he or she is stalled or blocked from getting at their meaning. Letters that jumped around on the page would, of course, make reading altogether impossible. In other words, the printed page leads one *away* from the form of its symbols and *toward* their meaning. The TV image, because it is interesting in itself and continuously changing, leads one *toward* the form of its symbols and *away* from their meaning. There is no more important observation to be made about the difference between the two media than this: Print is content-oriented; TV is form-oriented.

What does all of this mean? The best expression I know of the consequences of a shift from a word-centered to an image-centered curriculum was provided in 1935 by Rudolph Arnheim, who, I might add, knew rather more about visual literacy than Goldenson of ABC. Whereas Goldenson is optimistic about a culture of images and talks rather carelessly about the advance of civilization, Arnheim wrote the following:

> We must not forget that in the past the inability to transport immediate experience and to convey it to others made the use of language necessary and thus compelled the human mind to develop concepts. For in order to describe things one must draw the general from the specific; one must select, compare, think. When communication can be achieved by pointing with the finger, however, the mouth grows silent, the writing hand stops, and the mind shrinks.

I join with Arnheim in believing that an education dominated by concrete, dynamic visual images must weaken the abstracting powers of youths and erode their abilities in all modes of digital symbolism—that is, in all modes of conceptual thinking, particularly language and mathematics. Digital modes of symbolism are by their nature slow-moving, sequential, logical, continuous, and abstract. Whether writing or speaking, reading or listening, one must maintain a fixed point of view and a continuity of content; one must move to higher or lower levels of abstraction; one must follow to a greater or lesser degree rules of syntax and logic. This is not so in experiencing TV. Language and pictures are processed differently by the brain and produce entirely different responses, not to mention differences in the production of alpha and beta waves.

Here are some facts for skeptics to ponder. The only activity an American child engages in that occupies more time than televiewing is sleeping. Using the 1982 Nielsen Report, you can estimate that, between ages 6 and 18, an American child averages about 16,000 hours in front of a TV set; that same child will spend only about 13,000 hours in school. By my reckoning, in the first 20 years of his or her life, an American child will see approximately 700,000 TV commercials, at a rate of close to 700 per week. According to studies by Daniel Anderson of the University of Massachusetts, children begin to watch TV with sustained attention at 36 months, at which time they are able to interpret and respond to the imagery of the medium. They identify with characters, sing TV jingles, and begin to ask for products that they see advertised. TV, in other words, needs no equivalent of the McGuffey Reader. It is almost immediately accessible to the young and demands no prerequisite training. Which is why—again according to Nielsen—children have already clocked nearly 5,000 hours of televiewing before they ever show up at school. After they start school, they continue to watch every day of the week, around the clock. Unlike the school curriculum, TV does not give its students time off for weekends, summer vacations, or holidays. Indeed, according to Frank Mankiewicz's book on television, *Remote Control,* every day of the year approximately two million children are watching TV between 11:30 p.m. and 1:30 a.m.

Assuming that you will accept my assertions that television is a curriculum, that it competes with the traditional curriculum we call school, and that in this competition the school is losing, I would like to contribute two things to our speculations about school in the year 2000. First, I want to identify five of the most important characteristics of the TV curriculum and specify the attitudes and cognitive predispositions that each of them promotes. These attitudes and predispositions are, of course, antagonistic to what the school wishes to teach; therefore, as I see it, they define the battleground on which the struggle between two modalities of education is taking place. Second, I would like to make some proposals about what educators might do to preserve the best values of a traditional education.

The first characteristic of the TV curriculum is the most obvious one. Certainly it is the one from which most of the others are generated. Quite simply, the basic mode of discourse of the TV curriculum is the analogic, nondiscursive visual image. People *watch* television. They don't read it, and what they hear is almost always subordinate to what they see. And what they see are millions of pictures. Now, it is sometimes said that one picture is worth a thousand words. Perhaps so. But this does not mean that one picture is the *equivalent* of a thousand words. Or 200 or 20 or even one. Indeed, we might say that one word is worth a thousand pictures. For a word is a creation of the imagination in a way that a picture can never be.

A picture, for example, cannot convey the idea "cat" or "work" or "wine" or "conference." A picture can merely give you an example, a particularity, whereas a word gives a concept, a generality. It is well to remember that there is no such thing in the universe as "cat" or "work" or "wine" or "conference." Words, even of the most specific kind, are always several levels removed from reality and are therefore entirely responsible for whatever intellectual superiority we may claim to have over baboons. Therefore, a curriculum based on pictures is very different from one based on words. Moreover, the pictures seen on TV are in constant motion and are continuously changing their aspects. The average length of a shot on a network show is 3.5 seconds. This means that every 3.5 seconds, more or less, there is a new point of view, or angle of vision, and a new pictorial image to process. On commercials, the average length of a shot is 2.5 seconds. A child watching TV must process as many as 1,200 different shots every hour. That means about 30,000 per week for the average 8-year-old.

It is perfectly obvious that there is a fundamental antagonism between TV and language. Moreover, linguistic content must always lose when it competes with high-speed visual information. That is why, on such occasions as a Presidential address, the TV image must be kept fixed. Whenever complex language is to be processed, visual stimulation must be kept to a minimum. But a talking head is anathema to TV directors—and for good reason. Television is at its most engaging when it is showing, not telling. That is why even such intellectual programs as "Cosmos" show Carl Sagan riding a bicycle while he discusses the work of the Dutch astronomer Huygens. You see, the science of astrophysics, being little else but a linguistic construct, does not play well on television. And that is why "Cosmos" was not about astrophysics but about Carl Sagan. Had I been the director of "Cosmos," I would have done the same thing, if I wanted to hold my audience.

The second characteristic of TV is related to the first and, I believe, has not been extensively analyzed. Because TV consists of pictures and stories, its curriculum is mostly nonpropositional. That is, pictures do not make assertions about the world, as language does. Pictures are presentations of experience. not commentary about experience. Thus the TV curriculum is largely irrefutable. You can dislike television programs, but you cannot disagree with them. There is no way, for example, to refute Laverne and Shirley, or an Ajax commercial, or Carl Sagan's turtleneck sweater, or Dan Rather's good looks. There is no way to show that the feelings evoked by the imagery of a McDonald's commercial are true or false.

Such words as "true" and "false" come out of a different universe of symbolism altogether. They are applicable to the world of exposition, in which we confront statement and counterstatement, hypotheses, reasons, refutations, contradictions, explanations, verifications—above all, where we confront ideas expressed in the form of subjects and predicates. School, of course, is a world dominated by subjects and predicates, usually unfolded in 40- or 50-minute periods, during which even mediocre teachers welcome students' attempts at refutation. Television is a world dominated by stories, usually accompanied by music and segmented into eight-minute modules, that call for visceral, not cortical, responses. TV makes exposition irritating to students and renders them increasingly incapable of attending to it for long periods of time. The TV curriculum does not encourage the development of analytical abilities, which is the central purpose of most school subjects.

This leads to a third characteristic of the TV curriculum: It is easy. As I implied earlier, watching television requires no skills and develops no skills. This is why you will never hear of courses in remedial televiewing. It is also why you yourself are no better at watching TV today than you were 10 years ago. And if you believe that you are, I would submit that this is so because you learned something, somewhere else, that changed the quality of your mind.

Now, I am not about to argue that easy things are necessarily worse than hard things. But, in this case, the fact that no learning is required by the TV curriculum means that it is nonhierarchical, nongraded, and nondifferentiated. "Sesame Street" is not easier to watch than "Cosmos" or "Little House on the Prairie." Unlike books, which can be placed on a scale according to their lexical and syntactic complexity, and unlike school subjects, which can be placed on a scale according to their conceptual complexity, television demands no prerequisites, involves no sequential learning, and yields no intellectual or emotional growth. Television is the most egalitarian curriculum ever devised. Everything in it is for everybody, simultaneously. And thus there can be no standard of excellence, or of competence, or even of improvement. I need hardly dwell on the consequences of such an education. Suffice it to say that such an education mocks the ideas of deferred gratification, self-discipline, and intellectual achievement, without which education is mere entertainment.

This leads me to the fourth characteristic of the TV curriculum: namely, that it is nearly always entertaining. Partly because of its nondiscursive form, and partly because of its economic imperatives, and partly because it is unable to differentiate among its audiences, television considers unsuitable that which is not entertaining—which is another way of saying that television is an attention-centered curriculum. It has no purpose that takes precedence over keeping the attention of its student-viewers. Unlike the school, which selects its subject matter first and then tries to devise ways to attract interest, TV first selects ways to attract interest and allows content to be shaped accordingly. In the school curriculum, if a student repeatedly fails to pay attention, the teacher may remove him or her from the classroom. In the TV curriculum, if the student repeatedly fails to pay attention, the teacher is removed; that is, the show is canceled.

Obviously, no social institution is more jeopardized by the entertainment modality than education. Education has traditionally kept itself separate from entertainment. The TV curriculum all but wipes out that tradition. What TV teaches is not merely that learning is fun, which quite often it isn't, but that learning and entertainment are indistinguishable from one another. This is a very dangerous idea, not only because it is untrue but also because it makes schoolteaching increasingly difficult.

Teachers are forced by the expectations of their students to replicate in their classrooms the assumptions about learning that TV engenders. Students expect to be charmed and amused by their studies; above all, they expect that what they are to learn ought to be instantly accessible to them. This fact is painful to their teachers, who, naturally enough, want to engage the students' attention and to do so must model their lessons on TV. Indeed, it is not inconceivable that—if television is allowed to proceed unchecked—most teachers in the years ahead will be singing the entire curriculum to their students, interrupting their songs every eight minutes for a string of commercials. What this implies for the state of learning in the future is painful to contemplate. It is enough to say that, when there is no distinction between the tasks of the mind and the actions of the viscera, we have, by definition, come to the end of education.

The last characteristic of TV I want to mention is that its curriculum is entirely fragmented and discontinuous. Nothing on TV, for example, has very much to do with anything else on TV. There is no theme or coherence or order to what is presented. Both the school curriculum and the TV curriculum are windows to the world, but the world that TV reveals is made up largely of discrete events, which have no connection to anything that has gone before or will come after. You need only glance at the weekly syllabus (found in *TV Guide*) to confirm this fact.

The TV curriculum thus stands in sharp contrast to the school curriculum, which even at its worst has a rational order. The school curriculum always reflects an attempt to establish organizing principles. Courses, for example, may be organized by historical sequence, intellectual complexity, thematic similarity, logical progression, even vocational requirements. If the TV curriculum has such an organizing principle, it is merely the immediate, short-term psychological gratification of the student. Therefore, what is shown on TV requires no continuity and needs to have no implications beyond itself. That is one of the reasons why a commercial message, as it is called, can be inserted at any point during a program, even a program that might be thought of as "serious." On any news broadcast, for example, one may find a commercial for a detergent or a soft drink sandwiched between a story of mass murder and one on an earthquake in Chile. Now, if I had paused every few paragraphs in this article to insert a word or two on behalf of United Airlines or Jordache jeans, you might rightly think that I had no respect for my subject or for my readers—or, if you were in a generous mood, that I had lost my mind. Why, then, do we not think the same thing about those who design TV presentations? The answer is that we do not anticipate or require any logical, emotional, or ideational connections among events shown on TV. Each event, each program, each commercial stands alone.

Make no mistake about it: The TV curriculum embodies a clear and powerful philosophy concerning the nature of reality. Its axioms include that history is bunk, that hierarchies are arbitrary, that problems have no antecedents, that the future is not worth dwelling upon, that randomness is uncontrollable. I believe the word for these beliefs in philosophical discourse is nihilism. In aesthetic discourse, the word is Dadaism. In psychiatric circles, it is known as chronic depression.

As I see it, the teachings of television are hostile to language and language development, hostile to vigorous intellectual activity, hostile to both science and history, hostile to social order, and hostile in a general way to conceptualization. Television is a curriculum that stresses instancy, not constancy; discontinuity, not coherence; immediate, not deferred, gratification; emotional, not intellectual, response. The question is, What can we do about it? How do we prepare for the year 2000?

In the face of all of this, perhaps the most important contribution schools can make is to provide young people with a sense of purpose, of meaning, and of the interconnectedness of what they learn. At present, the typical school curriculum reflects far too much the fragmentation one finds in television's weekly schedule. Each subject, like each TV program, has nothing whatever to do with any other—and for reasons less justifiable than those that explain the discontinuity and incoherence of TV. After all, the major aim of TV is the psychological gratification of the viewer. Schools, on the other hand, offer what they do either because they have always done so or because colleges or professional schools "require" it. There is no longer any principle that unifies the school curriculum and furnishes it with meaning, unless it is the mission of preparing students for jobs, which is hardly a morally or intellectually worthy theme.

To suggest a single, plausible theme for a diverse, secularized population is to tread on shaky ground. Nonetheless, I propose as a possibility the theme that animates *The Ascent of Man,* by Jacob Bronowski. His is a book and a philosophy filled with optimism and suffused with the transcendent belief that the destiny of humanity is the discovery of knowledge. Moreover, although Bronowski's emphasis is on science, he finds ample warrant to include the arts and the humanities as part of our unending quest to gain a unified understanding of nature and our place in it. In other words, to chart the ascent of man—which I will here call the ascent of humanity—we must join art and science. But we must also join the past and the present, for the ascent of humanity is above all a continuous story.

The virtues of adopting the ascent of humanity as a scaffold on which to build a curriculum are many and various, especially in our present situation. For one thing, this theme does not require that we invent new subjects or discard old ones. The structure of the subject-matter curriculum as it now exists in most schools is entirely usable. For another, this is a theme that can begin in the earliest grades and extend through college in ever-widening and ever-deepening dimensions. Better still, it provides students with a point of view from which to understand the meaning of subjects, for each subject can be seen as a battleground of sorts—an arena in which fierce intellectual struggle has taken place and continues to take place. From this point of view, the curriculum itself can be seen as a celebration of human intelligence and creativity, not as a meaningless collection of requirements for a high school or college diploma.

Best of all, the theme of the ascent of humanity provides us with a nontechnical, noncommercial definition of education. This is a definition drawn from an honorable humanist tradition, and it reflects a concept of the purposes of academic life that counters the prejudices of television. I am referring to the idea that to become educated means to become aware of the origins and growth of knowledge and knowledge systems; to be familiar with the intellectual and creative processes by which the best that has been thought and said has been produced; to learn how to participate, even if only as a listener, in what Robert Maynard Hutchins once called The Great Conversation. You will note that such a definition is not student-centered, not training-centered, not skill-centered, not even problem-centered. It is idea-centered and coherence-centered. It is also other-worldly, in the sense that it does not assume that what one learns in school must be directly and urgently related to a problem of today. In other words, it is an education that stresses history, the scientific mode of thinking, the disciplined use of language, a wide-ranging knowledge of the arts and religion, and the continuity of the human enterprise. It is a definition of education that provides an excellent corrective to the antihistorical, nonanalytical, nonsequential, immediately gratifying biases of television.

As an example of what I mean, let us consider history, for history is in some ways the discipline central to the theme that I am proposing. It is hardly necessary for me to argue here that, as Cicero put it, "To remain ignorant of things that happened before you were born is to remain a child." It is enough to say that history is our most potent intellectual means of raising our consciousness.

But there are some points about history and its teaching that require emphasis, since they are usually ignored by our schools. The first is that history is not merely one subject among many that may be taught in school. Every subject—including biology, physics, mathematics, literature, music, and art—has a history. I propose, therefore, that every teacher be a history teacher. To teach, for example, what we know about biology today without also teaching what we once knew, or thought we knew, is to reduce knowledge to a mere consumer product. It is to deprive students of a sense of the meaning of what we know and of how we know it. To teach about the atom without Democritus, to teach about electricity without Faraday, to teach about political science without Aristotle or Machiavelli is to refuse our students access to The Great Conversation. It is to deny them knowledge of their roots, about which no other social institution—least of all television—is presently concerned. To know about your roots is not merely to know where your grandparents came from and what they had to endure. It is also to know where your ideas come from and why you happen to believe them—and to know from whence spring your moral and aesthetic sensibilities. To complete Cicero's thought, "What is a human life worth unless it is incorporated into the lives of one's ancestors and set in an historical context?" By *ancestors,* Cicero did not mean your mother's aunt.

Thus I recommend that every subject be taught *as* history. In this way, our students can begin to understand, as they now do not, that knowledge is not a fixed entity, but a stage in human development, with a past and a future.

The teaching of subjects as studies in historical continuities is not intended to make history as a special subject irrelevant. If every subject is taught with a historical dimension, the history teacher would be free to teach what histories are—which is to say, hypotheses about why change occurs. Of course, there is a sense in which there is no such thing as "history," for every historian, from Thucydides to Toynbee, has known that the stories must be told from a special point of view that always reflects a particular theory of social development. Historians also know that they write histories for some particular purpose: more often than not, either to glorify or to condemn the present. Thus there is no definitive history of anything; there are only histories, human inventions that do not give us *the* answers but only those answers called forth by the particular questions that the historians asked.

Historians know all of this; it is common knowledge among them. Yet it is kept a secret from our youths. Their ignorance of it prevents them from understanding how "history" can change and why the Russians, the Chinese, the Indians, and virtually all other groups see historical events differently from the authors of history textbooks.

The task of the history teacher, then, is to become a "histories" teacher. This does not mean that some particular version of the American, European, African, or Asian past should remain untold. A student who does not know at least one history is in no position to evaluate others. But it does mean that a histories teacher will be concerned, at all times, to show how histories are themselves products of culture.

Critics will object that this idea—history as comparative history—is too abstract for students to grasp. But this is one of several reasons why comparative history should be taught. To teach the past simply as a chronicle of indisputable, fragmented, and concrete events is to replicate the bias of television, which largely denies our youths access to concepts and theories, providing them only with a stream of meaningless events. Whatever events may be included in the study of the past, the worst thing we can do is to present them devoid of the coherence that a theory or theories can provide—that is to say, as meaningless. This, we can be sure, TV does daily. The histories teacher must go far beyond the "event" level into the realm of concepts, theories, hypotheses, comparisons, deductions, evaluations. In other words, the idea is to raise the level of abstraction at which "history" is taught.

This idea would apply to all subjects, including science. I have already mentioned the importance of teaching the history of science in every science course. But this is no more important than teaching its "philosophy," by which I mean that science be taught as an exercise in human imagination, something quite different from technology. Science, in other words, as natural philosophy. Would it be an exaggeration to say that not one student in 50 knows what *induction* means? Or knows what a scientific theory is? Or a scientific model? Or knows what are the optimum conditions of a valid scientific experiment? Or has ever considered the question, What is scientific truth?

Because I believe that our students do not address these questions, I propose that every school—elementary through college—offer and require courses in the philosophy of science. Such courses should consider the language of science, the nature of scientific proof, the source of scientific hypotheses, the role of the imagination, the conditions of experimentation, and, especially, the value of error and disproof. Such courses would try to dispel the notion that science is pharmacy or technology or magic tricks; they would teach science, instead, as a special way of employing human intelligence. It is important for students to learn that one does not become scientific by donning a white coat (which is what television teaches), but by practicing a set of canons of thought, many of which have to do with the disciplined use of language.

This leads me to propose that, in addition to courses in the philosophy of science, every school offer a course in semantics—the processes by which people make meaning. In this connection, I must note the gloomy fact that English teachers have been consistently obtuse in their approach to this subject, which is to say that they have mostly ignored it. This has always been difficult for me to understand in light of the fact that English teachers claim as their concern the teaching of reading and writing. If they do not teach anything about the relationship of language to reality—which is what the study of semantics is about—I cannot imagine how they expect reading and writing to improve.

Like history, semantics is an interdisciplinary subject; it is necessary to know something about semantics in order to understand any subject. It would be extremely useful to the growth of their intelligence if our young people had access to special courses in which fundamental principles of language were identified and explained. Such courses would deal not only with the various uses of language but with the relationships between things and words, symbols and signs, factual statements and judgments, grammar and thought. Especially for young students, these courses ought to emphasize the kinds of common semantic errors that are avoidable through awareness and discipline. I refer here to such tendencies as the misuse of either/or categories, misunderstandings of levels of abstraction, and the confusion of words with things.

In using the ascent of humanity as a theme, we would also, of necessity, elevate such subjects as literature, music, and art to prominence. Clearly, the subject matter of these disciplines contains the best evidence we have of the unity and continuity of human experience and feeling. For this reason, I propose that, in our teaching of the humanities, we should emphasize the enduring creations of the past. The schools, in my opinion, should stay as far from contemporary works as possible. Because of the nature of the communications industry, our students have continuous access to the popular arts of their own time—its music, rhetoric, design, literature, architecture. Their knowledge of the form and content of this art is by no means satisfactory. But their ignorance of the form and content of the art of the past is abysmal. This is one good reason for emphasizing the art of the past. Another is that there is no subject better suited to freeing us from the tyranny of the present than art history. Painting, for example, is more than three times as old as writing and contains in its changing styles and themes a 15,000-year-old record of the ascent of humanity.

In saying this, I do not mean to subsume art under the heading of archaeology, although I certainly recommend that the history of art forms be given a serious place in the curriculum. But art is much more than a historical artifact. To have meaning for us, it must connect with levels of feeling, and this raises the question, Is it possible for students of today to relate, through feeling, to the painting, architecture, music, sculpture, or literature of the past? The answer, I believe, is: only with the greatest difficulty. They, and many of us, have an aesthetic sensibility of a different order from that which is required to appreciate a Shakespeare sonnet, a Haydn symphony, or a Hals painting. Simply stated, a young man who believes the Led Zeppelin to have reached the pinnacle of musical expression lacks the sensibility to distinguish between the ascent and the descent of humanity. But that is an oversimplification, and, in any case, it is not my intention to further blacken the reputation of popular culture. The point I wish to make is that the products of the popular arts are amply covered by the media. The school must make available the products of classical art forms, precisely because they are not so readily available and because they demand a different order of sensibility and response. In our present circumstances, there is no excuse for the schools to sponsor rock concerts, when students have not heard the music of Mozart, Beethoven, Bach, or Chopin; or for students to have graduated from high school without having read, for example, Shakespeare, Milton, Keats, Dickens, Tolstoy, or Balzac; or for students not to have seen at least photographs of paintings by Goya, El Greco, David, and other great artists. It does not matter that many of these composers, writers, and painters were, in their own times, popular artists. What does matter is that they worked when they did, making artistic statements from a point of view different from, and yet continuous with, our own. These artists are relevant today not ony because they established the standards with which civilized people approach the arts. They are relevant because television tries to mute their voices and to render their standards invisible.

It is highly likely that students immersed in the popular arts of today will find such an emphasis as I suggest tedious and even painful. This fact will, in turn, be painful to teachers, who—naturally enough—prefer to teach content that will arouse an immediate and enthusiastic response. But our youths must be shown that not all worthwhile things are instantly accessible and that there are levels of sensibility previously unknown to them. Above all, they must be shown the artistic roots of humanity. And that task, in our own times, falls inescapably to the schools.

Speaking of roots, I want to close by including in the school curriculum the subject of religion, with which so much of our painting, music, architecture, literature, *and* science is intertwined. Specifically, I propose that the curriculum include a course on comparative religion. Such a course would deal with religion as an expression of the creativity of humankind—that is, as a total, integrated response to fundamental questions about the meaning of existence. The course would be descriptive, promoting no particular religion but illuminating the metaphors, the literature, the art, the ritual of religious expression.

I am not unaware of the difficulties that such a course would face, not the least of which is the belief that the schools and religion must on no account touch one another. But I do not see how we can claim to be educating our young people if we do not ask them to consider how different people of different times and places have tried to achieve a sense of transcendence. No education can neglect such sacred texts as Genesis, the New Testament, the Koran, the Bhagavad-Gita. Each of them embodies a style and a world view that tells as much about the ascent of humanity as any book ever written.

To summarize: I am proposing a curriculum in which all subjects are presented as a stage in the historical development of humanity; in which the philosophy of science, of history, of language, and of religion are taught; and in which there is a strong emphasis on classical forms of artistic expression. This kind of education may be considered conservative, although it is surely not what the back-to-basics advocates have in mind. Regardless of the label applied, this sort of school curriculum is justified by the fact that the TV curriculum is present-centered, attention-centered, image-centered, emotion-centered, and largely incoherent. Thus the TV curriculum is quite probably dangerous. Without the schools to teach the values that television ignores and even mocks, our students are disarmed, and their future is exceedingly bleak.

After Reading

In your journal, respond to the following:

1. In a paragraph, describe yourself as a TD, or as a TS, or as someone with characteristics of both.
2. Make a list of the characteristics of the TV curriculum as Postman explains it. On the basis of your own television viewing, to what extent do you agree with these?
3. Summarize Postman's proposed curriculum by making a chart or diagram that shows the basic theme and the subjects that would be included. What is your immediate response to the proposal?
4. In a focused free writing—two or three pages in your journal—write on the following topic:

   My Formal Schooling: What It's Been Like So Far

   Remember, once you start writing, do not lift your pen. You want to recall as much as you can about your own schooling, especially the curriculum. When you run out of something to write, just keep writing the word "school" until you think of something.

Before Reading

In the next selection, David Travis presents a vision of what he thinks the university might be like in the year 2004. As you read, think about your conception of higher education and those of your friends and classmates.

Higher Education 2004: A Fable

David L. Travis

Professor Frederick T. Cain looked out the window of his fifth-floor office in the rust-stained concrete "ivory" tower. Students milled in profusion below. He sighed as he checked his watch: 30 minutes before the next class period.

Once, only a few students would have been outside during a "prime time" class period. Some of those few would have been studying, perhaps even reading a book for pleasure. Now they were talking, laughing, and listening to or watching every conceivable style of piped and beamed entertainment. Not a book in sight. Most of the fluttering youths below were cutting classes. Most—probably all— would get credit for those classes. Certainly, all those who remained for four years would receive a degree. Many would do so without having read a single book.

The library budget was near zero. "They haven't read up the ones we got last year," joked one college "trustee."

Fred Cain glanced at his desk. On it were piled a dozen books, the stack almost hiding the screen to the computer console. Twenty years earlier, the desk would have been cluttered with memos from faculty colleagues or administrators. Now the memos rolled across the screen in greenish phosphor—as welcome and as ignored as ever.

Professor Cain peered out the window again at the students who never studied. Then he began to pack the books into two large cases.

His new course was waiting. His Waterloo? His Dunkirk? Why couldn't he think of any winning battles? Voices echoed in his head: "An *education*, Professor Cain? Define your terms!" from the curriculum committee. "You'll have to maintain enrollment levels!" from the dean. "You're crazy in the head!" from most of his colleagues.

He was a full professor with tenure, 59 years old, who had amassed 31 years of service to the college. Why was he tilting at windmills, despite his vital statistics? He knew that it was *because* of those statistics.

He had arrived on campus in 1972, just before it became effectively impossible to find an academic teaching position. Naturally, he had his Ph.D. He also had earlier degrees in other fields.

By perseverance and adaptability, he survived to tenure and promotion ("I can teach any one of half a dozen subjects or more"). The same qualities, and his willingness to fill an opening on any college committee, carried him through the RIFs of the Eighties.

He had watched standards slide—first and worst in the departments and divisions that were losing enrollments the fastest, but eventually in all of them. Professor Cain had slid down the tube with the rest.

Now he was making a stand. By law he could stay until he was 65. By custom he should have left when he was 55. If he failed today, the pressures to retire would become intense. He did not plan to resist.

The cases were heavy, and Fred Cain thumped them down gratefully on the broad counter of the lecture hall. He was astonished to find nearly all the seats filled, though he knew that most students were still shopping around for classes. He went to the chalkboard—he had deliberately chosen an old building without individual computer screens—and wrote the course title: "Human Knowledge: An In-Depth Survey."

How had he gotten the course scheduled? Through two years of writing proposals and testifying before committees. Through 30 years of experience with committee politics. By knowing where some bodies were buried and by calling in years of owed favors.

He checked his watch and faced the class. The hall was now full, with observers standing at the back. One or two "colleagues" were watching skeptically. He recognized one—a "Ph.D." in astrology.

Some of the students (*prospective,* he had to remember that) had never been in such an old-fashioned classroom; they fumbled in vain to plug in individual 'corders and tapers. With an oratorical throat clearing and a booming lecture voice that he seldom bothered to use anymore, Professor Cain began: "There will be no recording— visual or sound—of the lectures and discussions in this class."

Immediately, a shaggy product of 20 years of "student rights" stood up and began to speak. "Do you mean we're supposed to remember it all?"

Cain pointed a finger directly at the student. "You! Sit down!" Astonished, the youth did. More quietly, Cain continued, "I'm going to answer that question, but first I want to make one thing clear. In this class, you are not to speak without my permission. If you have something to say, you will indicate this fact by raising your hand. When the appropriate time comes, I will recognize you—and then you may speak."

In response to the shaggy student's question, Cain added, "In this class, I intend to revive an old custom called taking notes. In a notebook, you will write down as much of the discussion as you can. I want the information impressed on your mind by the motor action of writing it down."

He looked the group over. "Most of you are here because of an advertising campaign I mounted in the last few weeks—and personally paid for. I promised a kind of class you have never had. Eclectic, informative, exciting, different. I used all of those words, and they are quite accurate. This class will be organized and taught as it might have been 40 years ago. Believe me, you will find the approach novel. And challenging. You are going to be active participants."

The shaggy student got up and left, along with two or three others.

Professor Cain nodded grimly. He took out a sheaf of papers and faced the audience again. "This is a description of the procedures I will follow in this class. I will give each of you a copy later, after going over some of the provisions with you.

"First, attendance is compulsory. You will be dropped from the rolls after two absences."

An audible gasp followed this pronouncement, and several more students got up and left.

"Second, there will be four written examinations. Three will be one-hour essay tests, and the final examination will be a two-hour essay test."

More students got up and left.

"Third, the exams will be graded by me, using the letters A, B, C, D, or F. If I may say so, your opinion of the quality of your work is *not* as good as mine."

Some more students joined the exodus.

"Fourth, this is not a class where you automatically receive an A or a B."

A stream of students headed out the door. Cain noticed that the observers were gone as well. He suspected that some, maybe most, of the leave-takers were heading for the nearest comm-terminals to report, to complain, or simply to spread the word about the reactionary events in classroom 201B.

"Fifth, you will be expected to read some chapters in all of these books I have here—and all the chapters in some of them. Several copies of each book will be on reserve in the library." Dryly, he added, "I will give you a campus map, with the location of the library clearly marked."

No laughter. Just shuffling of feet as students left.

"Sixth, these books cover quite a cross section of human knowledge, though obviously not all of it. We have philosophy: Plato, Hegel, Kant. Physics: Newton and Einstein. Whitehead and Russell on the foundations of mathematics. Some literature— Joyce, Tolstoy. Toynbee on history. Darwin on evolution. And, for art and science, Gray's *Anatomy.* These authors use difficult vocabularies, and most are not—at least, immediately—fun to read."

More feet, echoing now as the room emptied.

"Seventh, under my close supervision, you will write a term paper on a topic that I have approved."

A final exodus.

Cain lowered the paper. Eleven wide-eyed students remained. He sighed, wondering whether he could blackmail the dean into letting a class proceed with only 11 students. He could try.

He spoke to the silent minority. "Why don't you all come down close to the front, and we can start some of the preliminary work. In the old days, a class of this size was often called a seminar, and. . . ."

He broke off. The 11 were approaching the front row, but a noise had begun outside the room—not just the usual loud music, but also a strident chant. His 11 potential students froze in listening attitudes. "Hey! Hey! Don't stay. Professor crazy; come away! Hey! Hey! Don't stay. Professor crazy; come away. . . ." The chorus grew louder and louder.

The 11 diehards looked at Professor Cain and at one another. Then, almost in unison, they turned and left the room.

Defeated, Cain continued numbly to function. He repacked the papers and books and erased the mocking words from the chalkboard.

As he walked slowly across the campus, he left as though he were running a gauntlet of sneering, jeering faces. Perhaps he was, for—though he didn't look up—he heard various voices and comments as he trudged along.

From the students: "Grades! How prehistoric can you get?" "Compulsory attendance?" "Failure? How are we supposed to get jobs if we fail?" "Research paper? What's *he* been sniffing?" And still the chorus: "Professor crazy; stay away. . . ."

From members of the faculty: "Arrogant elitist." "He's just trying to make the rest of us look bad. Do a good job of teaching, and you don't *have* failures." "He's too old. Out of touch. He ought to step aside and make room for new blood."

The union representative: "Drive students away. Lose jobs. Antagonize colleagues. Jeopardize negotiations. Censure. Retire!"

A dean: "Accountability. Loss of credibility. Outdated ideas. Retire!"

The voices blended into the chorus. "Professor crazy; stay away!" The tumult ceased only when he closed and locked the door of his office behind him. He carefully stacked the two cases in the corner, knowing that they would probably never be opened again.

Silently, Fred Cain left the office, crossed the campus to the electric scooter with the bubble top that he still thought of as his car, and drove home. To stay.

After Reading

In your journal, respond to the following question: From what you observe around you and from your own sense of what college should be like, how accurate do you think Travis' prediction is? Write about one page, citing specifics whenever possible. With your classmates, share your responses to the Postman and the Travis readings. Record in your journal responses that differ from your own.

Before Reading

The following chapter selection explores the relationships between undergraduate education and career preparation. As you read the selection, consider the following questions:

1. To what extent do the authors believe that preparation for work should be an integral part of a college education?
2. What do the authors claim as the benefits of general education?
3. What suggestions do the authors make about how colleges can make more clear their role in career education?

Undergraduate Education and the World of Work

Carnegie Foundation for the Advancement of Teaching

In the view of many Americans, preparing people for work is becoming the dominant function of education. R. Freeman Butts (1975, p. 21) has observed that "Despite the concern of the 1930s and 1940s for the values of nonvocational liberal education, the rush to the professions and the technical specializations has proceeded pell mell, interrupted for a time by the downgrading of scientific and professional training by the youth culture of the 1960s, but by common agreement now in full flood tide among college students of the present generation." By 1976, 95 percent of America's undergraduates considered training and skills for an occupation to be either "essential" or "fairly important" goals of their college education (Carnegie Council Surveys, 1975–1976).

There are two possible consequences of this interest that could distort the purposes of the college curriculum. One is that students may become so single-minded in their studies aimed toward specific jobs that they become overspecialized and perhaps inflexible. The other is that students and employers alike might overemphasize the importance of degrees and other certification for employment. The result of this emphasis is that the level of credentialing for the positions that are available spirals upward beyond the actual demands of the work to be performed. Those people caught up in this trend can become underproductive and dissatisfied employees, discontented citizens, and frustrated alumni who feel that their education has somehow failed them (O'Toole, 1974, pp. 19, 20).

For this reason, we believe that any discussion of the relationship between education and the world of work must go beyond specific job preparation and manpower needs of the moment. Although graduates of American colleges can, and hopefully will, derive independence and satisfaction in careers with promising futures, it is equally, if not more important that they match their skills and competences with a thorough understanding of work as a characteristically human enterprise. They should appreciate its role in building self-esteem and a sense of accomplishment; in ordering one's personal life; in contributing to the welfare and comfort of others; in participating in the productive activities of the enterprise, the profession, the community, and the nation. Only by understanding the role of work in all of its forms and in all of its many contexts can one fully understand humanity and some of the basic forces that shape our society. Failure to understand it could leave one oblivious to the full significance of what goes on in at least one-third of the lives of most adult Americans.

A thorough introduction to the world of work will also give students a sense of reality that may not always come through their academic studies and campus experiences. It will introduce them to the costs as well as benefits of activities and programs and will introduce them to the importance of basic processes that are encountered directly in the world of work but have implications for other parts of life as well. Among them would be planning, budgeting, supervision of the work of others, scheduling, and maintaining inventories and quality controls. Although it may be difficult to teach these processes in the classroom, they can be taught and learned as a part of an undergraduate experience that effectively combines classroom studies with experiences in work situations. . . .

The Roles of General Education

The fact that students place a high value on career preparation while they are still in college does not mean that the specialized studies involved in such preparation are all employers should care about. They should also value the results of the total undergraduate educational experience. If it is effective, it increases the likelihood that a prospective college-educated employee will be:

- **Appreciative of the local, national, and international contexts in which his or her occupational endeavors are pursued**
- **Aware of fields of knowledge that offer data and insights relevant to his or her occupation**
- **Capable of communicating effectively with coworkers, superiors, customers, and the general public**
- **Resourceful in adjusting personally and professionally to problems and unexpected developments and opportunities**
- **Able to learn quickly and independently**
- **Able to recognize excellence in products, performance of associates and competitors, and plans for future developments**
- **Experienced in working to meet specified standards and persevering to the conclusion of assigned tasks**
- **Able to set and meet standards of ethical behavior and morality**

These are not outcomes colleges should strive to realize solely, or even mainly, to satisfy prospective employers. They are consequences of a good total undergraduate experience that should be valued for their own sake and should "come with the deal" when employers hire college graduates.

Improving Chances for Employment

Undergraduates typically acquire the particular knowledge and skills they hope to offer to prospective employers in their major studies. But there is not always a close correlation between one's major and one's ultimate career. Opportunities may arise that lead one into an occupation for which one has not specifically prepared, and college-educated people may change careers several times during their working lives. Moreover, some students deliberately choose majors that prepare them for specific roles in careers or professions outside their major field. The student who plans to become a salesman and majors in psychology rather than business administration or the student who plans to become an attorney and majors in speech might be examples. Such uses of the curriculum are consistent with the fact that, in 1971, nearly two-thirds of American business administrators who were college graduates had not majored in business administration (Bisconti, 1975, p. 7). Virtually all academic disciplines provide an educational base for teachers, including (with advanced training) college faculty members, and some teacher-training institutions do not permit undergraduates to major in education. On the other hand, teaching careers may be among the few that are really compatible with the educational preparation of large proportions of graduates in the social sciences and humanities (which explains why the 1970s, with their reduced opportunities for educators at all levels, have been particularly difficult for graduates in these fields).

Colleges might improve the employment prospects of such students by offering, in addition to departmental major options, certain interdisciplinary majors defined by broad areas of occupational and professional endeavor. A major in ecology or environmental management, for example, could draw on the biological sciences, physical sciences, forestry, agriculture, geography, urban management, and other disciplines related to occupations in land management, environmental protection, urban and regional planning, irrigation development, and other such fields. A major in communications could draw on English, journalism, languages, art, music, mathematics, and electronic and computer technology and could prepare persons for employment in news and information media, data processing and analysis, publishing, advertising, and public relations. A major in public service could draw on political science, psychology, biological sciences, law enforcement, and business administration and could prepare persons for a wide range of positions in government and public service organizations. If such majors were more extensively available, concentrations offered by single departments could become, more frankly and perhaps more effectively, what many of them are now—preparation for advanced education or for narrowly defined occupations and professions. Such majors might also be beneficial to students who plan to become members of college or university faculties.

Students should have options to take joint majors and major-minor combinations that permit them to concentrate on subjects of special interest to them and, at the same time, to increase their potential value to employers. Joint majors in business education and a foreign language, or education and a foreign language are examples of combinations for which there is some demand at the present time.

At some institutions, it may not be possible for students to obtain the courses they need in order to balance majors that are in low demand on the job market with instruction that will increase their employability. For example, some liberal arts colleges may not have any technical or professional courses available. Universities may not have any occupational instruction in their curricula. In such cases, colleges might explore the possibility of cooperating with other institutions, including two-year colleges, universities, technical institutes, or professional schools, to provide such courses for their students.

The principle to be observed is not that every student should be encouraged to acquire a specialized marketable skill before graduation from college but that no student should be involuntarily penalized in the job market for electing to concentrate in college on a subject that is of great personal interest but has no obvious demand by employers.

In the absence of interinstitutional cooperative arrangements, undergraduates should themselves seek ways to enhance the attractiveness of low-demand majors to prospective employers by supplementing them with technical and vocational education or work experience during summers and stop-outs. Such experiences will be particularly valuable if they demonstrate to employers a student's early interest in certain long-term career goals. . . .

Conclusion

America's colleges have been reluctant to make explicit commitments to an education that is designed to help their students acquire a full understanding of the world of work. At some institutions, particularly two-year community colleges, students are able to obtain intensive, short-term training in skills needed for specific types of jobs.

For a more general education, they must rely heavily on what they learned in high schools or from their families or peers. At other colleges, students find great concern for the life of the mind, for individual adjustment to life experiences, to uses of leisure, and for preparing them for more advanced learning but little interest in relating all of that to the great bloc of time men and women devote to earning a living. For many, integration of education and the world of work does not really begin until after they graduate.

To fill this gap in undergraduate education, we believe colleges should become more explicit about their role in preparing students for occupations and professions. In addition, we support:

- More study of the place of work in human lives and in society and experimentation with courses and seminars that explore various aspects of the world of work
- Provision of opportunities for students to stop out of college periodically to alternate educational and work experience
- Scheduling of classes and courses to accommodate needs of students who work part-time
- Development of cooperative work and education programs, particularly when they include features that give students a chance to integrate work and classroom experiences
- Development of work-study programs on the campuses and in the neighboring communities
- More extensive use of computer technology for assessing student skills, interests, and aptitudes and for matching them with career fields and appropriate educational programs
- Improvement of occupational counseling services and making their availability better known on campuses
- Introduction of some of the instruction generally encountered only in general education into the courses offered in vocational programs and professional schools, so that students will become familiar with the human problems and ethical issues specifically encountered on the job or in practice

References

Bisconti, A. S. *College Graduates and Their Employers.* Bethlehem, Pa.: College Placement Council Foundation, 1975.

Butts, R. F. "The Search for Purpose in American Education." Paper presented at the 75th anniversary forum of the College Entrance Examination Board, Plenary Session, New York, October 27, 1975.

Carnegie Council Surveys, 1975–1976.

O'Toole, J. (ed.). "Work and the Quality of Life." Resource papers for Work in America, a special task force, Massachusetts Institute of Technology. Cambridge, Mass.: M.I.T. Press, 1974.

After Reading

In your journal, respond to the following:

1. Brainstorm all the skills you believe you have gained from your schooling so far. Include cognitive as well as physical and social skills. When you have thought of all the skills you can, try to divide them into several categories.

2. Now do the same with the subjects about which you believe you have knowledge (e.g., American history, woodworking).
3. Compose a journal entry in which you summarize both of these lists and sets of categories.
4. Review these journal entries in preparation for discussion. Think about what the material suggests about the purposes of your formal education thus far. Share these entries in class discussion.

Before Reading

In the following excerpt from Governor Hunt's article "Education for Economic Growth: A Critical Investment," he rather pointedly expresses a single purpose for education.

Education for Economic Growth: A Critical Investment

Governor James B. Hunt, Jr.

Americans believe in education. It is the public enterprise that is closest to the hearts and most important to the lives of Americans. Ultimately, education is crucial to success in everything we attempt as a nation.

Time and again in its history, the U.S. educational system has been challenged to meet the changing needs of a growing, complex society. Yet not since the Russian launching of Sputnik in 1957 has education in America faced a greater challenge than the one it faces today, for today America is in danger of losing the worldwide economic and technological leadership that it has built up over generations.

During the 1970s Japan, France, and West Germany began to outstrip the U.S. in the rate of growth of productivity.[1] Today we are told that we have become less competitive and that our factories are crumbling into obsolescence. Our economic future is in danger because our students, unlike those in other leading industrial nations, are not learning the fundamental skills they need in a modern economy.

Last May [1983] *Newsweek* reported that "on most levels, U.S. students suffer in comparison with those in other industrialized nations at a time when American standing in world markets, in terms of both products and ideas, is threatened."[2] Indeed, our curriculum, particularly at the primary and secondary levels, is much less demanding than that of other leading nations. For example, all high school students in the Soviet Union take four years of chemistry (including one year of organic chemistry)[3] and two years of calculus.[4] In contrast, half of all high school graduates in the U.S. take no science or math beyond the 10th grade.[5] Japan, now with the highest literacy rate in the world, graduates 95% of its teenagers from high school; only 74% of U.S. teenagers graduate from high school. Such statistics clearly indicate that, without a shift in our educational direction, America will soon have difficulty competing in a world that demands new knowledge and higher levels of skills from its workforce.

The U.S. economic system is undergoing fundamental change today. Technology greatly affects how we do our work, and other countries have become major competitors with the U.S. for the world market. The majority of workers in the United States are now engaged not in industrial production, but in service occupations such as trade, transportation, banking, public utilities, and so on. In 1950, 55% of the U.S. workforce was employed by industry; today that figure has fallen to 20%. In contrast, in 1950, 30% of our workforce held service and information jobs; today that figure has climbed to 70%.

This shift is sure to continue. In fact, it's fairly common to see estimates predicting that 15 million American manufacturing jobs will disappear in the coming decade. We must respond to this shift with a renaissance in education. We must educate our young people for the jobs of tomorrow, the jobs that will be available when they leave high school or college. And we must begin now to develop the skills that will be required tomorrow.

Certainly those jobs promising upward mobility will require the mastery of skills that go beyond today's definition of "the basics." To adequately prepare our young people for these jobs, we must expand our idea of the basics to include not only the abilities to read, write, and compute at a rudimentary level, but also the ability to put to creative use more complex skills.

Basic competence in reading, for example, must be expanded to include the ability to analyze, summarize, and interpret written passages. Competence in writing must encompass the ability to select, organize, and develop ideas. Competence in mathematics must include the ability to compute—with whole numbers, fractions, decimals, and percentages—and to use basic concepts of probability and statistics. Most important, students must acquire such "learning to learn" skills as analysis and problem solving, which will enable them to acquire new skills.

All jobs in the future will by no means require higher-order skills. Yet the growth of technology will change both job opportunities and job requirements, and jobs promising advancement will increasingly be those that require not just mastery of the more advanced skills, but also the ability to use them creatively in the workplace.[6]

Our American educational ethic demands that we provide all students, not just a selected elite, with the opportunity and encouragement to develop more sophisticated skills. We must give everyone both a choice and a genuine chance in life. We must begin immediately to invest more in our human resources by strengthening the education and training of *all* our students. To achieve sound economic growth, we must make these investments now.

We Americans want to insure that we can continue to compete in the world economy. We want our economic productivity increased, our technological capability enhanced, and our standing in the world restored.[7] Our quality of life and the future of our children depend on our ability to pursue this new ethic of educational excellence. We are, of course, concerned about the enormous task of training and retraining that lies before us. Clearly our educational system is being called upon to meet a new challenge. We must equip our citizens to be scientifically and technologically literate if our nation is to participate in a technology-based world economy. In short, we must "maximize human potential through education."[8]

Notes

[1]Three of the major reports are Education Commission of the States, *Action for Excellence: A Comprehensive Plan to Improve Our Nation's Schools* (Denver: ECS, 1983); Twentieth Century Fund Task Force on Federal Elementary and Secondary Education Policy, *Making the Grade* (New York: Twentieth Century Fund, 1983); and National Commission on Excellence in Education, *A Nation at Risk: The Imperative for Educational Reform* (Washington, D.C.: U.S. Government Printing Office, 1983).

[2]See Daniel Quinn Mills, "Decisions About Employment in the 1980s: Overview and Underpinning." and Michael Wachter, "Economic Challenges Posed by Demographic Changes," in Eli Ginzberg et al., eds., *Work Decisions in the 1980s* (Boston: Auburn House, 1982).

[3]"For example, while males 20 to 24 years old earned $73 for every $100 by prime-age males in 1955, they earned only $58 for every $100 in 1977," according to Wachter, p. 43.

[4]For a discussion of the Youth Employment Act of 1977, see Joel Spring, *American Education,* 2nd ed. (New York: Longman, 1982), pp. 117–21.

[5]"In fact, in the mid-1970s American manufacturing firms were cautious about capital investment, but relatively expansive about employment. . . . In the most telling comparison, American manufacturers and manufacturers in France, Japan, and Germany increased output between 1972 and 1978 by somewhat similar amounts. During the same period employment fell in France by 2.2%, in Japan by 4.7%, and in Germany by 12%; but in the United States, manufacturers increased employment by 61.5%," according to Mills, pp. 8–9.

[6]Ibid., p. 5.

[7]Wachter, pp. 35–42.

[8]Michael Timpane, *Corporations and Public Education*, report distributed by Teachers College, Columbia University (New York: Carnegie Corporation, May 1982), pp. 8–9.

After Reading

1. In a journal entry, record what Governor Hunt claims is the main goal of education. Express your agreement or disagreement with his view. Then, list your specific goals for your college education.
2. Review your journal response to the Postman article and paraphrase—or put into your own words—Postman's idea of the principal goal of education. Share your responses with the class.

Thus far in this chapter you have read selections focused on education and responded to them by writing in your journal and discussing them in your class; you have thought and written about your own formal education and what its purpose has seemed to be; you have compared others' notions of what education ought to be and what it should achieve. As countless others before them, Postman, Travis, Hunt, and the Carnegie Commission all express their opinions on this subject. You are in a position now to do the same in response to a specific writing situation.

Assignment

Most colleges have a general education requirement for all students, and it may comprise anywhere from one-quarter to one-half of the credits needed for graduation with the bachelor's degree. Typically, the requirement includes courses in the social sciences, humanities (literature, philosophy, art, music), and the natural sciences including mathematics. Assume that a faculty and student committee at your school has just completed a process of reevaluating its general education requirement. After extensive examination and work, the committee has proposed to the college that the requirement for all majors be increased to account for three-quarters of the hours required for graduation. These hours would consist of introductory courses distributed evenly among the humanities, the social sciences, and the natural sciences. The rationale of the committee's proposal is primarily that the college can no longer hope to train undergraduate students effectively in all the special skills that might be needed in the rapidly changing workplace and that it might as well concentrate its programs on what it can do well—that is, provide a solid background or core in liberal studies and teach students how to think, organize, and solve problems.

The committee putting forth the proposal is composed of the following: one professor of literature, one professor of business, one professor of biology, one professor of computer science, one junior student majoring in journalism, and one senior student majoring in art. The proposal has been shared informally around the campus with students and faculty and has triggered a variety of responses. Some are in favor of the proposal in principle, but others who oppose it argue that it does not allow much freedom of choice for students and that liberal studies do not prepare students for specific job markets upon graduation.

In an attempt to get a more comprehensive view of student response to this issue, your president has invited all students to submit to the committee a position paper on the proposal. Knowing that such a major curriculum revision would not take effect until after you have graduated, you are in a good position to be objective. You have a sense of your own educational goals and those of others, and you have thought about, read, and shared views on the purposes of higher education.

Write your position paper to the president and the members of the committee, who want no more than 500 words from each student. To give your audience confidence in your opinion, be sure to demonstrate your understanding of the variety of purposes for education that students and others may see, as well as your own considered opinion or point of view.

Generally, a position paper must include three parts.

1. It must state the issue or proposal clearly.
2. It must show that the writer has considered positions other than his or her own and why the other positions were rejected.
3. It must state and support the writer's own position.

Although position papers need not follow a specific format, they often do. They begin with a full statement of the issue or proposal and the position of the writer, then explore and refute other possible positions, and finally restate and support the writer's position. The number of paragraphs in a position paper may vary, but sections are normally devoted to each of the three parts listed above. Position papers typically include the use of the pronoun "I"—you are, after all, expressing your opinion. This is not to say that all your sentences will begin with "I think" or "It seems to me," but readers certainly expect your personal voice in this kind of writing.

HOW TO BEGIN

Let us consider the audience specified in the major writing project for this chapter, a committee composed of college faculty and students and, ultimately, the college president. What we know about these people both as a group and as individuals can help us in our attempt to convince them of our position on the proposal to increase the general education component to three-fourths of the hours required for graduation. Make a list in your journal of the characteristics of this audience. In doing so, try to address the following areas:

1. Age
2. Experience
3. Educational level
4. Fields of interest
5. Likely predispositions on the issue
6. Knowledge of the issue

Consider also the nature of the college, its capabilities and strengths as well as its deficiencies.

Once you have considered your audience, try a focused free writing in your journal, talking to yourself about the issue. This writing should help you discover your position and the various kinds of support that might prove useful. By the time you have finished this exploratory writing you will probably have decided on a position which, with work, you can support. As background for your position, use ideas from the readings of this chapter, from any additional readings if you wish, and from your own and others' experiences. Cite authorities if appropriate.

On another page in your journal, state the opposing position and list as many reasons as you can that could be garnered to support that position. These are the points you must counter in refuting the opposing position. Keeping these and your audience considerations in mind, write a draft of your position paper. Remember, your job is threefold:

1. Make clear the issue and state your position.
2. Present and refute the opposing view.
3. Restate and support your own position.

GENERALIZING

You may already know what you think about the proposed change in the general education requirements, or you may not. If you think you know what position you will take, your task will be to articulate the reasons for your position. If you do not yet have a position, you will have to consider your experience, your readings, and your class discussions to arrive at a position you can support. And, whether you begin with an opinion or develop one as you work, you may well find that you change your position on the issue as you sort out evidence and consider arguments. The position you ultimately take will reflect your personal values (see Chapter 6 for a detailed discussion of values) and your judgment of what *generalization* the arguments and evidence best support.

What is a generalization? Put simply, it is a statement that applies to more than one specific instance. There are many levels of generality. You can think of statements as being on a scale from specific to general:

specific	1. It was a dark and stormy night.
more general	2. Nights here are dark and stormy.
more general	3. The weather is bad here at night.
most general	4. The weather is bad here.
	AND
specific	1. On their late albums, the Beatles began to use the Moog synthesizer more.
more general	2. The Moog synthesizer became more popular in the late 1960s.
more general	3. Music changed from the early 1960s to the early 1980s.
more general	4. Many things changed from the early 1960s to the early 1980s.
most general	5. Things change.

Look at each of the following sets of sentences and arrange the sentences from most specific to most general.

1. (a) How much did your furniture cost?
   (b) How much does a valuable Chippendale cost?
   (c) How much did that chair cost?
   (d) How much is your personal property worth?
2. (a) Susan is very rude.
   (b) Yesterday Susan said, "Give me 50¢, will you?" And when I handed it to her, she just took it and walked away.
   (c) I can't stand Susan.
   (d) Susan never says please or thank you.
3. (a) Thou shalt not commit adultery.
   (b) Ms Miller should not make love to my husband.
   (c) No man or woman should make love to another's mate.
   (d) Follow my commandments saith the Lord.
   (e) Do unto others as you would have them do unto you.
4. (a) Repairs are needed at Sawyer Park.
   (b) County parks are deteriorating.
   (c) The baseball field at Sawyer Park is more mud than grass.
   (d) The county is broke and things are going downhill.
   (e) The baseball field at Sawyer Park is in disrepair.

Have you noticed that the most interesting sentences are the most specific? They give you something to visualize because very specific statements encourage concrete language (see p. 208). More general statements, however, are by nature more consequential. To say what something means, or to evaluate it, or to describe an ongoing condition, you need a fairly general statement. An interplay of generalizations and specifics is therefore what carries most writing.

When you clarify your purpose for writing a given piece, you ask, "What do I want my reader(s) to think or do or feel?" The answer to this question gives you the *major generalization* for that piece of writing. If you answer "I want the Dean to approve my petition to drop Chemistry 201," then your major generalization will be "I deserve to drop Chemistry 201." If you answer, "I want my readers to know how to adjust the brakes on a Raleigh bicycle," then your major generalization will be "to adjust the brakes on a Raleigh bicycle, you should do the following." If you answer "I want readers of my letter to the editor to share my attitude toward U.S. military involvement in Central America, then your major generalization will be "The U.S. should [not] be militarily involved in Central America." If you answer "I want my readers to share the peacefulness I felt while canoeing the boundary lakes," then your major generalization will be "canoeing the boundary lakes made me feel peaceful." If you answer "I want the readers of my short story to understand what a child may feel when his or her parents are divorcing," then your major generalization will be "a child can feel hurt and guilty and resentful and protective and independent in response to his or her parents' divorce."

In some kinds of writing, the major generalization (sometimes called a *thesis statement*) is explicitly stated. The intent of these forms—namely: position papers, research reports, editorials, letters to the editor, and most persuasive writing—is to make readers grasp certain information or think a certain way. In other types of writing the major generalization is usually left unstated. Short stories, for example, virtually never make explicit their generalization (often called a *theme*). Accounts of personal experience, intended to share a mood or feeling with the reader, are also likely to leave their major generalization unstated.

Whether explicitly stated or merely implied, the major generalization of a piece determines its content. When you are deciding whether to include a detail, you ask, "Will it help support my major generalization?" If it will, you include it; if it will not, you leave it out. Likewise, you ask, "Do I need more material to support my major generalization?" and then decide if you will add material. In addition to your major generalization, stated or implied, you will have other supporting generalizations. These, too, may be either stated or implied. If you take a look at the structure of paragraphs, you will find that most consist of relatively specific statements that support a generalization which, in turn, supports the major generalization of the writing. Notice how this pattern organizes the student's petition to drop Chemistry 201:

major generalization supporting generalization	{ I am petitioning to drop Chemistry 201 with a grade of W. I believe that I deserve a W rather than an F because circumstances beyond my control have caused me to miss class for the last three weeks.

specific
support {
On October 17, I was hit by a car while riding my motorcycle. I spent six days in the hospital and another two weeks at home because of leg fractures. A letter from my doctor is attached to this petition.

supporting
generalization {
specific
support {
Before the accident, I was in good standing in the class. I think my average would have been about a B− on tests and lab reports, and I had missed only one class before the accident.

Each of the following paragraphs is organized around one supporting generalization. Identify the generalization for each; if the generalization is implicit, write a sentence that could serve as the generalization.

A.   Realizing that things have names, that "w-a-t-e-r" meant "the wonderful cool something that was flowing over my hand," changed Helen Keller's life. Dead objects became living things; she was able to know for the first time that she had broken something, knowledge which, in turn, allowed her to experience sorrow and regret. This simple realization made possible seeing things in combinations and relationships, the essence of thought. Barriers were swept away, and in their places she found hope and joy and freedom.

B.   Roger Chillingworth, of *The Scarlet Letter,* had been isolated from humanity because of his scholarly pursuits and his deformed body even before he arrived in Boston. Though he had been married to Hester, there was a great gulf between them which widened after his decision early in the novel to determine her partner in sin. Once he made his discovery of Arthur Dimmesdale's guilt, he became isolated completely from others and from peace in his own soul and was "seized" as he said, "by some dark necessity to bring about the ruin of the soul of Dimmesdale." Chillingworth slowly became a pitiful creature possessing only the physical human characteristics; unlike a human being he was driven completely by a single motive, vengeance, the only reason for his existence.

C.   There is something in the mealy smell of fallen leaves and their dry scuttle along the pavement that makes me breathe more slowly. The mornings are foggy and in the evenings a dry dust hangs in the air. In the clear afternoons, whenever I look up, I think of Yeats's line about the "rook-delighting sky." Springtime makes me want to clean and plan; in October, I just what to stand and watch it all before it vanishes. I want to play old music, write letters, and look through the photo album.

D.   Transistors are made of special substances called semiconductors which in turn are made of highly purified silicon, germanium, and boron. Transistors are small and require little power; so they have replaced vacuum tubes in many cases and have made integrated circuits and silicon chips possible. Computers utilizing transistors have been greatly reduced in size and are used in space programs as well as in artificial intelligence.

Now consider the following paragraph:

Hitler attacked Denmark and Norway on April 9th of 1940. Denmark was under German control within a few hours, and Norway fell within a few weeks despite British aid to the Norwegians. These quick Nazi victories brought on political crisis in Britain; Chamberlain resigned as Prime Minister and Churchill took over on May 10. That day Hitler's forces invaded the Netherlands, Belgium, and Luxembourg. By June 22 of that year, France had fallen as well.

It would be very difficult to compose a generalization for this last paragraph because it is just a sequence of events, all specifics. Writing that is intended to tell a story—fiction or nonfiction—is likely to have many paragraphs made up entirely of specifics. The implied generalization for these would be something like "this is what happened next."

The fact that most of us like a good story should remind us how appealing specifics are. Look at the different proportions between generalizations and specifics in the following examples:

A.   I spent the summer of 1970 at my aunt's house, and I hated being there because she was sick and the town she lived in was depressing. My mother was taking care of my aunt and I had come along. Now, as an adult, I realize that that summer was harder for my mother than for me and I feel bad about not being more helpful or at least more cheerful.

B.   I spent the summer of 1970 in Newport. My aunt was ill and my mother had come to take care of her. I very much wanted to be with my mother, but I hated the old neighborhood with boarded-up stores and second-hand shops and gospel missions. I slept on a cot put underneath the dining room table, and the neighbors' radio played late with "Imagine There's No Heaven" and reports on the last illness of the last Civil War widow. There were no other children around, no yard, no grass. To get out of the stifling house, I spent as much of the time as I could outside, throwing a rubber ball against the wall of the dirty gothic brewery across the street and trying not to think about my aunt's life or how it had come to this. One night the ball took a bad bounce and went over my head, along the littered gutter, and down the sewer. Inside the house I could hear my mother running hot water for the laundry and my aunt calling "Elizabeth! Elizabeth!" She probably wanted the TV station changed, and I thought about going in, but instead I sat down on the curb and cried for everything I had not known was wrong with the world.

Although the sentences in the first version are not very general, they are still more general than those in the second. And most people find the second version more interesting and more affecting than the first.

Not only are specifics most likely to affect us, but they are also most likely to convince us. Specifics are the best support because they can be checked on. If you argue "Sawyer Park is deteriorating," someone can say, "It looks all right to me." But if you can support your claim with very specific details about broken water fountains, rotting picnic tables, roads with potholes, and baseball fields with more mud than grass, you win. The next part of this chapter will deal with the process of generalizing on specifics and with supporting a generalization adequately.

SUPPORTING A GENERALIZATION

Generalizing from Your Experience

Certain kinds of generalizations require no more than our own personal experience as support. Suppose a friend said to you, "I remember my childhood as a happy one." You might ask why and your friend might give you examples or reasons. But he does not have to; he is entitled to feel about his childhood any way he wants. If, however, he goes on to say, "I remember it as one long Little League game. I think there is no better experience for kids than playing in Little League," now he has generalized beyond his own experience and can be challenged.

Of course, you could let his generalization go unchallenged, as you probably would if you agreed with it or were just more interested in pursuing another part of the conversation. But, if you were interested and disagreed, you might offer a counterexample: "Do you remember Ken Kramer? He hated Little League. Spent all his time on the bench, and every time they lost, his father would go around yelling at everybody." To this your friend might answer, "Well, I guess you do have to like baseball and get some playing time and not have a macho lunatic for a father."

This exchange is in many ways a model of the process by which we come to our positions on various issues. We generalize on the basis of our own experience, and we modify our generalization when we find out about other people's experience that differs from ours. We may also have some other kind of data to consider, like responses to a questionnaire or case studies, which are really just formal means of learning about other people's experience and perhaps their reaction to it. This textbook repeatedly asks you to reflect on your own experience before it asks you to take a position on any issue. It does this because your experiences are unique and thus give you something uniquely valuable to contribute to any debate. But it is only on personal topics that you can legitimately generalize on the basis of your experience alone (e.g., "I remember my childhood as a happy one"). For this reason, this text always asks you to compare your experience and reflections with those of your classmates before taking a position. This process of formulating a generalization after considering instances is called *inductive reasoning*.

Evidence and Illustration

Retelling your own or someone else's experience can be a very effective way to lead your reader to accept your conclusion. The concrete and sensory language that comes easily when recounting an experience is likely to involve the reader's interest and emotions. Consider this example:

> Margaret Flaherty arrived at the hospital just in time to see her eighteen-year-old son, Steve, taken into surgery. "I suppose I should be grateful I never

really got to see him; he wasn't conscious and as it is, I'm haunted by the sight of the mangled car though I only saw it for an instant, lit by the flashing red lights of the police cars," says Ms. Flaherty. Stephen Flaherty died that night of injuries suffered when his car was hit head-on by a car which crossed the center line. The other driver was drunk. And that night Flaherty's mother joined the campaign to make jail sentences mandatory for even first offense drunk drivers.

Reading this, we share Ms. Flaherty's experience. The concrete language enables us to visualize what she saw, which, in turn, helps us to understand her position and, perhaps, inclines us to agree with it. But there is an old proverb that says, "An example isn't proof." The account of Ms. Flaherty's experience is a good and useful illustration, but it is not enough to support a generalization by itself.

What, then, does it take to support a generalization? Generally, you must demonstrate that you have considered all facets of the issue, have made good arguments in favor of your view, have shown why opposing arguments are less convincing, and have qualified your generalization to reflect the limits of your evidence. To get a better sense of this last point, imagine that your classmates fill out a questionnaire about their reasons for going to college and that 53 percent of them say that getting a good job was their chief motivation. On the basis of this data you could not legitimately say that "more than half of today's college students have come to college primarily to get a better job." Your evidence covers only *your class*, not all of today's college students or even a large enough random sample to support the generalization. Likewise, you could not legitimately say, "*Most* of our class members have come to college primarily to get a good job." *Most* implies a bigger majority than 53 percent. You could legitimately claim *more than half*, however, because that is accurate.

Deductive Reasoning

The opposite of inductive reasoning is *deductive reasoning*, whereby we come to our position on an issue by applying general principles or reasoning from accepted general statements. Here is an example.

> Burglary is the act of breaking into another's dwelling at night with intent to steal.
>
> Howard was caught inside the house at 2520 Lee Road at 9:40 p.m. on June 17, having entered by cutting a screen on a ground floor window; he was caught filling a suitcase with the owner's silverware.
>
> Therefore, Howard is guilty of burglary.

But is he guilty? Howard argues that it was still light at 9:40 on that June night and therefore it was not night and therefore he is not a burglar. Even with deductive arguments, there is usually a case to be made. Few deductive arguments are airtight; someone will argue that a different general principle should have been applied or that the general principle that was used should not per-tain to this instance. The First Amendment guarantees free speech, for example, but it has been successfully argued that citizens' right to be protected from unnecessary danger overrides the guarantee of free speech in the case of someone yelling "fire" in a crowded theater.

LOGICAL FALLACIES

In applying general principles to specific instances, there are some well-worn paths of error you can learn to recognize and avoid.

1. *Argument from ignorance:* Arguing that something must be true because it has never been proved false.

Example: There must be intelligent life on other planets because no one has proven there isn't.

2. *Ad Hominem (to the man) appeal:* Basing an argument on personalities or personal situations that are irrelevant.

Example: How can you take seriously Professor Smith's work in optics? He doesn't even believe in evolution!

AND

As an educated person, you must accept Smith's theories.

3. *Appeal to authority:* Citing some individual or group's belief in a conclusion to establish that the conclusion is probable or valid. The appeal to authority is fallacious *only* if the authority is not an authority in the relevant field or if the writer attaches too much weight to the authority's judgment.

Example: The track coach says that learning French is a waste of anyone's time.

AND

This study, produced by a very reputable and nationally known engineering firm, says that solar energy is this country's best hope of meeting its energy needs in the twenty-first century; therefore, there is no point in waiting for other studies and delaying development.

4. *Appeal to the people:* An appeal playing on the individual's desire to be "one of the crowd" or to have status within the crowd. It includes

advertising that associates its product with luxury or status or sex appeal but presents no evidence that the product will give these to its buyers. It includes variations of the "everyone believes it, so it must be true" argument.

Example: Our product is clearly a good one because it has been the best-selling brand for a decade.

5. *Hasty generalization*: Deriving a general principle from an insufficient number of instances and without considering other relevant factors.

Example: Every year hundreds of people are killed in auto accidents in this state; therefore, the state should protect its citizens by banning automobiles.

6. *Circular argument*: Using as a premise the very conclusion you are trying to prove.

Example: Free public education is desirable because everyone should have access to educational opportunities without having to bear the expense.

7. *Composition*: Ascribing to the whole the attributes of the parts.

Example: None of the components of the system is beyond my means; therefore, the system will be inexpensive enough for me to afford.

8. *Equivocation*: Using a term in two different senses in the same syllogism. (This is most often done by writers using vague and abstract terms.)

Example: Government *regulation of business* is undesirable. By passing consumer protection legislation, government is *regulating business*. Therefore consumer protection laws are undesirable.

9. *Post hoc ergo propter hoc (after that; therefore, because of that)*: Assuming that B was caused by A because B occurred after A.

Example: Maple leaves always turn red before they die; therefore, the red pigment must be lethal to maple leaves.

10. *False dilemma*: Setting up false alternatives as if they are the only possibilities and the choice must be made between them.

Example: We can either abandon nuclear energy and freeze in the dark or we can give free rein to its developers and assure a secure future for our children.

Some of the following arguments are deductive and some are inductive. Explain in your journal why each of the deductive arguments is valid (e.g., logically correct) or invalid, and, if invalid, why. Judge the probability of the conclusion of each of the inductive arguments. Indicate what evidence would be needed to make each more probable.

1. I must not know how to care for house plants; this is the second philodendron that has died in my custody.
2. Rising gasoline prices have not significantly reduced the consumption of gasoline; therefore, if the price of chocolate rises, consumption of it will not be significantly reduced.
3. This is the approved method of organization; it is the one used by professional writers.
4. A flood isn't likely to occur in this area; we've had this much rain before and the river didn't rise very far.
5. Americans are among the best-fed people in the world; so I doubt that my lack of energy can be attributed to a nutritional deficiency.
6. He's been drinking for years and feels no ill effects; so I suppose he might as well go on drinking.
7. Compulsory military service for all males between 18 and 36 is justified because all young men should have to serve their hitch in the armed services.
8. You might as well go ahead and buy products made from the skins of animals that are from endangered species; the animal is already dead by then.
9. This brand of luxury car will last you longer than any other make of car; it has the highest percentage of cars still in service after 10 years.
10. Our foundation can fund only one of these two proposals which seem equally worthy. We have chosen to fund Professor Bernstein's proposal because he has a record of distinguished research in the field of his proposal.

Examine the logic of the following argument. Point out any clues in the writing that may help you identify a logical flaw and name the kind of fallacy you find.

Legalize Marijuana

If someone wants to know why marijuana isn't being legalized, an investigation will reveal two issues. The first is the health issue. Is it possible that smoking grass is a serious danger to your health? Is it worse than cigarettes or liquor or air pollution? The second issue is profit. Government officials profit by keeping marijuana an illegal substance.

Back in the 1930s there was a campaign to make people think marijuana did serious damage to our health. The government supported this idea, and movies showed people going wild after smoking dope. But actually, marijuana leaves you with more control than alcohol.

Automobiles kill. Chemicals in food can kill. Cigarettes and liquor ruin us. But only marijuana is illegal. Who benefits from this? As in a murder investigation, it pays to ask, "Who benefits?" Criminals benefit because illegality keeps the price of marijuana high. And who are they paying off? To answer this you only have to ask who could legalize marijuana but hasn't. The last few years have shown us that legislators can be bought. Why should we be surprised that our government is keeping marijuana illegal, despite what the public wants, just to serve its own interests?

Appeals to the emotions of readers, the testimony of relevant authorities, and the good character of the writer are all elements that can help to convince. This section will help you distinguish between the correct use of these elements *with logical support* to further a conclusion and the incorrect use of them to *replace logical support*, as in many of the fallacies.

APPEALS TO EMOTION

While the foregoing discussion may make logic sound rather complicated, in reality it is not more than good common sense. Similarly, when a writer makes an emotional appeal, he or she simply takes advantage of those normal human feelings that an audience experiences. Such appeals can be very effective in rousing an audience to some needed action. For example, if it were your responsibility to urge citizens not to use lead paint, you would probably do well to give vivid, specific examples of the effects of lead poisoning in the hope of arousing a little healthy fear. A Red Cross poster that showed a disaster site and read "Blood Saves Lives" would be justified in its attempt to arouse sympathy because the slogan explains how the sympathy and the blood donation are related. And the newspaper writer who gave us such a vivid account of Ms. Flaherty's tragic experience (see pp. 166–167) did so to help us see why Mothers Against Drunk Driving (MADD) are so vehement.

Writers can also take advantage of other emotions, like envy, patriotism, and personal or civic pride. You can use such emotional appeals along with inductive or deductive reasoning. If used honestly, they can be a powerful tool in convincing an audience to accept your position. Sometimes, however, you will find such appeals used dishonestly: the writer tries to play on our feelings without making it clear how those feelings relate logically to the generalization. If, for example, someone were impassioned enough to argue "computerizing the library card catalogue is a betrayal of our special identity here at _____ College, where tradition has always been respected," he or she would be appealing to school spirit and respect for tradition. But this would be a dishonest appeal to emotions because the writer has never demonstrated *how* computerizing the card catalogue betrays any tradition worthy of respect.

Appeals to emotion are easy to identify once we are in the habit of watching for them: generally we can tell when we are being asked to think and when we are being asked to feel. Read the following letter to the editor and write a journal entry in which you analyze the letter's appeals to reason and its appeals to emotion. Share these entries with the class.

On the Defeat of the SST

It was with great regret that I witnessed the Senate's rejection of the bill that would have funded the building of the supersonic transport. I had the feeling that perhaps I was watching the moment that marked the waning of America's greatness.

America needs the SST. Britain and France have cooperatively designed, funded and built the Concorde, the prototype of which was extremely impressive at the recent Paris Air Show. The Russian SST prototype shown at this same exposition was eloquent testimony to what can be accomplished by a society that is not afraid of technology.

Indeed, it is precisely this antitechnology hysteria that was behind the defeat of the American SST. Perpetrated by environmental alarmists looking for a campaign issue, this hysteria was pandered to an uninformed public, and the issue became lost in a gush of rhetoric. It came as a surprise to no one that the campaign to kill the SST was spearheaded by Senator _____, whose legislative capabilities have long been questioned.

The demise of the SST means the demise of American primacy and it is doubtful whether it can ever be regained. Nevertheless, I urge all those who are aware of just how vital this issue is to initiate a campaign of letter writing to bring pressure to bear on their representatives to revive this most important issue.

CITING AUTHORITIES

In addition to basic reasoning and occasional and appropriate use of emotional appeal, how else do you strengthen your position on an issue? Above all, you want to seem as authoritative as possible. One way you can do this is to include in your case conclusions by certain authorities whose names are respected in the field about which you are writing. The expertise of such individuals can lend weight to your own argument. The citing of authorities and sources is necessary in many kinds of writing, in particular, the research report or a scientific treatise, but it can also be useful in persuasive writing such as a position paper. A carefully chosen quotation by a well-known scholar or thinker can reinforce or underscore your reasoning.

In citing the conclusions and opinions of experts in the field, you must take care that such inclusion is appropriate. To argue that good dental hygiene includes flossing and then to support that argument by calling forth the name of Victoria Principal is neither sound nor convincing. Perhaps the television star has a nice smile and *does* floss, but is she an appropriate authority on dental hygiene? If you are stating your position on nuclear disarmament, would quoting Julia Child, noted gourmet chef and writer of American cookbooks, be effective in winning an audience to your point of view? Probably not.

THE READER'S TRUST

Like appeals to emotion and the testimony of authorities, a sense of the writer's good character can do much to influence a reader; while appeals to emotion and to authority are merely helpful, trust in the writer is essential.

To carry your point, you must convince your audience that behind your words is a thoughtful, honest, and perceptive person, a consistent, tactful, and, above all, reasonable individual. You must refrain from resorting to unfair practices such as name-calling or other ridiculing techniques. Such techniques incline readers to suspect that there is insufficient support for your argument or that your position is little more than a casual opinion. Readers can be convinced only by writers they respect.

Considering your audience is essential if your persuasive writing is to have an impact. Many writers make consideration of their audience the first priority in planning any piece of writing. Treating your readers with respect, not condescending or patronizing, not sounding pompous or stiff, is the least you can do for any audience. (For a fuller discussion of the importance of audience, see Chapters 2 and 3.)

Revising Workshop

In small groups share your papers, assisting each other with responses to the following questions. Try not to pay attention to mechanical correctness at this stage. Each position paper should be reviewed by at least two students.

1. What is the writer's position on the proposal? Where is the position first stated? Is this an appropriate placement for the reader?
2. How does the writer back up his or her position (logic, authorities, statistics, emotional appeal, polls, relevant anecdotes, etc.)? Mark any support that seems questionable or needs expanding.
3. How does the writer refute the opposing view? Mark any passages that seem questionable or need expanding.
4. What seems to be the tone of the position paper? (Pompous, serious, humorous?) How will the specified audience respond? Mark any passages or words that you think might be inappropriate for the audience.
5. What seems to be the function of each paragraph? Is this the most effective order for the paragraphs?
6. If you were the intended audience, what questions would you raise in response to the paper? Is there any statement to which you would object? Is there any section of the paper where you would like more information?
7. Comment on the sentence structure in the paper. Are any sentences choppy? Any too long? Any weakened by unnecessary words?

Before writing the second draft of your position paper, take into consideration the responses of your classmates offered during the Revising Workshop. You are not compelled to act on every suggestion, but you do have a responsibility to think through their ideas.

Now write your second draft, making whatever revisions you deem necessary—for clarity, to improve the support of your position or your refutation of the opposing position, or for tone and organization.

Editing Workshop

Return to class with your second draft of the position paper for the Editing Workshop. Your aim in this session is to help each other review the position papers for mechanical flaws and problems with form. As in the Revising Workshop, each paper should be reviewed by at least two students. Use as guidelines the following questions and suggestions:

1. Are there any sentences or parts of sentences that confuse you or cause you to have to reread to grasp their meaning? If so, bracket these as needing reconsideration.
2. Place an *X* in the margin on any line in which you see what you perceive as an error in spelling or punctuation. Use as many marks as there are errors.
3. Put a *C* in the margin of any line in which you find a trite expression or a cliché.
4. Place a *G* in the margin of any line in which you find what you consider an error in grammar or usage. Use as many marks as there are errors.

Examine the responses to your draft. If there are sentences bracketed, try to decide what the problems are. If you find marks indicating spelling, punctuation, or grammar and usage errors, try to identify what those errors are and correct them. For help, see the Editing Guide (Chapter 12). Make notes in your journal on the kinds of sentence and mechanical errors you are making in your draft.

Make whatever revisions you feel need to be made for a clear, convincing, polished position paper and submit your final copy to your instructor.

CHAPTER 6

Clarifying a Situation

THEME *Conflicting Values*

SKILL FOCUS *Making Language Choices*

When people disagree with us it is satisfying to think that they do so just because they are wrong. Indeed, they may be wrong; they may have the wrong information or incomplete information or insufficient experience to judge the situation. Or it may be that their values differ from ours. Consider the following exchange:

> *Terry:* It's cold in here. I'm going to turn up the heat.
> *Chris:* Don't do that. We'll have a four-digit gas bill. I refuse to play into the hands of the gas company. We can live with 64 degrees.
> *Terry:* Maybe you can, but I can't. I'd rather save a few dollars on something else than walk around here with my coat on and see my breath in the air.

We cannot say that either of these people is right or wrong; rather, that our values are more like those of Terry, who thinks being warm is more important than keeping money away from the gas company, or more like those of Chris, who thinks that beating the gas company is worth some discomfort.

There are, of course, some values to which most human beings give priority, such as the preservation of human life. But there is much disagreement generally about which values are more important than others. Political debates in particular show us the conflict of values in action. Recognizing that someone's values differ from ours does not mean that we must simply agree to disagree and let it go at that. We may be morally outraged at the values of others and work very hard to change them. Recognizing the values that motivate our own and other people's actions is a constructive first step.

Before Reading

The following selection is an excerpt from Michael Silver's *Values Education* which will give you some background on values. As you read it, formulate in your own words a definition of the word "value" and decide how a *value* differs from a *rule* (e.g., always count your change).

Defining Values and Value Systems

Michael Silver

In the broadest sense, values can be defined as the preferred events that people seek. Values consist in or arise from needs and wants. But provided only with this simple definition, it would be impossible . . . to handle adequately the kinds of difficulty in communicating . . . about values. A clear understanding of human values can be gained by becoming familiar with some of the existing conceptual frameworks of values.

Milton Rokeach has provided a typology of human values.[1] According to him, a value is an enduring belief that a certain type of behavior or a certain condition of life is desirable. More specifically, he defines a value as "an enduring belief that a specific mode of conduct or end state of existence is personally or socially preferable to an opposite or converse mode of conduct or end state of existence."[2]

Rokeach claims that human beings the world over seem to share the same small group of values, although they often disagree about which ones are the most important. Rokeach divides the 36 basic values into two categories: eighteen that apply to goals or desired end states of human existence (terminal values) and eighteen that apply to means or desired modes of behavior (instrumental values). The values in alphabetical order are:

Terminal Values	*Instrumental Values*
A comfortable life	Ambitious
An exciting life	Broadminded
A sense of accomplishment	Capable
A world at peace	Cheerful
A world of beauty	Clean
Equality	Courageous
Family security	Forgiving
Freedom	Helpful
Happiness	Honest
Inner harmony	Imaginative
Mature love	Independent
National security	Intellectual
Pleasure	Logical
Salvation	Loving
Self-respect	Obedient
Social recognition (approval)	Polite
True friendship	Responsible
Wisdom	Self-controlled

A value system is the rank-ordering of values in terms of their importance with respect to one another. A person's value system represents a learned organization of values for making choices and for resolving conflicts between values. Rokeach also claims that values are determinants of social behavior. They are the internalized standards and criteria for guiding actions, developing and maintaining attitudes, and making moral judgments.

Jack Fraenkel has expanded Rokeach's definition of values by stating that values represent what a person considers important in life. "They are ideas as to what is good, beautiful, effective, or just, and therefore worth having, worth doing, or worth striving to attain. They serve as *standards* by which we determine if a particular thing (object, idea, policy, etc.) is good or bad, desirable or undesirable, worthy or unworthy, or someplace in between these extremes."[3]

Louis Raths, Merrill Harmin, and Sidney Simon have defined a value as something of worth or worth prizing in human existence.[4] Values constitute those ideas, ideals, or beliefs by which individuals (or groups) will guide their behavior by those ideas, ideals, or beliefs. Raths, Harmin, and Simon have summarized values into three general areas: choosing, prizing, and acting. To be a value, something must be consciously considered and deliberately chosen.

Defined operationally, a value may be described as a belief, attitude, purpose, feeling, or goal that is:

1. Chosen freely
2. Chosen from alternatives
3. Chosen after thoughtful consideration of the consequences of each alternative
4. Prized
5. Publicly affirmed willingly

6. Acted upon
7. Is recurring.

"Those processes collectively define valuing. Results of the valuing process are called values."[5]

Carl Rogers has defined values by distinguishing among three uses of the term.[6] "Operative values" are employed when one makes a preferred choice for one kind of object over another. "Conceived values" are the preferences one shows for a symbolized object, ideal, or goal. "Objective values" are what is objectively preferable, "whether or not it is in fact sensed or conceived of as desirable."[7]

The work of Harold Lasswell presents a framework of universal values prized in all cultures or groups.[8] According to Lasswell, the needs and wants of an individual or a group, when determined to be desirable, or of relative worth, or of importance, become values. Lasswell believes that these eight universal values permeate the lives of all peoples, are found in all places, and have been prevalent at all times. The truly unique feature of the framework is that virtually all needs and wants of human beings can be classified under these eight value categories.

> *Respect* refers to the degree of recognition given to, or the degree of discrimination against people in their capacity as human beings; it includes concern for authority, country, peers, adults, and self.

> *Wealth* is the ability to provide for one's needs adequately; to develop talents that increase one's productivity to appreciate and care for material objects with which one comes into contact.

> *Power* refers to participation in decision-making that affects self and group values; it refers to development of leadership and followship talents.

> *Enlightenment* is the process of improving one's ability to make intelligent decisions in a problem-solving situation, of understanding abstractions, and mastering problem-solving techniques.

> *Skill* is the development of potential talents in social, communicative, physical, mental, and aesthetic areas.

> *Rectitude* is the degree of concern one has for the welfare of others and the degree of responsibility one has for his own conduct in association with others.

> *Well-being* refers to the mental and physical health of the individual, and to his attitude toward fitness and ability to participate effectively in physical activities.

> *Affection* is liking others, being liked, and feeling love and friendship for persons in primary and secondary relationships. In this context, primary relationships are those involving one another; secondary relationships are those between an individual and an institution or group.[9]

The Lasswell classification model is not a set of norms but a framework of open-ended continuum categories based on comprehensive cross-cultural, psychological, and historical data as well as on wide-ranging historical studies. The list of categories is, by no means, the only useful scheme for classification. It is preferred for its contextuality, economy of terms, and precision in isolating fundamentally human goals. These eight value categories provide a holistic framework within which the various social, economic, political, and personal value systems can be more clearly understood. . . .

John Wilson has written extensively on moral values.[10] For Wilson moral values are basic ideas and beliefs about what is right or good and what is wrong or bad. Wilson has proposed a more complex system than simply subscribing to a set of values. He claims that the individual needs certain attributes in order to put his morality into effect. Morality is not something simply to be believed, but also something to be put into practice. Wilson sets forth six components, which can be regarded as indicating six different characteristics in the development of a person's moral abilities. Wilson gives these components Greek-derived names. They are:

- PHIL—the degree to which one can identify with other people
- EMP—insight into one's own and other people's feelings
- GIG—the mastery of adequate factual knowledge
- DIK—the rational formulation of principles concerning other people's interests
- PHRON—the rational formulation of principles concerning one's own interests
- KRAT—the ability to translate these principles into action; in a word, will-power.[11]

Lawrence Kohlberg has developed a developmental stage theory derived from his research on moral reasoning.[12] He has found developmental changes while studying individual conceptions of such universal values as life, law, roles of affection, property, contract and trust, liberty, social order and authority, and equity.[13] The six stages are:

I. Preconventional level

At this level, the child is responsive to cultural rules and labels of good and bad, right or wrong, but interprets these labels either in terms of the physical or the hedonistic consequences of action (punishment, reward, exchange of favors) or in terms of the physical power of those who enunciate the rules and labels. The level is divided into the following two stages:

Stage 1: *The punishment-and-obedience orientation.* The physical consequences of action determine its goodness or badness, regardless of the human meaning or value of these consequences. Avoidance of punishment and unquestioning deference to power are valued in their own right, not in terms of respect for an underlying moral order supported by punishment and authority (the latter being Stage 4).

Stage 2: *The instrumental-relativist orientation.* Right action consists of that which instrumentally satisfies one's own needs and occasionally the needs of others. Human relations are viewed in terms like those of the marketplace. Elements of fairness, of reciprocity, and of equal sharing are present, but they are always interpreted in a physical pragmatic way. Reciprocity is a matter of "you scratch my back and I'll scratch yours," not of loyalty, gratitude, or justice.

II. Conventional level

At this level, maintaining the expectations of the individual's family, group, or nation is perceived as valuable in its own right, regardless of immediate and obvious consequences. The attitude is not only one of *conformity* to personal expectations and social order, but of loyalty to it, of actively *maintaining*, supporting, and justifying the order, and of identifying with the persons or group involved in it. At this level, there are the following two stages:

Stage 3: *The interpersonal concordance or "good boy-nice girl" orientation.* Good behavior is that which pleases or helps others and is approved by them. There is much conformity to stereotypical images of what is majority or "natural" behavior. Behavior is frequently judged by intention—"he means well" becomes important for the first time. One earns approval by being "nice."

Stage 4: *The "law and order" orientation.* There is orientation toward authority, fixed rules, and the maintenance of the social order. Right behavior consists of doing one's duty, showing respect for authority, and maintaining the given social order for its own sake.

III. Postconventional, autonomous, or principled level

At this level, there is a clear effort to define moral values and principles that have validity and application apart from the authority of the groups or persons holding these principles and apart from the individual's own identification with these groups. This level also has two stages:

Stage 5: *The social-contract, legalistic orientation,* generally with utilitarian overtones. Right action tends to be defined in terms of general individual rights and standards which have been critically examined and agreed upon by the whole society. There is a clear awareness of the relativism of personal values and opinions and a corresponding emphasis upon procedural rules for reaching consensus. Aside from what is constitutionally and democratically agreed upon, the right is a matter of personal "values" and "opinion." The result is an emphasis upon the "legal point of view," but with an emphasis upon the possibility of changing law in terms of rational considerations of social utility (rather than freezing it in terms of Stage 4 "law and order"). Outside the legal realm, free agreement and contract is the binding element of obligation. This is the "official" morality of the American government and constitution.

Stage 6: *The universal-ethical-principle orientation.* Right is defined by the decision of conscience in accord with self-chosen *ethical principles* appealing to logical comprehensiveness, universality, and consistency. These principles are abstract and ethical (the Golden Rule, the categorical imperative); they are not concrete moral rules like the Ten Commandments. At heart, these are universal principles of *justice,* of the *reciprocity* and *equality* of human *rights,* and of respect for the dignity of human beings as *individual persons.*[14]

Notes

[1] Rokeach, Milton. *The Nature of Human Values.* New York: The Free Press, 1973.

[2] *Ibid.,* p. 8.

[3] Fraenkel, Jack. "Strategies for Developing Values." *Today's Education.* Vol. 63, No. 7, Nov./Dec. 1973. p. 49.

[4] Raths, Louis; Harmin, Merrill; and Simon, Sidney B. *Values and Teaching.* Columbus, OH: Charles E. Merrill Pub. Co., 1966.

[5] *Ibid.,* p. 30.

[6] Rogers, *op. cit.*

[7] *Ibid.,* p. 242.

[8] Lasswell, Harold. *The World Revolution of Our Time.* Stanford, CA: Stanford University Press, 1951.

[9] Arnspiger, Robert H., "Education in Human Values." *School and Community.* Vol. 57, May 1972. pp. 16–17.

[10] Wilson, John; Williams, Norman; and Sugarman, Barry. *Introduction to Moral Education.* London: Penguin Books, 1967.

[11] *Ibid.,* pp. 192–197.

[12] Kohlberg, Lawrence. "Development of Moral Character and Moral Ideology." *Review of Child Development Research. Vol. 1.* (Edited by M. L. Hoffman and L. W. Hoffman.) New York: Russell Sage Foundation, 1964. pp. 383–431.

[13] Kohlberg, Lawrence. "Developmental and Education Psychology," *Educational Psychologist.* Vol. 10, No. 1, Winter 1972, p. 6.
[14] Kohlberg, Lawrence. "The Claim to Moral Adequacy of a Highest Stage of Moral Judgment." *The Journal of Philosophy.* Vol. 70, No. 18, Oct. 25, 1973. pp. 361–362.

The following is a values clarification exercise, designed to help you recognize your own values. You may have done this exercise before, but that will not matter because there are no right or wrong answers. You will not be asked to share your responses unless you volunteer them.

Values Clarification

Sidney B. Simon, Leland W. Howe, and Howard Kirschenbaum

1. If you were with your family in a boat that capsized far from shore and there was only one life preserver would you
   _____ save your wife/husband?
   _____ save one of your children?
   _____ save yourself?

2. If you were stranded on a deserted island which would you rather have with you?
   _____ the Bible
   _____ the complete works of Shakespeare
   _____ the history of civilization

3. Which of these would be most difficult for you to accept?
   _____ the death of a parent
   _____ the death of a spouse
   _____ your own death

4. How would you break off a three-year relationship with someone you've been dating steadily?
   _____ by telephone
   _____ by mail
   _____ in person

5. Which of these jobs would you like most?
   _____ schoolteacher on an Indian reservation
   _____ director of an inner city project
   _____ coordinator of social action projects for a liberal suburban church

6. What is the worst thing you could find out about your teenager? (Does the sex make any difference?)
   _____ that he has been shoplifting
   _____ that he is a high school dropout
   _____ that he is promiscuous

7. Which would you be more concerned about as you grow older?
   _____ lung cancer
   _____ overweight
   _____ declining vision

8. Would you rather be a teacher in a classroom that was
   _____ teacher centered?
   _____ student centered?
   _____ subject-matter centered?

9. As a small child, which did you like least?
   _____ recess
   _____ show and tell
   _____ storytime

10. Which would you prefer to give up if you had to?
    _____ economic freedom
    _____ religious freedom
    _____ political freedom

11. If you needed help in your studies, whom would you probably go to?
    _____ your friend
    _____ your teacher
    _____ your parent

12. Which of these problems do you think is the greatest threat in the nearest future?
    _____ overpopulation
    _____ too much leisure time
    _____ water and air pollution
    _____ crime

13. During a campus protest where would you be most likely to be found?
    _____ in the midst of it
    _____ gaping at it from across the street
    _____ in the library minding your own business

14. Which would you rather see a cutback of federal expenditures for?
    _____ urban research
    _____ educational allotments
    _____ foreign aid

15. During what period in U.S. history do you think you would have been a most effective leader?
    _____ colonization of America
    _____ Civil War
    _____ the Industrial Revolution

16. How would you rather spend a Saturday evening?
    _____ at a good play
    _____ at a good concert
    _____ at a good movie

17. How would you rather spend a Friday evening?
    _____ at a nightclub
    _____ at home alone
    _____ at a party at a friend's home

18. Which would you least like your son or daughter to do?
    _____ marry out of necessity
    _____ marry outside of his/her race
    _____ smoke marijuana once a week

19. If you were about to be drafted into the army which would you do?
    _____ go willingly
    _____ leave the country
    _____ go to jail

20. Which is the most beautiful sight to you?
    _____ a sunset
    _____ a person giving blood
    _____ a baby taking his/her first step

21. Which do you like least?
    _____ an uptight indoctrinator
    _____ a cynical debunker
    _____ a dull, boring fact giver

22. Which would you most like to take a course in?
    _____ sex education
    _____ race relations
    _____ ecology

23. Which would you first join?
    _____ a woman's/man's consciousness-raising group
    _____ an environmental action group
    _____ a community food cooperative

24. Which of these people would you have the most trouble introducing to your friends?
    _____ a racially mixed couple
    _____ Christine Jorgenson [a transsexual]
    _____ the Grand Dragon of the Ku Klux Klan

25. Which best describes the way you handle money?
    _____ spend freely
    _____ always look for bargains
    _____ budget carefully

26. If one of your friends and your spouse were attracted to each other which would you prefer?
    _____ for them to be open about their relationship
    _____ for no one to know
    _____ for them to keep it a secret from you alone

27. Which would you want most in a best friend?

    _____ someone who will tell you that your fiancée isn't good enough for you

    _____ someone who will listen to your problems

    _____ someone who is aware of other people's needs

28. Your friend has written a book which you think is lousy. If he asks for your opinion what would you tell him?

    _____ the whole truth

    _____ as much as you think he can stand

    _____ what he wants to hear

29. *Men.* What kind of wife would bother you most?

    _____ one who interrupts her husband

    _____ one who spends too much money

    _____ one who keeps a messy house

30. *Women.* What kind of husband would bother you most?

    _____ one who interrupts his wife

    _____ one who spends too much money

    _____ one who keeps a messy house

31. *Teenagers.* Which do you think is the worst?

    _____ to become (or get someone) pregnant (unwed)

    _____ to be dependent upon hard drugs

    _____ to date someone from another race

After Reading

1. After you have answered the questions, consider what your answers tell you about your own values and write about this in your journal. You may want to begin by deciding what choices among values you are given by each question. What value would each choice represent? Do you see a pattern or patterns in the ones you select? What do you value most? What do you value least?

2. Look again at the exercise. Can you find any language that helps you make a good guess at how the authors of it would answer any of the questions? For example, in question 13, what can you say about the use of the word "gaping" rather than "watching?"

Before Reading

The short story "The Poor Are Always with Us" by Tobias Wolff presents a situation in which there are several conflicts of values. As you read it, ask yourself what values motivate Dave and which motivate Tom Groves. Where do Russell's values conflict with those of others? Do Russell's values change during the story?

The Poor Are Always with Us

Tobias Wolff

The trouble with owning a Porsche is that there's always some little thing wrong with it. At least it seemed that way to Russell. This time it was a sticky brake pedal. Russell had planned a trip for Easter weekend, so he left work early on Friday afternoon and drove up to Menlo Park to have Bruno, his mechanic, take a look at the car. Bruno was an Austrian. The wall behind his desk was covered with diplomas, most written in German, congratulating him on his completion of different courses in Porsche technology. Bruno's office overlooked the bay where he and his assistant worked on the cars, both of them wearing starched white smocks and wielding tools that glittered like surgical instruments.

When Russell pulled into the garage, Bruno was alone. He looked up, waved, and bent back down under the hood of a vintage green Speedster. Russell walked around the Speedster a couple of times, and then watched over Bruno's shoulder as Bruno traced the wiring with a flashlight whose thin silver beam looked as solid as a knitting needle.

"So?" Bruno asked. After Russell described the trouble he was having, Bruno grunted and said, "Sure, sure. No sweat, old bean." He said that he would get to it as soon as he was finished with the Speedster—forty-five minutes, maybe an hour. Russell could wait or pick it up on Monday.

Russell told him he would wait.

There were two men in Bruno's office. They glanced up at Russell when he came in and then went on talking above the noise of a radio that sat on Bruno's desk, playing music from the 1950s. Russell couldn't help listening to them. They were friends; he could tell that by the way they kept insulting each other. They never let up, especially the bigger of the two, a black guy who wore sunglasses and a safari jacket and who popped his knuckles steadily. Whenever the white guy got off a good line, the black guy would grin and shake his head and get off a better one. Twice Russell laughed out loud, and after the second time the white guy turned and stared at him. He had red-rimmed eyes that bulged as if some pressure were forcing them out. His skin was tight-looking, drawn so severely over the bones of his face that even now, unsmiling as he was, his teeth showed. He stared at Russell and said, "Little pitchers have big ears."

Russell looked down at the rug. He tried to mind his own business after that, until the two men began to talk about someone from Russell's company who had recently been arrested for selling information about a new computer to the Japanese. Russell had met the man once, and from what these two fellows were saying he gathered that they had both worked with the spy a few years back at Hewlett-Packard. Russell knew he should keep his mouth shut, but he decided to say something. He had followed the case and had strong opinions about it. Mostly, though, he just wanted to join in the conversation.

"We all got our price," the black guy was saying. "Shit, they'd put every one of us in stir if they could read our minds for an hour. Any hour," he added.

"As if everybody else in this town isn't doing something just as bad," the white guy said. "Bunch of piglets. They're just burned up because he got to the trough before they did."

"I see it differently," Russell said. "I think they should lock him up and throw away the key. He sold out the people who worked with him and trusted him. He sold out his team. As far as I'm concerned, he's a complete write-off."

The white guy fixed his eyes on Russell and said, "Groves, who is this weenie?"

"Now, now," Groves said.

"I swear to God," the white guy said. He pushed himself out of his chair and went to the window overlooking the garage, coming down hard on the heels of his boots as he walked. He stood there, hands clenched into fists, and when he turned away, Russell saw that his upper teeth were almost entirely exposed. He squinted at Russell. "A complete write-off," he said. "How old are you, anyway?"

Groves popped a knuckle. "Easy does it," he said. "Lighten up there, Dave."

Dave, Russell thought. He didn't know any Daves, but this one had something against him. "Twenty-two," he said, adding a year.

"Well, then, I guess you know it all. From the lofty perspective of your twenty-two years."

"I don't know it all," Russell said. "I know the difference between right and wrong, though." *I hardly ever talk like this,* Russell wanted to add. *You should hear me with my friends back home.*

The pants Dave wore looked too small for him, and now he made them look even smaller by jamming his hands into the back pockets. "Go away," he said to Russell. "Go away and come back later, okay?"

"We're all friends here," Groves said. He put a small silver bong on Bruno's desk and began to stuff it with brown marijuana from a sandwich bag. "Peace pipe," he said. He lit up and passed the bong to Russell. Russell took a hit and held it out to Dave, but Dave kept his hands in his pockets. Finally Russell put the bong back down on Bruno's desk. He wished that he had refused it too.

"While we're on the subject," Dave said, "is there anybody else you want to write off?"

"Unbelievable," Groves said, turning up the volume on the radio. " 'Runaround Sue.' Man, I haven't heard 'Runaround Sue' for about eighty years."

Dave looked gloomily out the window. "Is that your Targa?" he asked. Without waiting for Russell to answer he said, "How do you rate a Targa? Graduation present from Pop?"

"I bought it myself," Russell said.

Dave asked Russell where he worked, and when Russell told him, he said, "That outfit. Nothing but Jap spies and boy wonders. I swear to God they'll be hiring them out of first grade next."

"I do dearly love a Porsche," Groves said. "There isn't anything I wouldn't do to get me a Porsche."

Dave said, "Why don't you buy one?"

"Ask my wife."

"Which wife?"

"You see my problem," Groves said. He fired up the bong again and offered it to Russell. "Go on, child, go on," he insisted when Russell shook his head, and kept pushing it at him until Russell took another hit. Russell held the smoke in his mouth and then blew it out and said, "*Gracias.* That's righteous weed."

"Righteous!" Dave said. He grinned at Groves, who bent over and made a sound like air escaping from a balloon. Groves began to drum his feet on the floor. *"Gracias!"* Dave said, and Groves threw his head back and howled.

Bruno came into the office carrying a clipboard. "You chaps," he said. "Always laughing." He sat down at the desk and started punching away at a pocket calculator.

Groves said, "Oh, Lord. Lord, Lord, Lord." He pushed up his sunglasses and rubbed his eyes.

Bruno tore a sheet off the clipboard. "Seventy-two fifty," he said to Dave.

"Catch you tomorrow," Dave said.

"Better now," Bruno told him. "Tomorrow something bad might happen."

Dave slowly counted out the money. He was putting his wallet in his pocket when Groves pointed at him and said, "Name that tune!"

" 'Turn Me Loose,' " Dave said. "Kookie Byrnes. 1959."

"Fabian," Russell said.

"What do *you* know?" Dave said. "You weren't even born when this song came out."

Russell said, "It's Fabian. I'll bet you anything. I'll bet you my car."

Dave studied Russell for a moment. "Boy, you do bad things to me, you know that? Okay," he said. "My Speedster against your Targa."

Russell turned to Bruno. "You heard that."

"Get your papers," Bruno said.

Russell had his in his wallet. Dave's were in the glove compartment of the Speedster. While he was down in the garage getting them, Groves stood up and began to walk around the office. "I don't believe this," he said. Dave came back and handed the papers to Bruno, and they all waited for the song to end. But when it ended, two more songs played back-to-back—"My Prayer" and "Duke of Earl." Then the deejay came on and gave the names of the recording artists.

"Nuts," Dave said. Then, to Russell, "You little weenie."

The whole thing caught Bruno on his funny bone. He laughed until tears came to his eyes. "You crazy chaps," he said. "You crazy, crazy chaps."

Russell agreed to let Dave bring the car over to his apartment later that afternoon. He had legal title now; if Dave didn't show up, Russell could have him arrested for grand theft auto. Bruno was the one who made this point. Still laughing, Bruno got his Polaroid camera out of the desk and took several pictures of the Speedster to keep as souvenirs of the event.

Russell waited alone in the office while Bruno put the Targa right; then he drove home and ate a sandwich beside the pool in the courtyard of his apartment building. He had the place to himself. All the other tenants were still at work, and none of them had children. Some owned dogs, but they'd been trained not to bark, so the courtyard was quiet except for the sigh of traffic from Page Mill Road and the tick of palm fronds above the chair where Russell sat.

He hated to think of giving the Speedster back. He wanted to keep it, and he could give himself reasons for keeping it, reasons that made sense. But all of them sounded like lies to Russell—the kind of lies you tell yourself when you already know the truth. The truth was that he'd been certain Fabian was the singer, and certain that Dave would take his bet. He had smoked marijuana in the middle of the afternoon like some kind of junior-high dropout, and lied about his age, and generally made a fool of himself. Then, because his feelings were hurt, he had goaded a man into gambling away his car.

That was how the truth looked to Russell, and it had nothing to do with his dream of being a magnanimous person, openhearted and fair. Of course, not everyone would see it this way. Russell knew that most people would think he was being fussy.

Russell lived alone now, but when he first arrived in town he had roomed with a fellow from his company, an MIT graduate whose ambition was to make a bundle in a hurry, invest it, and then become a composer. He wrote moody violin pieces, which he played for Russell. Russell thought that they sounded great and that his roommate was a genius. But his roommate was also a swinger. He had girls in the apartment every weekend and sometimes even during the week, different girls, and one night he and Russell got into an argument about it. Russell hadn't said anything up to then, but his roommate knew that he disapproved. He wanted to know why. Russell told him that it seemed cheap. His roommate said, "You're completely uptight, that's your problem," and left the room, but he ran back a moment later yelling that nobody, but nobody, called him cheap and got away with it. He waved his long white hands in Russell's face and said, "How would you like a knuckle sandwich?" Russell apologized, and apologized again the next morning, and after that the two of them lived together on terms so polite that they would excuse themselves after coughing. Russell understood that his roommate had written him off.

Russell moved out at the end of the month. For a long time afterward, until he got used to living alone, he made up conversations with his old roommate in which he laid bare his soul and was understood and forgiven. "Listen," Russell would say, "I know you think I'm uptight because I don't sleep around or do many drugs or party a lot. But I'm not uptight, I'm really not. I just don't want to end up like Teddy Wells. I don't want to end up fifty years old and getting my sixth divorce and wearing gold chains and putting half my salary up my nose and collecting erotic art and cruising El Camino for teenagers."

And Russell's roommate would answer, "I never looked at it that way before, but I see what you mean and you're absolutely right."

Russell just wanted to keep his bearings, that was all. It was easy to lose your bearings when you were three thousand miles from home and making more money than you needed, almost twice as much as your own father made after thirty years of teaching high school math. "I'm doing the best I can," Russell would say. "I'm only twenty, for Christ's sake!"

And his roommate would answer, "Of course. Of course."

Dave brought the Speedster by at five-thirty, half an hour later than he'd promised. Russell was waiting outside the apartment building when Dave drove up. A dark-haired woman in an old station wagon pulled in behind the Speedster and sat there with the engine running. Dave rolled his window down. "Did you call the heat yet?" he asked.

"I knew you'd come," Russell said. He smiled, but Dave did not smile back.

"That's funny," Dave said. "A throw-away-the-key guy like you, I figured you'd have my picture in the post office by now." He got out and closed the door gently. "Here," he said, and tossed Russell the keys. "What are you going to do with it? Sell it?" He looked at the car, then back at Russell.

"No," Russell said. "Listen—"

Dave said, "You listen." He crossed the strip of grass to the sidewalk where Russell stood. Russell felt the man's hatred and took a step backward. The woman in the station wagon revved the engine. Dave stopped and looked back at her, and then put his hands in his pockets, as he had done earlier that day. Russell understood the gesture now: it was what Dave did with his hands to keep them from doing something else.

"I wish this hadn't happened," Russell said.

Though Dave was a couple of inches shorter than Russell, he seemed to be examining him from a height. "You're nothing special," he said. "You might think you have ideas, but you don't. No one has had an actual idea in this business for about five years. You want to know how I got the Speedster?" When Russell didn't answer, he said, "I'll tell you. They gave it to me for an idea I had, actually a lot of ideas put together. They just handed me the keys and told me where it was parked and that was that. No speeches or anything. No plaque. Everything was understood."

The woman in the station wagon revved the engine again. Dave ignored her. He said, "You little snots think you're on the cutting edge, but all you're doing is sweeping up, collecting our stuff. The work's been done. You're just a bunch of janitors."

"That's not true," Russell said.

"You're a janitor," Dave repeated. "No way in hell do you rate a car like that. A car like that is completely out of your class." He took a quarter from his pocket and said, "Flip me for it."

"Flip you? Flip you for what?"

Dave looked down the street to where the woman sat watching them. "The wagon," he said.

"Come on," Russell said. "What kind of deal is that?"

Dave flipped the quarter. "Call it."

"This is baloney," Russell said. Then, because he was afraid of Dave and wanted to be done with him, he said, "What the hell. All right. Tails."

"Tails it is," Dave said, and threw the coin into Russell's face. It struck him below the eye and fell to the sidewalk. Dave walked back to the station wagon. He knocked on the window, and when the woman rolled it down, he reached past her, turned off the engine, and dropped the keys into the gutter.

"Hey," she said.

"Get out," Dave told her, and held the door open until she obeyed him. She was thin and pale. She had liquid brown eyes like a deer's eyes, and like a deer she looked restlessly around her as if unsure of everything.

"I'll send Groves over with the papers," Dave said. He turned and started down the street toward Page Mill Road. The woman watched him walk away, and then looked at Russell.

"I'm sorry," he said. "It wasn't my idea."

"Oh, no," she said. "Wait a minute, Dave!" she called, but Dave kept walking and didn't look back. "Don't go anywhere," she told Russell. "Just wait here, okay?" She took a couple of steps and gave a loud scream. Then she broke into a run, stopping once to scream again—no words, only the pure sound rising between the tiled rooftops into the cloudless blue sky.

Russell ate dinner at a Chinese place near the freeway. When he got home, he found Groves leaning back in one of the chairs by the pool. The woman who managed the building was sitting beside him. She was a widow from Michigan. The other tenants complained about her because she was snoopy and enforced all the rules. In the eight months since Russell had moved in he had never seen her smile, but when he stepped into the courtyard she was laughing.

"That's gospel," Groves said. "I swear."

She laughed again.

It was dark, but Groves still had his sunglasses on. His hands were folded behind his head. When he saw Russell, he pointed one foot at him and said, "Here come de champ."

"Sorry I made you wait," Russell said. "I didn't know you'd be coming tonight."

"See?" Groves said. "I'm no perpetrator." He pushed himself up from the chair and said to Russell, "Emma here thought I was a perpetrator."

"No, I didn't!" she said.

Groves laughed. "That's cool. Everybody gets one mistake." He clapped his hand on Russell's shoulder. "Champ, we got to talk."

Russell led Groves up the stairs and along the walkway to his apartment. Groves followed him inside and looked around. "What's this number?" he asked. "You in training to be a monk or something?"

"I just moved in a while ago," Russell said.

"No pictures, no sounds, no box," Groves went on. "No nothing. You sure you live here?" He took an envelope from his pocket and dropped it on the counter that divided the living room from the kitchen. "Candygram from Dave," he said. "Crazy Dave. Champ, we got a problem." Groves began to pace the small room, deliberately at first, then faster and faster, wheeling like a cat in a cage, the unbuckled straps of his safari jacket swinging at his sides. "We got a priority situation here," he said, "because you just got yourself all tied up in something you don't understand, and what you don't understand is my man Dave isn't in *no* condition to go laying off his automobiles at this point in time. He isn't what we say *competent,* you dig? What we're talking about here is some serious post-Vietnam syndrome. I mean, serious head problems."

Without slowing down, Groves lit a cigarette. Then he went on talking, waving his hands and scattering ash onto the carpet. "What we've got here is a disturbed veteran. We've got a man who's been on the big march through the valley of the shadow of death, you follow me? I'm talking about Khe Sanh, champ. The Pit. Here's how it went down. Dave's company is sitting out on the perimeter or whatever, and the Cong come pouring over, you with me? There's mortars going off and all that shit and rifles and whatever, and a whole bunch of Dave's friends, I mean his special dudes, get shot up. I mean they're hanging out there on the wire and so on. Now, my man Dave, he's been hit too, but he crawls out there anyway and drags his buddies in. All of them. Even the dead ones. And all the time old Charlie Cong is just *raining* on him. I mean, he's got holes in places you never even *heard* of."

Groves shook his head. "Two years in the hospital, champ. Two years all wrapped up like some kind of horror movie, and then what do they do? They give him the Congressional Medal of Honor and say Sayonara, sucker. He don't think straight anymore, that's not their problem, right?"

Groves walked around the counter. He ran water on the butt of his cigarette and dropped it in the sink. "What I'm saying is, you got any self-respect, you don't go ripping no automobiles off of no disturbed veterans with the Congressional goddamn Medal of Honor. That's what I'm saying here tonight."

Groves leaned forward against the counter and smiled at Russell. "Child," he said, "why don't you just give the man his cars back?"

"My name is Russell. And I don't believe that story. I don't believe that Dave was even in Vietnam."

"Damn!" Groves said. "Where's your imagination?" He took his sunglasses off, laid them on the counter, and began to rub his eyes in a way that made Russell think they were causing him pain—slowly, with his fingertips. "I don't know," he said. "All right. Let's take it again. We're talking about Dave."

Russell nodded.

"Dave's a good head," Groves went on. "I admit he's not that great with the general public, but he's okay. Lots of smarts, too. I mean, I'm smart, but Dave is *smart*. It used to be just about everybody in town wanted a piece of him. Dave was centerfold material for a while there, but nowadays things just keep messing up on him. It's like the well went dry. Happens to plenty of people. It could happen to you. I mean, you might be coming up with sweet stuff today, but there's no law says it's got to be there tomorrow, and just maybe it won't be. You ought to think about that."

"I do," Russell said.

"Now his wife's gone and left him. No concern of yours, but Lord, what a business."

"I tried to give the car back to him," Russell said. "He didn't give me a chance. He wouldn't even let me talk."

Groves laughed.

"It wasn't funny," Russell said. "I've had the willies all night. He really scared me, Groves. That's why I can't give him the car back now. I'd always wonder if I did it just because I was afraid of him. I wouldn't ever feel right about it."

Groves said, "Russell, I never saw no eighty-year-old man looked like you before."

"What I'm going to do is give the Speedster to you," Russell said. "Then you can give it to Dave. That's something I can live with. But I'm going to keep the station wagon," Russell added. "I won that fair and square."

"Well, now," Groves said. He seemed about to go on, but finally he just shook his head and looked down at the counter.

Russell had the papers in his pocket. He spread them out. "How do I write your name?" he asked.

"Just like it sounds. Groves. Tom Groves." As Russell took the cap from his pen, Groves said, in a quiet voice, "make that Thomas B. Groves, Junior."

Russell never saw Groves again, but from time to time he felt a shadow on his back and looked around to find Dave watching him from another line in the market where he shopped, or through the window of the bank where he kept his money. Dave never said anything, never accused, but Russell began to think that he was being followed and that a showdown was soon to come. He tried to prepare himself for it. Sometimes at night and even at work Russell made angry faces, and shook his head, and glared at things without seeing them, as he rehearsed again and again the proofs of his own decency. This went on for almost a year.

Then, in April, he saw Dave on El Camino. Russell had parked in the customer lot of a liquor store and was waiting for his date to come out with some wine for a party they were going to. He was sitting there, watching the cars go by, when he caught sight of Dave standing on the curb across the road. Russell felt sure that Dave had not seen him, because Dave was giving all his attention to the traffic. He swung his head back and forth as the cars rushed past him—looking, Russell supposed, for a chance to cross. Sometimes the line of cars heading north would thin out, and sometimes the line heading south, but never both together. There was no light nearby and no pedestrian crossing, because on El Camino there were no pedestrians. You never saw anyone on foot.

Dave went on waiting for a break to come. Twice he stepped into the road as if to test his luck, but both times he changed his mind and turned back. Russell watched for Dave to bare his teeth and scream and shake his fists. Nothing like this happened. He stood there and waited for his chance, leaning into the road a little as he looked each way. His face was calm. He accepted this situation, saw nothing outrageous in it—nothing to make him go home and come back with a gun and shoot every driver on the road.

Finally Dave spotted an opening and made a run for it. He moved heavily but for all he was worth, knees flying high, arms flailing the air, and Russell's heart went out to him. At that moment he would have given Dave everything he had—his money, his car, his job, everything—but what was the point? It didn't make sense trying to help Dave, because Dave couldn't be helped. Whatever Russell gave him he would lose. It just wasn't in the cards for him to have anything.

When Dave reached the curb, he stopped and caught his breath. Then he started south, in the direction of Mountain View. Russell watched him walk past the parking lot, watched him until he disappeared from sight. The low sun burned in the windows of a motel down the street. Above the motel rooftop, against the blue sky, hung a faint white haze like the haze of chalk dust on the blue suit Russell's father wore to school. Blurred shapes of cars flashed back and forth. Russell felt a little lost, and thought, *I'm on El Camino.* He was on El Camino. Just a short drive down the road some people were having a party, and he was on his way there.

After Reading

In your journal, try to sum up the conflicts of values in "The Poor Are Always with Us." Record also how you feel about the story. What do you think of the main characters? Can you imagine someone else judging them differently? What do you think of Russell at the end of the story?

As a separate journal entry, do a free writing for three minutes, focused on what either Dave or Russell would tell the other if they were to have a conversation at the end of the story. Write as if you were the character and explain why you did what you did.

Before Reading

The Harvard Negotiating Project was begun in 1980 to find more effective means of carrying out various kinds of negotiations: labor, sales contracts, committee decisions, and so on. The book *Getting to Yes,* by Roger Fisher and William Ury, is based on its authors' work in that project. In the chapter reprinted here, the authors stress the usefulness of recognizing what interests lie behind each position. As they use the term "interest," it is something more specific than a value. For example, one of your interests in negotiating your work schedule (if it is negotiable) might be that the schedule leave you time to study. This interest would reflect the higher value you place on education than on extra pocket money. Ultimately, you may have opted for education because you value learning or because education increases earning power or both. Thus, different values can give rise to the same interest.

As you read this excerpt, try to determine how Fisher and Ury characterize their audience. How do you react to the exclusively male pronouns in the last paragraph of the section entitled "Realize That Each Side Has Multiple Interests," p. 197? To the assumption that the negotiator has a wife? Do you think the authors' characterization of their audience is accurate?

Focus on Interests, Not Positions

Roger Fisher and William Ury

Consider the story of two men quarreling in a library. One wants the window open and the other wants it closed. They bicker back and forth about how much to leave it open: a crack, halfway, three quarters of the way. No solution satisfies them both.

Enter the librarian. She asks one why he wants the window open: "To get some fresh air." She asks the other why he wants it closed: "To avoid the draft." After thinking a minute, she opens wide a window in the next room, bringing in fresh air without a draft.

For a Wise Solution Reconcile Interests, Not Positions

This story is typical of many negotiations. Since the parties' problem appears to be a conflict of positions, and since their goal is to agree on a position, they naturally tend to think and talk about positions—and in the process often reach an impasse.

The librarian could not have invented the solution she did if she had focused only on the two men's stated positions of wanting the window open or closed. Instead she looked to their underlying interests of fresh air and no draft. This difference between positions and interests is crucial.

Interests Define the Problem

The basic problem in a negotiation lies not in conflicting positions, but in the conflict between each side's needs, desires, concerns, and fears. The parties may say:

"I am trying to get him to stop that real estate development next door."

Or "We disagree. He wants $50,000 for the house. I won't pay a penny more than $47,500."

But on a more basic level the problem is:

"He needs the cash; I want peace and quiet."

Or "He needs at least $50,000 to settle with his ex-wife. I told my family that I wouldn't pay more than $47,500 for a house."

Such desires and concerns are *interests*. Interests motivate people; they are the silent movers behind the hubbub of positions. Your position is something you have decided upon. Your interests are what caused you to so decide.

The Egyptian-Israeli peace treaty blocked out at Camp David in 1978 demonstrates the usefulness of looking behind positions. Israel had occupied the Egyptian Sinai Peninsula since the Six Day War of 1967. When Egypt and Israel sat down together in 1978 to negotiate a peace, their positions were incompatible. Israel insisted on keeping some of the Sinai. Egypt, on the other hand, insisted that every inch of the Sinai be returned to Egyptian sovereignty. Time and again, people drew maps showing possible boundary lines that would divide the Sinai between Egypt and Israel. Compromising in this way was wholly unacceptable to Egypt. To go back to the situation as it was in 1967 was equally unacceptable to Israel.

Looking to their interests instead of their positions made it possible to develop a solution. Israel's interest lay in security; they did not want Egyptian tanks poised on their border ready to roll across at any time. Egypt's interest lay in sovereignty; the Sinai had been part of Egypt since the time of the Pharaohs. After centuries of domination by Greeks, Romans, Turks, French, and British, Egypt had only recently regained full sovereignty and was not about to cede territory to another foreign conqueror.

At Camp David, President Sadat of Egypt and Prime Minister Begin of Israel agreed to a plan that would return the Sinai to complete Egyptian sovereignty and, by demilitarizing large areas, would still assure Israeli security. The Egyptian flag would fly everywhere, but Egyptian tanks would be nowhere near Israel.

Reconciling interests rather than positions works for two reasons. First, for every interest there usually exist several possible positions that could satisfy it. All too often people simply adopt the most obvious position, as Israel did, for example, in announcing that they intended to keep part of the Sinai. When you do look behind opposed positions for the motivating interests, you can often find an alternative position which meets not only your interests but theirs as well. In the Sinai, demilitarization was one such alternative.

Reconciling interests rather than compromising between positions also works because behind opposed positions lie many more interests than conflicting ones.

Behind Opposed Positions Lie Shared and Compatible Interests,
as well as Conflicting Ones.

We tend to assume that because the other side's positions are opposed to ours, their interests must also be opposed. If we have an interest in defending ourselves, then they must want to attack us. If we have an interest in minimizing the rent, then their interest must be to maximize it. In many negotiations, however, a close examination of the underlying interests will reveal the existence of many more interests that are shared or compatible than ones that are opposed.

For example, look at the interests a tenant shares with a prospective landlord:

1. **Both want stability. The landlord wants a stable tenant; the tenant wants a permanent address.**
2. **Both would like to see the apartment well maintained. The tenant is going to live there; the landlord wants to increase the value of the apartment as well as the reputation of the building.**
3. **Both are interested in a good relationship with each other. The landlord wants a tenant who pays the rent regularly; the tenant wants a responsive landlord who will carry out the necessary repairs.**

They may have interests that do not conflict but simply differ. For example:

1. **The tenant may not want to deal with fresh paint, to which he is allergic. The landlord will not want to pay the costs of repainting all the other apartments.**
2. **The landlord would like the security of a down payment of the first month's**

rent, and he may want it by tomorrow. The tenant, knowing that this is a good apartment, may be indifferent on the question of paying tomorrow or later.

When weighed against these shared and divergent interests, the opposed interests in minimizing the rent and maximizing the return seem more manageable. The shared interests will likely result in a long lease, an agreement to share the cost of improving the apartment, and efforts by both parties to accommodate each other in the interest of a good relationship. The divergent interests may perhaps be reconciled by a down payment tomorrow and an agreement by the landlord to paint the apartment provided the tenant buys the paint. The precise amount of the rent is all that remains to be settled, and the market for rental apartments may define that fairly well.

Agreement is often made possible precisely because interests differ. You and a shoe-seller may both like money and shoes. Relatively, his interest in the thirty dollars exceeds his interest in the shoes. For you, the situation is reversed: you like the shoes better than the thirty dollars. Hence the deal. Shared interests and differing but complementary interests can both serve as the building blocks for a wise agreement.

How Do You Identify Interests?

The benefit of looking behind positions for interests is clear. How to go about it is less clear. A position is likely to be concrete and explicit; the interests underlying it may well be unexpressed, intangible, and perhaps inconsistent. How do you go about understanding the interests involved in a negotiation, remembering that figuring out *their* interests will be at least as important as figuring out *yours?*

Ask "Why?"

One basic technique is to put yourself in their shoes. Examine each position they take, and ask yourself "Why?" Why, for instance, does your landlord prefer to fix the rent—in a five-year lease—year by year? The answer you may come up with, to be protected against increasing costs, is probably one of his interests. You can also ask the landlord himself why he takes a particular position. If you do, make clear that you are asking not for justification of this position, but for an understanding of the needs, hopes, fears, or desires that it serves. "What's your basic concern, Mr. Jones, in wanting the lease to run for no more than three years?"

Ask "Why not?" Think about Their Choice

One of the most useful ways to uncover interests is first to identify the basic decision that those on the other side probably see you asking them for, and then to ask yourself why they have not made that decision. What interests of theirs stand in the way? If you are trying to change their minds, the starting point is to figure out where their minds are now.

Consider, for example, the negotiations between the United States and Iran in 1980 over the release of the fifty-two U.S. diplomats and embassy personnel held hostage in Tehran by student militants. While there were a host of serious obstacles to a resolution of this dispute, the problem is illuminated simply by looking at the choice of a typical student leader. The demand of the United States was clear: "Release the hostages." During much of 1980 each student leader's choice must have looked something like that illustrated by the balance sheet below.

AS OF: Spring 1980
Presently Perceived Choice of: An Iranian student leader
Question Faced: "Shall I press for immediate release of the American hostages?"

IF I SAY YES	**IF I SAY NO**
− I sell out the Revolution.	+ I uphold the Revolution.
− I will be criticized as pro-American.	+ I will be praised for defending Islam.
− The others will probably not agree with me; if they do and we release the hostages, then:	+ We will probably all stick together.
	+ We get fantastic TV coverage to tell the world about our grievances.
− Iran looks weak.	+ Iran looks strong.
− We back down to the U.S.	+ We stand up to the U.S.
− We get nothing (no Shah, no money).	+ We have a chance of getting something (at least our money back).
	+ The hostages provide some protection against U.S. intervention.
− We do not know what the U.S. will do.	
BUT:	**BUT:**
+ There is a chance that economic sanctions might end.	− Economic sanctions will no doubt continue.
+ Our relations with other nations, especially in Europe, may improve.	− Our relations with other nations, especially in Europe, will suffer.
	− Inflation and economic problems will continue.
	− There is a risk that the U.S. might take military action (but a martyr's death is the most glorious).
	HOWEVER:
	+ The U.S. may make further commitments about our money, nonintervention, ending sanctions, etc.
	+ We can always release the hostages later.

If a typical student leader's choice did look even approximately like this, it is understandable why the militant students held the hostages so long: As outrageous and illegal as the original seizure was, once the hostages had been seized it was not irrational for the students to *keep* holding them from one day to the next, waiting for a more promising time to release them.

In constructing the other side's presently perceived choice the first question to ask is "Whose decision do I want to affect?" The second question is what decision people on the other side now see you asking them to make. If *you* have no idea what they think they are being called on to do, *they* may not either. That alone may explain why they are not deciding as you would like.

Now analyze the consequences, as the other side would probably see them, of agreeing or refusing to make the decision you are asking for. You may find a checklist of consequences such as the following helpful in this task:

Impact on my interests
- Will I lose or gain political support?
- Will colleagues criticize or praise me?

Impact on the group's interests
- What will be the short-term consequences? The long-term consequences?
- What will be the economic consequences (political, legal, psychological, military, etc.)?
- What will be the effect on outside supporters and public opinion?
- Will the precedent be good or bad?
- Will making this decision prevent doing something better?
- Is the action consistent with our principles? Is it "right"?
- Can I do it later if I want?

In this entire process it would be a mistake to try for great precision. Only rarely will you deal with a decision-maker who writes down and weighs the pros and cons. You are trying to understand a very human choice, not making a mathematical calculation.

Realize That Each Side Has Multiple Interests

In almost every negotiation each side will have many interests, not just one. As a tenant negotiating a lease, for example, you may want to obtain a favorable rental agreement, to reach it quickly with little effort, and to maintain a good working relationship with your landlord. You will have not only a strong interest in *affecting* any agreement you reach, but also one in *effecting* an agreement. You will be simultaneously pursuing both your independent and your shared interests.

A common error in diagnosing a negotiating situation is to assume that each person on the other side has the same interests. This is almost never the case. During the Vietnam war, President Johnson was in the habit of lumping together all the different members of the government of North Vietnam, the Vietcong in the south, and their Soviet and Chinese advisers and calling them collectively "he." "The enemy has to learn that *he* can't cross the United States with impunity. *He* is going to have to learn that aggression doesn't pay." It will be difficult to influence any such "him" (or even "them") to agree to anything if you fail to appreciate the differing interests of the various people and factions involved.

Thinking of negotiation as a two-person, two-sided affair can be illuminating, but it should not blind you to the usual presence of other persons, other sides, and other influences. In one baseball salary negotiation the general manager kept insisting that $200,000 was simply too much for a particular player, although other teams were paying at least that much to similarly talented players. In fact the manager felt his position was unjustifiable, but he had strict instructions from the club's owners to hold firm without explaining why, because they were in financial difficulties that they did not want the public to hear about.

Whether it is his employer, his client, his employees, his colleagues, his family, or his wife, every negotiator has a constituency to whose interests he is sensitive. To understand that negotiator's interests means to understand the variety of somewhat differing interests that he needs to take into account.

The Most Powerful Interests Are Basic Human Needs

In searching for the basic interests behind a declared position, look particularly for those bedrock concerns which motivate all people. If you can take care of such basic needs, you increase the chance both of reaching agreement and, if an agreement is reached, of the other side's keeping to it. Basic human needs include:

- security
- economic well-being
- a sense of belonging
- recognition
- control over one's life

As fundamental as they are, basic human needs are easy to overlook. In many negotiations, we tend to think that the only interest involved is money. Yet even in a negotiation over a monetary figure, such as the amount of alimony to be specified in a separation agreement, much more can be involved. What does a wife really want in asking for $500 a week in alimony? Certainly she is interested in her economic well-being, but what else? Possibly she wants the money in order to feel psychologically secure. She may also want it for recognition: to feel that she is treated fairly and as an equal. Perhaps the husband can ill afford to pay $500 a week, and perhaps his wife does not need that much, yet she will likely accept less only if her needs for security and recognition are met in other ways.

What is true for individuals remains equally true for groups and nations. Negotiations are not likely to make much progress as long as one side believes that the fulfillment of their basic human needs is being threatened by the other. In negotiations between the United States and Mexico, the U.S. wanted a low price for Mexican natural gas. Assuming that this was a negotiation over money, the U.S. Secretary of Energy refused to approve a price increase negotiated with the Mexicans by a U.S. oil consortium. Since the Mexicans had no other potential buyer at the time, he assumed that they would then lower their asking price. But the Mexicans had a strong interest not only in getting a good price for their gas but also in being treated with respect and a sense of equality. The U.S. action seemed like one more attempt to bully Mexico; it produced enormous anger. Rather than sell their gas, the Mexican government began to burn it off, and any chance of agreement on a lower price became politically impossible.

To take another example, in the negotiations over the future of Northern Ireland, Protestant leaders tend to ignore the Catholics' need for both belonging and recognition, for being accepted and treated as equals. In turn, Catholic leaders often appear to give too little weight to the Protestants' need to feel secure. Treating Protestant fears as "their problem" rather than as a legitimate concern needing attention makes it even more difficult to negotiate a solution.

Make a List

To sort out the various interests of each side, it helps to write them down as they occur to you. This will not only help you remember them; it will also enable you to improve the quality of your assessment as you learn new information and to place interests in their estimated order of importance. Furthermore, it may stimulate ideas for how to meet these interests.

Talking about Interests

The purpose of negotiating is to serve your interests. The chance of that happening increases when you communicate them. The other side may not know what your interests are, and you may not know theirs. One or both of you may be focusing on past grievances instead of on future concerns. Or you may not even be listening to each other. How do you discuss interests constructively without getting locked into rigid positions?

If you want the other side to take your interests into account, explain to them what those interests are. A member of a concerned citizens' group complaining about a construction project in the neighborhood should talk explicitly about such issues as ensuring children's safety and getting a good night's sleep. An author who wants to be able to give a great many of his books away should discuss the matter with his publisher. The publisher has a shared interest in promotion and may be willing to offer the author a low price.

Make Your Interests Come Alive

If you go with a raging ulcer to see a doctor, you should not hope for much relief if you describe it as a mild stomachache. It is your job to have the other side understand exactly how important and legitimate your interests are.

One guideline is *be specific.* Concrete details not only make your description credible, they add impact. For example: "Three times in the last week, a child was almost run over by one of your trucks. About eight-thirty Tuesday morning that huge red gravel truck of yours, going north at almost forty miles an hour, had to swerve and barely missed hitting seven-year-old Loretta Johnson."

As long as you do not seem to imply that the other side's interests are unimportant or illegitimate, you can afford to take a strong stance in setting forth the seriousness of your concerns. Inviting the other side to "correct me if I'm wrong" shows your openness, and if they do not correct you, it implies that they accept your description of the situation.

Part of the task of impressing the other side with your interests lies in establishing the legitimacy of those interests. You want them to feel not that you are attacking them personally, but rather that the problem you face legitimately demands attention. You need to convince them that they might well feel the same way if they were in your shoes. "Do you have children? How would you feel if trucks were hurtling at forty miles per hour down the street where you live?"

Acknowledge Their Interests as Part of the Problem

Each of us tends to be so concerned with his or her own interests that we pay too little heed to the interests of others.

People listen better if they feel that you have understood them. They tend to think that those who understand them are intelligent and sympathetic people whose own opinions may be worth listening to. So if you want the other side to appreciate *your* interests, begin by demonstrating that you appreciate *theirs.*

"As I understand it, your interests as a construction company are basically to get the job done quickly at minimum cost and to preserve your reputation for safety and responsibility in the city. Have I understood you correctly? Do you have other important interests?"

In addition to demonstrating that you have understood their interests, it helps to acknowledge that their interests are part of the overall problem you are trying to solve. This is especially easy to do if you have shared interests: "It would be terrible for all of us if one of your trucks hit a child."

Put the Problem before Your Answer

In talking to someone who represents a construction company, you might say, "We believe you should build a fence around the project within forty-eight hours and beginning immediately should restrict the speed of your trucks on Oak Street to fifteen miles an hour. Now let me tell you why. . . ." If you do, you can be quite certain that he will not be listening to the reasons. He has heard your position and is no doubt busy preparing arguments against it. He was probably disturbed by your tone or by the suggestion itself. As a result, your justification will slip by him altogether.

If you want someone to listen and understand your reasoning, give your interests and reasoning first and your conclusions or proposals later. Tell the company first about the dangers they are creating for young children and about your sleepless nights. Then they will be listening carefully, if only to try to figure out where you will end up on this question. And when you tell them, they will understand why.

Look Forward, Not Back

It is surprising how often we simply react to what someone else has said or done. Two people will often fall into a pattern of discourse that resembles a negotiation, but really has no such purpose whatsoever. They disagree with each other over some issue, and the talk goes back and forth as though they were seeking agreement. In fact, the argument is being carried on as a ritual, or simply a pastime. Each is engaged in scoring points against the other or in gathering evidence to confirm views about the other that have long been held and are not about to be changed. Neither party is seeking agreement or is even trying to influence the other.

If you ask two people why they are arguing, the answer will typically identify a cause, not a purpose. Caught up in a quarrel, whether between husband and wife, between company and union, or between two businesses, people are more likely to respond to what the other side has said or done than to act in pursuit of their own long-term interests. "They can't treat me like that. If they think they're going to get away with that, they will have to think again. I'll show them."

The question "Why?" has two quite different meanings. One looks backward for a cause and treats our behavior as determined by prior events. The other looks forward for a purpose and treats our behavior as subject to our free will. We need not enter into a philosophical debate between free will and determinism in order to decide how to act. Either we have free will or it is determined that we behave as if we do. In either case, we make choices. We can *choose* to look back or to look forward.

You will satisfy your interests better if you talk about where you would like to go rather than about where you have come from. Instead of arguing with the other side about the past—about last quarter's costs (which were too high), last week's action (taken without adequate authority), or yesterday's performance (which was less than expected)—talk about what you want to have happen in the future. Instead of asking them to justify what they did yesterday, ask, "Who should do what tomorrow?"

Be Concrete but Flexible

In a negotiation you want to know where you are going and yet be open to fresh ideas. To avoid having to make a difficult decision on what to settle for, people will often go into a negotiation with no other plan than to sit down with the other side and see what they offer or demand.

How can you move from identifying interests to developing specific options and still remain flexible with regard to those options? To convert your interests into concrete options, ask yourself, "If tomorrow the other side agrees to go along with me, what do I now think I would like them to go along with?" To keep your flexibility, treat each option you formulate as simply illustrative. Think in terms of more than one option that meets your interests. "Illustrative specificity" is the key concept.

Much of what positional bargainers hope to achieve with an opening position can be accomplished equally well with an illustrative suggestion that generously takes care of your interest. For example, in a baseball contract negotiation, an agent might say that "$250,000 a year would be the kind of figure that should satisfy Cortez's interest in receiving the salary he feels he is worth. Something on the order of a five-year contract should meet his need for job security."

Having thought about your interests, you should go into a meeting not only with one or more specific options that would meet your legitimate interests but also with an open mind. An open mind is not an empty one.

Be Hard on the Problem, Soft on the People

You can be just as hard in talking about your interests as any negotiator can be in talking about his position. In fact, it is usually advisable to be hard. It may not be wise to commit yourself to your position, but it is wise to commit yourself to your interests. This is the place in a negotiation to spend your aggressive energies. The other side, being concerned with their own interests, will tend to have overly optimistic expectations of the range of possible agreements. Often the wisest solutions, those that produce the maximum gain for you at the minimum cost to the other side, are produced only by strongly advocating your interests. Two negotiators, each pushing hard for their interests, will often stimulate each other's creativity in thinking up mutually advantageous solutions.

The construction company, concerned with inflation, may place a high value on its interest in keeping costs down and in getting the job done on time. You may have to shake them up. Some honest emotion may help restore a better balance between profits and children's lives. Do not let your desire to be conciliatory stop you from doing justice to your problem. "Surely you're not saying that my son's life is worth less than the price of a fence. You wouldn't say that about your son. I don't believe you're an insensitive person, Mr. Jenkins. Let's figure out how to solve this problem."

If they feel personally threatened by an attack on the problem, they may grow defensive and may cease to listen. This is why it is important to separate the people from the problem. Attack the problem without blaming the people. Go even further and be personally supportive: Listen to them with respect, show them courtesy, express your appreciation for their time and effort, emphasize your concern with meeting their basic needs, and so on. Show them that you are attacking the *problem,* not them.

One useful rule of thumb is to give positive support to the human beings on the other side equal in strength to the vigor with which you emphasize the problem. This combination of support and attack may seem inconsistent. Psychologically, it is; the inconsistency helps make it work. A well-known theory of psychology, the theory of cognitive dissonance, holds that people dislike inconsistency and will act to eliminate it. By attacking a problem, such as speeding trucks on a neighborhood street, and at the same time giving the company representative positive support, you create cognitive dissonance for him. To overcome this dissonance, he will be tempted to dissociate himself from the problem in order to join you in doing something about it.

Fighting hard on the substantive issues increases the pressure for an effective solution; giving support to the human beings on the other side tends to improve your relationship and to increase the likelihood of reaching agreement. It is the combination of support and attack which works; either alone is likely to be insufficient.

Negotiating hard for your interests does not mean being closed to the other side's point of view. Quite the contrary. You can hardly expect the other side to listen to your interests and discuss the options you suggest if you don't take their interests into account and show yourself to be open to their suggestions. Successful negotiation requires being both firm *and* open.

After Reading

1. In your journal, make a list of Fisher and Ury's principles for identifying the interests at work in a negotiation. Make a second list, giving their precepts for negotiating once you have identified the interests.
2. In your journal, write a response to this reading. What situations in your own life does it bring to mind? Do you think Fisher and Ury's precepts will work in your situation?
3. Write a journal entry about a situation in your personal or family life or issues in our society in which you see a conflict of values.

Having read material on the theory of values and on negotiating, and having done some writing about your own values and value conflicts and those in "The Poor Are Always with Us," you are well prepared for the following assignment:

Assignment

Traditionally the Student Government Association (SGA) gave three full-tuition scholarships each year to freshmen. For years, these were awarded on the basis of academic excellence alone. Then, beginning in 1966, the SGA began awarding them strictly on the basis of financial need and disregarding grades as long as the students were in good standing. But the money for the scholarships has not been available in the SGA budget since 1977. Now, amazingly, there is again money in the budget for the three scholarships. The SGA must decide what criteria it will use for awarding them. The decision will be made by a committee, composed of a faculty representative, another student, and you. You are the chair.

The first meeting was an outright disaster. Professor Rothman began by declaring it immoral to ignore financial need, and Steve, the other student, went on at some length about the meritocracy and how society must reward those who achieve or there will be no incentive to work hard. Professor Rothman kept saying, "It's important that we be rational about this," which Steve, rationally enough, took to imply that he was not. Walking out with you after the meeting, Steve confided that, in his view, "Professor Rothman has forgotten that there is a real world beyond the campus."

You are not looking forward to the next meeting. You can't imagine it being worse, but you have no reason to think it will be better unless you can change the tone of the next meeting and get the parties to stop thinking of each other as wicked or stupid. You decide to write a memo to Steve, whom you've known since high school, and another memo to Professor Rothman. In each memo you will try to explain what values you think prompt the other to take an opposing position. Point out the values they share on this issue, and include suggested procedures the committee might use to resolve the conflict. Remembering how different your two audiences are, write two effective memos. (See Appendix B for an example of memo format.)

HOW TO BEGIN

Before you begin to write these memos, you will need to think of the probable values and interests motivating each party, and you will need to have some procedures to recommend. It will be critically important for you to know how you want to sound to each of your very different audiences. For the values, interests, and procedures, use one or more prewriting strategies of your choice (see pp. 100ff). The following discussion of language choice will help you address your audiences.

LANGUAGE CHOICE

The Way We Sound on Paper

In June of last year, the Public Works Department announced that it had filled all of the potholes it had money to fill and the rest of them would just have to stay there. The following letters are some the department received in response:

A. Who the hell do you think you are? I pay taxes and I don't pay you guys to tell me what you can't do. I want to see the street fixed fast or I'll be asking where the money's going.

B. You people are wonderful. I thought you couldn't top that stunt where you painted new lane lines before blacking out the old ones (how well I remember what fun we had guessing which lane "counted" and wondering if the oncoming traffic would have a different guess). But I have to give you credit: this pothole business is even better. Don't tell me, you're going to wait until a car falls in and then cement around it, right?

C. I write to urge that you reconsider your decision to stop repairing potholes. These holes not only ruin the front end alignment of our cars, but they are now getting so deep as to be a serious danger. The steering wheel is jerked out of the driver's hand and the car fishtails. Surely it will only become more expensive to repair these problems if they are left to

> grow. Can you not use some of the money set aside for
> leaf pick-up in the fall? The leaves are harmless,
> but the potholes are not.

D. I think it is really kind of stupid not to fix the
   potholes. I mean, when you're driving along and hit
   one of those things, it screws up the whole car. People who come from out of town will think this is a
   dumb city with big holes in its roads.

E. Enclosed please find a statement from my dental surgeon. I find it altogether appropriate to forward
   said statement, unpaid, to you, as my recent adventure in dentistry was necessitated entirely by the
   condition of the roads, a condition for which you are
   accountable to the citizens of this metropolis.

In your journal, describe each of the letter writers. What type of person would write each of these letters? Try to note which language choices in each letter created the impression you have of each writer. When you and the class have compiled a list of the words, phrases, and figures of speech that characterize each writer, try to generalize about the features of each writer's language that lead us to an impression. For example, the use of words that derive from Latin (e.g., reconsider) rather than Old or Middle English (e.g., think) is one key indicator.* Which others can you identify?

When we speak or write, we each have certain characteristics that identify us as individuals. Even if you could not tell by the handwriting which friend wrote a particular note or letter, the content or the way it was written would probably give it away. Notice how each of the people who wrote to the Public Works Department sounds distinctly different, even though all of them are saying "fix the potholes." They sound different because of the way in which they make their argument and because they have different sentence structure, vocabulary, and tone.

Even though we each have a voice that is characteristically ours, we are

---

*The modern English language has acquired vocabulary from the Anglo-Saxon tongues spoken in England before the Norman invasion of 1066, from the French of the Norman conquerors, and from Latin, the international language of educated individuals throughout the Middle Ages and the Renaissance. After the Norman invasion, the Anglo-Saxons did most of the manual labor, and therefore most of our words that apply to manual labor come from Anglo-Saxon. The Normans were an aristocracy, and thus many of our words for luxuries and high living come from French (e.g., gourmet, boudoir). The famous illustration of the difference between the Anglo-Saxon and French vocabularies is that the words for meat on the plate (beef, pork, mutton) all derive from French, but the words for meat on the hoof (cow, pig, sheep) come from the Anglo-Saxons, who tended the animals. Latin, as the language in which educated people wrote, supplies us with many more abstract than concrete terms—words for ideas rather than things. When we have an Anglo-Saxon derivative and a Latin derivative that mean the same thing, the Latin derivative nearly always sounds more formal and distanced and is more likely to sound pretentious than the Anglo-Saxon one. The endings -ate, -tion, -al often indicate a Latin derivative. (See also "Pretentious Diction" in George Orwell's "Politics and the English Language," Chapter 8.)

able to vary it when we choose. We can sound elated or furious and still sound like ourselves. We can sound sarcastic or slangy and casual or serious and respectful. We shift these gears, mostly without thinking about it. We naturally shift to the kind of language that seems to us most appropriate for the situation. There is nothing dishonest about this; it is like our choosing different clothes for different occasions. We are still ourselves, dressed up or in T-shirt and jeans. In both speaking and writing, our language can reflect our mood or attitude and can be more or less formal, depending on the audience and purpose.

Degrees of Formality and Distance

The English language, for our purposes here, can be divided into three kinds:—stilted English, formal English, and informal English—which differ in the degree of distance they establish between the writer and the audience.

Stilted English is either very official or merely pompous and pretentious. It is the language of official proclamations and engraved invitations—it is also the language used by butlers in old movies to discourage anyone from talking to them. Stilted English is characterized by the use of abstract words and archaic constructions or expressions.

Examples: 1. We have come to the determination that the firm will no longer require your services.
2. I shall thank you never to darken my doorway again.
3. By these presents be it here known that David Alexander has fulfilled all of the requirements leading to the degree of Bachelor of Science in Aerospace Engineering. . . .

Formal English sets up a respectful but not exaggerated distance between the writer and the reader. One mark of this respect is the absence of any usage that the reader might not understand. It is a good language in which to write to people you do not know personally. Formal English is characterized by a mixture of Anglo-Saxon and Latinate words and by a mixture of simple, compound, and complex sentences.

Examples: 1. Although I am intrigued by the work of the Campaign for Animal Suffrage, I am sure that I will never be in a position to make a contribution. Please remove my name from the mailing list.
2. As Bishop of the diocese, I must support your pastor's decision not to allow "Benny and the Jets" to be sung at your wedding. It is not in keeping with the tone of the ceremony.

Informal English is the language most of us think in and use to talk and write to our family and friends. It puts little distance between writer and reader, and it is characterized by a majority of Anglo-Saxon words and simple constructions, including sentence fragments. Even in writing, informal English sounds like speech. When someone uses informal English in a situation that calls for formal English, the effect is often that the writer sounds young and naive.

Examples: 1. Hi Mom,
                 Having a swell time in Istanbul! If the consulate calls you, don't believe a word of it (ha, ha).
                 Love ya,
                 Lori
              2. It was an awful morning. The phone was ringing off the hook and the dog had the meter reader cornered. There was Biff, screaming like a Banshee.
              3. *Don't touch* Bake Sale cake in fridge. Ice cream in freezer.

None of the varieties of English is better than any other. Nor is formal English inherently better than informal English. A tuxedo is not *better* than jeans and a T-shirt; it would just be *inappropriate* to wear to a baseball game. Similarly, the maid of honor who wore her softball uniform to a formal wedding would distract and possibly offend the bride and groom, who might think she did not take the occasion seriously. In writing, your audience and your purpose will determine what variety of English and what degree of formality are appropriate. Your first question should be, "Will the reader know what this means?" Your second question should be, "Is this a formal situation?"

Sometimes, even when we write to people we know, the occasion or the purpose for writing are ones that call for formality. If, for example, you are writing a job application letter, you should use formal English, even if the prospective employer is a family friend. Even though you and the employer may "speak the same language," job application letters are formal documents that live on in files and may be read by people other than your friend. Likewise, weddings and funerals are ceremonies that prompt formality, even among close friends and family members. Cousins we have always called by their first names may send us engraved cards requesting the honor of our presence at their weddings.

The impression you give of yourself on paper will depend to a great extent on the language you use. People who do not know you will form an opinion about you based on the language you use to communicate. It is certainly in your interest, therefore, to learn to use different varieties of language in your writing and to practice judging which variety suits which audience and purpose.

You should respond to the following exercises in your journal.

1. Returning to the samples on p. 205, rewrite each of the examples of stilted English so that they will be formal English and then informal English. Try translating each of the examples of the formal and informal into the other two varieties.

2. Fill in the missing equivalents:

Stilted	Formal	Informal
_____	_____	a crook
_____	to telephone	_____
_____	study	_____
_____	plant a garden	_____
_____	a good meal	_____

Create more lists of your own like these.

3. Read each of the following letters and make notes about the appropriateness of specific language choices. How would you characterize each of the writers? Why? Both letters are "open letters" to a newspaper columnist and were written to persuade readers that the columnist's position is wrong.

   A. Dear Mr. Pierce:
       This is about your article saying in this state we spend too much money on basketball and not enough on education. What's wrong with basketball, if people like it? Who ever said education's sacred? The same amount of money devoted to education wouldn't make people as happy as basketball. Only a wimp could think basketball is a waste. You need to reconsider your position and change your mind.

   B. Dear Mr. Pierce:
       I disagree with your claim that this state spends money on basketball that it should spend on education. The people of this state repeatedly vote against school levies, but they continue to buy basketball tickets. In this way, they set the priorities they want the state to follow. Democracy means that the people rule. I think it is kind of crazy for you to bad mouth support for basketball. Think about it.

4. Both of the following letters are requests for a job. What specific changes would you make in each letter to improve it?

A. Dear Ms. Stoner:

 I'm writing because I found out you need a law clerk during the summer. Next year will be my last year of law school, and I want the job. My grades are good and I know how to do the job. . . .

B. Dear Ms. Stoner:

 I write to apply for the position of law clerk which you have recently advertised as available. I have completed my penultimate year of legal studies and have amassed requisite credentials for the position. My transcript documents my academic achievement. . . .

Technical Jargon

When you write for readers who are members of a particular profession, you will find yourself using many technical terms. This is appropriate because your audience of professional peers understands the terms. Some writers have a tendency, however, to write as if everything were technical and could not possibly be written in plain English. And when the jargon of one field invades another, as in "the registration process is user friendly," absurdity hovers near. See if you can translate the following examples into formal English.

> The analog to digital converter will be refabricated to implement improved designs and materials and ruggedize the existing AD12-3 converter so that is has a greater capability of withstanding extreme climatic conditions.

> Operationalization of the plan for apportioning the wilderness area into recreational and preservational sectors cannot be optimized without the inflow of funds.

This kind of inflated writing is what many people have in mind when they bemoan the state to which writing ability has sunk in America. You can avoid writing like this if you remember not to use pseudotechnical language when there is a way to say the same thing in ordinary English. In your journal, make a list of the other features of this writing that make it so hard to read.

Concrete and Sensory Language

Which of the two paragraphs below do you prefer?

> One experience which has been important to me occurred during my last year at boarding school. One night two of my friends, Lynn and Jan, and two of the boys who worked on the farm, Terry and Doug, and I jumped on the freight train that passed the school. We must have looked pretty funny—all five of us and a guitar. We just rode along on the train as it wound through all the small

towns in the area. We left about ten o'clock at night and just got back in time to sneak in for chapel. That night, no one said or did anything very significant but it was an experience I'll always remember.

During my last summer at boarding school, I was eighteen years old, and because I was in the "senior form" I was charged with seeing that the six- and seven-year-olds were packed off to bed by 8:30. After that, I and two other girls from senior form would sit on the wooden back porch of the century-old motherhouse and wait for the two boys who helped with the farm work to come in with the horses. One of them would play the guitar and he would be alternately good or bad at it and nobody cared which, and the pleasure of it was mixed with the smell of honeysuckle and forsythia in its second blooming, and the clay of the near field which was just turned over. Out on the Anderson State Road there was a pickup truck kicking up dust on the gravel road and it seemed to move so slowly. There was no hurry. The only sound was the low whistle of the milk train as it came to the Georgetown crossing. All at once, we decided to ride the train and we ran laughing through the near-dusk and I could feel the wet leaves brush my face and hear the twigs brush against my starched uniform blouse as we ran. I wasn't out of breath; I think I could have run forever. Inside the train I could feel the wheels bouncing on the rails and a split second later I would hear the clack. I knew we would have to be back early the next morning before the line formed to go to chapel, but I thought that even if the sisters found out, they just couldn't help but feel that it was the only thing to do on a June night like that.

Most readers prefer the second version of this student's paper because it makes them feel closer to the experience she is describing and they can understand better and share the feeling she is remembering. Both versions have details; in fact, the first has some details that the writer dropped in the second. But the difference in effect comes from the number of concrete and sensory words in the second version. When a writer recreates the sight, sound, smell, taste, and feel of something, the reader can share the experience. Indeed, the use of sensory language is one of the best strategies a writer has for involving the reader directly and emotionally. Consider the following example:

There are people who want to eliminate school sports programs on the ground that they do nothing but foster competitiveness. These must be people who have never experienced the sheer joy of sport. When you have run until your throat is raw from the intake of air and your muscles are knots and you are hot and cold and dizzy and you know you can't run one more yard, then, sometimes, you bring your foot down and it doesn't hurt, and you realize you've "hit the wall" and gone past it. There is no more muscle pain, your breath is free and painless, and you don't even feel the pavement below you. You can see the horizon up ahead and know you will run until you step into it. All you hear is the rush of the wind past your ears. It's the closest to free flight that a human being can get. This is the same "high," the same sense of infinity, a baseball player knows when he's hit a ball perfectly, the same sense the hurdler feels when she is in perfect stride. There's a lot more to sport than winning and losing. Athletes know this, even if the critics do not.

Does this paragraph make you want to run? If you want a reader to share your point of view, there is nothing as effective as sharing the experience that led you to that point of view. And concrete and sensory language is the best means of sharing that experience.

Euphemisms and Abstract Language

An abstract term denotes something you cannot see, hear, feel, taste, or smell. Most kinds of writing require both specific, concrete language to help the reader share the experience and more general, abstract language to offer conclusions or implications to the reader. It is possible to generalize without abstraction (e.g., "This is the worst hamburger in the world"), but most generalizations do involve some abstracting. Consider the following example:

> Commonly, national cuisines developed in response to environmental conditions. The Chinese, for example, had scarce fuel for cooking and therefore developed a style of preparing food in which meat is chopped or sliced before cooking and all ingredients are cooked in one vessel. In Mediterranean countries, fresh meats, fruits, and vegetables dominate the cuisine because the climate made it impractical to store many types of foodstuffs. In colder northern climates, salted meats and dried fruits take precedence because fresh food is not available.

Though essential to most kinds of writing, abstract language necessarily lacks sensory appeal, and thus is less immediately attractive to the reader. Whenever you can, choose a concrete word over an abstract one to engage the reader's interest.

Because abstract language distances the reader from the subject and discourages emotional involvement, it can be not only dull but also deceptive. Certainly we can picture a plane crash more easily than a "controlled flight into terrain," as some crashes are now called by the National Transportation Safety Board. And we are likely to be horrified by the number of civilian casualties projected in a nuclear war, but when the Pentagon uses the term "collateral damage" for such casualties, it tends to blunt our perception. A *euphemism* is a word or phrase that is used because it sounds less harsh than the word or phrase it replaces. We say that someone "passed away" because it is less harsh than "died." We use the word "obituary" because its Latinate ring sounds better to us than "death notice." These are fairly harmless euphemisms, intended to cushion us from our mortality. Other euphemisms, like "rectification of boundaries" and "collateral damage," keep us distanced from the things that can happen to our fellow human beings and are therefore dangerous. An honest writer will use euphemisms only to spare someone's feelings on a topic, like death or taxes, that nothing can be done about. An intelligent reader will question abstract terms and imagine their human consequences.

Denotation and Connotation

The *denotation* of a word is its meaning as given in the dictionary. The *connotation* is the shade of additional meaning it has acquired because of the way in which our society has characteristically used it. A pair of $13 running shoes may be either "cheap" or "inexpensive." Which word would you use to advertise them? A four-year-old may be "articulate" or "talky." Which word would his parents choose to describe him? It is worth a writer's trouble to be aware of connotations because they are part of the message the reader receives. Indeed, the attitudes and biases of the writer are reflected in the choice of words he or she makes among synonyms. Read the following sonnet by George Barker and describe his attitude toward his mother. What kind of woman is she, in his eyes? What words convey this information through their connotations?

To My Mother

George Barker

Most near, most dear, most loved and most far,
Under the window where I often found her
Sitting as huge as Asia, seismic with laughter,
Gin and chicken helpless in her Irish hand,
Irresistible as Rabelais, but most tender for
The lame dogs and hurt birds that surround her,—
She is a procession no one can follow after
But be like a little dog following a brass band.

She will not glance up at the bomber or condescend
To drop her gin and scuttle to a cellar,
But lean on the mahogany table like a mountain
Whom only faith can move, and so I send
O all my faith and all my love to tell her
That she will move from mourning into morning.

The bias of a writer can subtly shape a report, so readers, for their own protection, should get in the habit of noticing "loaded" words—ones that have positive or negative connotations that reveal the writer's bias. In 1965, John Merrill, a journalism professor, published a study of bias in *Time* magazine.* He demonstrated that, among other expressions of bias, *Time* chose words with strong connotations as synonyms for the word "said," which itself has neither positive nor negative connotations. When reporting what President Harry

Reprinted by permission of Faber and Faber Ltd. from *Collected Poems: 1930–1955* by George Barker.

*John C. Merrill, "How *Time* Stereotyped Three U.S. Presidents," *Journalism Quarterly,* Autumn 1965.

Truman said, *Time* was inclined toward synonyms with negative connotations (e.g., Truman "barked" or "sputtered"); *Time* favored synonyms with positive connotations (e.g., "chatted amiably") for what President Dwight Eisenhower said; reporting on President John Kennedy, *Time* usually used the neutral "said" because the magazine neither opposed nor supported Kennedy.

Remember as you write to choose words with appropriate connotations, ones that truly reflect your attitudes, that will not offend your reader, and that do not insert bias in a piece that is supposed to be objective. For practice in recognizing and using connotative language, try to decide whether the following account is more likely to have been written by a supporter of Israel or a supporter of Egypt:

> On the eve of Yom Kippur, holiest of Jewish religious holidays, Egyptian tanks invaded the Sinai. Israeli forces, caught off guard by this nocturnal sneak attack, sustained heavy losses.

Now rewrite the paragraph as it might have been written by one who favored the *other* side. Remember to convey the same information; choose synonyms but ones with different connotations.

Clichés

A *cliché* is an expression that has become so familiar that most people no longer think about it when they hear it. Many clichés are metaphors that have long since lost their freshness or vividness. The first recorded use of the expression "dead as a doornail" (What *is* a doornail?) occurs in the 1377 version of the poem *Piers Plowman*. Whoever created the expression no doubt delighted his or her listeners, who thought about just how dead a doornail was. But now we have heard the expression so often that we don't picture the doornail any more. The phrase "as a doornail" is just a group of useless words in a sentence. So are "clean as a whistle," "tight as a tick," "happy as a clam," and any other metaphor you have frequently heard. Similarly, "to put it in a nutshell" is fit for retirement because everyone has heard it so often that no one ever really thinks about it. The recently overheard comment by a registration worker, "They're dropping that class like flies," illustrates how easy it is to pick up clichés and use them without thinking about what they might mean. In your journal, list every cliché you can think of.

Choice of Pronouns: I, You, He or She

Perhaps you have been advised not to use "I" in an academic paper. Sometimes teachers ask students not to use "I" or "me" because they want to stress that a particular paper calls for objective analysis rather than the expression of opinion or report of personal experience. They prefer "The images of rotting food in *Hamlet* suggest corruption" to "The images of rotting food in *Hamlet* made me think of corruption." Recently, however, there has been greater interest in the way individual readers respond to literature, and the use of "I" and "me" may be acceptable if you are asked for your *response* to a literary work. It is still a good idea to delete phrases like "I think" and "I believe" and "in my opinion" from academic papers, because most such papers call for you to support an assertion rather than advance an opinion.

There was a time when technical writers were advised not to use the first person, but as long ago as 1960 the *Style Manual For Biological Journals* broke this taboo:

> Biological publications now cost almost six cents a word. But more than money is at stake. Economy of communication and reading time is the major concern. Economy of words also yields clarity. *I found* costs less than half as much as *it was discovered,* and identifies the discoverer immediately. When *experiments were conducted,* the reader cannot tell whether the author or his predecessor conducted them. If you use *I* or *we* (*we* for two or more writers, never as a substitute for *I*), you easily avoid the passive voice, at least in that one sentence.*

In 1972, the *American National Standard for the Preparation of Scientific Papers* dictated:

> When a verb concerns action by the author, he should use the first person, especially in matters of experimental design ("to eliminate this possibility, I did the following experiment"). Constant use of the first person is not advisable, however, since it may distract the reader from the subject of the paper.†

Despite the last sentence, which advises the researcher not to make himself or herself appear the star of the experiment, the scientific community read this as a strong endorsement of the first person pronoun. In the past two decades, this usage has become more common in scientific writing. It is best, however, to check with your science instructors about using it in the papers you write for them.

In technical writing, it is best to avoid the second person—"you"—because the paper is not about the reader. Even phrases like "as you know" are inappropriate because academic papers traditionally establish a wide distance between writer and reader to maintain the objectivity of the thesis, and "as you know" violates this formal distance. In an academic paper it sounds downright folksy.

In other kinds of writing, however, the "you" pronoun is perfectly acceptable. When magazines offer "Ten Cures for Your Insecurities," they want

---

*Conference of Biological Editors, Committee on Form and Style, Washington, D.C.: American Institute of Biological Sciences, 2.

†Quoted in American Psychological Association, *Publication Manual,* Washington, D.C., 1972, 28.

you to think it is truly your very own insecurities that they have been worrying about. And in business correspondence, the "you" is almost inevitable (e.g., "Dr. Michelle Hill, my mathematics professor, suggested that I write to *you* about an internship").

Sometimes writers fall into using "you" because it is easier than keeping track of the original agent of the action or because it seems like a convenient way to avoid repetition. As a result, their writing sounds confused, and readers may have to backtrack to figure out the sense. Consider the following excerpt:

> Potential blood donors must be screened to determine their suitability as donors, and they have a right to have the donation procedure explained to them in advance. The health professional will reject you if you have certain chronic diseases or if. . . .

The writer began to substitute "you" for "potential blood donors," probably because he or she just got careless. A switch like this indicates that the writer does not have much control.

It has not been so very long since writers were advised to use "he" to represent "someone," even if it were equally likely that the someone were female. The reader was supposed to understand that "he" really meant "he or she." In recent years, however, women have objected because the exclusive use of male pronouns made them invisible. If doctors and engineers and politicians are always referred to as "he," little girls will get the message that certain kinds of jobs are men's jobs, and the society generally will have reinforced the idea that women doctors, engineers, and politicians are exceptions to the norm. A similar misimpression is fostered when nurses, teachers, and cooks are referred to as "she." The use of "he or she" and "his or her" may sound awkward to us now because we are not accustomed to it yet, but these alternatives are much fairer and more honest than using just "he" or just "she."

Revising Workshop

Bring drafts of your memos to class for a Revising Workshop. In small groups, share your papers with each other, assisting each other by responding to the questions below in relation to each paper. Each person's paper should be responded to by at least two other students.

1. What are some differences in the language in the memo to Steve and the memo to Professor Rothman?
2. Has the writer chosen appropriate language for each memo? In the margin, mark any language that you think may be inappropriate.
3. Where in the paper are the language choices particularly good?
4. Imagine in the assignment that you are, in turn, Steve and Professor Rothman. Write a few lines describing your response to the memo. Let the writer know how you respond to his or her explanation and proposals and to his or her attitude as reflected in the memos.

5. Comment on the sentence structure in each memo. Are any sentences choppy? Any too long? Any weakened by unnecessary words?

Before you write the second draft of your memo, consider the responses of your classmates in the Revising Workshop. You may not agree with everything they tell you, but their responses should help you understand how your memos affect readers.

Editing Workshop

The purpose of this workshop is to help each other find any mechanical problems or difficulties with form in your memos. Each person's paper should be read by at least two students.

1. How closely does the paper follow the memo format as shown in appendix B.
2. Are there any sentences or parts of sentences in the memo that confuse you or cause you to have to reread to grasp the meaning? If so, bracket these as needing repair.
3. Place an *X* in the margin of the paper on any line in which you see what you perceive as an error in spelling or punctuation. Use as many marks as there are errors.
4. Place a *C* in the margin of any line where you find a trite expression or cliché.
5. Place a *G* in the margin of any line where you find what you think is an error in grammar or usage. Use as many marks as there are errors.

Examine the responses of your classmates to your paper. If sentences are bracketed, try to decide what the problems are with those sentences. If you find marks indicating grammar, spelling, punctuation errors, or clichés, identify the errors and correct them. For help, consult the Editing Guide. Make notes in your journal about the kinds of errors you seem to be making. Finally, edit again to correct any errors and submit your papers.

CHAPTER 7

Responding to a Specific Request

_____ THEME *Money, Money, Money*

_____ SKILL FOCUS *Revising and Editing*

It has been said that money makes the world go round, that time is money, and that love of money is the root of all evil. The theme of this chapter, "Money, Money, Money," invites you to consider the role of money in your life. How much money does your life style require? What "things" do you spend your money on? What do you want money for in the future? What are the relationships between your values and the ways in which you spend your money? What is your idea of a necessity and a luxury? How do your classmates' ideas of luxuries and necessities differ from your own? You will consider all these questions and more as you read, respond, think, and interact with your class in preparation for the major writing assignment of this chapter.

The writing assignment will ask you to respond to a specific request with a formal letter on the subject of money. In order to write the letter you will need to integrate your own ideas from your reading, your journal entries, and your discussions with your class.

In your journal, respond to the following questions:

	Agree	Disagree
1. I am good at managing my money, however much I have.	____	____
2. I spend appropriately the money I have at the present time.	____	____
3. Education will help me earn more money in the long run.	____	____
4. I am confident that in the future I will have enough money to enjoy the life style I desire.	____	____
5. If I needed to, I could manage at a subsistence level to stay in school.	____	____
6. I would prefer to drop out of school and work for a while than to live at subsistence level as a student.	____	____
7. Different people have different money needs; what is a necessity for one person is a luxury for another.	____	____
8. Money problems could keep me from completing my college education.	____	____
9. I prefer to work while attending school.	____	____

Examine your responses to the nine items and compose a journal entry (at least two pages) in which you explore your responses to several of the items. Your aim is simply to clarify your own thoughts and feelings about the importance of money in your life now. Consider also your specific needs as an individual in thinking about how you spend your money. Your entry *need not be shared* with the class unless you choose to share.

Before Reading

Before reading "Some Emotional Uses of Money" by William Kaufman, jot down responses to the following questions in your journal:

1. What factors influence the symbolic meaning individuals attach to money and the manner in which they use money?
2. On their way to adulthood, what stages do children go through in their sense of money and money concepts? Compare this development with your own as you remember it.

Some Emotional Uses of Money

William Kaufman

Although money is an important stimulus for many different patterns of normal and abnormal behavior, little systematic attention has been given to this subject by most psychologists and psychiatrists. This despite the fact that most people, rich and poor, are more or less continuously concerned—consciously or unconsciously—with the solution of their private money problems.

In my study of over a thousand patients from three to eighty-four years of age whom I have seen in the course of my private practice of internal medicine during the past twelve years, it has been possible to trace how concepts of money and money transactions are integrated into our lives, unconsciously or consciously influencing our conduct, our aspirations, and emotional reactions to ourselves, our families, and other people.

The symbolic meaning of money to the individual and the manner in which he uses it are determined by his culture, religion, by the attitudes of parents and teachers, by his life experiences (including the impact of the media of mass communication), by example of the people he knows, and by his personal short- and long-term goals.

Money can be translated into many of the things and services we really want. Much of what we call emotional security is soundly backed by the proper uses of money. Even part of what we call love and affection in parents stems from their ability to spend wisely for the benefit of their children.

The emotionally well-balanced use of money requires that the individual plan realistically for his present and future. His work effort must be translated into an income which will do more than support a mere subsistence level of living. If he has no emotional blocks to earning an ample income, then each expenditure he makes in a sense further tests his reality function, measures his attitudes toward himself and others, and indicates fluctuations in mood and affect.

The proper use of money creates within the individual a sense of well-being and emotional security. The inappropriate use of money becomes a serious emotional threat when the person is faced with the conflict between his desires and his conscience and with the consequences of his aberrant money-behavior. Deep unconscious motivations may prevent him from spontaneously using his money in constructive ways. Such people, regardless of income or economic reserves, often develop one of the most common psychosomatic illnesses of our time: *money-sickness*.

To delineate the complexity of the emotional aspects of money transactions in adults of our culture, I will review briefly the growing child's adjustments to money and money concepts.

A child's notions about money are usually vague until he reaches his fifth year. His first knowledge of money may come accidentally as he secretly explores his mother's pocketbook and finds a small hoard of coins and paper money. He looks at the money, clinks the coins, feels the bills. Then he may stuff some money into his mouth and quickly decide that he doesn't like its taste. Thereupon, he spits it out and throws the rest away. If strangers scramble for it, it amuses him. His emotional satisfaction comes from literally throwing money away.

From the age of three to five by passing coins to salespeople under the direction of a parent, the child gradually learns that by giving money to the right person at the right time and in the right environment, he can get some things more desirable than money. It is at this stage that a child believes that money has magical properties, since his parents, merely by putting their hands into the right pocket, can draw on what seems to be an inexhaustible store of money and buy with it anything they want.

From the age of five to nine, the youngster learns to manipulate the pennies, nickels, and dimes at his disposal, and begins to develop some of his most important emotional reactions to the symbolic meaning [of] money transactions. He learns to his pleasure that he can buy certain reward foods such as ice cream, candy, and cookies. Later he realizes that money can obtain for him toys, comic books, special clothes—and admission to the movies or circus.

Because money becomes associated with pleasures in the child's mind, parents can now use it as a reward to reinforce habit development of various desirable forms of behavior. It is at this time that a child first makes the connection between love and money.

A child's income in the form of allowance or gifts is fixed by his parents. Often, when a parent refuses to give him additional money, a youngster may blurt out: "You don't love me any more!" At this point, the child still believes that his parents have unlimited supplies of money, but that for their own reasons they are withholding it from him. Depending on the way the parent handles this situation, the child may make either a good or bad adjustment to the initial situation of not having as much money as he wants.

When a child learns that he has monetary limitations, he has to solve one of the basic dilemmas in the emotional uses of money: What to do with it? One little boy, aged six, told me: "Money is nice to have—but it's nice to spend, too!" Each child must find his own solution to this ambivalent situation—to save or to spend—and this will determine some of his adult patterns of money-use.

At about this time, he may learn that he can increase his income by running errands or doing simple jobs. He may wheedle money from his parents by nagging them till they give in—or by making such a nuisance of himself that he is paid to behave.

As the child's social life develops, he learns disquieting things. Some kids have more money than he has—and he is envious. He may have to accept as a reality the fact that he cannot have as much money as others—or he may fight it. However, he has some emotional balm when he discovers that other children may have even less money at their disposal than he has—and this gives him a sense of superiority. His already formed feelings about money will determine whether he prefers playing with children who have more money than he, or less—and this sets the stage for future relations with people whom he may always react to in terms of their economic status.

Gradually, a child's ideas of "mine and thine" become more sharply differentiated. He may share his money with others only on a this-for-that basis. But even at this early age, a child may try to buy love and friendship by giving his money to others in his play group.

As he becomes increasingly aware of the desirability of material possessions, he may wonder aloud why his parents can't have as many wonderful things as the parents of his friends. Then he learns what is a fundamental, traumatic, and almost catastrophic truth: his parents are not omnipotent. There is a limit to their buying power. This realization often creates in the growing child strong feelings of anxiety and anger.

Since his father is usually the chief wage-earner, the child's anger lashes out chiefly against him. He may kick, bite, or punch his father. Or he may try to run away from home. Parents usually do not recognize the cause of the child's anger, anxiety, mild depression, rage, temper tantrums, deep insecurity feelings, and other psychosomatic illnesses.

What this agitated child needs most is reassurance, love, and the gradually taught understanding that there is enough money to take care of all his basic needs, and even for some luxuries; and that there is no real cause for worry, since he will be well taken care of by his loving parents.

But what happens most frequently is that a parent is enraged because his child has made an unfavorable economic comparison between him and a neighbor, friend, or stranger. The father retaliates by becoming harsh and punitive toward his child. He may so criticize every money use of his child that the youngster becomes an anxious and frightened user of money. It is during this time that the parents' unconscious anxieties about money and economic security are transferred to children. From this point onward, children may develop abnormal attitudes toward the uses of money which adversely affect them the rest of their lives.

The emotionally insecure child of five to nine may try to solve his conflict about money by withdrawal from wealthier children, by subservience to them in expectation of monetary favors, by aggressive behavior intended to wrest what he wants from the richer child or to punish him for his wealth. He may limit his friendships to those having equal or lesser amounts of money than he has at his disposal. Or he may try to save or earn as much as he can to be more independent than if he had only the parental allowance available. He may feign indifference to money, emphasizing as one boy did: "What do I want money for? . . . If you don't have it, you can't lose it." A few day-dreamy children escape from realistic solution of their basic money problems by fantasying the great wealth of imaginary relatives, and savoring the pleasure of unlimited make-believe buying power.

However, a child may be tempted to solve his money problems by committing minor money crimes when he finds money that belongs to his parents or siblings, and diverts it to his own uses. To some extent these children are within their rights when they do this. Since they use so many things in common with other members of the household, they can easily assume that money too is common property within the family. To some extent, many of these children who steal money unconsciously feel rejected by their parents and substitute the things they can buy with money for the love which they believe parents have withheld from them. Formerly, most of these children could be taught over a period of time to develop a sense of honesty which precluded stealing other people's money or possessions.

However, today there is an alarming tendency in youngsters under the age of nine who, influenced by radio, television, movies, and comic books, have solved their basic money conflicts by entering into criminal activity of both amateur and professional caliber. The amateurs rob other children, short-change people they run errands for, or do minor shoplifting in stores. But some have planned and successfully executed complex and daring robberies, even opening safes, to get the money they feel they need, which their parents are unwilling or unable to give them.

The way in which a child's first money crimes are handled by his parents, teachers, or correction officers will have a marked bearing on the individual's ability to make for himself ultimately a socially acceptable life.

As the youngster grows into adolescence, he becomes increasingly aware of economic class distinctions. His increased need for money is part of his sex-awakening. The adolescent eventually spends much of the money available to him to increase his attractiveness to the opposite sex. Since he is dependent on parents, and yet desires to assert his growing independence, there is a reactivation of his earlier anger against his parents for not being able to give him all the money he thinks he needs.

The various solutions which the adolescent has at his disposal are mostly variants of those already described for younger children. The one who has developed constructive solutions of his money-problems earlier in childhood faces his contemporary adolescent money-problems with good reality function and formulates workable plans for his future education and employment. The adolescent with faulty emotional solutions to his money-problems will almost surely have a troubled adult life.

My discussion of the emotional uses of money in adults which follows assumes that the individual has at his disposal more than a minimum subsistence level of income. The major classifications indicate the predominant money behavior of the individual at the time of observation. Such behavior may be fixed for one's lifetime, or altered either spontaneously or through psychotherapy.

Some Emotional Uses . . .

A. Emotionally Well-Balanced Uses of Money
B. Compulsive Nonspending
   1. conservative
   2. economical
   3. dollar-stretcher
   4. stingy
   5. tight-wad
   6. miser
C. Compulsive Spending
   1. infantile
   2. childish
      a. passive-dependent
      b. hostile-aggressive
      c. security-buying
   3. dreamy
   4. narcissistic
      a. self-adornment
      b. show-off spending
      c. socially competitive
      d. affection-buying
   5. expense-account
   6. self-pitying, self-rewarding
   7. gambling
   8. bargain-hunting
   9. scrimping to splurge
D. Indecisive or Frightened Uses of Money
E. Denial of Economic Status
   1. pretended wealth
   2. pretended poverty
F. Use of Money as Reward
   1. constructively, to encourage socially useful activity
   2. destructively, to encourage unethical, illegal activity
G. Punitive Uses
H. Charitable Uses

I. Guilty Uses
J. Fetish Uses
K. . . .
L. Money Uses by Older People
M. Psychotics

Mood	Psychosis	Result
1. Euphoric	Manic	Excessive spending
2. Sad	Depressed	Decreased spending
3. Suspicious	Paranoic	Decreased spending
4. Dreamy	Schizoid	Spotty, unpredictable spending

A. Emotionally Well-Balanced Uses of Money

This individual may be in the low, medium, or high income bracket. He budgets his income for short- and long-term goals in a manner which shows good reality function. There is food-money, clothing-money, rent-money, money to be saved—and as an emotional safety valve, extra money set aside to be spent without guilt for trifles that seem desirable at the moment.

This person maintains as high a standard of living as possible, while allowing for reasonable savings and insurance. Fluctuations in his income are met by realistic adjustments in his spending, borrowing, and saving. His credit is good but he does not abuse it. Although he is willing to take reasonable business risks, he doesn't speculate. He is not stampeded into miserly or spendthrift uses of money. He shares his monetary resources equitably with other members of his family. Should it be necessary to do so, he can make economic sacrifices for the benefit of others.

Usually he has had a good relationship in childhood with his parents and siblings, and is free from crippling anxieties and tensions. His parents taught him reasonable ways of solving money problems, and in adulthood he has formulated his own flexible but reachable economic goals and is willing to compete fairly with others to attain these. He accepts without jealousy that there are many who have more money than he has, and often helps deserving people who are economically less fortunate than he.

B. Compulsive Nonspending

This individual makes enough money to maintain a decent standard of living within his low, medium, or large income bracket. But he has such a great inner fear of economic insecurity that his spending is inhibited. He tries to combat his unconscious fear by finding some minimal level of spending, and maximal rate of saving, which satisfy him. This he continues even though as time goes by both his income and monetary reserves may become so large that there is no longer any realistic basis for his inner fear of economic insecurity.

This emotionally rigid mode of inhibited spending leads to such descriptive terms as: conservative, economical, dollar-stretcher, stingy, tight-wad and miser.

The *conservative spender* is interested in getting his money's worth and no more, but limits his buying to necessities and few luxuries. The *economical* one is bargain-minded, spending much time and effort in finding goods and services he wants at the lowest prices. He is willing to sacrifice quality for price. The *dollar-stretcher* buys nothing that he can possibly make, and is constantly working during his free time to avoid spending either for finished products or services of others. The *stingy* person is self-punitive by depriving himself of things he needs or would enjoy, and which he certainly could afford. The *tight-wad* satisfies his physical needs by spending only when he must, regretting each dollar that he takes out of his purse as if it were a dear, departed friend whose loss he would never cease to mourn. The *miser* cares more for money than he does for the satisfaction of his physical needs—and gets immense satisfaction from actual contact with his money, deposit slips, bank books, and other symbols of wealth which he tries to conceal from other people.

The compulsive nonspender forms poor relationships with other people, since he unconsciously fears that they will deprive him of his money. The descending scale of warmth, scope, and frequency of human contacts starts with the conservative and ends with the miser, who often is content to lead a hermit-like existence.

These unconsciously love-hungry, money-hungry men and women set up their interpersonal relationships in a manner which causes their ultimate rejection. Their unconsciously determined notion that it is more blessed to *receive* than to *give* identifies them socially as "chiselers" or "spongers." Rejection reaffirms their belief that no one really cares for them—which is true—and this in turn makes their emotional isolation from other humans more complete than ever.

Most of these people were deprived in their early lives of love and affection, and experienced poverty, punishment, and regimentation. Symbolically, money represents the love, affection, and security which they never had and for which they have an insatiable craving.

Often anything which forcibly dislocates a compulsive nonspending pattern may cause severe anxiety, panic, depression, and many different kinds of psychosomatic illness, as well as a total breakdown in the person's capacity to adapt realistically to even minor economic reverses.

Compulsive nonspenders are especially vulnerable to confidence-men who promise them the only form of love they can understand—a sudden, large increase in monetary reserves at small expense to themselves. When the swindle is consummated, the victims turn with increasing bitterness to an even lower level of disbursement than previously.

(A few persons who originally had emotionally well-balanced uses of money became compulsive nonspenders after having lost their economic resources during the economic depression of 1929.)

C. Compulsive Spending

Emotionally the compulsive spender is comfortable only when he is able immediately to satisfy his slightest desire for spending. Often there is no realistic need for buying either the things or services which he purchases. Some spend their money merely for the sake of spending, and others spend compulsively for specific self-gratifying items, such as antiques, jewelry, clothing, or unusual food. If a compulsive spender is forced to save some of his money, he may become uneasy or even sick until he can resume spending at will.

These people have small, medium, or large incomes. Their main trouble in life is that they can never obtain all the spending money they need. Some work hard to earn huge salaries, and spend everything they make. Others go into debt. Still others have to resort to unethical, immoral, and illegal activities to get the money they require.

There are many emotional reasons for compulsive spending, and many kinds of compulsive spenders. Often a spendthrift gets rid of his money to obtain transient sensual gratification from the power of his money and from what is to him—unconsciously—much more important: to return to a passive-dependent status as a result of self-inflicted poverty. Many such compulsive spenders maintain a reliable economic relationship with a member of the family or a friend, who comes to his financial rescue whenever this help is needed.

The history of many of these compulsive spenders indicates that they were overprotected in their early childhood by an overindulgent parent who guiltily substituted liberal money gifts for love and affection. Usually one parent was strict, but the other one overcompensated for his severity. The child's allowance was constantly augmented by secretly given additional sums from his indulgent parent. The child learned to spend all he had, since this was sure to bring him more money to spend. And at the same time he could punish his parents for not loving him by creating parental anxiety about his rate of spending. The constant replenishment of spending money prevented him from learning to tolerate the frustration of having to make a choice between two purchases. He never learned that money could be saved for future use.

Other compulsive spenders had neither money nor love in childhood. Their selfish spending in adulthood is an unconsciously overdetermined means of giving themselves something akin to love and at the same time creating debts which their relatives have to repay. This spending behavior is a frequent source of domestic trouble when a husband spends money needed for household expenses to gratify his own needs and to punish his wife and children.

Many compulsive spenders like charge accounts and time-payment buying even better than money itself, since this equates to temporarily unlimited spending power. The pleasurable excitement from spending exceeds the pleasure obtained from their purchases.

Many compulsive spenders have such pleasing personalities and glib tongues that it is easy for them to ingratiate themselves with others. If they need money for spending, they borrow without intention of repaying—and frequently victimize the same person over and over again. When this fails, they may have to fall back on their sex-attractiveness to get the money they need for spending. This may necessitate prostitution or marrying a bank-account.

There is the honest type of complusive spender who suffers as he undergoes voluntary periods of great scrimping and saving until he has available the sum he needs. Periodically he goes on a spending binge, enjoying the intense sensual pleasure of being able to buy anything he wants—until his money runs out.

Not all compulsive spenders are willing to work. Some are aggressive, hostile individuals who ultimately acquire their spending money by force. These people are rarely seen in private practice, but often in court. This is the type: He is an immature, sadistic individual, who has little patience for earning a living. He can never earn as much as he thinks he needs. He likes to live as if he were rich. Rather than face the discomfort of holding down a steady job, he flits from one job to another, hoping to find an employer who will give him a high salary. Eventually he gets his money from all sorts of unethical, immoral, and illegal ventures.

He enjoys flashy cars, flashy clothes. But what he likes most is the intense pleasurable excitement of taking money away from those who have. In the process of robbing people, he enjoys beating his victims up—sometimes even murdering them in his assaultive rage. Stealing, armed robbery, procuring, prostitution, gambling, blackmail, dope-peddling, extortion are his kind of crime.

As long as he is successful in his asocial ventures and eludes the law, he has the money and excitement he craves. He has emotional gratification of his unconscious needs, since he has symbolically attacked the parent-surrogate from whom he forcibly wrested the money he wanted.

If caught, tried, and jailed, he is actually supported and protected by the society he has harmed—and these individuals have ambivalent feelings toward incarceration. In a way it gives them a sense of security and belonging. But finally jailing acts as a further stimulus for increased antisocial activity, so that when he has served his sentence he embarks on even more vicious crimes, often culminating in murder. These individuals are sometimes described as having character disorders, as being psychopathic personalities, and some are actually psychotic.

Their history often shows rejecting parents, poverty, upbringing in a slum environment—but not always. Some come from families of high income levels in which strictness was substituted for love.

Some emotionally immature individuals are willing to work hard, but they compulsively spend all their money by giving it on payday to a parent or parent-surrogate, expecting in return to get taken care of in a manner which is symbolically equivalent to that of the passive-dependent child. An unmarried man—or woman—earning an excellent salary may be content to receive for personal use only a token sum of spending money. His parents may buy his clothes, feed him, pay his doctor's bills—and require that he spend most of his time at home keeping them company. If he marries, which he usually does after his parents die, he tries to establish the same type of relationship with his spouse. In essence, these people are willing to spend all their money as soon as they get it to buy a facsimile of the childhood type of emotional security, and when this is attained, they are satisfied.

A number of dreamy individuals who have a rich fantasy life, try to deny their poverty by compulsive spending. They have a certain hauteur which fools unwary creditors. These persons in their youth were often deprived of money and love, and were rejected and punished excessively by their parents. They are recurrently in trouble with the law because they cannot pay for what they buy. Finally, to obtain spending money, they may pass worthless checks, commit petty crimes, gamble, or give themselves sexually for money. As they deteriorate, alcoholism and increasingly prominent schizophrenic reaction patterns appear in their behavior. Many become chronic offenders who fill our city jails. Some finally are institutionalized and treated in mental hospitals. A few even commit crazy murders.

The *narcissistic* compulsive spender may disburse his money for clothes, jewelry, beauty treatments, or plastic surgery. All he is interested in is enhancing his appearance and attracting the admiration of others. The *show-off* spender must have a large audience, since what he enjoys most is astonishing people by the lavishness or unusualness of his spending. He likes to give money to institutions or organizations which will give him the publicity he craves. The *competitive* spender disburses his money to retain social prestige by outspending others in his social group. The *affection-buying* compulsive spender tries to buy love wherever he can bolster up his own feelings of inferiority. His efforts are self-defeating because he often befriends immature individuals who, instead of giving him the affection he craves, are ever-insistent for larger handouts. This compulsive spender often lapses into periodic alcoholism, during which time he throws money away to watch people scramble for it.

Some salesmen and executives who have emotionally well-balanced uses of the money they earn obtain special gratification from compulsive spending of their company's accounts. They enjoy the feeling of being lavish hosts—at someone else's expense.

The self-pitying individual spends compulsively only when he is mildly depressed—sometimes for good reason. At such times, he may feel that no one loves him. He may shower gifts on himself till his spirits improve. I know of several patients who during hospitalization for surgical procedures secretly sent themselves flowers, fruits, and other gifts, with self-directed, self-written, effusive get-well wishes.

Sometimes a woman who has had a quarrel with her husband feels so low that she has to reward herself by buying several expensive hats which she doesn't need, and may never wear. When she makes her purchases, her anger at her husband disappears, as does her depression.

Gamblers are compulsive spenders who get excitement at the prospect of losing what they already have. They basically have the desire for big income with little work. By losing money, they punish themselves for these desires. When they win, they spend money liberally, enjoying particularly the pleasures of alcohol, tobacco, food, and sex.

Bargain hunters are often compulsive spenders, in the sense that they buy things they don't need merely because they are cheap.

The *infantile* spender is a person who literally throws money away. This behavior is normal for infants and very young children. Some alcoholics, psychotics, and senile individuals get gratification from throwing their money away and watching the furor this causes.

D. Indecisive or Fearful Uses of Money

Sometimes an individual has the history of having been so frustrated by his early money experiences that he has developed poor problem-solving ability in relationship to spending money. Usually, no matter how he spent money as a child, he was told he was wrong; and at unpredictable intervals he was punished for making mistakes in his use of money even when he didn't think he had done anything wrong.

In adulthood, he is often a cringing, insecure individual who is afraid to spend the money at his disposal. He wants to please others by the way he spends his money—and buys mainly to please salespeople. He deprives himself of things he wants because he fears that his spending money for this purpose would cause others to ridicule him. He usually is underpaid for his work, fearful of losing his job, and willing to lend others money in an attempt to gain their approval.

All of his money behavior tends to perpetuate his habit of making mistakes in the use of money, and thus further justifies his lack of self-confidence.

E. Denial of Economic Status

Pretended wealth   These people are often ashamed of their origins. Sometimes they come from well-to-do families who have lost their fortunes. They spend money to make others feel that they are wealthy, hoping thereby to attract genuinely wealthy people to them in order to gain fair or unfair advantage. Matrimony is often the object of such people who want to "better" themselves. Of course, they are seriously limited by their lack of funds, and must resort to subterfuge or illegality to maintain their front.

Pretended poverty   These individuals want to be pitied and have a passive-dependent status. They want to be given handouts so that they can conserve their own money. They secretly enjoy the potential power of their hidden monetary reserves. Many have paranoid fears that mysterious enemies are threatening to deprive them of their wealth. They believe that by seeming to be poor they will be protected against robbery. They distrust banks and often hide their money on their persons or in their homes. They are self-punitive and self-denying.

F. Emotional Uses of Money as Rewards

The possessor of money can manipulate the behavior of other human beings for constructive or destructive purposes through the use of monetary rewards.

When used constructively, monetary rewards encourage socially desirable activities in individuals and groups. Such a reward may reinforce desirable behavior traits in a child. It keeps adults at their daily work. It can be used to improve education, raise standards of living, improve health and welfare, and encourage creative activities in the arts and sciences. The proper uses of monetary rewards can even become an effective way of helping mentally sick patients to become rehabilitated. (In an excellent study, *Dr. Peter A. Peffer* has given a concise picture of the remarkable benefits which occur when properly selected patients in a mental institution are permitted to work for money rewards.)

Unfortunately, monetary rewards can also be used destructively to encourage unethical, illegal, or immoral activity. Bribery is often used to break down an individual's resistance to antisocial acts—and as the sum involved becomes large enough, many previously upright people succumb to the temptation. This leads to the cynical idea that every man has his price. The point of breakdown in terms of dollars and cents is a measure of the sturdiness of an individual's ethical and moral training, and of the strength of his conscience in opposing his desire for illegitimate economic gain.

G. Emotionally Punitive Uses of Money

Some parents control their adult children by threatening to disinherit them for disobedience. Many a passive-dependent personality will allow himself to be controlled in this way.

Sometimes gifts of money are used to disrupt the normal incentives conducive to competitive work behavior.

A grandparent may attempt to wean a grandchild's affections away from his parents by plying him with money and with luxuries that money buys. This struggle for dominance favors the moneyed grandparent and permits him to punish his own children, when symbolically buying the love and affection of his grandchildren.

A girl who learned that her father had a mistress, suddenly went on spending sprees, unconsciously desiring to punish her father and at the same time to rectify symbolically the wrong done to her mother. She opened many new charge accounts and bought expensive gifts for her mother which were charged to her father.

H. Charitable Uses

Many give to charity because they believe it is the duty of those who have money to share it with the needy or the sick. Some do so to gain the approval of others, and to get publicity for themselves. Many give to charity to assuage their feelings of guilt.

I. Guilty Uses

An individual may consciously or unconsciously wish to make symbolic or actual restitution for some real or imagined antisocial act he has committed. To do so, he may give small or large sums of money to a charity, institution, or individual—or he may even pay some of his evaded back taxes. He may do this anonymously, or he may want to have his name associated with the gift or restitution even though no one suspects his motivation.

J. Fetish and Ritual Uses

Some particular coin or sum of paper money may be used as a good-luck piece, and the individual's self-reliance and peace of mind seem contingent on his having the monetary fetish always with him. Sometimes the individual associates a particularly auspicious event with having this money—including having found it originally. At other times a person may carry a specific, sufficiently large sum of money to ward off possible recurrence of a previously embarrassing situation which occurred when he lacked sufficient funds for some particular purpose.

Some people are impelled to count their money repeatedly in times of stress. When the crisis in their lives is solved in a manner acceptable to them, they no longer have the need to count their money. . . .

L. [Money Uses by] Older People

Older people may find it increasingly difficult to manage successfully their economic resources, and often become emotionally disturbed when they have to solve even minor problems relating to the use of money.

Sometimes an older person of this sort desires to assume a passive-dependent relationship with others, who take over his care so that he will not need to concern himself with money matters. Such an individual may be willing to turn over all his economic resources to others in return for lifelong care.

Some older people become anxious, fearful, and depressed if they have to relinquish control of their funds to others. These people have always enjoyed the power money gave them, and even though others manage their affairs, they like to feel that they always make their own final decisions.

Some senile individuals develop intense fear reactions when they imagine that their families are trying to do away with them, either to save expenses or gain control of their funds. These fears may in turn inspire self-defensive behavior which is difficult to manage in the family setting.

A few older people may literally throw their money away, sign blank checks, or give gifts to strangers. They may make punitive wills disinheriting children or relatives, for real or fancied slights.

Some older people who are well-off financially feel so insecure that they are impelled to hoard their resources to the point of miserliness. Others suddenly increase their scale of spending in order to enjoy in their declining years many of the pleasures and luxuries they formerly denied themselves.

M. Psychotics

The first indication of the breakdown in reality function of an adult may be his inappropriate uses of money or money transactions.

An elated or manic individual is a wild person in his spending. His interest jumps from one thing to another, with breaks in the continuity of his thinking. He tends to buy everything big, but even before a deal is consummated he is interested in carrying out some other money transaction. He cannot be induced by pleas of family or friends to be more circumspect in his spending. In fact, this angers him and may increase the rate of his disbursement of money. Sexual promiscuity, heavy eating and drinking are an important part of his spending orgies. As long as his income and spending are in equilibrium, he is not likely to have legal difficulties. Occasionally during a manic phase a man may launch a successful business project. More often he merely dissipates his resources. He may recover from his manic phase with or without treatment, and may again have better-balanced uses of money, perhaps becoming economy-minded. Or he may go into a depressive phase.

The depressed spender may spend little or nothing, and becomes more depressed with every expenditure. Sometimes, immediately before depression sets in, the patient guiltily uses some of his money to make symbolic restitution for his real or fancied anti-social acts. The depressed individual cannot continue working and earning. He feels impoverished, unworthy and unloved, and may often refuse to eat. A few seem to equate money to excreta or dirt. If the depressed individual recovers spontaneously or through therapy, he will gradually redevelop his prepsychotic uses of money.

The paranoid may spend money in a manner which indicates that he thinks someone may overcharge or rob him. He may secrete money in various pockets, in shoes, sew it into secret hiding places in his outer clothes or underwear. His spending is greatly restricted, since he fears that any display of his buying power may lead to attacks from powerful imaginary enemies. As paranoid delusions get more fixed, he is less able to get along with other people. Some emotionally sick people in this group become frankly schizophrenic paranoids.

The schizophrenic individual has erratic uses of money. He may have no recollection of what he does with his money, and may appear indifferent to the consequences of what he does with it. He may buy an expensive and wholly useful object which he adores—or may buy a piece of junk and adore it just as much. He may give money to a person whom he later assaults and kills. Or he may attack and rob a stranger. His spending behavior is unpredictable, and without recognizable reality function. Those schizophrenics in remission try to maintain a passive-dependent relationship to some person whose advice about money matters they try to follow. But even so, inexplicable expenditures occur.

Beginning with an individual's early life experiences, his use of money becomes subject to various instinctual, emotional, and intellectual reactions which ultimately lead either to socially acceptable or unacceptable money behavior. Aberrant money behavior, in turn, may create many varieties of psychosomatic illness. Moreover, mental illness may cause an individual to develop inappropriate uses of money.

Money-sickness is a clinically evident disturbance in the individual's psychosomatic health which is initiated by his excessive reaction to the stress of psycho-economic problems. It may take such forms as: headaches, anxiety states, hysterical paralysis, obsessional reaction patterns, panic reactions, depression, behavior disorders, and dysfunctions of gastrointestinal, cardio-respiratory and musculoskeletal systems.

One reason why money-sickness is not often detected is that most doctors have not been interested in studying the psycho-economic behavior of individuals. A doctor himself may have unresolved emotional problems regarding his own uses of money which unconsciously prevent him from recognizing or investigating his patient's abnormal psycho-economic behavior. He may consider it indelicate or unnecessary to ask how his patient uses money, and he certainly doesn't want to offend his patient, who may resent and misinterpret such questions as being "too personal." For these reasons, a doctor is usually content to send his bill and receive payment for his services without looking further into the psycho-economic processes of his patient. Unless the patient spontaneously talks about his financial problems during therapy sessions, this matter may never be explored. Instead, the patient may talk interminably about symptoms, troubled interpersonal relations, unhappy sex life, and dreams—all of which may be secondary to his psycho-economic problems.

In instances of money-sickness, the doctor cannot be his patient's banker or financial advisor. But he can help direct his patient's attention to the money-roots of his stressful contemporary life problems. When good rapport between patient and therapist can be established, it is surprising how rapidly progress toward recovery can be made by discussing the broad money problems of the patient at the very start of treatment. If the patient can be helped to get a new viewpoint and gain insight into the nature of his money problems and how these affect him psychosomatically, he is often able to develop good solutions leading to a cure of his basic emotional problems. This may require a change in job, a change in saving, borrowing, lending, or spending habits, a change in financial relations with members of his family, a change in his economic goals—or any other type of appropriate psycho-economic adjustment.

The psycho-economic aspects of the patient's emotional disorder must always be considered by the doctor in relation to other noxious causes which may simultaneously contribute to ill-health. The doctor should try to evaluate all the factors contributing to his patient's ill-health, so that these will appear in proper perspective and be given proper weight in the treatment of the patient as a person.

But instead of focusing all of our attention on diagnosis and treatment alone, our goal should also be prevention of the development of abnormal psycho-economic patterns of behavior in children. This can be done by helping parents to understand and resolve their own psycho-economic problems and to learn how to help their children to develop healthy patterns of money behavior.

If we could be successful in these undertakings, we might find that our world would be a much better place to live in—not only because of improvement in individual health, but also because there would be a corresponding resolution of many of the unsolved sociologic problems which plague us today. . . .

After Reading

Write a second journal entry in which you consider the extent to which you are "emotionally balanced" in the way you deal with money. Explore, too, the occasions or times in your life when you have been a compulsive spender or a compulsive nonspender, a person who uses money as a fetish or as an emotional punishment, and so on. Consider any or all of the categories Kaufman presents. This entry will be shared with the class only if you desire. Try writing for two to three pages.

Before Reading

Now that you have expressed your thoughts about yourself as an individual user of money and begun to consider your own financial situation, read John Ciardi's column "Is Everybody Happy?" for his view of money and happiness.

Is Everybody Happy?

John Ciardi

The right to pursue happiness is issued to Americans with their birth certificates, but no one seems quite sure which way it ran. It may be we are issued a hunting license but offered no game. Jonathan Swift seemed to think so when he attacked the idea of happiness as "the possession of being well-deceived," the felicity of being "a fool among knaves." For Swift saw society as Vanity Fair, the land of false goals.

It is, of course, un-American to think in terms of fools and knaves. We do, however, seem to be dedicated to the idea of buying our way to happiness. We shall all have made it to Heaven when we possess enough.

And at the same time the forces of American commercialism are hugely dedicated to making us deliberately unhappy. Advertising is one of our major industries, and advertising exists not to satisfy desires but to create them—and to create them faster than any man's budget can satisfy them. For that matter, our whole economy is based on a dedicated insatiability. We are taught that to possess is to be happy, and then we are made to want. We are even told it is our duty to want. It was only a few years ago, to cite a single example, that car dealers across the country were flying banners that read "You Auto Buy Now." They were calling upon Americans, as an act approaching patriotism, to buy at once, with money they did not have, automobiles they did not really need, and which they would be required to grow tired of by the time the next year's models were released.

Or look at any of the women's magazines. There, as Bernard DeVoto once pointed out, advertising begins as poetry in the front pages and ends as pharmacopoeia and therapy in the back pages. The poetry of the front matter is the dream of perfect beauty. This is the baby skin that must be hers. These, the flawless teeth. This, the perfumed breath she must exhale. This, the sixteen-year-old figure she must display at forty, at fifty, at sixty, and forever.

Once past the vaguely uplifting fiction and feature articles, the reader finds the other face of the dream in the back matter. This is the harness into which Mother must strap herself in order to display that perfect figure. These, the chin straps she must sleep in. This is the salve that restores all, this is her laxative, these are the tablets that melt away fat, these are the hormones of perpetual youth, these are the stockings that hide varicose veins.

Obviously no half-sane person can be completely persuaded either by such poetry or by such pharmacopoeia and orthopedics. Yet someone is obviously trying to buy the dream as offered and spending billions every year in the attempt. Clearly the happiness-market is not running out of customers, but what is it trying to buy?

The idea "happiness," to be sure, will not sit still for easy definition: the best one can do is try to set some extremes to the idea and then work in toward the middle. To think of happiness as acquisitive and competitive will do to set the materialistic extreme. To think of it as the idea one senses in, say, a holy man of India will do to set the spiritual extreme. That holy man's idea of happiness is in needing nothing from outside himself. In wanting nothing, he lacks nothing. He sits immobile, rapt in contemplation, free even of his own body. Or nearly free of it. If devout admirers bring him food he eats it; if not, he starves indifferently. Why be concerned? What is physical is an illusion to him. Contemplation is his joy and he achieves it through a fantastically demanding discipline, the accomplishment of which is itself a joy within him.

Is he a happy man? Perhaps his happiness is only another sort of illusion. But who can take it from him? And who will dare say it is more illusory than happiness on the installment plan.

But, perhaps because I am Western, I doubt such catatonic happiness, as I doubt the dreams of the happiness-market. What is certain is that his way of happiness would be torture to almost any Western man. Yet these extremes will still serve to frame the area within which all of us must find some sort of balance. Thoreau—a creature of both Eastern and Western thought—had his own firm sense of that balance. His aim was to save on the low levels in order to spend on the high.

Possession for its own sake or in competition with the rest of the neighborhood would have been Thoreau's idea of the low levels. The active discipline of heightening one's perception of what is enduring in nature would have been his idea of the high. What he saved from the low was time and effort he could spend on the high. Thoreau certainly disapproved of starvation, but he would put into feeding himself only as much effort as would keep him functioning for more important efforts.

Effort is the gist of it. There is no happiness except as we take on life-engaging difficulties. Short of the impossible, as Yeats put it, the satisfactions we get from a lifetime depend on how high we choose our difficulties. Robert Frost was thinking in something like the same terms when he spoke of "The pleasure of taking pains." The mortal flaw in the advertised version of happiness is in the fact that it purports to be effortless.

We demand difficulty even in our games. We demand it because without difficulty there can be no game. A game is a way of making something hard for the fun of it. The rules of the game are an arbitrary imposition of difficulty. When the spoilsport ruins the fun, he always does so by refusing to play by the rules. It is easier to win at chess if you are free, at your pleasure, to change the wholly arbitrary rules, but the fun is in winning within the rules. No difficulty, no fun.

The buyers and sellers at the happiness-market seem too often to have lost their sense of the pleasure of difficulty. Heaven knows what they are playing, but it seems a dull game. And the Indian holy man seems dull to us, I suppose, because he seems to be refusing to play anything at all. The Western weakness may be in the illusion that happiness can be bought. Perhaps the Eastern weakness is in the idea that there is such a thing as perfect (and therefore static) happiness.

Happiness is never more than partial. There are no pure states of mankind. Whatever else happiness may be, it is neither in having nor in being, but in becoming. What the Founding Fathers declared for us as an inherent right, we should do well to remember, was not happiness but the *pursuit* of happiness. What they might have underlined, could they have foreseen the happiness-market, is the cardinal fact that happiness is in the pursuit itself, in the meaningful pursuit of what is life-engaging and life-revealing, which is to say, in the idea of *becoming*. A nation is not measured by what it possesses or wants to possess, but by what it wants to become.

By all means let the happiness-market sell us minor satisfactions and even minor follies so long as we keep them in scale and buy them out of spiritual change. I am no customer for either puritanism or asceticism. But drop any real spiritual capital at those bazaars, and what you come home to will be your own poorhouse.

After Reading

Ciardi states that "the mortal flaw in the advertised version of happiness is in the fact that it purports to be effortless. . . . Happiness . . . is neither in having nor in being, but in becoming." He refers to the "pleasure of difficulty" as opposed to the buying of easy happiness. Write an entry in your journal in which you try to delineate your current sense of happiness and the part money plays in that. As a college student, how much money do you require to achieve happiness? Exclude the money you or someone pays for tuition, but include all other money you feel you need. Try to indicate the items that you feel are necessary and those that are luxuries for you. Share this entry only if you wish.

Before Reading

Before reading the following excerpts from Thoreau's *Walden,* discuss in class the kinds of items or expenses that some people consider necessities and luxuries. How much discrepancy is there among class members as to what is necessary and what is luxurious?

Economy

Henry David Thoreau

When I wrote the following pages, or rather the bulk of them, I lived alone, in the woods, a mile from any neighbor, in a house which I had built myself, on the shore of Walden Pond, in Concord, Massachusetts, and earned my living by the labor of my hands only. I lived there two years and two months. At present I am a sojourner in civilized life again.

I should not obtrude my affairs so much on the notice of my readers if very particular inquiries had not been made by my townsmen concerning my mode of life, which some would call impertinent, though they do not appear to me at all impertinent, but, considering the circumstances, very natural and pertinent. Some have asked what I got to eat; if I did not feel lonesome; if I was not afraid; and the like. Others have been curious to learn what portion of my income I devoted to charitable purposes; and some, who have large families, how many poor children I maintained. I will therefore ask those of my readers who feel no particular interest in me to pardon me if I undertake to answer some of these questions in this book. In most books, the *I,* or first person, is omitted; in this it will be retained; that, in respect to egotism, is the main difference. We commonly do not remember that it is, after all, always the first person that is speaking. I should not talk so much about myself if there were anybody else whom I knew as well. Unfortunately, I am confined to this theme by the narrowness of my experience. Moreover, I, on my side, require of every writer, first or last, a simple and sincere account of his own life, and not merely what he has heard of other men's lives; some such account as he would send to his kindred from a distant land; for if he has lived sincerely, it must have been in a distant land to me. Perhaps these pages are more particularly addressed to poor students. As for the rest of my readers, they will accept such portions as apply to them. I trust that none will stretch the seams in putting on the coat, for it may do good service to him who it fits. . . .

Some of you, we all know, are poor, find it hard to live, are sometimes, as it were, gasping for breath. I have no doubt that some of you who read this book are unable to pay for all the dinners which you have actually eaten, or for the coats and shoes which are fast wearing or are already worn out, and have come to this page to spend borrowed or stolen time, robbing your creditors of an hour. It is very evident what mean and sneaking lives many of you live, for my sight has been whetted by experience; always on the limits, trying to get into business and trying to get out of debt, a very ancient slough, called by the Latins *aes alienum,* another's brass, for some of their coins were made of brass; still living, and dying, and buried by this other's brass; always promising to pay, promising to pay, tomorrow, and dying today, insolvent;

Excerpted from the essay "Economy" in *Walden* by Henry David Thoreau.

seeking to curry favor, to get custom, by how many modes, only not state-prison of-fenses; lying, flattering, voting, contracting yourselves into a nutshell of civility, or dilat-ing into an atmosphere of thin and vaporous generosity, that you may persuade your neighbor to let you make his shoes, or his hat, or his coat, or his carriage, or import his groceries for him; making yourselves sick, that you may lay up something against a sick day, something to be tucked way in an old chest, or in a stocking behind the plastering, or, more safely, in the brick bank; no matter where, no matter how much or how little. . . .

One farmer says to me, "You cannot live on vegetable food solely, for it furnishes nothing to make bones with"; and so he religiously devotes a part of his day to supply-ing his system with the raw material of bones; walking all the while he talks behind his oxen, which, with vegetable-made bones, jerk him and his lumbering plough along in spite of every obstacle. Some things are really necessaries of life in some circles, the most helpless and diseased, which in others are luxuries merely, and in others still are entirely unknown.

. . . It would be some advantage to live a primitive and frontier life, though in the midst of an outward civilization, if only to learn what are the gross necessaries of life and what methods have been taken to obtain them; or even to look over the old day-books of the merchants, to see what it was that men most commonly bought at the stores, what they stored, that is, what are the grossest groceries. For the improvements of ages have had but little influence on the essential laws of man's existence: as our skeletons, probably, are not to be distinguished from those of our ancestors.

By the words, *necessary of life,* I mean whatever, of all that man obtains by his own exertions, has been from the first, or from long use has become, so important to human life that few, if any, whether from savageness, or poverty, or philosophy, ever attempt to do without it. To many creatures there is in this sense but one necessary of life, Food. To the bison of the prairie it is a few inches of palatable grass, with water to drink; unless he seeks the Shelter of the forest or the mountain's shadow. None of the brute creation requires more than Food and Shelter. The necessaries of life for man in this climate may, accurately enough, be described under the several heads of Food, Shelter, Clothing, and Fuel; for not till we have secured these are we prepared to entertain the true problems of life with freedom and a prospect of success. . . .

Most of the luxuries, and many of the so called comforts of life, are not only not indispensable, but positive hinderances to the elevation of mankind. With respect to luxuries and comforts, the wisest have ever lived a more simple and meagre life than the poor. The ancient philosophers, Chinese, Hindoo, Persian, and Greek, were a class than which none has been poorer in outward riches, none so rich in inward. We know not much about them. It is remarkable that *we* know so much of them as we do. The same is true of the more modern reformers and benefactors of their race. None can be an impartial or wise observer of human life but from the vantage ground of what *we* should call voluntary poverty. Of a life of luxury the fruit is luxury, whether in agricul-ture, or commerce, or literature, or art. There are nowadays professors of philosophy, but not philosophers. Yet it is admirable to profess because it was once admirable to live. To be a philosopher is not merely to have subtle thoughts, nor even to found a school, but so to love wisdom as to live according to its dictates, a life of simplicity, independence, magnanimity, and trust. It is to solve some of the problems of life, not only theoretically, but practically. The success of great scholars and thinkers is com-monly a courtier-like success, not kingly, not manly. They make shift to live merely by conformity, practically as their fathers did, and are in no sense the progenitors of a nobler race of men. But why do men degenerate ever? What makes families run out?

What is the nature of the luxury which enervates and destroys nations? Are we sure that there is none of it in our own lives? The philosopher is in advance of his age even in the outward form of his life. He is not fed, sheltered, clothed, warmed, like his contemporaries. How can a man be a philosopher and not maintain his vital heat by better methods than other men?

When a man is warmed by the several modes which I have described, what does he want next? Surely not more warmth of the same kind, as more and richer food, larger and more splendid houses, finer and more abundant clothing, more numerous incessant and hotter fires, and the like. When he has obtained those things which are necessary to life, there is another alternative than to obtain the superfluities; and that is, to adventure on life now, his vacation from humbler toil having commenced. . . .

A man who has at length found something to do will not need to get a new suit to do it in. For him the old will do, that has lain dusty in the garret for an indeterminate period. Old shoes will serve a hero longer than they have served his valet—if a hero ever has a valet—bare feet are older than shoes, and he can make them do. Only they who go to soirées and legislative halls must have new coats, coats to change as often as the man changes in them. But if my jacket and trousers, my hat and shoes, are fit to worship God in, they will do; will they not? Who ever saw his old clothes,—his old coat, actually worn out, resolved into its primitive elements, so that it was not a deed of charity to bestow it on some poor boy, by him perchance to be bestowed on some poorer still, shall we say richer, who could do with less? I say, beware of all enterprises that require new clothes, and not rather a new wearer of clothes. If there is not a new man, how can the new clothes be made to fit? If you have any enterprise before you, try it in your old clothes. All men want, not something to *do with,* but something to *do,* or rather something to be. . . .

I thus found that the student who wishes for a shelter can obtain one for a lifetime at an expense not greater than the rent which he now pays annually. If I seem to boast more than is becoming, my excuse is that I brag for humanity rather than for myself; and my shortcomings and inconsistencies do not affect the truth of my statement. Notwithstanding much cant and hypocrisy,—chaff which I find it difficult to separate from my wheat, but for which I am as sorry as any man,—I will breathe freely and stretch myself in this respect, it is such a relief to both the moral and physical system; and I am resolved that I will not through humility become the devil's attorney. I will endeavor to speak a good word for the truth. At Cambridge College the mere rent of a student's room, which is only a little larger than my own, is thirty dollars each year, though the corporation had the advantage of building thirty-two side by side and under one roof, and the occupant suffers the inconvenience of many and noisy neighbors, and perhaps a residence in the fourth story. I cannot but think that if we had more true wisdom in these respects, not only less education would be needed, because, forsooth, more would already have been acquired, but the pecuniary expense of getting an education would in a great measure vanish. These conveniences which the student requires at Cambridge or elsewhere cost him or somebody else ten times as great a sacrifice of life as they would with proper management on both sides. Those things for which the most money is demanded are never the things which the student most wants. Tuition, for instance, is an important item in the term bill, while for the far more valuable education which he gets by associating with the most cultivated of his contemporaries no charge is made. . . .

This spending of the best part of one's life earning money in order to enjoy a questionable liberty, during the least valuable part of it, reminds me of the Englishman who went to India to make a fortune first, in order that he might return to England and live the life of a poet. He should have gone up garret at once. "What!" exclaim a million Irishmen starting up from all the shanties in the land, "is not this railroad which we have built a good thing?" Yes, I answer, *comparatively* good, that is, you might have done worse; but I wish, as you are brothers of mine, that you could have spent your time better than digging in this dirt. . . .

There is a certain class of unbelievers who sometimes ask me such questions as, if I think that I can live on vegetable food alone and to strike at the root of the matter at once,—for the root is faith,—I am accustomed to answer such, that I can live on board nails. If they cannot understand that, they cannot understand much that I have to say. For my part, I am glad to hear of experiments of this kind being tried; as that a young man tried for a fortnight to live on hard, raw corn on the ear using his teeth for all mortar. The squirrel tribe tried the same and succeeded. The human race is interested in these experiments, though a few old women who are incapacitated for them, or who own their thirds in mills, may be alarmed.

After Reading

In your journal respond to any of the excerpts of Thoreau. Choose one that has particular meaning for you at the present time. You might want to explore his comments on the meaning of necessities and luxuries. You might want to argue with Thoreau's views or explain to him how times have changed. Or you might simply write whatever the passage makes you think of. Make this entry at least one page long. Share this entry with your class.

Now review the Kaufman article and what you have learned about Thoreau's attitudes toward money from the excerpts you have read and from others in your class. Share ideas about how Kaufman's categories of money users might relate to Thoreau's ideas.

Before Reading

Naomi Wolf, who graduated from Yale University in the spring of 1984, poses an interesting question about her own experience at the university where she found an "invisible line" between herself and other, more well-to-do students. Make some notes in your journal about any situation you have ever been in when you felt out of place either because others had more money than you or less. How did you cope? These notes will be shared *only if you wish.*

The Psychic Expense of an Elitist Campus

Naomi Wolf

It didn't take long to feel the invisible line. It was the first frantic week of freshman year, and my new friends and I were crowded around a solid oak table in the dining hall, filling each other in, creating for each other and ourselves the histories and identities that were so important in that new place. All around me were images, textures, extravagances I'd never imagined: the light bearing down from huge, mock-Gothic windows; moose heads, crested china, formal portraits, even the abundance of flowers, wine, the cuts of meat we never had at home. My new friends seemed all to have gone to the same prep schools, and we all laughed at the antics and hazards of private school life—the "three-feet-on-the-floor" rule, the debauched graduation parties. I began to tell the story of my own graduation from a San Francisco public school, with a thousand classmates in red rayon robes filing across the Cow Palace, a cavernous space used for livestock shows that still smelled of a thousand prize heifers. The conversation stopped. I'd thought it was a laugh; here, apparently, it wasn't so funny.

The invisible line was new and hard for me to understand. Perhaps if I'd come from a working-class background, I'd have felt at once that kind of pride. But I was a teacher's daughter, raised to believe in the classlessness of the intellect. My family wasn't poor enough to be defiant, or wealthy enough to forget about money; not ethnic enough to be Ethnic, but too Jewish to be anything else. No injustices grave enough to rally round, nor the freedom of unquestioned security. It was my need for carefulness—at such a careless place—that I felt so acutely throughout my four years.

I looked around and saw that I wasn't the only one. I also saw that class pressure had its casualties; kids who felt the need to camouflage, or felt shame at where they came from and what their parents did. I saw it was a great temptation—it was also too expensive as well as being psychic bad news. And the institution too often fell short of its own ideal of being a great intellectual equalizer, a "meritocracy." It was frustrating to see that aid students who worked 20 hours a week in the kitchen were competing with those who could afford that much more study time; that the appealing summer internships were really only open to those who didn't have to work summers to pay tuition. Suddenly it was my home, that humming feudal village: vast lawns and their gardeners; formal receptions with red-jacketed black bartenders; liquor flowing from gold-labeled bottles and janitors cleaning up the inevitable vomit in the courtyards the morning after. We all lived in it together, but some of us were struggling with the upkeep payments. And some were not.

And I was struggling with the guises—and disguises—that seemed bound to express a relationship to those payments. My parents had packed me off with three Sears buttondown oxford shirts, the likes of which I had never worn in my life. We took a gamble that that was standard. Pink, blue, yellow; polyester blend. I never unpacked them. It looked as if you went all the way, or you didn't go at all. "All the way" was a uniform with a code so petrified and exquisite that I couldn't begin to consider it—"rich girl" hair, skin, teeth. Blunt "classic" cuts. I let my hair get wilder and started to wear costumes, to make believe and invent. Whatever came my way, cheap or free. I went Baroque; fake everything. Fake fur, rhinestones, and secondhand satin and tweed on top of my mother's 1960s *shmattas*. If I could never be perfectly well bred, I could certainly be perfectly brash. And the disguises went both ways: the Bloomingdale's prole look was its own statement, but on Parents' Weekend, when the station wagons and Labradors arrived, Talbot's Fair Isles and the family pearls came out of the closet.

Playing that way was the easy part; the harder part was what you might expect. Jealousy, I was discovering, could be as crippling as bitterness. But sometimes anger is appropriate: a callous or ignorant comment deserves no justification. I remember mentioning my worry about paying tuition to a classmate, who responded, "Oh, I'd love to be poor. It would be so romantic." It was a drag to be teased because I'd never heard of the Vineyard, and I got tired of explaining why I didn't speak French. The assumptions were often ill-thought-out, rather than mean spirited. I knew of a working-class freshwoman who was asked to pay a share of the new couch that her suitemates had decided to buy; feeling too ashamed to confess that she simply didn't have the money, she wrote them an explanation in the college daily. "I can't afford it" can be one of the hardest phrases to say when you're in college—and also one of the most necessary. I was lucky to have found a group of friends who were mature enough to respect that.

And sometimes I had to shake myself out of my own embarrassment to simply take care of business: to apply for endless grants and scholarships, which added the pressure of having to understand my transcript in economic terms to the burden of knowing what my parents were sacrificing to keep me here. Worst of all was the dreaded annual conference with the Financial Aid Overlord to explain why, in fact, my family was not as well off as we were expected to be. *Charlatan!* I could hear the portraits above me murmur.

Year by year, I saw how being unmoneyed at a moneyed institution tended to force a dichotomy: either you got radical fast (realizing that the wrought-iron gates didn't separate you in any material way from the problems of the city beyond them—that the gates were part of the problem) or you gave in and got over, imitating and accumulating.

Four years later, we were sitting again around a table, discussing the news story about a young black man who had talked himself into the homes and lives of New York's "best" families. He'd done this by claiming to be Sidney Poitier's Andover- and Harvard-educated son. My friends—whose families had been taken in—were laughing at the absurdity of the story: "I wonder how he thought he'd get away with it!" As I laughed with them from "inside" the wrought-iron gates, I felt suddenly uneasy. Boy, I thought, he must have wanted to get in pretty bad. And I was there, with him, in the night outside, looking up at the bright arched windows, looking in.

After Reading

Generate a list of questions that you would like to ask Wolf if you could have a conversation with her. Three to four questions would be suitable, but list more if you choose. Be sure to avoid questions that can be answered with *yes* or *no*. Use questions that ask the *hows* and *whys*. When you have generated your list, exchange your questions with a classmate and in writing respond to that person's questions as if you were Wolf. You may not have enough material in the article to be at all sure how the author would respond. You are assuming her role—try to respond as you think she might. Share these questions and responses in group or class discussion.

No doubt, in your discussion you touched on the issue of what is a necessity and what is a luxury for college students. The writing assignment coming up invites you to consider this issue in more detail.

Assignment

The faculty sponsors of the newspaper at your high school have asked you to write an open letter to students telling what, beyond tuition, it costs to live as a student at your college or university. The sponsors want information in the article about books, rent on or off campus, transportation to and from campus, food, clothes, entertainment, and so on, but they also want you to help the students to think about how much they as individuals *need*. A student could *live* on macaroni in a room with a hot plate and a bare light bulb; he or she could check out all textbooks from a library and never attend an athletic event or concert. In this way, expenditures could be very small indeed, but how many students could *afford* emotionally or psychologically to live this way? If designer clothes are considered necessary, expenditures would certainly be greater. What need is met with such purchases? Your job in writing the open letter to high school students is to suggest how much different life styles cost at your university and what is gained and lost with each one. You may want to use yourself as an example. Your letter should be formal, suitable for publication, and readable by high school students. Though it may ultimately be cut for space considerations, the letter will be the featured piece in one issue of the newspaper and should range from 750 to 1000 words.

Your preparation for this writing assignment should probably begin with your review of your journal entries and the readings in this chapter to remind yourself of your and others' attitudes toward money and its value. Then a detailed listing of your expenses on a weekly basis will provide you with a starting point for thinking about the content of your letter. Use any other prewriting strategies that seem appropriate. Now write the first draft of your letter. The next section of this chapter will help you improve this draft.

REVISING

Writer-Based Revision

Except for simple notes, personal letters, and some journal entries, nearly everything you write will need revision. You may find it helpful to think of two kinds of revision: *writer-based* and *reader-based*.* If you are doing *writer-based revision,* you are changing your draft so that it reflects what you really want to say. When you deal with complex material, you cannot sort it out in your head. Writing some drafts is the best way to sharpen your understanding of the material and discover what you think about it and want to say. There is great value in stopping often as you draft to read over what you have written. Some drafts are never finished because you get so far along and then realize that you no longer believe in your main idea. You rethink your main idea and begin a new draft. Or sometimes it is just a paragraph or two you cross out and rewrite; sometimes it is just the last sentence you wrote. Successful writers produce messy drafts, with much scratched out, lines written between the lines and in the margin, arrows going from one paragraph to another, and notes like "here insert paragraph on back of page." The following is the first draft of an article by a student, Mike, who was invited to write for the campus paper on the question, "Should society censor pornography?"

---

*Linda Flower, *Problem-Solving Strategies for Writing,* 2nd ed. (San Diego: Harcourt Brace Jovanovich, 1985).

I oppose censorship because it is a basic American right
to read what we please. Censorship and blue laws only
drive pornography underground; they don't end it.

When Mike had written this much he realized that it did not say exactly what
he meant, and he began again.

              very disturbed
    Although I am ~~worried~~ by the research indicating

that pornography leads to an increase in violent crimes
               not yet willing
against women, I am ~~unwilling~~ to support censorship as a

solution to this problem. I fear that censorship will

only drive pornography underground. First, we should try

to educate the public so that they know that pornography

is based on the debasement of women and promotes violent

crime. We need to make people realize that pornography

is not just harmless racy entertainment that only old-
                  object to
fashioned moralists ~~dislike~~. People say we all should

have the right to read anything we choose. It is true

that the first amendment protects free speech. Many peo-

ple say it's no one else's business what anyone else

reads. But pornography featuring children <u>does</u> involve

people (the children) who don't have a choice in the

matter.

    In 1983 an amendment defining pornography and making

it a civil rights violation was passed by the Minneapo-

lis City Council, but it was vetoed by the mayor. None-

theless, Indianapolis used the amendment as a model for

its own legislation, which eventually passed. But law is

```
not the best answer. First we should make a real effort

to make people realize that to think porn is OK is to

think violence and exploitation are OK.
```

Mike realized as he began his first draft that he was on his way to saying "I oppose censorship despite my feelings about pornography." As he thought about it, he realized that such a statement did not represent his feelings exactly. He then began again, this time focusing on his case against pornography, suggesting education as a better solution than censorship, but not finally closing the door on censorship as an option. The second draft represents his feelings much more accurately. Notice that even as he wrote this second draft he revised it, changing "worried" to "very disturbed" for example, because the latter more accurately describes how he feels.

Reader-Based Revision

When you have a draft that says what you want to say, you can concentrate on preparing it for your reader. You first thought about your reader in the prewriting stage when you asked questions like, "What kind of people am I writing to?" "How do they feel about the subject?" and "What do they need to know?" When you drafted, you thought about your readers as you decided on your organization and asked yourself what kind of words and sentences would be appropriate. When you do reader-based revision, you check on how well you have acted on the answers to these questions. More specifically, you may ask yourself the following questions:

1. Did I give my readers the material they need in order to do (or think or feel) what I meant them to?
2. How will my tone affect my readers? Is it too flippant? Too serious?
3. How might the readers answer me when they've finished reading?
4. Is my paper so long that readers won't persevere to the end? If so, is there anything I can cut?
5. Will the readers be certain to see how each paragraph is related to the one before and after it and why I put them in this order?
6. Is my paper dull?
7. Is there any way my readers can miss my point?
8. Is there any way someone could misinterpret what I'm saying?
9. Have I used any words that may have a connotation I do not intend?

Notice that we began with questions focusing on what material is given and how effective it is for the writer's audience and purpose, the next questions center on the organization, and the last questions focus on sentence structure and word choice. It makes sense to divide the job of reader-based revising into these three large divisions (what points are made, how are they developed and organized, how effective are the words and sentences) and to tend to each in a separate reading. Begin with a check on what material you have included. Then when you feel confident about what point you will make, you can settle on ways to develop and organize it. Only when you are pleased with your development or organization is it worth your while to improve sentence structure and word choice. If you follow this system, you will be revising your paper three times, looking in each revision at a different aspect of its effect on your readers.

Sometimes it is enough just to ask these questions and, based on your answers, make changes in your draft. You may, for example, decide that your paper is too long and that there is a section you can cut. But at other times you may be frustrated because you have identified problems in your draft but do not know how to fix them or because you just cannot decide how the readers will react to your tone or your organization. Fortunately, there are some strategies you can learn and use to help you revise.

Checking Content: Outlining for Summary

When you are ready to begin reader-based revision, it is helpful to know just exactly what your draft says in its present form. A summary outline can help you see what you have said.* The first step is to write a summary sentence for each paragraph in the margin next to the paragraph. Here is Mike's summary outline:

I am very disturbed by research indicating that pornography leads to violence against women but believe we should try education on the issue before censorship.	Although I am very disturbed by the research indicating that pornography leads to an increase in violent crimes against women, I am not yet willing to support censorship as a solution to this problem. I fear that censorship will only drive pornography underground. First, we should try to educate the public so that they know that pornography is based on the debasement of women and promotes violent crime. We need to make people realize that pornography is not just harmless racy entertainment that only old-fashioned moralists object to.
The First Amendment protects free speech. Children in pornography may be exploited without their consent.	People say we all should have the right to read anything we choose. It is true that the First Amendment protects free speech. Many people say it's no one else's business what anyone else reads. But pornography featuring children *does* involve people (the children) who don't have a choice in the matter.

*Kenneth A. Bruffee, *A Short Course in Writing,* 2nd ed. (Boston: Little, Brown & Co., 1980).

Porn is not about sex but violence, and people feel they have to pretend to like it.	Most people's impression of pornography is that it's about sex and good times, but this isn't true. It's about violence. During pledge week, a lot of the fraternities invited most of the freshmen guys on campus to beer parties. They thought they had to show these movies, and it was supposed to be cool to think they were great. But what was on the screen was really kind of sick. I'm sure I wasn't the only one who thought so.
There have been attempts to legislate against porn on the grounds that it violates women's civil rights, but it will be better to try to educate people.	In 1983 an amendment defining pornography and making it a civil rights violation was passed by the Minneapolis City Council, but it was vetoed by the mayor. Nonetheless, Indianapolis used the amendment as a model for its own legislation, which eventually passed.
Summary of Summary Sentences: Pornography encourages violence against women but educating the public is a better solution than censorship.	But law is not the best answer. First we should make a real effort to make people realize that to think porn is OK is to think violence and exploitation are OK.

As you write your summary sentence for each paragraph, be sure that it reflects all of the material in that paragraph. In other words, be sure that you are summarizing the whole paragraph and not just part of it. In the example above, Mike had trouble writing a summary sentence for paragraph two. When he tried to reflect all of the material in the paragraph, he found he had two summary statements with no real connection between them: "The First Amendment protects free speech" and "Children in pornography may be exploited without their consent." From this he could tell that this paragraph needed revision. If you find a paragraph or several paragraphs like this in your paper, put an R (for revise) in the margin next to them, and write the summary statements in the margin, even though the paragraph needs work.

The next step is to write a sentence that summarizes all of your summary sentences. Try to do this honestly, reflecting what is on the paper and not what is in your head. This general summary sentence is the main idea or major generalization of your paper.

The third step is to review for yourself who your readers are and what you want them to do or think or feel. What do they know or think or feel about the subject now? What do they need to know? Now, compare your answer to this last question with the thesis sentence you wrote for your paper. Do they match? If they do, your paper is responsive to your audience and purpose. In reviewing his paper, Mike discovered that his summary statement did answer the question he was asked, "Should society censor pornography?" If yours does not, you will want to revise it.

The best way to begin this revision is to find the paragraphs in your draft that give unneeded material or to decide what material is needed but missing. Put an R in the margin next to a paragraph that includes unnecessary material; put an R in the margin where you think additional material is needed. The final step is to rewrite, making the additions and deletions and reconstructing the paragraphs you have marked. The paragraphs that required two summary sentences may be divided into two paragraphs with additional development and a good strong transition between them. Or you may decide to solve the problem by moving a portion of the paragraph to another part of the paper where it fits better. Mike rewrote his second paragraph as follows.

```
     People say we all should have the right to read any-

thing we choose. It is true that the First Amendment

protects free speech. The theory has been that society

can regulate what people do but it should not try to

regulate what people read or say or think because these

can't hurt anyone else. We have thought of pornography

as affecting no one but the reader and therefore pro-

tected by the First Amendment. But this defense is weak-

ened if we realize that people are affected against

their will: not only are women more at risk of violence

but children below the age of consent are exploited in

"kiddie porn." We must balance First Amendment rights

against the civil rights of pornography's victims.
```

To discover how your reader is likely to react to your draft, nothing is more helpful than having someone else try to take the role of the intended reader and give you a reaction. This is not just a strategy used in writing classes; it is a practice used both formally and informally by most writers. Drafts of documents are submitted to committee members for them to comment on the content and the tone. Business and technical reports are nearly always read by someone other than the writer before they are submitted. And most of us have been asked by our friends, "Listen to this and tell me how it sounds." When you have the opportunity to revise your paper with a partner or a group, have someone else do a summary outline of your paper after you have done yours. See how well they match and talk honestly about differences. Remember that it is the writer's job to make the reader understand. The high school students to whom you are writing in this chapter are likely to be less sophisticated as readers than your classmates are. If your classmates have any trouble under-standing you, your intended audience will probably find it even harder. The solution may be to make your generalizations in each paragraph explicit rather than implicit. You could simply work your own summary sentence into the paragraph. For example, the data in the following paragraph leads to a gener-alization, but the generalization is never explicitly stated:

> More than 40 percent of the students at this college are evening students, attending classes between 5:30 and 8:30 P.M. The bookstore, however, closes at 5:00 and the snack bars in the academic buildings close at 3:00. The Admissions, Registrar's, and Financial Aid offices close at 4:30.

A good summary sentence for this paragraph would be, "Although more than 40 percent of the students at this college are evening students, such students are not receiving adequate academic or support services." If the writer discov-ered that readers kept missing this point, she could solve the problem by working this explicit generalization (the summary sentence she wrote in her outline) into the paragraph itself.

Checking Development and Organization: Outlining for Function

When you planned your paper you probably worked from a list of topics you wanted to cover or things you wanted to include. And your list indicated the order in which you would include things. But as you drafted, you probably discovered other things to say and saw new connections in the material; and now your draft does not match your list. To see accurately how your draft is developed and organized, make an outline showing the function of each para-graph. Here are some examples of functions various paragraphs might per-form:

Give background.
Provide evidence in support of the main idea or thesis.
Refute possible objections.
Give descriptive detail.
Criticize previous theories or interpretations.
Tell what happened next.
Summarize.
Give an example or illustration.
Point out implications.

You will probably find other functions to add to the list. In the margin of your paper, next to each paragraph, write the function of that paragraph. It may help to think of "function" as the purpose each paragraph serves in relation to the major generalization. For example, a paragraph in a story may help to convey the theme by advancing the plot, fleshing out the characters, or giving the setting. A paragraph in a persuasive essay may support the thesis by giving evidence or refuting counterarguments or explaining implications. You will get a better sense of the paragraph's function if you ask not "What does this paragraph do?" but "How does this paragraph serve the thesis?" This is what Mike did for his article on censorship and pornography.

States the
thesis

Although I am very disturbed by the research indicating that pornography leads to violent crimes against women, I am not yet willing to support censorship as a solution to this problem. I fear that censorship will only drive pornography underground. First, we should try to educate the public so that they know that pornography is based on the debasement of women and promotes violent crime. We need to make people realize that pornography is not just harmless racy entertainment that only old-fashioned moralists object to.

Explains and
attacks
a counter-
argument

People say we all should have the right to read anything we choose. It is true that the First Amendment protects free speech. The theory has been that society can regulate what people do, but it should not try to regulate what people read or say or think because these can't hurt anyone else. We have thought of pornography as affecting no one but the reader and therefore

protected by the First Amendment. But this defense is weakened if we realize that people <u>are</u>
affected against their will: not only are women
more at risk of violence but children below the
age of consent are exploited in "kiddie porn." We
must balance First Amendment rights against the
civil rights of pornography's victims.

Makes an assertion based on experience

Most people's impression of pornography is
that it's about sex and good times, but this
isn't true. It's about violence. During pledge
week, a lot of the fraternities invited most of
the freshman guys on campus to beer parties. They
thought they had to show these movies, and it was
supposed to be cool to think they were great. But
what was on the screen was really kind of sick.
I'm sure I wasn't the only one who thought
so.

Gives history and restates the thesis

In 1983 an amendment defining pornography
and making it a civil rights violation was passed
by the Minneapolis City Council, but it was vetoed by the mayor. Nonetheless, Indianapolis used
the amendment as a model for its own legislation,
which eventually passed. But law is not the best
answer. First we should make a real effort to
make people realize that to think porn is OK is
to think violence and exploitation are OK.

What Mike can tell by looking at his outline of functions is that he has not provided much support for his main idea. In a short article, he has stated his thesis twice, attacked a counterargument, and given some history and some support based on his own experience. This may be enough to account for his position, but will it be enough to convince his readers? Some readers may ask, "What research demonstrates the connection between pornography and violence?" or "How do you know that pornography generally is like the films you've seen?" or "Why not censor it now and not waste time trying education first?" These are questions Mike will want to forestall since his goal is not just to express his opinion but to try to convince others to share it. His organization, however, seems all right so far.

After you have done an outline of functions for your own paper, trade with a partner and see how well his or her outline matches yours. Exchange it with those of one or two more people and see how their outlines of your paper match yours. Remember that it is the reader's perception that counts. If more than one of your classmates fails to see a paragraph as serving the function you think it serves, try making the transitions between paragraphs explicit rather than implicit. A transition tells the reader how each paragraph is related to the one above or below it and makes it much easier for a reader to follow the organization. Likewise, if your readers do not believe you have given enough support, you will benefit from listening to their questions and objections and strengthening your development.

Improving Sentence Construction and Word Choice

When you have a draft that gives the appropriate information in the right tone and is developed and organized effectively, then it is worth your while to look specifically at sentence construction and word choice. Most drafts use more words than are needed to say what they say. Richard Lanham, a researcher who has examined much contemporary writing, reminds us that too many sentences are loaded with excess words.* He recommends some strategies for making your writing stronger:

1. Circle the prepositions and see how many you can eliminate.
2. Circle the forms of the verb *to be* and see how many you can eliminate.
3. Make the agent of the action the subject of your sentence.
4. Don't waste time on mindless introductions.

The goal is to eliminate all unnecessary words and produce a stronger, clearer sentence. Notice what happens when Mike tries this on one of his sentences:

Original
sentence

In 1983, an amendment defining pornography
and making it a civil rights violation was passed

---

*Richard Lanham, *Revising Prose* (New York: Charles Scribner's Sons, 1979).

```
                    by the Minneapolis City Council, but it was ve-
                    toed by the mayor.
Rewritten                In 1983 the Minneapolis City Council passed
sentence            an amendment defining pornography and making it a
                    civil rights violation, but the mayor vetoed it.
```

This sentence is at least as clear as Mike's original version, and it is four words shorter.

If you find and try to eliminate all of the prepositions that you can do without, you will be focusing on some of the following wordy formulas that have much simpler equivalents:

due to the fact that	because
at that point in time	then
at this point in time	now
until such time as	until
in the neighborhood of 350	approximately 350

This is not, of course, a complete list. As you find more such phrases, add them to the list. To indicate that something is "green *in color*" or "octagonal *in shape*" or located "in *the state of* Arkansas" is to say the same thing twice. (If you are writing about New York, you should specify whether you mean the city or the state if the context does not make it clear.) A hard look at all of your prepositions will also bring you face to face with constructions like these that may be taking up space in your paper.

Try Lanham's strategies on the following sentences:

A. The reason that this is a problem is because it is easy to buy beer across the county line even if you are not 21 and don't have an ID.

B. There are two sides to the question of draft registration: the country must be prepared for war by registering potential soldiers; and it is considered unfair to register men and not women.

C. It is because refrigerators use electricity and may cause fires by overloading the circuits that they are not allowed to be used in dorm rooms, according to Edward Rosen, vice president for student services.

You can prevent confusion and make your prose livelier by making the agent of the action the subject of your sentence. Consider a sentence like the one a campus club printed on its recruiting poster: "If you are currently a member or have recently expired, please indicate on your application." We all know that the writer meant "If you are currently a member or if your membership has recently expired. . . ." If the writer had looked at the verbs "are" and "have expired" and asked "who's doing these actions," he or she would have rewritten the sentence.

Often, making the agent of the action the subject of the sentence is crucial to the reader's understanding. Look at the following sentences.

It is a nurse's responsibility to monitor what medications are given to the patient, even though they may be delivered by another health professional. Whenever a medicine is administered, it is registered on the patient's chart.

Who is responsible for making the entry on the chart? The nurse? The other health professional who may deliver the medicine? The phrase "it is registered" does not tell us.

Now use these strategies to improve your own sentences. Remember that they are meant only to help you focus your rewriting: they are not absolute rules. You may find a sentence that you believe is stronger with the passive voice than it would be with an active construction. For example, at the beginning of this section we wrote the sentence, "Richard Lanham, a researcher who has examined much contemporary writing, reminds us that too many sentences are loaded with excess words." The last phrase could have been rewritten "too many sentences have excess words," which would have eliminated a passive verb and a preposition. But we prefer "are loaded with" because it is easier to visualize. So use Lanham's strategies to help you find places in your writing where you have choices to make and then decide what construction you prefer.

How Does This Sound?

How do you react to the sound of Mike's sentence, "First we should try to educate the public so they know that pornography is based on the debasement of women and promotes violent crime"? Do you hear "based" and "debasement" too close together? There are no rules to help you decide when a sound recurs too quickly. Likewise, there are no rules to help you decide when you have used the same word too much. Your best guide is your ear; try reading your work aloud. If you are in doubt and can get advice from a friend, take advantage of a second opinion.

Mike can make his sentence sound better by substituting "pornography exists to portray the debasement of women" for "pornography is based on the debasement of women." Such rephrasing is fairly simple in this case because Mike found another way of saying the same thing. If he could not have found a way of rephrasing, he may have been tempted to settle for saying something just a little different from what he meant. He might, for example, have settled for "pornography portrays the debasement of women." He would not have been happy with this substitution, however, because it is not as strong a statement. If you cannot find another way to say exactly what you want to say, stick with your original, even if it sounds a bit clumsy. You have a right and a responsibility to say what you mean.

It is to your benefit, however, to develop skills in rephrasing because readers will be affected by the sound of your writing as well as by its content. Sometimes you can substitute a synonym for a word you want to replace. Be careful, though, not to confuse your reader, who might not be able to figure out whether the synonym is just a substitute to improve the sound or a new term being introduced. This problem occurs most often in technical writing. Consider the following sentences:

> Certain chemicals change the form of the protein. The following is a list of those which alter protein structures.

"Alter" has replaced "change" presumably for the sake of variety, but are "form" and "structures" intended to by synonymous? We cannot be sure. To avoid confusing your reader this way, it is best not to introduce synonyms for the major technical terms. You are better off if you can reconstruct some of your sentences to solve the problem. The example given above could have been rewritten: "Certain chemicals change the form of the protein and these are listed below" or "certain chemicals (listed below) change the form of the protein."

In your last revision, you should be checking for any remaining problems in word choice or sentence construction that may weaken your paper. Remove any clichés (see p. 212). Make sure your reader can tell to whom each of the pronouns refers.

Here is Mike's revised draft, much stronger than his original version:

Although I am very disturbed by recent research demonstrating that pornography fosters violent crimes against women, I am not yet willing to support censorship as a solution to the problem. Recent studies support the conclusions of Donnerstein and Hallam at Iowa State University (1978) and of Fishback and Malamuth at University of California at Los Angeles (1978) that pornographic films increase the likelihood of violent aggression against women. But I believe that censorship will only drive pornography underground. First, we should try to educate the public so they know that pornography exists to portray the debasement of women. We need to make people realize that pornography is not just harmless racy entertainment that only old-fashioned moralists object to.

People say we all should have the right to read anything we choose. It is true that the First Amendment
protects free speech. The theory has been that society
can regulate what people do but it should not try to
regulate what people read or say or think because these
can't hurt anyone else. We have thought of pornography
as affecting no one but the reader and therefore protected by the first Amendment. But this defense is weakened if we realize that people <u>are</u> affected against
their will: not only are women more at risk of violence
but children below the age of consent are exploited in
"kiddie porn." We must balance First Amendment rights
against the civil rights of pornography's victims.

Most people's impression of pornography is that it's
about sex and good times, but this isn't true. It's
about violence. During pledge week, a lot of the fraternities invited most of the freshman guys on campus to
beer parties. They thought they had to show these movies, and it was supposed to be cool to think they were
great. But what was on the screen was really kind of
sick. I'm sure I wasn't the only one who thought so.
Films can be sexually explicit without degrading either
partner. That's the difference between sexually explicit
and pornographic.

In 1983 the Minneapolis City Council passed an
amendment defining pornography as any depiction debasing

```
to women and making it a civil rights violation, but the

mayor vetoed it. Nonetheless, Indianapolis used the

amendment as a model for its own legislation, which

eventually passed. But law is not the best answer. First

we should make a real effort to make people realize that

to think porn is OK is to think violence and exploita-

tion are OK.
```

EDITING

Editing is the final sprucing up of your paper before your readers see it. When you edit you check spelling, punctuation, grammar, and usage. These are the last things a writer checks but the first thing the reader sees. Incorrect spelling or punctuation distract the reader: he or she is thinking "this writer hasn't learned that there is *a rat* in 'separate' " rather than concentrating on what you say. And readers do judge writers on how well they spell and punctuate. If the writer hasn't bothered to check the spelling of *preceding,* did he or she check these statistics? Writers lose credibility with every mistake they fail to catch in editing. There are, however, some strategies you can use to edit more effectively.

Read from Last to First

It is notoriously difficult to edit your own prose because you are very familiar with it. You read what you expect to see rather than what is actually there. To edit effectively, then, read your final draft beginning with the last sentence. Then read the second to the last sentence, then the third to the last, and so on. Reading this way will disrupt the flow of your paper and force you to look at sentences, words, and punctuation.

Focus Your Suspicions

Even if you are not a good speller, there are still hundreds of words you spell correctly. Even if you have trouble punctuating accurately, there are still many kinds of punctuation that you generally use correctly. For example, you may never forget or misplace the apostrophe in "Dr. Jablonski's classes," but maybe when it is "Dr. Jones's classes," you cannot trust yourself to get it right, because of the final *s.* All writers have certain spelling, grammar, and punctuation errors to which they are particularly susceptible.

If you can identify the problems that trip you up, you can focus particular attention on these when you edit. Do you have problems marking sentence boundaries? Getting your verbs to agree with their subjects? Placing commas in compound or complex sentences? Placing the apostrophe in *its* and *it's?* Use the Editing Guide (Chapter 12) to help you characterize your errors. When you edit, then, focus special attention on the areas where you know you are likely to have problems. Now look at your list of misspelled words, write the correct spelling next to each, and see if you notice any patterns. Do you characteristically reverse *i* and *e* when they occur together? Forget to double consonants? You may not find any pattern at all, but if you can find one in your errors, you will know to focus particular attention on words that fit your pattern. Similarly, if there are any common homonyms like *their* and *there* or *here* and *hear,* add these to the list of words and punctuation you should watch out for.

The practice of keeping a list of punctuation, grammar, and spelling errors to check for should help you notice those you might otherwise miss. Do not rely on the list, though, to catch every error for you. Read your entire paper with suspicion and verify every item you are not sure of.

Consult the Best Reference Book

Any complete dictionary will give you a correct spelling. The advantage of using an up-to-date dictionary is that it will also tell you if a modern spelling is acceptable. For example, *dialog* is now acceptable for *dialogue.*

Checking your spelling in a dictionary will work most of the time, but it may not work when you do not know the first few letters of a word (e.g., "gnawing," "gauge"). If you cannot find the word you need in the dictionary, look up a synonym in a thesaurus. If you look under "chew," you will find "gnaw" given as a synonym; looking up "meter" will give you "gauge."

Revising Workshop

Before you bring the draft of your article on college expenses to the Revising Workshop, make sure you have done writer-based revisions until you feel comfortable that your draft says what you believe. Then, to prepare for the workshop, write a summary outline of your paper.

In the workshop, have two other students do a summary outline of your paper. When they finish, compare their outlines with yours. If you think they have probably understood your point but may just be phrasing it differently, discuss it with them to be sure. When their summary sentences for a given paragraph do truly differ from yours, find out what in your paragraph led them to their summaries. Ask your readers also to comment on your tone. After this workshop, revise your paper on the basis of the readers' responses. You will probably find it helpful to write more explicit generalizations.

Bring your revised draft to a second workshop. Also bring an outline of the functions of the paragraphs. Have two students write an outline of functions for your paper and compare their outlines with yours. Discuss the paragraphs about which you disagree. Remember that there is no point in convincing your readers that they are wrong; your goal is not to get agreement but to discover how your work reads. Find out what in any disputed paragraph led them to assign it the function they did. Then have your readers do the following:

1. Respond as you think the intended audience would respond. What questions would they raise? What might they object to?
2. Indicate any generalization (including the major generalization) that requires more support.

Based on what you learned in this Revising Workshop, rewrite your paper to strengthen its support and organization. Pay particular attention to your transitions. Then return to your workshop group for answers to the following questions:

1. Are there any confusing sentences or parts of sentences? Any sections you could not understand on first reading? If so, bracket these as needing repair.
2. Are there any sentences that are too long to read easily? Any sections that sound choppy? If so, put a line in the margin next to these.
3. Is there variety in the sentence patterns used? Indicate repetitious patterns.
4. Are there any words or phrases that seem inappropriate? If so, mark these by underlining.

After this last Revising Workshop, make any changes you think would improve your paper. Then give your paper a thorough editing and take it to the Editing Workshop.

Editing Workshop

Your paper should be read by at least two other students, who will answer the following questions:

1. Are there any sentence fragments, run-on sentences, or comma splices? If so, bracket these.
2. Are there any spelling or punctuation errors? If so, put an X in the margin on the line in which the error occurs. Put as many marks as there are errors.
3. Put a C in the margin of any line in which you find a trite expression or cliché.
4. Put a G in the margin of any line in which you find an error of grammar or usage. Use as many marks as there are errors.

Edit again to fix any problems your classmates discovered and submit the final copy to your instructor.

CHAPTER 8

Summarizing Texts

THEME Language and Power
SKILL FOCUS Reading Critically,
Paraphrasing, and Quoting

The twentieth century has been intrigued with the power of language to shape and limit what can be expressed. To what extent does our language reinforce the social status quo and maintain stereotypes? What happens to a minority group whose language is not well understood by the majority? At what cost is a minority language abandoned? What are the implications for society if *Miss* and *Mrs.* are replaced by *Ms?* Why would a politician prefer to say "I misspoke" rather than "I lied"? To what extent does language *relate* things as they are and to what extent does it *make* things as they are? These are all *political* questions.

Before Reading

The British writer George Orwell (1903–1950) was interested in the ways in which language could be used to deceive and oppress people and also with the ways he saw the governments of his own time using language to keep the populace unaware of what they, the political organizations, were doing. Before you read his essay "Politics and the English Language," make a list of all the clichés you can think of. Then make a list of all the euphemisms (words or phrases we use to replace harsher words or phrases) that come to mind. You might begin with "obituary," the euphemism for "death notice." When you have a list, try to categorize the items. For what subjects, besides death, do we create euphemisms? Write a short journal entry about why you believe we create the euphemisms we do. You can then compare your analysis with Orwell's as you read his essay.

Politics and the English Language

George Orwell

Most people who bother with the matter at all would admit that the English language is in a bad way, but it is generally assumed that we cannot by conscious action do anything about it. Our civilization is decadent and our language—so the argument runs—must inevitably share in the general collapse. It follows that any struggle against the abuse of language is a sentimental archaism, like preferring candles to electric light or hansom cabs to aeroplanes. Underneath this lies the half-conscious belief that language is a natural growth and not an instrument which we shape for our own purposes.

Now, it is clear that the decline of a language must ultimately have political and economic causes: it is not due simply to the bad influence of this or that individual writer. But an effect can become a cause, reinforcing the original cause and producing the same effect in an intensified form, and so on indefinitely. A man may take to drink because he feels himself to be a failure, and then fail all the more completely because he drinks. It is rather the same thing that is happening to the English language. It becomes ugly and inaccurate because our thoughts are foolish, but the slovenliness of our language makes it easier for us to have foolish thoughts. The point is that the process is reversible. Modern English, especially written English, is full of bad habits which spread by imitation and which can be avoided if one is willing to take the necessary trouble. If one gets rid of these habits one can think more clearly, and to think clearly is a necessary first step towards political regeneration: so that the fight against bad English is not frivolous and is not the exclusive concern of professional writers. I will come back to this presently, and I hope that by that time the meaning of what I have said here will have become clearer. Meanwhile here are five specimens of the English language as it is now habitually written.

These five passages have not been picked out because they are especially bad—I could have quoted far worse if I had chosen—but because they illustrate various of the mental vices from which we now suffer. They are a little below the average, but are fairly representative samples. I number them so that I can refer back to them when necessary:

>   (1) I am not, indeed, sure whether it is not true to say that the Milton who once
>   seemed not unlike a seventeenth-century Shelley had not become, out of an ex-

perience ever more bitter in each year, more alien *[sic]* to the founder of that Jesuit sect which nothing could induce him to tolerate.

Professor Harold Laski (Essay in *Freedom of Expression*).

(2) Above all, we cannot play ducks and drakes with a native battery of idioms which prescribes such egregious collocations of vocables as the Basic *put up with* for *tolerate* or *put at a loss* for *bewilder.*

Professor Lancelot Hogben *(Interglossa).*

(3) On the one side we have the free personality: by definition it is not neurotic, for it has neither conflict nor dream. Its desires, such as they are, are transparent, for they are just what institutional approval keeps in the forefront of consciousness; another institutional pattern would alter their number and intensity; there is little in them that is natural, irreducible, or culturally dangerous. But *on the other side,* the social bond itself is nothing but the mutual reflection of these self-secure integrities. Recall the definition of love. Is not this the very picture of a small academic? Where is there a place in this hall of mirrors for either personality or fraternity?

Essay on psychology in *Politics* (New York).

(4) All the "best people" from the gentlemen's clubs, and all the frantic fascist captains, united in common hatred of Socialism and bestial horror of the rising tide of the mass revolutionary movement, have turned to acts of provocation, to foul incendiarism, to medieval legends of poisoned wells, to legalize their own destruction of proletarian organizations, and rouse the agitated petty-bourgeoisie to chauvinistic fervor on behalf of the fight against the revolutionary way out of the crisis.

Communist pamphlet.

(5) If a new spirit *is* to be infused into this old country, there is one thorny and contentious reform which must be tackled, and that is the humanization and galvanization of the BBC. Timidity here will bespeak canker and atrophy of the soul. The heart of Britain may be sound and of strong beat, for instance, but the British lion's roar at present is like that of Bottom in Shakespeare's *Midsummer Night's Dream*—as gentle as any sucking dove. A virile new Britain cannot continue indefinitely to be traduced in the eyes or rather ears, of the world by the effete languors of Langham Place, brazenly masquerading as "standard English." When the voice of Britain is heard at nine o'clock, better far and infinitely less ludicrous to hear aitches honestly dropped than the present priggish, inflated, inhibited, school-ma'amish arch braying of blameless bashful mewing maidens!

Letter in *Tribune.*

Each of these passages has faults of its own, but, quite apart from avoidable ugliness, two qualities are common to all of them. The first is staleness of imagery; the other is lack of precision. The writer either has a meaning and cannot express it, or he inadvertently says something else, or he is almost indifferent as to whether his words mean anything or not. This mixture of vagueness and sheer incompetence is the most marked characteristic of modern English prose, and especially of any kind of political writing. As soon as certain topics are raised, the concrete melts into the abstract and no one seems able to think of turns of speech that are not hackneyed: prose consists less and less of *words* chosen for the sake of their meaning, and more and more of *phrases* tacked together like the sections of a prefabricated henhouse. I list below, with notes and examples, various of the tricks by means of which the work of prose-construction is habitually dodged:

Dying Metaphors

A newly invented metaphor assists thought by evoking a visual image, while on the other hand a metaphor which is technically "dead" (e.g., *iron resolution*) has in effect reverted to being an ordinary word and can generally be used without loss of vividness. But in between these two classes there is a huge dump of worn-out metaphors which have lost all evocative power and are merely used because they save people the trouble of inventing phrases for themselves. Examples are: *Ring the changes on, take up the cudgels for, toe the line, ride roughshod over, stand shoulder to shoulder with, play into the hands of, no axe to grind, grist to the mill, fishing in troubled waters, on the order of the day, Achilles' heel, swan song, hotbed.* Many of these are used without knowledge of their meaning (what is a "rift," for instance?), and incompatible metaphors are frequently mixed, a sure sign that the writer is not interested in what he is saying. Some metaphors now current have been twisted out of their original meaning without those who use them even being aware of the fact. For example, *toe the line* is sometimes written *tow the line*. Another example is the *hammer and the anvil,* now always used with the implication that the anvil gets the worst of it. In real life it is always the anvil that breaks the hammer, never the other way about: a writer who stopped to think what he was saying would be aware of this, and would avoid perverting the original phrase.

Operators or Verbal False Limbs

These save the trouble of picking out appropriate verbs and nouns, and at the same time pad each sentence with extra syllables which give it an appearance of symmetry. Characteristic phrases are *render inoperative, militate against, make contact with, be subjected to, give rise to, give grounds for, have the effect of, play a leading part (role) in, make itself felt, take effect, exhibit a tendency to, serve the purpose of,* etc., etc. The keynote is the elimination of simple verbs. Instead of being a single word, such as *break, stop, spoil, mend, kill,* a verb becomes a *phrase,* made up of a noun or adjective tacked on to some general-purposes verb such as *prove, serve, form, play, render.* In addition, the passive voice is wherever possible used in preference to the active, and noun constructions are used instead of gerunds *(by examination of* instead of *by examining).* The range of verbs is further cut down by means of the *-ize* and *de-* formations, and the banal statements are given an appearance of profundity by means of the *not un-* formation. Simple conjunctions and prepositions are replaced by such phrases as *with respect to, having regard to, the fact that, by dint of, in view of, in the interests of, on the hypothesis that;* and the ends of sentences are saved from anticlimax by such resounding common-places as *greatly to be desired, cannot be left out of account, a development to be expected in the near future, deserving of serious consideration, brought to a satisfactory conclusion,* and so on and so forth.

Pretentious Diction

Words like *phenomenon, element, individual* (as noun), *objective, categorical, effective, virtual, basic, primary, promote, constitute, exhibit, exploit, utilize, eliminate, liquidate,* are used to dress up simple statements and give an air of scientific impartiality to biased judgments. Adjectives like *epoch-making, epic, historic, unforgettable, triumphant, age-old, inevitable, inexorable, veritable,* are used to dignify the sordid processes of international politics, while writing that aims at glorifying war usually takes on an archaic color, its characteristic words being: *realm, throne, chariot, mailed fist, trident, sword, shield, buckler, banner, jackboot, clarion.* Foreign words and expressions such as *cul de sac, ancien régime, deus ex machina, mutatis mutandis, status quo, gleichschaltung, weltanschauung,* are used to give an air of culture and elegance. Except for the useful abbreviations *i.e., e.g.,* and *etc.,* there is no real need for any of the hundreds of foreign phrases now current in English. Bad writers, and especially scientific, political and sociological writers, are nearly always haunted by the notion that Latin or Greek words are grander than Saxon ones, and unnecessary words like *expedite, ameliorate, predict, extraneous, deracinated, clandestine, subaqueous* and hundreds of others constantly gain ground from their Anglo-Saxon opposite numbers.[1] The jargon peculiar to Marxist writing (*hyena, hangman, cannibal, petty bourgeois, these gentry, lacquey, flunkey, mad dog, White Guard,* etc.) consists largely of words and phrases translated from Russian, German or French; but the normal way of coining a new word is to use a Latin or Greek root with the appropriate affix and, where necessary, the *-ize* formation. It is often easier to make up words of this kind (*deregionalize, impermissible, extramarital, non-fragmentary* and so forth) than to think up the English words that will cover one's meaning. The result, in general, is an increase in slovenliness and vagueness.

Meaningless Words

In certain kinds of writing, particularly in art criticism and literary criticism, it is normal to come across long passages which are almost completely lacking in meaning.[2] Words like *romantic, plastic, values, human, dead, sentimental, natural, vitality,* as used in art criticism, are strictly meaningless, in the sense that they not only do not point to any discoverable object, but are hardly ever expected to do so by the reader. When one critic writes, "The outstanding feature of Mr. X's work is its living quality," while another writes, "The immediately striking thing about Mr. X's work is its peculiar deadness," the reader accepts this as a simple difference of opinion. If words like *black* and *white* were involved, instead of the jargon words *dead* and *living,* he would see at once that language was being used in an improper way. Many political words are similarly abused. The word *Fascism* has now no meaning except in so far as it signifies "something not desirable." The words *democracy, freedom, patriotic, realistic, justice,* have each of them several different meanings which cannot be reconciled with one another. In the case of a word like *democracy,* not only is there no agreed definition, but the attempt to make one is resisted from all sides. It is almost universally felt that when we call a country democratic we are praising it: consequently the defenders of every kind of regime claim that it is a democracy, and fear that they might have to stop using the word if it were tied down to any one meaning. Words of this kind are often used in a consciously dishonest way. That is, the person who uses them has his own private definition, but allows his hearer to think he means something quite different. Statements like, *Marshal Pétain was a true patriot, The Soviet Press is the freest in the world, The Catholic Church is opposed to persecution,* are almost always made with intent to deceive. Other words used in variable meanings, in most cases more or less dishonestly, are: *class, totalitarian, science, progressive, reactionary, bourgeois, equality.*

Now that I have made this catalogue of swindles and perversions, let me give another example of the kind of writing that they lead to. This time it must of its nature be an imaginary one. I am going to translate a passage of good English into modern English of the worst sort. Here is a well-known verse from *Ecclesiastes:*

I returned and saw under the sun, that the race is not to the swift, nor the battle to the strong, neither yet bread to the wise, nor yet riches to men of understanding, nor yet favour to men of skill; but time and chance happeneth to them all.

Here it is in modern English:

Objective consideration of contemporary phenomena compels the conclusion that success or failure in competitive activities exhibits no tendency to be commensurate with innate capacity, but that a considerable element of the unpredictable must invariably be taken into account.

This is a parody, but a very gross one. Exhibit (3), above, for instance, contains several patches of the same kind of English. It will be seen that I have not made a full translation. The beginning and ending of the sentence follow the original meaning fairly closely, but in the middle the concrete illustrations—race, battle, bread—dissolve into the vague phrase "success or failure in competitive activities." This had to be so, because no modern writer of the kind I am discussing—no one capable of using phrases like "objective consideration of contemporary phenomena"—would ever tabulate his thoughts in that precise and detailed way. The whole tendency of modern prose is away from concreteness. Now analyse these two sentences a little more closely. The first contains forty-nine words but only sixty syllables, and all its words are those of everyday life. The second contains thirty-eight words of ninety syllables: eighteen of its words are from Latin roots, and one from Greek. The first sentence contains six vivid images, and only one phrase ("time and chance") that could be called vague. The second contains not a single fresh, arresting phrase, and in spite of its ninety syllables it gives only a shortened version of the meaning contained in the first. Yet without a doubt it is the second kind of sentence that is gaining ground in modern English. I do not want to exaggerate. This kind of writing is not yet universal, and out-crops of simplicity will occur here and there in the worst-written page. Still, if you or I were told to write a few lines on the uncertainty of human fortunes, we should probably come much nearer to my imaginary sentence than to the one from *Ecclesiastes*.

As I have tried to show, modern writing at its worst does not consist in picking out words for the sake of their meaning and inventing images in order to make the meaning clearer. It consists in gumming together long strips of words which have already been set in order by someone else, and making the results presentable by sheer humbug. The attraction of this way of writing is that it is easy. It is easier—even quicker, once you have the habit—to say *In my opinion it is not an unjustifiable assumption that* than to say *I think*. If you use ready-made phrases, you not only don't have to hunt about for words; you also don't have to bother with the rhythms of your sentences, since these phrases are generally so arranged as to be more or less euphonious. When you are composing in a hurry—when you are dictating to a stenographer, for instance, or making a public speech—it is natural to fall into a pretentious, Latinized style. Tags like *a consideration which we should do well to bear in mind* or *a conclusion to which all of us would readily assent* will save many a sentence from coming down with a bump. By using stale metaphors, similes and idioms, you save much mental effort, at the cost of leaving your meaning vague, not only for your reader but for yourself. This is the significance of mixed metaphors. The sole aim of a metaphor is to call up a visual image. When these images clash—as in *The Fascist octopus has sung its swan song, the jackboot is thrown into the melting pot*—it can be taken as certain that the writer is not seeing a mental image of the objects he is naming; in other words he is not really thinking. Look again at the examples I gave at the beginning of this essay. Professor Laski (1) uses five negatives in fifty-three words. One of these is superfluous, making nonsense of the whole passage, and in addition there is the slip *alien* for akin, making further nonsense, and several avoidable pieces of clumsiness which increase the general vagueness. Professor Hogben (2) plays ducks and drakes with a battery which is able to write prescriptions, and, while disapproving of the everyday phrase *put up with,* is unwilling to look *egregious* up in the dictionary and see what it means; (3), if one takes an uncharitable attitude towards it, [it] is simply meaningless: probably one could work out its intended meaning by reading the whole of the article in which it occurs. In (4), the writer knows more or less what he wants to say, but an accumulation of stale phrases chokes him like tea leaves blocking a sink. In (5), words and meaning have almost parted company. People who write in this manner usually have a general emotional meaning—they dislike one thing and want to express solidarity with another—but they are not interested in the detail of what they are saying. A scrupulous writer, in every sentence that he writes, will ask himself at least four questions, thus: What am I trying to say? What words will express it? What image or idiom will make it clear? Is this image fresh enough to have an effect? And he will probably ask himself two more: Could I put it more shortly? Have I said anything that is avoidably ugly? But you are not obliged to go to all this trouble. You can shirk it by simply throwing your mind open and letting the ready-made phrases come crowding in. They will construct your sentences for you—even think your thoughts for you, to a certain extent—and at need they will perform the important service of partially concealing your meaning even from yourself. It is at this point that the special connection between politics and the debasement of language becomes clear.

In our time it is broadly true that political writing is bad writing. Where it is not true, it will generally be found that the writer is some kind of rebel, expressing his private opinions and not a "party line." Orthodoxy, of whatever color, seems to demand a lifeless, imitative style. The political dialects to be found in pamphlets, leading articles, manifestos, White Papers and the speeches of under-secretaries do, of course, vary from party to party, but they are all alike in that one almost never finds in them a fresh, vivid, home-made turn of speech. When one watches some tired hack on the platform mechanically repeating the familiar phrases—*bestial atrocities, iron heel, bloodstained tyranny, free peoples of the world, stand shoulder to shoulder*—one often has a curious feeling that one is not watching a live human being but some kind of dummy: a feeling which suddenly becomes stronger at moments when the light catches the speaker's spectacles and turns them into blank discs which seem to have no eyes behind them. And this is not altogether fanciful. A speaker who uses that kind of phraseology has gone some distance towards turning himself into a machine. The appropriate noises are coming out of his larynx, but his brain is not involved as it would be if he were choosing his words for himself. If the speech he is making is one that he is accustomed to make over and over again, he may be almost unconscious of what he is saying, as one is when one utters the responses in church. And this reduced state of consciousness, if not indispensable, is at any rate favorable to political conformity. . . .

The inflated style is itself a kind of euphemism. A mass of Latin words falls upon the facts like soft snow, blurring the outlines and covering up all the details. The great enemy of clear language is insincerity. When there is a gap between one's real and one's declared aims, one turns as it were instinctively to long words and exhausted idioms, like a cuttlefish squirting out ink. In our age there is no such thing as "keeping out of politics." All issues are political issues, and politics itself is a mass of lies, evasions, folly, hatred and schizophrenia. When the general atmosphere is bad, language must suffer. I should expect to find—this is a guess which I have not sufficient knowledge to verify—that the German, Russian and Italian languages have all deteriorated in the last ten or fifteen years, as a result of dictatorship.

But if thought corrupts language, language can also corrupt thought. A bad usage can spread by tradition and imitation, even among people who should and do know better. The debased language that I have been discussing is in some ways very convenient. Phrases like *a not unjustifiable assumption, leaves much to be desired, would serve no good purpose, a consideration which we should do well to bear in mind,* are a continuous temptation, a packet of aspirins always at one's elbow. Look back through this essay, and for certain you will find that I have again and again committed the very faults I am protesting against. . . .

I said earlier that the decadence of our language is probably curable. Those who deny this would argue, if they produced an argument at all, that language merely reflects existing social conditions, and that we cannot influence its development by any direct tinkering with words and constructions. So far as the general tone or spirit of a language goes, this may be true, but it is not true in detail. Silly words and expressions have often disappeared, not through any evolutionary process but owing to the conscious action of a minority. Two recent examples were *explore every avenue* and *leave no stone unturned,* which were killed by the jeers of a few journalists. There is a long list of fly-blown metaphors which could similarly be got rid of if enough people would interest themselves in the job; and it should also be possible to laugh the *not un-*formation out of existence,[3] to reduce the amount of Latin and Greek in the average sentence, to drive out foreign phrases and strayed scientific words, and, in general, to make pretentiousness unfashionable. But all these are minor points. The defence of the English language implies more than this, and perhaps it is best to start by saying what it does *not* imply.

To begin with, it has nothing to do with archaism, with the salvaging of obsolete words and turns of speech, or with the setting up of a "standard English" which must never be departed from. On the contrary, it is especially concerned with the scrapping of every word or idiom which has outworn its usefulness. It has nothing to do with correct grammar and syntax, which are of no importance so long as one makes one's meaning clear, or with the avoidance of Americanisms, or with having what is called a "good prose style." On the other hand it is not concerned with fake simplicity and the attempt to make written English colloquial. Nor does it even imply in every case preferring the Saxon word to the Latin one, though it does imply using the fewest and shortest words that will cover one's meaning. What is above all needed is to let the meaning choose the word, and not the other way about. In prose, the worst thing one can do with words is to surrender to them. When you think of a concrete object, you think wordlessly, and then, if you want to describe the thing you have been visualizing you probably hunt about till you find the exact words that seem to fit it. When you think of something abstract you are more inclined to use words from the start, and unless you make a conscious effort to prevent it, the existing dialect will come rushing in and do the job for you, at the expense of blurring or even changing your meaning. Probably it is better to put off using words as long as possible and get one's meaning as clear as one can through pictures or sensations. Afterwards one can choose—not simply *accept*—the phrases that will best cover the meaning, and then switch round and decide what impression one's words are likely to make on another person. This last effort of the mind cuts out all stale or mixed images, all prefabricated phrases, needless repetitions, and humbug and vagueness generally. But one can often be in doubt about the effect of a word or a phrase, and one needs rules that one can rely on when instinct fails. I think the following rules will cover most cases:

1. Never use a metaphor, simile, or other figure of speech which you are used to seeing in print.
2. Never use a long word where a short one will do.
3. If it is possible to cut a word out, always cut it out.
4. Never use the passive where you can use the active.
5. Never use a foreign phrase, a scientific word or a jargon word if you can think of an everyday English equivalent.
6. Break any of these rules sooner than say anything outright barbarous.

These rules sound elementary, and so they are, but they demand a deep change of attitude in anyone who has grown used to writing in the style now fashionable. One could keep all of them and still write bad English, but one could not write the kind of stuff that I quoted in those five specimens at the beginning of this article.

I have not here been considering the literary use of language, but merely language as an instrument for expressing and not for concealing or preventing thought. Stuart Chase and others have come near to claiming that all abstract words are meaningless, and have used this as a pretext for advocating a kind of political quietism. Since you don't know what Fascism is, how can you struggle against Fascism? One need not swallow such absurdities as this, but one ought to recognize that the present political chaos is connected with the decay of language, and that one can probably bring about some improvement by starting at the verbal end. If you simplify your English, you are freed from the worst follies of orthodoxy. You cannot speak any of the necessary dialects, and when you make a stupid remark its stupidity will be obvious, even to yourself. Political language—and with variations this is true of all political parties, from Conservatives to Anarchists—is designed to make lies sound truthful and murder respectable, and to give an appearance of solidity to pure wind. One cannot change this all in a moment, but one can at least change one's own habits, and from time to time one can even, if one jeers loudly enough, send some worn-out and useless phrase—some *jackboot, Achilles' heel, hotbed, melting pot, acid test, veritable inferno* or other lump of verbal refuse—into the dustbin where it belongs.

Notes

[1] An interesting illustration of this is the way in which the English flower names which were in use till very recently are being ousted by Greek ones, *snapdragon* becoming *antirrhinum, forget-me-not* becoming *myosotis,* etc. It is hard to see any practical reason for this change of fashion: it is probably due to an instinctive turning-away from the more homely word and a vague feeling that the Greek word is scientific.

[2] Example: "Comfort's catholicity of perception and image, strangely Whitmanesque in range, almost the exact opposite in aesthetic compulsion, continues to evoke that trembling atmospheric accumulative hinting at a cruel, an inexorably serene timelessness. . . . Wrey Gardiner scores by aiming at simple bull's-eyes with precision. Only they are not so simple, and through this contented sadness runs more than the surface bittersweet of resignation." *(Poetry Quarterly.)*

[3] One can cure oneself of the *not un-* formation by memorizing this sentence: *A not unblack dog was chasing a not unsmall rabbit across a not ungreen field.*

After Reading

In your journal, write your response to "Politics and the English Language." What do you think of Orwell's ideas? How do you feel about them?

This topic of language and power comes to the fore in every civil rights struggle. Racial and ethnic minorities and women all confront the stereotypes as well as the cultural assumptions embodied in the American language. The following assignment will ask you to focus your reading, thinking, and writing on this topic.

Assignment

Your college sponsors a series of informal seminars designed to inform members of the community about contemporary issues. Most of the people who attend these seminars are college graduates; all are thinking people, concerned about the world they live in and eager to understand the many facets of contemporary issues. One seminar meeting will be on the topic "Language and Power." Assume that you are the student assistant to the professor who is leading this seminar. Your responsibility is to prepare summaries of relevant articles: "Politics and the English Language," " 'Vive la Différence!' and Communication Processes," and " 'What Go Round Come Round': *King* in Perspective" (each of which is presented in this chapter). The summaries, which will be sent to each participant before the seminar, should be approximately two hundred words each.

AUDIENCES AND PURPOSES

A summary is a shortened version of one or more documents. Some summaries are written for publication or presentation to another reader. Technical reports and research studies commonly are submitted with a summary—or abstract—attached so the publications manager or administrator can quickly get the gist of the document. Other summaries are written to help the writer gain control of a mass of material and are written for the writer alone. Researchers, for instance, read everything in print on the topic of their research and many synthesize their notes into an informal summary so they can get a clear picture of what has been done and what needs to be done in their field. Many students summarize their reading to help them understand it.

The assignment in this chapter calls for you to summarize each of the readings. As you plan each summary, you will have to make decisions about the complexity of your language and the degree of detail you should include. Here is a passage from Jacob Bronowski's *The Ascent of Man,* followed by a college student's summary of it for himself and one that a middle school teacher might write to present to her geography class.

"Nomads"

Jacob Bronowski

It is not possible in the nomad life to make things that will not be needed for several weeks. They could not be carried. And in fact the Bakhtiari do not know how to make them. If they need metal pots, they barter them from settled peoples or from a caste of gipsy workers who specialise in metals. A nail, a stirrup, a toy, or a child's bell is something that is traded from outside the tribe. The Bakhtiari life is too narrow to have time or skill for specialisation. There is no room for innovation, because there is not time, on the move, between evening and morning, coming and going all their lives, to develop a new device or a new thought—not even a new tune. The only habits that survive are the old habits. The only ambition of the son is to be like the father.

It is a life without features. Every night is the end of a day like the last, and every morning will be the beginning of a journey like the day before. When the day breaks, there is one question in everyone's mind: Can the flock be got over the next high pass? One day on the journey, the highest pass of all must be crossed. This is the pass Zadeku, twelve thousand feet high on the Zagros, which the flock must somehow struggle through or skirt in its upper reaches. For the tribe must move on, the herdsman must find new pastures every day, because at these heights grazing is exhausted in a single day.

Every year the Bakhtiari cross six ranges of mountains on the outward journey (and cross them again to come back). They march through snow and the spring flood water. And in only one respect has their life advanced beyond that of ten thousand years ago. The nomads of that time had to travel on foot and carry their own packs. The Bakhtiari have pack-animals—horses, donkeys, mules—which have only been domesticated since that time. Nothing else in their lives is new. And nothing is memorable. Nomads have no memorials, even to the dead. (Where is Bakhtyar, where was Jacob buried?) The only mounds that they build are to mark the way at such places as the Pass of the Women, treacherous but easier for the animals than the high pass.

The spring migration of the Bakhtiari is a heroic adventure; and yet the Bakhtiari are not so much heroic as stoic. They are resigned because the adventure leads nowhere. The summer pastures themselves will only be a stopping place—unlike the children of Israel, for them there is no promised land. The head of the family has worked seven years, as Jacob did, to build a flock of fifty sheep and goats. He expects to lose ten of them in the migration if things go well. If they go badly, he may lose twenty out of that fifty. Those are the odds of the nomad life, year in and year out. And beyond that, at the end of the journey, there will still be nothing except an immense, traditional resignation.

Who knows, in any one year, whether the old when they have crossed the passes will be able to face the final test: the crossing of the Bazuft River? Three months of melt-water have swollen the river. The tribesmen, the women, the pack animals and the flocks are all exhausted. It will take a day to manhandle the flocks across the river. But this, here, now is the testing day. Today is the day on which the young become men, because the survival of the herd and the family depends on their strength. Crossing the Bazuft River is like crossing the Jordan; it is the baptism to manhood. For the young man, life for a moment comes alive now. And for the old—for the old, it dies.

What happens to the old when they cannot cross the last river? Nothing. They stay behind to die. Only the dog is puzzled to see a man abandoned. The man accepts the nomad custom; he has come to the end of his journey, and there is no place at the end.

The college freshman's summary, written to help him learn:

> There can be virtually no progress in nomadic life be-
> cause the need to keep the flock or herd moving each day
> to new pasture means that they haven't time for anything
> but the journey. "There is no room for innovation," and
> the nomads cannot even carry anything they don't need
> each day. Except for having pack animals now, they live
> as nomads did 10,000 years ago.

Notice that this summary omits many details about the lives of the Bakhtiari that are specific to them alone (e.g., how many mountain passes they cross each year). The student has concentrated his summary on the features of nomadic life in general, because he knows that this is what he should learn.

Summary for the middle school geography class:

> Nomads are always moving to find new fields where their
> animals can eat. Because they are always moving, they
> don't have time to invent new things to change their
> lives. The Bakhtiari tribe are nomads who herd goats.
> They live simple lives, owning only the things they can
> carry with them each day, like simple tools and cooking
> equipment. They have pack animals now, but otherwise
> they live as their ancestors did 10,000 years ago.

Notice that this summary covers most of the same information that the college student included, but it uses simpler language. The middle school summary includes some details (the simple tools and cooking equipment) that the college student's did not. For middle school children, these details make the picture more vivid and memorable and therefore easier to learn.

HONEST SUMMARIES

The two summaries above were written for very different audiences, but both are faithful to Bronowski's original in that they reflect all of Bronowski's major points and his emphases, they do not add additional information or interpretation, and they reflect the tone of the original. Each of these characteristics deserves some detailing.

The Balance and Emphases of the Original

It would be unfair to Bronowski to summarize his writing by omitting his point that nomadic life is unchanging and stressing in great detail his point that the Bakhtiari now have pack animals. The summary would be conveying a different message from the original. An honest summary reflects the major generalization of the original with any qualifications the author makes, and as much of the support as is useful or that you have room for.

No Outside Material

A summary is intended to make its readers familiar with the original document, and not primarily to teach them about the subject. The college student and the middle school teacher may both have been able to think of other nomadic tribes and how they live, but it would not be legitimate to include these in the summary because Bronowski did not include them.

It *is* legitimate to include a generalization if the piece you are summarizing leads the reader *inevitably* to this conclusion but never states it explicitly. There would be no way to summarize a piece that has only specifics, unless you were allowed to provide the generalization.

When you are writing a summary, it is tempting to get involved in the subject, add interesting information, argue with the author, comment on what the author says, evaluate the author's work, or raise questions. These are healthy impulses because they mean that you are reading actively and not just thoughtlessly accepting the author's words. But remember that a summary is not a dialogue between you and the author; it is just a reflection of the author's work. There are some types of writing, like the evaluative summary and the review, in which you combine summary with comment and judgment. These, however, are variations of the basic summary. (When you are assigned to write a summary, it is a good idea to be sure you know whether it is a simple summary, an evaluative summary, or a summary-plus-comment that you are being asked for. This chapter calls only for basic summaries.) When writing a basic summary, you reflect the original without comment.

The Tone of the Original

If the original is serious, the summary should be serious. A summary that began "Don't become a nomad!" would be flippant and disrespectful of the nomadic peoples. Bronowski does not use that tone. If the original is flippant or sarcastic, you can either reflect that tone or summarize the writer's points and note that they are made in a flippant or sarcastic voice. If the original is pompous and stuffy, you need not be pompous and stuffy in your summary. (In fact, it will be a mercy if you are not.) It is enough to reflect serious writing seriously or to let the reader know if satire, parody, sarcasm, or flippancy characterize the original.

READING CRITICALLY

To summarize effectively, you must have a clear understanding of what you have read. Reading critically means asking yourself where the writer is going. When you read short stories or novels, you unconsciously ask, "What happens next?" and you find out as you read on. When you read essays, reports, memos, or formal letters, you ask—consciously or unconsciously—"What is the point the writer is making?" and "What am I being asked to understand or feel or do?" You begin guessing the answer to these questions as soon as you begin reading. Read the opening paragraphs of the next two selections ("Jackson Plays by the Rules" and "Museums, No") and write down what point you believe the author is making or where the story seems to be going and why it is being told.

Sometimes, as in "Jackson Plays by the Rules," it is easy to guess where the writer is going because he or she has provided a generalization in the first paragraph as is often the case in news reports. In other cases, such as "Museums, No," it is more difficult to guess because the writer is saving the generalization and building toward it. This guessing is no mere game. It is a strategy for understanding what another person is trying to say.

Once you have made a guess about the writer's point, the rest of the article will either confirm it or cause you to change it. Read on in each of the selections you began before, and see how or if the body of the article alters your earlier guess.

Jackson Plays by the Rules

Kurt Andersen, Staff Writer for *Time* Magazine

He has not lost his touch. Preaching before mostly black audiences in Pine Bluff, Ark., Lexington, Ky., and Savannah, Ga., last week, he had them cheering and chanting after just a few minutes. But Jesse Jackson, no longer pursuing his own candidacy, is now stumping on behalf of Walter Mondale, his erstwhile opponent. If Jackson spent last spring and summer grandstanding, hectoring his party, demanding that it pay him respect, this fall he is out to show the Democratic establishment that he is a politician who can play by the rules too.

What happened to the political crusader who, it was thought, would spend the fall on some renegade course of his own, perhaps pulling blacks from the mainstream of the Democratic Party? Jackson did not change so much as adapt, strategically, to new circumstances: if he was to accumulate significant power within his party, he knew, he had no choice but to campaign actively for the ticket. Furthermore, since an overwhelmingly Democratic vote by blacks was inevitable, Jackson realized that it suited his own purposes if the turnout seemed partly Jackson-inspired. "Jesse has a future," says one Democratic National Committee official. "He has been anxious to demonstrate his loyalty to the party, and he has been doing just that."

He has indeed. Since Labor Day, Jackson has made almost 50 appearances in 16 states encouraging blacks to register and vote Democratic. The D.N.C. has picked up his $230,000 in expenses, including salaries for four aides, and a week ago lent him a Learjet so that Jackson and company could make an intense get-out-the-vote tour of the South and big Northern cities for the remainder of the campaign. "The record will show that I've spoken more times to more people and convinced more people to vote for Mondale and Ferraro than anybody else in the field," he boasts, "perhaps including the ticket itself."

When he showed up at the Pleasant Green Baptist Church in Lexington on Wednesday, he delivered his standard autumn rap with passion. "There are thousands of reasons for us to vote in this election and no reason not to," Jackson told the crowd of 600. "Mondale ever, Reagan never! Give peace a chance, give Reagan the ranch!" As ever, the rhyme was punctuated by cries of affirmation from the crowd. Jackson reminds his audiences that Mondale is an ally from the epochal civil rights fights of the 1960s, when it counted.

Jackson's role in the campaign was arranged during a meeting at Mondale's Minnesota home in August. Yet Mondale, he complains, has failed to fulfill his part of the bargain, including a pledge to deliver a major speech on southern Africa and U.S. relations with developing countries. Jackson is also upset that the few blacks appointed to nominally high positions in the Mondale campaign are virtual tokens, seldom consulted. Many lower-level Jackson workers have been absorbed fully into the Mondale campaign operation, but Jackson feels that the party establishment has not sufficiently addressed black concerns.

Even so, he has not proved to be a politically divisive figure in the presidential campaign, as many Democrats feared and Republicans hoped last summer. Jackson, however, has been careful to avoid provocative gestures. In June he disavowed Nation of Islam Leader Louis Farrakhan's various venomous remarks, and Jackson has not appeared with his former ardent supporter since last spring. Farrakhan still delivers his disturbing messages at meetings and on the radio, but most now sink into well-deserved obscurity. In addition, Jackson offered a moving apology in his Democratic Convention speech to those, including Jews, whom he had offended. Thus while Jackson is still deeply mistrusted by Jewish voters, he seems not to have provoked anything like a serious anti-Mondale backlash.

In large part, moreover, the emotional temperature has gone down because Jackson is no longer running for President; reporters and the public now have more important demands on their attention. Jackson's appearances on behalf of voter registration have received little national notice, and he has made only a few appearances alongside Mondale. "If Jesse just does his thing, it's better for Mondale," says a Democratic Party official who deals with the black leader. "Mondale doesn't need to be too closely identified with Jesse Jackson. And you know something? Jesse knows that would be disastrous for Mondale. He's smart."

Of course, Jackson still heads straight for the spotlight when it is available. Against the opinion of some advisers, he was host of NBC's *Saturday Night Live*. He brought along his own censor, Harvard Psychiatry Professor Alvin Poussaint, to vet the scripts; Jackson excised at least one joke from a funny monologue about people who are unwelcome to join his Rainbow Coalition. (The rejected line: that "really, really, *really* poor people" were not included.)

Jackson's good soldier phase may be temporary. Part of his motivation is a sincere desire to help discredit Ronald Reagan. Yet since a G.O.P. defeat seems unlikely, Jackson's more real hope is that a large black turnout will result in more clout for blacks—

and for Jesse Jackson—within the party. "We intend on Nov. 6 to break a record and prove a point," he says. "Black voters are more loyal and disciplined than any other interest group in the Democratic Party. A new relationship is going to have to take into account new people."

For Jackson, the new relationship would entail an end to runoff elections. He also wants the few white Democrats who represent predominantly black congressional districts to give up their seats in favor of black candidates. With Mondale trailing so badly, there has been little point in blacks' asserting their demands aggressively. But after next Tuesday, Jackson's own agenda, as well as the hopes and resentments he has aroused within the party, could bubble forth again. "There's some lack of trust and some anxiety" between him and party leaders, he admits. "I'll have something to say about that on Nov. 7."

Museums, No

Robert M. Strozier

A friend once said to me, "The trouble with a museum is that, well, it's a *museum.*" I know exactly what he was driving at. A longtime New Yorker, I go to museums fairly often, but I've been rethinking the whole thing lately. I don't know about you, but I become instantly aimless and kind of floppy upon entering a museum. With good intentions I set out to do, say, Greek friezes, but then I make a wrong turn and suddenly find myself in a room filled with Flemish tapestries or early New Brunswick furniture or little Aztec tools. Searching blindly for the original path, I stray yet more: wander into the Triptychs Wing, perhaps never to return, or end up standing in line for the All the Chinese Vases exhibition.

In New York a person lives with a constant dark presence, and it's called the Metropolitan Museum of Art. It stares down at you from its august height, saying: ENTER NOW AND DON'T RETURN TO YOUR OTHER LIFE. Cradled in its vast bosom are some *three million* items of art, each more important than the last. Even if you finally come to terms with the Met, you won't have begun to make a dent in the museum world.

This museum thing affects everyone, not just city dwellers. Jot down the first ten words that come to mind when I say: THE LOUVRE. I bet they all have to do with inadequacy and loneliness and desperation and physical exhaustion. Let's start with the last. People talk about "museumitis," and it's a real affliction, all right. Confronted by anything hanging on a wall, the body starts to sag. I think it has to do with a tension between the two parts of the trunk: the lower half says "Move on," the upper, "Stand and absorb the beauty."

All other art forms—literature, concerts, operas, movies—allow us to sit down. Not a museum, no way. You're lucky to find an occasional hard, backless bench, its tiny surface occupied by about fifteen people, their behinds fighting for a grip. Usually I just plunge on, but at the Met's Vatican Collections exhibition last year I got really tuckered out about halfway through. For ten minutes I staked out the one bench in the vicinity and then darted in when a corner spot became vacant, just beating out a heavyset woman in her fifties. In retrospect I can see how truly undignified it was to fight for a seat in the New Directions in Papal Patronage Room.

Something else happens to me when I enter a museum: my body starts whining and asking for something to eat. I crave something that I can stuff into my mouth and relate to at the most elemental of levels. Sometimes I take a bag of M&M's along and pop them as I go, even as I spend more and more time in front of paintings titled *Still Life of Bowl of Fruit* and *Study of Asparagus.* Museums also immediately make me want to go to the bathroom, which is unfortunate, because, huge as these buildings are, they have only two bathrooms. All the great museums of the world have only two bathrooms. And two water fountains. And these are usually roped off.

It's a tribute to New Yorkers that they go to museum shows, but the downside of this commitment is that they do go—lots of them. Every morning thousands of them wake up, stretch, and say, "Let's go block some views of art today." Part of me actually likes the crowds: I'm reminded that we're all in this together. And it certainly beats being the only one there. Surely there is no greater loneliness in the world than being by yourself in a room filled with gigantic paintings by the masters. The masters were not a fun, lighthearted group, and the gloomier and more anguished they got, the bigger they painted. Enormous, unforgiving saints, dark, brooding cardinals, and great winged things stare down at you, reproaching you for being such an ignoramus.

It's even worse if there's a guard around. Bad enough that he thinks you may steal something, but you also know that he's got your number. Under the assumption that I'm being watched, I usually scrutinize each masterpiece in turn for a long time, cock my head left and right, murmur appreciatively, form a church steeple with the fingers to help frame the different elements, jot things down in a notebook if I remembered to bring one, pretend to be smitten by the sublimity of it all.

Anyway, crowds. I visited the Met's Manet exhibition a while ago, and it was packed. I kept expecting a hostess to come by and say, "Okay, let's all mingle, everybody." The painting that most struck my fancy was *Boating,* but I had to take a slow boat myself to get there. I kept poling nearer, catching glimpses now and then, through the jungle of napes, of what appeared to be blue sky, but then my sextant went on the blink or something, because when I finally hit a clearing the sky turned out to be a cloud cover of blank wall just left of a vent. At another point I got turned completely around and arrived at a painting only to find myself facing the opposite direction.

Museums also sorely lack dramatic guideposts. No curtain goes up; you never get to applaud; nothing has a clear-cut beginning, middle, and end. When reading a book, you come to the last page, savor the conclusion, snap the volume shut, and get on with your life. Art won't allow you that pleasure: everything is kind of mushy and undefined and paralyzing. When you do finally take those first uncertain, shuffling steps on to the next room, the slighted *objet d'art* pushes off and follows you home, perches on the headboard of your bed, and says bad things about you all night in a kind of mournful hiss.

To make sure you have someone to turn to at all times, it is best to go to a museum with a friend, but the choice must be made with great care. Museums have been known to destroy friendships and dissolve marriages in a single afternoon. At the Manet show I heard a woman say to her husband, very irritatedly, "I am *not* just wandering around, I am *looking* at the paintings." Maybe states should even require that couples go to a museum together before they get married. In any case, proceed with caution in choosing a companion. You certainly don't want someone who moves faster than you do, because then you'll both be out on the street in ten minutes, nursing terrible anxieties. Nor, God knows, do you want someone who pokes along at an impossibly conscientious pace. I once went to an exhibition with a woman friend who examined each *oeuvre* at length, read all the inscriptions at least four times, lingered over every single item, even if it was only a doodle on a sketch pad, and recited sections of Collingwood's *Principles of Art* under her breath, caressing the words with her tongue. This woman was having a love affair with a museum.

I like to move out fast, hit four or five rooms, and then circle back and rejoin my partner for a while before taking off again. This must be very unnerving for the person, but it's all I know. You certainly don't want to *be* with someone the whole time. That requires, among other things, that you make conversation and offer trenchant views. The less said about art the better, I submit. If the aesthete in you tries to get out, *hurt* it and make it want to go back in.

Now and then you do have to say something, of course; otherwise your companion will think you're a total dodo. My approach is a feigned deep, silent communion with the work, punctuated by flip and offhand remarks: "Un-be-liev-able."/"I wouldn't want to be alone with him in a dark alley."/"These boys [the Popes] sure knew how to live, didn't they?" The image I hope to project is of someone so sophisticated that he can afford to be cute, though some might argue that I'm living beyond my means. But the real risk one runs is of simply being *wrong*. A friend of mine who attended a Calder exhibition overheard a woman providing instruction to four companions, who hung intently on every word. "The sculpture can be divided into two categories," she explained with great solemnity. "Stabiles, which are free-floating, and mobiles, which are stationary."

I see my time is nearly up, but I keep hearing that museums are great places to meet singles. Maybe that is the way to go. On second thought, I think I'll pass. This has got to represent a nadir of some kind: getting all dolled up to go hang out in the Etruscan Room.

In this process of guessing and modifying your guess, you are also adding support and qualifiers. For example, after reading the first paragraph of "Jackson Plays by the Rules," your guess might have been "Jesse Jackson is campaigning for the Democratic ticket, and this demonstrates that he wants to be seen as loyal to the party." After reading the second paragraph, you could have added "He wants to be associated with the significant black support of the ticket, and his demonstration of loyaltiy should help him gain power in the party." Thus the second paragraph would have led you to fill in specific support for the general guess you made after reading the first paragraph. And each successive paragraph might give you further support or qualification.

When you finish reading the article, your guess will be a statement of the writer's point. Most often it will be a restatement of the writer's major generalization and of the support and qualifications the writer provided. Your summary will be much shorter than the original article and will lack detail, but it will reflect all of the important ideas in the writing.

Before Reading

As you read the following essay by Alleen Pace Nilsen, consciously keep track of the guess you make and the way you modify it.

"Vive la Différence!" and Communication Processes

Alleen Pace Nilsen

Back in the 1960s and '70s, when most of us first heard the word *sexism,* we had the experience a hundred times over that our students have when they learn a new word and then are amazed at how many places they meet it. Once we became aware of sexism, we saw it everywhere—in the language, in the mass media, in our teaching materials, in department meetings, and even in the ways we related to our families and friends. But just knowing that it was there didn't make it go away.

This has been frustrating to many of us and has caused us to probe into factors that promote and contribute to sexism. The article that follows is one such probe. It looks at the circular way in which sexism is fostered by four different but related processes of communication: first overgeneralization, then exaggeration, followed by metaphorical extension, and finally by people adapting their behavior to fit the exaggerations and metaphors that grew out of the overgeneralizations.

Overgeneralization

The success of today's mass media works against the accurate presentation of individuals. The environment is filled with so many messages that creators are forced to compete in trying to tell their stories in the fewest possible words. Writers and philosophers worry that we have become a nation of bathroom readers. Anything too long or too complex to be read in small snatches will never make it to the mass consciousness of a people who get their philosophies from the cryptic messages on bumper stickers, T-shirts and campaign buttons. Within the last decade, novels for leisure reading have grown substantially shorter. One researcher investigating the new brevity in mystery stories found that the change was in characterization, especially of less important roles where authors could rely on stereotypes. A somewhat comparable change has occurred with television commercials. Companies who used to have 60-second commercials are now paying for shorter time slots—30 or 45 seconds—which forces the creators to rely on stereotypes viewers already have in their heads.

Political cartoonists are even more restricted. Since they have only a single frame to tell a story, they must rely on stereotypes. For example, a cartoon about the increasing problem of malpractice suits in medicine pictured an operating table with two surgeons, an anaesthesiologist, two nurses, and a person labelled "Patient's Attorney" and another labelled "Surgeon's Attorney." What the cartoonist wanted to point out was the presence of the attorneys. He wanted everything else to be as typical as possible. Since 90% of the surgeons in the United States are male, he drew the surgeon as male. Since 85% of the nurses are female he drew the nurses as females. He made the patient on the table old, the anaesthesiologist male, the attorneys male, and the hospital room clean and well equipped.

With this kind of instant story, illustrators, creators of commercials, cartoonists, and writers are tempted to rely on whatever is most typical, so they won't take any attention away from the one original point being made. The cumulative effect is overgeneralization. Roles and professions that in real life are usually filled by one sex are shown in the mass media always filled by that sex.

A related factor that encourages people to overgeneralize is what Marshall McLuhan called the global village. We have people in our own physical environment to keep track of, plus all those people we read or hear about in the news media. Since we can't possibly keep everyone straight, we group or classify them. Once we've categorized people and given them labels, then we aren't so bothered by their differences from us because, in our minds, we have exiled them to an outer circle. This is why people find comfort in labelling people they do not like with such sexist terms as *women's libber, militant, chauvinist, male chauvinist pig, wimp, bitch,* etc.

A somewhat different kind of overgeneralization is forced on us by the lifestyles we live as we move from rural to urban societies. For example, in a single day I may meet more strangers than did my grandparents in a year of ordinary living. My father-in-law is among those rare Americans maintaining a rural lifestyle similar to that of his parents. He lives on a farm in the house in which he was born. He knows the genealogy and personal beliefs of every property owner within a five-mile radius. The doctor he goes to is the son of the doctor who treated his parents, the mayor of the nearest town grew up on the farm across the road, and the mechanic who fixes his car was in the graduating class with my husband.

In contrast, although I have lived in the same house for ten years, I do not know the names of my neighbors. I am a member of a health plan so I seldom see the same doctor. I have no personal knowledge of the politicians for whom I vote, and I go through the yellow pages searching for a mechanic to whom I can trust my car.

When my father-in-law needs help, he calls on a neighbor he has known all his life or on one of his nearby relatives. But when I need help, I am probably among strangers. If I fall ill at a shopping center or have car trouble on a freeway and someone offers me a ride home or to a service station, I have to decide instantly whether the convenience outweighs the risk. In making this decision I call into play all the stereotypes I've learned. I will be sexist, ageist, and ethnocentric as I decide to accept a ride from a white middle-class woman with two little children. I will overgeneralize that all mothers are trustworthy and that someone who looks like me will indeed behave as I would in a similar situation.

On any given day in most schools, an observer could find examples of sexist overgeneralizations in both methods and materials used for instruction. Librarians who provide books expressing personal feelings to girls only and adventure and sports books to boys only are overgeneralizing. So are English teachers who choose to teach only novels and stories with male protagonists because they have heard that girls will read books about either boys or girls while boys will enjoy books only about boys. Counselors who encourage girls to enter only care-giving professions, such as teaching, nursing, waitressing, and mothering while encouraging boys to be doctors, lawyers, scientists, and engineers are overgeneralizing as are authors of history textbooks who focus on *masculine* or war related aspects of history and ignore ordinary people surviving at home.

Researchers who, no matter what they are studying, automatically split a group into male and female limit the potential worth of their studies. And English teachers who ignore sexism in language and teach students to address business letters to *Dear Sirs* or *Gentlemen* and to use masculine pronouns as if they refer equally to females miss opportunities to show students that grammar and usage are living subjects.

Exaggeration

A look at today's mass communication—as well as a historical glance backwards—shows how commonly people exaggerate an idea once it is firmly established. Cartooning is the art of caricature, exaggeration, and hyperbole, and in a different sense so is advertising when store owners promise "unsurpassed value," "an absolutely unforgettable sale," and "the finest . . . the world has ever known."

From a historical standpoint, one theory about the creation of folktales featuring "little people" or the "wee folk" is that when the ancestors of today's northern Europeans took over the land, the indigenous tribes were slightly smaller in build. As these conquered people fled to live in the hills, they alternately conducted guerilla warfare and made tentative attempts at friendship. They did not know how to smelt iron as did the newcomers so they would occasionally come out to trade for kettles and weapons. Over the centuries as stories were told about these exchanges, tellers made the characters smaller and smaller resulting in today's stories about elves and fairy folk.

This contrasts with what happened in American folklore where the process was similar except in the opposite direction. Here the characters started out big and grew bigger. Paul Bunyan, Pecos Bill, Old Stormalong, Casey Jones, and John Henry grew in people's imaginations to become giants.

People's minds work much the same today. Once we overgeneralized the differences between males and females, we began to exaggerate them. For example, names given to baby girls have far different meanings than the names given to baby boys. Girls get names taken from small, aesthetically pleasing items: *Daisy, Ruby, Stella, Pearl, Fawn, Flora, Angel,* and *Iris.* Boys are more likely to get names connoting strength and power. *Barry* means sword; *Gerald,* spear ruler; *Roger,* famous spear; *William,* resolute protection; *Ward,* guard; *Harold,* chief of the army; *Martin,* god of war; and *Leo,* lion.

Slang terms and clichés we use in referring to males and females also reflect exaggeration. For example, the contrast in size and strength between men and women is exaggerated many times over when we compare the sizes of animals whose names are attached more to one sex than the other. For example, a woman will be "weak as a kitten" while a man will be described as "strong as an ox." Women are called *social butterflies, birds, chicks, lambs, vixen,* and *bunnies* and described as being *kittenish, catty,* and *mousey,* while men are called *tigers, wolves, beasts, jackasses,* and *loan sharks,* and described as being *bullheaded.* A similar contrast in size is seen in reference to plants. Women can be referred to as *wallflowers, shrinking violets,* or *clinging vines,* but if a man is referred to as a small plant, i.e., a *pansy,* the message is that he is not playing his masculine role. A plant metaphor for a "real man" must be based on something big, for example, a tree as when Andrew Jackson was called *Old Hickory.*

Approximately 100 common words include some masculine marker which would appear to make the words refer to males only, but through overgeneralization many of them are used to refer to females as well as males, for example, *chairman, bachelor's degree, master's degree, fellowship, upperclassman, craftsmanship, gentleman's agreement, masterful,* and *workmen's compensation.* In contrast to these hundred masculine sounding words sometimes used generically to include both sexes, I could find only three feminine sounding words that are used generically to refer to males as well as females: *ladybug, black widow spider,* and *seacow.*

The reason that the feminine form of these words took hold of people's imaginations and caused an unusual kind of overgeneralization is that they represent three points on a triangle of exaggerated stereotypes of women. The ladybug is the darling, little girl—harmless, sweet, and appealing. In the virgin-whore dichotomy, she is the virgin. The black widow spider is the whore—evil, conniving, and sexy. She is the woman who entices men only to bring them harm. The third extreme is the most unappealing of the three. She is the large, old, overweight, and unattractive woman—the one who suffers from the misogyny of the world.

Other examples of exaggeration are given below under metaphor and symbolization. The nature of the metaphorical process exaggerates the particular features being compared between the root of the metaphor and what it now refers to.

Extension through Metaphor and Symbolization

Extension happens deep within speakers' and writers' minds when they take an idea they consider well established and extend it to communicate something not so well established. They use the established idea as the basis of a metaphor or symbol through which they can communicate unknown ideas or abstractions.

As the world gets smaller through travel and increased communication, the value of universal symbols goes up. For example, some symbols that speakers in the continental United States take for granted do not communicate the same messages to speakers in other parts of the world. Here in Arizona the metaphor of a *snake in the grass* is wonderfully communicative, but it probably says little to someone living in the Arctic Circle where there are neither snakes nor grass. And the symbolization that goes throughout much of Western literature in which spring is equated with birth, summer with childhood, fall with adulthood, and finally winter with old age and death does not have the same communication value to a person living on the equator where there are no seasons.

Probably the best example to illustrate how denotations and connotations are extended through the metaphorical process are language usages centered around left-handedness. Because in every culture left-handed people are in the minority and it is the majority or the more powerful people who make language decisions, we would expect metaphors based on left-handedness to have negative connotations. The most literal of the metaphors express the concept of awkwardness because to the majority of speakers the left hand is less skilled than the right hand. This awkwardness is implied when a poor dancer is said to have two left feet. The word *dextrous* which means skilled comes from Latin meaning right. *Ambidextrous* literally means two right hands. *Adroit* meaning skilled and graceful is French for right while *gauche* meaning clumsy and awkward is French for left.

An important point is that while these words began as literal references to the difference in skill for the right-handed majority, they have now been extended beyond the concept of physical skill vs. awkwardness. For example, a social faux pas may be described as "a gauche remark" while a witness in court may keep from indicting a friend by answering the prosecuting attorney's questions "adroitly." Throughout the world, examples can be found in which metaphors based on left-handedness are used to communicate negative feelings while metaphors based on right-handedness are used to communicate positive feelings. The most vivid example is the word *sinister* meaning evil. It is the Latin word for *on the left* or *unlucky*. The reason wedding and other religiously symbolic rings are worn on the left hand is to protect the evil side of the body. In the Book of Genesis there are 19 references to being "on the right hand of God." "My right-hand man" is a complimentary way to refer to someone—just the opposite of "giving a left-handed compliment." Some primitive tribes believe that left-handed girls will grow up to be witches while those babies who refuse to nurse at the left breast instinctively recognize evil and therefore will grow up to be saints. One Australian tribe believes that females are born from sperm from the left or weaker testicle.

Just as left- and right-handedness are universal concepts upon which metaphors are based, so is the obvious fact that approximately half the people in the world are born female and the other half male. And in much the same way, metaphors and symbols have developed that go far beyond male and female differences, even beyond the exaggerations discussed above.

The pervasiveness of such symbolic extension is widespread. For example, there are no physical differences in the coloring of males and females, yet most of us would agree that "soft, pastel" colors—pink, baby blue, lime green, and sunshine yellow—are feminine while "bold, and solid" colors—black, maroon, brown, navy blue, steel gray, and dark green—are masculine. A Stuart Anderson steak house is a masculine restaurant while ice cream parlors, tea rooms, and salad bars are feminine restaurants.

A world-wide example is the assigning of masculine or feminine gender to all nouns in such languages as French and Spanish, and masculine, feminine, or neuter gender to nouns in such languages as German and Latin. In 1784 John Fell attempted to do something similar for English when he wrote in *An Essay Towards English Grammar:*

> The passions must be determined according to their different natures: the fiercer and most disagreeable are masculine—the softer and more amiable are feminine. *Mind* is masculine, *soul* feminine; for in the latter term more of the affections are frequently implied than in the former. The *sun* is masculine, the *moon* feminine, the *Heaven* neuter—the *earth* is feminine; the mountains and rivers are commonly masculine; countries and cities are feminine—and *nature* as comprehending all, is feminine.

Fell's essay revealed more about cultural attitudes than about English grammar.

A more contemporary example of symbolic extension is the *Alpha One* and *Alpha Time* Reading Programs (Plainview, New York: New Dimensions in Education, 1969) whose creators personified the alphabet making the consonants boys and the vowels girls. Their reasoning was that young children already understand differences between boys and girls, and this knowledge could be used to help them comprehend how vowels and consonants differ.

Another example are these lines from an essay, "My Lady the Furnace" printed in the *Baltimore Sun:*

> [furnaces] are extremely human and possessed of no end of temperament. A furnace should be spoken of as "she" for its traits are distinctly feminine. Like a woman, a furnace requires constant attention and prefers to be handled by a man. Like a woman, a furnace has moods of warmth and coldness. . . . When properly treated, they are capable of irradiating warmth throughout the home. But their glow subsides when a damper is put upon them.

Adaptation to Fit the Metaphors

This last stage is not so much one of communication as it is behavior, but communication leads to behavior, and it is impossible to delineate clearly how much behavior is influenced by communication processes vs. other factors. Human nature is such that people do not want to be misfits so just as some parents try to force their children to be right-handed, males and females try to match themselves to whatever they consider appropriate sex-role images regardless of whether or not there is a natural fit. The process is easiest to illustrate on a physical, visible level, but it happens even more with mental characteristics.

I'll begin with the example of height—the idea that males are taller than females—since that is an issue I have lived with and pondered over ever since I discovered that I was the tallest child in the first grade. All through elementary school, I noticed I wasn't the only girl taller than most of the boys in class even though all the pictures in the textbooks and the picture on the caution sign at the school crosswalk showed boys to be taller than girls.

My paternal grandparents died before I was born, but as a young teenager I remember looking at their wedding portrait and being told that grandmother was sitting down so no one would know that she had married a man shorter than she was. A few years ago my parents and their six adult children with their respective spouses went to a photo studio for a family portrait. The photographer had a phalanx of stools, wooden boxes, and pillows he used to make sure that in this portrait for posterity every male would look taller than every female.

These examples show how the idealized view of males as taller than females is communicated, but closely related is taking steps to make reality fit the portrait. The easiest way is for women to restrict themselves to dating men who are taller. Most young women accept this restriction as a matter of course without considering the fact that for many women the practice arbitrarily cuts out between 50 and 80 percent of their potential suitors. A more extreme instance occurred when I took my eleven-year-old daughter for her annual check-up with her pediatrician. While he was doing the typical things, listening to her heart and looking into her ears, he casually asked if I wanted him to start her on birth control pills to make her begin menstruating and thereby stop growing. I was too stunned to reply before he had a second thought, "Oh, never mind. She's diabetic and we wouldn't want to mess around with anything like that." As we left the office, my daughter understandably inquired, "Am I too tall?"

Related to the idea that boys should be taller than girls is the idea that they should be bigger and heavier, hence the body-building kits and diets guaranteed to turn "90-pound weaklings" into "150-pound he-men." For girls, the exercise and diet books promise to turn "150-pound slobs" into "90-pound darlings."

It's only a tiny step further to say or think that boys should be not only bigger and taller but also stronger. And since strength is a male characteristic, then it must not be a female characteristic. An exemplification of this idea appears in the introduction to a book marketed to high school libraries, *Gymnastics for Girls* (Viking, 1976) by Frank Ryan, the gymnastics coach at Yale University:

> **During the last generation gymnastics for girls has broken away from imitating the activities of the men. Special events have been developed. No longer is there a premium on great physical strength. Instead a show of strength is discouraged. Emphasis is now on the graceful feminine activity. So the great appeal of girls' gymnastics results from its history, the deliberate and intelligent effort to modify it. For this reason gymnastics has become the most appropriate sport for girls.**

Relevant to my point is that phrase, "deliberate and intelligent effort to modify it." The modification was based on people's preconceived idea of what was innately feminine, that is, grace rather than strength.

From the idea of greater physical size and strength for males, it is only a small step to the notion that males should also have greater mental and emotional strength. Again there is a two-pronged effort, first to promote the image and second to make reality match the image. In the promotional part, boys are taught to be strong, silent types so they do not show either their ignorance or their emotional vulnerability. Girls who want to make boys feel good are encouraged to talk about *"his* subjects." And boys and men show a preference for associating with girls and women who are younger than they are, giving them the advantage of a few more years of experience from which to draw the kind of knowledge and sophistication they are expected to have. To make reality match the image, boys go to school longer, study *deeper* or *harder* subjects, and continue in-service education as part of challenging careers.

We are surrounded by many other illustrations of society taking arbitrary measures to increase differences between men and women and thereby fulfill the exaggerated idea that males and females are exact opposites of each other, rather than being quite similar. We start at birth when girls are dressed in pink and boys in blue. From there we go on to say that girls should wear dresses while boys wear pants, females should have long hair while males have short hair, females should wear clothing that reveals their body while males should not, female clothing should lap right side over left while male clothing should lap left side over right, females should wear make-up while males should not, females should be smooth shaven while males should have body hair, and on and on and on and on.

After Reading

Respond in your journal to Nilsen's observations about stereotyping and language. Can you think of an example, from your own experience, of adaptation to fit the metaphors?

Before Reading

Geneva Smitherman has written many articles on bilingualism and on Black English. Before reading " 'What Go Round Come Round': *King* in Perspective," write a journal entry in which you do one of the following:

1. Relate an incident in which you remember having your language corrected by some adult other than your parents. How did you feel? Did the correction change your language from that point on?
2. Speculate about the importance you think your language will have in later life. Will your work be affected by the way you talk and write?

Then, as you read Smitherman's article, practice the guessing strategy as you go along.

"What Go Round Come Round": *King* in Perspective

Geneva Smitherman

That teacher, he too mean. He be hollin at us and stuff. Browny, he real little, he six, and he smart cause he know how to read.

—Two of the plaintiff children in *King*

The children are the future and the hope of black America. Therefore, it is fitting and proper to begin with the words of those children who brought the federal lawsuit in the nationally prominent but widely misunderstood case of *Martin Luther King Junior Elementary School Children v. Ann Arbor School District Board*. Although this case

Geneva Smitherman, " 'What Go Round Come Round': *King* in Perspective," *Harvard Educational Review,* 51:1, pp. 40–56. Copyright © by President and Fellows of Harvard College.

has come to be known as the "Black English Case," it was as much a case about black children as about black English. As Judge Charles W. Joiner himself said, "It is a straightforward effort to require the court to intervene on the children's behalf to require the defendant School District Board to take appropriate action to teach them to read in the standard English of the school, the commercial world, the arts, science and professions. This action is a cry for judicial help in opening the doors to the establishment. . . . It is an action to keep another generation from becoming functionally illiterate" (473 F. Supp. 1371, E.D. Mich. 1979).

The precedent established by the *King* decision represents the first test of the applicability of 1703(f), the language provision of the 1974 Equal Educational Opportunity Act, to black English speakers. The case suggests new possibilities for educational and social policies in our struggle to save children and develop future leadership. As the plaintiff children's chief consultant and expert witness during the two years of litigation, I shall provide an analysis of *King* and its implications for public policy and black community development in light of the stark reality of white racism and class contradictions among blacks in the United States.

Background

Briefly, the background facts of the case are as follows. On July 28, 1977, Attorneys Gabe Kaimowitz and Kenneth Lewis of Michigan Legal Services filed suit in Eastern District Court located in Detroit, Michigan on behalf of fifteen black, economically deprived children residing in a low-income housing project on Green Road in Ann Arbor, Michigan. By the time the case came to trial in the summer of 1979, one family with four children had moved out of the school district, leaving eleven plaintiff children to litigate the case.

Initially, the plaintiffs' action was directed against the State of Michigan, the Ann Arbor School District, and officials at Martin Luther King Junior Elementary School, where black children comprised 13 percent of the school population of predominantly white, upper-class children. The allegation was that the defendants had failed to properly educate the children, who were thus in danger of becoming functionally illiterate. Specifically, plaintiffs charged that school officials had improperly placed the children in learning disability and speech pathology classes; that they had suspended, disciplined, and repeatedly retained the children at grade level without taking into account their social, economic, and cultural differences; and that they had failed to overcome language barriers preventing the children from learning standard English and learning to read. Actions taken by school officials, such as labeling the children "handicapped" and providing them with museum trips and other types of "cultural exposure," had failed to solve the academic problems of the children. The attitude of school officials was that the school had done its job, and that perhaps the children were uneducable. Yet close scrutiny of the academic records and psychological and speech-language evaluations failed to uncover any inherent limitation in the children's cognitive or language capacities. Further, the children's mothers were not persuaded that the academic and behavioral problems were due to slowness or mental retardation. The mothers' intuition was corroborated by professional judgment: their children were normal, intelligent kids who could learn if properly taught.

The Trial

During the pretrial stages of *King,* Judge Joiner tried to settle the case out of court, perhaps wary of the precedent that would be set. The "Friends of *King,*" as we, the children's advocates, came to call ourselves, prepared a reading program which the officials rejected. The Complaint was revised and amended several times to comply with Joiner's orders. For the course of future litigation in this area, the most critical revision was that all claims relative to economic, social, and cultural factors were dismissed. Joiner contended that there is no constitutional provision guaranteeing the right to educational services to overcome unsatisfactory academic performance based on cultural, social, or economic background. To put it more pointedly, the U.S. Constitution can provide protection on the basis of being black, but not on the basis of being poor.

In Judge Joiner's reasoning, it was necessary to focus the issues in *King* on a decidedly narrow set of arguments. He dismissed all of the plaintiffs' claims except one which forced the lawsuit to be tried solely on 1703(f), which reads in part: "No state shall deny equal educational opportunity to an individual on account of his or her race, color, sex, or national origin, by . . . the failure to overcome language barriers that impede equal participation by its students in its instructional programs." Restricting the case to the issue of language barriers, Joiner instructed plaintiffs to specify the nature of the barriers, the lack of appropriate action to overcome them, and the resulting denial of educational opportunity based on race. What began as much more than a "Black English Case" would now focus narrowly on language issues, and its outcome would depend on the interpretation of a single sentence. For the plaintiffs and their "friends of *King*," it was clear that the trial would depend on expert testimony. During the four-week trial, a biracial team of expert witnesses in the fields of psychology, education, linguistics, and reading testified on behalf of the plaintiff children. The members of this team advised the court of the extensive research in their respective fields, the relationship of this knowledge to language barriers, and the obligation of schools to overcome these barriers.

Significantly, the defendant school board called no expert witnesses. Its attorney simply relied on cross-examination of the plaintiffs' experts—a strategy consistent with the community's self-righteous posture. Ann Arbor prides itself on being a liberal community, and ranks among the country's top six public school systems in academic achievement. It is also the home of the prestigious University of Michigan and a multi-million dollar research program that has included the study of race, language, teaching, and learning. Indicative of its presumed enlightenment, Ann Arbor had decided to promote racial and economic integration by opting in the 1960s for scattered-site, low-income housing; poor blacks live in the same neighborhood and attend the same school as affluent whites and blacks. The Ann Arbor defendants, reflecting a blame-the-victim methodology, contended that their school district could not possibly have failed to practice equal educational opportunity. Although apparently confident about being vindicated, the school district nevertheless employed the expensive Detroit law firm that had successfully defended Detroit's suburbs before the U.S. Supreme Court in the *Bradley v. Milliken* school desegregation case.

The trial proceedings established that the school district had failed to recognize the existence and legitimacy of the children's language, black English. This failure of the teachers to recognize the language as legitimate and the corresponding negative attitudes toward the children's language led to negative expectations of the children which turned into self-fulfilling prophecies. One critical consequence was that the children were not being taught to read. On July 12, 1979, Judge Charles W. Joiner, a resident of Ann Arbor himself, issued what he later described as a "rather conservative" ruling: on the basis of failing to overcome language barriers, the Ann Arbor School District had violated the children's right to equal educational opportunity. *Though black English was not found to be a barrier per se, the institutional response to it was a barrier.* In short, this ruling affirmed the obligation of school districts to educate black children and served to establish, within a legal framework, what has been well documented in academic scholarship: black English is a systematic, rule-governed language system developed by black Americans as they struggled to combine the cultures of Africa and the United States. The district was given thirty days to devise a remedy.

The intent of the Equal Educational Opportunity Act (EEOA) is fairly clear. Initiated by President Nixon and passed by Congress at the height of the antibusing crusades, the EEOA shifted the policy emphasis from desegregation to quality education, and thus, in classic U.S. fashion, attempted to reconcile the two contradictory forces of white racism and black aspirations. Therefore, much of the impetus behind the new legislation was related to racial issues. Because bilingual legislation had already been in existence for four years, however, the inclusion of 1703(f) within the EEOA raises the question of whom this obscure language provision was originally designed to protect. In fact, once Joiner had ruled this a language case, the Ann Arbor School District immediately filed a motion to dismiss on the grounds that 1703(f) did not apply to black English speakers but only to those with foreign language backgrounds. Had this reasoning prevailed, of course, there would have been no case, since this was the only remaining claim of the plaintiffs that Joiner had allowed to stand. Emphasizing former HEW Secretary Elliott Richardson's interpretation that the statute protected the "legal right of any child [with] a language handicap" (118 Congressional Record 8928, 1972), Joiner denied Ann Arbor's motion and issued the following ruling that represented our first victory in the case:

> The President's [Nixon's] list of persons covered by his proposal is only merely illustrative but could well include students whose "language barrier" results from the use of some type of nonstandard English. . . . The statutory language places no limitations on the character or source of the language barrier except that it must be serious enough to impede equal participation by . . . students in . . . instructional programs. Barring any more legislative guidance to the contrary, 1703(f) applies to language barriers encountered by students who speak German (451 F. Supp. 1332, E.D. Mich. 1978).

The court's ruling in this regard meant that the case would not have to be based on the theoretical problem of differentiating a language from a dialect, nor consequently, on specifically determining whether black English is a language or a dialect. Yet it was an issue that really was not—and, in fact, cannot be—dismissed, for the lack of theoretical clarity and intellectual consensus on the question presented serious difficulties formulating our legal arguments and pedagogical remedies. Further, this confusion serves to account, in part, for the broad misinterpretations of *King* and the continuing ambivalence about black English in the lay community.

Language or Dialect

In categorizing linguistic phenomena, a commonly applied test is that of mutual intelligibility. If speech data from Community A can be understood by Community B, and vice versa, with relative ease, requiring only slight adjustment on the part of each group of speakers, we can generally conclude that the two sets of speech data derive from the same source, that is, they are variations of the same language. Since there is an overlap between Africanized (black) English and Euro-American (white) English, mutual comprehension exists between blacks and whites, suggesting that black English is a dialect. There are also areas of significant linguistic differentiation between the two speech communities, however, which can lead to a lack of understanding and confusion, and can contribute to the conceptualization of black English as a language. (See Dillard 1972; Fasold and Shuy 1970; Labov 1971; Smitherman 1977, 1980; Valdman 1977.)

A few examples will serve to more fully illuminate the nature of the language-dialect controversy. An often-cited characteristic of black English, strikingly distinguishing it from standard white English, is the use of *be* as a full verb form, as in the opening quotation "He be hollin at us and stuff." This use of the verb "to be" derives from an aspectual verb system that is also found in African Pidgin English, and in the Gullah Creole spoken by blacks living on the Sea Islands along the southeastern seaboard of the United States. Its use conveys the speaker's meaning with reference to the qualitative character and distribution of an action over time. In the case of "He be hollin at us," the speaker indicates habitual action. The standard English verb system of past, present, and future tenses cannot accommodate this type of construction, while the black English usage has captured all three tenses simultaneously. The closest standard English equivalent would be: he is always (or constantly) hollering at us; he frequently (or often) hollers at us; or, he sometimes (or occasionally) hollers at us. Other examples of aspectual *be* collected from taped interviews with the plaintiff children are: *When school is out dis time, uhma be going to summer school; They be hitting on peoples;* and *I like the way he be psyching people out.* Black English also allows for sentences without any form of the copula, as in *He real little; He six; My momma name Annie; She my teacher;* and *They always fighting.*

In black English, possession does not require the inflectional *z* (written as *s* preceded or followed by an apostrophe), but rather, is indicated by juxtaposition, as in these examples from the children: *She took him to his grandmother house; Popeye girlfriend;* and *My daddy name John.* Consider the potential for linguistic confusion to the nonblack English speaker that can result from the co-occurrence of two or more features of black English within a single statement, as in the following item from the "Black Language Test" (Smitherman 1975): *"She the girl momma."* Does this mean that she is the mother of the girl in question; that she is a very young girl who is the mother of a child; or, that she is a girl being pointed out to somebody's mother?

It is not only in phonology (sound) and morpho-syntax (grammar and structure) that critical differences between the black and white speech communities occur. Intelligibility can be affected by the lack of familiarity with the rhetorical and semantic strategies of black English. For example, Muhammad Ali, hero and rapper par excellence to virtually the entire black English-speaking community, nearly caused an international diplomatic disaster by using the rules of "talkin black" when he said: "There are two bad white men in the world, the Russian white man and the American white man. They are the two baddest men in the history of the world." Although the Tanzanians, to whom Ali was speaking at the time, apparently understood his meaning perfectly well, the standard white English-speaking world did not. He was castigated for using a term interpreted in the Websterian tradition as evil, wicked, negative, or not good. In the semantics of inversion used by the descendants of African slaves, however, "bad" can mean powerful, omnipotent, spiritually or physically tough, outstanding, wonderful, and with emphasis, very good. For this feature of language use in black English, Dalby (1969; 1972) cites linguistic parallels in Mandingo and several other African languages. His work remains the most rigorous treatment of the lexico-semantic system of black language from a diachronic perspective. (See also Dillard 1977; and Major 1970.)

I have deliberately chosen the example of Muhammad Ali because the contrasting black and white American interpretations of his verbal showmanship place the language-dialect controversy in bold relief. Although Ali's language appears to be English—and fairly standard English at that—the correct interpretation of his meaning requires the listener to have access to sociocultural data outside the realm of standard English. Ali represents the bad man of words in the black oral tradition. Through boastful talk, pungent rhymes, verbal repartee, and clever "signifyin" (indirect language used to tease, admonish, or disparage), the rapper establishes himself or herself (but more generally himself) as a cultural hero solely on the basis of oral performance. Preachers, politicians, and other black leaders reflect this tradition. A clever rapper can talk himself out of a jam, and in sessions of ritual insult such as "playing the dozens" (talking about somebody's momma of other kinfolk), tension is relieved and fights often avoided. Those who are verbally adept at the art of "selling woof [wolf] tickets" (boasting) often do not have to prove anything by action. It is believed that the African concept of *Nommo,* word power, can indeed "psych your opponent out." Thus, when Ali engages in the art of black braggadocio, the louder and badder he talks, the more blacks applaud him, but the more whites, lacking cultural experience in this tradition, censure him. Ali symbolizes a cultural value manifested in black language behavior, suggesting that we are dealing with more than surface dialect differences.

The black English language-dialect controversy reflects a fundamental contradiction within linguistics itself as to how language is to be defined, conceptualized, and studied. The classic dichotomy between *langue* and *parole* (loosely, speech and language) is evident in the differences between Chomskyian theoretical linguistics and Hymesian "socially constituted" linguistics. Chomsky (1966, 1972) abstracts language from social context and focuses on its structure—sound patterns, grammatical structure, and vocabulary. Hymes (1974) more broadly conceptualizes language within the framework of culture and society, and focuses on the use and users of language: their history, culture, values, world views, and social structure are considered basic to understanding a given language. The former is the more popular view of language and that taken by Judge Joiner when he demanded that we identify language barriers without reference to the children's cultural characteristics, which he deemed "irrelevant to a cause of action under the language barrier statute" (463 F. Supp. 1027 at 1030, E.D. Mich. 1978).

. . . The point is that the semantics within which one formulates a general theory of language can determine whether one views the issue as black language or as black dialect. If one considers only words, grammar, and sounds as the essence of language, then black speech data might tend to look more like a dialect of English. If one also considers the history and social rules that govern the use, production, and interpretation of the words, grammar, and sounds, then black speech data more nearly resemble a different language. Applying this to *King,* if black English is a dialect, then the language barriers are mere surface differences that do not impede communication between teacher and student, nor between student and material written in standard English. If the barriers are not in language per se, we must look elsewhere for impediments to the children's access to equal educational opportunity. In this case they were found in attitudes of teachers and other school personnel toward language. On the other hand, if we are dealing with a language, then the barriers reside not only in attitudes, but also in actual linguistic interferences that hamper communication. Since linguistics cannot offer the definitive word on language-dialect differentiation, it ultimately comes down to who has the power to define; or as Max Weinreich once put it, the difference between a language and a dialect is who's got the army (1931). . . .

Attitudes about Language

Research on sociolinguistics in the education process has been most fruitful and convincing in uncovering underlying attitudes about language. Specifying the nature of these nonstructural barriers proved to be our most powerful legal strategy. In the educational context, negative linguistic attitudes are reflected in the institutional policies and practices that become educationally dysfunctional for black English-speaking children. Research on language attitudes consistently indicates that teachers believe black English-speaking youngsters are nonverbal and possess limited vocabularies. They are perceived to be slow learners or uneducable; their speech is unsystematic and needs constant correction and improvement (Esselman 1978; Shuy and Fasold 1973; Williams 1972; Williams, Whitehead, and Miller 1971). These beliefs, though linguistically untenable, are essentially those held about black English speakers.

Myths and misconceptions about language and negative attitudes toward language diversity are fostered in the school and perpetuated in the general populace of the public school experience (Pooley 1974). Schools and teachers are seen as guardians of the national tongue. Condemned as immoral, ignorant, and inferior are all those who depart from the idealized norm of standard English which, as Pooley's research (1969) so powerfully demonstrates, teachers themselves preach but do not practice. It was this type of mental set that led King School teachers to correct constantly, to the point of verbal badgering, some of the plaintiff children's speech, thereby causing them to become truly nonverbal; to exclude them from regular classes in order to take speech remediation for a nonexistent pathology; to give them remedial work since "that's the best they can do"; and to suspend them from class for trivial and inconsequential acts of so-called misbehavior.

The use, or rather misuse, of standardized tests is a prime example of institutional policy detrimental to the educational success of black English-speaking children. Intelligence tests and other diagnostic and assessment tools used in the schools have been normed on white, middle-class, standard English speakers and are obviously linguistically and culturally biased against poor black children. For example, standard speech articulation and language assessment tests measure forms and distinctions that do not exist in black language. One set calls for the distinction between "Ruth" and "roof," which in black English are pronounced the same. Examples of this feature of black English in the speech data from the King School children include: "maf" ("math") work; "birfday" ("birthday"); "bof" ("both"). Another set of test items calls for the singular/plural distinction to be made by changing the verb form, as in the task requiring children to match pictures with the examiner's spoken sentences: "The cat is playing" vs. "The cats are playing." In black English, each sentence would be expressed without the verb and without the morphemic indication of plural. Plurality is generally realized by context in black English. Examples from the plaintiff children include "Two captain," "a few cartoon," and "two year." In sum, what we were able to show is that these linguistically biased instruments of educational institutions cannot possibly validate the problems nor the promise of a black English-speaking student (Bliss and Allen 1978; Green 1975; Taylor 1971; Williams 1972; Williams, Rivers, and Brantley 1975).

This impressive array of social science research on attitudinal language barriers led the court to conclude that "if a barrier exists because of language used by the children in this case, it exists . . . because in the process of attempting to teach the students how to speak standard English the students are made somehow to feel inferior and are thereby turned off from the learning process" (473 F. Supp. 1371, E.D. Mich. 1979).

Since black English is viewed negatively by standard English-speaking teachers, it is not difficult to reconstruct the process whereby this language barrier impeded the educational success of the plaintiff children. King School teachers denied that the plaintiff children even spoke black English, contending that "they talk like everybody else." In contradiction, however, were their own formal commentaries on the children's school records indicating the use of black English forms, test data showing low verbal ability in standard English, and the taped samples of the children's speech, excerpts of which were cited in the final amended complaint and detailed during the trial. Because teachers did not even acknowledge the existence, much less the legitimacy, of the plaintiff children's language, they obviously failed to "take it into account" in teaching standard English. It is not, then, black language in and of itself that constitutes the barrier, but negative institutional policies and classroom practices relative to black English that were, and are, key causes of black children's reading problems. Since reading is crucial to academic achievement in all school subjects, the inability to read at grade level prevents equal participation in the educational programs of the school.

The Decision

What, then, was the appropriate action the defendant school board had failed to take? It had not instituted policies to assist King School teachers and personnel to handle the linguistic and educational needs of the plaintiff children. As Joiner indicated: "The court cannot find that the defendant School Board has taken steps (1) to help the teachers understand the problem; (2) to help provide them with knowledge about the children's use of a 'black English' language system; and (3) to suggest ways and means of using that knowledge in teaching the students to read" (473 F. Supp. 1371, E.D. Mich. 1979).

In his opinion, Joiner refers to the crucial data from social science research on effective schools for poor black children (Brookover and Beady 1978; Edmonds 1979; Weber 1971; Edmonds and Fredericksen 1978). This research has established that appropriate action by schools can result in educational achievement despite pupil characteristics. Educational climate is the critical variable, not the race or class of the children.

Finally, the relationship between the district's lack of appropriate action and race lies in the manner in which black English has developed and is maintained as a unique speech system. The speech patterns of black Americans developed from an African linguistic and cultural base which was transformed by their experience in the United States, and reinforced and sustained by racial oppression and segregation, on the one hand, and by the response to racism, in the form of ethnic solidarity, on the other. The institutionalization of racism in America, through both *de facto* and *de jure* mechanisms, has meant exclusion of blacks from participation in the dominant culture, and has resulted in the continuance of two separate societies and two distinct, if not entirely separate, languages.

Blacks, however, have been differentially affected by white racism, and that has created class distinctions within the black community. Differing degrees of competence in standard English is one way these distinctions are manifest. Not all black children suffer from language barriers. Indeed, at King, the only black children having great difficulty were those from the Green Road Housing Project, who were both black and poor. The other black children attending King were from middle-class, professional families. Though these middle-class children spoke black English, they were also competent in standard English: they were skilled at code-switching and, hence, "bilingual." This is precisely the case among those blacks who have successfully negotiated the educational system and become middle class. Thus, it may be said that a black speaker's ability to code-switch is a behavioral manifestation of the interaction of race and class. Not being adequate code-switchers, the economically deprived plaintiff children experienced language-based problems in school. The language barriers for the Green Road children were thereby directly related to racial, as well as economic, discrimination, but Joiner had ruled out the latter as a consideration.

Put more succinctly, negative language attitudes are directed toward the "blackness" of black English; the attitudes and the language itself are the consequences of the historical operations of racism in the United States. To the extent that the district failed to take appropriate action, such failure was connected to the race of the plaintiff children by virtue of their speaking black English, and the barriers created are therefore directly related to race. This, in turn, obligates the district to take appropriate action under the Equal Educational Opportunity Act of 1974 to eliminate the discrimination. Such action would consist of an educational plan designed to help teachers identify black-English speakers to help these children learn to read standard English.

The educational plan approved by Joiner, however, falls far short of the mark. As Attorney Kenneth Lewis noted, the plan "amounts to no more than yet another shot in the arm of teacher inservice programs [which] only travels halfway to a full solution to overcome language barriers impeding learning" (Lewis 1980). Clearly, a teacher inservice program is desirable and needed to alter teacher attitudes toward black English. Programs of this nature are not uncommon, particularly among school districts undergoing desegregation. Yet such programs are pitifully inadequate as a remedy to eliminate barriers to equal educational opportunity. Inservice training should simply be a component of a more comprehensive education remediation plan that would have as its central theme the teaching of reading and other communication skills. In sum, with no assessment of teacher behavior and actual classroom practice, the Ann Arbor approach is premised on the theory that benefits will accrue to the children after teachers are properly trained and thereby develop new attitudes. This remedy is too slow and too limited for the immediate educational crisis facing poor black youth in schools in the United States.

Based on the procedural strategy and the outcome of *King,* there are several additional approaches to the formulation of public policy that would address this crisis. First, judicial processes are critical in shaping educational policy and practice. Joiner was reluctant to tread these waters, and partly for that reason. Ann Arbor's education plan is woefully inadequate. Despite the lament that the courts are too involved in the management of social institutions, the judiciary can promote the just and humane administration of large social bureaucracies that seem incapable of righting themselves. As the custodian and protector of values, the judiciary should be more involved, not less, in social management. The public school, more so than any other institution, directly involves and affects every citizen of the United States. Education is everybody's business—including the judge's.

Second, we need a school effectiveness policy monitored and enforced by the courts and by appropriate citizens' bodies. Accountability must be demanded and delivered. Race and class cannot be used to justify miseducation. There is now an overwhelming body of data to demonstrate that, as Edmonds put it, "some schools work, and more can" (1979). Further, schools must be willing to adopt policies to overcome cultural and economic handicaps. This is a basis for future litigation since this claim was dismissed early on in *King.* An argument could be made that culture and class are handicaps just as are physical infirmities. As Kaimowitz (1981) later put it, "Economic, social, and cultural factors, as well as the racial factors . . . and the language factor, must be taken into account."

Third, there should be a national moratorium on tests—standardized, employment, and other such assessment instruments. All evidence points to the cultural and linguistic biases of such tests. *King,* along with *Larry P. v. Riles* No. C-712270 RFP (N.C. Cal. October 1979), attests to the inadequacy of tests for evaluating and diagnosing black children. These rulings reinforce the call for such a moratorium, already issued by a number of professional and concerned citizens' groups.

Fourth, one outcome of Joiner's ruling was clearly to give legalistic legitimacy to a speech form spoken at times by 80–90 percent of the black community in the United States. (Dillard 1972; Smitherman 1977). As a corollary to *King* and coincident with the goals of the Bilingual Education Act, we need a national public policy on language that asserts the legitimacy of languages and dialects other than standard English. As recommended by the Task Force on Language Policy and National Development (in press), a parallel tactic might be the development of awareness campaigns on black English conducted in communities throughout the country.

Fifth, just as *King* reaffirms the viability and appropriateness of black English, it also demands that students gain competence in standard English. As sociolinguists have maintained, effective speakers, writers, and readers have a highly de·eloped level of communicative competence, that is, using language forms in socially appropriate contexts. Such competence allows one to manipulate a variety of speech forms, adapted to various audiences, media of communication, intention, and other social variables. There is not simply one form of standard English, but varieties of standard English—formal, informal, and colloquial. Similarly, there are varieties of black English conducive to communicating in various social situations; black church language, proverbs, and street raps are examples. The recognition of black English alongside standard English reinforces the call for a curriculum policy that would mandate and facilitate teaching of communicative competence.

Sixth, because of the distortions of *King* perpetrated by the media, a potential weapon for black child advocacy has been grossly misunderstood. There were over three hundred newspaper and magazine articles and editorials (Bailey 1981) along with numerous television and radio broadcasts. Yet media sensationalism prevented the issues from being clearly and fully delineated. There was a persistent attempt to discredit the plaintiffs' mothers and to exonerate the school district, and survey results indicate that many people received negative views of black English from media coverage of *King* (Wilks 1981). Black and other nonmainstream communities have traditionally been the victims of biased media coverage. Communities must rally to force the media to adhere to a standard of ethics and to establish media clearinghouses to counter the dissemination of inaccurate and distorted information (Task Force on Media and Information Dissemination 1981).

Seventh, in some circles it has become fashionable to disavow the need for and utility of academic research. *King,* however, reaffirms the need for more, not less, research, of the kind that is responsive to the needs of black and other similarly dispossessed communities. Joiner also commented in his ruling on the value of research in informing the court (473 F. Supp. 1371, E.D. Mich. 1979).

He noted the efficacy of the personal appearance and involvement of experts as advocates for the children. Research efforts of this kind should be encouraged, and blacks should be involved from the beginning. Creative ways must be found to encourage the allocation of funds for research on black children and youth. At the very least, blacks should vigorously monitor all such research to insure that only projects with policy implications for improving the education of black children and youth receive top priority.

To complete our analysis of *King,* I shall briefly examine the issues of black double-consciousness and class contradictions which were raised during the legal proceedings. "Double-consciousness" was first described by Du Bois when he said:

After the Egyptian and Indian, the Greek and Roman, the Teuton and Mongolian, the Negro is a sort of seventh son, born with a veil, and gifted with second-sight

in this American world—a world which yields him no true self-consciousness, but only lets him see himself through the revelation of the other world. It is a peculiar sensation, this double-consciousness, this sense of always looking at one's self through the eyes of others. . . . One ever feels his twoness—an American, a Negro: two souls, two warring ideals in one dark body. . . . The history of the American Negro is the history of the strife—this longing to attain self-conscious manhood, to merge his double self into a better and truer self. In this merging, he wishes neither of the older selves to be lost (Du Bois 1903/1961, 44).

With respect to black speech, I describe the manifestation of double-consciousness in language as "linguistic push-pull": the push toward Americanization of black English counterbalanced by the pull of its Africanization (Smitherman 1977). Both linguistic forms have been necessary for black survival in white America—standard English in attempts to gain access to the social and economic mainstream, black English for community solidarity, deception, and "puttin on ole massa." In "If Black English Isn't a Language, Then Tell Me What Is?" (*New York Times,* July 29, 1979) written shortly after the *King* trial, Baldwin spoke eloquently of the role of black English in the black experience: "There was a moment, in time, and in this place, when my brother, or my mother, or my father, or my sister, had to convey to me, for example, the danger in which I was standing from the white man standing just behind me, and to convey this with a speed, and in a language, that the white man could not possibly understand, and that, indeed, he cannot understand, until today."

With the beginnings of education for blacks in the late nineteenth century, linguistic push-pull became more pervasive in the Afro-American community. As Woodson (1936/1969) tells us, that education has always been away from—not toward—black culture, language, and community. Relating his critique specifically to language, Woodson noted that: "In the study of language in school, pupils were made to scoff at the Negro dialect as some peculiar possession of the Negro which they should despise rather than directed to study the background of this language as a broken down African tongue—in short to understand their own linguistic history, which is certainly more important for them than the study of French Phonetics, or Historical Spanish Grammar" (1933/1969, 19).

This ambivalence about a dimension of blackness so close to personal identity explains the mixed reactions of blacks to *King.* Despite the decidedly forward advancement in black pride during the 1960s, there continues to be a lingering self-consciousness about the value of black culture and black language, even among those who speak it most frequently and who, in their more culturally chauvinistic moments, decry "nigguhs who talk all proper and white."

This linguistic push-pull also serves to account, in part, for the paucity of research on black speech by contemporary black scholars. Seeing the value and distinctive African character of black English, white researchers have produced a sizable body of data attesting to the systematicity, use, and functions of black English. Not all of this research has been to our betterment. In particular, blacks have decried treatments such as Folb's *Runnin' Down Some Lines* (1980) and Jackson's *Get Your Ass in the Water and Swim Like Me* (1974) because they focus on the sensational words and phrases in black speech. Black language is, after all, more than "jive-ass" lingo of ghetto teenagers or the "pussy-coppin" raps of prisoners. The "more than" awaits the treatment of black scholars who can continue in the black intellectual tradition of Frederick Douglass, W. E. B. Du Bois, Carter G. Woodson, and Lorenzo Turner. All wrote positively about—and in Turner's case, thoroughly analyzed—black English long before post-1960 white scholars. In fact, Turner's *Africanisms in the Gullah Dialect* (1949) was quoted, while still in manuscript form, by white anthropologist Herskovits in *Myth of the Negro Past* (1941), surely one of the rare instances in which a white scholar acknowledges an intellectual debt to a black scholar.

Black teachers and educators are often more negative toward black English-speaking children than are white educators. This reaction of educators and other black leaders to *King* serves to remind the black community that our class contradictions were never resolved in the 1960s era of black progress ("What go round come round"). Briefly, their fear is that black speech will prevent blacks from getting a share of the rapidly shrinking pie—a threat, as Baldwin indicated in his keynote speech to the National Invitational Symposium on Black English and the Education of Black Children and Youth, that is no longer in the power of the United States to give, as the Third World continues to cut off America's historically free and ready access to resources (Baldwin 1981). Several editorials by noted black columnist Rowan (*Detroit News,* July 11, 1979) are representative of the disturbing reaction of many members of the black middle class. Stating that *King* was one of the "silliest and potentially most destructive" cases to affect the education of black children, he argued that this approach would "consign millions of ghetto children to a linguistic separation [as if it doesn't already exist!] which would guarantee that they will never make it in the larger U.S. society." Note that it is not high unemployment, or the shifting balance in world economic power, or the crises caused by a highly advanced, technological capitalist society in the United States but "linguistic separation," mind you, that will keep black children and youth from making it in the United States.

The language, education, and other public policies typically proposed by black middle-class leadership will not serve the needs of the black underclass. Their programs only ensure that a few blacks slide past the gatekeepers. Limited by an analysis based solely on race, without considering issues of class, they are unable to propose solutions that address the broader structural crises that affect all groups in United States society, but affect poor blacks with disproportionate severity. While *King* reminds us that standard English is a *sine qua non* of survival in our complex society, the harsh reality is that if all blacks commanded the language of textbooks and technocracy, the system, as it is presently constructed, could not accommodate all of us. Further, if our society could solve the problem of black unemployment—and that's a big if—it would only shift the burden to some other group. It would do nothing to address the fundamental cause of unemployment.

There are no spoils to the victors in *King*. Though the ruling set a legal precedent establishing that black English falls within the parameters of the statutory language of 1703(f), it is an acknowledged reformist strategy. But it is a tool now available to other communities for manipulating the legal system to obtain a measure of redress from our continuing oppression.

The fate of black children as victims of miseducation continues to be the bottom line in the "Black English Case." *King* gives us yet another weapon in our struggle to save the children and develop future leadership. The case began with a claim of institutional mismanagement of education for children from the Green Road Housing Project. It ended with a claim of institutional mismanagement of the children's language. For those who know that language is identity, the issue is the same: *the children's language is them is they mommas and kinfolk and community and black culture and the black experience made manifest in verbal form.*

References

Bailey, R. "Press Coverage of the Black English Case." In *Black English and the Education of Black Children and Youth: Proceedings of the National Invitational Symposium on the King Decision,* edited by Geneva Smitherman. Detroit: Center for Black Studies, Wayne State University, 1981.

Baldwin, J. "Black English: A Dishonest Argument." In *Black English and the Education of Black Children and Youth: Proceedings of the National Invitational Symposium on the King Decision,* edited by Geneva Smitherman. Detroit: Center for Black Studies, Wayne State University, 1981.

Bereiter, C., and S. Engelmann. *Teaching Disadvantaged Children in the Preschool.* Englewood Cliffs, N.J.: Prentice-Hall, 1966.

Bliss, L., and D. Allen. Language Screening and Assessment Test for Preschool Children of Diverse Backgrounds. (Interim report to National Institute of Health. Research Project NIH-NINCDS-76-03) Detroit: Wayne State University, 1978.

Brookover, W. B., and C. Beady. *School Social Climate and Student Achievement.* New York: Praeger, 1978.

Chomsky, Noam. *Cartesian Linguistics.* New York: Harper & Row, 1966.

———. *Language and Mind.* New York: Harcourt Brace Jovanovich, 1972.

Cooper, G. "Black Language and Holistic Cognitive Style." Paper presented at the Association for the Study of Afro-American Life and History Conference, New Orleans, October 1980.

Dalby, David. *Black through White: Patterns of Communication in Africa and the New World.* Bloomington, Ind.: Indiana University Press, 1969.

———. "The African Element in American English." In *Rappin' and Stylin' out: Communication in Urban Black America,* edited by T. Cochman. Urbana, Ill.: University of Illinois Press, 1972.

Deutsch, M. "The Disadvantaged Child and the Learning Process." In *Education in Depressed Areas,* edited by A. Passow. New York: Columbia University Press, 1963.

Dillard, J. L. *Black English: Its History and Usage.* New York: Random House, 1972.

———. *Lexicon of Black English.* New York: Seabury, 1977.

Du Bois, W. E. B. *The Souls of Black Folk.* Chicago: A. C. McClurg, 1903. Reprint. New York: Fawcett, 1961.

Edmonds, Ronald, and J. R. Fredericksen. "Search for Effective Schools: The Identification and Analysis of City Schools That Are Instructionally Effective for Poor Children." Cambridge, Mass.: Center for Urban Studies, Harvard University, 1978. Photocopy.

Edmonds, R. "Educational Policy and the Urban Poor: Search for Effective Schools." In *Black English and the Education of Black Children and Youth: Proceedings of the National Invitational Symposium on the King Decision,* edited by Geneva Smitherman. Detroit: Center for Black Studies, Wayne State University, 1981.

———. "Some Schools Work and More Can." *Social Policy* 9 (1979): 28–32.

Esselman, B. "An Investigation of Third and Fourth Grade Reading Teachers' Perceptions as Related to Those Who Speak Black Dialect in the School District of the City of Highland Park, Michigan." (Ph.D. diss., Wayne State University, 1977). *Dissertation Abstracts International* 39 (1978): 1320A.

Fasold, Ralph W., and Roger Shuy, eds. *Teaching Standard English in the Inner City.* Washington, D.C.: Center for Applied Linguistics, 1970.

Folb, Edith A. *Runnin' Down Some Lines.* Cambridge: Harvard University Press, 1980.

Green, R. L. "Tips on Educational Testing: What Teachers and Parents Should Know." *Phi Delta Kappan* (October 1975): 89–93.

Herskovits, M. *Myth of the Negro Past.* Boston: Beacon Press, 1941.

Hymes, D. *Foundations in Sociolinguistics.* Philadelphia: University of Pennsylvania Press, 1974.

Jackson, B. *Get Your Ass in the Water and Swim Like Me.* Cambridge: Harvard University Press, 1974.

Kaimowitz, G. "Commentary on the *King* Case." In *Black English and the Education of Black Children and Youth: Proceedings of the National Invitational Symposium on the King Decision,* edited by Geneva Smitherman. Detroit: Center for Black Studies, Wayne State University, 1981.

Labov, W. "The Notion of Systems." In *Pidginization and Creolization of Languages,* edited by D. Hymes. New York: Cambridge University Press, 1971.

Lewis, Kenneth. "Analysis of the *King* Case." Detroit, 1980. Photocopy.

Major, Clarence. *Dictionary of Afro-American Slang.* New York: International Publishers, 1970.

Pooley, Robert C. "The Oral Usage of English Teachers." In *Language and Teaching: Essays in Honor of W. Wilbur Hatfield,* edited by V. McDavid. Chicago: Chicago State College, 1969.

———. *The Teaching of English Usage.* Urbana, Ill.: National Council of Teachers of English, 1974.

Shuy, Roger and Ralph W. Fasold. *Language Attitudes: Current Trends and Prospects.* Washington, D.C.: Georgetown University Press, 1973.

Simpkins, G. "Cross-Cultural Approach to Reading." (Ph.D. diss., University of Massachusetts–Amherst, 1976.) *Dissertation Abstracts International* 37 (1976): 5669A.

Simpkins, Gary, G. Holt, and C. Simpkins. *Bridge: A Cross-Culture Reading Program.* Boston: Houghton Mifflin, 1976.

Smitherman, Geneva. "Black Language Test." Detroit: Center for Black Studies, Wayne State University, 1975. Photocopy.

———. *Talkin and Testifyin: The Language of Black America.* Boston: Houghton Mifflin, 1977.

———. "White English in Blackface, or Who Do I Be?" in *The State of the Language,* edited by L. Michaels and C. Ricks. Berkeley and Los Angeles: University of California Press, 1980.

———. *Black English and the Education of Black Children and Youth: Proceedings of the National Invitational Symposium on the King Decision,* Detroit: Center for Black Studies, Wayne State University, 1981.

Taylor, O. "Recent Developments in Sociolinguistics: Some Implications for ASHA." *American Speech and Hearing Association Journal* 13 (1971): 340–47. Task Force on Language Policy and National Development. In *Black English and the Education of Black Children and Youth: Proceedings of the National Invitational Symposium on the King Decision,* edited by Geneva Smitherman. Detroit: Center for Black Studies, Wayne State University, 1981.

Turner, Lorenzo Dow. *Africanisms in the Gullah Dialect.* Chicago: University of Chicago Press, 1949.

Valdman, A. *Creole and Pidgin Linguistics.* Bloomington, Ind.: University of Indiana Press, 1977.

Weber, G. *Inner-City Children Can be Taught to Read: Four Successful Schools.* Washington, D.C.: Council for Basic Education, 1971.

Weinreich, M. "Tsveyshprakhikayt: Mutershpracht un tsveyte shprakh." *Yivo-Bleter* 1 (1931): 301–16.

Weinrich, U. *Languages in Contact.* The Hague: Mouton, 1963.

Wilks, M. "Black English and the Media." In *Black English and the Education of Black Children and Youth: Proceedings of the National Invitational Symposium on the King Decision,* edited by Geneva Smitherman. Detroit: Center for Black Studies, Wayne State University, 1981.

Williams, F., J. Whitehead, and L. Miller. *Attitudinal Correlates of Children's Speech Characteristics.* Austin: Center for Communication Research, University of Texas, 1971.

Williams, R. L. *The BITCH 100: A Culture-Specific Test.* St. Louis: Washington University, 1972.

Williams, R. L., L. W. Rivers, and M. Brantley. "The Effects of Language on the Test Performance of Black Children; Developing Cultural Specific Assessment Devices: An Empirical Rationale; Disentangling the Confusion Surrounding Slang, Nonstandard English, Black English and Ebonics." In *Ebonics: The True Language of Black Folks,* edited by R. Williams. St. Louis: Institute of Black Studies, 1975.

Wilson, R. "A Comparison of Learning Styles in African Tribal Groups with Afro-American Learning Situations and the Channels of Cultural Connection: An Analysis of Documentary Material." Ph.D. diss., Wayne State University, 1971. *Dissertation Abstracts International,* 1971, 32/5A, p. 2497.

Woodson, Carter G. *The Mis-Education of the American Negro.* New York: AMS Press, 1933. Reprint. Washington, D.C.: Associated Publishers, 1969.

———. "The Education of the American Negro." In *The African Background Outlined or Handbook for the Study of the Negro,* edited by Carter G. Woodson. Washington, D.C.: Negro Universities Press, 1936. Reprint. New York: New American Library, 1969.

After Reading

Write a one- to two-page response to the ideas and feelings in the Smitherman article. What did it make you think?

CRITICAL READING AND PREWRITING

Good critical reading is the best preparation for writing an effective summary. Before you begin writing, you need to find the generalization that governs the piece (or the purpose for which a story or description was written) and identify its qualifications and major support. With short readings, you can keep track of these things, building them into your guess as you read. With longer material, however, you will probably find it necessary to mark the text or take notes as you read. And you will have to read the selection more than once. Here are some strategies for keeping track of the generalization, qualification, and support as you read.

First, look in the first paragraph of a selection for a generalization that the rest of the paragraph seems to support. Often there will be one sentence that sums up the rest. For an example, turn back to the Sontag article on p. 57 and read the first paragraph. What sentence in that paragraph seems to be the generalization?

The last sentence in Susan Sontag's "The Double Standard of Aging" sums up or generalizes the examples that fill the rest of the paragraph. It would be the sentence you would note as being the generalization of the whole piece.

What sentence would you choose as the generalization for the following paragraph?

The Jazz Tradition

Martin Williams

"All I ask of popular songs," a journalist once wrote, "is that they be beautiful"— which is to ask everything or nothing. Pretty they may sometimes be, but beautiful they often are not. And if they were beautiful, an artist like Billie Holliday might have nothing to do. Her repertory abounded in trivial melody, in ugly melody, in merely pretty melody. To be sure, a part of the meaning of jazz comes from its spontaneity—improvisation and variation have meanings of their own. But in another sense there would be no point in Miss Holiday's changing a melody if it were already beautiful. Her particular musical talent was that she could find emotional and melodic beauty in banality.

Second, if there are several statements that you think could be the major generalization of a paragraph, try to keep track of all of them, either by marking or remembering them. By doing this, you are actually making several guesses. As you read on, you will be able to discard some of these and keep the ones that still fit as the generalization of the whole reading. Some of the statements may end up as qualifiers of the generalization you finally construct. Read the first paragraph of the following selection and pick out the sentences you feel are the major generalization. Then finish the reading and write down what you believe Friedenberg's premise is for the chapter that this is excerpted from.

Adolescence in an Open Society

Edgar Z. Friedenberg

What is most extraordinary about youth today is that adults everywhere should be so worried about it. I do not mean to suggest that this concern is groundless; on the contrary. A great many young people are in very serious trouble throughout the technically developed and especially the Western world. Their trouble, moreover, follows certain familiar common patterns; they get into much the same kind of difficulty in very different societies. But it is nevertheless strange that they should. Human life is a continuous thread which each of us spins to his own pattern, rich and complex in meaning. There are no natural knots in it. Yet knots form, nearly always in adolescence. In American, British, European, Japanese, Australasian, and at least the more privileged Soviet youth, puberty releases emotions that tend toward crisis. Every major industrial society believes that it has a serious youth problem.

Adolescence is both a stage and a process of growth. As such it should proceed by doing what comes naturally. Instead, there is a widespread feeling that it cannot be allowed to proceed without massive intervention. The young disturb and anger their elders, and are themselves angered and disturbed, or repelled and depressed, at the thought of becoming what they see their elders to be. Adults observe and condemn the "teen-age tyranny" of "the adolescent society," over which they seek to establish and maintain hegemony by techniques of infiltration and control.

Adolescents are among the last social groups in the world to be given the full nineteenth-century colonial treatment. Our colonial administrators, at least at the higher policy-making levels, are usually of the enlightened sort who decry the punitive expedition except as an instrument of last resort, though they are inclined to tolerate a shade more brutality in the actual school or police station than the law allows. They prefer, however, to study the young with a view to understanding them, not for their own sake but in order to learn how to induce them to abandon their barbarism and assimilate the folkways of normal adult life. The model emissary to the world of youth is no longer the rough disciplinarian but the trained youth worker, who works like a psychoanalytically oriented anthropologist. Like the best of missionaries, he is sympathetic and understanding toward the people he is sent to work with, and aware and critical of the larger society he represents. But fundamentally he accepts it, and often does not really question its basic values or its right to send him to wean the young from savagery.

How is the statement you have written related to the sentences in the first paragraph that you had identified as possible themes?

Third, if the first paragraph of a selection does not appear to have a generalization, try composing one of your own, either in your head or on paper. Practice by writing a general statement that sums up this paragraph:

> In 1976 when the remedial writing program was instituted on campus, 496 students (20 percent of the freshman class) were required to take at least one remedial writing class. Of these, only 12 percent had completed a baccalaureate degree by the end of 1980. In 1980, 380 students (16 percent of the freshman class) were required to take a remedial writing class. Of these, 22 percent had earned a baccalaureate degree by the end of 1984.

Fourth, it may be more difficult to compose a generalization for an article that tells a story and/or describes something, yet efficient readers routinely do this, even if unconsciously. Read the following portion of a narrative and try to compose a generalization.

> On the Saturday of her fourteenth birthday, Connie Jackson spent the day cleaning and recleaning the five-room duplex she called home. She shared these cramped quarters with her ten brothers and sisters who were stairsteps, two

years apart, the youngest, two, the oldest, twenty. She was planning to have her first birthday party in the two front rooms of the house, and with all those younger brothers and sisters around constantly living in those rooms while she was trying to clean, Connie had had an exhausting day. As soon as she had mopped the worn linoleum, dusted, and straightened one room, the three youngest, all energetic boys, would come racing in to wreck the neat room, tossing comic books, sofa pillows, Tinkertoys, and shoe boxes around the room.

By seven o'clock in the evening, Connie had given the house a final check to see that everything was as neat as possible. She stepped into the steamy hot kitchen to check with her mother about the food.

"Have you got the cupcakes iced yet?" Connie asked impatiently.

Mother looked up from the table where she rested her body heavily as she worked. She was wearing a clean but plain rose print housedress whose buttons were trying to pop at her bosom and around her stomach. She was perspiring and daubed at her forehead with a handkerchief.

"No, but don't worry; I'll git 'em done in plenty a' time."

"It's already after seven. Can't you hurry?"

"They'll git done, I said," Mother calmly replied. With her table knife, she swirled the yellow icing onto a plump chocolate cupcake in its pale pink paper, admiring this first cupcake briefly. She smiled broadly and extended the cupcake in her chubby icing-flecked fingers toward Connie for a sign of pleasure.

"And what about the dip? Is it ready?"

Mother placed the little beauty on an empty plate on the table.

"Yes, Connie," said Mother, mildly stern. "Settle down and git yourself ready now. Your friends are gonna be here in a few minutes, I'll tend to the food."

In arriving at your generalization you probably discovered that you could not include all the separate actions that are related in the piece. For example, you could not include all of Connie's activities in cleaning the house or all of her mother's actions as she worked with the cupcakes. Nor could you include exact quotations that pass between the two characters. In addition, you could not use the specific nouns and adjectives that help bring the narrative to life (Mother's "rose print house dress," "the steamy hot kitchen," Mother's "chubby icing-flecked fingers," or the "cramped quarters" of the home).

Which of the following generalizations comes closest to yours? Which of them most accurately represents the narrative?

1. Connie Jackson and her mother work together to prepare a party for Connie's fourteenth birthday.
2. After working hard all day, Connie Jackson becomes impatient with her mother who is kind and in control of the situation.
3. Connie Jackson and her overweight mother talk about the food for Connie's birthday party.

Fifth, as you finish reading the first paragraph of a selection, keep in mind not only what generalization will be developed but also any qualification of that generalization and the major kind of support given for it. Often you can incorporate the qualification into a single summary sentence that has one of these basic forms:

1. _____ , but _____ .
2. Although _____ , _____ .

Consider again the first paragraph in the Jesse Jackson article (p. 270). The paragraph can be summarized in two ways:

> Jesse Jackson is still an exciting campaigner, but now he is campaigning for Mondale and Ferraro to demonstrate that he is loyal to the party.

> or

> Although Jesse Jackson is no longer campaigning for himself in 1984, he is still working hard to elect the Democratic ticket; one motive is to demonstrate party loyalty.

Notice that you could not delete the qualification (the section following "but") and still give an honest and comprehensive summary.

In the following paragraph, it would be worth marking or noting as support the four groups of medical complications.

> The accounts so far in this chapter illustrate the severe psychological problems that may accompany bulimia. But this is not all: Bulimia can lead to serious medical complications as well. Bulimia-associated medical complications fall into four groups: problems due to (1) self-induced vomiting, (2) laxative abuse, (3) use of diuretics ("water pills"), and (4) binge eating per se.*

The four groups are supporting detail for the generalization that bulimia is associated with medical complications. They are worth noting because there is a very high probability that the rest of the chapter will consider each complication in turn. (In fact, it does.) Writers often proceed this way, stating their generalization and its support and then developing the support in succeeding paragraphs.

Sixth, after reading each successive paragraph of a selection, decide whether you want to modify your generalization. It is not unusual for writers to think of each paragraph as a unit that supports or qualifies the major theme of the piece. Mark the section of the paragraph that caused you to modify your guess or that added support, or write a sentence that sums up the paragraph.

Seventh, sometimes the last paragraph of an article will include a sum-

---

*Harrison G. Pope and James I. Hudson, *New Hope for Binge Eaters: Advances in the Understanding and Treatment of Bulimia* (New York: Harper & Row, 1984), 25.

mary. Compare this with your interpretation to see how well they match. The conclusion of the piece should match your generalization, but your interpretation may be more defined by including more support and qualification.

WRITING A SUMMARY

Drafting a Summary

When you feel confident that you understand the reading, you are ready to begin a draft of your summary. Try using the following steps:

1. When you have read and understood the piece, your guess will now be a paraphrase of the major generalization. Write this generalization as the opening of your summary. Include any qualification or support given in the first paragraph.
2. Paraphrase the generalization of each subsequent paragraph, or write a sentence that sums up the support or qualification in each paragraph.
3. Write transitions to indicate how each sentence in your summary relates to the ones before and after it. These transitions will help your reader understand how the author has developed his or her point.

Length of a Summary

The appropriate length for a summary depends on the purpose for which it is written and the audience for whom it is intended. If you are writing a summary of a text or an article for yourself in order to learn the material, you probably want a reasonably full summary. You will probably want to review or study it before a test or in preparation for a discussion rather than returning to the original material. On the other hand, if you are creating a summary for other readers, before deciding how long the summary should be you need to ask yourself just how much complexity and detail the audience requires and what they need the material for.

Depending on the needs of the audience, a full book could be summarized in two pages, two paragraphs, or even two sentences. Examine these student summaries of John Naisbitt's *Megatrends: Ten New Directions Transforming Our Lives.**

A Two-page Summary

    In <u>Megatrends: Ten New Directions Transforming Our
Lives,</u> John Naisbitt proposes that we can gain control
over the future by understanding the present. The author

---

*New York: Warner Books, 1982.

claims that trends in our between—era society "are gen—
erated from the bottom up, fads from the top down" (p. 3).
To understand the nature of our society and where it
seems to be going, we need to look to local events and
behavior in cities and communities other than New York
or Washington, D.C., namely in California, Florida,
Washington, Colorado, and Connecticut. Through his
analysis of 2 million local newspaper and magazine arti—
cles, Naisbitt offers an outline of the 10 directions in
which our society is moving.

The first megatrend Naisbitt discusses is the shift
of our society from an industrial to an informational
one. As early as the 1950s this trend was observable,
but then only about 17 percent of employed Americans
worked in information jobs; now that percentage is up to
60. By contrast, only 13 percent of our current labor
force works in manufacturing, and this percentage will
continue to decrease. One of the most important implica—
tions of this shift is the need for everyone to become
computer—literate in order to survive in the work world.
Related to this first megatrend is the second——a shift
from "forced technology to high tech/high touch" (p. 39),
Naisbitt's way of saying that whenever new technology is
brought into our society there occurs a parallel devel—
opment in human response or else the technology is re—
jected. The author has observed the growth of the human
potential movement as a reaction to high tech. As medi—
cal technology has increased, for example, so has the
personal human response, such as more reliance on the
family practitioner, home—like atmosphere for birthing,
and out—patient centers. The more we are surrounded by
technology, the more we feel the need to express and
look for the spiritual and human touch.

Naisbitt's third megatrend is the shift from a na—
tional economy to a world economy: "Never again will a
single country dominate the world the way the United
States did after World War II" (p. 57), says Naisbitt.
Realizing that we are no longer an industrial nation
means that we must accept the idea of an economically
interdependent world, a positive step toward peace. The
author's fourth megatrend is the short—term to long—term
shift, the change Naisbitt sees beginning to occur in
America's business, cultural, and political life. Ameri—
cans are beginning to engage in long—term planning and
to think of the future of their companies and institu—
tions. Only through developing a "strategic vision"
(p. 94) of the future and engaging in "strategic planning"
(p. 94) can individuals, companies, or institutions hope
to survive the multitude of changes in American society.

From "centralization to decentralization" (p. 97)

and from "institutional help to self-help" (p. 131) are
Naisbitt's fifth and sixth megatrends. Government and
industry have moved toward decentralization since 1950
as have our social and cultural institutions. Local action on all kinds of issues and renewed interest in regional concerns have reflected this pattern. Grass-roots
movements create the power to effect meaningful social
change. This sense of power given back to the people is
seen also in the shift from "institutional help to self-
help." According to Naisbitt, it was during the 1970s
that "after four decades of trusting in institutional
help, Americans began to disengage from the institutions
that had disillusioned them and to relearn the ability
to take action on their own" (p. 131). This emerging
self-reliance can be seen in the physical fitness and
nutrition movements and other kinds of medical "self-
help" programs. Equally important are the responses to
the disillusionment with public schools: increased parent involvement, the establishment of alternative
schools, and even home education. Other indicators of
this megatrend include local crime prevention organizations, consumer self-help programs, and food co-ops and
urban gardening.

A shift toward "participatory democracy" (p. 159)
also reflects this emerging self-reliance for it describes how Americans want to be involved in governing
themselves. "Representative democracy" (p. 159) left
people with little voice in decisions and has outgrown
its usefulness because of the information or communication explosion. One result of the growth of participatory democracy will be the extinction of the two-party
structure of our political system and a new emphasis on
local parties and initiatives. The effective leader in
the future will be a "facilitator, not an order giver"
(p. 188), claims Naisbitt. Just as government was always
structured in hierarchies, so were corporations,
churches, schools, and other institutions. The 1970s
brought the failure of hierarchies and the introduction
of networking as a way of organizing and communicating.
The trend away from hierarchies toward networking has
helped create and sustain the women's movement and other
groups that encourage self-help, the improvement of society, and the sharing of resources and knowledge.

According to Naisbitt, the 1980 census "uncovered a
massive shift not just in population but in wealth and
economic activity from North to South" (pp. 207-8). This
shift, the ninth megatrend, is related to three other
trends: "the change from an industrial to an information
society, the move from a national to a global economy,
and the reorganization from a centralized to a decen-

tralized society." The importance of the North to South shift lies in its economic implications and irreversibility. The decline of northern and eastern cities as industrial centers has created bankruptcy, unemployment, and reduced services. Boomtowns such as Houston are having a difficult time providing adequate services for their new populations.

Naisbitt's tenth megatrend, "from either/or to multiple option" (p. 231), characterizes a basic shift in our society from white bathtubs and black telephones to the Baskin-Robbins society with everything available in at least 31 flavors. Multiple-option society describes the choices we have in everything from brands of cigarettes and shampoo to types of families and living arrangements, kinds of music, and religious denominations. America no longer considers itself a melting pot but rather a nation of cultural and ethnic diversity. Naisbitt concludes by reminding us that the past is not yet dead. Our desire to cling to it instead of anticipating a new era is based on fear which can be overcome only by using brains and courage.

A Two-paragraph Summary

John Naisbitt's <u>Megatrends: Ten New Directions Transforming Our Lives</u> warns readers that unless we are aware of the important changes occurring now in our between-eras society and plan for the future accordingly, we will continue to be victimized by the past and unable to survive. The 10 new directions Naisbitt articulates are all shifts that he derives from careful analysis of media coverage of local events and behavior in what he calls the bellwether states: California, Florida, Washington, Colorado, and Connecticut. Events in these states demonstrate his proposition that trends come from the bottom up, not the top down. The 10 shifts are the following: "from an industrial to an information society, from forced technology to high tech/high touch, from a national economy to a global economy, from short term to long term, from centralization to decentralization, from institutional help to self-help, from representative to participatory democracy, from hierarchies to networking, from North to South, and from an either/or society to a multiple option one" (p. 1-2). Understanding the nature of these shifts can give Americans a framework for making sense of the world today.

Acknowledging that our society is predominantly an information society rather than an industrial one demands a change in the way we look at the world of busi-

ness and at our own individual technological skills for
survival. The fact that high tech always brings an increase in human response is a reminder that technology
can never solve all our problems. The shifts from institutional help to self-help, from centralization to decentralization, from representative to participatory
government, and from hierarchies to networking all reflect the basic desire of Americans to assume renewed
responsibility for their own destiny. Recognition that
we are moving toward a global economy which demands cooperation for survival and realization of the importance
of "strategic planning" (p. 94) for the future are two
more critical directions which Naisbitt analyzes. Ac-
knowledgement that the geographic pattern of growth in
America has generally been from North to South and is an
irreversible trend will force us to consider both national and local economics and social implications which
will continue to affect us in the twenty-first century.
Finally, the shift from an "either/or to a multiple option society" has created America's rich and ethnically
diverse population and made us a nation that is less of
a melting pot and more of a conglomerate of differing
tastes, beliefs, life styles, and cultures. This multiple-option reality in America will provide the setting
for the making of crucial decisions by America and by
each American individual in the years to come.

A Two-sentence Summary

In <u>Megatrends: Ten New Directions Transforming Our
Lives,</u> John Naisbitt defines the time in which we live
as between eras and focuses on the 10 trends he sees
America experiencing, trends that actually are shifts
between the past and the future, trends that we must understand if we are to thrive in the future. The 10 megatrends are as follows: (1) from an industrial to an
information society, (2) from forced technology to high
tech/high touch, (3) from a national economy to a global
economy, (4) from short term to long term, (5) from centralization to decentralization, (6) from institutional
help to self-help, (7) from representative to participatory democracy, (8) from hierarchies to networking, (9)
from North to South, (10) from an either/or to a multiple option society.

How do these summaries differ? For what purpose might each summary be
useful? For what audience might each be useful?

Notes versus Summary

Of course, not all material that you read to learn requires a formally written summary. Often careful notes in outline or list form will suffice to help you remember key points and details of a text or article. For example, in preparing for an objective test on *Megatrends,* making a list of the trends with some supporting descriptors and studying that list may be effective. Still, taking the time to put someone else's ideas into your own words in fully formed sentences and paragraphs can help immeasurably in giving you control over the reading. Not only will you be more comfortable with the ideas because you have put them in your own language, but you will also be better able to compose responses to essay questions or to discuss the ideas with others.

Revising Your Summary

As you revise, you will be trying to improve your summary in two ways: (1) by making it more faithful to the original; and (2) by making it clearer for yourself and your reader. When you read over the draft of your summary, ask yourself whether the message and the emphases and the tone are the same as the original. It is not unusual to discover that your draft will be slightly out of kilter; early drafts usually distort the original document in some way and have to be brought into line by some revising. Keep tinkering with the draft and rereading the original until you are confident that they say the same thing. If the emphasis seems different in your draft, add and delete material until the major points of the original are reflected as major points in your draft and so on. If the tone does not match that of the original, ask yourself whether you have reflected the author's attitude toward his or her subject. If the author is outraged or thrilled or mystified, the summary should either duplicate that tone or make note of it. If you have tried to duplicate the author's attitude but the tone still sounds wrong, focus on the parts that sound wrong and look at your individual word choice. Perhaps you have made the wrong choice among stilted English, formal English, and informal English (see Chapter 6). Or perhaps you have chosen a word with a connotation that gives it a different meaning from the original.

Editing Your Summary

In editing a summary, check your spelling and punctuation as you would in other writing tasks. Remember to check the spelling of the author's name and to give the title exactly. If it is "The Implications of Sneezing in Scandinavia," that is how it must appear in your summary, not "Sneezing in Scandinavia" or even "Implications of Sneezing in Scandinavia," but every word exactly as it appeared in the original and with the same spelling. If the author gave "Theatre" or "Colour" or "Centre" these British spellings in the title, you do the same.

One very important part of editing a summary is checking quotations and paraphrases. The next section of this chapter will be devoted to these two important topics.

Paraphrase and Quotation

To paraphrase something is to restate it in your own words. Sometimes, however, you will want to use some of the author's language because it is particularly effective or because it is virtually impossible to paraphrase accurately. Read the introductory paragraph from the Neil Postman article, "Engaging Students in the Great Conversation" on p. 138, and decide which part or parts you would quote rather than paraphrase.

If you were to try to paraphrase the next passage, you might be hard-pressed.

> What did the Weavers contribute to popular music? They did not invent folk songs, but they can be said to have invented folk music. They took regional songs and made them an American idiom. They took songs of local struggles and gave us songs that are metaphors for all struggles.

Your logical decision might be to quote the entire passage or at least the last three sentences because the ideas would be nearly impossible to paraphrase accurately.

There is no such thing as "sort of quoting" or "half paraphrasing." The material within quotation marks must be the *same* words and the *same* punctuation the author used. If you use *three or more consecutive words* taken directly from the source, you are quoting, in which case you must put the borrowed material in quotation marks and quote it *exactly*. This insistence on exact quotation may seem pointlessly strict, but it is reasonable, if you consider that authors have a right to be represented accurately and readers have a right to expect accuracy. If you wrote, "I am petitioning to have English 102 waived because it covers the same material as the English 132 course I took at _____ University," you would not want that quoted as "I am pettitioning to have English 102 waived because it covers the same material as English 131 at _____ University." The misspelling of "petitioning" would not improve your chances of getting the waiver, the misquoted number would direct the committee to the wrong course description, and the rephrasing of the last portion makes it unclear whether you have already had the course at the other university or are perhaps thinking of picking it up in the summer. Any one of these changes in your text would probably be enough to make you cry "foul," and to make you agree that close is not good enough when you are quoting. Even a change that seems completely insignificant to you may not seem so to the author.

Read the following brief excerpt from Gordon Allport's *The Language of Prejudice,* and comment on the correct and incorrect use of quotation and paraphrase in each of the three summaries that follow the selection.

The Communist Label

Gordon W. Allport

Until we label an out-group it does not clearly exist in our minds. Take the curiously vague situation that we often meet when a person wishes to locate responsibility on the shoulders of some out-group whose nature he cannot specify. In such a case he usually employs the pronoun "they" without an antecedent. "Why don't they make these sidewalks wider?" "I hear they are going to build a factory in this town and hire a lot of foreigners." "I won't pay this tax bill; they can just whistle for their money." If asked "Who?" the speaker is likely to grow confused and embarrassed. The common use of the orphaned pronoun *they* teaches us that people often want and need to designate out-groups (usually for the purpose of venting hostility), even when they have no clear conception of the out-group in question. And so long as the target of wrath remains vague and ill-defined specific prejudice cannot crystallize around it. To have enemies we need labels.

Until relatively recently—strange as it may seem—there was no agreed-upon symbol for "communist." The word, of course, existed but it had no special emotional connotation, and did not designate a public enemy. Even when, after World War I, there was a growing feeling of economic and social menace in this country, there was no agreement as to the actual source of the menace.

A content analysis of the *Boston Herald* for the year 1920 turned up the following list of labels. Each was used in a context implying some threat. Hysteria had overspread the country, as it did after World War II. Someone must be responsible for the postwar malaise, rising prices, uncertainty. There must be a villain. But in 1920 the villain was impartially designated by reporters and editorial writers with the following symbols:

> **alien, agitator, anarchist, apostle of bomb and torch, Bolshevik, communist, communist laborite, conspirator, emissary of false promise, extremist, foreigner, hyphenated-American, incendiary, IWW, parlor anarchist, parlor pink, parlor socialist, plotter, radical, red, revolutionary, Russian agitator, socialist, Soviet, syndicalist, traitor, undesirable.**

From this excited array we note that the "need" for an enemy (someone to serve as a focus for discontent and jitters) was considerably more apparent than the precise "identity" of the enemy. At any rate, there was no clearly agreed upon label. Perhaps partly for this reason the hysteria abated. Since no clear category of "communism" existed there was no true focus for the hostility.

But following World War II this collection of vaguely interchangeable labels became fewer in number and more commonly agreed upon. The out-group menace came

From *The Nature of Prejudice* by Gordon W. Allport, pages 183 and 184. Copyright © 1979 by Addison-Wesley, Reading, Massachusetts. Reprinted with permission.

to be designated almost always as "communist" or "red." In 1920 the threat, lacking a clear label, was vague; after 1945 both symbol and thing became more definite. Not that people knew precisely what they meant when they said "communist," but with the aid of the term they were at least able to point consistently to "something" that inspired fear. The term developed the power of signifying menace and led to various repressive measures against anyone to whom the label was rightly or wrongly attached.

Logically, the label should apply to specifiable defining attributes, such as members of the Communist Party, or people whose allegiance is with the Russian system, or followers, historically, of Karl Marx. But the label came in for far more extensive use.

What seems to have happened is approximately as follows. Having suffered through a period of war and being acutely aware of devastating revolution abroad, it is natural that most people should be upset, dreading to lose their possessions, annoyed by high taxes, seeing customary moral and religious values threatened, and dreading worse disasters to come. Seeking an explanation for this unrest, a single identifiable enemy is wanted. It is not enough to designate "Russia" or some other distant land. Nor is it satisfactory to fix blame on "changing social conditions." What is needed is a human agent near at hand: someone in Washington, someone in our schools, in our factories, in our neighborhood. If we feel an immediate threat, we reason, there must be a near-lying danger. It is, we conclude, communism, not only in Russia but also in America, at our doorstep, in our government, in our churches, in our colleges, in our neighborhood.

> A. Gordon Allport argues that human beings have a certain amount of fear and hostility that makes them feel threatened by some unnamed malicious force or group. Whenever something goes wrong we need to blame someone, not just conditions beyond our control. Until the post–World War II era, Americans did not focus their accusations on any one group but blamed the "foreigner" or "anarchist" or "alien" or "communist" or "laborite," among others. But after World War II, we settled our fear and hostility on the label "communist," even though many people who use it don't know exactly what it means.

> B. According to Gordon Allport, "The common use of the orphaned pronoun *they* teaches us that people often want and need to designate out-groups (usually for the purpose of venting hostility), even when they have no clear conception of the out-group in question." Americans had no particular label for a feared out-group until the years after World War II when they came to be designated almost always as *communist* or *red*.

> C. Gordon Allport asserts that people always choose some out-group to blame for all their problems, even though the problems may be caused not by enemies but by changing social conditions or economic conditions. Until the end of World War II, there was no clearly agreed upon label, and partly for this reason the hysteria abated. But "after 1945 the thing became more definite" and people blamed their problems on the Communists.

There are some circumstances in which you will find you have to make some changes in a quotation to meet the needs of your reader. You may find that some material that deserves quoting is part of a long sentence, and it is not worth quoting all of the long sentence. Here is a passage from the conclusion of Orwell's "Politics and the English Language."

If you simplify your English, you are freed from the worst follies of orthodoxy. You cannot speak any of the necessary dialects, and when you make a stupid remark its stupidity will be obvious, even to yourself. Political language—and with variations this is true of all political parties, from Conservatives to Anarchists—is designed to make lies sound truthful and murder respectable, and to give an appearance of solidity to pure wind.

A writer wishing to quote a main idea but not an entire sentence wrote the following:

> Orwell sums up his notion of political language when he claims that it ". . . is designed to make lies sound truthful and murder respectable, and to give an appearance of solidity to pure wind."

When you excerpt from a quotation, you ask the reader to take it on faith that you have not changed the sense of the original. The following is Vincent Canby's review of the movie *Angel:*

Angel in School, Outside the Law

Vincent Canby

Fifteen-year-old Molly, a pigtailed student at an exclusive Los Angeles prep school, is told by her faculty adviser, "You know there's more to life than straight A's."

Molly knows only too well. As the advertisements say, Molly is both an honor student and a Hollywood hooker known as Angel.

"Angel" . . . is another fearless "problem film." It asks how Molly can do her homework, which one night includes reading the entire first act of "King Lear," and turn enough tricks to pay her school tuition. It's not easy, especially when there's also a killer preying on Molly and her winsome associates of the street.

The film comes very close to being so consistently ridiculous that it's not unentertaining. You simply can't imagine the heights that inappropriate dialogue can attain until you hear Molly say to a couple of street friends, "Gee, I'm glad I found you two. I'm on my way to the morgue."

Even as she picks up clients, and her friends are being dismembered by the not-so-mysterious killer, Molly talks like Winnie Winkle.

As played by Donna Wilkes, who looks to be an extremely mature 15, Molly behaves like a dirty old man's idea of a nymphet. The film pretends to be somewhat more shocked than it really is by Molly's unusual behavior, which is explained by the fact that she was abandoned by her parents.

The killings are shown in some unpleasant detail, and Molly is often seen passing through the crowded girls' shower room at the school. Apparently it's the only way to get to the library.

The cast is all quite bad, if good-humored. Dick Shawn, in full drag, plays Molly's aging transvestite friend as if he were trying to imitate Jack Lemmon in "Some Like it

Hot." Rory Calhoun, wearing enough fake hair to stuff a sofa, plays an old-time cowboy actor.

An unscrupulous promoter might excerpt this review as follows:

> Vincent Canby writes "Angel is another fearless problem film" and "You can't imagine the heights that . . . dialogue can attain until you hear Molly. . . . The cast is all quite . . . good."

You may also want to quote a part of a sentence that will not make complete sense out of context. It is up to you, in this case, to supply the needed information, putting it in brackets to show that the insertion is not the author's own (e.g., "According to Samuels, 'it was hardly to be expected that he [Pasteur] would have known about the experiment.'").

Whenever you include a direct quotation in your writing you must introduce the quotation into your own sentence. It cannot simply stand alone in the middle of a paragraph. As the writer, you can introduce the quotation into your writing in a number of ways:

1. Robertson states that "_____."
2. According to Paulsen, "_____."
3. "_____," claims Whittington.
4. McVickers offers two alternatives to the adoption of the proposed amendment: "_____."

As you have seen in the several examples in the preceding paragraphs, writers adhere to certain conventions in punctuating quotations. Refer to your Editing Guide for enumeration of those conventions.

Revising Workshop

When you have good drafts of your summaries, bring them to class for a Revising Workshop. In a small group, share your paper with your classmates. Everyone's paper should be read by at least two other students, who will answer the questions below:

1. Is each summary faithful to the original in emphasis and tone? Does each convey the same message as the original? In the margin, mark any places that seem to distort the original. Note at the conclusion of each summary anything that seems to have been slighted.
2. Is the word choice in each summary appropriate for the audience? Note any words or passages you question.
3. Indicate any place in each summary where you think the transition between sentences should be made clearer.
4. Have any of the quotations been distorted by either the addition or deletion of material? Mark any that have.
5. Comment on the sentence structure in each summary. Are any sentences choppy? Any too long? Any weakened by unnecessary words?

Editing Workshop

When you have revised the drafts of your summaries, bring them to an Editing Workshop, where at least two other students will read them and respond to the following questions.

1. Are there any sentences or parts of sentences that confuse you or cause you to have to reread to grasp the meaning? If so, bracket these as needing repair.
2. Place an *X* in the margin of the paper on any line in which you see what you believe to be a spelling or punctuation error. Use as many marks as there are errors.
3. Is the author's name spelled correctly? Is the title given *exactly* as in the original? If not, place an *X* in the margin next to the error.
4. Has the writer used three or more consecutive words from an original without putting the material in quotation marks? If so, place a *Q* in the margin on the line where you find the problem.
5. Are all the quotations *exact?* Put an *X* in the margin by any that are not.
6. Has the writer used correct capitalization, quotation marks, ellipses, and other punctuation in each summary? Put a mark *C* in the margin by any line in which you find such an error.
7. Put a *G* in the margin of any line in which you see an error of grammar or usage. Use as many marks as there are errors.

Examine the responses of your classmates to your summaries and make the appropriate corrections. Note in your journal the types of errors you seem to be making and read the summaries once again for a final edit. Submit the finished papers to your instructor.

CHAPTER 9

Demonstrating What You Know, I

Perspectives on Humanity

Using Formulas and Patterns

Imagine that you are taking an interdisciplinary course called Perspectives on Humanity. What does it mean to be human? Are human beings rational beings, free to choose the greatest good? Or are we driven by chemicals in our bodies or genetic drives to violence? Why do we enjoy the company of others? What makes us hurt others? These are all variations on the question, "What makes us do what we do?" Social scientists, natural scientists, philosophers, and theologians have been intrigued by this question and the implications of various answers. Different opinions about how criminals should be treated, for example, can be traced to different views about what made the criminals become criminals. And in our everyday life, most of us wonder about our own behavior and that of those around us. Is it our true selves or our worst selves that come out when we have had too much alcohol? Can we cure a head cold by putting mind over matter? What does it mean for an athletic team to be "psyched up" to win? What is the source of those spiteful impulses we hate to recognize in ourselves? This chapter will give you an opportunity to read, think, talk, and write about some of the many contemporary perspectives on humanity and theories about our behavior.

This theme provides good subjects on which to practice writing essay tests and exams. It offers many theoretical considerations for you to balance, and it is a topic on which you will not have any trouble generating examples of your own. Of course, this chapter cannot deal exhaustively with perspectives on humanity, and it cannot even approximate the range or considerations that essay exams might cover, but the strategies it will give will be effective even when you are responsible for much more material.

AUDIENCE AND PURPOSE

Writing an essay exam is an exercise in telling someone what he or she already knows. This lends a certain artificiality to the enterprise from the very start. Essay exam answers look as though they were meant to inform, but in fact they are intended to *demonstrate* that you know the material, can manipulate the concepts, and, perhaps, can bring your knowledge to bear on a hypothetical situation. Because your purpose is to demonstrate knowledge, you cannot omit the obvious. Instead of asking "What does the reader need to know?" ask "What is the instructor asking me to prove I know?" It might be helpful when writing essay exam answers to imagine that you are writing *as the instructor* and as if you were presenting the material to the class for the first time. This will prompt you to take nothing for granted and to include all the necessary explanations.

ADAPTING THE WRITING PROCESS TO A TIMED WRITING SITUATION

The most important thing to remember about essay exams and tests is that you have to answer the question, the whole question, and nothing but the question. (Many of the writing tasks on essay tests and exams are not questions at all, but the academic community seems to find it convenient to call them "questions" nonetheless, and this text will follow that practice.) A good strategy for helping yourself do this is to note how many parts there are to the question. How many things does it ask you to do? Your answer should include that many parts. Consider the following question from an American literature test:

> The publication of Upton Sinclair's *The Jungle* in 1906 was very influential in promoting passage of the Pure Food and Drug Act. In the novel, Sinclair attacks

> more than the corrupt practice of the meat-packing industry. What other forms of corruption and exploitation does he depict? How does his view of American society place him in the tradition of literary naturalism? Include in your answer a definition of naturalism.

This question gives the writer three concerns: (1) "What other forms . . ."; (2) "How does his view . . ."; (3) "Include in your answer. . . ." A successful answer must deal with all three parts of the question.

If you match the parts of your answer to the parts of the question, you will be less tempted to include material the question does not ask for. Professors are usually annoyed rather than impressed when an essay answer includes material the question did not ask for. Including extra material, either because you have wandered off the topic or because you learned the material and are determined to use it, takes up your valuable writing time and adds to the professor's reading time. It is more likely to hurt than to help you. If there is a motto to repeat to yourself while waiting for the exams to be distributed, let it be "Answer the question, the whole question, just the question."

Because there are time limits on tests and exams, there is always a temptation to forget most of what you know about an efficient writing process and just to start in writing. Of course it does make sense to get your ideas on paper before you lose them, and having something in writing can do much to reduce anxiety. But it is important not to confuse this prewriting—in which you make notes and lists—with the writing of the answer itself. Take time to plan your answer from beginning to end before you begin writing. Make a list of the topics you will have to cover. This will save you from discovering while you are writing that you have left out something important. It will also help you avoid including any irrelevant material. The list does not need to be fancy; just a few words to jog your memory will do.

When you are ready to write your answer, you need not agonize over how to begin. It is safest and most efficient to begin your answer by making a statement that rephrases and answers the question or begins to answer it. For example, if the question asks you to define Jacksonian optimism, you are on solid ground if you begin your answer, "Jacksonian optimism is the spirit of confidence in American righteousness and in the American future that characterized the country during Andrew Jackson's presidency." Of course, you could have begun by describing the spirit in America during the 1930s, compared that to the spirit in America during Jackson's presidency, and then ended your essay with a definition. This would be legitimate but very risky. You would be taking the chance that you would get sidetracked into including irrelevant material and not have time to get to the definition itself. Beginning your essay with a statement built on the question may seem unimaginative, but it is the most reliable strategy.

You will probably have time to write the full essay only once, so it is important to read what you have written each time you complete a paragraph to make sure you are still answering the question that was asked. Your revisions will be mostly the scratch out, write in the margin, follow the arrows kind. Of course, your paper must be legible, and neatness pleases the eye of the reader, but between neatness and an improved answer there is no contest. Read your paper over and make the revisions that will give it more accuracy, more exactness, more depth, and more specificity. As you read to revise, remember that you are writing to demonstrate your knowledge and you do not want to slight anything.

After you have revised, give your paper one more reading. This time, check your spelling and punctuation. Even in classes other than English, competence and carefulness make a positive impression, and the easier your paper is to read, the more it will recommend itself to the professor.

COMMON FORMS OF ESSAY QUESTIONS

Think back over the essay exams you have taken. How did the questions begin? Have you reached a point where you can guess what the questions are likely to be? If you can, you have a great advantage, because you can study with these questions in mind. It is likely that many of the questions you will encounter will fall into one of these patterns.

1. *Define* _____. Asks for a definition and usually for some development by example or comparison.

   Example: Define sonata form.

2. *Compare* _____ *with* _____. Asks you to tell how two things are alike with respect to relevant points. Even if the question does not explicitly ask you to contrast them as well, you are usually expected to include an explanation of how they differ.

   Example: Compare the styles of Ernest Hemingway and F. Scott Fitzgerald.

3. *Trace the development of* _____. Asks you to relate in chronological order the events that led to _____ and to tell what each event contributed to the development.

   Example: Trace the development of the English Parliament from the Norman invasion up to the death of Henry III.

4. *[statement:] Agree or Disagree.* Asks you to provide support for the statement or to provide evidence that proves the statement false.

   Example: Critics claim that Hawthorne's *The Scarlet Letter* is a perfect novel. Agree or Disagree.

   Note that this question implicitly requires you to define what a perfect novel is.

5. *Describe the process of* _____. Asks you to tell what the process does and what the steps in the process are.

Example: Describe the process of photosynthesis.

6. *Interpret* _____. Asks you to tell what _____ means.

Example: Interpret the election statistics given in the accompanying chart.

7. *Discuss* _____. This can be the trickiest kind of question because it sometimes leaves it up to you to decide exactly what is wanted.

Example: Discuss the prevailing view of the world held by the English in the early sixteenth century.

Such a question asks you to decide what are the most important things to say about the view of the world held by the English in the early sixteenth century. A good answer would probably describe the view, give some examples that demonstrate it, explain its origins, and compare it to the period that preceded or followed it. You as student would have to know that this constituted a good discussion of the topic.

Sometimes, however, the question is more focused and therefore easier to answer.

Example: Discuss the contribution of Rosalind Franklin to the discovery of the structure of DNA.

This question asks you to tell what Rosalind Franklin contributed, and it also invites you to comment further on the contribution. The verb *discuss* is the clue that further comment is asked for; if the professor wanted you only to tell what Franklin contributed, the question would probably have read *"Describe* the contribution. . . ." When you are asked to *discuss,* your knowledge of the material will help you decide how to elaborate.

FORMULAS FOR ORGANIZING YOUR ANSWERS

Because of the time pressure in an exam, it is convenient to have some formulas for organizing your answers to the common forms of questions. Formulas are conventional patterns with standard sections that come in a set order. They are based on the common patterns of thought (see Chapter 2) and therefore guide you to do all of the mental operations necessary to answer the question. Because professors are often faced with time limits when they grade exams, most are happy to see an exam that has been written in an appropriate formula: the professor knows where to look in it for the thesis, the support, and the conclusion and is not likely to have trouble reading the exam.

Comparison and Contrast

There are two conventional patterns for comparison and contrast: subject by subject and point by point. In the subject-by-subject pattern, you first consider subject A with respect to points x, y, and z and then consider subject B with regard to the same points. This pattern is usually best for comparing the subjects as wholes. In the point-by-point pattern, you consider subject A and subject B with respect to point x, then to point y, and finally to point z. This pattern is usually best when you want to focus on individual points. Here is an example of an exam answer written in the subject-by-subject pattern:

> *Q.*   Compare the underlying social principles of modern architecture with those of postmodern architecture.
>
> *A.*   Modern architecture assumed that it could change people for the better by changing their buildings. Modern architects built modern functional buildings with no attempt to make them blend into the surrounding neighborhood. They assumed that eventually modern architecture would replace the old and therefore it didn't need to fit in. Modern architects wanted a complete break with previous architectural and social traditions and designed buildings that deliberately did not look like any previous style of building. They assumed also that architecture should be unornamented and that the function of a building should determine its form. The idea was that decorated buildings had been the luxuries of aristocrats, but for the new democratic age buildings should be functional and make it easy for people to do their work.
>
> In contrast, postmodern architecture does not try to change people's social values. It promotes buildings that are designed to fit into their surroundings because it does not imagine that its style will eventually replace the previous styles. It does not try to break with tradition but often incorporates bits of previous styles (Greek columns, carpenter Gothic trim). It allows ornamentation because ornamentation is attractive.
>
> Modern architecture set about to change people and society but postmodern architecture has simple goals of providing pleasant, convenient buildings.

Notice how easy it is to follow this student's comparison (actually, it contrasts rather than compares because it concentrates on the differences). This answer is effective and easy to read because it follows a basic rule of the subject-by-subject comparison and contrast pattern: it compares the two subjects on the basis of the same points and takes up the points in the same order each time. In this example, the student wrote a paragraph about modern architecture, considering the following points: its social goal, relation to neighborhood, relation to tradition, attitude toward decoration. In her paragraph on postmodern architecture, she considered *the same points in the same order.*

The next example uses the point-by-point pattern, which in this case is better than subject-by-subject because the question requires the student to begin by listing the points at issue.

> *Q.* What were the major issues of the U.S. presidential campaign of 1840 and how did the Whig and Democratic parties differ in their stands on these issues?
>
> *A.* The major issues of the 1840 presidential campaign were tariffs, the national bank, and to a lesser degree slavery. The Democratic Party, led by Martin Van Buren, favored lower tariffs, whereas the Whig Party, led by William Henry Harrison, favored higher, protectionist tariffs. On the issue of the national bank, the parties disagreed again. The Democrats opposed the idea of a banking policy that would have the federal government financially backing a banking system. Van Buren proposed instead to create an independent Treasury in which the government would keep its money. Harrison himself never spoke publicly on the issue of the national bank, but the Whig Party itself favored a national bank.
>
> The issue of slavery was one that neither the Democrats nor the Whigs wanted to make much of because any stand was bound to alienate a large part of the nation. Van Buren is on record as opposing extension of slavery into the territories but agreeing to protect it in the states that had it already. The Whig Party did not come right out and endorse slavery, but the party was generally supported by those who favored slavery. The only candidate to oppose slavery—and to make it the major campaign issue—was James G. Birney of the Liberty Party.

Definition

In some courses, the exam questions that ask for definitions will ask for ones that were given in the textbook, ones you could memorize rather than construct. In other courses, however, you may be asked to construct definitions of your own. This is particularly likely in courses beyond the introductory level.

The conventional pattern for definition is first to indicate the general group to which the subject you are defining belongs and then to tell how it differs from other members of the group. On a biology exam, you might write "a passive deterrent is a pest-control system that works by luring pests away from the plants that are to be protected." Here the general group is "pest-control system," and "that works by luring pests away from the plants that are to be protected" tells how a passive deterrent differs from other pest-control systems. If the general group were "a gardening device," you would have to use more qualifiers to tell how the passive deterrent differs from all other gardening devices. This broader general group would be necessary if the context had not already made it clear that the subject was gardening. Generally it is advisable to use as narrow a general group as the context will permit; imagine the number of qualifiers you would have to construct if you began "a cocker spaniel is an animal. . . ."

One temptation to avoid when writing definitions is the error of *circular definition* such as "a respiratory infection is an infection of the respiratory system." Obviously, this does not demonstrate much knowledge to the reader. The circular definition can be avoided if you are careful not to repeat the term being defined. One exception to this rule is the compound term, such as "isosceles triangle," in which only the first term requires definition. There is no point in confusing the issue with unnecessary words just to avoid repeating the term "triangle." A definition such as "an isosceles triangle is a triangle with two equal sides" or "an isosceles triangle is one with two equal sides" is quite acceptable.

Often, essay questions will ask you to go beyond definition and provide an example. Sometimes, although the question asks only for a definition, you can tell from the weight given the question or the space allotted for your answer that the instructor wants the definition developed beyond the bare bones. In these cases it is still a good idea to begin with a sentence that tells the general group and how the thing being defined differs from other members of the group. After that, the definition can be developed by example, description, comparison, contrast, or a combination of these. Notice how the following definition is made clearer with the use of example:

> *La nouvelle cuisine* is a variety of French cooking that relies heavily on fresh vegetables and fruits, lean meats, and small portions, rather than the richer and more caloric ingredients and larger portions associated with traditional French cuisine. A typical nouvelle cuisine entrée could include thinly sliced veal with a light sauce, crisp steamed vegetables, and fresh fruit garnishes.

Exemplification

When a question asks you to "illustrate," you are expected to provide supporting examples. Also, when a question gives you a descriptive statement (e.g., "Benjamin Franklin's *Autobiography* epitomizes American values") and asks you to agree or disagree, it is inviting you to provide examples that support the statement or examples that undercut the statement.

The strategy of exemplification often gives rise to a general support–specific support pattern. To use this pattern, you choose statements as your general support that are less general than the one given in the question and then choose specific examples that illustrate the general points. In outline form, the pattern looks like this:

General Proposition	A restatement of the question.
General support 1	A statement less general than the proposition, giving an example to support or deny the proposition.
Specific support 1.1	A specific example of general support 1.
Specific support 1.2	A second specific example of general support 1.
General support 2	A second statement less general than the general proposition, giving a second example supporting or denying the general proposition.
Specific support 2.1	A specific example of general support 2.

(There may be any number of general and specific supports.)

Here is an example of an answer that uses the general support–specific support pattern for exemplification.

	Q.	Agree or disagree with the following statement: Benjamin Franklin's *Autobiography* epitomizes traditional American goals and values.
General Proposition	*A.*	I agree that Franklin's *Autobiography* epitomizes traditional American goals and values. It chronicles Franklin's campaign for self-improvement morally and financially. The belief that people are responsible for constantly remaking themselves into more
Major support		virtuous people is not an exclusively American idea, but when moral improvement is seen as promoting financial gain, it is recognizable as an important idea of American culture: the virtuous
Specific support 1		prosper. We can see Franklin's belief in this idea when he tells of insisting on paying his fare to the boatman who brought him to Philadelphia, even though he helped to row. He comments about this that he was generous when he had very little money, as people often are because they don't want to be thought poor. Thus the desire to seem prosperous is what makes him act virtuously. And when he reports on the success of his campaign for
Specific support 2		moral perfection he notes that Industry and Frugality helped him amass a fortune. He is proud of having a fortune and implies that it is the result of his virtue. This belief that virtue is rewarded with prosperity is central to American life, and only in this century has it been challenged by those who note that virtue isn't enough if you are disadvantaged and that concern for the poor is a virtue Americans haven't had enough of.

The question allowed the student to choose any value or goal she thought of as American. She did not provide any specific support for her generalization that the identification of virtue with prosperity is characteristically American.

This does not weaken her answer, however, because the test is on Franklin's *Autobiography.* Other students may have chosen other American values or goals, and their answers would be equally acceptable as long as they could relate these specifically to the *Autobiography.*

Chronological Narration

When a question asks you to "describe the process of photosynthesis" or "describe what happens when the Federal Reserve Bank allows the money supply to increase" or "describe what happens when Beowulf enters the mere," it is asking you to narrate events in chronological order. The question that requires you to "trace the development" of something is also asking you to use chronological narration to organize your answer. This is a simple pattern, requiring that you note the events in the order in which they occur or occurred. In answering a "trace the development" question, you are also asked to explain how each event contributed to the development of something. This adds a step that other types of chronological narration do not require. Notice how the following example uses the two-step, event-plus-explanation pattern. Notice too that this is one type of question that you cannot answer even generally in the opening sentence.

> *Q.*   Trace the development of photography from its beginning to the mid-nineteenth century.
>
> *A.*   The *camera obscura* was developed as early as the fifteenth century, but *the photochemistry capable of holding the image was not developed until* the end of the eighteenth century, when Carl Scheele discovered that ammonia can slow the effects of light on silver salts. Around 1826, Joseph Niepce *was the first to combine the camera obscura and Scheele's chemical discoveries.* The problem was that Niepce's process took eight hours of exposure. Niepce's partner, Louis Daguerre, then developed the daguerreotype, which used a copper plate that was coated with a layer of photosensitive silver oxide. *This was an improvement over Niepce's process because it reduced the exposure time to minutes.* By the mid-1840s, William Henry Fox Talbot had developed the calotype, *which enabled photographers to use paper negatives. This was important because paper negatives produced photographs in which the image was not reversed, mirror-image, as those on daguerreotypes had been. It also allowed for the production of many copies from one negative. This meant that books and magazines could now include photographs.*

The italics indicate the portion of this answer that explains how each refinement furthered the development of photography. As you can see, there is no event whose significance is not explained. Notice too that sometimes, as in the first sentence, the explanation of significance comes *before* the event itself. There is nothing wrong with this. All that you have to remember is to explain the significance of *each* event to the development of your subject.

SOME SAMPLE QUESTIONS AND ANSWERS

Trying to figure out what questions you will be asked on an exam is not only a good survival strategy but also a good learning strategy. By identifying the questions you think will be asked, you will be singling out the most important ideas and the major relationships among those ideas. Your list of probable questions can then guide your study. You are well prepared to take an exam when you have thought out the probable questions and how you would answer them.

Below are an article, a selection from a book, a textbook chapter, a poem, and a copy of a painting, all of which might be distributed in an interdisciplinary course called Perspectives on Humanity. Assume that the first test will be an essay test and will cover only the article by Vance Packard. Read the article several times and make a list of the questions that might appear on the test.

Images of Man

Vance Packard

. . . What is Man? How should humans be treated by their fellow humans? Is Man something special, a being set apart from other creatures, or not? Are humans essentially self-directed or is their behavior essentially determined by other forces? What paths should future human development ideally follow? What is a reasonable model of Man for tomorrow?

The image of Man we hold today and the model of Man we want to realize in the future are important. They substantially influence how people perceive themselves. And they help determine what goals are desirable.

Man's nature has been a source of argument for at least 30 centuries, and there have recently been some significant shifts in emphasis.

Judeo-Christian doctrine generated the widespread belief that God created man in His own image. That was comforting, if ambiguous, and implied that unspoiled man had only good qualities. Judeo-Christian theologians also had great success in promoting the idea that humans, and only humans, had a touch of divinity. The popularity of this image largely explains why the first reports of Darwin's theory that humans evolved from animals created such widespread consternation.

In the seventeenth century the philosophers Thomas Hobbes and John Locke took up radically different positions on the nature of Man. In Hobbes's view, Man was an elaborate machine controlled by outside stimuli. Individual humans were so irresponsible, aggressive, and ego-driven that they needed an absolute monarch to control their lives in detail.

Locke believed that each individual deserved to be accepted as a rational, responsible, tolerant, self-directed being until proven otherwise. Rather than being in the grip of instincts, an individual grew from experience and awareness and should concede only limited regulation of his affairs to government.

In the eighteenth century two influential shapers of the new nation in America—Alexander Hamilton and Thomas Jefferson—paired off in much the same way as Hobbes and Locke did, except that Hamilton was not as arrogant or pessimistic as Hobbes. Jefferson's view was that people normally will be sensible and fair in dealing with each other and with any government, and deserve to be trusted. This view became accepted by most officials and laymen alike during the early decades of the American Republic.

The life roles people are expected to play have had their impact on some latter-day images of Man. For example:

- **With industrialization, people often became valued only to the extent that they were efficient units of production.**
- **More recently, with the superabundance of goods made possible by mass production in many countries, families have become esteemed by business and government leaders only to the extent that they are ardent consumers.**
- **In those societies experimenting with Marxism or Maoism, the individual is valued only to the extent that he selflessly contributes to the group effort.**

In recent decades, scientists have come up with a number of novel images of Man. Six of them are described in highly abbreviated form in the next paragraphs. Most have substantial contemporary support.

Man Is a Bad Animal

This image, which got some support from Freudian views about the often ugly subconscious side of Man, was recently revived. Archaeologists claimed to have uncovered evidence that very early Man began as a meat-eating hunter. From this it was extrapolated that aggression was a part of Man's biological nature. Experts in animal behavior (ethologists) pointed out that almost all species except Man have a built-in prohibition against killing their own kind if they can possibly help it. In quarrels over mates and territory, they try to keep contention as bloodless as possible. Only Man is a systematic murderer of his own kind. In wars he often kills wantonly and sometimes with seeming enthusiasm.

The best-known ethologist, Konrad Lorenz, has argued that the discovery of weapons made it easy for men to kill each other. The adoption of weapons was so rapid that inhibition against their use did not have time to evolve. Lorenz's theory may account for the beginning of Man's homicidal habits. But since we have had effective weapons for hundreds of thousands of years now, we have certainly had time to evolve an inhibition if we really wanted to. It is more plausible to suggest that weapons have made people-killing more tempting.

On the other side of the fence are a number of critics who consider the view of Man as a bad animal overblown. They have observed, for example, that Man has never been just a carnivore. He has eaten everything he could get. Time and time again, men have demonstrated that they can be altruistic and cooperative, that they abhor violence. According to one hypothesis about Man the Hunter, altruism and cooperation had survival value. And if Man were restricted to killing the hard way, by tooth and claw, without weapons, as animals must do, we surely would see a spectacular decline in intentional homicide.

The important point is that scientists in many fields are coming up with strategies to remove the alleged inborn aggressiveness of Man.

Man Is Controlled by His Genes

This tendency to physiological predestination has been known to college freshmen for decades. Recent argument has centered around the contention of two educational psychologists that scores on intelligence tests are primarily determined by genes. They have asserted further that consistent differences in the scores were related to race or social class. Their conclusions upset those who believe that basically we start off with a fairly clean slate and that major differences arise from the way we are reared. (As of late 1976, the Genetics Society of America was contending that it had no convincing evidence of any appreciable genetic difference in intelligence among races.)

One of the educational psychologists cited above, Arthur Jensen, has maintained that 80 percent of IQ differences are based on genes, not on the effects of environment. His claims have been denounced. Several leading geneticists have advanced rebuttals or strong reservations. One, Theodosius Dobzhansky, pointed out that you don't find an 80-percent degree of heritability in far simpler matters, such as chicken-egg production.

In late 1976 the genetic dogmatists were subdued by evidence that an early English pioneer in educational testing who had tied intelligence to genes by studying twins had apparently invented some of his data.

Whatever the facts, the big new thing is that genes are now considered manipulatable, not immutable. The genetic engineers have a host of plans, some already tested, for modifying Man by modifying his genetic patterns.

Man Is Shaped by Primal Instincts and Early Childhood Experiences

This view, pioneered by Sigmund Freud, remains the cornerstone of one of modern psychology's three major schools of thought about the nature of Man, the other two being the humanistic and the behaviorist.

The instincts that concerned Freud were those of sexuality, aggression, pleasure-seeking, and so on. They may be masked by people, but they remain in force and influence behavior. The challenge is to cope with these debilitating urges so that civilization can stay on the track.

Modern neo-Freudians continue to use Freud's terms and some of his concepts, but most do not see Man as essentially base. And they give credit to the way we live as a shaping influence.

Man Is Captain of His Fate

Humanists such as Abraham Maslow, Carl Rogers, and Rollo May have seen Man as possessing a considerable amount of free will despite genes, instincts, and the environment. The individual can size up his situation, weigh alternatives, and decide upon courses of action. Some humanists from the existential wing, notably Jean-Paul Sartre, have insisted that Man can be a *totally* free agent. Those from the vitalist wing believe there is no physical accounting for the inspired behavior of some people. The historian-philosopher Arnold Toynbee, for example, has contended that there is a spark of "creative spiritual power in every human being."

Humanists in general hold that life provides the greatest satisfactions if people largely manage their own affairs. They work to enhance our capacity for self-fulfillment, creativity, open communication, and psychological growth.

Man Is a Mere Reactor to Prods from the Environment

This proposition is assumed by most behavioral psychologists. For some years behaviorism has been in the ascendancy.

Behaviorists tend to see themselves as far more scientific than the humanists or psychoanalysts. They deal only with observable behavior and are wary of the "mind," since what goes on in it is not observable. They measure behavior, sometimes with stopwatches, and design precise testing strategies. Often they aim for, and get, quick, visible results. The more ardent behaviorists argue that real progress for Man can come only if people rid themselves of prescientific ideas about freedom, will, consciousness, and dignity.

As a general rule behaviorists are fascinated with techniques of control. Many favor using conditioning techniques. They modify the behavior of humans by shifting factors in the environment and manipulating incentives. Many believe that Man can progress fastest by permitting his environment to be systematically managed.

In short, they tend strongly to the view that Man is highly malleable and needs molding.

Man Is an Adjustable, Chemically Controlled Machine

The most forthright spokesman of this still marginal view is a neo-Hobbesian and a radical behaviorist, H. L. Newbold. He is a New York orthomolecular psychiatrist, and thus is a believer in using chemicals to enhance the success of behavioral therapy.

Behaviorists have often been described by critics as being mechanistic. Newbold goes further and calls Man a machine. In his book *The Psychiatric Programming of People,* which is addressed to psychiatrists, psychologists, and those preparing to be psychiatrists, he says of Man's nature: "Man is, for psychological purposes, a computer. . . . This computer can fail to function properly if the hardware (central nervous system) is physically or chemically damaged or if the software (Biologically Programmed Computer or Socially Programmed Computer) is abnormal. . . . It follows then that, if damaged or abnormal, the computer must be, insofar as is possible, normalized . . . with psychochemicals" to get it to function more effectively.

Newbold is not alone in his opinions. One of the speakers of the Master Lecture Series at the 1976 convention of the American Psychological Association alluded to the Man-is-a-machine concept. He said that the flowering of behavior modification has forced people to take the concept seriously. The approach is to modify Man in a desired direction by pressing social and biological levers.

So where do we stand? If we ponder the underlying assumptions of most of the scientific images of Man cited, a common thread emerges. The same thread appears when we consider assumptions of pioneering activists from such diverse fields as reproductive biology, psychosurgery, and molecular biology.

What emerges is a pervading assumption that humans are creatures of almost limitless plasticity.

People are raw material that needs perfecting, modifying, or at least improving, either for their own good or to suit the wishes of others. Malleable people are more likely to be controllable people.

Whereas the old believers in the perfectibility of people thought primarily in moral terms, the new revolutionists want to change people physically, emotionally, mentally. Often their efforts are underwritten by the government.

If their view prevails, people will indeed become different. The revolutionary brain prober José Delgado suggests that the main question is no longer "What is Man?" but rather, "What kind of man are we going to construct?"

Under expert management, some scientists feel, people will benefit by becoming more efficient and predictable. Quite probably as a side effect people will also lose some of what we think of as humanness.

The ascent of Man as described by Jacob Bronowski covered tens of thousands of years. The reshaping of Man now under way can occur within a few decades.

Rage

Melvin Konner

Many of our intellectuals rush to quell our fears by telling us that theoretically none of this has to happen, that violence is not part of human nature, that it occurs only because of evil intentions and circumstances that we can eradicate. They are the Christian Scientists of sociology; and they have not as yet solved the paradox: if we are not by nature violent creatures, why do we seem inevitably to create situations that lead to violence?

—Lionel Tiger and Robin Fox,
The Imperial Animal

On July 8, 1977, Richard James Herrin, a twenty-three-year-old Yale senior, went to the bedroom of Bonnie Jean Garland, a classmate and sometime girl friend in whose home he was then a guest, and bludgeoned her to death in her sleep with a claw hammer. He then fled from the scene in a car, driving from White Plains, New York, where the slaying took place, to Coxsackie, New York, where he surrendered himself to a priest and confessed his crime. He told the arresting officer that he had planned to kill the young woman and then commit suicide. The precipitating cause was romantic rejection; Garland had evidently broken off with Herrin.[1]

At the trial, he pleaded not guilty by reason of temporary mental defect or disease. Evidence concerning the relative poverty he lived in as a child was introduced (by his mother) as a mitigating factor. Herrin testified that he did not know why he committed the slaying. Two psychiatrists testified that he was psychotic at the time of the alleged murder, and two other psychiatrists testified that he could not be considered to have been psychotic at the time of the alleged murder. It became evident during the trial that Herrin was a well-brought-up, well-behaved, even religious young man who had never done anything that would in the slightest way suggest that he was capable of homicide. Because of this, there was support of his defense in the Yale community. On the third day of deliberation by the jury, Herrin was convicted of manslaughter, and he was subsequently sentenced to the maximum term of eight and one-third to twenty-five years. The jurors, confused by conflicting psychiatric testimony among

From *The Tangled Wing: Biological Constraints on the Human Spirit* by Melvin Konner. Reprinted by permission of Holt, Rinehart & Winston, Publishers. Footnote numbers have been revised.

other complex matters, had almost reported to the judge that they were deadlocked—three of the twelve had been holding out for a second-degree murder verdict; instead, they requested that they be allowed to go to mass on Sunday in the hope of "some divine inspiration." However, they reached their verdict without this source of inspiration.[2] Citing Herrin's evident premeditation, they also took into account the depth of his and Garland's dependence on and love for each other (as evidenced by their love letters) and the extreme emotional disturbance influencing Herrin during his crime: his two-year intimacy with Garland was to have ended in marriage, but instead she decided that she wanted to date other men and broaden her social life, plunging him into despair and the belief that "I could not live without her."[3] The judge, in delivering the maximum sentence, said, "Even under the stress of extreme emotional disturbance, the act of killing another is inexcusable,"[4] therefore, in effect, refusing to consider the argument of the defense attorney that Herrin's crime had been "totally inconsistent with his conduct before and after the act."[5]

On November 18, 1978, while Richard James Herrin awaited trial, Wang Yungtai, a twenty-four-year-old warehouse worker at the Materials Recuperation Company in Peking, sought out Hu Huichin, a fellow worker whom he had wanted as his girl friend, and, near their lockers at the factory, struck her seven or eight times in the head with a hammer. She was to survive this assault, but barely, after months of intensive care and with permanent brain damage. Wang Yungtai left the scene of his crime on foot, but only after swallowing a substantial amount of mercury, which he had prepared for his planned suicide attempt. He became ill, but not seriously so, and the next day confessed to his father. His father recommended that he go to the police, but withdrew this recommendation when he realized that if the victim died his son would get the death sentence. He was arrested several months later and subsequently confessed. The precipitating cause was romantic rejection; Hu Huichin had refused to become his girl friend, after he had requested her to do so several times, with all due respect, in writing.

At the trial, the defendant was asked by the judge what he was thinking while he hit the victim with the hammer. He said, "I was thinking that she made me lose face by telling everything to someone or everyone. . . . I was very angry and I wanted revenge. I wanted to teach her a lesson, to let her suffer. I didn't think of the consequences." The defense attorney pointed out that the defendant showed every sign of contrition, including contributing a substantial sum of money to aid in the victim's recovery, and that he had been, prior to his crime, a model worker guilty of no other criminal acts. After summary by the defense and prosecution, Wang was permitted to make a summary statement of his own, and he reiterated sentiments he had expressed earlier in the trial: "I would like to repeat that when I struck her I did not intend to kill her. I only wanted to vent my anger. I had no other thoughts. The cause of my crime is my low political consciousness. I didn't study very much; I knew nothing about the rights of citizens and of the law and I have very bourgeois thoughts." In his previous statement, a reply to a patently leading question from the judge, he added that he had come under the influence of Lin Biao and the Gang of Four during the Cultural Revolution. "I don't know what the law is and I have bourgeois ideas. Because I could not achieve my personal aims, I did not consider the interests of the state or of other people, so I threw everything to the wind and did what I wanted." In the final statement by the judge, "in order to implement the law, preserve revolutionary order, protect the safety of all citizens, insure the smooth progress of socialist modernization and strike at criminal activity, in order to strengthen the proletarian dictatorship," Wang was sentenced to life in prison.[6]

The juxtaposition of these two cases makes them striking—even more so than each is on its merits. Two modern societies professing completely different beliefs and, indeed, acting on those beliefs with different systems of child training, education, work, and justice, confront in effect the same crime and respond to it in the same way, while giving radically different explanations of the crime and the punishment. In one, the individuals sitting in judgment listen to expert testimony by psychiatrists as to whether the criminal was capable of controlling his actions and distinguishing between right and wrong; they are impressed by the romance between the criminal and his victim, take into consideration his impoverished childhood, and attempt to consult "divine inspiration" to aid in their decision. The defendant says "I could not live without her," and gives himself up to a priest after his crime. In the other, the defendant says "She made me lose face," and confesses his crime to the head of his family, his father. The judges appear to believe that the crime can be explained by ideological inadequacy on the part of the defendant, particularly his "bourgeois ideas" and the influence of the Gang of Four, a viewpoint with which the defendant, after some encouragement, concurs.

But consider the similarities. In each case a young man is enamored of a young woman, is rejected, "loses control" of his emotions, and, after at least some premeditation, brutally bludgeons his beloved to death or near death with a hammer held in his hand, striking many hard blows. One contemplates, one attempts suicide, each relates his crime to a culturally appropriate confessor, each is very contrite, neither has ever committed a crime or "lost control" in an unusual way before. Both report having acted under an extreme of emotional agitation, despite relatively calm preparations. Both introduce culturally appropriate explanations at the respective trials and both receive the maximum sentence allowable given the nature of the charge. Both face judges who react, finally and primarily, to the brutality and injustice of the assault, giving all other factors minor consideration. Both end up in prison, not because anyone believes they are likely to commit such crimes again, but because of the sense of justice common to the social orders to which the young men and their victims belong, and as a warning to all others to respect and fear the law.

This is, of course, not an everyday series of events. Nevertheless, in many societies, including so-called primitive ones, young women occasionally meet death at the hands of men who supposedly love them, and in a wide range of these societies such crimes make up a substantial percentage of homicides. Frequently there is a motive of rejection and/or jealousy, there has been no other criminal behavior, there is suicide or attempted suicide, and there is contrition. Certainly it is not the only, or even the principal course of events leading to homicidal or near-homicidal violence, but it is interesting because, of all situations that tend to violence, this one covers and exemplifies the widest range of human—or, indeed, nonhuman—emotions.

The young man experiences lust, of course; he has had, and/or wants to have, sexual intimacy with the young woman who is to become his victim. But in these cases, to be perfectly fair, the lust is held in check within the context of a much more respectful feeling, one which, except with the easy wisdom of hindsight, we would not be able to distinguish from what we usually are willing to call love: a desire to be close, a desire to stay with, a desire to care for, a desire to share with, a desire, we may suppose, to possess. In the context of this feeling, and as a product of it, there must usually be a deep sense of joy that attends the thought of the prospect of shared life, the contemplation of the innumerable rewards of that life. When the young woman's affections begin to be alienated, or when she is disinclined to return those of the man, he experiences fear—of loss, of loneliness, of humiliation—a fear that must sometimes be close to terror. There arises from this fear a feeling of rage, a desire to take revenge upon, to punish the object of the fear; in these cases, the rage is sufficiently strong to produce homicidal violence. And mixed with the fear and rage, supplanting them in the end, is grief, a mourning for the losses—after the rejection, the loss of love, companionship, pride, sexual release, hope; and, after the crime, the loss of the very person of the beloved.

It is only because this gamut of the emotions is run that such cases compel our interests more than does many another homicide. Conflict is more moving than unalloyed motive—however horrible—and we are able to sympathize with the conflict in question because we have, however moderately, shared it. It touches every corner of the human unconscious. . . .

Rage is the name we give to the emotion that sometimes underlies the behaviors we call aggressive, although each can exist without the other. In characterizing such behaviors and emotions and their causation, it is generally useful to begin descriptively. To get an idea of the magnitude of the problem, consider the following pattern of behavior. Many species in the cat family exhibit a sequence of predatory behaviors that are as close to constituting an instinctive sequence of motor action patterns as mammals are likely to get. It includes lying in wait, crouching, stalking, pouncing, seizing between the paws, and directing a "killing bite" quite specifically at the nape of the neck of the prey, where it will do mortal damage to the brain stem.[7] A cat with no experience of prey will not do this properly at first, but with a few repeated opportunities, especially under conditions of playful excitement, the sequence "clicks into place" and it does so in a tiny fraction of the time required for cats to learn comparably complex sequences that do not draw on phylogenetic preparation.

The gulf between the acts of these cats and the human acts described at the beginning of the chapter is vast, the list of differences long. First, the behavior just described is normal for all wild cats, the behavior described for humans, rare and abnormal. Second, the cat behavior necessarily involves the motor action sequence described, with little variation, while the specific motor action sequence in the human cases of homicide, though they happen to be parallel, was incidental. Third, the cat behavior serves the obvious adaptive purpose of food getting, while the human behavior, if it is functional in any sense at all, is certainly much more obscurely so, and perhaps is a case of function gone awry; in any event it has nothing to do with food. Finally, the cat sequence is carried out in a spirit of playful excitement, even in a subdued mood, while the young men who attacked their friends did so in a mood of intense rage.

Nevertheless, behavioral scientists, sometimes with important and confusing consequences, classify both these very distinct sequences of behavior under the general rubric of "aggressive" because they both have the effect, in some sense intended, of inflicting damage upon another creature. The category "aggressive behavior in animals" includes at least the following: serious fights that can inflict real damage; play fights, or rough-and-tumble play, that generally cannot; dominance hierarchies that eventually result from a settling out of winners and losers into a temporarily stable social pattern; threats of violent action, which can begin fights, play a role in them, or prevent them; and predation. Threat, attack, and fighting can serve a wide range of adaptive functions: competition between individuals for mates, food, and other scarce resources; play and exercise; enforcement of sexual intercourse, and defense against such enforcement; defense of the young; elimination of the young, either one's own or those of others, for purposes relating to the reduction of competition; competition between groups for territory and other scarce resources; exploitation of prey species, for the purpose of obtaining food; and action against members of another species, one's own species, even one's own family, for purposes of self-defense. To these must be added an unknown quotient of functionless aggression that surely must emerge, the inevitable misfirings of so complex a system of hurtful acts.

Some distinctions of kind must now be made. Playful fighting, or perhaps more properly "rough-and-tumble play," is a universal characteristic of the mutual behavior of young mammals and also occurs among many mammalian adults. It is not violent, it is usually not damaging, and it involves different behaviors of threat, attack, defense, and especially expression from those involved in real fighting. Nevertheless, it can sometimes grade into real fighting, it provides exercise for real fighting, and it helps to establish the dominance hierarchy that will regulate real fighting.

Predatory "aggression" involves members of another rather than one's own species, is usually done in a playful mood or a mood of skilled challenge, and is motivated by hunger rather than anger or competitiveness. Nevertheless, it inflicts mortal damage using at least some of the same motor actions and fighting apparatus that the predator may use against conspecifics—members of its own species.

To further complicate matters (or perhaps to help explain some of the complexities) rage and fighting behavior can be dissociated from one another in experimental animals in the laboratory, using appropriate different brain lesions. Cats may have real rage, as shown by expressive signals under sympathetic nervous system control—widening of the eyes, growling and hissing, arching of the back, and erection of the fur—which appears as a prelude to attack; but after an appropriate brain lesion they will have only "sham rage," the same expressive signs never followed by attack. Cats may kill their prey with all expressive signs following stimulation of one part of the midbrain, but stimulation of another midbrain location produces only quiet-biting attack, the unemotional killing characteristic of cat predation in the wild.[8]

The various forms of aggressive behavior and their emotional concomitants, if any, may have varying degrees of unlearned and learned components. Every such behavior, in every species without exception, has some of both. But in some, genetically determined fixed action patterns and releasing mechanisms play a powerful role, in others little or none, with the innate factors reduced to some characteristics of motive and mood. Adapting for our purposes a scheme originally put forward by the Dutch ethologist Niko Tinbergen, we may say that to ask the question, What causes aggressive—or indeed any—behavior? is really to ask a series of questions, and we will be greatly aided in our attempt to provide an answer if we make ourselves aware of the different questions in advance, and indeed organize our explorations in accord with them. This is not the series of questions engendered by our usage of the word "aggressive" to denote so many categorically different behaviors, but rather by the variety of things we can mean by the word "cause."[9]

First, we mean, What events in the individual's environment immediately or recently preceded the behavior, and seem to have precipitated it? These are called by ethologists "releasing stimuli" and they may be learned or unlearned. Second, we are asking about fast-acting physiological causation: the neural circuitry and associated neurotransmitters whose activation preceding or concurrent with the behavioral output produced it. Third, slower-acting physiological determinants within the organism, such as hormone levels or disease processes, must be considered. Fourth, environmental events of fairly recent vintage, such as training or observation, though not the immediate precipitating factors, may have had a strong influence on the behavior by altering the organism's response tendencies, just as hormones and disease do.

Fifth, we want to know the events of gene coding and embryonic development—

really a sort of remote physiology of the behavior, which tells us something about the raw materials of the organism—in relation to the particular behavior. Sixth, we are interested in environmental causation of a remote sort: "sleeper effects" that may arise from experience, nutrition, or insults in early life, including life before birth or hatching. Seventh, Why did the organism do that? can mean, What adaptive function does it serve? To a pre-Darwinian such as Goethe, this might have meant, Why did God give it that behavior? but to us it means, What were the forces of natural selection that favored it, given the environment inhabited by the creature and its recent ancestors?

Eighth and finally, we want to know the phylogenetic history of the animal. The wings of flies come from the thorax; those of birds, from forelimbs; of bats, from fingers; and the "wings of man" from Eastern Airlines. In each case the same adaptive function is served: flight, which in various ways enhances survival. But these very different creatures must solve this problem in very different ways, each consistent with its own unique phylogenetic history. That history directs and constrains the animal in its evolutionary response to the adaptive problem posed by the environment.

In this framework, and only in this framework, is it possible to give a more than partial, more than trivial account of the causation of behavior, including aggressive behavior. It would be misleading, perhaps even dangerous, to suggest that behavioral biology can provide a satisfactory explanation for the homicides described at the start of this chapter. Although it might do better than the court psychiatrists, its findings would be no more useful to the court, which in the end must decide on the basis of simpler, more human, and perhaps more brutal principles. Indeed, I doubt whether another hundred years of research in behavioral biology will make possible the prediction or control of individual acts of passionate homicide.

What I do expect from such research, however, is a more comprehensive understanding of anger and violence in general; an understanding of the sort that could lead to a better prediction, management, and prevention of conflict of a more ubiquitous sort, from marital fights to child abuse to international warfare. Many of the components of these latter forms of conflict reflect those of the two homicides discussed. But to approach the sort of comprehensive explanation of human conflicts that we will need, we must first proceed to a much more detailed kind of analysis—one that carries us from the physiological laboratory through the field setting of the natural historian to the annals of human history. These components will give us, in the end, at least an outline of what will one day be a nearly complete explanation of violent and other conflict-related behavior, drawing on all the eight categories of causes mentioned earlier—from the immediate precipitating cause, through the physiological mediators, to the phylogeny. And in the process we will have evolved a method for explaining behavior that is more balanced and eclectic than any that has been previously devised; an outline for the understanding not only of rage and conflict, but all human emotional behavior. . . .

There are powerful genetic effects on aggressive behavior and rage, and powerful environmental effects on them. Any answer to the question, Why did that act of aggression occur? must include both. It would trivialize the bitter experiences of Richard James Herrin and Wang Yungtai—and even more, that of their victims—to presume to explain what they did on the basis of what has been learned in all these studies. Nevertheless, one can see certain common threads of causation. Both were men, and such crimes are overwhelmingly committed by men rather than women—partly, at least, for genetic and hormonal reasons. Both were well bred in the moral sense, but both also lived in societies that traditionally glorified violence, including violence by men against women designed to make them submit. Both were exposed to one of ordinary life's worst stresses, that of romantic rejection, and both were young enough perhaps to be experiencing this stress for the first time. Both were probably exposed to the activation of testosterone in connection with their sexual feelings toward the women they attacked, but this is of course much more speculative. All of these factors are at times present in millions of individuals who do not commit homicide, and so do not help very much in explaining these cases. Nevertheless, the presence of such factors makes them slightly more comprehensible—not, I must stress, more excusable—than, say, the random shooting of motorists on a highway. . . .

I would only add to this account a brief summary of a recent shift in outlook affecting many behavioral biologists, a shift owing largely to a successful challenge to classical ethology by the newly developed field of sociobiology. According to the classical view, identified especially with the name of Konrad Lorenz, a principal function of aggressive behavior is to distribute members of a group over an area of resource availibility.[10] This way, the group as a whole benefits, and individuals are not getting in each other's way. Furthermore, the existence of aggressive displays, such as threats, serves to reduce actual violence by spacing individuals and arranging them in a hierarchy.

Field observations of wild animals for a long time seemed to support this view. It used to be said that humans are almost unique among animals in that they kill members of their own species; this was explained by reference to the fact that our use of weapons renders less effective our normal mechanisms for limiting the damage we do to each other.

This is now known to be simply false. It was pointed out by some observers that if a troop of baboons had the same homicide rate as people in New York City, the baboon troop would have to be watched constantly for hundreds of years before the observer would be likely to see a homicide with his or her own eyes. It was only after thousands of person-years of field observations were logged by animal behaviorists that it became clear that intraspecific (within-species) homicide exists in many species other than humans—and this is now an incontrovertible finding. In other words, "natural" mechanisms for the limitation of violence do not work much better in nonhuman animals than they do among humans.[11] . . .

The problem of violence among humans, of course, looms darkly over any such discussion as this one. Since it is obvious that I believe in the existence of innate aggressive tendencies in humans, the easy way out for me would be to describe the most violent of human societies: the Yanomamo of highland Venezuela, the Dani of highland New Guinea, the Plains Indians of the United States, the Zulu of southern Africa, the Germans of the Third Reich. But it will be more interesting to look at the least violent. Differences in the degree of violence among cultures and societies are real and large, and an understanding of the basis of those differences will help us to develop a strategy for reducing violence. But it is first important to abolish the myth that there are societies in which people are incapable of violence.

The !Kung San of Botswana are frequently used as a textbook example of the least violent end of the human cultural spectrum.[12] They are. But this is very far from being equivalent to total nonviolence. They have a homicide rate shown by Richard Lee (who had originally subscribed to the view that they were nonviolent) to be equal to or greater than the rate for most American cities, and not very different in character.[13] Most people among the !Kung are perfectly capable of violence, and there are many nonlethal acts of violence in addition to the recorded homicides. While the !Kung, like most hunter-gatherers, do not have war or other organized group conflicts, their explicitly stated contempt for non-San people, for San people speaking languages other than !Kung, and even for !Kung in other village-camps who are not their relatives, makes it perfectly clear that if they had the technological opportunity and the ecological necessity to make war, they would probably be capable of the requisite emotions, despite their oft-stated opposition to and fear of war.

The Semai of Malaysia are a society almost as simple as that of the !Kung. They have been the subject of a study by anthropologist Robert Knox Dentan. Violence is said to be virtually nonexistent among them and abhorrent to them. "Since a census of the Semai was first taken in 1956," Dentan writes, "not one instance of murder, attempted murder, or maiming has come to the attention of either government of hospital authorities."[14]

> People do not often hit their children and almost never administer the kind of beating that is routine in some sectors of Euro-American society. A person should never hit a child because, people say, "How would you feel if it died?" . . . Similarly, one adult should never hit another because, they say, "Suppose he hit you back?". . .
>
> It should be clear at this point that the Semai are not great warriors. As long as they have been known to the outside world, they have consistently fled rather than fight, or even than run the risk of fighting. They had never participated in a war or raid until the Communist insurgency of the early 1950s, when the British raised troops among the Semai, mainly in the west. Initially, most of the recruits were probably lured by wages, pretty clothes, shotguns, and so forth. Many did not realize that soldiers kill people. When I suggested to one Semai recruit that killing was a soldier's job, he laughed at my ignorance and explained, "No, we don't kill people, brother, we just tend weeds and cut grass." Apparently, he had up to that point done nothing but grounds duty.[15]

But when the Semai were lured by the British into counterinsurgency activities against Communist rebels in the 1950s, they gave evidence enough of violent capability. Dentan goes on:

> Many people who knew the Semai insisted that such an unwarlike people could never make good soldiers. Interestingly enough, they were wrong. Communist terrorists had killed the kinsmen of some of the Semai counterinsurgency troops. Taken out of their nonviolent society and ordered to kill, they seem to have been swept up in a sort of insanity which they call "blood drunkenness." A typical veteran's story runs like this. "We killed, killed, killed. The Malays would stop and go through people's pockets and take their watches and money. We did not think of watches or money. We only thought of killing. Wah, truly we were drunk with blood." One man even told how he had drunk the blood of a man he had killed.[16]

Astonishing as this description is, it is in some respects less astonishing than the adaptation that followed the Semai experience with warfare:

> Talking about these experiences, the Semai seem bemused, not displeased that they were such good soldiers, but unable to account for their behavior. It is almost as if they had shut the experience in a separate compartment, away from the even routine of their lives. Back in Semai society they seem as gentle and afraid of violence as anyone else. To them their one burst of violence appears to be as remote as something that happened to someone else, in another country. The nonviolent image remains intact.[17]

Despite this bleak reversal of a nonviolent cultural tradition, there is some evidence that cultural contexts can be constructed so as to reduce the likelihood of certain kinds of violence. One finding of anthropologists John Whiting and Beatrice Blyth Whiting is of interest here and strikes a much more positive note. They discovered in a wide-ranging cross-cultural study that husband-wife intimacy is apparently not compatible with organized group conflict.[18] Societies in which husbands and wives eat together, sleep together, and take care of children together are among the least violent; while the ones that have organized themselves around constant or at least intermittent warfare find it necessary to segregate men away from influence by women and children, in separate men's houses for eating and sleeping, and in men's societies in which even young boys are severely stressed and actively trained for warfare. The Whitings' study established on a quantitative basis a set of hypotheses put forward in a different form by Lionel Tiger in his book *Men in Groups.* Something happens when men get together in groups; it is not well understood, but it is natural, and it is altogether not very nice.[19]

The Whitings' version of the theory gives substance to the popular slogan "make love, not war"; and actually it improves it, giving it new and interesting depth, since that slogan probably did not mean "love" at all.

Whatever cultural conditioning we may do, we must remain cognizant of the fact that human beings who have been trained and conditioned to be nonviolent retain the capacity for violence; as constrained as that capacity may be in certain contexts, it can come out in others. It is subdued, reduced, dormant, yes. But it is never abolished. It is never nonexistent. It is always there.

This is the lesson of the experience of the Semai, the nonviolent people of Malaysia; and in a more personal way, that of Richard James Herrin and Wang Yungtai. Yet to recognize the impossibility of erasing the tendency to violence is not to throw up our hands and let the blows fall as they may. The Semai have returned to nonviolence; perhaps if they had never been recruited and trained by the British, or if their relatives had never been killed by the Communists—if they had never been exposed to the whole horror of modern war—they would have remained nonviolent permanently. Perhaps, just perhaps, if the two young men who so violently attacked their lovers had not been exposed to folk traditions in which violence done by men against women was deemed at least understandable, they would have swallowed their pride—and grief—and not taken up their hammers.

What seems certain to me, though, is that no cultural training, however designed, can eliminate the basic core of capability of violence that is part of the makeup of human beings.[20] The continued pretense by some social scientists and philosophers that human beings are basically peaceable has so far evidently prevented little of human violence—which latter achievement would be the only possible justification for its benighted concealment of the truth. Perhaps we could let it go for a while and see if the other assumption gives us a better understanding; if it does, it will give us a better chance at control.

Notes

[1] Initial report of killing of Bonnie Jean Garland: Ronald Smothers, "Yale Senior Slain in Scarsdale; Boyfriend Surrenders to Priest," *The New York Times,* July 9, 1977, pp. 1 and 30.

[2] Facts of the case from the following sources: Ronald Smothers, "Mother Testifies at Son's Trial in Murder of Student," *The New York Times,* June 6, 1978, section 2, p. 8; Ronald Smothers, "Defendant Takes Stand in White Plains Murder Trial," *The New York Times,* June 7, 1978, section 2, p. 5; Ronald Smothers, "Herrin Jury Recalls Tortuous Path It Took Trying to Reach a Verdict," *The New York Times,* June 22, 1978, section 4,

p. 18; Ronald Smothers, "Herrin Given Maximum Jail Term in Bludgeoning Death in Scarsdale," *The New York Times,* July 28, 1978, pp. 1 and 10.

[3]Richard Herrin quoted in Smothers, "Herrin Given Maximum Jail Term."

[4]Judge Daronco quoted in Smothers, "Herrin Given Maximum Jail Term."

[5]Jack Litman quoted in Smothers, "Herrin Given Maximum Jail Term."

[6]Trial of Wang Yungtai: All quotes are from Barrie A. Chi and Emile C. Chi, "Trial of Wang Yungtai," *The New York Times Magazine,* Oct. 7, 1979, p. 48.

[7]Konrad Lorenz and Paul Leyhausen, "On the Function of the Relative Hierarchy of Moods," in *Motivation of Human and Animal Behavior: An Ethological View* (New York: Van Nostrand Reinhold, 1973).

[8]J. Flynn, H. Venegas, W. Foote, and S. Edwards, "Neural Mechanisms Involved in a Cat's Attack on a Rat," in *The Neural Control of Behavior,* ed. R. F. Whalen, M. Thompson, M. Verzeano, and N. Weinberger (New York: Academic Press, 1970).

[9]Niko Tinbergen, "On the Aims and Methods of Ethology," *Zeitschrift für Tierpsychologie* 20 (1963), pp. 410–33.

[10]Konrad Lorenz, "What Aggression is Good For," in *Animal Aggression: Selected Readings,* ed. Charles H. Southwick (New York: Van Nostrand Reinhold, 1970).

[11]Baboons and Homicide: E. O. Wilson, *Sociobiology: The New Synthesis* (Cambridge, Mass.: Harvard University Press, Belknap Press, 1975), pp. 246–47.

[12]Elizabeth Marshall Thomas, *The Harmless People* (New York: Knopf, 1959).

[13]Richard B. Lee, *The !Kung San,* chapter 13.

[14]Robert Knox Dentan, *The Semai: A Nonviolent People of Malaysia* (New York: Holt, Rinehart and Winston, 1968).

[15]Ibid., p. 58.

[16]Ibid., pp. 58–59.

[17]Ibid., p. 59.

[18]John Whiting and Beatrice Blyth Whiting, "Aloofness and Intimacy Between Husbands and Wives," *Ethos* 3 (1975), pp. 183–207.

[19]Lionel Tiger, *Men in Groups* (New York: Random House, 1969).

[20]The viewpoint I express here is not, by any means, universally accepted. For an eloquent statement of the diametrically opposite view, see Montagu, *The Nature of Human Aggression.*

Behavior Therapy and Behavior Modification

F. Kanfer and J. Phillips

. . . Although the principles of learning and conditioning had been studied since the 1920s and behaviorism had become a dominant force in academic and theoretical psychology, it was not until the mid-1960s that large numbers of clinicians began to use behavioral techniques. There had been, during those earlier decades, several demonstrations that these techniques could be used to effect clients' behavioral change. As early as the 1920s, various investigators have used Pavlovian conditioning to curtail the drinking of alcoholics. O. Hobart Mowrer had devised a conditioning apparatus that cured bed-wetting. And Mary Cover Jones had combined elements of classical and operant conditioning to modify a little boy's fears. Why, then, did it take so long for practicing psychotherapists to take note of and adopt these techniques?

In the discussion of successive modifications of psychotherapeutic techniques presented in the preceding chapter, it is stated that major changes in the way of dealing with patients usually followed major changes in the general cultural climate. This phenomenon is also true of behavior therapy. In the 1960s in the United States the mood was one of discontent coupled with optimism: There was widespread discontent with social institutions, which seemed to be failing large segments of the population. Still, there was optimism that by a massive application of technology, training, and environmental engineering, these institutions could be revitalized. Thus, discontent with the results of psychoanalysis coupled with the belief in the efficacy of technology and training inspired numbers of clinicians to attempt the modification of behavior through conditioning techniques. . . .

Behavior clinicians differ from other therapists both in the methods they use and in the way they conceptualize the therapeutic process. Several important assumptions guide and distinguish all of their clinical work.

Basic Assumptions

Basic to the behavioral approach is the belief that *the same learning principles govern all behaviors, "normal or deviant."* Other theories apply learning principles only to the acquisition of knowledge and have a specific explanation for the development of each type of personality deviation. Behavior therapists regard psychological problems simply as learned responses that have harmful consequences for the client or for his environment. They interpret problem behaviors not as symptoms of unconscious conflicts that must be uncovered but as the primary and legitimate targets of therapy. Treatment is tailored to the individual's problems without regard to diagnostic labels such as "neurotic" or to presumed personality traits such as "passive-aggressive."

Behavior therapists believe that *the environment plays a crucial role in determining behavior and that problem behaviors are specific to given types of situations.* Consequently, behavioral diagnosis requires accurate descriptions of **observable behaviors** and the **environmental events** that accompany them. These descriptions omit speculation about such matters as the individual's "ego state" or the meaning of the events to the individual. Although behavior therapists do not deny the importance of behaviors they cannot observe or of a person's self-descriptions and descriptions of past events, their aim is to modify present behaviors by changing the environmental conditions that currently control them.

Behavior therapists reject the notion that psychological difficulties and their treatment are not subject to the same rigorous scientific analysis and verification used to study other areas of human behavior. They use empirical data not only to assess the client's difficulties but also to formulate a treatment plan, to monitor progress and guide changes during treatment, and to evaluate the outcome. [The] table . . . summarizes the major points of difference between psychoanalytic psychotherapy and behavior therapy. Although the terminology is classical or Pavlovian, the points apply equally well to operant behavioral treatments.

At times, behavior therapists discuss their work as if the description of a given conditioning technique covers the entire clinical process. Actually, no matter how well-defined the specific techniques may be, their application to individual cases still requires ingenuity. The ability to relate to others and a high level of skill in face-to-face interaction usually are essential qualities in a behavior therapist. Far from being the mechanistic robot some people fear, the behavior therapist often deals with the client in traditional ways during most phases of the therapeutic process, from initial interview to the client's discharge.

Nevertheless, the basic elements used to describe the therapeutic process come from the learning laboratory. The behavioral clinician examines the **stimuli that control behavior** and its **consequences** rather than its internal motivation or meaning.

COMPARISON OF PSYCHOTHERAPY AND BEHAVIOR THERAPY

	Psychotherapy	*Behavior Therapy*
Theory	Theories usually derived from clinical observations.	Theory derived from experimental studies.
Symptoms	Considers symptoms as visible signs of unconscious conflicts and evidence of repression.	Considers symptoms as learned responses that are unadaptive.
	The symptoms each patient displays are determined by defense mechanisms.	The symptoms each patient displays are determined by his conditionability and his environmental circumstances.
	If only symptoms are treated, they will be replaced by other symptoms because underlying conflict was not resolved.	Treatment of symptomatic behavior brings permanent cure.
Treatment	Treatment is often based on patient's history. The interpretation of symptoms, dreams, acts, and the like is an important element of treatment.	Treatment is concerned with habits existing at present, how the habits developed is usually irrelevant. Interpretation is irrelevant.
	Cure is obtained by resolving the underlying conflicts, not by treating the symptomatic behavior or trait.	Cure is obtained by treating the symptomatic behavior, that is, by extinguishing maladaptive habits, having the patient learn adaptive ones, or altering the environment.
	Relationship with therapist is an essential part of treatment, in psychoanalysis, transference is necessary.	Personal relationship with therapist not essential for cure but may be useful.
	Treatment generally consists of dialogue between therapist and patient.	Treatment uses techniques of conditioning and manipulation of environmental variables.
Goal	To modify present personality.	To modify present behavior.

He finds, for instance, that a child's temper tantrums become more frequent when they are followed by parental attention or giving in; he does not attribute them to the acting out of an Oedipus conflict. To understand how the therapist arrives at his formulation, it is necessary to reexamine, from a clinical viewpoint, some elements of behavior. . . .

The Behavioral Formula: S-O-R-K-C

Behavior is a continuous interaction of the individual with his social and physical environment. Out of this ongoing flow, several events may be identified as surrounding a particular problem behavior. By artificially stopping and segmenting this flow, the behavioral clinician can determine the role of each event. The behavioral formula S-O-R-K-C symbolizes this task:

S   stands for **stimuli,** the immediately preceding events.
O   stands for the biological state of the **organism.**
R   stands for the target **response,** or problem behavior.
K   stands for the **contingency relationship** between the response and its consequence.
C   stands for the **consequence,** the events that follow the response.

This formula preserves the time sequence of the crucial events and covers both **elicited (classically conditioned) behaviors** and **emitted (operantly conditioned) behaviors.** Classical conditioning, however, is concerned with only the first three elements, S-O-R, with S and R standing for both unconditioned and conditioned stimuli and responses. Operant conditioning emphasizes the last three elements, R-K-C, because emitted responses are controlled by the events that follow them. However, because antecedent stimuli may signal which consequences are likely to occur, the S element is important in operant behaviors also. For example, a child learns to read his parents' moods: He may curb his temper tantrum (R) when Father's grouchiness (S) signals that a spanking (C) is the most probable result.

In assessing a problem behavior, the clinician must fill in each part of the formula. He usually begins with R, the target behavior, and then asks: What are the consequences (C) of this behavior, and how are they delivered (K)—intermittently, continuously, or inconsistently? What events (S) usually precede this behavior? Under what circumstances (S) does the behavior fail to appear? Is there anything special about the client's biological state (O) that might play an important role in this behavior? The clinician's assessment of the function of each event is called a functional analysis of the problem behavior.

Behavior therapy always seeks to increase the frequency of responses that are deficient or to reduce the frequency of responses that are excessive. Although the ultimate goal is to change the target behavior, the source of the difficulty may lie in one of the other elements in the formula. It is by modifying these environmental factors that the clinician modifies the target behavior. A more detailed examination will show the importance of each element in producing and treating problem behaviors.

S: Stimuli and Stimulus Control

Almost any behavior is acceptable under some circumstances: Nakedness is fine in the shower but not usually on crowded beaches. A major part of a child's socialization process involves learning to match the various circumstances with the appropriate behaviors. These environmental circumstances come to control the person's behaviors by signaling the probable consequences of a behavior.

Problem behavior may arise because stimulus control is too weak. Obese people tend to eat under all sorts of circumstances: when watching television, reading, cooking, studying, or just sitting alone and bored. Behavioral weight reduction programs aim to reduce these occasions—and the fat person—by bringing the problem behavior, eating, under much narrower stimulus control. The dieter's first instruction usually is to eat only when sitting at a particular table and to do nothing else at that time but eat. A reduction in food intake comes only after this rule is firmly established. Indeed, because overweight people often exercise great restraint at mealtimes but snack recklessly in between, stimulus-control training may begin with an increase in the amount of food eaten at regular meals, along with the rule prohibiting snacks.

Similarly, a person who studies ineffectively may be instructed to designate a place where he does nothing but study. If he slips into fantasy or any other behavior that disturbs his study, he must move to another spot. When the dieter or the student follows this rule consistently, the place comes to set the occasion for eating or studying and for nothing else.

Stimulus control that is too strong and restricted also may produce problems. Some children ignore their parents' quiet requests to do some task but obey their shouts because they have learned that shouts usually precede important consequences such as a spanking, whereas quiet requests do not. Similarly, some people develop sexual fetishes when their arousal and performance come under increasingly narrow stimulus control, such as a specific set of events or a specific piece of wearing apparel. In sexual problems as in other emotional responses, antecedent stimuli play a crucial role, because sexual responses are elicited responses and are therefore governed by the principles of classical conditioning. For this reason, behavior clinicians generally follow the classical-conditioning model in treating emotional problems.

Learning appropriate stimulus control also is an important feature in the acquisition of any new behavior. For instance, behavior modification programs designed to help a shy person increase his assertive behavior must include discrimination training so that the newly outspoken client learns when he may safely assert himself. Otherwise, he might end up in jail, out of a job, or in the divorce courts.

O: The Organism

Temporary changes in a person's biological state and the more enduring features of his physical capacities may influence his behavior. A person who has eaten nothing all day usually responds to food as a potent reinforcer. Blind persons cannot respond to visual stimuli that control the behavior of other persons. And some children with minimal brain damage tend to be hyperactive; in behavioral language, they emit behavior at a very high rate.

Anxiety is a particularly important aspect of the organism's state. As already noted, therapies that draw on a Pavlovian model are especially concerned with such emotional states. A later section in this chapter describes systematic desensitization, a treatment approach designed to cure handicapping anxieties or phobias—morbid fears that have no realistic basis.

Biological factors may give rise to problem behaviors, as in some cases of hyperactivity, or they may make a problem worse, as in smoking, drinking, and other such habits. They also may facilitate therapy. For example, autistic children by definition do not respond to other people. But they do respond to food, and in order to begin treating these children—teaching them language, play, self-care, and all the other social skills they lack—the therapist usually uses food as a reinforcer and schedules training sessions shortly before mealtimes. After repeated pairings with this powerful **primary reinforcer,** the therapist becomes a **conditioned reinforcer,** able to reward responses from the children by praise and affection even in the absence of food.

R: The Response

Ultimate success or failure of treatment depends on altering the response, the problem behavior. Often the choice of which behavior to change is quite straightforward: Parents want their child to stop having temper tantrums. Even so, several factors may complicate the selection of a **target behavior.**

A first challenge is to achieve a clear, precise definition of the behavior. People customarily describe themselves and others in terms of traits rather than behaviors. Parents who complain that their child is "stubborn" or "smart-alecky" may have difficulty specifying the behavioral components of their complaints. Only when the parents, with help from the clinician, are able to pinpoint exactly what behaviors, in what situations, are covered by these terms can the clinician select an appropriate target.

Target selections also may require compromises. For example, parents seeking help with their child usually want quick modification of undesirable behaviors. The clinician knows, however, that the best strategy for the child's development and for the family's long-run equilibrium would be to work on increasing the child's desirable behaviors, many of which the parents may not even be aware of. Clinical experience has shown that because these behaviors are likely to be incompatible with the undesirable behaviors, the latter would gradually be reduced. Nevertheless, to gain and keep the parents' cooperation, the clinician may focus first on the undesirable behaviors.

The selection process becomes more complicated and at the same time more exciting when the clinician considers the total ecology of a person's behavior. One behavioral intervention can have snowballing effects. For example, curing a twelve-year-old boy's bed-wetting will likely affect many other aspects of his behavior in favorable ways. He probably will get along better with his mother as a result of his cure because she no longer will be burdened with his extra laundry, and his cure will free him to stay overnight with friends or go to summer camp without fear of embarrassment.

The clinician can enhance this snowball effect by choosing as the target a behavior that will gain the client entry into a "behavioral trap"—an environment in which positive reinforcement occurs naturally. Such an environment will support the behaviors established in therapy and help shape other desirable behaviors. A shy and fearful nursery-school boy who clings to his teacher might be trained to play near other children by using the teacher's attention and encouragement as reinforcement. Once he starts interacting with the other children, their company becomes a behavioral trap, spontaneously taking over the delivery of reinforcement.

K: The Contingency Relationship

This element of the behavioral formula refers to the schedule by which a consequence such as reinforcement or punishment follows a particular behavior. This relationship usually is the most difficult element to grasp, and yet it is often at the root of the problem behavior. Anyone who has had a hangover or broken a diet knows all too well that the immediate positive reinforcement of being high or of eating can easily override the delayed and less predictable unpleasant consequences.

Because different patterns, or schedules, of reinforcement have different (and sometimes quite powerful) effects, they can be crucial in obtaining the desired therapeutic results. . . . Schedules may be continuous or intermittent. A **continuous schedule,** in which the same consequence occurs immediately after each target response, is ideal for delivering punishment: It is the quickest and surest way to stop an undesirable behavior.

Most parents punish their children on an **intermittent schedule,** which can be less effective than no punishment at all. Like the slot machine player, children will continue a behavior such as temper tantrums despite occasional punishment so long as a payoff comes once in a while. Indeed, when parents try to end a child's tantrums by sometimes ignoring the child's behavior but then, occasionally, giving in, they usually make the problem worse. "Ignoring" is a valid technique for curtailing—or, in behavioral language, extinguishing—a behavior, but . . . an intermittent schedule produces

resistance to extinction. In the case of tantrums, resistance to extinction can be expected if the parents do give in from time to time. Often they actually shape the behavior to a higher degree of aversiveness, because they tend to give in when the child's screams become more intense than usual.

Sometimes the only change needed for successful therapy is a change in K: Consequences that had been freely available, such as a weekly allowance, may be made contingent on the performance of certain tasks. Even when K is not the main focus, any therapy program must take it into account. With a client who is acquiring new assertive responses, the clinician at first gives massive social reinforcement each time the client attempts an assertion. Gradually this schedule is shifted until it approximates the variable way in which the natural social environment reacts to assertive behavior.

The contingency relationship may play a fundamental role in psychological health. Two clinicians, Roberta Ray and Ernest Swihart, have detected a kind of "contingency hunger" in weeks-old infants. They found that "colicky" infants, who cry for long periods, were not deprived of attention, as might have been expected, but were given massive quantities of hugging and cuddling by ever-attentive parents. This attention apparently was not a reinforcer, however, because its removal did not extinguish the colic symptoms. Quite the opposite was found to be the case: The parents were giving their attention noncontingently; rather than engaging in a behavioral give-and-take with their infant, they emitted their behaviors without regard to what the baby was doing at the moment. Instead of playing *with* the baby, they were dumping large amounts of play *on* him. When the clinicians trained the parents to make their own responses contingent upon the behaviors of the baby, the baby gradually recovered and the colic disappeared.

C: The Consequence

The consequence of an act is what reinforces or diminishes it, and it is this element of the behavioral formula that most people associate with behavior modification. The problem that clinicians face is identifying for each person the objects or events that actually do function as reinforcers and, if the range is too small, enlarging the number of things that can serve to reinforce desired behaviors. An example might help in understanding this problem. Imagine a little boy who has a school phobia; he is terrified of going to school. A careful analysis of what serves the child as a social reinforcer might show that up to this point, his mother has been the only person to perform that function in his life. Thus, instead of devising a treatment that consisted of some kind of massive reinforcement for the act of going to school, treatment might better be aimed at increasing the child's range of social reinforcers to include other children.

People who have lived for a long period in institutions often have the problem of no longer responding to a variety of naturally available reinforcers. To help them adjust to life outside the institution, it is necessary to help them learn to respond to a normal variety of reinforcers. Because in certain institutional settings naturally occurring reinforcement is limited, clinicians set up systems to provide positive reinforcement beyond that ordinarily available. For example, tokens (poker chips, slips of paper, or points) are awarded for desired behavior; the tokens are exchangeable for material goods such as cake, candy, games, toys, and books, or for access to preferred activities, such as watching television, participating in games, and spending time away from the institution. The tokens are called **conditioned reinforcers,** because the recipients have learned that they are associated with such primary reinforcers as food and games.

Clinicians attempting to identify naturally occurring events that can serve as reinforcers often use the **Premack principle** as a guide. . . . Premack says that any behavior a person or animal naturally engages in relatively frequently will serve to reinforce a behavior with a lower relative probability of occurrence. And the particular context and circumstances will determine which of two behaviors can serve to reinforce the other. In certain circumstances, children will choose to play with pinball machines rather than to eat candy. In this case, pinball playing will reinforce candy eating. If the children are hungry or have been playing with the machines for a long time, candy eating can serve as a reinforcement for pinball playing.

Clinicians can make use of the Premack principle in hospitals. For example, hospital staff members may observe each patient, identify his or her more probable behaviors, and then require the performance of a less probable target behavior before the patient may engage in a preferred one. A socially withdrawn patient may be required to spend time talking with others to earn time alone in his room. A patient who likes to talk over his troubles with staff members may be required to *buy* therapy time with tokens earned by engaging in more direct attacks on his problems, whereas a patient who lacks skill in observing and labeling his own feelings may be *paid* tokens for discussing them with staff members.

A more elaborate form for exchanging reinforcements is the **contract.** In place of tokens given by one person to another, the two parties agree on behaviors each desires in the other. These behaviors, along with the rewards and sanctions they agree to exchange contingently, are stipulated in written form and both parties sign the contract. . . . Contracts are especially useful in the treatment of marital and family conflicts because they involve each person in a mutual effort to provide reinforcements and to change problem behaviors.

Therapies Based on Classical Conditioning

The examples used thus far, for each element of the behavioral formula, have been based primarily on the operant-conditioning model. It is necessary to consider further some of the ways in which behavior therapists have applied the classical-conditioning model to emotional and behavioral problems.

Aversive Conditioning

The clearest example of a therapeutic technique based on the Pavlovian model is that of aversive conditioning. This technique aims to reduce the frequency of a response such as smoking cigarettes by pairing an aversive stimulus—a mild electric shock, for example—with the natural stimulus that usually precedes the response until the therapy causes the natural stimulus itself to become aversive.

In the treatment of alcoholism by this method . . . , the presentation of alcohol (conditioned stimulus), including its taste and smell, is paired with an electric shock (unconditioned stimulus)—a stimulus that is tied innately to a pain reaction (unconditioned response). To promote generalization, the setting for this treatment may be highly realistic, with a bar, a bartender, and the client's favorite drink. To take advantage of the termination of shock, which is negative reinforcement, and to avoid the positive reinforcement of swallowing alcohol, the client usually must spit out the alcohol before the shock ends. After a sufficient number of pairings, alcohol takes on a stimulus function similar to the shock: The client comes to react with aversion and fear to the sight, smell, and taste of alcohol (conditioned response). Between conditioning trials, the client sips soft drinks or juices—without being shocked—to prevent generalization to all drinking behavior and to promote the use of substitutes for alcohol.

A number of investigators have reported success in using imagined unpleasant events in place of shock, a technique termed **covert sensitization,** or **aversive imagery.** For example, the therapist may instruct a smoker to close his eyes, relax, and picture himself taking out a cigarette. As he imagines himself lighting up and taking his first puff, he is told to imagine that he feels nauseated, starts gagging, and vomits all over the floor, the cigarettes, and finally himself. The details of this scene are conjured up with excruciating vividness. The client also rehearses an alternative, "relief," scene in which the decision not to smoke is accompanied by pleasurable sensations. This technique, using no special equipment, has obvious advantages; for instance, the client may carry out conditioning sessions on his own at home.

Systematic Desensitization

This therapy was first introduced by Joseph Wolpe under the name reciprocal inhibition but now most clinicians call it systematic desensitization. It is a therapy designed to decrease handicapping anxiety and unrealistic fears, or phobias. In systematic desensitization, a desirable response is substituted for an undesirable one. The anxiety-producing stimulus is presented at a low intensity while the opportunities for an incompatible response to occur are enhanced.

Most commonly, deep muscle relaxation is used as the response incompatible with anxiety. The first step in desensitization is to teach the client how to alternately tense and relax gross muscle groups, so that he can eventually reach a state of deep calm. The second step is to construct a graded hierarchy of the stimuli that make the patient feel anxious. . . . A hierarchy for test anxiety . . . was constructed by interviewing the client, a medical student, about the situations in which he felt anxious; he then rated, from 0 to 100, the intensity of the anxiety he felt in each situation so that the situations could be listed in ascending order. In this hierarchy, both type of test and amount of time before tests were to occur varied, so that the stimuli could be listed in ascending degrees of intensity. Ratings around 90 meant that the student had indicated he would feel faint, weak, unable to think, and so nauseated that he would have to leave the examination room. At lower levels, his anxiety would be severe enough to disrupt his efforts to study.

The final step in desensitization is the systematic presentation of the hierarchy items to the relaxed client. Most often, the clinician asks the client to imagine the situations rather than presenting them to the client in reality. There are practical advantages to this arrangement: Some items would be difficult to present in reality in a controlled fashion, and those dealing with internal events such as "thinking about . . ." could be accomplished only by instructions to imagine them. In this final step, when the client has reached a state of deep muscle relaxation, the clinician asks him to imagine the lowest hierarchy item first, then the next-to-the-lowest item, and so on, and to give a signal the moment he reaches an item that causes any slight tension. When the client signals, the clinician instructs him to stop visualizing that item and to relax himself again. The client then returns to a lower item and works back up to the tension-producing one. If he does not signal, he continues to visualize the scene for several seconds, then has a short period of deep relaxation alone. After this period of relaxation, he repeats the item several more times. In this fashion, he progresses gradually through all the items until none of them any longer elicits anxiety.

As clinicians have become more experienced in using techniques like systematic desensitization, they have come to have a more sophisticated appreciation of the assessment process that must precede their application. A person's initial complaint may not be the most relevant place to start. The client represented by the hierarchy . . . is a good case in point. He was failing in medical school because of his extreme anxiety before and during exams. He was given both help with his study habits and a series of systematic-desensitization sessions on the hierarchy illustrated, from which he derived only moderate relief. At first, it seemed that treatment was being seriously hindered by his ongoing exposure to real exams before he had progressed far enough in the hierarchy. Further assessment, however, indicated that the therapist was probably working on the wrong hierarchy!

This young man belonged to a very large Polish family; he had worked in construction, had married, and had had several children before deciding to go to medical school. Significantly, he was the only person in his whole extended family who had graduated from college. All the cousins, aunts, and uncles inquired with interest at weekly clan gatherings into what he was doing and learning and what his grades were. They asked his advice about all their aches and pains and generally vicariously relished his medical career. Meanwhile, his wife struggled with their reduced budget and resented his absence from home because of all his studying. With this information, therapy was altered. He was given desensitization for his fear of failing and disappointing his family; his wife was helped to find satisfactions of her own; and the family members were persuaded to remove their intense pressure on him. After these procedures, the medical student's test anxiety improved dramatically. . . .

The Draft Horse

Robert Frost

With a lantern that wouldn't burn
In too frail a buggy we drove
Behind too heavy a horse
Through a pitch-dark limitless grove.

A man came out of the trees
And took our horse by the head
And reaching back to his ribs
Deliberately stabbed him dead.

The ponderous beast went down
With a crack of a broken shaft.
And the night drew through the trees
In one long invidious draft.

The most unquestioning pair
That ever accepted fate
And the least disposed to ascribe
Any more than we had to to hate,

We assumed that the man himself
Or someone he had to obey
Wanted us to get down
And walk the rest of the way.

L'Angelus by J. F. Millet, reprinted courtesy of the Louvre Museum. © CNMHS/ SPADEM.

The following are some good and bad examples of answers written in response to some of the questions the Packard article could generate.

> *Q:*   Distinguish between Thomas Hobbes's and John Locke's views of humankind and describe in detail one modern view that is compatible with each of these.
>
> *1:*   Hobbes believed human beings to be irresponsible, but Locke believed we are rational. Hobbes believed we need a despot to rule us because we are not capable of ruling ourselves. One modern view that resembles Locke's is the existential view of Jean-Paul Sartre, which holds that man is totally free and in fact that the meaning in life is there because individuals invest life with meaning. A view like Hobbes's is the modern view that people are computers and can be programmed to do anything their society wants them to do.

This is not an irredeemably bad answer, but it is not a good one. The writer knew her material—at least, nothing she says is wrong. But she fails to demonstrate that she really has control of the material and knows it in depth. Let us look at some of the weaknesses in the answer.

The comparison between Hobbes and Locke is inexact because "irresponsible" and "rational" are not necessarily contradictory.	Hobbes believed human beings to be irresponsible, but Locke believed we are rational.
This statement is true but does not further the comparison because it is not matched by a statement about Locke's politics.	Hobbes believed we need a despot to rule us because we are not capable of ruling.
The account of Sartre's belief is accurate, and it is true that Locke and Sartre share many ideas about humankind, but the writer here does not explain how believing people to be rational (Locke's idea) is like believing people to be totally free (Sartre's idea).	One modern view that resembles Locke's is the existentialist view of Jean-Paul Sartre, which holds that <u>man is totally free</u> and in fact that the meaning in life is there because individuals invest life with meaning. A view like Hobbes's is the modern view that people are computers and can be programmed to do anything their society needs them to do.

Here is a better answer.

2: John Locke believed that human beings are rational and responsible and capable of getting along in a society that allows much individual freedom. In contrast, Thomas Hobbes believed that human beings are driven by aggressive impulses, irresponsible, and in need of a despotic ruler to keep peace among them. Those in the twentieth century who believe that human beings are captains of their fates are in agreement with Locke's view. These people include Jean-Paul Sartre, the existentialist, and Abraham Maslow and Rollo May. All of these believe that despite genetic and social and economic and chemical influences on human beings we are still capable of making free, rational decisions. People who, like H. L. Newbold, think that our behavior is determined by chemical elements within our body, are much closer to Hobbes's view.

This answer is stronger because it is more specific (identifies Sartre, Maslow, May, and Newbold with their respective viewpoints), has more depth (fuller explanation of each viewpoint), and is more exact (notice how the three beliefs of Locke are paralleled by three exactly contrasting beliefs of Hobbes and how the word "rational" is repeated in line 11 to show how some twentieth-century thinkers are in agreement with Locke).

Assume that the next test in the interdisciplinary Perspectives on Humanity class would cover both the "Images of Man" article and the selection "Rage." Read the selection several times and then list the questions you think would be likely to appear on the test covering it and the article.

Evaluate the following two responses given when students were asked to "discuss Konner's view of humankind and relate it to the 'man is a bad animal' school of thought discussed in the article."

> *1:*   Konner describes humankind as being naturally violent. We keep our tendency to be violent even when we may live nonviolently for years. He tells of a Malaysian tribe that had no violence until the British turned them into warriors. This is like the case of the two men who were not criminals until they felt betrayed and rejected and became violent. Konner doesn't believe that we are naturally peaceful. We can be either peaceful or violent, and Konner believes that the way we live can be very important in determining whether we become violent. So we do have some control.

> *2:*   Konner describes human beings as always having a capability for violence, but he does not just condemn us as "bad animals." He points out that some societies can have traditions of peaceful living, like the Malaysian people he describes, and can live without violence unless something very unusual happens to make them violent. Culture can be extremely influential in restraining our tendency for violence. For example, Konner says that violence is reduced when husbands and wives eat, sleep, and care for their children together. Konner believes that violence is natural to human beings but can be culturally controlled.

Now assume that the Perspectives on Humanity course will have two more tests and a final exam. The first test will cover the article "Images of Man," "Rage," and the textbook excerpt "Behavior Therapy and Behavior Modification"; the second will cover the Packard article, Millet's painting "The Angelus," and Robert Frost's poem "The Draft Horse." The final exam will be cumulative. List the questions you think likely to appear on each test and those likely to appear on the final. Then, using only the time you would have for the tests or final, write effective answers to questions the class or the instructor chooses. Following are some guidelines to help you in writing your answers.

Reminders When Taking Essay Tests and Exams

1. In studying, try to anticipate all of the questions you think you might be asked, study with these in mind, and think in advance how you would answer them.

2. When you are given the test, note how many parts there are to each question. Remind yourself to answer all the parts of the question and not to include material that does not answer the question.

3. Before you begin writing an essay, think through your answer and make notes. Make a list, in order, of the ideas or topics you want to cover. Check to make sure your list answers all the parts of the question.

4. Remember that you are writing to demonstrate that you know the material. Do not hesitate to state the obvious.

5. Adapt your writing process on the assumption that you may have time for only one draft. If you are a writer who usually does more drafting and less planning, you should make a conscious effort to plan more thoroughly, knowing there will not be time for many drafts.

6. Begin your answer by rephrasing and answering the question or beginning to answer it.

7. When you have finished a question, read over your answer, checking to make sure that you have answered all the parts of the question. Make any changes that will make the answer clearer, fuller, or more specific.

8. Read over your answer one final time to correct spelling, sentence, and punctuation problems.

CHAPTER 10

Demonstrating What You Know, II

THEME *Food as a Symbol*

SKILL FOCUS *Organizing a Draft*

How do you view food? Is it simply fuel to keep your body functioning effectively and efficiently? Is it a comfort when you are feeling low? Does the sight of a Baked Alaska or a Chocolate Mousse give you aesthetic pleasure that has little to do with nutritional value? Does fancy gourmet cooking delight you? Are you a fast-food fanatic, wanting your meals quickly without much concern for variety or fanciness? Do you eat health food? The food we eat and the way we regard it may say something about us. Dieting seems to be an extremely popular hobby in the twentieth century; in fact, as Hegsted, one of the authors in this chapter, reminds us: "You can count on a never-diminishing group of 30 or 40 million overweight people, always ready to try something else." Obesity and anorexia are severe problems in our culture. But even individuals without such problems seem obsessed with weight control. In this chapter—

through reading, responding, and interacting—you will be considering the various meanings people attach to food, the ways food can control people, and the ways people can control food.

Before Reading

Write in your journal about your own eating habits and attitudes toward food. You might want to ask yourself the following questions before or as you write.

1. How do I view food? What is my usual diet? What special foods do I enjoy? Favorite meals?
2. To what extent do I enjoy cooking? For myself? For others? How do people respond to my cooking?
3. Do I go on diets? If so, what types of diets do I follow? What are the results of my dieting?
4. How have my attitudes toward food and my eating habits changed since I have become an adult?
5. What do others (family, friends) think of my eating habits or attitudes toward food?

Make your entry at least a couple of pages long. It will be shared only if you choose.

In the following article, Nancy Stedman of *Health* magazine shares research about the possible meanings of what people eat and how they eat it. Keep your own journal entry in mind as you read the article, and let the following questions guide your reading:

1. How seriously should we take the notion that our diet may be a reflection of our personalities?
2. How can food be a reflection of our individual moods?
3. To what extent might the way we eat say something about the kind of people we are?

Food Foibles:

What secrets do your eating habits reveal about you?

Nancy Stedman

Does food, like clothing, make the man? *Are* we what we eat? Can you *really* read a person like a menu—based on his or her eating habits?

Sure, say several experts, as long as you take the whole matter with a grain of salt. For instance, your Uncle Willard's alarming habit of pouring ketchup over everything, including your famous Beef Wellington, could have a number of causes. Maybe he grew up in a household of ketchup worshippers or owns stock in Heinz. Still, chances are the habit also says something about his personality. Explains Martin Wayne, MD, a psychiatrist in private practice in Tarrytown, New York, "In general, personality traits affect *all* behavior. What you eat, how rapidly you eat it and with what pleasure—these reflect the kind of person you are."

Uncle Willard, for example, could be an unadventurous sort. "People who use a great deal of condiments like salt, pepper or ketchup may be trying to drown the unexpected with familiar tastes," says Robert D. Martin, MD, a psychiatrist who directs the Psychosomatic Clinic of the Long Island Jewish-Hillside Medical Center in New York City. On the other hand, they may just really like the taste of the condiments.

The following might help you sift through the personality ingredients of your friends, your loved ones and yourself.

You Are What You Eat?

Your first step is to think about food in terms of what statements it makes. "In large part, people consume food because of its symbolic significance," says Edward Sadalla, PhD, assistant professor of psychology at Arizona State University. A prize fighter who devours a bloody steak just before a title match to "prove" his ferociousness, for example, is trying to convince himself as much as his public.

Rather remarkably, studies by Sadalla and a team of researchers in Arizona suggest that we tend to agree on what certain people's diets mean. Moreover, the stereotypes of these eaters—vegetarians, gourmets, health food nuts, fast food fans and synthetic food users—seem to be a fairly accurate reflection of their own self images.

Suppose your daughter brings home a new boyfriend—a vegetarian who relishes brown rice with snow peas and avocado sandwiches with bean sprouts. Look out the window. According to Sadalla's research with Arizona students, odds are the fellow drives a foreign car. Even if he doesn't, your best guess is that he's non-competitive, sexual, serious and pacifistic. Meanwhile, what if your new babysitter turns out to be a health food nut who shows up laden with wheat germ and yogurt—is this someone you want to take care of your children? That depends on how you feel about a nuclear-power-plant foe and solar-energy advocate who's also a hypochondriac.

If your new beau's idea of culinary bliss is fast food (burgers, fries and shakes) or synthetic food (liquid margarine and cheese food spread), what does that imply? In all probability, you've stumbled across a "regular guy"—religious, competitive and family oriented. On the other hand, if you've been dating a gourmet—someone whose taste runs to lobster Newburg and freshly ground French-roast coffee—you've picked the recipe for adventure. Sensual and cultured, gourmets prefer sailing, riding and gambling. But think twice before you marry one—they tend to be self-oriented.

The Meaning of Munching

Even if you don't fall into a clear-cut diet group, many experts believe that your very attitude toward food reflects your approach to life. "An ordinary eater often is an ordinary person," says Dr. Martin. "Those more interested in wines and foods are more likely to be complex people, sensual explorers." Adds Dr. Wayne, "In general, people who like food enjoy pleasures in many things. But someone with a languid, flaccid attitude toward life won't see the value of food."

What you reach for at any given moment, however, may be as much a reflection of your mood as of your disposition. It's widely believed that a craving for crunchy food means you're angry, for example. Instead of venting your anger directly at its source, you let off steam by biting down on something hard. Some people also handle anger by devouring sweets. In *Fat Is a Feminist Issue,* author and therapist Susie Orbach recounts this story: "One woman I was seeing ate candy inexplicably during the day while she was at work. The intake of sweets had to do with an attempt to sweeten herself, to make herself 'nice' when indeed she was quite angry." Sweets are also often eaten as a reward—a practice carried over from childhood.

Certain foods are particularly comforting if you're depressed or anxious. A yen for creamy foods, which are associated with milk and hence mother's care, may indicate a need for love and reassurance. Similarly, when you reach for soft carbohydrates like bread or muffins, you may be trying to recreate the softness of mother.

People who repeatedly overeat may have a chronic need for comfort, according to current psychiatric thinking. "Many of the obese never felt adequately nurtured by their mothers, and they learned, instead, to nurture themselves with food," says Martin. Wayne agrees: "People who have a general feeling of being deprived—either financially, sexually or because of a neurotic childhood—often, rather than squarely facing that feeling, eat to get rid of it."

The bingeing that results often centers around carbohydrates. Recently researchers have found a possible physiological basis for this connection: Consuming carbohydrates can increase the amount of serotonin, a brain chemical that seems to relax people and raise their spirits. "It's likely that early in life people make associations between the consumption of certain foods and changes in how they feel," says Richard J. Wurtman, PhD, a neuroendocrinologist at the Massachusetts Institute of Technology. "Then, later on, they unconsciously turn to those foods to recreate the desired feelings."

Mom's Apple Pie

"Like sex and poetry, food is extraordinarily emotional," says Martin. That's why many of our quirkier tastes can be traced back to emotionally charged relationships or situations from the past. Take, for instance, the case of a man whose mother always insisted he drink orange juice with breakfast and who grew up to loathe it. Even if he initially liked the taste, nowadays when he's offered the juice he unconsciously calls up the hostility he felt when his mother made him drink it. Or look at the normally mild-mannered Connecticut man who went bananas when he realized his coffee had been lightened with condensed milk. The canned milk, he explained to his shaking daughter, reminded him of being at the front during World War II.

Private symbolism can also evoke positive feelings. Christine, a New York photographer, can never resist buying Swedish crackers and smoked eels when she sees them in a deli. Why? "Eating food that reminds me of my Swedish grandmother makes me feel warm and pleasant," she says. Another New Yorker, Susan, says that the nicest thing Stouffer's ever did for her was to come up with frozen Welsh rarebit: She had eaten this cheese dish virtually every Sunday during her childhood in England. "Whenever I feel nostalgic, I pick up some at the supermarket," she says.

For some people, ethnic food brings up bigger issues: It can be a way of expressing ethnic identification or disidentification, according to Arizona State University's Sadalla. While immigrants may rely on the food they were raised with because it is familiar, their children may reject it as a way of proving they are Americans. One woman, a librarian in Wisconsin, tried to resolve her feelings about her ethnic upbringing through her diet. Brought up as an Orthodox Jew, she rejects what she sees as the narrow focus of that world, but appreciates its sense of community. Her compromise: She keeps a kosher kitchen but will eat non-kosher food (except pork) when out of the house.

The moral of these stories: Don't jump to conclusions before you get a person's eating history.

Beyond Manners

How you eat is as meaningful as *what* you eat, say many experts. Here are some questions to ask yourself:

Do you eat like you're trying to set a world speed record? Then you're probably an impatient person, says Wayne. On the other hand, if you're a notorious slowpoke, then you might be a bit depressed, he adds. Do you finish everything on your plate? You're probably just following your childhood training. But if you always leave something over, you're either rebelling or trying to feel wealthy.

If you always leave the crust when you eat a piece of bread, you may want to get to the substance of things and avoid their periphery, says Wayne. And if you play with food in a slightly repulsive way you may be rebelling and thus expressing unresolved anger toward authority figures.

Order counts, too: If you mush all your food together, Martin says, you may have a jumbled attitude toward life and may lack an esthetic sense. But if you eat the things on your plate one at a time, you're probably cautious and like to complete one job before starting a new one. On the other hand, if you move from one food to another for variety, you're probably flexible and can deal with change.

What happens when a dawdler meets a gobbler, or when *his* meat is *your* poison? Things may well go sour. "Food incompatibility could mean that there are more widespread incompatibilities in the way you see the world," says Sadalla. Adds Martin, "If one party is pedestrian and the other adventurous and creative, it's possible that someone is going to get hurt."

Fortunately, you often see a person's eating habits early in a relationship—because eating out is a common first date. However, don't get *too* nervous if your dinner partner keeps grabbing for the soft, warm-as-a-womb bread: He may simply like the way it tastes. After all, to paraphrase Freud, sometimes a pickle is really just a pickle.

After Reading

Write your response to the article in a journal entry of about one page. What did the article make you think of? To what extent do you believe that any human behavior, such as eating, reflects an individual's personality? Share your responses to the article with your classmates—not in an attempt to reach agreement or consensus but merely to share reactions and ideas.

ORGANIZATION

Notice how Stedman organizes her article and try to answer the following questions about her method.

1. How does the author try to capture your interest in reading the article?
2. How is the article divided into parts? What effect does this organization have on you as a reader? Are the subheads effective? Are they necessary?

3. In addition to the subheads, what devices does the author employ to arrange her ideas for the reader?
4. How does the author tie things together in the last paragraph so that you know the article has come to an end?

Your responses to these questions should help you toward an understanding of the kinds of organizational decisions a writer makes.

When you write for yourself, as in a personal journal entry, you are probably not much concerned about organization. In fact, unfocused free writing often makes sense only by associations that exist in the writer's mind. Accounts of personal experience may have only a loose chronological structure. In writing to learn, you may well organize a subject after the pattern presented in the material you are learning, or you may put the material together in a way that is easier for you to remember. In writing for audiences other than yourself, however, organization becomes one of the important means of getting your message across for a specific purpose to a specific reader or group of readers. Decisions you make about organizing your work may be particularly critical when you want to share information with others or influence them in some way.

Try to characterize the audience Stedman is addressing in "Food Foibles." Who reads *Health* magazine? What seems to be the purpose of the article? To what extent does the organization of the article seem suitable given its purpose and audience?

Before Reading

Reread the journal entries you wrote before and after the Stedman article. Think seriously for a few moments about your own diet and that of your family and friends. How many people do you know who have been on weight reduction diets? What kinds of diets have these weight-conscious people tried? How have they worked? If millions of Americans are dieting at any one time, you probably know someone who is dieting even if you are not dieting yourself or never have. What should a person know before embarking on a weight reduction diet? In the reading that follows, Mark Hegsted raises basic questions about eight diets—questions that he believes need to be answered by anyone considering a weight reduction plan. Read "Rating the Diets," and respond in your journal to the questions that follow the article.

Rating the Diets

D. Mark Hegsted, Ph.D.

There are dozens of ways to lose weight; that's why so many diet plans succeed in making money. What a great business to be in! No matter what the immediate results of any diet may be, most people seem to regain the weight after a while, so you can count on a never-diminishing group of 30 or 40 million overweight people, always ready to try something else, always hoping for the one great gimmick that will make it easy.

But losing weight and maintaining proper weight are obviously *not* easy in our society. If they were, the problem would long since have been solved, and the market for new diets would disappear along with obesity. In fact, we can be sure that when there are many solutions offered for the same problem, none of them is very satisfactory.

Given that fact, and the fact that there is a lot that is not known about obesity, what can we be sure of? That to lose body fat you must see to it that your total calorie intake is less than the amount of energy you expend. Since some bodies are much more efficient at storing fat than others, some people get fat without being gluttons or sloths while others seem able to eat anything, do nothing and stay thin. Because individual energy needs vary so much, I will not comment on the amounts of weight you might expect to lose in any given period of time on any of the diets I am going to discuss. Even on a low-calorie diet (1,000 calories a day or less) on which practically everybody will lose weight, they will do so at different rates. I *will* try to answer six basic questions about eight popular diets in such a way that you can decide whether one of them is appropriate for you—when and if you want to take off some weight and (the hard part) keep it off for a lifetime.

The Never-Say-Diet Diet from *The Never-Say Diet Book* by Richard Simmons

What Is this Diet's Underlying Principle?

The principle is the basic one that to lose weight you must eat less or exercise more, preferably both. If you want exhortations and pep talks you'll find them here, as well as what is supposed to be a rather clever exposé of the evils of obesity and how you got that way. Whether this will turn you on or turn you off, I have no idea. The whole thing is a bit too slick for me.

A substantial portion of the book is devoted to the exercise program. Although you can't be against exercise (or motherhood), I would be surprised if much of this— taking deep breaths, stretching the facial muscles, etc.—does a lot for you. It certainly won't use up many calories. Maybe it puts you in a better frame of mind.

The author speaks of his "volume food plan" and says that if you are too fat you eat too much. He is correct about eating too much, but volume has nothing to do with it. In fact, *increasing* the actual volume while lowering the calories by substituting voluminous salads for more compact high-calorie foods is the basis for many weight control programs—including this one.

There is nothing unusual about the diet, which includes breakfasts of fruit, cereal and skim milk; lunches of salad with cottage cheese or chicken and a low-calorie dressing; dinners of lean meat, a small salad, one vegetable and, on occasion, half a baked potato or a glass of wine.

Is It Safe to Follow this Diet?

There are no known problems with this approach.

Is the Diet Easy to Stick to?

This is a sensible, moderate plan which should be acceptable to a well-motivated dieter.

Are the Required Foods Inexpensive, Easy to Find, Easy to Prepare?

There is nothing unusual about the foods. You can undoubtedly spend money and time trying to improve them but they require no special skills.

Can the Whole Family Eat What the Dieter Eats?

The foods are suitable for the family, making a nice change from diets proposed by authors who always seem to think that you live alone and only have to feed yourself.

Does this Diet Help Establish Good Permanent Eating Habits?

This is the type that should serve that purpose in the long run. It is rather low in sugar, salt, fat and cholesterol, and over the long haul each individual will have to modify the diet to fit his own needs, but it is a reasonable start.

The Beverly Hills Diet from *The Beverly Hills Diet* by Judy Mazel

What Is this Diet's Underlying Principle?

This is really gimmicky. It is an all-fruit diet with weird and generally nonsensical instructions about which fruits should be eaten and when. The only "principle" involved is that fruits are about 90 percent water and usually provide 50 to 100 calories per serving. If you need 1,500 calories to maintain your present weight, you would have to eat 20 to 30 cups of fruit per day to get them. It should surprise no one to find that if you eat all the fruit you can hold, you will still lose weight.

Is It Safe to Follow This Diet?

It's a sure recipe for malnutrition if you stay on it long enough. For example: One serving of fruit usually provides about one gram of protein, so even if you ate 20 to 30 cups you would get only about half of the protein you need. No diet of one food—fruit or anything else—is really safe.

Is the Diet Easy to Stick to?

I haven't tried the diet (and I don't expect to) but I think you are going to be hungry (no matter how much fruit you eat) and bored and disgusted (or disgusting) after a few days. I presume that after a couple of days every meal will be a "special occasion" but not the kind you look forward to.

Are the Required Foods Inexpensive, Easy to Find, Easy to Prepare?

If you really stick to the menus given, with their emphasis on papaya, mangos, watermelon, etc., you will have difficulty obtaining the foods you want in some places or at some times of the year. And if you can eat enough, it will cost you plenty. Most restaurants have fruit, of course, but what's the point in eating out if you insist on only fruit for breakfast, lunch and dinner?

Can the Whole Family Eat What the Dieter Eats?

Well, there is nothing wrong with fruit. Fruit is low in calories, and many people can increase their intake with profit, particularly by substituting fruits for high-calorie desserts. An all-fruit diet, however, makes *no* nutritional sense and should certainly not be imposed upon the family or anyone else.

THE DIETS AT A GLANCE

Diet	What Principle Is Involved?	Is the Diet Safe?	Is the Diet Easy to Stick To?	Are the Foods Inexpensive, Easy to Find, Etc.?	Can the Whole Family Eat this Diet?	Will It Give You Good Long-term Eating Habits?
The Never-Say-Diet Diet	Reduced calories, limited choice, more exercise	Yes	Yes	Yes	Foods yes, amounts no	Yes
The Beverly Hills Diet	Fruit only	No	No	Expensive and at times hard to obtain	No	No
The University Diet	Two low-calorie meals, one low-calorie supplement drink per day	Yes	No	Yes	No	Probably not
The Cambridge Diet	330 calories per day	No	No	Yes	No	No
The Atkins Diet	High-fat, low-carbohydrate intake; ketosis	Not nutritionally balanced; too much fat	Not very easy	Easily available, possibly costly	No	No
The Stillman Diet	High protein intake	Not nutritionally balanced	Not very easy	Demands careful shopping, a lot of meat purchases	No	No
The Scarsdale Diet	Reduced calories, limited choice	Yes	Not in the long run	Easy to find, easy to prepare, but costly	Foods yes, amounts no	Maybe
The Pritikin Diet	Radically reduced intake of calories, fats, protein, sugar, salt	Yes	Not very easy	Inexpensive and easy to find but calls for whole new approach to shopping, cooking	Maybe	Yes

Does this Diet Help Establish Good Permanent Eating Habits?

Obviously, this diet leaves you nowhere in terms of what you should eventually eat. What is most distressing to me is that practically every page offers statements that are not only wrong but ridiculous. For example, the author explains that "anything that can't be digested is fattening." This is exactly wrong. Things that are not digested are *not* fattening. Or how about this one: "God created us with a thymus gland which secretes the enzyme necessary to digest milk." The thymus has nothing to do with the digestion of milk or anything else. Or, "Remember that milk is a protein. So a little drop in your coffee will make all of the carbohydrate that follows it undigested and fattening." Simply untrue on every count. Similar fantasies occur everywhere.

I expect that this book, like many miracle-diet books, will make a lot of money for the author (for reasons that elude me). Anyone who enjoys reading it should then file it under fiction and let it sink into the oblivion it so richly deserves.

The University Diet

What Is this Diet's Underlying Principle?

This is another gimmick that may or may not work. The University Diet offers six reasonably well-balanced menus providing about 1,000 calories a day. The gimmick is that for lunch you can eat only the 110-calorie University Diet Supplement Blend. There is nothing unique about this—instant breakfasts and other meal replacements that avoid temptations and choices have been around for a long time. If taking a meal of this kind once a day helps you control your total calorie intake, there is not much to be said against it. You can't, however, eat this for lunch and then overindulge for dinner.

Is It Safe to Follow this Diet?

There is no reason to think otherwise. The 110-calorie supplement is almost a negligible amount of food, but contains 27 vitamins and essential minerals. When food intake is severely restricted, no matter how it is done, it becomes more difficult to get a full complement of essential nutrients, and a vitamin-mineral supplement is often recommended as a kind of insurance. It should be emphasized, however, that taking a vitamin-mineral supplement—as far as anyone knows—will not keep you from feeling hungry.

Is the Diet Easy to Stick to?

I expect that the supplement will not be very exciting after a few days but that is really not the point. The question is whether taking it and forgetting about a meal will help keep your caloric intake down. If so, a glass of skim milk, a slice of bread and a vitamin-mineral pill would do the same thing. Does the fact that the manufacturers of the supplement provide only a one-week menu mean that this regimen generally proves unacceptable after a few weeks?

Are the Required Foods Inexpensive, Easy to Find, Easy to Prepare?

The cost of the supplement is not unreasonable, but then it shouldn't be since it is mostly skim milk powder, casein (a protein from milk) and soy flour, plus vitamins and minerals. There is nothing particularly unusual or expensive about the diet given— it's very limited in meat and consists mostly of fruits and vegetables.

Can the Whole Family Eat What the Dieter Eats?

This is a rigid 1,000 calorie diet made somewhat more rigid by the use of a single supplement for lunch. It has all the difficulties inherent in rigid diets when it comes to feeding the family, and one should not impose it on them.

Does this Diet Help Establish Good Permanent Eating Habits?

As I have already mentioned, meal replacements have been around for a long time without taking the country by storm or solving the obesity problem. They may provide some assistance to some people but seem certain not to be the longed-for long-term solution.

The Cambridge Diet

What Is this Diet's Underlying Principle?

The Cambridge Diet drink and the University Diet supplement appear to be very similar, which emphasizes a problem that plagues the manufacturers of diet supplements. Their products are rarely patentable, so once they are developed, anyone can copy and sell them.

But although they use the same material, the similarity between the Cambridge and University diets ends there. Whereas the University Diet uses the supplement to replace one meal, the Cambridge Diet consists of *only* the supplement, taken three times a day. It is one thing to replace a meal with a 110-calorie supplement. It is quite another thing to go on a 330-calorie diet. This is close to starvation.

The Cambridge mixture consists of skim milk powder, with casein and soy flour as protein sources. The carbohydrate is fructose, a fruit sugar which is now made from corn syrup. The mixture contains almost no fat. It is supplemented with 27 different vitamins and minerals and comes in 10 different flavors.

Is It Safe to Follow this Diet?

I am reluctant to discuss this diet since I think you should simply avoid it. The use of very low calorie, near-starvation diets has been subject to considerable research in the last 10 years or so. Such diets may possibly have a legitimate role in the treatment of gross, intractable obesity, but even in such cases there is considerable argument about the appropriate composition, the level of calories, and the safety of the procedure. When these diets were first introduced a number of deaths resulted. Presumably the products have been improved since then but many physicians still warn against them. Many believe that if they *are* used, it should be only under "continuous medical supervision"—in other words, in a hospital.

The warning label on the Cambridge product should be sufficient to scare most people off. It reads: "Consult your doctor before starting this diet. In particular, individuals who have heart and cardiovascular disease, stroke, diabetes, gout, hypoglycemia, chronic infections; the very elderly, growing children, adolescents or anyone under medical care for any other condition should diet only under direct medical supervision. Your doctor can advise you whether you have any of the above conditions or if for any reason you should not be on this or any diet. Pregnant and nursing mothers should not be on any weight-loss program."

I wonder if any of us (or our doctors) can be sure that our hearts, kidneys and everything else are in perfect condition. It is worth emphasizing, too, that although the label is presumably there to protect you, it also has another purpose: It provides some protection for the company. If anything untoward happens, you have been warned.

Is the Diet Easy to Stick to?

Weight loss will be maximal on this diet—probably the same as if you didn't eat at all. Although the manufacturers claim that users tolerate the diet well and after the first few days are not hungry, it is obvious that this is not an easy regime. And there is no relief. You are either on it or off it.

Are the Required Foods Inexpensive, Easy to Find, Easy to Prepare?

The three meals will cost you about $3, which is not much. But then, you are not getting much. Of course, if you try this diet under "close medical supervision"—as you should—you won't be worrying about the price of the supplement. You'll worry about the cost of the medical care.

Can the Whole Family Eat What the Dieter Eats?

The family certainly can*not* participate in this.

Does this Diet Help Establish Good Permanent Eating Habits?

This diet doesn't teach anyone how to eat. The important question, of course, is what happens afterward—assuming you have the fortitude to go through several weeks of this. There isn't much data on long-term results, and what is available is not encouraging. Even Alan N. Howard, PhD, of the University of Cambridge, the principal developer and chief defender of this plan, found that about 80 percent of users had regained 50 percent or more of their lost body weight 15 months later. Only about 30 percent were sufficiently motivated to continue attending a follow-up clinic. It sounds as though one attempt at this diet was enough for most of them, and few may have ended up any better off.

People who are concerned about their weight—even those who are 10 to 20 percent above desirable weight—may have a problem, but it is uncertain whether the risks of being obese are any greater than the risks associated with this kind of regime (particularly when it appears that most people regain a lot of weight). A very grossly obese person might want to try this diet under a physician's supervision, but I think it should not be promoted to the public.

The Atkins Diet from *The Atkins Diet Revolution* by Robert C. Atkins, MD

What Is this Diet's Underlying Principle?

This is an extremely low carbohydrate diet. You are allowed no foods containing sugars or carbohydrates except for small salads of very low calorie vegetables. There are no limitations on protein foods (meats, fish, poultry) and none on fat. Pile on as much as you can!

The presumed secret of this diet is ketosis, a condition that occurs in diabetes and in starvation. When the body is forced to use fat as its major source of calories, some fat will be incompletely oxidized, and the acidic products are called ketones. You test your urine for ketones, and if it doesn't have any, you are not adhering to the diet. If, on the other hand, your ketosis is sufficiently severe, you feel sick and lose your appetite, which most people assume is the reason this diet works—if it does. However, recent research at the University of Vermont showed no real differences in hunger or appetite in people on this kind of diet versus people on a more balanced one. In all probability, simply eating nothing but fat and meat is enough to discourage food consumption.

Is It Safe to Follow this Diet?

The plan has been very severely criticized. Many diets are specifically designed to *prevent* ketosis, which is considered bad for you. High-fat, high-cholesterol diets are also associated with high serum cholesterol levels, heart disease, hypertension, diabetes and cancer. Furthermore, very high protein diets induce calcium losses from the bones, and this diet is already low in calcium. Finally, the diet is low in fiber. The long-term consequences have not been tested, of course, but they don't look good.

Is the Diet Easy to Stick to?

It sounds unpalatable to me, but I may be influenced by my conviction that high-fat diets should be avoided.

Are the Required Foods Inexpensive, Easy to Find, Easy to Prepare?

The cost will depend on what you choose and how much you eat. If it's prime steak and lobster, the cost may be high enough to further depress your appetite; if it's fatty hamburgers and other inexpensive meats, your pocketbook won't hurt. Clearly, most restaurants can provide these kinds of foods, if you have the fortitude to avoid the potatoes, bread, desserts, etc.

Can the Whole Family Eat What the Dieter Eats?

This kind of extreme diet should *never* be imposed upon the rest of the family or your friends—and certainly not on your children.

Does this Diet Help Establish Good Permanent Eating Habits?

Even the author of this diet proposes it only as a way to lose weight, not to be followed for long periods of time. He offers suggestions for making a transition toward something more sensible, but the diet itself is a far cry from what you should eventually eat.

The Stillman Diet from *The Doctor's Quick Weight-Loss Diet*

by Irwin Maxwell Stillman, MD, and Samm Sinclair Baker

What Is this Diet's Underlying Principle?

Here's the other extreme of the high-protein diets. You are allowed only *lean* meat, fish and poultry, and both fat and carbohydrates are severely restricted. All meat is broiled or boiled and eight glasses of water a day are prescribed. The presumed justification is what has been called the "specific dynamic action of protein." After a meal, the bloodstream absorbs sugars, fats and amino acids, the last derived from protein. Fats can be stored in the adipose (fatty) tissue; carbohydrates, in the liver or muscles, or they can be converted to additional fat. Later, we use these reserves as sources of energy after absorption is complete. If we didn't have this capacity we would have to eat continuously in order to have a continuous source of energy.

The body, however, has only limited capacity to store protein, or to convert it to fat or carbohydrate. When we eat a lot of protein, some of the amino acids are simply "burned" and disposed of as heat. So, in theory at least, if we eat only protein some of the calories don't count. The idea is intriguing, of course, but its importance is under considerable debate.

Is It Safe to Follow this Diet?

Lean meat does *not* constitute a balanced diet. It is very low in dietary fiber and calcium, and the high protein intake stimulates calcium losses. Just how safe this extreme diet (or any other) is depends on how long you follow it. Most extreme diets have considerable "built-in" protection since you probably can't stick to them very long. However, if your daily intake falls as low as 300 to 500 calories (and it might), you could be in real trouble.

Is this Diet Easy to Stick to?

Since this diet is even stricter than the Atkins, I would expect it to be even harder to adhere to. The choice of meats is very limited—broiled or boiled and very low in fat. What do you do about special occasions like holidays or parties? I expect you either avoid them or break the diet.

Are the Required Foods Inexpensive, Easy to Find, Easy to Prepare?

Since only very lean meat is allowed, you have to be extremely careful in shopping and in eating at restaurants. I suppose this raises the cost, but since you won't eat much, it will probably turn out to be not very expensive. You certainly don't have to have much cooking skill to prepare the foods—even I can broil a steak.

Can the Whole Family Eat What the Dieter Eats?

Like the Atkins diet, this should not be imposed on the rest of the family or anyone else! I expect you are going to be eating alone.

Does this Diet Help Establish Good Permanent Eating Habits?

This is strictly a weight-loss diet. Any shopping or eating patterns you establish on this diet will not be very helpful in making the transition to normal eating that must come.

The Scarsdale Diet from *The Complete Scarsdale Diet* by Herman Tarnower, MD,

and Samm Sinclair Baker

What Is this Diet's Underlying Principle?

This is a more sensible diet than the Atkins and Stillman diets. As prescribed, it provides 43 percent of your total calories as protein, 22 percent as fat, and 35 percent as carbohydrate. (This is about double the proportion of protein and half the proportion of fat calories in the average American diet.) The *amount* of protein, fat and carbohydrate you actually eat will be low, because every menu is strictly prescribed, the calorie intake is strictly limited, and you are instructed, "Eat exactly what is assigned: Don't substitute." You don't have to count calories because you have no choices.

Is It Safe to Follow this Diet?

This is a reasonably well-balanced low-calorie diet. Although the proportion of protein is high, the total intake is restricted.

Is the Diet Easy to Stick to?

It may be about as acceptable a low-calorie diet as can be developed. Of course, there are no particular merits in the menus given—many others could be equally effective, but many people may find it easier to follow instructions exactly than to make choices at the table. The problem with this diet is universal with weight reduction—you *do* have to limit your intake.

Are the Required Foods Inexpensive, Easy to Find, Easy to Prepare?

The goal is to prepare attractive, low-calorie menus and dishes. This will probably turn out to be expensive, but I'm told the recipes are not difficult. The author does provide some dos and don'ts ("Don't use sugar. Don't use cream. Don't use whole milk.") as a guide for eating on special occasions when the diet cannot be strictly followed.

Can the Whole Family Eat What the Dieter Eats?

This diet, although reasonably balanced, is much too spartan for children or adolescents. A lunch of fruit salad and a slice of protein bread won't provide enough food for a growing youngster, even if you serve him double helpings. This, of course, is one reason that many women have so much difficulty with reducing diets. If they have to feed the rest of the family a well-balanced, nutritionally adequate diet, the temptation to eat forbidden foods is always there.

Does this Diet Help Establish Good Permanent Eating Habits?

Although there is nothing magical about the menus, this diet does provide foods many people may find helpful in establishing long-range dietary plans.

The Pritikin Diet (from *The Pritikin Permanent Weight-Loss Manual*
by Nathan Pritikin)

What Is this Diet's Underlying Principle?

Of all the diets discussed, this one demands the most radical permanent changes in your eating habits and would perhaps be the most successful—if it were followed. It requires, however, a whole new approach to food and practically a new way of life. The original Pritikin Diet was aimed at controlling chronic diseases, especially heart disease. It was a vegetarian diet—low in fat, cholesterol, sugar and salt, very high in starches and complex carbohydrates (fruits and vegetables)—and was combined with a rather vigorous exercise program. It has been relaxed a bit here, but only a bit, to allow a little lean meat, fish or poultry. Sugar and salt are still rigorously excluded. Different dietary plans for 700, 850, 1,000 and 1,200 calories a day are included. Real exercise—swimming, walking, jogging if you are up to it—is encouraged.

Is It Safe to Follow this Diet?

I have little doubt that it is safe. The real question is whether it is *necessary*. Many health organizations, including the American Heart Association, the National Academy of Sciences, and the U.S. Departments of Agriculture and Health and Human Services, have recommended that Americans reduce their consumption of fat, especially saturated fat. We are also authoritatively advised to reduce our intake of sugar and salt, and increase our consumption of fruits, vegetables and cereal products, especially whole-grain cereals. This sound advice is obviously consistent with the Pritikin diet. All these organizations, however, recommend *moderate* reductions. Pritikin goes the whole way.

Is the Diet Easy to Stick to?

Well, as I have implied, it requires a completely new approach to shopping and food preparation. You will have to throw away most of your recipes and start fresh. To help you, Pritikin provides a large number of recipes to make the essentially vegetarian diet more palatable and avoid salt and sugar. I recognize that there are a lot more vegetarians around now than there used to be, so maybe vegetarianism is not as bad as it might seem.

Are the Required Foods Inexpensive, Easy to Find, Easy to Prepare?

Once you have made the transition, I suppose this is really a cheaper way to eat. If you are eating out, of course, you will have difficulties unless you go to vegetarian restaurants. The few times I have tried them, they were better than I expected but didn't convince me that I wanted to make vegetarianism a permanent way of life.

Can the Whole Family Eat What the Dieter Eats?

Like virtually all popular diets, this one is aimed at adults. Many nutritionists are somewhat skeptical about the value of vegetarian regimes for children. In the past some ridiculous and dangerous diets have been recommended—the brown rice diet, for example. On the other hand, near-vegetarian groups like the Seventh Day Adventists have a better health record than most American communities and obviously raise healthy children. Nutritionally adequate diets of this kind are certainly possible for the family.

Does this Diet Help Establish Good Permanent Eating Habits?

There is no doubt in my mind that shifting the American diet in this direction would improve our health. But do we need to go to this extreme? Whatever the benefits, probably relatively few people will make this kind of commitment. This being the case, the regimen will not solve the general health problems of the country. If, on the other hand, a less rigorous diet were equally effective, it should be much more acceptable to much larger numbers of people and, therefore, a much better solution to widespread problems.

After Reading

Respond in your journal to the following:

1. To what extent do Hegsted's six questions match the kinds of questions you or those you know would ask about a reducing diet?
2. Check Hegsted's analysis of two or three of the diets with friends or family (or yourself) who have tried them. To what extent do others with personal experience agree with the author's analyses?
3. Respond to Hegsted's statement that "you can count on a never-diminishing group of 30 or 40 million overweight people, always ready to try something else, always hoping for the one great gimmick that will make it easy." What does this statement imply about a good portion of the American population?

4. What conclusions does Hegsted reach after his rating of the diets?
5. What is the principal technique Hegsted used to organize his article? How does he introduce his ratings, and how does he bring the article to a close? Of what value is Hegsted's chart?

Before Reading

While millions of Americans may diet to lose weight, obesity is only one kind of problem associated with food consumption. Of recent interest to the general public is the condition known as anorexia nervosa. While anorexia has been identified and dealt with for some time by the medical community, it was the 1983 death of Karen Carpenter, popular American singer of the 1970s and 1980s, that brought this disease to the attention of Americans.

In Chapter 1 of *The Best Little Girl in the World,* Steven Levenkron creates a portrait of teenaged Francesca who is on the road to anorexia nervosa. As you read, notice how Levenkron creates his character and the family situation in which she lives.

The Best Little Girl in the World

Steven Levenkron

At the barre the girls moved and stretched, pointed and arched in time to Madame's precise cadence. One, two, three, four. . . .

I must be perfect, Francesca thought. She compared her own leg to the outstretched limb of the next girl and straightened her knee. "Five, six, seven, eight . . ." Madame continued to count, her pointer echoing the staccato beat. Francesca checked her leg against the girl on the other side. Straighter. The pleasure in her triumph dulled the pain behind her knee. Surely Madame would notice the perfection of her movements.

The studio was lined with mirrors. No matter where Francesca looked she could see legs stretching, arms arching, torsos bending, backs straightened in time to Madame's constantly demanding beat. In the mirror a black leotard, taut and slim and straight, caught Francesca's attention. She was perfect. Not an awkward gesture. Not an extra ounce of flesh. The figure was pure movement, all energy and strength for the dance.

Francesca turned from the girl's image to her own. Her thighs were grotesque bulges under the leg warmers. Above them her buttocks protruded offensively. Her torso seemed to be all flab. Her breasts hung uselessly, obscuring the straight line that should have risen above her ribs. She was fat. Worse than that, she was a monster. A five-foot-four, ninety-eight-pound monster.

"One, two," Madame continued to count, and as she passed Francesca the staccato beat came out "well done." Had Francesca heard correctly? And if she had, were the words directed at her? The leg on her right reached higher. The girl on her left was slimmer and straighter. Francesca had to know. Had the words been said? Had they been meant for her? She wouldn't leave the studio until she found out.

When class was over Francesca stayed at the barre pretending to practice a last exercise until the handful of girls who normally clustered around Madame after each class had drifted off to change. She was not looking at the teacher but was acutely aware of her presence. Madame was gathering up her things. Soon she would be out of the room, and Francesca would never know. But how did she dare ask? The words echoed in her head foolishly. "Did you mean me when you said well done?" Impossible. "How was I today?" Sophomoric. A true dancer knew how she had performed. "Am I getting any better?" Worse than sophomoric. Babyish. And then, as if God or Madame or someone had answered her prayers, the teacher was standing beside her. Her dark reflection in the mirror next to Francesca's own blond one dazzled her. All the light that filtered in through the high windows seemed concentrated in the teacher's proud, bright eyes. Her body was straight and thin and firm. Without realizing it, Francesca drew her small slender frame up in imitation of the woman.

"A good class, Francesca. You're showing progress." The tones were as clipped and precise as her movements. "Now stay slim—perhaps even a pound less here." She touched Francesca's rear lightly. "And firm up." She patted the girl's stomach. "Slim and firm. It isn't enough to make you a dancer, but without it you'll never be a dancer." The words echoed in Francesca's head as she stared into the mirror at the woman's receding reflection. *Slim, firm, slim, firm.* They made a rhythm of their own. Like the *well done, well done* the teacher had thrown out during class.

Francesca had felt tired, but now she began to exercise again in time to the chant. She counted *slim, firm, slim, firm* to herself as Madame did the more conventional cadences. As she moved she observed herself closely in the mirror, still feeling where the teacher had touched her. It was as if her buttocks and stomach burned with the stinging rebuke. In the mirror her body seemed to swell and sag with every movement. She was worse than grotesque. There were no words for the slovenliness of Francesca's body, no words for the failure that was Francesca.

The idea came to her with a flash of excitement. Francesca was fat. Francesca was dead. She quickened her movements. *One, two, slim, firm, three, four, well, done,* and then, as if it came from the beat itself, the new girl was born, *Kes-sa, Kes-sa.* It matched the beat of Madame's stick. Better than that, it matched the beat of Madame herself. *Kes-sa, Ma-dame, Kes-sa, Ma-dame.* The name was brief, firm, and hard, just as Kessa would be. The name was born. The body would follow. The useless flesh and layers of revolting fat would fall away, and like her model, Madame, she would be pure strength and energy and movement. Fat Francesca was dead, had died giving birth to perfect Kessa.

The changing room was a bedlam of practice clothes and dance shoes and young, high-fluted voices. Giggles, shouts, whispered confidences. "I don't think she's all that good." This last, murmured just as she passed, Kessa was sure was said about her. For a moment she felt like crying. Then she remembered Madame. What did the opinion of some silly girl her own age matter against the superior wisdom.

"Hey, Francesca," the blond girl who had whispered the dire comment shouted, "we're going to Charlie's Soup Burg for something to eat. Want to come along?"

Reactions raced through Kessa's mind. They didn't mean me after all. They couldn't have meant me or they wouldn't ask me along. But of course they meant me, and now they're trying to make it up. Or they want me to come along so they can laugh at me. *Kes-sa, Kes-sa.* Her clenched fists beat in time against her thighs. But how could Kessa live if Francesca kept stuffing her with hamburgers and french fries and disgusting, fattening food?

"I'm not hungry," she lied, and turned her back on the girls to change. The battle had been joined, the first skirmish won.

Her step as she walked along Fifty-second Street was light. *Kes-sa, Kes-sa, Kes-sa.* She moved in time to her own rhythm now. She felt light and full of energy. How silly people were to eat. They thought they needed food for energy, but they didn't. Energy came from will, from self-control. Kessa, almost skipping now in time to her new name, was proof of that. She stopped at the corner waiting for the light to change. From the newsstands a dozen models smiled up at her from a dozen magazine covers, smiled in thin-faced, high-cheekboned agreement to Kessa's new discovery. They knew the secret too. They knew thin was good, thin was strong, thin was safe.

The windows were open, and the breeze from the park sent the curtains billow-ing into the living room like swirling dancing girls. From the kitchen Kessa could hear the faint sounds of the radio. She thought of going straight to her room but knew her mother had heard the sound of the front door closing.

As Kessa entered the kitchen, her mother looked up from the letter she was reading. "How was class?" It was clear from the speed with which Grace Dietrich re-turned to the letter that she had anticipated her daughter's answer.

"Fine," Kessa said.

"Anything unusual?"

"Francesca Louise Dietrich died! Kessa lives!" She wanted to scream the words that would tear her mother from the letter—it would be from her sister or brother, Kessa knew—but she merely murmured, "Nothing special."

Kessa watched her mother's face as she read. From the way her complexion, normally pale against the blond hair, flushed as her eyes traveled down the page, Kessa guessed the letter was from Susanna. Gregg's letters from Harvard always made her mother beam with pride. He had gotten another A, won another award, been elected to another office. In fact, the only thing about Gregg's letters that didn't please her mother was their frequency, or rather, infrequency. Grace never said a word to anyone, but Kessa knew her mother waited for Gregg's calls and letters with the eagerness of a young girl waiting for an invitation to a prom. And they came with about as much regularity.

"What does Susanna have to say?" Kessa asked.

"She's thinking of leaving this commune and moving to another near Big Sur. She says she's beginning to get 'bad vibes' at this one." Grace was wondering whether the "bad vibes" were drug-induced.

When Susanna had quit college and gone to live in a California commune, Grace Dietrich had told herself she was through worrying about her older daughter. She had always been a problem, always the child contemptuous of her advantages. But, of course, Grace couldn't stop worrying about her any more than she could stop breathing. Even in her absence, Susanna dominated her attention. And though she wouldn't admit it to herself, she had a certain grudging respect for Susanna's spunk. Francesca, on the other hand, was never a problem. She looked at the slight, fair girl before her.

"You must be hungry, Francesca. There's some apple pie from last night in the fridge."

Kessa went cold at the words. "I had something to eat after class." The lie was a suit of armor that might crack any minute, and she felt the need to get away from her mother immediately. "I think I'll get started on my homework. I've got an English test tomorrow."

There's no doubt about it, Grace thought as she watched the slim, straight back disappear down the hall. Francesca's too good to be true. I never even have to remind her to do her homework. She's so independent I don't even know she's there sometimes. Not like Susanna, and the endless battles over what seemed to be everything. She turned back to the letter.

Kessa closed the door to her room. She knew her mother would not bother her until dinner was ready. As she put her books on her desk, she noticed that the cleaning woman had rearranged her blotter and the pencils in the small Harvard mug Gregg had sent her two years ago. Kessa could feel the rage rising within her. She had told her mother again and again that she would take care of her own room. She didn't want that old cow shuffling around and getting her things out of order. Every time the cleaning woman rearranged her possessions, Kessa felt as if her whole life were out of order, as if she had no control over anything. She moved the blotter to the exact center of the desk and placed the small mug to the upper right-hand side of it. Then she walked to the mirror on the back of the closet door. She stood very close so that her nose was almost touching its reflection. Turning so that she could see her face in profile, she touched one cheek, then turned to view the other cheek and probed that with her fingers. Where were the bones, the ones those models on the magazine covers had? Despite her exhaustion she was glad she had walked the thirty blocks home. That must count for something.

Kessa took a step back from the mirror and pulled her leotard down to her waist. Her breasts were small enough so that she did not have to wear a bra, but they were still too large. *Useless fat,* Kessa thought. *They'll have to go.* She remembered the lamb chops she had seen defrosting on the kitchen counter, the peeled potatoes soaking in water. They were the enemy, but she had beaten the enemy once today and she would do it again. Francesca may have given in to Charlie's Soup Burg and meat and potatoes, but Kessa would not. She began to plan. She would eat no potatoes and only one chop. Kessa raised her arms above her head and took a deep breath. Her ribs made prominent ridges in the smooth skin. The sight was reassuring.

Kessa thought she might study for the English test—she was determined not to lose her A average—but after the long walk uptown the bed looked inviting. She took off her shoes and arranged herself precisely in the middle of the bed. *Just a little nap before dinner,* she thought. At least it would stop her from thinking about food.

"Dinner." The word sliced into Kessa's sleep and brought her back to the nightmare ahead. She turned over on her back and slid her hand down to her stomach. Flat. But not flat enough. It had to be concave. She had to have a margin for error, the error of eating too much.

"Francesca, dinner's ready!" Her mother's voice came down the hall like a call to battle. Kessa found the panic rising within her. They were going to force her to eat. Her stomach would swell grotesquely, her ribs would recede into a mass of flesh, and there was nothing she could do about it. But that was silly. Kessa was in control. They couldn't make Kessa eat. She marched down the hall toward the dining room to her own beat. *Kes-sa, Kes-sa, Kes-sa.*

Her parents were already at the table. "You must have been awfully engrossed in that English," her mother said. "That was the third time I called you."

Kessa rubbed her eyes and said nothing.

"It looks as if Francesca was sleeping instead of studying." There was no harshness in Hal Dietrich's loud voice—he knew he did not have to worry about his younger daughter's grades—but neither was there any kindness. Kessa heard the tone, saw the drink next to his plate, and knew her father had come home angry. She wondered what it was this time.

"I tell you, Grace," he said as he began to heap food onto Kessa's plate, "I have half a mind not to send her any more money."

Kessa watched the scalloped potatoes mount with a rising sense of alarm. She had to have a battle plan. *Kes-sa, Kes-sa.* It beat in her head. *One, two, three, four.* The magic number. She'd chant her name twice between each bite. She began to beat against the side of her chair with her fingers. *Kes-sa, Kes-sa.*

"Stop fidgeting, Francesca," her father snapped. "I work hard, Grace, and she doesn't do *anything*. Back to the land, she says. She's not back on the land. She's living on my money." He wanted his wife to know he couldn't be fooled.

"You're not going to change her by not sending money, Hal."

"She always cashes the checks."

Kessa heard her parents' voices as if from a distance. She saw their mouths going, her father's working angrily around the words, around the food he shoveled into it, her mother's pouting slightly, nibbling daintily, and felt as if she were watching them through a glass wall. She felt no connection with them, the words they were spewing out, or the food they were taking in. She was disconnected, miles away, safe.

"Francesca!" Her father's voice shattered the protective wall. "Are you going to eat or are you just going to sit there in a daze all through dinner?"

"I am eating." She began to push the food around her plate.

"You may be moving the food around," her father said, "but you are definitely not eating."

"I don't like lamb chops." Kessa felt her mother's sudden attention.

"What do you mean, you don't like lamb chops? You used to love lamb chops."

"Well, I don't care whether you like lamb chops or not. Your mother made lamb chops for dinner and you'll eat lamb chops for dinner."

Kessa cut a minuscule piece of meat and raised it to her mouth. As she chewed, her fingers tapped out the magic formula on the side of her chair. *Kes-sa, Kes-sa.*

Kessa felt her father's eyes on her. "One mouthful does not a dinner make. I said you're going to eat your lamb chops, and you're going to eat them."

"Perhaps she doesn't feel well, Hal."

Now both parents had focused their attention on her, and Kessa began to eat rapidly. The chant now accompanied the tiny portions that she raised to her mouth in quick staccato movements. Suddenly she wiped her mouth with her napkin and stood.

" 'Scuse me," she mumbled, and walked quickly down the hall to the bathroom.

Kessa closed the door behind her and turned on both water faucets. Bending over the toilet, she stuck out her tongue and reached as far back in her throat as she could with her index finger. The first two times she merely gagged. On the third attempt she felt her stomach heave. Despite the pain, there was a surge of relief as the undigested dinner spewed out of her. *Empty again,* she thought, and flushed the toilet with a feeling of satisfaction.

"What's for dessert?" she asked as she returned to the table. The question, typical of the old fat Francesca, would hide the new Kessa from them.

"First you won't eat at all, then you gobble it down as if we're going to grab it away from you, and you can't wait for the next course." But there was no real anger in her father's voice. Francesca had followed his dictates and eaten her dinner. She was once again the obedient Francesca he knew. Kessa waited for him to bring up Susanna again.

"The trouble with that kid is that she has no idea what an honest day's work is. We gave her everything, and she couldn't throw it away fast enough."

"Gregg didn't have to work for any of his advantages, and he appreciates them," Grace said.

"Gregg's different. Kid's got common sense besides being smart."

Kessa heard the old familiar praises dully.

"Always had a summer job at Harvard," Harold continued. "Even before he could get one in his own field, he found a way to make money."

Ah, yes, Kessa thought, tapping the spoon against her dessert dish rhythmically. *That's our Gregg. Not only the smartest one in the family, but a money-maker just like Daddy.*

"Would you please stop fidgeting, Francesca!" Hal snapped.

Kessa's spoon halted in midair, and for a moment the old panic returned.

"But Susanna," Harold continued, "when has Susanna ever made a cent? . . ."

Silently, surreptitiously, Kessa returned to her counting, and her father seemed to grow smaller and smaller until she couldn't hear his words at all.

The following night victory came so easily Kessa was almost disappointed. She had prepared herself for another battle of the dinner table, but the contest was called on account of her father's absence.

"Your father won't be home until late, Francesca." Kessa could hear the rage her mother was trying to control.

Grace Dietrich never got angry. That was her husband's prerogative. Over the years, in a thousand subtle ways, Grace had taught Kessa exactly what she thought of showing anger. The lessons ranged from "A lady doesn't raise her voice, Francesca" to "You get more bees with honey than vinegar, Francesca." Kessa wasn't the only one who had received such instructions, but it seemed only she had taken them to heart. Susanna had screamed and Gregg had ignored them. Only she seemed to struggle and end up confused. Suddenly a picture of Madame came to mind. It must have been more than a month ago now, sometime in February. Not sometime, Valentine's Day. Two girls in the class had been behaving badly, whispering, giggling, not working seriously at all. Kessa remembered the fire in Madame's eyes, and she could still see the veins in her lower arm as she gripped the pointer she had stopped in mid-count. Madame stood there sending out messages of rage as surely as a homing beacon sends out directions. She stood there staring until the silence in the room became almost palpable. When she finally spoke, her voice was coldly depreciating. "I have room in my class and time in my life only for serious dancers. Miss Miller, Miss Denman, I would like you both to leave my class."

The scene had terrified Kessa, and for the next several classes she had worked twice as hard to please. Then she had gradually forgotten it, but it came back to her now as she stood watching her mother struggling to stifle her anger. For one crazy moment she put Madame in her mother's place. "Mr. Dietrich, I do not accept your excuse for dinner. Will you please leave my kitchen."

"And I was going to make veal and fettucini."

Her mother's words burst the fantasy of her father's being called to task and sent a bolt of fear through Kessa. Fettucini. Butter and cream and pasta and a million calories conspiring to suffocate Kessa. Even the word was revolting.

"Of course, I can still make it for you now. I'm going to wait and eat later with your father."

The old dutiful Francesca merged with the new Kessa. "Don't bother, Mom. I'm not hungry now. I'll get started on my homework and make myself a sandwich later."

After her parents had eaten dinner and were in the living room in front of the television, her mother with her needlepoint, her father with his paper, Kessa went into the kitchen. She opened and closed the refrigerator several times, took a plate, a glass, and silverware noisily from the cupboards, filled the glass with water, and sat down at the table. She lifted the glass to her mouth, took a sip, and replaced the glass on the table. She repeated the procedure six times until she had drunk the entire glass. Suddenly Kessa felt happy, overwhelmingly, powerfully happy. *Water. Drink water. No calories, no preservatives, no carcinogens. No nothing. Drink water, water, and more water.* She'd never get hungry, and she'd never get fat. Water. The magic formula. Kessa's salvation.

She sang as she carried the plate, knife, fork, and glass to the sink and put them in the dishwasher. She rejoiced at the squeaking noise the machine made as it closed. The sound would carry to the living room.

Kessa moved down the hallway to her room with small ballet steps in time to her name. She closed the door and carried the movement into three turns, perfectly executed turns, she thought. Then, flinging herself face up on the bed, she ran her hand over her stomach. Flat. She inhaled and looked down. There was at least an inch between her stomach and the waistband of her jeans. She reached beneath the jeans. The elastic waistband of her underpants lay flat against her stomach. Kessa felt a lurching panic. That shouldn't be. There should be a space between her stomach and underpants just as there was between her stomach and jeans. She would be more careful tomorrow. She had eaten nothing for lunch yesterday, but this afternoon as the girls had wandered out to the little grocery store to buy sandwiches and ice cream and doodles and cokes, one of them had noticed that Kessa was not eating for the second day in a row. "Hey Francesca," she called over the noise of the crowd, "what's wrong with you anyway?"

The words sounded sharp and insistent in Kessa's ears. She wasn't like the rest of the girls. Something was "wrong with her."

"Nothing." Kessa laughed and bought a container of peach yogurt.

"You on a diet?" another girl asked.

"Kind of."

"But you don't have to diet. You're so thin." The girl's voice was heavy with envy, and suddenly Kessa felt much better. She ate the yogurt slowly, repeating the words in her head. *So thin. So thin. So thin.*

When the bell rang, summoning them back into the building, the container was still half full. Kessa tossed it into the trash basket with a feeling of irrepressible joy. But the joy was gone now as she felt the elastic tight against her stomach. There would be no yogurt tomorrow. Tomorrow she'd think up some excuse not to go with the girls to the store at lunchtime.

Later that night, as Grace Dietrich made her last tour of the apartment to turn out the lights, she noticed that there were no dishes in the sink. How many teenage girls would bother to put dishes in the dishwasher? When Gregg and Susanna lived at home, the kitchen had looked like the rummage table of Bloomingdale's dishware department, with pots and pans and glasses and plates tumbling over each other in a cascade of half-eaten snacks. Even then, Grace remembered, Francesca had been neat. What pleasure to have a child who showed some consideration for the rest of the family. What a pleasure to have a child who allowed you to worry about other things.

Kessa sat in the last row of the study hall, slumped low with her head held forward, as if the low profile would make her invisible. She was smarting from Mlle. Boulanger's reprimand. Kessa still didn't know what the question had been, but when

Mlle. Boulanger had called Kessa's name three times and still received no answer, she had launched into a sarcastic tirade in rapid-fire French. It was only when every head in the class had turned to her that Kessa realized the teacher's diatribe was directed against her.

Kessa was stung by the words, only half of which she could comprehend through her own embarrassment and Mlle. Boulanger's perfect accent. French was one of Kessa's best subjects, though she did well in all of them. But more important, she admired Mlle. Boulanger, who was young and attractive and so wonderfully sophisticated with her French accent and her French clothes, and she wanted Mlle. Boulanger to admire her. But now Mlle. Boulanger thought she was a fool, a fool and a failure like the girls who never had their papers in on time and anglicized their *r*'s. Well, to hell with Mlle. Boulanger. *Merde* on Mlle. Boulanger. Francesca might have needed her approval, but Kessa did not.

Kessa tossed her French grammar into her book bag and took out a copy of *Glamour* she had bought during lunch while the other girls were stuffing themselves with pizza at the little stand across the street. She began to work her way through the magazine, tearing out the photographs of the thinnest models. When she reached the last page of the issue, she had a dozen pictures. Kessa's standards for thinness were strict. She arranged them in order of their weight, with the heaviest on top. Kessa decided that as she surpassed each model she would throw that picture away. *Soon I'll be thinner than all of you,* she swore to herself. *And then I'll be the winner. The thinner is the winner.* She felt a contraction in her stomach, almost as if it were echoing her words, but she would not be intimidated by hunger pangs, despite the fact that it was two o'clock and she had eaten nothing so far today but half a grapefruit. *The thinner is the winner,* she repeated, and smiled menacingly at the models, who grinned back at her in vacant pride at their own appearance.

After Reading

Write a journal entry in which you respond to the Levenkron chapter using the following questions as a guide:

1. What are the cultural and family factors introduced in this chapter as background for the case of Francesca?
2. How do you react to the character of Francesca? To what extent is the young woman a sympathetic character? To what extent is she like anyone you know?
3. What does food mean to Francesca? What does it mean to Kessa?
4. On the basis of this first chapter of the novel, what can you predict will happen in the remainder of *The Best Little Girl in the World?* What clues support your predictions?

Before Reading

Although Levenkron's story is fiction, it is an accurate portrayal of the psychological type and family situation of a "classic" anorexic. The following selection from a medical text describes the characteristics of anorexic patients as recorded by a therapist. Notice the generalizations that Palazzoli makes about the patients and their families.

The General Picture of Anorexia Nervosa

Mara Selvini Palazzoli, Trans. by Arnold Pomerans

Patients suffering from anorexia nervosa are easily identified, even on first acquaintance: their attitude to the therapist, to whom they are often brought by members of their family against their will, is generally studied, cold and forbidding, though quite a few are fatuous, loquacious, hypocritical and inconsistent. But no matter what particular stance they adopt, all alike seem determined to discourage or exasperate the physician. They all insist that they are perfectly well and appear to be completely unconcerned about their grave physical condition or their amenorrhoea. (It is only when the disease has persisted for many years that some of them realize that all is not well and make up their own minds to visit a physician, but even then they never co-operate with him.)

The relatives usually tell the same monotonous story. They claim that the patient suddenly changed from a normal and peaceful girl into a hostile and solitary character. She refuses to make new friends and has dropped all her old ones. In particular she has no friends of the opposite sex let alone any sexual relationships (some of these patients express completely fanciful wishes for Platonic friendships). At work or school she is completely withdrawn, and tends to be shunned by others. She is reported to be overactive in whatever she does, but her expression is doleful, her lack-lustre eyes are usually glazed and her bearing is stiff. The physician, too, is immediately struck by the rigidity of these patients, and by the length of time that they maintain any one posture. They never lean back in their chairs, and rarely gesticulate or change their facial expression.

In conversations with their family, and quite especially with their mothers, they show intense irritability about all sorts of matters. They are often hypocritical of their brothers and sisters, whom they keep under constant observation, and whom, strangely enough, they often accuse of not eating enough; or of eating the wrong food. Many will try to force food down the unwilling throats of their mother, brother or sister—their chosen victim. They themselves are extremely intolerant of critical remarks about their own dietary habits and even resent any compliments about their looks. In spite of this professed attitude, they spend a good deal of time mirror-gazing, and are strangely preoccupied with their general appearance, their hairstyle and dresses, of which some can never have enough though they only wear one and leave the rest untouched in the wardrobe. Many of them are social snobs: they admire the upper classes but fear any contact with them.

Almost without exception and despite the obvious family tension, they resolutely refuse to leave home. The whole family is usually deeply disturbed by, and involved in, the pathological situation, in a kind of *folie à deux ou à plusieurs*.[1] The entire household revolves round the patient. Nevertheless, the parents and even the family doctor generally resist all attempts to bring the underlying emotional conflict into the open. They insist that the home environment is 'perfectly normal' and that the patient is the sole disturbing factor.

Whatever spurious explanations the patient herself may give for her refusal to eat, the result is always the same: a drastic reduction in the food intake. This is usually a gradual process, and some time may elapse before it is noticed. The patients say that they have lost their appetite, that they feel bloated and replete, and complain of stomach aches, indigestion and nausea. They claim that they only like certain foods, particularly sweets, and this is especially so in the stable phase of the disease. Some crave exotic or monotonous dishes. Fatty foods are rejected with disgust, and farinaceous[2] foods are spurned. There is no longer any question of regular meals; the patients take a mouthful of this or that at irregular intervals. In some, especially in chronic, cases there are occasional bouts of voracious eating interspersed with periods of fasting. During such bouts these patients will raid the refrigerator and gorge themselves with whatever cold titbits, sweets and unsavoury mixtures they can lay their hands on.

They never discuss what they eat, preferring to make a great mystery of the matter. No one can ever tell just how much or when they have last eaten. They never sit down voluntarily at table with others. They prefer to eat alone, standing up in the kitchen or their bedroom while nibbling casually at a snack. (One of my patients lived exclusively on food scraped out of saucepans.) They are often revolted by the sight of a fully-laden table. If they are made to eat, they will secrete their food, and later give it away to animals or throw it into the dustbin. At times, however, they will steal food and hoard it in their wardrobe. The thought of not having free access to food terrifies them, even though they have not the least intention of eating it.

All these patients are stubbornly self-willed and rarely worry about the effects of their behaviour on other members of the family. They are always ready with excuses, and will tell you the most far-fetched lies. They readily burst into tears at the least sign of opposition, often sobbing their hearts out in the privacy of their rooms, but occasionally causing dramatic scenes.

At the inception of the disease the patients simply refuse to eat enough, but during the subsequent, active phase they swallow enormous doses of laxatives and give themselves enemas. They will also make themselves vomit repeatedly, at first with great and painful effort and later almost at will.

The uncontrollable impulse to keep moving about, to do secret gymnastics is a common feature of anorexia nervosa especially during the initial stages. Some patients seem to have a fakir-like insensitivity to painful sensations: to cold (they are inadequately dressed in winter, have an obsession with keeping their overcoats unbuttoned and scorn underclothes); to fatigue (they always stand while studying, working, knitting or travelling by public transport, and even when they do sit down they are perched on the edge of their seats; they go to bed late and rise very early). Later, when the disease begins to take its toll, the fakir-like attitude disappears: they become highly sensitive to cold and complain constantly of this and that. Moreover, as Bliss and Branch have so rightly observed, their overactivity is more apparent than real: they seem overactive merely because the least activity in such skeletal people takes the uninformed observer completely by surprise.

Notes

[1] Folly of two or more.
[2] Made from grain.

After Reading

Respond in your journal to the following:

1. What connections can you make between this medical discussion of anorexics in general and what you read of *The Best Little Girl in the World?*
2. How do these two selections differ? In amount of information about anorexia? In style and tone? In degree of reader participation invited?
3. How are the two selections organized?

Before Reading

Both the anorexic and the extremely obese person face genuine and severe problems related to food. To a lesser extent most of us use eating at times to help us satisfy needs that we perceive can be met, in part at least, by food. As Stedman reminded readers in "Food Foibles," "what you reach for at any given moment . . . may be as much a reflection of your mood as of your disposition."

Nora Ephron, in her novel *Heartburn,* elaborates on this notion of the relationship between food and mood or state of mind as she describes her own eating habits and their relationship to romance.

Potatoes and Love:

Some Reflections

Nora Ephron

The Beginning

I have friends who begin with pasta, and friends who begin with rice, but whenever I fall in love, I begin with potatoes. Sometimes meat and potatoes and sometimes fish and potatoes, but always potatoes. I have made a lot of mistakes falling in love, and regretted most of them, but never the potatoes that went with them.

Not just any potato will do when it comes to love. There are people who go on about the virtues of plain potatoes—plain boiled new potatoes with a little parsley or dill, or plain baked potatoes with crackling skins—but my own feeling is that a taste for plain potatoes coincides with cultural antecedents I do not possess, and that in any case, the time for plain potatoes—if there is ever a time for plain potatoes—is never at the beginning of something. It is also, I should add, never at the end of something. Perhaps you can get away with plain potatoes in the middle, although I have never been able to.

All right, then: I am talking about crisp potatoes. Crisp potatoes require an immense amount of labor. It's not just the peeling, which is one of the few kitchen chores no electric device has been invented to alleviate; it's also that the potatoes, once peeled, must be cut into whatever shape you intend them to be, put into water to be systematically prevented from turning a loathsome shade of bluish-brownish-black, and then meticulously dried to ensure that they crisp properly. All this takes time, and time, as any fool can tell you, is what true romance is about. In fact, one of the main reasons why you must make crisp potatoes in the beginning is that if you don't make them in the beginning, you never will. I'm sorry to be so cynical about this, but that's the truth.

There are two kinds of crisp potatoes that I prefer above all others. The first are called Swiss potatoes, and they're essentially a large potato pancake of perfect hash browns; the flipping of the pancake is so wildly dramatic that the potatoes themselves are almost beside the point. The second are called potatoes Anna; they are thin circles of potato cooked in a shallow pan in the oven and then turned onto a plate in a darling mound of crunchy brownness. Potatoes Anna is a classic French recipe, but there is something so homely and old-fashioned about them that they can usually be passed off as either an ancient family recipe or something you just made up.

For Swiss potatoes: Peel 3 large (or 4 small) russet potatoes (or all-purpose if you can't get russets) and put them in cold water to cover. Start 4 tablespoons butter and 1 tablespoon cooking oil melting in a nice heavy large frying pan. Working quickly, dry the potatoes and grate them on the grating disk of the Cuisinart. Put them into a colander and squeeze out as much water as you can. Then dry them again on paper towels. You will need more paper towels to do this than you ever thought possible. Dump the potatoes into the frying pan, patting them down with a spatula, and cook over medium heat for about 15 minutes, until the bottom of the pancake is brown. Then, while someone is watching, loosen the pancake and, with one incredibly deft motion, flip it over. Salt it generously. Cook 5 minutes more. Serves two.

For potatoes Anna: Peel 3 large (or 4 small) russet potatoes (or Idahos if you can't get russets) and put them in water. Working quickly, dry each potato and slice into 1/16-inch rounds. Dry them with paper towels, round by round. Put 1 tablespoon clarified butter into a cast-iron skillet and line the skillet with overlapping potatoes. Dribble clarified butter and salt and pepper over them. Repeat twice. Put into a 425° oven for 45 minutes, pressing the potatoes down now and then. Then turn up the oven to 500° and cook 10 more minutes. Flip onto a round platter. Serves two.

The Middle (I)

One day the inevitable happens. I go to the potato drawer to make potatoes and discover that the little brown buggers I bought in a large sack a few weeks earlier have gotten soft and mushy and are sprouting long and quite uninteresting vines. In addition, one of them seems to have developed an odd brown leak, and the odd brown leak appears to be the cause of a terrible odor that in only a few seconds has permeated the entire kitchen. I throw out the potatoes and look in the cupboard for a box of pasta. This is the moment when the beginning ends and the middle begins.

The Middle (II)

Sometimes, when a loved one announces that he has decided to go on a low-carbohydrate, low-fat, low-salt diet (thus ruling out the possibility of potatoes, should you have been so inclined), he is signaling that the middle is ending and the end is beginning.

The End

In the end, I always want potatoes. Mashed potatoes. Nothing like mashed potatoes when you're feeling blue. Nothing like getting into bed with a bowl of hot mashed potatoes already loaded with butter, and methodically adding a thin cold slice of butter to every forkful. The problem with mashed potatoes, though, is that they require almost as much hard work as crisp potatoes, and when you're feeling blue the last thing you feel like is hard work. Of course, you can always get someone to make the mashed potatoes for you, but let's face it: the reason you're blue is that there *isn't* anyone to make them for you. As a result, most people do not have nearly enough mashed potatoes in their lives, and when they do, it's almost always at the wrong time.

(You can, of course, train children to mash potatoes, but you should know that Richard Nixon spent most of his childhood making mashed potatoes for his mother and was extremely methodical about getting the lumps out. A few lumps make mashed potatoes more authentic, if you ask me, but that's not the point. The point is that perhaps children should not be trained to mash potatoes.)

For mashed potatoes: Put 1 large (or 2 small) potatoes in a large pot of salted water and bring to a boil. Lower the heat and simmer for at least 20 minutes, until tender. Drain and place the potatoes back in the pot and shake over low heat to eliminate excess moisture. Peel. Put through a potato ricer and immediately add 1 tablespoon heavy cream and as much melted butter and salt and pepper as you feel like. Eat immediately. Serves one.

After Reading

Respond in your journal to the idea of food and romance. Have you ever connected any particular food with love or romance? Have you ever noticed others making this connection? To what extent do you or others you know believe that "the way to people's hearts is through their stomachs"? Is this connection one that females make more often than males? To what extent is the way to a person's heart through his or her stomach?

Share your ideas from these journal entries and consider the following questions:

1. In addition to its nutritional value, how important is food in American life? On what occasions does food play an important role?
2. How much meaning is attached to food in other countries? What is necessary for a person or a culture to see food as something other than simply nutrition for survival?
3. How is Ephron's selection organized?

Before Reading

Russell Baker, noted *New York Times* columnist, who satirizes modern culture, here spoofs the "real men don't eat quiche" syndrome.

Comment

Russell Baker

Yes, I craved power. Had always craved power. Always wanted to exude power. Strong men and forceful women buckling to my iron will—that was my craving, and yet. . . .

I shall be frank. Life had come to a dead end. Confronted with strong men, challenged by forceful women, I was the one who did the buckling. People who had power invited me to lunch for the pleasure of seeing me buckle.

The most sadistic was Buck Backbreaker, whose power was such a legend in the board rooms of eight continents that no one dared tell him there were only seven continents. Twice each month he commanded me to lunch for the sheer joy of seeing me buckle to his iron will.

I might be buckling still but for a book titled "Power Lunching," by E. Melvin Pinsel and Ligita Dienhart. It is subtitled "How You Can Profit From More Effective Business-Lunch Strategy." A more accurate subtitle would be "Everything You Always Needed to Know About Power but Machiavelli Wouldn't Tell You."

I had scarcely opened it when the explanation for my constant buckling to Buck Backbreaker's will leaped from the pages. I had been lunching on wimp food, whereas Backbreaker ate nothing but power food.

Of course! No wonder the waiters sneered as they took my lunch orders for quiche, prune salad, cottage-cheese soufflé and date-nut bread. No wonder they trembled in awe as Buck ordered raw oysters, uncooked leeks and 32-ounce sirloins.

Buck was ordering power foods; I was ordering wimp foods. The man who wants to have his way orders power food, and in big quantities. "The bigger the steak, the more *macho* it becomes"—that is the principle. Fortified with new knowledge, I was ready to spring a surprise on Mr. Backbreaker when next we lunched.

"I suppose you'll have the watercress salad and sautéed bean sprouts," he said, winking at the waiter, then adding, "By the way, while waiting for the food to come, take my shoes across the street to the cobbler like a good fellow and have them shined."

Ignoring the waiter's cackling, I said, "I'll have two pounds of chopped mutton, extremely rare, and an order of raw turnips on the side." Eating things raw is the very essence of power lunching, according to Pinsel and Dienhart. It is also "a very high power play to order the same thing as your guest in food and drink."

"Now if you'll give me your shoes," I said.

"Never mind my shoes," snarled Buck Backbreaker, suddenly aware that he was in for the power struggle of his life. "Let's talk merger."

"Order first," I suggested. What else could he do? Needing a very high power play, he could only order the same thing his guest had ordered. His complexion's shift from ruddy to gray betrayed a deep distaste for extremely rare chopped mutton, even in minute quantities, but it was not for nothing that he was called a legend in the board rooms of eight continents. He ordered the two-pound serving, complete with raw turnips.

"You mentioned merger," I said as he reached the half-pound point.

"Not right now," he gasped, dashing from the table. I mercifully ordered the waiters to remove his uneaten mutton during his absence and, when he returned, offered to take his necktie and vest across the street to the cleaner to have the stains removed.

His reply was the challenge of a wounded giant: "Lunch tomorrow at high noon. Be on time."

I arrived early to talk to the chef.

"I'll order first today," Buck announced. The entire corps of waiters surrounded us, aware that they were witnessing a battle of titans.

"I'll start with six raw abalones on the half shell, unpounded," Buck said. "Followed by rabbit tartare."

The waiter recoiled. "You mean rabbit meat raw and finely ground?"

"Not just rabbit meat. I want it made with jack-rabbit meat."

Buck leered in triumph. Then the chef appeared. "I hope you won't think me unsporting for not emulating your order," I said to Buck, "but I was afraid you wouldn't feel like eating very powerfully today, so I had the chef do me something a little special."

"M'sieur," said the chef, lifting the lid from his concoction, "just as you ordered— a whole roasted alligator basted with a gallon of hog lard and garnished with cloves of raw garlic."

"Can I take your shoes out for a shine?" Buck asked. I had brought a second pair of shoes, anticipating this gambit, and a wise move it was. He still hasn't returned.

After Reading

Discuss the following questions with your classmates:

1. To what extent are we what we eat?
2. How effective is Baker's satire?
3. What is the principal technique Baker uses to create his satire?
4. How is Baker's column organized?

The reading and responding you have done thus far in this chapter and the discussions you have had with your classmates have provided you with a wide variety of ideas about what food can mean to people. Look over your readings and your responses before examining the writing assignment below.

Assignment

Assume that you are enrolled in an introductory anthropology course which your instructor, Dr. Benjamin, has taught according to the premise that human behavior reflects or makes statements about the values, beliefs, and attitudes of a given culture as well as the individual human being. By observing human behavior carefully, he says, we can learn about people and cultures and what individuals may not be able to articulate, or articulate honestly, about themselves. In addition to direct observation, we can also read what others have discovered. In your first writing assignment in Benjamin's class you are asked to provide an overview of what food and eating habits may say about human beings. While the writing you would do for a real anthropology course might necessitate library research and direct observation, for this assignment you are asked to use only the reading selections in this chapter and your own experience and that of your classmates as your resource material. You are writing both to learn the material and to demonstrate your knowledge. Professor Benjamin also expects to see your skill in generalizing from reading material and experience, and he requests that your paper be no longer than 1,000 words.

HOW TO BEGIN

First, consider your purpose and audience for this writing assignment.

Purpose

The assignment specifies that you are writing to demonstrate your knowledge and your skill in generalizing and supporting your generalizations. In other words, you are asked to take raw material (both readings and responses) and derive your own generalizations and support that will show Professor Benjamin that you know the subject and can write about it effectively.

Audience

Your audience—your professor—knows a great deal more than you do about anthropology. He has read considerably more than you have and has done extensive field research. He is probably not going to learn anything new from you about this subject of "food as a symbol" even though it is a relatively new field that he has not studied thoroughly. Your professor wants to see what you know and how you can put it together.

Knowing that you are writing for a professor rather than family members or fellow students can help you automatically make certain decisions. First, Professor Benjamin is a scholar and, as such, respects clear, direct prose that is well organized and supports its generalizations effectively. He expects writing that is neither rigidly formal nor too casual and informal. Like any academic audience, Benjamin is concerned that papers submitted to him be edited carefully so that mechanical and spelling errors do not disrupt his reading.

Second, your readings, writings, and discussions with classmates have provided you with background for preparing this assignment. One way to begin is to make a list of the reading selections and to summarize in a few words what each selection says about the symbolic meanings of food and food habits. Take into consideration your own and your classmates' responses to the readings.

Third, look over these summaries and see what categories you might make out of them. The categories could provide you with the major sections of your paper. At least, they can be useful as you begin to draft. In your first draft, you are trying to get your generalizations (categories) down and to support them with specifics—illustrations, examples, personal experiences. Take the generalizations one by one and draft the paragraphs that support them. At this stage, do not be concerned with introductions, conclusions, style, or correctness. Get your information down on paper.

Fourth, once you have drafted the paragraphs based on your categories, read them over for completeness and clarity. Ask yourself whether your generalizations seem valid and whether the support you offer is strong and sufficient.

Finally, think about your audience again. What are the various ways your paragraphs could be put together to make a whole and unified paper for a reader? What order would be the most effective for Professor Benjamin?

ORDERING PARAGRAPHS

When we put paragraphs in order we may follow one of several ordering principles:

1. We may begin with the least important paragraphs or arguments and build to the most important, or vice versa.
2. We may proceed chronologically, as in a personal narrative or a how-to kind of paper.
3. We may proceed spatially if we are describing a setting.
4. We may utilize conventional patterns of organizing that relate to the way the human mind works (e.g., comparison and contrast, definition, classification, exemplification; see Chapter 9).

No matter which ordering principle we choose, our prime goal is to proceed as logically as we can for the benefit of the reader. We need to ask ourselves, "What will the reader expect next?" "What makes the most sense after this paragraph?" "Do my paragraphs seem to follow one another logically?"

Note the beginning of this student's paper. The student was asked to write an article for a popular women's magazine about a subject of interest to women and one about which she had had considerable experience. With your class, see if you can raise the questions that readers would logically have after reading thus far in the paper. Where is the writer probably going from here? Consider, then, how the student was likely to proceed to answer the reader's questions.

Choosing a Child Care Facility

Carole Kirby

Do you feel guilty as you deliver your pre-schooler to the day care center each morning? Have the problems of scheduling, transportation, unexpected illness, and frustration created stress in you as a parent that is affecting your happiness in your job as well as in your home life? More mothers of small children are employed outside the home than ever before in the history of America. While some of them have relatives, housekeepers, or sitters who come into the home daily as the women go off to their jobs, many must rely on day care centers to provide proper supervision and care of their young children. The number of day care centers and nursery schools has increased in the last ten years, but if you are a parent who needs this kind of service, how are you to decide on the right center or pre-school for your child or children?

Though you might think that location of a facility is not extremely important, it is one of the considerations you should have in mind in selecting a day care center or pre-school. If you live in a large city with many facilities to choose from, you probably do not want to choose one that requires forty-five minutes of driving time and a dollar's worth of gasoline each way. Not only will you be wasting money, you will also be shortening the time that your children have at home. And anyone knows that forty-five minutes in an automobile with small, tired children can be a nightmare, especially in rush-hour traffic in the morning or at the end of a work day. While location is surely not the most important factor in your decision, you should try to select a place that is within a reasonable distance from your home. . . .

After reading this much of the article, discuss the direction you think the piece will take from here on. How has the writer let you know what you can expect to follow these paragraphs? How does the writer try to interest her readers? What logical pattern would you expect that the writer will follow as she proceeds through the article? How do you think she will conclude the paper?

The following are sections of an academic paper written by a college student for a course, Introduction to Communications. The class had been studying the verbal language of advertising, and students were assigned to review several of the principles of language use in ads in the print or the electronic media and to illustrate them with examples from their own reading and/or viewing.

Arrange the paragraphs of this paper in an order that seems logical and effective.

Language Strategies in Advertising

Gregory Greathouse

An understanding of language strategies in advertising will probably not prevent us from buying products we are exposed to in the various media. It may, however, make us suspicious of the manipulative power in ads and commercials so that we do less impulsive buying and give more thoughtful consideration to the facts about the products we do buy.

Like similes, the double entendre is not found exclusively in poetry, but it is a poetic device that ad writers utilize rather often. The Kentucky Fried Chicken folks assure us the we "have a right to chicken done right," and in regard to another new pain reliever that pharmacists recommend most, we are reminded that we are "probably painfully unaware of it." Writers know that poetic techniques with the imagery, sound, and cleverness they create can appeal to viewers and readers in a way that straight literal language rarely does.

Another language strategy that is apparent to any astute viewer or reader is exaggeration. The Ford Company advertises its Ranger Truck as having "unbeaten quality." Not only does such a description use language so general that the claim probably can't be measured, but it also exaggerates what a little truck can be and has the power to do. In trying to capture the fast food hamburger market, Wendy's based their "Where's the Beef?" campaign on exaggerating how dreadful and skimpy the burgers were at other competitive franchises. And the producers of a new pain reliever make the ridiculous claim that it is the medicine "that's over a hundred million prescriptions strong." Shell Oil promotes its SU-2000 [as the] "New Gold Standard Gasoline." While the gold standard may do little more than suggest the price to thinking buyers, the intent, of course, is to make them feel that they're buying a gasoline far beyond the everyday variety. When a cereal is recommended as "100% delicious," we know as intelligent persons that exaggeration is at work here. In addition, *delicious* is hardly a descriptor that can be measured in percentages.

Not only do ads or commercials use language to address general groups of people rather than individuals, the language they use in describing a product also tends to be general. The proposal that Nice 'n Easy Hair Color "lets me be me," in addition to its obvious irony, is so general as to be meaningless. Sanka Coffee, "lets you be your best," and More Cigarette is touted as "more you," while Seagrams V.O. is "everything you never expected," and Vantage Cigarettes offer the "taste of success." Examples of general language that says nothing about the product abound in all the media. Perhaps the reason such general language is used is that products like coffees, hair care products, cigarettes, or hundreds of others, essentially differ very little.

Advertising on television and radio and in print, such as in newspapers and magazines, accounts for a significant portion of the space or time used by these news and entertainment media. Although great use is made of visual impressions and images on television and in print, the more important component in all advertising is verbal language. We are bombarded at every turn by attempts to manipulate us into buying the products that sponsors want to sell us, and we need to be aware of these attempts in order to keep from being victimized by them. Just what are the language strategies that ad persons are using on us innocent viewers/readers?

One of the most common verbal strategies found in advertising is the use of general language to characterize potential buyers. Because sponsors want to appeal to a wide market, their ads or commercials tend to aim themselves at groups of people such as arthritis sufferers, teens with complexion problems, housewives with kitchen floors ruined by ground-in dirt, and adventurous men who "go for the gusto." While one individual, often a star in some field or other, may do the talking about a product, the appeal is always to a large group who sponsors hope will see themselves in the individual—beautiful women everywhere, choosy mothers, hemorrhoid sufferers, world travelers, denture wearers, or wise food shoppers.

Certain language devices found in advertising are of the same nature as those found in poetry. One strategy that advertisers and poets depend on is the use of connotative words. In advertising, writers seem especially to like using words whose connotations are intended to make the potential buyer feel good—words such as youth, wealth, protection, Mom, home, classic, health, fresh, light, and so on. But ad writers use a whole range of poetic devices. From the simple alliteration in "Players [cigarettes] Go Places" to the use of rhyme in "Cream and Rum, Yum" in the ad for Meyer's Original Rum Cream, writers use poetic techniques to promote their products. Metaphors are everywhere in advertising; a 6½ gallon container of gourmet popcorn is called "canned happiness," while the apricot is referred to as the "beauty fruit." And with similes we are told that certain cookies are "just like Mom made" and that Sterling is "*only* a cigarette like Bang & Olfsen is *only* a stereo."

When you have ordered the paragraphs in a way which you find sensible and effective, share your order with the class, attending to the following questions.

1. What helped you decide which paragraphs go where?
2. What alternate patterns are possible?
3. How helpful to the reader is (are) the pattern(s) or order(s) that the class discovered?

INTRODUCTIONS

It is rarely wise to write an introduction before drafting your ideas. Setting down exactly what the piece of writing will do may restrict you unnecessarily and prevent you from discovering everything you have to say on a subject. After you have drafted your ideas, you are in a better position to decide what your readers may need to know in an introduction. Depending on the type of writing, its purpose and audience, an introduction *may* need to serve the following purposes.

First, an introduction may provide the context within which the piece of writing is presented. Just as in introducing a speaker, we give some background of the occasion for the speech, the scope of the topic, the qualifications of the speaker, the nature of the gathering or audience, and the purpose of the speech, so in introducing certain pieces of writing we *may* provide such material.

Second, it may present the writer's experience and knowledge of the topic. The reader should know that an article in the school newspaper about the parking situation is presented by a student who has had considerable difficulty in locating parking spots for her car. In addressing effective teaching methods, teachers with several years of experience will enjoy more credibility with readers than a prospective teacher will.

Third, introductions inform the reader of what is to come in the remainder of the paper. In addition to a title, an introduction may set up the reader's expectations for the piece. In a memorandum, this information may be given in a general way in the heading of the memo.

> *Example:*   To: All Employees
>   From: Bob Brophy, General Manager
>   Subject: Changes in Sick Leave Policy
>   Date: September 13, 1985

In formal writing, introductions *may* spell out quite elaborately what the topic is, how it is limited, and precisely what the reader can look forward to in succeeding paragraphs or sections of the paper or article.

A Note on Titles
The title of a paper, article, or book can be extremely useful to a reader. For example, if you are using *The Readers' Guide to Periodical Literature,* scouting for articles on Duran Duran or the Washington Redskins, you appreciate titles that specifically include the names of these groups rather than just terms such as Rock Groups or Athletic Teams. General titles may seem bland and may fail to create interest in what may be a very thought-provoking, informative, or entertaining piece to read. Therefore, select your title carefully with an eye toward being accurate and toward hooking your reader.

Fourth, an introduction should generate a reader's interest in the remainder of the piece. You as writer want to feel assured that your audience will read your entire paper. Stirring the curiosity of your readers, motivating them to read on, is one of your aims as a writer. But how can you accomplish this aim? Below are some strategies you can try.

A. Include an introductory statement that explains how your topic pertains to the reader either as an individual or as part of a group. Notice, for example, the introductory paragraph of the selection "Language Strategies in Advertising" (p. 384) and how it attempts to involve the reader personally in the content of the essay. Sometimes readers are not aware that they need to know what you may have to share with them, or they need to be assured that their lack of knowledge is not unusual. Suppose you were to write an article for a general audience about the dangers of poisonous substances that can be found in most homes. Some readers, maybe most readers, might not realize that they need to be informed about such matters. The title of your paper, and more importantly, its opening, must convince readers that their ignorance can be harmful.

B. Include statements or questions that invite the reader as an individual to identify personally with the material you are about to present. This identification might be created by addressing readers directly as *you* and putting them into a situation that you, as writer, feel sure they might have experienced. Look at the opening of the student article, "Choosing a Day Care Facility" and the opening of the Stedman article, "Food Foibles."

C. Contradict a well-known assumption or truth to shock your readers into reconsidering their position or understanding of a subject. This strategy is useful especially in writing that is intended to move readers to thought, feeling, or action—that is, persuasive writing.

D. Begin with a quotation from a well-known person that sets the tone for what you want to say, that supports your position on an issue, or that provides background for information you want to convey.

E. Share a brief anecdote that involves your readers immediately in an event that points out the direction of the writing to come.

INTRODUCING AN ACADEMIC PAPER

This chapter's writing assignment asks you to demonstrate your knowledge of a subject for a professor. Remember that Professor Benjamin will be reading thirty or more essays on a similar subject. His goal will be to determine how well students have learned and how effectively they can generalize from their reading, writing, thinking, and discussions.

Your goal then, in your introduction, must be to make as clear as possible what your overall thesis is and how you will proceed to support that generalization. In most academic papers, you would surely want to follow the third and fourth suggestions above. The contradiction and quotation strategies might be very useful in creating an introduction that would stimulate your professor to read your paper with interest. The other strategies might be more appropriate for other kinds of audiences.

Following are two examples of poor introductory paragraphs, the first found in an academic paper for which the student was asked to define ecology; the second a paper in which the student was to analyze the impact of the invention of the printing press. With your class, examine the weaknesses of the paragraphs and the titles of the papers.

Ecology

Ecology is an interesting topic in our society today. There are many different views of what ecology really is. The term is used by just about everyone these days, scientists, laypersons, politicians, and they all use it to mean what they want it to mean. When a variety of people use a term and put different meanings on it, the end result is confusion for everyone. What is needed is one single definition that everyone should abide by.

The Printing Press

The invention of the printing press constituted an event of major importance. The importance of this invention has been remarked upon by numerous scholars and is of great interest to all educated people. In fact, it would be hard to overestimate the effect that the press has had on human existence and our society in the last 500 years. Not everyone recognized the importance of the printing press.

CONCLUSIONS

Whether you should write a separate conclusion depends on the type of writing. In news articles, for example, a piece may be chopped from the bottom up according to its allotted space on a page. This practice explains why the most important aspects of a story generally come in the first paragraphs and why stories often seem just to stop rather than conclude, but it also suggests the futility of including a formal conclusion. In friendly letters you signal the end of the letter with brief remarks such as "That's all for now. Gotta run" or "Write soon." In formal letters, you may conclude with a brief expression of gratitude or request for response and always with formal closings. A memo meant simply to inform generally has no separate conclusion except perhaps for a conventional statement, such as "If you have further questions, please call Ms. Bartel at 971-5644" or "I look forward to working with you on this project."

Research reports and academic papers of most kinds generally have conclusions that may summarize and/or discuss the implications of the information that has been presented. Similarly, in columns or magazine articles a writer often chooses to tie things together in a final paragraph. Notice how Stedman concludes her article "Food Foibles." What does she try to accomplish in her final paragraph? How about Hegsted in "Rating the Diets"?

Beginning writers may find it helpful to omit writing conclusions altogether while they are learning to write. This practice forces a writer to pack as much meaning as possible into the body of the paper, not to save *important* points until the final paragraph. If you follow the advice not to write conclusions at all when practicing, you may tighten up your writing considerably, but the way you conclude most papers depends on the form of the writing you are doing, its purpose, and your audience. You must ask yourself,

1. What is the convention in regard to conclusions for this particular kind of writing?
2. What is my purpose?
3. What does my audience need?

In writing that does seem to require a formal conclusion, the functions of such conclusions may include one or more of the following:

1. Reviewing what has been said
2. Applying the material that has been presented
3. Suggesting the general implications of the points discussed
4. Underscoring to individual readers the importance of what has been said
5. Inviting readers to apply knowledge or insight gained to their own lives
6. Predicting the future on the basis of the information presented

But how do you sound finished? We have all read papers or articles that just seem to stop, to fall off the edge of a cliff, as it were. If we think about the purpose of the piece we are writing and about our specific readers and their involvement with what we have to say, we will be in a good position to decide which of the above functions our conclusion should fulfill. But having made that decision, how do you write that last sentence (or those closing sentences) that will make your paper sound finished? Here are some strategies that can lend finality to your conclusion.

1. Make sure your final sentence concludes with its main clause rather than with a subordinate clause or clauses.

   Example: Although space exploration costs the United States millions and millions of dollars, it changes significantly how all of us view ourselves and the potential of life in general.

(Reverse the order of these clauses to see what happens as you read the sentence aloud.)

2. Try for shorter final sentences using active verbs.
   Example A: This university must revise its grading system.

   Example B: "Women should tell the truth." (Susan Sontag, "The Double Standard of Aging," p. 57.

3. Try parallel constructions and repetitions for rhetorical effectiveness, especially in persuasive writing.

   Example A: In a campaign speech to B'nai B'rith in September 1984, presidential candidate Walter Mondale concluded with the following warning:

   Family must not become a code for intolerance. Religion must not become code for censorship. Neighborhood must not become code for discrimination. Law must not become code for repression. Work must not become code for callousness. Flag must not become code for jingoism. Peace must not become code for war.

   Example B: In Jesse Jackson's address to the Democratic National Convention in July 1984, he employed both parallel structures and simple repetition in his moving and powerful conclusion:

   Our time has come. Our faith, hope and dreams have prevailed. Our time has come. Weeping has endured for nights but that joy cometh in the morning. Our time has come. No grave can hold our body down. Our time has come. No lie can live forever. Our time has come. We must leave the racial battleground and come to the economic common ground and moral higher ground. America, our time has come. We come from this grace to amazing grace. Our time has come. "Give me your tired, give me your poor, your huddled masses who learn [sic] to breathe free," and come November, there will be a change because our time has come. Thank you and God bless you.

4. Try ending with a question that asks your readers to think beyond your argument to the future or to the effect of an issue or situation on their own personal lives.

Example A: "How long will you wait until something is done about water pollution in your community?"

Example B: "What will it take before those in charge of hospitals realize that the public can no longer endure the high cost of medical care?"

TRANSITIONS

Much of the writing you do in your journal has only its own natural logic, and there is little need to be concerned with transitions. Indeed, journal entries of the free writing sort often leave others completely in the dark about the connections between parts. See an example of this lack of transition in the free writing sample on p. 100. Since you are your own audience for journal entries, there is no need for concern about how they read. But assume that you have drafted several paragraphs on a specific topic for an article, a formal letter, or an academic paper. You have then gone back to write an introduction that carefully provides a context for your ideas and prepares your reader for what is to come. You have also concluded it in a way that is appropriate to the form and purpose of the paper. As you reread your draft, you want to see if the paragraphs follow each other smoothly. Transitional words and phrases help your readers move from one paragraph to the next so they are not pulled up short wondering what the connection is between one paragraph and the next. What are the various techniques you can use to connect your paragraphs for your readers?

One of the simplest ways to provide a transition for readers is to indicate in your introduction that there are several aspects to an issue (or steps in a process, or factors to consider, or questions to be explored or answered) and then to discuss each methodically. It is a simple matter to begin paragraphs with markers such as *first, second, third;* or *first, next, then, finally.* Many subjects and forms lend themselves to this systematic approach, but deciding on and depending on this kind of easy organization and numerical transition marking can become so formulaic as to restrict your thinking and to bore your readers as well. Nevertheless, it does have its place. If you are called upon to produce a finished paper in a class period—a timed writing, for example—this formula may serve you well. A similar device is the use of chronology. Observe how Feingold demonstrates this technique in the first six paragraphs of "Emerging Careers: Occupations for Post-Industrial Society" in Chapter 11.

Other devices for creating transition between paragraphs may be less obvious but may also result in writing that is less boring for your readers:

1. Repeat key words from the last sentence of one paragraph in the first sentence of the next paragraph. In the Greathouse paper on the language of advertising, you can see how this technique holds the parts of the paper together when its paragraphs are in the proper order. (Using key words in subheadings to help indicate a shift in subject is common in textbooks, magazine articles, and research reports, but they are never a substitute for transitions, only an added convenience for the reader.)
2. Use words that show a contrast between what is presented in one paragraph and what is presented in the next ("however," "on the other hand," etc.). The ninth and tenth paragraphs of the Stedman article in this chapter illustrate the effectiveness of this device.
3. Use words to introduce illustrations, anecdotes, or definitions of terms or concepts presented in the previous paragraph ("It may be necessary at this point to define _____," or "To illustrate the point more vividly, . . .").

Providing transitions in your writing is a courtesy to your readers and encourages them to read to the end of your paper. Your ears are often extremely important here, for as you read your work aloud to yourself or to a classmate, you will probably be able to hear where transitions are needed.

Now, return to the assignment and work on organizing your paper for the anthropology class.

Revising Workshop

Bring your draft to class for a Revising Workshop. In small groups, share your papers and assist each other by responding to the questions below in relation to each draft. Each person's draft should be responded to by at least two other students.

1. How does the writer categorize what our food and eating habits may say about us?
2. How does the writer illustrate the categories? Mark any paragraph that needs additional illustration.
3. How does the writer organize the paper? How does the writer introduce the subject? How does the writer conclude the paper?
4. To what extent do all the paragraphs hang together? Mark any places where transitions need improving.

5. If you were the intended audience, what questions would you raise in response to the paper? Is there any statement you would object to? Any section of the paper where you would like more information?
6. Comment on the sentence structure in the paper. Are there choppy sentences? Any sentences too long? Any weakened by unnecessary words?

Before you write the second draft of your paper, take into account the responses your classmates offered during the Revising Workshop. You are not compelled to agree with their ideas, but you should think about and treat them seriously. With your classmates' responses to these questions in mind, write the second draft of your paper, making whatever revisions you have decided are necessary to improve the clarity, support, and organization of the paper.

Editing Workshop

Return to your small group with your second draft for an Editing Workshop. In this group session, your purpose is to assist each other in reviewing the papers for mechanical flaws and problems with form. Each person's paper should be reviewed by at least two students using the following questions:

1. Are there any sentences or parts of sentences in the paper that confuse you or cause you to have to reread to get the meaning? If so, bracket these as needing repair.
2. Place an *X* in the margin of the paper on any line in which you see what you perceive as an error in spelling or punctuation. Use as many *X*s as there are errors.
3. Put a *C* in the margin of any line of the paper in which you find a trite expression or cliché.
4. Put a *G* in the margin of any line in which you find an error in grammar or usage.

Then, examine these editing marks on your draft. If sentences are bracketed, try to decide what the problems are with such sentences. If you find marks indicating spelling or punctuation errors, identify the errors and correct them. For help, consult the Editing Guide (Chapter 12). Add to your list in your journal the editing errors you seem to make. Make note also of those you are not making this time around that you have made in other papers.

Make the final revisions and corrections that you deem necessary for a solid and polished paper and submit your final copy to your instructor.

CHAPTER 11

Reporting Information

THEME Career Decisions

SKILL FOCUS Using the Library and Interviewing

In working through this chapter on career decisions you will be involved in all stages of the writing process. The skills you will focus on are using the library and interviewing, two important means of gathering information. Much of the information gathering we do in our daily lives is quite informal. When we are in the market for a VCR or a microwave oven we may shop around, look at ads in the media, call stores, and generally compare the quality of brands and the prices. We may even read *Consumer Reports* for a thorough study of competing brands of individual items. In planning a trip, we may also gather information about routes to travel, modes of transportation, cost of living in the location where we are going, and so forth. For major trips, this information gathering may be done more systematically, shopping through travel agents for the best deal. We also gain information informally from our friends when we choose a restaurant, select a college class, or decide whether to see a certain film. In all these kinds of daily information gathering, our goal is to make a decision, and we feel more secure with our decisions when we have not relied solely on others or on impulse to make them for us.

Other kinds of information gathering are more formal than those just described. Perhaps in high school English or social studies classes you produced a formal research paper for which you read a number of books and articles trying to discover what you could about a subject or what your informed opinion really was on that subject. In this chapter you will learn how to gather information and put it together about an area that is of vital interest to you as an individual: your career.

You have already expressed an interest in having a career simply by being present in a college classroom. You have made the decision that college is a prerequisite for the work you want to do in your life. In this last quarter of the twentieth century, more and more jobs require an education beyond high school, so it is not surprising that the percentage of high school graduates going on for some kind of postsecondary education has increased steadily.

Future work is not the only reason for attending college. Developing your intellect and broadening your knowledge and awareness are admirable goals in and of themselves, but you still have to make a living. As a student, you will probably find yourself in one of the following categories:

1. Tentatively committed to a career choice made prior to coming to college
2. Thinking about your first career choice
3. Thinking about changing a career you have been in for some time
4. Satisfied with a career you are engaged in now

In whichever category you place yourself, chances are you can profit from exploring in this chapter your needs, aptitudes, interests, expectations, and career opportunities.

Though you will complete several journal entries for this chapter, your final writing project will be a research report for a general student audience. This research report may not be like any you may have written in high school English or in other courses. It is primarily an informational report rather than an attempt to create new knowledge.

In many research papers—whether you use only a few select resources or all the literature that is available on a certain topic—your aim is to synthesize views, interpretations, opinions, or knowledge and perhaps to add to that synthesis your own personal insight or new interpretation. In the research report required in this chapter, most of the information you gather will not be disputable, so you are really just reporting and perhaps summarizing information.

Write a journal entry, at least two to three pages, in which you explore your own notions of the meaning of work and the place it has in your present life, your past, and your future. Write whatever occurs to you as you reflect on this topic or use the following questions as a guide:

1. What part has work played in my life in the past? What part does it play now? In the future?
2. What satisfactions do I get from doing work?
3. How do I define work? What are the differences for me between work and leisure?
4. What kinds of work have I enjoyed most of my life?

From Powell, *Career Planning Today,* copyright © 1981 by C. Randall Powell. Reprinted by permission of Kendall/Hunt Publishing Company.

Before Reading

In the selection from an Education Resources Information Center (ERIC) document, the authors review the variety of meanings that have been attached to the word *work* and conclude by proposing a set of factors to be considered in using any definition. As you read, note how the various definitions compare with your own.

Ambiguity in the Meaning, Value, and Definition of Work

H. C. Kazanas, G. E. Baker, F. M. Miller, and L. D. Hannah

The term "work" means many different things to different people. Its usage in modern language can reflect a variety of these meanings. Therefore, any investigation into the meaning of work must be based upon the specific definition of the work involved. Not only must the specific definition be identified, but the specific time in history must be specified since the usage of the word "work" has changed down through the ages (Mills, 1953; Weber, 1958a and 1958b; Tilgher, 1958, 1962; Wrenn, 1964; "The Land the Poor Built", 1972; Borow, 1973; Mosse, 1969).

Work to an artist may mean the creation of an original and beautiful piece of art. To a coal miner, "work" may mean long hours of physical toil. To a lawyer in the defense of a client before a jury, "work" may involve a variety of reacting and writing activities that are mostly mentally and not physically demanding. The *Concise Oxford Dictionary of Current English* (Fowler and Fowler, 1970) contains a number of explanations for the word which exceeds a full dictionary page. On the other hand, the *American College Dictionary* (Barnhart, 1959) contains a mere 46-word definition.

Work has both sociological and scientific definitions. In the field of physics, work refers to the rate of transfer of energy as a result of the application of a force. However, in the physiological sciences, it refers to the amount and type of muscular activity promoted. In the sociological sense, it refers to the expenditures of human energies as they produce goods or services (Vroom, 1964; Dubin, 1958).

Many other definitions are given for work. Work is a human activity which one is impelled to undertake as a result of internal or external pressures, or is man's effort to master the environment (Menninger, 1964). Work is the replacement of a primitive problem in history with a less primitive problem, or any effort by man to intentionally modify his environment (Udy, 1970; Schaw, 1968). Man's work is to produce the necessary food and shelter for survival (Goodman, 1960). Work is the only way for man to wrest from the environment the necessary elements to satisfy his needs (Wolfbein, 1971). Wrenn stated that *"Work* is activity calling for the expenditure of effort toward some definite achievement or outcome. Paid or not, hard or easy, it is always effort toward a specified end" (1964:27).

Russell identifies work in two forms: ". . . first, altering the position of matter at or near the earth's surface relatively to other such matter; second, telling other people to do so. The first kind is unpleasant and ill paid; the second is pleasant and highly paid" (1958:97).

Webster's New World Dictionary of the American Language (Guralnik, 1970) defines work as bodily or mental effort exerted to do or make something. However, the dictionary, while providing a very sterile definition, does not reflect many of the assumptions and meanings conveyed by the use of the term in the living language. Quey (1968) has defined work as purposeful mental and physical human activity which deliberately points beyond the present by creating economic products or values to be consumed in the future, thus adding the dimension of the future to the definition of work. Quey (1971), in a later publication, adds to his earlier concept by stating that work in its most universal form represents man's attempt to improve human purpose in his environment. However, this definition is based on his earlier definition by describing work as purposeful mental and physical activity oriented into the future which is designed to produce economic goods and values to satisfy man's needs.

Parker (1971) notes the problems in assuming a definition of work and categorizes work into four broad groupings: (1) production, (2) effort, (3) labor, and (4) employment. The category of employment was expanded by Dubin (1958), who defined work as being *continuous* employment in the *production* of goods and services for *remuneration.*

Work as a continuous concept is reflected in several ideas. Parker (1971) recognizes that work need not necessarily be employment in the narrow sense that it produces income, but states that work has a biological and psychological meaning which must involve purposeful and sustained action. Thus, Parker imparts a social and psychological relationship to the definition of work. The continuous nature of work is also supported by Henry (1971), who stated that work is a continuing engagement with the human community; this lends credence to the sociological involvement of work. Schaw's (1968) concept of work regards the continuing application of energies as evolving a problem in history from a more primitive to a less primitive state of being. This evolution requires that existing work lead to further work, thus stressing the continuous nature of work.

Other controversial aspects of work include differences of words with similar meanings, such as "work" and "labor." Arendt (1958) uses the word "labor" to denote necessary activity that would assure the survival of the individual and the word "work" to denote other activities that provide artificial or unnatural states of an unnecessary, but preferred, state. Berger states that "To be human and to work appear as inextricably intertwined notions. To work means to modify the world as it is found" (1964:211). Thus, work is seen not necessarily as the exertion of physical labor but the application of energies to the improvement of man's status over nature.

Work has religious connotations as well as sociological and psychological meanings. Work (or to work) is seen by some as a religious duty and involves anguish and suffering as a part of man's natural fate in the universal order of being. Tilgher (1958) supports both the religious and sociological positions of work. Tilgher promulgated the ideas that work is effort done not merely for the pleasure of doing but with the interest or intent to provoke an occurrence that would not otherwise happen, be the intent religious or aimed toward the enhancement of man's environment.

Another aspect of the definition of work is the implication that work is a result of exterior pressures which make the activity required of the individual in order to accomplish the stated objectives or purposes. This aspect of work is supported by studies of employed workers conducted in Detroit by Weiss and Kahn (1960). Weiss and Kahn found four different ways that workers defined work:

1. Work is an activity which must be *performed* even though it may not be enjoyed.
2. Work is an activity which requires either physical or mental *exertion.*
3. Work is an activity which is *productive* in goods or services.
4. Work is a *scheduled* and/or paid activity.

The concept of work as a productive activity requiring physical exertion or resulting in remuneration (monetary or psychological) corresponds to findings earlier cited. However, the concept of work as an activity which is performed or required by some *external pressure* is believed by some researchers to be one of the major elements in the meaning of work which distinguishes it from non-work activity or play. For example, the work of a professional tennis player is to play the game of tennis. On the other hand, the same activity by a person making the same physical exertion for recreation is considered a non-work activity or play. Friedmann (1962) sees all work as requiring the elements of pressure and restraint and believes that contradiction between freedom and constraint is the distinguishing element between work and non-work activities. This same distinction is also supported by Meyerson (1951) and Hearnshaw (1954) who agree that the distinguishing characteristics as to the meaning of work must require constraint, obligation and description.

In contrast to the preceding definitions of work, Brien (1966) regards work as an invention of the devil. Brien states: "It is work which makes the hours limp and the years run" (1966:392). Thus, Brien regards work as something undesirable that man could easily exist without. However, he does not take a position regarding the sociological aspects that range from the providing of man's basic necessities to his meaningful existence in a modern society.

Most researchers, however, regard work and its various synonyms as having no fine distinctions. Words such as effort, labor, and employment all have the same meaning in various situations and this concept is supported by the number of synonyms listed in reference books such as the *New Roget's Thesaurus in Dictionary Form* (Lewis, 1961) which lists 21 noun and 23 verb synonyms for the term "work". However, there is an ambiguity that is implied in these factors with the use of descriptive adjectives in conjunction with the term "work". Terms such as "meaningful", "noble", "ignoble", "productive", "anomic", "alienated", "physical", "mental" and "interesting" are used in abundance along with other variations of these terms to describe work in the literature. Although some researchers and writers use the terms "meaningful" and "interesting" work interchangeably, "meaningful" work actually implies that the person doing the work may understand the relationship of what he is doing to the total product or service being produced, and, therefore, may have a personal interest or satisfaction, whereas the term "interesting" work does not necessarily include having personal meaning. The term "noble" has a similar meaning in that it refers to work that provides opportunity for self-identification and self-commitment for the personal fulfillment of the worker. On the other hand, "ignoble" work threatens both the self-identification and dignity of the worker. Udy (1970) refers to these descriptive terms as the conditions of work and not as a part of the meaning of work itself.

P. Berger (1964) cites Karl Marx as the originator of the term "alienated" work which describes the situation where man works from necessity in order to survive rather than for self-fulfillment. Marx's "alienated" work corresponds to Durkheim's (1964) term "anomic" work which, according to Berger, refers to a condition where work does not provide the worker with a sense of social attachment or identification. Thus, the eclectic might accept either the term "anomic" or the term "alienated" work as being derogatory to the social and personal significance of the activity.

The term "productive" work is used to describe work that produces economic goods or services which can be used by society. Parker (1971) feels that the term "productive" work is misleading since the effort expended to produce something is work regardless of the result of the effort. Thus, Parker feels that effort may be work although it may disagree with the needs of a particular society. On the other hand, Hoyt (1973) pointed out that the " . . . trend is clearly toward an increasingly service- and information-oriented occupational society in which machines produce products while man services the machines and serves his fellow man. This trend holds many serious implications for the meaning of work" (1973:34).

D. Riesman (1958) recognized the variations of such meanings and suggested that everyone is forced to accept to a certain degree these cultural definitions of work. The socialization process that researchers undergo in our society forces them to categorize definitions relative to the phenomenon (or phenomena) being investigated. In addition, each worker also makes distinctions about the meaning of work based on his perceptions, experiences or point of reference. While a worker may recognize the variations and categories of distinctions, he must also draw an overall conclusion as to the general "goodness" or "badness" of the work being performed.

Three aspects which appear to be stressed in any sociological analysis of work include: (1) the overall structure of the work performed in relation to the worker's immediate associates and location; (2) the worker's function in the total society; and (3) the social and psychological aspects which deal with the worker's interpretation of his place, his status and his relationships as a result of the work performed (Berger, 1964). This last aspect is the ideological aspect and infers that society, or a part of society, must depend upon the work performed. Thus, the ideological aspect of work is the degree of dependence, usually distorted, that the workers believe the society has upon the particular work which they perform.

From the various sources reviewed this far, it appears that several factors may prescribe a pragmatic definition of work. Included among these generally recognized factors are:

1. Work is continuous and leads to additional activity.
2. Work results in a production of goods and/or services and in some instances carries the connotation of the "efficient" production of goods or services.
3. Work is performed for a personal purpose, but these purposes may be: (a) *intrinsic*-performed for self-satisfaction; (b) *extrinsic*-performed for pay or to secure other forms of remuneration.
4. Work requires physical and/or mental exertion.
5. Work is performed on a regular or on a scheduled basis.
6. Work has socio-psychological aspects in which certain relations must exist. Among those are: (a) the macro-sociological aspect which deals with the relations of the worker to the society as a whole; and (b) the micro-sociological aspect which relates to the worker's relationships within his immediate society of fellow workers.
7. Work involves a degree of constraint which is either externally or internally applied.

From these qualifications, it is evident that the meaning and definition of work is not a simple, clearly discernable matter. For the researcher, therefore, the meaning and definition of work he uses must recognize this fact and try to categorize and weigh the various factors involved in an attempt to satisfy the research problem under consideration.

References

Arendt, Hannah. *The Human Condition.* Chicago: University of Chicago Press. 1958.

Barnhart, Clarence L. *The American College Dictionary.* New York: Random House, Inc. 1959.

Berger, Peter L., ed. *The Human Shape of Work.* New York: The Macmillan Company. 1964.

Borow, Henry. "Shifting Postures Toward Work: A Tracing." *American Vocational Journal.* Vol. 48, No. 1 (January, 1973), 28–29, 108.

Brien, Alan. "A Word of Four Letters." *New Statesman.* Vol. 72, No. 1853 (September 16, 1966), 391–392.

Dubin, Robert. *The World of Work.* Englewood Cliffs, NJ: Prentice-Hall, Inc. 1958.

Durkheim, Emile. *The Division of Labor in Society.* New York: The Free Press. 1964.

Fowler, Henry W., and Fowler, F. G., eds. *The Concise Oxford Dictionary of Current English.* Oxford: Clarendon Press. 1970.

Friedmann, Georges. *The Anatomy of Work: Labor, Leisure, and the Implications of Automation.* New York: The Free Press. 1962.

Goodman, Paul. *Growing Up Absurd.* New York: Random House, Inc. 1960.

Guralnik, David B., ed. *Webster's New World Dictionary of the American Language.* New York: The World Publishing Company. 1970.

Hearnshaw, L. S. "Attitudes to Work." *Occupational Psychology.* Vol. 28, No. 3 (July, 1954), 129–139.

Henry, W. E. "The Role of Work in Structuring the Life Cycle." *Human Development.* Vol. 14, No. 2 (1971), 125–131.

Hoyt, Kenneth B. "What the Future Holds for the Meaning of Work." *American Vocational Journal.* Vol. 48, No. 1 (January, 1973), 34–37.

"The Land The Poor Built: A Review of America at Work." *American Vocational Journal.* Vol. 47, No. 7 (October, 1972), 59–70.

Lewis, Norman. *The New Roget's Thesaurus in Dictionary Form.* New York: G. P. Putnam's Sons. 1961.

Menninger, William C. "The Meaning of Work in Western Society." *Man in a World at Work.* Edited by Henry Borow. Boston: Houghton Mifflin Company. 1964.

Meyerson, I. "Comportement, Travial, Experience, Oluvre." *Lannee Psychologique.* Hommagea Henri Pieron. 1951.

Mills, C. Wright. *White Collar.* New York: Oxford University Press. 1953.

Mosse, Claude. *The Ancient World At Work.* Translated by Jane Lloyd. London: Chatto and Windus. 1969.

Parker, Stanley. *The Future of Work and Leisure.* New York: Praeger Publishers, Inc. 1971.

Quey, Richard L. "Toward a Definition of Work." *Personnel and Guidance Journal.* Vol. 47, No. 3 (November, 1968), 223–227.

———. "Structure of Work as Purposeful Activity." *Vocational Guidance Quarterly.* Vol. 19, No. 4 (June, 1971), 258–265.

Reisman, David. "Leisure and Work in Post-Industrial Society." *Mass Leisure.* Edited by Eric Larrabee and Rolf Meyersohn. Glencoe, IL: The Free Press. 1958.

Russell, Bertrand. "In Praise of Idleness." *Mass Leisure.* Edited by Eric Larrabee and Rolf Meyersohn. Glencoe, IL: The Free Press. 1958.

Schaw, Louis. *The Bonds of Work.* San Francisco: Jossey-Bass Inc., Publishers. 1968.

Tilgher, Adriano. "Work Through The Ages." *Man, Work and Society.* Edited by Sigmund Nosow and W. H. Form. New York: Basic Books, Inc. 1962.

———. *Homo Faber: Work Through the Ages.* Translated by Dorothy Canfield Fisher. Chicago: Henry Regnery Company. 1958.

Udy, Stanley H., Jr. *Work in Traditional and Modern Society.* Englewood Cliffs, NJ: Prentice-Hall, Inc. 1970.

Vroom, Victor H. *Work and Motivation.* New York: John Wiley and Sons, Inc. 1964.

Weber, Max. *From Max Weber: Essays in Sociology.* New York: Oxford University Press. 1958a.

Weiss, D. J. *The Protestant Ethic and the Spirit of Capitalism.* Translated by Talcott Parsons. New York: Charles Scribner's Sons. 1958b.

———, and Kahn, Robert L. "Definitions of Work and Occupation." *Social Problems.* Vol. 8, No. 2 (Fall, 1960), 142–151.

Wolfbein, Seymour L. *Work in American Society.* Glenview, IL: Scott Foresman and Company. 1971.

Wrenn, C. Gilbert. "Human Values and Work in American Life." *Man in a World at Work.* Edited by Henry Borow. Boston: Houghton Mifflin Company. 1964.

After Reading

With your class, formulate two or three specific questions that you can use to find out how individuals define work. For example, "How do you distinguish between work and leisure?" Then, using these questions, interview three working adults—friends outside your class or family members—to find out how they regard their work. Compile the information gained through your interviews and this selection in your journal. Share your ideas with your classmates.

WORK VALUES

In your first journal entry in this chapter, you considered what work means to you and what its value is (or has been or will be) in your life. Following is a list of work values that people might hold. Each is a redeeming quality about work, a specific kind of work, or a reward in doing the work.

1. the work environment
2. supervisors and associates
3. working hours
4. material gains
5. pride, prestige, dignity
6. therapy, solace
7. service, pursuit of truth

Review your journal entry and write another entry focused specifically on the work values that you feel are important to you. If you are satisfied in a career now, consider what reward keeps you there. If you are thinking of the future, project what reward you expect to enjoy in a career. Then return to the people you interviewed about the meaning of work. Ask those same people about what rewards they enjoy from their work, and use the seven work values listed above as the focus for your questioning.

Share your own entry on this issue of work values and the information you have gathered from your interviewees in class discussion. What generalizations, if any, can you derive on the basis of the combined data from the class and its interviews outside the class?

Before Reading

In John Updike's poem "Ex-Basketball Player," Flick Webb is introduced as the person "who helps out" at Berth's garage. As you read the poem, try to notice Flick's attitude toward his work, his talent and its relationship to his job, and the narrator's attitude toward Flick.

Ex-Basketball Player

John Updike

Pearl Avenue runs past the high school lot,
Bends with the trolley tracks, and stops cut off
Before it has a chance to go two blocks,

At Colonel McComsky Plaza. Berth's Garage
Is on the corner facing west, and there,
Most days, you'll find Flick Webb, who helps Berth out.

Flick stands tall among the idiot pumps—
Five on a side, the old bubble-head style,
Their rubber elbows banging loose and low.
One's nostrils are two S's, and his eyes
An E and O. And one is squat, without
A head at all—more of a football type.

Once, Flick played for the high school team, the Wizards.
He was good: in fact, the best. In '46,
He bucketed three hundred ninety points,
A county record still. The ball loved Flick.
I saw him rack up thirty-eight or forty
In one home game. His hands were like wild birds.

He never learned a trade; he just sells gas,
Checks oil, and changes flats. Once in a while,
As a gag, he dribbles an inner tube,
But most of us remember anyway.
His hands are fine and nervous on the lug wrench.
It makes no difference to the lug wrench, though.

Off work, he hangs around Mae's Luncheonette.
Grease-gray and kind of coiled, he plays pinball,
Sips lemon cokes, and smokes those thin cigars;
Flick seldom speaks to Mae, just sits and nods
Beyond her face towards bright applauding tiers
Of Necco Wafers, Nibs, and Juju Beads.

After Reading

Respond in your journal to any aspect of the poem that you choose—to Flick as a character or as a type, to the images that Updike uses to create the character and the setting, to the statement the poem may be making about the relationships between schooling and work or careers. Share these responses with your class.

ATTITUDES TOWARD WORK AND OCCUPATIONAL CHOICE

In discussing the Updike poem and in sharing responses to it, you could hardly have avoided commenting on Flick's attitude toward his work at the garage. Attitudes toward work vary for individuals depending on the kind of work they are engaged in. While you might really enjoy greatly the work you do in school, your feelings toward housework or childcare might be quite negative, or vice versa. Or you might hate the work you do part time at the fast food outlet while your work at a local hospital as a volunteer gives you great pleasure. What makes the difference?

Select three different working adult friends or family members to interview for the next assignment. Make notes about what they say when you ask them how they feel about their work. You might structure the interview with questions such as the following:

1. What kind of work do you do?
2. What is a typical day like on your job?
3. How much do you enjoy your work?
4. What makes the work rewarding or not rewarding?
5. If you could change to another job or profession, what change would you make?

After completing each interview try to place each interviewee according to Scale One* in terms of his or her "liking" for work:

Scale One
1. *Strong disliking:* "Work is boring and dull. I hate to work; there is no good in working at all. There is nothing to gain in work; I would never work."
2. *Mild disliking:* "There is not much good in working. I am not eager to work. I wish I didn't have to work."
3. *Neutral, accepting:* "Work is necessary. Everybody works; I will work, too. One has to work in order to eat."
4. *Mild liking:* "I would rather work than stay home. Sometimes I would like to go to work. Work doesn't hurt; there are some good things to get from it."
5. *Strong liking:* "Work is wonderful. I love to work: I would never like to stop working. I would like to go to work every day and work hard. I feel fine that way. Work is something I really like to do."

Liking for Work	Interviewee	Kind of Work
_____	Interviewee #1	_____
_____	Interviewee #2	_____
_____	Interviewee #3	_____
_____	Myself	_____

Make any additional notes about your response and those of the interviewees. Ask the interviewees how they feel about occupational choice. To what extent do they believe that as individuals they can be anything they want to be or can pursue any careers they choose?

Scale Two
1. Affirms the possibility of occupational choice
2. Affirms the possibility of occupational choice but accepts limits
3. Negates the possibility of occupational choice, accepts the inevitable, fate, or destiny

---

*This scale, Index IVC, Liking for Work, was originally created for the interview procedures of Donald E. Super and Phoebe L. Overstreet in their study, *The Vocational Maturity of Ninth Grade Boys* (New York: Bureau of Publications, Teachers College, Columbia University, 1960).

Interviewee	Attitude about Occupational Choice
Interviewee #1	
Interviewee #2	
Interviewee #3	
Myself	

After you have rated your three interviewees, mark the first scale for yourself on the basis of your current or past work. If you have never worked for pay or as a volunteer, use "school work" as the basis for marking the scale. Mark the second scale for yourself as well as for your three interviewees. Make additional notes on the responses of your interviewees and also on your own response.

Before Reading

In the early 1970s, Studs Terkel's book *Working* caught readers' attention all over the country. Through intensive interviews the author captured the voice of American workers talking about their work, what it means to them, does for them and to them. His portraits include a wide range of workers from spot-welders and stockbrokers to lawyers, teachers, and waitresses. In the following selection, Terkel introduces a dentist who talks about his work.

Dr. Stephen Bartlett

Studs Terkel

He is a dentist who has practiced for nineteen years in an upper-middle-class suburb just outside Detroit. He is forty-six, divorced. It was a late start for him; he enrolled at dental school at the age of twenty-eight.

He comes from Tennessee. "I worked for three years in the mines, digging thirty-inch coal" for his brother, who was an operator. "I was in one cave-in." He drove a truck. He worked in the world of outdoor advertising: "There was a lot of corruption, a lot of the under-the-table bit. That took all the fun out of it for me."

One day a week he teaches at a hospital in the city. He rides a motorcycle to and from his office, which is five blocks from his home.

Dentistry is very precise. No matter what you do, sometimes things just don't go right. One of the big diseases dentists have is stress. It's physically hard because you're in an uncomfortable position most of the day. With techniques today, young fellows are sitting down. I wish I'd sit down more, but I'm not accustomed to it. So I stand most of my day.

The mouth you work on usually is not in an ideal condition. If the patient is not cooperating, moving their mouth or salivating a lot, it's hard to get the job done. You're nervous. If you're not satisfied when you've completed your work, nobody else knows, but you do. You're your own worst critic.

The patients are in a tense position too. There is stress on both sides. The consciousness of pain is always with you. There are two categories of people: those that are more scared of the needle than the drill, who don't want Novocain, and those more scared of the drill. If you get those who don't want Novocain, you're under more stress, because the equipment today is high powered, fast. All they have to do is jerk once on you and they've damaged themselves.

You don't make money unless you have your hand in somebody's mouth. It's not like any other business where you can get income by being away. Any time you're not working on a patient, you're losing money. Your overhead continues.

What appeals to me here is that I can practice the dentistry I like. I couldn't be happy practicing in an area where a guy comes in and says, "Come on, doc, pull it, it hurts." Rather than pull a tooth, we could fix it with endodontics or root fill or put a gold crown on it. You don't have to really lose your teeth. When someone loses teeth, it's a traumatic experience. It's getting more so with all the TV ads. With toothpaste and mouthwashes and all this, people are getting a lot more conscious of their teeth.

I insulted a girl last night, a young, beautiful child. I noticed the corners of her mouth turned down a little bit. I asked if I could see her teeth. I wanted to see what kind of work she had there. She was missing a lot of teeth. The mouth closes like a person who's a denture wearer, and she will get old before her time. That's one of the first things I look at.

I went to see *Fiddler on the Roof.* When I saw a closeup of Topol and his teeth, he had partials. To me, this made him human. Did you know that Clark Gable for a number of years had only one tooth here in front? And no one saw it. When you're close to it, it's your life.

Teeth can change a person's appearance completely. It gives me a sense of satisfaction that I can play a role. The thing that bugs me is that you work hard to create, let's say, a good gold bridge. It requires time, effort, and precision. Before I put them in place, I make the patient look at them. An artist can hang his work on the wall and everybody sees it. No one sees mine except me. A dentist is creative too. It requires a certain skill, a certain art. If you do a good job, damn it, you're proud of it. And you want other people to appreciate it.

I don't think a patient knows whether you're a good dentist or a bad one. They know one of two things: he didn't hurt and I like him or he's a son of a bitch. It's strictly a personality thing. I tried to change my personality when I first started in and I did myself more damage than good. My first cards I had printed when I became a dentist were S. Harrison Bartlett. It was ridiculous, I dropped it. I'm not a formal type. I tell jokes, I make notes and remember things of interest to them. I try to say something personal to each of my patients. I don't antagonize people.

I've had some patients who did not stay with me. There are some people who are used to deference. This is not my way. They're always demanding. If you run a little late, they get upset—or if you don't hand them the napkin properly. They get irritated and raise their voice or they try to tell you what they want done and what they don't want done. Damn it, when they're in my office, I'm the boss.

Some tried to put me down when I was trying to establish myself. It hasn't bothered me for a number of years. Some people are chronically late, and that's all right. But if you're late with them once, they're upset. Sometimes they call up a half-hour before the appointment and say, "I forgot." I make adjustments now. My girl has a list of people who can come in immediately. So when somebody doesn't show, we start down the list. Otherwise, that's time lost which cannot be made up.

I have people who pay me once a year for income tax purposes, or they're waiting to clip coupons. I have people that drive Cadillacs but can't pay their dental bills. It's not because they don't want to. Dentistry is one of the first areas in business cut back in a recession, that people tend to ignore, unless they have a toothache.

When a person walks into the office, it's an instinct. You know who's gonna pay and who isn't gonna pay. I've never used a collection agency. I should, 'cause I have an awful lot on the books. But this bothers me. I don't want to do it.

My life is entirely different since my divorce. If someone told me of these opportunities as a married man, I would have called them a liar to their face. It is really unbelievable. The banter. When you're in a dental chair, you're under stress, I don't care who you are. As a consequence, your guard is down. People reveal more of themselves and their true nature than at other times.

Fantasies about women come before and after work. The schedule is set up that you're operating against time. You have a half-hour to get this done. Now in the evening or going back over the day I might think, "Goddamn, she was good looking!" Or, "I wonder what she meant when she said that?" Or, you know, "Hmm!" Draw your own conclusions.

I like girls. And women. I'm called a dirty old man lots of times in a joking situation. That's part of my image too. But you don't eat and play where you work, this bit. I not only work here, I live here. So I'm very careful. Reputation is very important in a small community such as this one.

Dentistry as a whole feels it's a second-class citizen. I know a lot of dentists who wanted to be physicians and couldn't get into medical school, so they went to dental school. I personally don't feel second-class because I spend every third month in the emergency room of the hospital. Believe me, medical men don't know the first thing in the world about dentistry.

People say, "Oh, he's a dentist." That doesn't bother me. When I first got my D.D.S. and I was a new doctor, hell yes, I was very proud and I wanted everybody to recognize that. Remember, I was older when I got out than most fellas, so it doesn't bother me as it might the others.

I wouldn't be a physician if they gave it to me, to be honest with you. I don't know any profession in the world that is better than dentistry. You're your own boss, you set your own hours, you can go anywhere in the world and practice. You don't have the burden of life and death over your head at every decision. Your working conditions are ideal. Okay, they're physically hard, but there's nothing wrong with that.

There are supposed to be peak years for a dentist, I've been told. I don't know what they are. My predecessor was an old man, his hands were shaking and all this bit. I know that will be a factor in time to come. But I think if you keep your image up-to-date, you'll decrease the age factor. I've seen many young men who are old and I don't propose to go that route.

The next selection offers several contrasts to the Bartlett portrait. Ralph Werner is considerably younger and shows a different attitude and outlook toward occupational choice.

Ralph Werner

Studs Terkel

"I'll be twenty tomorrow." His parents are divorced and have since remarried. He lives with his stepfather and mother in the area of the steel mills, where most families own their own homes; the archetype, a frame bungalow. "We're one of the last neighborhoods in the city that is just about all white. There is a fear of black people. Why, I don't really know. They bus a lot of kids in from the West Side, but there hasn't been any trouble at school. I do have certain questions about them, but I try to view things from a Christian standpoint . . ."

He graduated from high school as "an average student. My initiative didn't carry me any further than average. History I found to be dry. Math courses I was never good at. I enjoyed sciences, where I could do things instead of just be lectured to. We called it labs. Football was my bag in high school. My senior year I made all-city halfback."

He is small, wiry, agile, intense. He wears an American flag pin on the lapel of his suit coat.

In my neighborhood the kids grow up, they get married right after high school, and they work in the mills. Their whole life would revolve around one community and their certain set of friends. They would never get out and see what the world's like. It seemed terrible to me.

I was planning to go to Western Illinois on a football scholarship. I didn't get it. My attitude was kind of down. I couldn't really see myself working in the mills. I did, when I was a junior, full-time after school for about two months. I would work from two in the afternoon to eleven at night. Fortunately I never had much homework. I hated it. It's dirty. It's the same old routine day in and day out, and it's your whole life.

I was a laborer. That's where everybody starts in the mill unless you have a college education. I worked on the scarfing dock. We would burn the shavings off the steel. I would shovel 'em up and put 'em in a big tub, which would be carried off and remelted and made into steel again.

It wasn't that the work was so hard. You had a lot of time to rest. It was just demoralizing. I consider my morals high. Their whole life revolved around the mills, the race track, the tavern. They talked about sex in a very gross way. The language was unheard of in a public place. *(Laughs.)* It just wasn't my kind of living.

After five o'clock all the important people had gone home. The office people left, and things would kind of darken after that. By six o'clock the mills were pretty well run by the foremen. Those two months heightened my awareness of what the neighborhood was like.

I can remember as a child I was scared of the mills. I used to see pictures on a steel mill calendar of a big strong guy shoveling coal. Big pits where there was fire. I wanted to get in. I found out it's not a nice place. There are foremen and something new called sub-foremen. The mills used to be rough, but now they're getting wild. It's racial tensions. It's not where I want to spend my life.

As I knew a few white-collar workers, I associated with them on breaks. I was afraid to get too close to those that worked labor. Not because I was afraid of them themselves. They were all nice to me. It was just that I didn't care for their conversation. So I stayed with the white-collar workers. There were different cliques all over the mill, like I found in high school. There's cliques just about everywhere you go.

I think a lot of people who are in a higher position, the upper-class people with a lot of money, who don't have calloused hands, don't have quite the appreciation of a dollar as someone who has worked in a mill, who knows what it's like to earn your money by physically working. And if you're sick, you know it's gonna hurt you. And if something happens to you where you no longer have your capabilities, they're gonna get rid of you. They have a deeper concern for life. They have a deeper feeling for the political system than someone who's upper class. Because they've worked, they keep our nation moving, they turn the steel out. They put their hearts and their fists behind it. They don't sit there and let the brain do their work. I think they have a little stronger character.

Yesterday was my last day of working as a salesman in a store in the big shopping center. I worked there six months. An expensive store, high class. You don't come in there looking for a pair of socks. People are expected to spend a lot. It goes from upper class to middle, several doctors, execs, important people who have a lot of money.

We had cards that were color-coded depending on how good the credit rating is of the person. Naturally the best being gold. They were a higher quality of people. I myself would only shop there because I needed dress clothes to work. Otherwise I wouldn't shop there.

There was a gray card or silver, which was a good credit rating, but these people weren't as financially well off as the gold. Then there was a blue card, which they'd pass on to the employees or those with new accounts, where we would call downtown every time they would buy something. Most people would dress alike, so it was hard to tell what somebody did by the color of their card.

With the blue card, they wouldn't release any merchandise until we would call downtown. Several times we couldn't get through on our phones. There was a constant waiting. So we would tell 'em, "We can't release the merchandise to you. We'll have to send it out." I saw several occasions where people with blue cards as well as silver cards would tear them up and throw them. I didn't feel it was right to classify people like that. If you give 'em a credit card, whether they can work in a mill or can be a doctor, I feel everybody should be on an equal scale.

When I got out of high school, I thought I'd go into retailing. That's what my father did, my real dad. He was a salesman. This is what he's been all his life. But I didn't care for it. It's too seasonal. A lot of standing around.

My stepfather works in the mill. He used to be a pipe inspector. He's gone to be a clerk now, a better job. He's a lot more satisfied with life than my natural father. He gets along fine with the guys in the mill. He's happy when he comes home. He knows exactly what he's got to do in life. He talks very little about it. He doesn't express feelings, but he seems content. He's never said anything against it. It's a good paying job. He's looking for retirement in a number of years. Ten years, something like that. He's just going to last out his time until he can, which I think is great.

He also has a part-time job, which helps him waste his time anyway—collecting on a paper route for a news agency. The pay isn't that good, but it's something he likes to do. It gives him money which he uses on a fishing trip every year. Oh, he's good at home. He likes to clean up the garage, cut the grass, take care of the house, keep it clean. I believe he's forty-five, give or take a year or two. This is how old my real dad is, too.

My real dad, up in Minnesota, he's constantly traveling. He does sales. Constantly having to talk his way to his next dollar. I have a little brother and sister which are ten and eleven, which he wishes he could spend more time with. He longs to just get a cabin up at the lake and just relax in life. But he knows that won't come for a long time. He seems very tired for his age, very worn out.

This past summer, I spent quite a bit of time with him, and he's had many inspiring words for me. He's told me several things that have echoed in my mind as I found depressing things in life. He told me: "Sometimes you have to make a decision in life, right or wrong." Those few words have kept my head above water several times. Nobody's gonna take your hand and walk you through life. My dad has a lot of intelligence about things like that. He knows what life's about. He knows what you have to do in life to get ahead. This is why he's so successful as a salesman. Even though he's tired.

He doesn't—*(a pause)*—he no longer can really appreciate his job. Again, he's been at it for an awful long time. He's been with several firms, he's restless. He wants to be an individual. But he's growing older. He's growing older than he should. Time's catching up with him. He's caught up in his environment as well as somebody who got caught up in the mill.

My stepfather doesn't express himself. The other day he put an American flag sticker on his car—which some people might think a big deal. When he put that flag on his window, it kind of classed him. There he is, a typical middle-class American. I joked around with him about it, telling him he's become a capitalist and things like this. But he doesn't take an open stand. He's a quiet person who enjoys the natural beauty of life. This can be reflected on these fishing trips he goes on up to Canada, Wisconsin, Minnesota. He enjoys the outdoors.

I thought, I gotta make a goal for myself in life. I have to try to reach something. In my junior year I got interested in photography as a hobby, which I eventually put quite a bit of money into. This is what I want, something I can enjoy doing, something I can express myself. And it won't be a drag of a nine-to-five job five days a week for the rest of my life.

He is about to enroll for a forty-week course at a photography school. "They can't guarantee a job, but she said they place every one of their students within two days after they leave."

It's something where I'll be able to take my camera . . . I hope I get in advertising. I can develop the pictures myself. I can see the result of my work. I'll know if I'm good, if I'm doing bad. I enjoy taking pictures of scenes, of people, of creating moods. I want to create a better mood than the next guy, so they'll use my pictures. If I'm put in as a photographer for a certain company and there's no competition—no matter how the picture comes out, they'll have to use 'em if I am the only one—this is what I don't want. Because you're caught up in a rut. I have nothing to strive for, no one to beat. And if I can't beat no one, I don't want to play. *(Laughs.)*

Competition has always been an aspect in my life. I hate to lose and I love to win. Competition has been involved in me since grammar school. It gives a person a goal. It makes you push yourself to be better. Some people are satisfied with placing second or third in life. I don't. I want to be the best at it and I don't want to be overtaken.

I was short in football and many people thought I wouldn't make it. But I didn't let that take advantage against me. I worked hard. I put a lot of time into it. All year round we were constantly playing football. When I got on the varsity team, I weighed about 130. I felt it an advantage to be small. I turned what a lot of people thought was a handicap into an advantage. I worked on speed, on brain over brawn. I'm not gonna knock that big guy over, so I'm gonna work on how I'm gonna get around him. It was almost like a business. You had to know what you have to do, what your opponent can do, and try to beat him at his weakness. Knowing your enemy is half the battle.

You noticed the American flag on my lapel, which I wore every day for a year now. I got four stickers all over my car. I think America is the greatest country in the history of the world. One of the reasons? Free enterprise. You can go to your heart's content in life. You can set your goals anywhere you want to set 'em in America. This is all part of the American spirit, to compete, to be better, to be number one. To go as far as you can. If the next man can't go that far, don't stop and wait for him. Life will pass you up.

There are times when I shoot my mouth off and times when I shouldn't. I don't want to create hard feelings about me, expecially at the store. I was careful what I'd say and who I'd say it to. The length of my hair, I kept it clean, I kept it combed, it didn't fall in my eyes. But it was covering my ears a bit. I was classified right away as a radical. Management didn't come right out and attack me, but I couldn't help feel something behind closed doors was going on about it.

And I was wearing a conservative suit, and I had the flag on my lapel. But I was still heckled about my hair. I didn't wear my hair to be a leftist, I'm a right-winger. But I wanted to see what it was like. I enjoyed it for a while, but last Friday I got a haircut. Now it's straight where I had it most of my life. I like it better. At the store I felt a warmer feeling.

Oh, yes, I can see myself in the future with a family, with a home, being called a typical middle-class American. I don't see myself going up to the upper class. I would like to stay just middle class. I feel you can get a better taste of life.

My—quote—dream girl—unquote—has long brunette hair, doesn't have to wear a lot of make-up or put a lot of spray on her hair, because she's going to be naturally pretty. She'll be natural in the way she's dressed. I want her to have a lot of personality, because when she's fifty and I'm fifty and we're going up the ladder *(laughs),* there's going to have to be a lot more than just looks. It's going to be someone I can communicate with, who needs my guidance and my leadership. And she's someone I can depend on. And she'll be a good mother. At first she'll probably be working. She can stay home for our first child and from that time on. I feel that her place is to take care of the house, to have my dinner ready when I come home. I hope to have three children, two boys and a girl. And I hope my daughter will grow up like her. My daughter will be protected by the two boys. She'll have security in them if I shouldn't be around. Plus I think it's great to have two boys in sports.

Competition I hope is one of the things I can communicate to 'em. It creates a feeling of pride in yourself. When I've been beaten in a sport, I respect the guy. It's important that when you're beaten you should be gracious about it. But I really don't think about losing. Winning's the only thing.

I would like a colonial house of some sort, possibly one that leans toward a Mediterranean style. I like a lot of bold things in my house. I'd like a nice recreation room in the basement, possibly a pool table. I hope my wife can play pool.

Eventually, I'd probably go into my own business. Once I get into something I'll strive to be the leader in it. I want to be in command. Like the football team. I strived to be a captain. My junior year I was. I enjoyed being looked up to, to be expected to come up with the answers. I don't want to be on the bottom. I want to go for the top. I want to win.

After Reading

Write a journal response to either or both of the Terkel selections. Write what you might say to either Stephen Bartlett or Ralph Werner should you have an opportunity to talk to them. Share these responses with your class. Then, compose a journal entry in which you summarize what you have learned from your reading, interviewees, and from the thinking you have done about your own ideas on work, the values of work, and occupational choice. Share this entry with your class.

Now that you are thinking in terms of the meaning of and attitudes toward work, you are prepared to begin considering your own expectations for your future in the work world. In addition to your understanding of work and your attitudes toward it, what else do you need to consider before making even tentative career choices? Every individual is a unique blend or composite of talents, abilities, interests, needs, and personality characteristics, and any serious self-assessment must take all these factors into account. In your journal, start lists of what you think your talents, abilities, and interests are. You may be adding to these lists later.

Now, play the Party Game.*

The Party

Following is an aerial view (from the floor above) of a room in which a party is taking place. At this party, people with the same or similar interests have (for some reason) all gathered in the same corner of the room—as described below.

After you have made your decisions, separate into small groups according to the decisions you and your classmates made. Share your reasoning for the choices you made and exchange ideas about your career interests. Then examine the table which identifies characteristic interests, personal traits, and typical occupations. Discuss with your group how John L. Holland's analysis and matching of the different categories compares with your previous notions of the fields you are interested in and suited for. Review the Holland table only after playing the Party Game.

*Both the "Party Game" and the chart were adapted by Dr. Peggy Leiterman-Stock (of University of Hartford) from material that originally appeared in ACT Research Report No. 29, *An Empirical Occupation Classification Derived from a Theory of Personality and Intended for Practice and Research* by John Holland et al. Copyright © 1969 by The American College Testing Program. Used with permission.

PARTY ROOM

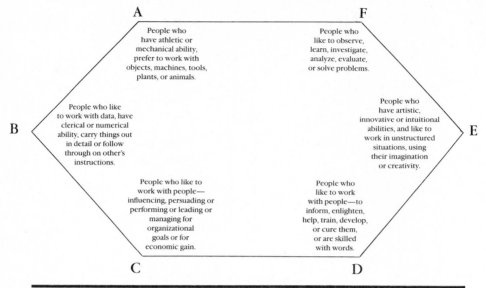

FIGURE 11.1   *Holland's Group Characteristics*

Realistic (Party group A)	Activities that involve the precise, ordered use of objects, tools, machines, and animals and include agricultural, electrical, manual, physical, and mechanical things and activities. Example: Working on cars
Investigative (Party group F)	Activities that involve the exploration and examination of physical, biological, and cultural things to understand and control them; sometimes includes scientific and mathematical activities. Example: Reading fiction
Artistic (Party group E)	Activities that involve the use of physical, verbal, or human materials to create art forms or products; includes activities and things related to language, art, music, drama, and writing. Example: Listening to music
Social (Party group D)	Activities that involve interaction with other people for enjoyment or to inform, train, develop, cure, and educate. Example: Entertaining guests
Enterprising (Party group C)	Activities that involve interaction with other people to reach organizational goals or economic gain; leadership, interpersonal, and persuasive activities included. Example: Working for a community action or political organization
Conventional (Party group B)	Activities that involve the precise, ordered use of data, i.e., keeping records, filing materials, organizing numerical and written data; clerical, computational, and business. Example: Working as a treasurer for a political campaign

PARTY GAME

1. Which corner of the room would you instinctively be drawn to, as the group of people you would most *enjoy* being with for the longest time? (Leave aside any question of shyness, or whether you would have to talk with them.) Write the *letter* for that corner below:	2. After fifteen minutes, everyone in the corner you have chosen leaves for another party crosstown, except you. Of the groups *that still remain* now, which corner or group would you be drawn to the most, as the people you would most enjoy being with for the longest time? Write the letter for that corner below:	3. After fifteen minutes, this group too leaves for another party, except you. Of the corners, and groups which remain now, which one would you most enjoy being with for the longest time? Write the letter for that corner below:
_____	_____	_____

Characteristic Personal Traits	Characteristic Occupations
Present-, thing-oriented (rather than people or data), conforming, physical, shy	Engineering, skilled trades; agricultural, technical
Analytical, abstract, rational, critical, intellectual, introverted	Scientific, analytical; some technical
Creative, expressive, rely on feelings, imaginative, nonconforming, idealistic	Musical, artistic, literary, dramatic
Sensitive to others' needs, friendly, outgoing, persuasive, tactful	Teaching, ministry, social welfare; other "helping"
Aggressive, self-confident, ambitious, sociable, persuasive	Sales, supervisory, leadership
Practical, conforming, efficient, orderly, set in ways	Accounting, computational, secretarial, clerical

Before Reading

In this article, S. Norman Feingold projects how occupations and careers will be different by the year 2000. As you read, consider how his projections might affect you and your tentative choices.

Emerging Careers

Occupations for Post-Industrial Society

S. Norman Feingold

Once upon a time Ben Franklin could take his son for a walk through the streets of Philadelphia and point out all the jobs that were available. Today there are more than 30,000 different job titles.

Careers have changed from time immemorial. First, food gathering was done by women, while men did the hunting. Then came a period when most people were subsistence farmers, growing plants and animals to meet their needs for food, clothing, and shelter.

In the Middle Ages, the emerging careers were those of craftsmen and artisans. These workers made a living in the villages by serving the needs of the upper classes. The serfs continued to grow food for themselves and the overlords and to provide military service.

During the Renaissance, a whole class of artists and craftsmen, assistants and guilds developed. Business, trade, and manufacturing expanded. People worked in jobs that never existed in the preceding agricultural age.

Next, the Industrial Revolution expanded the number and types of jobs and careers. Boosted by science and technology, the expansion of jobs has intensified.

We are now entering the post-industrial period. In 1980, just 28% of the work force was in manufacturing, and it will probably be only 11% in the year 2000 and 3% in the year 2030. More people now work at McDonald's than at U.S. Steel. Businesses are adapting by diversifying their operations. Today, for example, sewing machines make up only 1% of Singer's business; the rest is in electronics.

New occupations and careers emerge all the time while others become obsolete. In comparing a past *Dictionary of Occupational Titles,* published by the U.S. Department of Labor, with the most recent one, many changes are readily observed. Numerous job titles have been added, and many hundreds of others have been deleted.

One career, for example, of short duration in the nineteenth century was that of the pony express rider, though vestiges reappear in today's courier and messenger services. The elevator operator, the bowling pin setter, the milkman, and hundreds of other jobs and careers have virtually disappeared, and others will follow them into oblivion. The meter-reader will soon be extinct; instead of somebody reading the gas meter at your home, gas meters can be tied in to a computer and monitored more cost effectively. In 1977, the *Dictionary* added 2,100 titles while dropping 3,500.

All of us are in occupations and careers that are in transition. For some, the job titles will remain the same while the work tasks and concepts change. For some, there will be new titles and new tasks.

An emerging career has all of the following characteristics; it is one that:

- **Has become increasingly visible as a separate career area in recent years.**
- **Has developed from pre-existing career areas, such as medical care and personal or business services.**
- **Has become possible because of advances in technology or actual physical changes in our environment. For example, home computers, solar industries, satellite television, and water pollution equipment are a few of the many areas that have engendered new, emerging careers.**
- **Shows growth in numbers of people employed or attending emerging education and training programs.**
- **Requires skills and training.**
- **Does not appear and then disappear in a very short period of time.**

Careers in the Information Industry

One of the biggest areas of emerging careers is the information industry. Today, 55% of the workers in the United States are in information industries. More people are involved in information and communication than in mining, agriculture, manufacturing, and personal services combined. Some experts are calling the changes an "information revolution." By the year 2000, 80% of the work force will be information workers.

Here are some of the emerging career areas in the information industry:

Operation of Information Systems

Abstractor-indexers process the intellectual content of documents for convenient retrieval. Bibliographic searchers use modern computerized information systems and data bases to identify or retrieve pertinent publications. Information brokers perform specialized information retrieval services for a fee.

Management of Information Systems

Information center managers supervise facilities that organize knowledge of a specific subject area.

Design of Information Systems

Application or systems programmers write large-scale computer programs or modify existing programs in order to solve information problems in business, science, education, and other fields.

Research and Teaching

Computational linguists analyze word and language structure to determine how the computer can manipulate text for indexing, classification, abstracting, search, and retrieval. Information scientists conduct basic research on the phenomenon of information. Teachers of information science educate others in the planning, design, management, evaluation, and use of the total information process.

Consulting (or the Selling of Information)

There has been an explosive growth of consultants of all kinds. For example, image consultants work with clients on a variety of problems such as dress, speech, and color. One of the earliest types of image consultant was the public relations consultant, who handles information and communications problems for a variety of organizations.

Information is a limitless resource. Unlike finite industrial resources such as oil, ore, and iron, there is an inexhaustible supply of knowledge, concepts, and ideas as people gain further education.

Robotics Careers

Robots are to manufacturing and mining jobs as calculators are to white-collar jobs. Each takes the monotony of repetition out of the job. Additionally, robots can do the hazardous tasks—with bottom-line effectiveness, no retirement pay, no vacations, no coffee breaks, and no strikes.

Robotics means that people will have to be trained for new skills or remain unemployed—and this includes thousands of people who formerly worked in the automobile and steel industries.

In addition to the new jobs for scientists, mechanics, and technicians that the development of robotics has created, there will be an increasing need for such workers as robots' supervisors in new, largely automated factories. But whether the development of robotics will create more jobs than robots displace is unknown at this point.

Robots are taking away thousands of blue-collar jobs. The jobs they are creating are not in these fields. The changes are of a magnitude comparable to those the Industrial Revolution created.

Overall employment in robotics is small but will grow with the increasing demand for robots. The three general types of jobs now available in the robot industry are:

Planning

Robotic engineers select jobs a robot could perform based on a thorough knowledge of the robot's capacities and of the tasks to be performed and the environment in which they are done.

Installation

Technicians install the robots and adjust them to the specific tasks involved. These people could be technical-school graduates with a special interest in robotics.

Monitoring

Supervisors check the operation of the robot on the line and keep it supplied with any needed raw materials, such as wire for a welding gun.

Ocean Industry Careers

The ocean industry is growing, with new careers ranging from catching new kinds of fish to finding ships that have sunk at sea carrying gold and other precious items. We are now cultivating the ocean the way we do the land. And researchers have discovered new kinds of sea-grown food that could have tremendous value to feeding the world's people.

Fishing and other occupations exploiting the sea are almost as old as the human race, but marine technology is making possible many exciting emerging careers, such as ocean mining, fish farming, oil prospecting, treasure hunting, and underwater archaeology.

Now let's take a closer look at some of these emerging career areas.

Ocean Mining

Scientists and engineers work to solve the problem of how to retrieve and process the millions of tons of undersea minerals. Marine ecologists study how ocean mining operations could affect the ocean's environment. International sea-mining claims and law-of-the-sea treaties are new specialties for maritime lawyers.

Other areas such as off-shore drilling and deep-sea exploration require people with knowledge in more than one area, including oceanography, geology, seismology, marine engineering, and meteorology.

Underwater Archaeology and Treasure Hunting

Until recently, no technology was available to recover artifacts from sunken ships. Now, treasure hunting using the most modern underwater techniques can be profitable, although the chances of making a fortune are small. Among the positions relating most directly to underwater exploration are project directors, professional divers, crew members, equipment handlers, sonar operators, and television camera operators.

Aquaculture

As fish supplies diminish and world population increases, scientific farming of fish and other seafoods will expand. One technique used with increasing effectiveness is polyculture, or the raising of several species together, which maximizes utilization of food and water.

Fish farming requires workers skilled in land and water management and in the care, feeding, managing, harvesting, and marketing of fish.

Exploring New Frontiers

Space, "the final frontier," has already opened up undreamed of occupations and will demand many new kinds of pioneers in the future.

Exploring space and developing its resources will require highly skilled technicians in addition to the astronauts and pilots now serving in U.S. and other space programs. Specialists in communications, computers and electronics, energy, and pharmaceuticals, for example, will work on the space shuttle or Skylab.

Eventually, as humans can remain in space for longer and longer periods of time, space programs will require miners, mechanics, ecologists, geologists, and other technicians to explore extraterrestrial materials and energy resources; to mine raw materials on lunar bases; to build and staff industrial facilities, factories, processing plants, and

---

OCCUPATIONAL TITLES OF THE FUTURE

Here is a list of job titles that might appear in a *Dictionary of Occupational Titles* of the future:

Aquaculturist
Armed courier
Artificial intelligence technician
Arts Manager
Asteroid/lunar miner
Astronaut
Battery technician
Benefits analyst
Biomedical technician
Bionic medical technician
Cable television auditor
Cable television salesperson
CAD/CAM technician
Career consultant
CAT scan technician
Certified alcoholism counselor
Certified financial planner
Child advocate
Color consultant
Communications engineer
Community ecologist
Community psychologist
Computer:
    analyst
    camp counselor/owner
    designer
    graphics specialist
    lawyer
    microprocessor technologist
    programmer (software writer)
    sales trainee
    security specialist
    service technician
Contract administrator
Cosmetic surgeon
Cryologist technician
Cultural historian

Cyborg technician
Dance therapist
Dialysis technologist
Divorce mediator
EDP auditor
Electronic mail technician
Energy auditor
Ethicist
Executive rehabilitative counselor
Exercise technician
Exotic welder
Family mediator/therapist
Fiber-optics technician
Financial analyst
Financial consultant
Forecaster
Forensic scientist
Fusion engineer
Genetic biochemist
Genetic counselor
Genetic engineer technician
Geriatric nurse
Graphoanalyst
Hazardous waste technician
Health physicist
Hearing physiologist
Hibernation specialist
Home health aide
Horticulture therapy assistant
Hotline counselor
House- and pet-sitter
Housing rehabilitation technician
Image consultant
Indoor air quality specialist
Information broker
Information research scientist
Issues manager

OCCUPATIONAL TITLES OF THE FUTURE *(continued)*

Job developer
Laser medicine practitioner
Laser technician
Leisure counselor
Licensed psychiatric technician
Market development specialist
Massage therapist
Materials utilization technician
Medical diagnostic imaging technician
Medical sonographer technician
Microbial geneticist
Microbiological mining technician
Mineral economist
Myotherapist
Naprapath
Neutrino astronomer
Nuclear fuel specialist
Nuclear fuel technician
Nuclear medicine technologist
Nuclear reactor technician
Nurse-midwife
Ocean hotel manager
Ombudsman
Oncology nutritionist
Orthotist
Paraprofessional
Peripheral equipment operator
PET scan technician
Physician's assistant
Planetary engineer
Plant therapist
Plastics engineer
Pollution botanist
Power plant inspector
Protein geometrician
Radiation ecologist

Recombinant DNA technologist
Relocation counselor
Retirement counselor
Robot:
  engineer
  salesperson
  scientist
  technician (industrial)
  trainer
Security engineer
Selenologist (lunar astronomer)
Shrimp-trout fish farmer
Shyness consultant
Software club director
Software talent agent
Soil conservationist
Solar energy consultant
Solar energy research scientist
Solar engineer
Space botanist
Space mechanic
Sports law specialist
Sports psychologist
Strategic planner
Systems analyst
Tape librarian
Telecommunications systems designer
Thanatologist
Transplant coordinator
Treasure hunter
Underwater archaeologist
Underwater culture technician
Volcanologist
Waste manager
Water quality specialist
Wellness consultant

solar-power stations; to build space habitats and work in closed-ecology agricultural production; and to develop transportation systems connecting a growing number of space facilities.

Health Careers

Breakthroughs in genetics, bionics, cryology, laser surgery, and other medical sciences are creating exciting new career possibilities. The replacing of body organs with transplants or artificial parts represents a marriage of medical and engineering fields that has engendered such emerging careers as bionic-electronic technicians; orthotists or prosthetists, who develop surgical devices to activate or supplement weakened limbs or functions; spare-human-organs technicians; and many other previously unimagined occupations.

Electronic devices activated by voice, the blink of an eye, or a puff of breath have enabled mobility-impaired people to open doors and windows, use the telephone, eat. Closed-captioned television and movies allow the deaf to "hear."

Other new health-related careers result from changes in society, population, and lifestyles. As the population ages, for example, there will be a greater need for geriatric nurses and social workers, home health aides, nursing home counselors, stroke rehabilitation nurses, and thanatologists.

Unemployment and other economic social ills call for mental health professionals in new specialties such as certified alcoholism counselors, family therapists, licensed psychiatric technicians, mental-health nurses, corrective therapists, and community psychologists.

Emerging Energy Careers

After the Arab oil embargo of 1974, people began to think about energy conservation, and new career opportunities appeared:

Nuclear Energy

All kinds of new jobs are emerging in the area of nuclear fission and fusion. Construction of nuclear energy plants requires thousands of skilled workers ranging from boilermakers, pipefitters, welders, and sheet metal workers to office workers, laborers, and truck drivers.

Emerging careers for operating personnel include engineers specializing in ceramics, human factors, materials, reactor safety, systems, and standards development.

Technician jobs include power-plant inspectors, nuclear fuels specialists, quality assurance specialists, instrument servicepersons, and systems reliability analysts.

Scientists needed include those specializing in health physics and the environment as well as chemists, soil and air specialists, radio chemists, and geochemists.

Fossil Fuels

Though few new careers are emerging in this field, which has been automating many traditional jobs, there is a big demand for people who combine skills and knowledge in more than one area. For example, engineering geologists are crucial to coal mining, as are mineral economists, who combine knowledge of mining, petroleum, and geology with skills in economics, management science, and business.

Alternative Energy

Generation of power from water, the sun, organic wastes, the wind, and geothermal resources; from co-generation using two or more of these sources; and through energy conservation and recycling has expanded the need for workers with old-fashioned skills: electricians, pipefitters, plumbers, carpenters, and builders.

Small Business: Going Out on Your Own

From the end of World War II until the mid-1970s, small business was not looked upon favorably by the mass of young entrants into the labor force. Ten years ago, one study showed that while 27% of the parents of high-school students owned their own small business, only 3% of the children were willing to enter the same business.

This has changed. In the past five to ten years, the number of self-employed rose significantly. Small business is the key to high employment today and in the year 2000.

Twelve hundred new businesses are formed each day in the United States. In an era of bigness, more and more people are now starting to see that small is beautiful and that they can turn their interests, potential, and abilities into salable products and services. The root of American economic success has been in entrepreneurship. Today, high schools and colleges all over the United States are offering courses in small business.

Women are more involved than ever before in starting their own small businesses. Many are entering small business for self-actualization, growth, and development. Though money is still important to them, more and more people want to be able to control their lives and to believe that they are making some sort of contribution to society.

Many new small businesses are at the cutting edge of new career developments, such as communications, aids for the handicapped, and the information industry. But there are all kinds of people needs. Creative people can translate them into a successful small business.

For example, one man who earned a high salary but just couldn't get along with his supervisors decided to start his own chauffeur business because he loved to drive a car; he now has a Rolls-Royce and drives it for anyone who wants to rent it for a special event. He is busy every day and is now on the way to buying another Rolls.

What kind of economic impact does small business have? Plenty. Of all nonfarm businesses in the United States, 97% are considered "small" according to the Small Business Administration's definition. Small business accounts for nearly $7 out of every $10 in sales made by retailers and wholesalers annually. Nearly 80% of all U.S. businesses (excluding farms) employ fewer than 10 people. The small business part of the economy creates more jobs than any other; it provides, directly or indirectly, the livelihood of more than 100 million Americans—that's almost half of the current U.S. population.

Small business has been growing at the rate of 2.4% annually for the past couple of years. With more sophisticated financial planning and action by entrepreneurs, the failure rate will undoubtedly drop during the next five years.

Computers and the Changing Workplace

Computers and the information revolution are changing the workplace in many ways, and these changes affect how people work, relax, travel, think, and feel.

Recently I visited a paperless office in Washington, D.C. Most of the staff worked at home with their computers and came together only once every three or four weeks. They got their instructions for the day or week via their computers.

Computers may markedly change human behavior by altering the ways people relate to each other. Over the phone, you hear the other person's tone of voice. Face to face, you see a person's smile or anger. You also see who takes the head seat at a meeting. When people use a computer to communicate, they lack nonverbal cues since they cannot see or hear the other person. There are no cues as there are when you meet someone in person or talk to someone on the phone.

Over the next 20 years, there will be more pressure to increase job satisfaction by changing the content of jobs; today, few people seem to deeply enjoy their work and to have real psychic satisfaction. At the same time, people are likely to spend less time at work, either through shortened workweeks or through absenteeism.

While there is likely to be greater employee participation in decision-making, loyalty to one's company will probably continue to decrease. More people will change jobs or even careers more often. Training policies will be reassessed to meet an increasing need to train and retrain people. The proportion of women in the work force is likely to increase, and more of them will be career-oriented.

More people will work at home. There will probably also be more work for people in neighborhood work centers. These centers will be similar to the firms that offer a business address, an answering service, and an office to rent on an hourly or daily basis. There also can be community communication centers for sharing particularly expensive facilities, including video telephone booths, rooms for electronic meetings, etc.

While sophisticated technical skills will be needed in the twenty-first century, I believe we need to add life- and love-enhancing skills or our technology will accelerate alienation.

The concept of Win-Lose must be replaced by a Win-Win ideal. Rather than "King of the Mountain," the game we must learn now is "People of the Mountain."

When people are made to feel that their self-image and worth depend on their being on top, complex problems are created. They experience high levels of anxiety, display destructive tendencies, and show increased insensitivity to the feelings of others. They lie, cheat, hurt, maim, and kill to make it to the top. In the process, some people destroy not only their colleagues but their families and themselves.

We need to develop a special kind of sensitive balance for cooperation and individualism that allows people to live and work in harmony. People can compete in a psychologically healthy way.

We can enhance individual initiative and creativity and, at the same time, stimulate the ability or potential to work well as a team.

After Reading

On the basis of what you have discovered about yourself through Hollands's game and analysis and what you have learned from Feingold's article, write a journal entry in which you explore the kinds of work that you think you would like to do and would be suited for in the future. Then narrow your choice down to one job or profession. Tell what you think that job will be like—what the pay might be, the hours, the work environment, the rewards other than money, the disadvantages and advantages. Think about the life style you would expect to enjoy in this job. Make this entry three to four pages long.

In class, share these entries in small groups made up of students interested in similar career areas. After sharing the entries, work as a group to make up a list of possible questions that you could use in gathering information from the library about your tentative career choice. Use the following questions for getting started:

1. Where would I need to live if I entered this field? Would I have to travel?
2. What might salary expectations be in this field?
3.
4.

With your entire class, compile a grand list from the questions generated in your small groups. Categorize and refine your individual questions until you have a set of 8 to 10 that will provide the structure for gathering the information you want about your particular career choice.

Assignment

Assume that your campus library or career center is developing a file of student reports on various careers. Although those in charge have excellent resources on hand (many books and films on career development in general and some sources with a more specific focus), they have nothing written by students for students. And they have nothing that integrates factual information with more personalized data gathered through interviews. Your job is to write a research report on one particular career choice that would be inserted in this file and would be available to all students on campus. Your report will utilize both library research and one in-depth interview as sources of information. Your report is to be kept to about 1,000 words, or about four typewritten pages, and must be clearly focused on one particular career. Your report should be documented according to the *Publication Manual of the American Psychological Association*. Consult the Documentation Guide (Appendix A).

Now examine your list of questions to determine which are answerable through research in books and articles and which will need to be answered through the interview. Beginning with the library research rather than the interview is probably a good idea. It will give you the background information you will need in order to ask intelligent questions during the interview. If your college has a career counseling center or placement office, chances are additional material is available there. Remember, your aim in this research is to find answers to your basic questions about a specific career choice. Naturally, this choice is tentative, because you may change your mind in the years to come. Nevertheless, you will have discovered some resources and practiced some skills that will be useful to you in future library research, regardless of the topic.

Some basic books you may want to consult as you begin to look for information on your career choice are listed below:

1. *Careers Encyclopedia* by Craig T. Norback (ed.), Homewood, IL: Dow Jones-Irwin, 1980.

2. *The Dictionary of Occupational Titles,* Washington, DC: U.S. Dept. of Labor, 1981.
3. *Directory of Career Resources for Minorities* by Victoria B. King and Michael A. Mayhak, Santa Monica, CA: Ready Reference Press, 1980.
4. *The Hidden Job Market for the Eighties* by Tom Jackson and Davidyne Mayleas, New York: Times Books, 1981.
5. *The Men's Career Book: Work and Life Planning for a New Age* by Joyce Slayton Mitchell, New York: Bantam Books, 1979.
6. *Occupational Opportunities for Everywoman* (no author), New York: Sterling Publ., 1978.
7. *The Occupational Outlook Handbook,* Washington, DC: Government Printing Office, annual.

And, of course, there are many volumes on specific career areas which cover such topics as qualification and training or education requirements. Many also include case studies and discussions of the rewards inherent in individual professions or jobs. See, for example,

1. *Accent on Home Economics* by Nancy B. Greenspan and Elaine P. Davis, New York: Messner, 1978.
2. *Blue-Collar Jobs for Women* by Muriel Lederer, New York: E. P. Dutton, 1979.
3. *Breakthrough: Women in Archaeology* by Barbara Williams, New York: Walker & Co., 1981.
4. *Breakthrough: Women in Writing* by Diana Gleasner, New York: Walker & Co., 1980.
5. *Broadcasting for Beginners* by I. G. Edmonds and William H. Gebhardt, New York: Holt, Rinehart & Winston, 1980.
6. *Career Choices in Psychology* by Sarah Splaver, New York: Messner, 1976.
7. *Careers in Computers* by Lila B. Stair, Homewood, IL: Dow Jones-Irwin, 1984.
8. *Careers in Conservation: Profiles of People Working for the Environment* by Ada and Frank Graham, New York: Charles Scribner's Sons, 1980.
9. *Careers in State and Local Government* by John W. Zehring, Garrett Park, MD: Garrett Park Press, 1980.
10. *Careers: Working with Animals* by the Humane Society of the United States, Washington, DC: Acropolis, 1979.
11. *Challenging Careers in Urban Affairs* by Sterling McLeod, New York: Messner, 1976.
12. *Doctors for the People: Profiles of Six Who Serve* by Elizabeth Levy and Mara Miller, New York: Alfred A. Knopf, 1977.
13. *Getting into Film* by Mel London, New York: Ballantine, 1977.
14. *Here is Your Career: Banking, Money and Finance* by April Klimley, New York: G. P. Putnam's Sons, 1978.

15. *Here is Your Career: The Building Trades* by C. William Harrison, New York: G. P. Putnam's Sons, 1979.
16. *Here is Your Career: The Law* by George Coughlin, New York: G. P. Putnam's Sons, 1979.
17. *Jobs for English Majors and Other Smart People* by John L. Munschauer, Princeton, NJ: Peterson's Guides, 1981.
18. *Lawyers for the People: A New Breed of Defenders and Their Work* by Elizabeth Levy, New York: Alfred A. Knopf, 1974.
19. *Ms. Architect* by D. S. Fenten, Philadelphia: Westminster Press, 1977.
20. *Ms. Engineer* by Margaret Harmon, Philadelphia: Westminster Press, 1979.
21. *Ms. Veterinarian* by Mary Price Lee, Philadelphia: Westminster Press, 1976.
22. *Police Careers for Women* by Diane P. Muro, New York: Messner, 1979.
23. *The Salary Handbook* (no author), New York: Grosset & Dunlap, 1980.
24. *Saleswoman: A Guide to Career Success* by Barbara Fletcher, New York: Pocket Books, 1980.
25. *The Solar Jobs Book* by Kay Ericson, Andover, MA: Brick House, 1980.
26. *Teaching Exceptional Children: A Special Career* by Carol T. Anker, New York: Messner, 1978.
27. *What Can I do With a Major in . . . ?* by Lawrence R. Malnig and Sandra L. Morrow, Jersey City, NJ: St. Peter's College, 1975.
28. *Women Lawyers at Work* by Elinor P. Swider, New York: Messner, 1978.
29. *Work As You Like It: A Look at Unusual Jobs* by John Ott and Rosemary Stroer, New York: Messner, 1979.
30. *Yesss! Marv Albert on Broadcasting* by Marv Albert and Hal Bock, New York: New American Library, 1979.
31. *Your Career in Journalism* by M. L. Stein, New York: Messner, 1978.
32. *Your Career in Nursing*, rev. ed., by Mary W. Searight, New York: Messner, 1977.
33. *Your Career in Public Relations* by Robert Weinstein, New York: Arco, 1982.
34. *Your Career in Travel* by Janet and Joe Hollander, New York: Arco, 1981.
35. *Your Future in More Exotic Careers* by S. Norman Feingold and Alice Fins, New York: Rosen Press, 1980.
36. *Your Future in Religious Work* by Steven Herrup, New York: Rosen Press, 1980.

New books with general career information and those with a more specific focus are being published almost daily; so the preceding lists should be only a starting place. When you begin your library research, you need to discover what material exists in your particular library and career office. The best first step you can take is the building of a working bibliography.

A WORKING BIBLIOGRAPHY

The purpose of a working bibliography is to identify the material that looks, on the basis of title or author, most promising. The size of a working bibliography can vary greatly, not only according to how much material is available on a subject but also according to how much you want to know. If, for example, a zoology student thinks that he has observed an unexplained behavior in mallard ducks he has been studying, the first thing he wants to know is whether anyone else has observed this behavior and what explanations have been offered. At this point he does not need to know all there is to know about mallard ducks. From his literature search he will compile a working bibliography that is very specific, including only those reports, books, and articles that deal with the behaviors of mallard ducks or which have titles that lead him to believe that they contain the behavior he is interested in. He can then skim each of the items in his working bibliography and learn what is known and has been published in his specific area of interest.

When you are trying to decide whether to include an item in your bibliography, sometimes it is useful to consider its date of publication. There is no point in reading information that is bound to be outdated. Excluding by date is tricky, however, because it is always possible that an older article may include information that is not available in any recent work. Generally it is wise to be very careful about checking all the recent material and, if you have to cut corners somewhere, skimp on the earlier material. Nevertheless, if you are in doubt about whether to include a title, include it.

As your search progresses, materials you read will refer to or list other materials that you will want to check. In this way, your bibliography may grow as you become more familiar with the subject. To begin compiling a bibliography, familiarize yourself with the card catalogue and the *Readers' Guide to Periodical Literature*.

THE CARD CATALOGUE

A library's card catalogue lists the materials it owns. By checking the catalogue, you can tell if the library owns the material you are looking for and, if so, where you can find it. If you discover that the library does not have what you want, ask the interlibrary loan office to borrow the material you need from the nearest library that has it. Obviously, an interlibrary loan can take weeks to get your material to you; such requests are pointless if you must have the material very quickly. Also, since interlibrary loans impose on the goodwill of another library, they should be requested only when the material is truly important to your research or when you must be certain that you have checked *everything* available. This would be true, for example, if you were intending to publish your work.

Although some libraries have computerized their catalogues, most still retain card catalogues. In these, books are listed three times, according to title,

FIGURE 11.2   *Standard Card Catalogue Items for a Book*

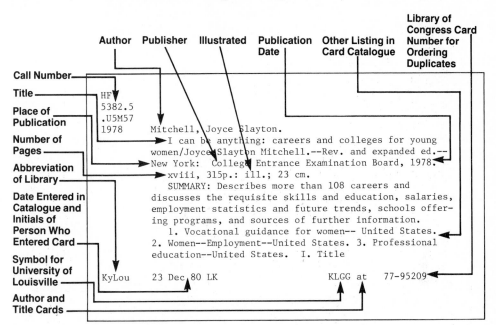

author, and subject. In some libraries all three categories are filed together in one alphabetical listing; in others, the title and author listings are interfiled, but the subject listings are separate. All libraries post large signs to tell you what system they use. If you want a specific book and know either its title or its author's name, it is easier to find it listed by these than by its subject because it is difficult to know just how the subject will be listed. (You may, for example, look up "hydroelectric plants" in the subject catalogue and be referred to "waterpower electric plants.") If, however, you want to know what books the library has on a certain subject, then finding its listing in the subject index and sifting through the cards is the quickest way.

The catalogue card itself includes information that can be useful to you. Figure 11.2 identifies standard items.

SERIALS

Serials are publications that appear at regular intervals, such as journals and magazines. Some libraries include serials in the regular card catalogue; others have a separate serials listing. Figure 11.3 is an example of a serials card. Some of the numbers and abbreviations along the bottom of both the author card and the serials card are peculiar to each individual library. An article in a magazine or journal will be listed in different formats in different biblio-

FIGURE 11.3   *Standard Card Catalogue Items for a Serial*

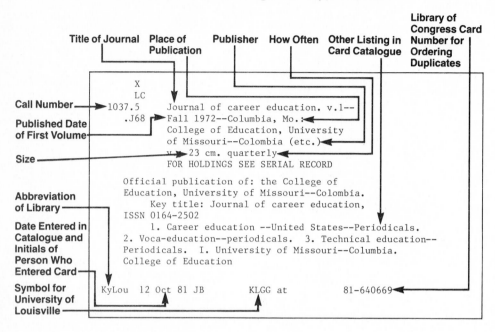

graphic guides, but the information that should always be included is the name of the author (if the article is signed), the name of the magazine or journal, the volume number, year, and page numbers.

READERS' GUIDE TO PERIODICAL LITERATURE

This resource remains one of the most commonly used tools in any library and can be found in the reference section. Over 180 journals and magazines are indexed in this reference collection, and the guide is updated monthly.

FIGURE 11.4   *A Sample Entry from the Readers' Guide*

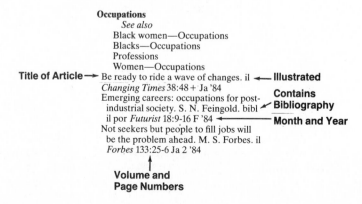

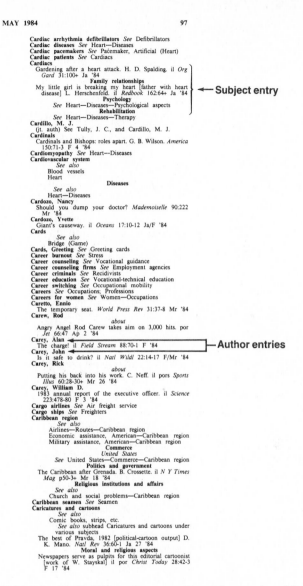

Copyright © 1984 by the H. W. Wilson Company. Material reproduced by permission of the publisher.

Entries are arranged by subject categories and authors as shown below. One may also locate reviews of books, dramas, ballets, musicals, operas, films, recordings, and television programs as well as fiction in the guide. Consult the first page in each issue for suggestions on locating such items. Figure 11.4 explains a sample entry in the *Readers' Guide*.

FIGURE 11.5   *The Catalogue Card*

```
HF
5382.5
.U5M57
1978     Mitchell, Joyce Slayton.
             I can be anything: careers and colleges for young
         women/Joyce Slayton Mitchell.--Rev. and expanded ed.--
         New York:  College Entrance Examination Board, 1978.
             xviii, 315p.: ill.; 23 cm.
             SUMMARY: Describes more than 108 careers and
         discusses the requisite skills and education, salaries,
         employment statistics and future trends, schools offer-
         ing programs, and sources of further information.
             1. Vocational guidance for women-- United States.
         2. Women--Employment--United States. 3. Professional
         education--United States.  I. Title

KyLou    23 Dec 80 LK                KLGG at    77-95209
```

RECORDING THE BIBLIOGRAPHY

There is always a great temptation to save some time by copying only part of
the citation for a book or article: it may not seem worth our while to record
the book's publisher or both the date and volume number of a journal article.
We assume that we will not need those to locate the book or article. Experienced researchers, however, know that copying the complete citation eventually saves time. If you are planning to list the item in the bibliography of your
report, you will need the full citation, and you will be wasting a great deal of

FIGURE 11.6   *Your Bibliography Card for a Book*

FIGURE 11.7 *Your Bibliography Card for an Article*

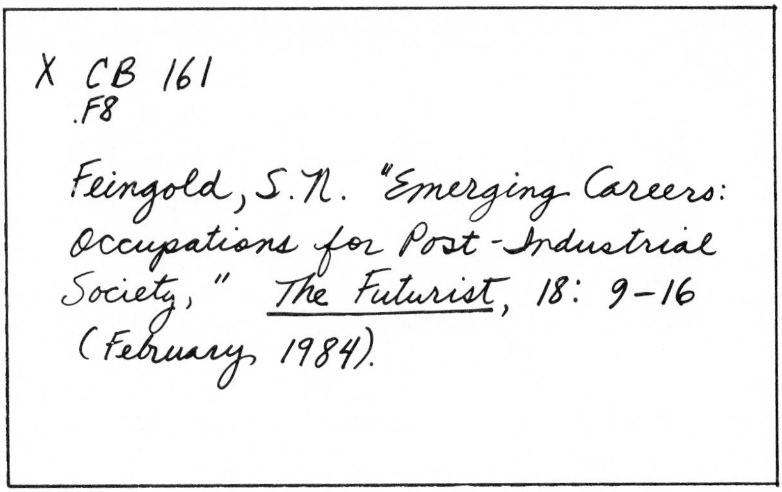

X CB 161
.F8

Feingold, S.N. "Emerging Careers:
Occupations for Post-Industrial
Society," *The Futurist*, 18: 9–16
(February 1984).

time if you have to return to the catalogue just to get a date or place of publication. Likewise, if you find you must request material from interlibrary loan, you will need the complete citation.

The most efficient way of recording the items in the working bibliography is on note cards (usually 3×5 or 4×6). If you record only one entry per card, you can then sort them into appropriate groups such as "not in library," "delete," and "completed." Then, later, when you are about to type the bibliography for your report, you can arrange the cards in alphabetical order. The following are examples of a library catalogue card and the researcher's bibliography card taken from it (Figures 11.5, 11.6, 11.7).

READING AND TAKING NOTES

Once you have compiled a working bibliography that you think includes the necessary items, you can begin working your way through your stack of bibliography cards, taking notes on the books that turn out to be most useful.

Order of Reading

In all fields, current study builds on previous research. This does not mean that newer work is always better than older work, or that newer theories are always more correct than older theories. In fact, most fields can offer an example of an older idea that was temporarily discarded but later proved correct. Because the general pattern, however, is one of advancement, it is best to read the literature in reverse chronological order. It would be a waste of time to take extensive notes on information compiled in 1920 if an article in 1970 demonstrated that the information is no longer valid. Of course, if recent work acknowledges some older work as indispensable and assumes familiarity with it, then you should read the older study early on.

Reading and Skimming

Realistically, the first thing you want to find out from a book, article, or report is whether you have to read any more of it. Is it relevant or was the title misleading? What does the study cover and in what depth? Does it duplicate information you already have? What are the author's credentials? Is this material to be looked over or to be studied? The following list provides an overview of what you should look for.

1. *The preface* (at least up to the point where the author begins thanking his or her editors and close relatives): Here the author defines the scope of his or her book.
2. *The table of contents:* Chapter titles generally give a fair indication of what will be covered, how the subject will be developed, and what specific applications may be discussed.
3. *The abstract* (if there is one)
4. *The introductory chapter:* Not only does this introduce the subject, but it should also give you an idea of the author's general competence.
5. *The list of figures or illustrations:* This should give you some idea of how theory or information is applied and to what.
6. *Notes on the author or sponsor:* It is often helpful to know what else the author has written, what his or her primary field is, what institution he or she is affiliated with; it is also helpful to know who financed or sponsored the research. Specifics about the author and sponsor are usually to be found in the preface, on the title page, or on the copyright pages of a book or report. For articles, they are usually on the first or last pages or, if they appear in a collection of essays, in a separate part of the volume called "Notes on Contributors" or the like.

After making this preliminary assessment of a work, you may decide that it is not worth further reading. But do not throw away the corresponding note card; simply mark it "checked" or "no needed information"—something to indicate that you have examined it. This same work may appear in the bibliography of another study and you will want to know that you have looked at it already.

If you decide that the article or book is worth further reading, the next step is to skim it. Beyond looking at the items listed above, skimming involves reading the following:

1. The first and last paragraphs of chapters and of sections within chapters.

2. The first sentence of each paragraph in an article or report. (If a first sentence of a particular paragraph is merely a transition or an example, read the last sentence of that paragraph, which may be a generalization or summary.)
3. All headings or subheadings and any words or phrases emphasized by italics or boldface type.
4. Any section or chapter called "conclusion" or "summary."

If, while skimming, you find that you have lost the thread of the discussion or explanation, backtrack to the point where you became lost and read a bit more thoroughly. The point of skimming is to follow the bare bones of the material; there is no point in skimming further if you are not getting enough information to make it worthwhile. Skimming should help you find the part of the work, if any, that contains information useful for your assignment. This is the material that you will want to read completely and write notes from.

As you do your research, read critically, even a bit skeptically. Do not assume that an assertion is true just because it appears in print. Even the "facts" may be disputable. There are, for example, widely varying numbers given for the percentage of the English population killed by the bubonic plague in the fourteenth century; one writer gives 20 percent, another estimates one-third, and another gives 60 percent. Every field of study offers similar examples of disagreements over factual information. Ideally, a writer will acknowledge that his or her facts conflict with those of other researchers, perhaps with a sentence such as "Although Professor Hengist estimates a 20 percent mortality rate and Professor Horsa estimates one-third, it now appears that 60 percent is a more likely figure, because. . . ." In this example, the writer has not only acknowledged that other estimates exist, but will go on to give the reader a reason for accepting the 60 percent figure. Different readers may or may not be convinced by the reason or reasons. Not all authors are this helpful, however. Sometimes, several works on the same subject appear at about the same time, and they may give conflicting factual information and not acknowledge the conflict because their writers did not know that the other books were in press. The moral of all this is that readers should look at all facts with some suspicion, always asking "Where did or how did the writer get that information?" and "Do other writers accept this information as true?" When several of your sources give conflicting information, you can judge among them by evaluating the methods through which the information was obtained. If they do not tell you how they got their information, you must simply report the disagreement in your paper.

Think for a moment about the ways in which the subject of UFOs would be treated by *National Enquirer,* the *National Lampoon,* and the *National Observer.* To which would you go for entertainment? Or amusement? Or information? It is helpful to think about the intentions of the publications you read in your research. In deciding how much you will believe a publication, you should determine whether reporting accurate information is a higher priority to the periodical than entertaining.

In evaluating what you read, it can be helpful to know who, if anyone, sponsored the research. If a study demonstrating no harmful effects of smoking were funded by the Tobacco Growers' Association, we would *not* be justified in assuming that the article is discredited by bias, but we would do well to remember that the sponsor was not a disinterested party. We should be interested in their research methods and in other studies that came to other conclusions.

Finally, as you read a book or article, you should be aware of how adequately the author is supporting the generalizations and whether he or she is reasoning logically (see Chapter 5). This is a critical test in determining how much faith to put in a source.

Note Taking

There is no single "correct" way to take notes. Ideally, the process of note taking should preserve the information you uncover, assure that later documentation is easy and accurate, and start you on your way to organizing and writing the first draft of your paper. The best way to ensure that you will be recording the most *useful* information is to have formulated your research questions in advance. For this chapter's assignment you can use the list of questions you developed in class (see p. 425). Read with these questions in mind, taking notes on the answers you find. If you discover some information that you think your audience would find useful and interesting (e.g., that persons in a certain career have the lowest suicide rate or the highest divorce rate or some such fact), make a note of that too. With some complex research projects, you are likely to find that you can only write very general questions before you begin reading. It is only after you have done some reading on the topic that you know what the issues are. For example, if you were assigned a research paper on the church versus state controversy in Norman England, it would take some reading before you could frame the specific question "To whose advantage did the Statute of Provisors operate?" The point is, however, to remember that you are looking for information to answer your readers' questions; you are not just summarizing the article or book for its own sake.

Whether you make notes on index cards or in a notebook or photocopy relevant pages from your sources, there are two things to keep in mind: (1) every piece of information recorded should be identified as to source and page number; and (2) even in notes it is crucial to distinguish among quotation, paraphrase, and your own contribution (see Chapter 8). If you take notes on index cards, either you can write a note on an index card and copy the author's name and the title on the top of the card (Figure 11.8), or you can number the cards in your working bibliography and then use these numbers to identify the source of a particular note (Figure 11.9). Obviously, with either method, it is *essential* to record the page number on which the information was found. Also, since the advantage of using index cards when you take notes is that you can sort them into different categories later on, be sure to record

FIGURE 11.8   *Referencing the Note Card to the Bibliography Card*

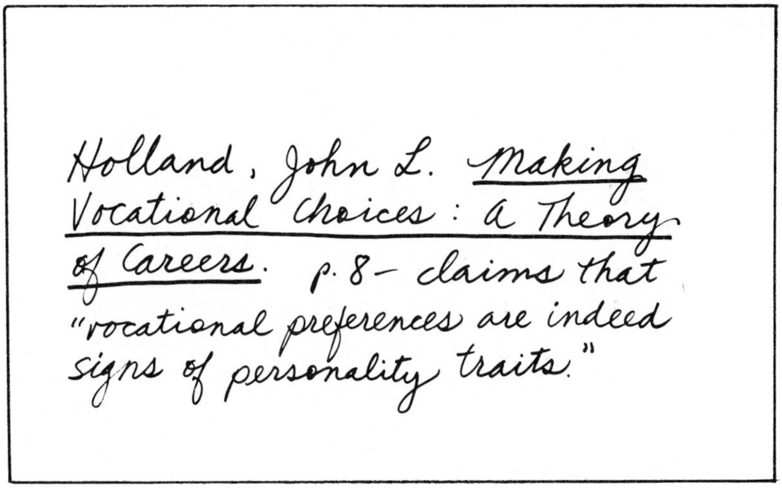

> Holland, John L. *Making Vocational Choices: A Theory of Careers.* p. 8 — claims that "vocational preferences are indeed signs of personality traits."

FIGURE 11.9   *An Alternative Method of Cross-Referencing the Notes to the Bibliography*

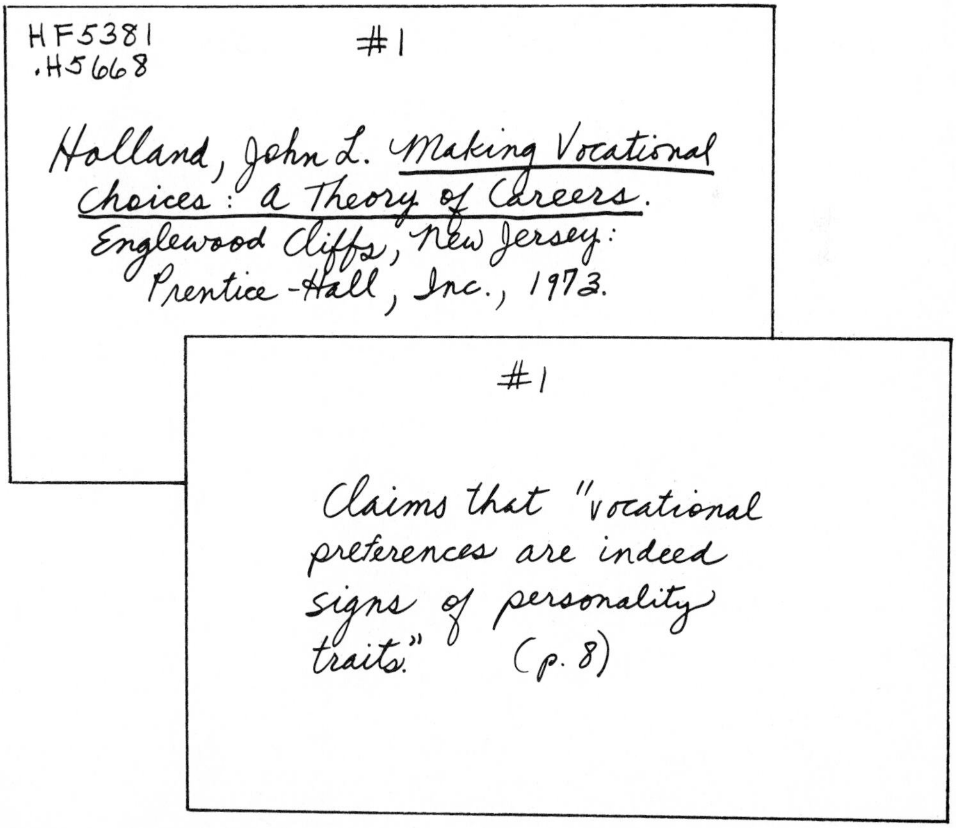

> HF5381
> .H5668   #1
>
> Holland, John L. *Making Vocational Choices: A Theory of Careers.* Englewood Cliffs, New Jersey: Prentice-Hall, Inc., 1973.

> #1
>
> Claims that "vocational preferences are indeed signs of personality traits."   (p. 8)

only *one* "idea" or one "bit" of information on each card. If you have more than one note on a card, you will probably be unable to sort the cards into categories.

INTERVIEWING

When you have finished your library research and have organized your notes according to your research questions, you are ready to conduct your interview. Select a person who works in the career area you have researched. If this is not possible or if you are interested in college teaching or research, seek someone at your college who is working in the general field in which you are interested. For example, if your tentative career choice is to work as an ocean-ographer but there are no oceanographers around, perhaps you could inter-view a professor of marine biology. Make arrangements for the interview at the convenience of your interviewee, and make sure that you and the inter-viewee have sufficient time to devote to the interview.

Early in this chapter you briefly interviewed three adults on the subject of the meaning of work and the values they find in their work. In interacting with those interviewees, you had a specific question in mind, as you did when you approached three different persons to question them about their attitudes toward work and their beliefs in regard to occupational choice. You probably based these brief interviews on questions provided for you in those sections of the chapter.

Now, you will plan and conduct a more in-depth interview with a person in your selected career field. Through this interview, you want to gather data or information that generally cannot be found in books or articles. You want your interviewee to be as comfortable and relaxed as possible but you also want him or her to be as honest and detailed as possible. Getting your ques-tions together is the first step in preparing for the interview. Without good questions, an interviewee may talk a good deal but not to the point you are interested in; or the interviewee may find it difficult to talk at all, not being sure of exactly what you want to know or simply because he or she is reserved. You can choose your interview questions from among those offered earlier in this chapter and add some that are specific to the career the interviewee is practicing.

To ensure a good interview, first, *be on time* and *respect the time limit.* If the interviewee has allotted thirty minutes for the interview, do not try to keep the interview going overtime. Second, *do your homework.* You should *know your subject*—in this case, the career. Having done your library work first is a must. Make sure also that you *know your interviewee.* Find out whatever you can about the person that will help you make him or her comfortable. Once you have done your homework, you as interviewer will be able to relax and feel confident.

Third, try to take notes unobtrusively. Getting down key words on a small pad is probably best. Instead of trying to write every word down, you can be looking at your interviewee and listening intently. Fourth, avoid questions that can be answered with *yes* or *no.* Instead, use *how, what, why,* and *to what extent* questions. Be willing to forget about your next question if the interviewee pursues a related and interesting point. Fifth, follow up on interesting leads your interviewee gives you in what he or she says rather than abruptly turning to the next question.

Finally, if the interviewee seems to run out of something to say in answering your questions, offer a statement that he or she might be able to respond to. This technique clearly demands that you know your subject (the career field) well enough to make a statement that might be slightly controversial and apt to provoke a response. Immediately after your interview, review your notes and write out those parts that are really in "shorthand."

With the notes from your library research and your interview, you have all the raw material you need for drafting your research report. Now it is time to think about putting the material together. One way to organize your report would be to include two major divisions, for example:

> Part I: Computer Programming as a Career
> Part II: One Computer Programmer Speaks

Part I might well be organized on the basis of your original 8 to 10 questions, Part II on the basis of your interview questions or other key themes that arose from your interview.

A second way to organize this material would be to integrate the information you gathered in the interview with the library research. In this way, the more personal data would be spread throughout and might liven up the report. You might still use your questions as organizers.

SYNTHESIZING AND PRESENTING RESEARCH DATA

A research report may make extensive use of other people's contributions to knowledge, but it is still your communication with the reader. You, as writer, decide how much your readers already know and what they need to know. You evaluate the sources and deal with conflicting data, you decide what organizational strategy to use, and you make the language choices. The rest of this section will give you some guidance in doing these things.

Prewriting

Before you began your research, you phrased specific questions you wanted the research to answer. In this case, the assignment gave you the general question, but you developed the specific subquestions by deciding what your audience needs to know about the career you are researching. These specific questions guide your note taking and you can use them now to plan the organization of your report. Remember to organize in a manner that suits your audience; do not be bound by the organization of your sources. For example, if the person you interviewed did not answer your questions but instead did something of a monologue on "How I Found My Niche as a Lightning Rod Salesperson," you would not want to adopt your interviewee's chronological narration. Instead, you would want to select and rearrange information from the narrative.

Another prewriting task is that of generalizing from your data. Assume that one of your research questions was, "Is the demand for poodle clippers increasing or decreasing?" None of your sources directly answered the question, but several of them noted that the number of poodles in America has increased yearly for a decade. In addition, one of your sources mentioned that membership in the American Poodle Clippers Professional Organization has declined in recent years, and your interviewee admitted to some fears that more and more poodles are going unclipped. You have, in fact, noticed that you are seeing shaggier poodles lately, but you realize that you cannot base much of a generalization on the limited sample you have observed. One of the issues you should settle during your prewriting would be how to answer the question from the data you have. What kind of a generalization do they support? Probably the best you could do in this case would be something like, "I could not discover whether there is increased or decreased need for poodle clippers. The number of poodles in the country has increased yearly for a decade, but. . . ."

When you think you know how you will answer each of the questions and when you have an idea of the order in which you will present your data, you are ready to begin drafting.

Drafting

Working from sources complicates the drafting process in two ways: you must constantly check that you are generalizing fairly from your data, and you must remember to indicate to your readers the sources for your data. In practice, the latter requires that you identify your sources in the body of your text. A reader has a right to know the source of every quotation without having to turn to the notes. Consider the following sample:

> By what standards is poodle clipping judged? "One hopes to see the creation of an overall 'look.' Beyond the obvious things like symmetry and proportion, one likes to think that each poodle will be a 'statement.'"

Who is answering the question? Is this one person's opinion or a statement with greater authority behind it? The writer should have identified the speaker:

> *According to Skipper Davis, president of the American Poodle Clippers Professional Organization,* "One hopes to see. . . ."

This not only gives the speaker's name but the information that the reader needs to judge the speaker's credibility. Quotations should never float free in the text, but should be *ascribed* through the use of common forms like "according to," "said," or "in the words of." Paraphrased material must also have its source indicated, but this can be done by use of a parenthetical reference. (See Appendix A for citation forms and formats.)

Beyond these considerations, your drafting process for the research report will be much like the drafting you have done for other writing tasks. You will be conscious of answering the questions your readers might have and of choosing language appropriate for them and for your purpose. In this assignment, for example, your primary audience is fellow students rather than the instructor, so your language may be a bit more conversational, though still within the general confines of formal English because you are writing for readers whom you do not know personally.

Revising

Revising a research report is much like revising any other writing task, but it is complicated by the need to make sure you represent all sources accurately and do not ignore any conflicting data. These are things with which a reader of your draft cannot help you unless he or she has also read your sources. Therefore, even if you know you will have the benefit of a Revising Workshop, you still have a responsibility to be particularly careful about your use of sources because the nature of a research report requires that the reader *trust* you in these matters. So begin your revising by rereading your notes on each issue about which you generalize. Does your generalization take into account *all* of the data? Have you represented conflicts fairly? Have you paraphrased or summarized each source accurately?

Editing

Begin your editing by making sure that you have identified all of the sources you have quoted or paraphrased and by checking the spelling of all names and titles and checking all dates and page numbers. These may seem like small matters, but readers quickly lose faith in a writer whose citations are not correct. If a writer cites page 331 as the source of a quotation and the reader discovers that the quotation is not on the page, the reader rightly loses confidence in the report. Beyond this, edit your research report as you would any other paper.

When you have a completed draft of your paper, you can prepare the bibliography that will be included with it. This will differ from your working bibliography in that it will include only the sources you consulted and found relevant. Consult Appendix A for further information about the final bibliography.

A Sample Synthesis of Data from Sources

One student, who was asked to report on proprioceptors to his physiology class, found the following two sources: "The Physiology of Acceleration" from *Car and Driver* and "Proprioception" from the *McGraw-Hill Encyclopedia of Science and Technology*. Read each of these sources critically and make notes in your journal about the credibility, the intended audience, and the purpose of each article. Make notes also about the audience and purpose for the student's report. List some questions you think the writer should be trying to answer.

The Physiology of Acceleration

Getting Off on Speed, and Other Thrills.

John Jerome

When I was on the staff of C/D, back in the mid-1960s, acceleration puzzled me. In those days I was a member of a kind of loyal opposition to generally available technology. (We were the ones who knew we would lose on the straights but were still talking about catching up on the turns.) I followed road racing rather than drag racing, finding handling more interesting than all that zero-to-sixty stuff. But the quarter-mile sport had a powerful if unacknowledged effect on the way all of us thought about automobiles.

It wasn't that I was prejudiced against acceleration; I just thought it was a bit simple-minded. I was comfortable enough with its technical aspects. I understood its uses, and definitely relished using it. I loved that surge as much as anyone. At *C/D* we were just beginning to get interested in motorcycles, and I was perfectly willing to admit how much fun they were. Most of that fun seemed to have to do with their vigorous acceleration. I wondered why that sensation was so stimulating, but I could never quite figure it out.

We were also fascinated by pure power and the control thereof. Hand over control of a running engine to someone and, I guarantee you, he will blip the throttle. He will press the pedal, work the control, toy with the power surge. But speed alone turns out not to be enough. We get jaded; we want the push of acceleration, the rising curve.

I suffer from a reductive turn of mind. Looking at motorcycles, for example, I always discounted noise and wind as mere side effects. (Acceleration in quiet, enclosed vehicles is also fun.) Therefore, I thought, the pleasurable sensations of acceleration had to be a product of the stimulation of the pressure receptors in the butt—the sense of touch in those parts of you that make contact with the accelerating vehicle—and of minor disturbances to the balance mechanism of the semicircular canals of the inner ear. But these seemed to me to be awfully minor neural hardware to generate the kind of sensation you get from a large engine attached to a short gear. How could receptors that are such physiological pipsqueaks create so much fun—and therefore so much mechanical sport?

I was overlooking muscle, and its sensory power. Skeletal muscle is the largest sensory organ we have, and it reads acceleration throughout the whole body. I never dreamed such a thing was possible. You can—you *do*—read acceleration right down in your little finger. Acceleration is one of the most massive sensory experiences we ever have.

The sensors that count, accelerationwise, are the *proprioceptors*—the "self-sensors"—little specialized nerve endings that are embedded in the muscle, the tendons, and the joints, that read and report on body position, movement, and loading. They are the memory banks your coach was talking about when he spoke of "muscle memory" (although that term is misleading). They are the neural devices that weigh and judge and perceive whatever you do with your musculoskeletal system, from guiding a forkful of pasta safely into your gob to catching the rear end of your Indy car when it starts to break loose at 220 mph. Some of us get very good with our proprioceptors. The ones who do are usually called athletes, of which racing drivers—drag, road, or round-and-round—are one special subcategory. Those of us who don't get good at proprioception are called spectators.

The way human muscle acts as a sensor requires a kind of neural rigging that would have made the late Colin Chapman proud. Muscle stays alive by means of a complex neural loop that connects sensory (afferent) nerve endings to the central nervous system and in turn to effector (efferent) nerve endings. This loop maintains in the muscle a steady state of low-grade contraction that keeps it ready for use: muscle tone. (Muscle tone has been likened to the idle of a car's engine.) Snip the loop at any point and the muscle that it innervates will atrophy like that of a limb in a cast.

Muscle tone in turn maintains the stretch reflex, which is the muscle's automatic resistance to the displacement of the limb. When the doctor taps your kneecap, he's really stretching the tendon that connects the kneecap to the thigh muscles. That stretch fires proprioceptors in the muscles that tell the spine there's a mismatch in the length of those muscles. The spine in turn sends signals back to the muscles to match up their length, which signals make you kick your foot.

When you twist the throttle on a motorcycle, you're changing the loadings on most of your musculoskeletal system. Acceleration snaps your head back: your neck and shoulders contain perhaps the richest bed of proprioception in your body, charged with the task of keeping your eyes level and your balance perfect, so that you will be ready to take action no matter what kinds of upset the rest of your skeleton is being put through.

Acceleration snaps *everything* back; you feel it just the way your face felt the pull of gravity plus centrifugal force at the bottom of the arc of the playground swing. At that moment gravity tugged harder at the mass of your facial flesh, and that attempted dislocation of the mass fired thousands of proprioceptor endings in the facial muscles. It was an unusual feeling and you experimented with it. (Kids are the ultimate sensualists, doing everything just to find out what each new experience feels like. This helps explain everything from roller coasters to teen-age pregnancies.) The same force at work on your facial muscles was also at work on the rest of you, of course, giving you that sweet little, perceptual thrill, almost a sexual thrill, that you get when your entire body is being worked upon by forces larger than usual.

Hard acceleration is the playground swing times ten, times a hundred, the same category of forces raised to breathtaking new heights. Every ounce of mass on your body is under a dislocating force that seems to want to pull the muscle from your bones, to pool your blood and your flesh on the backside of your skeleton. Your proprioceptors light up your central nervous system like those rows of control panels at Mission Control in Houston.

I'm thinking of acceleration in the drag-strip sense, as a straight-ahead push. *C/D*'s technical editors, who know a lot more about physics than I do, will tell you that in any kind of driving there are accelerations in every direction, accelerations in vectors and angles, side loadings and (heart-stopping) unloadings. There is no end to the ways you can find to get your frame tossed about and titillated by external forces and changes of direction. Every one of them carries this kind of proprioceptive thrill. Every one of them cranks on all those nerve endings, pleasuring you with new sensations.

Imagine the neural fireworks for a Formula 1 driver practicing his craft, taking all that horsepower through as complex a series of patterns as the course can dish up. (Looked at this way, aerodynamic bodywork is a complicated way to increase the possible loadings, to boost the forces at work right up to the breakaway point.) Imagine the balancing act, the vectoring that's going on, as the driver works those tiny little controls—steering, gas, brakes, gears—to cut a way through all that sensation, to come up with the alignments and arrangements that will keep the car (and his body) moving in the chosen direction at the fastest possible speed.

Skill at that balancing act is usually credited to *kinesthetic sense,* which is a rather vague term for the capacity to read and react to the signals from the proprioceptors. It's a sense that can be improved with practice. At its higher levels it is a very acute sense indeed. It's the sense that allows the diver to come out of his tuck—after three and a half somersaults from 33 feet in the air—at the precise instant that will enable him to enter the water absolutely vertical and with minimum splash. It's the sense that tells the trout fisherman just when and how hard to set the hook—on the basis of information gathered from no sources other than the muscles of the hand, wrist, and arm. It's the sense that allows the good tennis player to read—from the torque on the racket handle—just how far off-center the ball has met the racket face (and, on the basis of that information, to fire enough muscle fibers of the wrist and forearm to compensate and slam the forehand winner two inches inside the cross-court line). It is the sense that enables the racing driver to make sure that there is somewhere very close to 11,500 rpm (and third gear) available to the drive wheels—and that the accelerator pedal has just started *down*—at the precise instant the drive wheels drift out to the last inch of useful traction on the exit of the turn.

(It is equally involved in deceleration, of course. Braking a car in racing has always seemed to me to be one of the most elegant problems in sports. You have to select the latest possible moment that you can apply the brakes to slow the car just enough to go through the corner at the fastest possible speed. You must apply the brakes as hard as possible for the shortest possible time that will bring the tire surfaces to the point just short of sliding. Your job is to approach, but not exceed, these values. You can't tell when you exceed any of them until you do so. It is a problem of adjustable negatives, of going faster by decreasing less. Done right it is a demonstration of major-league powers of proprioception.)

Sounds like fun to me. Anyway, that, I think, is why acceleration is such a kick. It's a great deal more than some touch sensors on your butt and your semicircular canals (but it's also that, too, some *outrageous* signaling from those dumb organs). It's fun because of that entire great, thrusting sensory load, all those neurons crackling away, telling you how alive you are. Acceleration is a sensory intensifier.

Most sports—at least the high-effort, all-out ones that require that you do something as hard or fast or long as you can—are routinized ways of firing off every neuron you can summon up. That's where the fun lies, where the thrill comes in. Even in high-risk sports such as motor racing, the thrill isn't from exposing yourself to danger (ABC's "Wide World of Sports" to the contrary notwithstanding), but from the bombardment of sensory stimuli. It may not be socially redeeming, but it also is not the acting-out of some Freudian death wish. It's just enjoying your nerve endings. Cigar smokers and brandy sniffers can make the same claim.

The risk itself is only another vivid little intensifier, a psychological enhancer that further sharpens the sensory message. Maybe that's why many racing drivers and other high-risk athletes and performers can be so blasé about threats to their lives and limbs. They're having too much fun—experiencing too much in the way of sensory fire-works—to pay much attention to inconsequential matters like risk. That may not be very *smart*—and also may not be socially redeeming—but it's a lot less scary than the idea that our heroes have this secret lust to crisp themselves in a ball of flame.

Proprioception

Robert Lamotte

The sense of position and movement of the limbs and the sense of muscular tension. The awareness of the orientation of the body in space and the direction, extent, and rate of movement of the limbs depend in part upon information derived from sensory receptors in the joints, tendons, and muscles. Information from these receptors, called proprioceptors, is normally integrated with that arising from vestibular receptors (which signal gravitational acceleration and changes in velocity of movements of the head), as well as from visual, auditory, and tactile receptors. Sensory information from certain proprioceptors, particularly those in muscles and tendons, need not reach consciousness, but can be used by the motor system as feedback to guide postural adjustments and control of well-practiced or semiautomatic movements such as those involved in walking.

Sensory Discriminations

Position and movement of limbs can be sensed either when the muscles are relaxed and movement is passive or during active muscular contraction (the latter sense called kinesthesis). In the former case, the threshold for sensing small changes in the angle of the joints, as measured experimentally, depends upon the extent and velocity of the change in angle and is considerably better at proximal joints such as hip or shoulder joints than at more distal joints such as those in the fingers. For example, thresholds vary roughly between 0.2° for the hip to 0.7° for the main joint of the big toe when the speed of displacement is 10°/min. If passive movements of a joint are superimposed, by the experimenter, on active movements of the same joint, discriminatory capacity is improved. Human observers can also identify precisely the absolute position of a limb (placed either actively by the subject or passively by an experimenter) by actively matching the position with the corresponding limb on the opposite side of the body. Humans are also accurate in judging the amount of force exerted by their muscles in making a movement or in maintaining the position of a joint against an opposing force. The latter capacity can be assessed from discriminations between the active forces required to compress springs of different stiffness held between the thumb and finger. In fact, discriminations analogous to these can be made to a lesser degree without any information from proprioceptors, indicating that there is a "sense of effort" by which the motor system sends a copy of information sent to the muscles to higher sensory processing centers. In normal conditions such central feedback enables the nervous system to determine which proprioceptive information resulted from intended movements and which came from stimuli externally applied.

Proprioceptors

Receptors for proprioception are the endings of peripheral nerve fibers within the capsule or ligaments of the joints or within muscle. These endings are associated with specialized end organs such as Pacinian corpuscles, Ruffini's cylinders, and Golgi organs (the latter resembling histologic Golgi structures in the skin), and muscle spindles. *See* CUTANEOUS SENSATION.

Pacinian corpuscles are found mainly in the connective tissue surrounding the joint and are sensitive to vibrations or abrupt changes in position of the joint. Joint receptors, such as the Ruffini and Golgi types, within the capsule are compressed or stretched when the joint moves, and signal the direction and velocity of movement as well as the steady position of the joint. There are also Golgi organs located at the junction between a muscle and its tendon. When the muscle is lengthened and the ends of a muscle are fixed, then active muscle contraction will shorten the contractile part of the muscle, thereby stretching the inelastic tendon fascicles and exciting the Golgi receptors. Thus, these receptors are excited by muscle tension or force.

Two other stretch receptors are located within the muscle spindle, the latter consisting of small (intrafusal) muscle fibers attached at each end to the main (extrafusal) fibers of skeletal muscle. Each spindle is supplied with two types of sensory nerve endings. One type is excited mainly by changes in the length of the muscle, while the other is sensitive not only to changes in length but also to the velocity of muscle elongation. In addition, the muscle spindle is supplied with axons from neurons called gamma motoneurons, excitation of which causes the intrafusal fibers to contract. Whenever the intrafusal fibers are contracted more than the extrafusal fibers, the sensory endings of the spindle are excited. Stretch receptors are included in many reflexes involving the spinal cord and higher centers in the central nervous system. These reflexes have roles in the control of movement and posture. For example, when a static muscular contraction (such as that occurring in the legs during standing) is subjected to an added load, muscle spindles are stretched, resulting in a reflexive increase in contraction of extrafusal fibers (and relaxation of intrafusal fibers) to maintain the load. Activity in the gamma motoneurons then serves to re-adjust the length of the muscle spindle (via contraction of the intrafusal fibers) to its previous value in order to maintain the muscle spindle's sensitivity to subsequent varying conditions.

One or more types of muscle receptors may also contribute to the sense of movement and position of the joints since this sense is still possible, although impaired, following local anesthetization of joint receptors or after replacement of the joint with a prosthesis. Conversely, the sense of movement and position also remains, albeit impaired, after elimination of sensory signals from muscle receptors.

Cutaneous receptors may provide some relevant information (particularly in signaling that limb movement has occurred), although the results of experiments in which the skin is anesthetized indicate that this information is not essential. Thus, the sense of movement and position of the limbs probably depends upon the central integration of information from several different types of proprioceptors. *See* NERVOUS SYSTEM (VERTEBRATE); SENSATION; SOMESTHESIS.

One of the questions that you may have listed is, "What do propriocep-tors do?" Here is the section of the student's paper that answers that question. Notice how he has used information from both of his sources and synthesized it with additions of his own, organizing and choosing language to suit his own audience and purpose.

```
     Proprioceptors sense the position of the body, its
movement, and the strength of forces weighing on it.
This information allows the central nervous system to
react to the environment. For example, when we acceler-
ate quickly in a car or on a motorcycle, the propriocep-
tors sense the additional force on our bodies and send a
quick stream of signals to the central nervous system.
John Jerome, in an article in Car and Driver magazine
(May 1983), says that it is this heightened flow of sig-
nals from the proprioceptors that accounts for the at-
traction of acceleration. But signals from the
proprioceptors do not have to become conscious. The mo-
tor system uses these signals to guide the position of
the body in even simple activities, like walking ("Prop-
rioception" in The McGraw-Hill Encyclopedia of Applied
Science and Technology, 1982).
```

In your journal, practice synthesizing material from sources by answering the other questions you identified as belonging in the student's class report.

Revising Workshop

Bring your draft and bibliography to class for a Revising Workshop. In small groups, help each other by responding to the questions below in relation to each paper. Each person's paper should be read by at least two other students.

1. What are the sections of the report? What questions and subtopics does the writer address about the chosen career?
2. How does the writer illustrate the subtopics or the answers to key questions? Mark any sections that seem to need additional illustration.
3. Why do you think the writer put the paragraphs in this order? Comment on any paragraph that seems to be out of order.
4. What tone and style does the writer use in the report? How will an audience of other students respond to this tone and style?
5. After reading the report, what questions do you have left about this career?
6. How accurately does the title reflect the content of the report?
7. Comment on the sentence structure in the paper. Are any sentences choppy? Any too long? Any weakened by unnecessary words?
8. Is there any information for which no source is given?

Before you write the second draft of your report, take into account the responses your classmates offered during the Revising Workshop. You do not have to agree with others' responses, but you should think about their ideas seriously, particularly in this assignment in which your specific audience is other students.

Now write the second draft of your report, making whatever revisions you have decided are necessary—for clarity, to illustrate more, to keep your tone and style consistent throughout, to make your organization as effective as possible.

Editing Workshop

Return to your small group with your second draft for an Editing Workshop. In this session your aim is to help each other review the reports for mechanical flaws and problems with form. Each person's paper should be responded to by at least two students using the following questions:

1. How accurately is the paper documented according to the APA style as shown in the ERIC document in this chapter. Place a *?* in the margin on any line where you think you perceive an error in the body of the report and in the bibliography.
2. Are there sentences or parts of sentences that confuse you or cause you to reread to grasp the meaning? If so, bracket these as needing repair.
3. Place an *X* in the margin of any line in which you see what you perceive as an error in spelling or punctuation. Use as many marks as there are errors.
4. Put a *C* in the margin of any line in which you find a trite phrase or a cliché.
5. Put a *G* in the margin of any line where you see an error in grammar or usage. Put as many marks as there are errors.

Now make whatever revisions you feel are necessary for a polished report and submit your final copy to your instructor.

ONE MORE READING

Despite your work, reading, and interaction in this chapter and all the thoughtful consideration you may have given the important matter of career decision making before this course, you must know that there are always factors that cause us to change our minds, take new directions, and reevaluate our decisions. Ellen Goodman comments on the element of luck:

To Help a New Generation, Admit Luck's Role in Successful Careers

Ellen Goodman

BOSTON—The three women on the panel described their work histories in a nice orderly sequence—jobs, titles, dates.

They appeared to be the very model of proper career women, the well-organized success stories of five-year plans and life-management courses. Their autobiographies would have impressed any personnel manager or editor of Who's Who. Surely they impressed the college audience.

Yet later, when they talked alone, different words crept into their résumés. The first woman sheepishly confessed to "luck," the second woman admitted "chance," the third talked about "accident."

Not one of these women had tipped her hat to luck in her public job description. After all, they were enlightened women. They had all read the research.

Hadn't it been proved that most women attributed their success to luck, while most men attributed it to their own effort, skills, talents? They knew that trap and wanted to avoid it, and so, had expunged luck from their curriculum vitae. At least, said one of the women, the younger generation could be spared their self-doubt.

It was the first of two conversations that I heard about luck. The next one occurred last week when a woman who had started out in English criticism and ended up in political research confessed she, too, felt awkward explaining the role of accident in her peculiar progression. One wasn't supposed to talk about that anymore. It had become a cliché, a stereotype to shatter.

But this time, it occurred to me that I wasn't sure anymore. I wonder if "planning" isn't just as much of a cliché and "control" as much of a stereotype to shatter. I wonder which point of view is more realistic?

I know that when assorted studies about the differences between men and women filter into our popular language we usually begin by seeing men as the norm and women abnormal. If the topic is success and more men are successful, then we begin by worrying about the female success psyche. We assume that women need to change.

But if more men believe they made their own way deliberately, purposely, skillfully, is it because these men plan better or because they rationalize better? Is it because of their skills or egotism? Were their lives more in their control or are they more reluctant to admit a lack of control?

And if more women see fate, luck, accident as a central force in their work lives is it because they are passive, slow to see and reluctant to admit their own skills? Or is it because they are quick to see and comfortable to admit the reality of chance?

The answers depend less on our perception of men and women than on our perception of the truth. It depends on how we determine the tricky equation of luck and skill in a life.

I know there are many things we can't do without acquiring the skills, making the plans. We cannot, blessedly, do brain surgery without medical training. Few people "luck" into medical school.

But there are many things we can't do with planning. We cannot chart a course from English critic to political researcher. We cannot figure out how our interests will change and skills will grow. We don't know when chances will come, including the chance to throw over all our previous plans.

It is always easier to plot our lives backward and discover a straight line than to plot them forward on that line. To make a life, we need a peculiar combination of energy and persistence, skills that make readiness—and a lot of luck.

I don't say this as any kind of revelation but because luck has got this bad rap. Those who acknowledge luck as a mentor are tempted to believe that their experience has no meaning for others. It was just luck after all. Women in particular are tempted to hide the happenstance behind a timetable.

But we're dealing with a younger generation full of anxieties about the future, a generation longing to be told the one true path. Maybe what they really need is people who will give them first-hand accounts of chance. Maybe they need our experience and our wishes for good luck.

Part III

AIDS IN THE PROCESS

Chapter 12, Editing Guide, is designed as a reference for you as you edit your own writing and as you work in the Editing Workshops. You will find solutions to problems of sentence structure, punctuation, and grammar and usage. Chapter 13, Sentence Workshops, provides exercises that can help you develop more sentence variety in your writing. Although participating in these exercises with your class will be more beneficial, there is nothing to prevent you from trying some on your own.

CHAPTER 12

Editing Guide

This guide is included to assist you in editing your papers. The chapter is divided into three sections: sentence construction, punctuation, and grammar and usage.

SENTENCE CONSTRUCTION

If the readers in your Editing Workshop have bracketed any of your sentences as needing repair, you can consult the following section to learn how to recognize when there is a problem with one of your sentences, to identify what the problem is, and to learn one or more ways of solving the problem.

The basic element of a sentence is the *independent clause* (the subject and the verb).

     subject   verb

The announcer choked.

Sometimes the main clause may have only an implied subject (you), when the verb is a command.

     verb

Get out of here!

We seldom have any problem understanding who is being told to get out; for this reason the subject of a sentence like this is said to be *understood.*

The verb in the main clause must not be an infinitive (a verb with *to* in front of it: *to be, to seem*), must not be a present participle or a gerund (which end in *ing*), and must not be a past participle (a verb used as an adjective, usually ending in *ed:* the *potted* palm, the *stewed* tomatoes).

Along with independent clauses, sentences can have *dependent clauses.* These are clauses that are not sentences by themselves, but must be attached to an independent clause. Dependent clauses may begin with one of the following words: *after, although, as, as if, as long as, as soon as, because, before, if, in order that, since, so that, though, until, when, where, whereas, while.*

dep. clause   indep. clause

While you're in the kitchen, get me a sandwich.

dep. clause   indep. clause

As soon as I start to write, the phone rings.

indep. clause   dep. clause

Get me a sandwich while you're in the kitchen.

indep. clause   dep. clause

The phone rings as soon as I sit down to write.

Sometimes *who, which,* and *that* can also introduce dependent clauses.

indep. clause   dep. clause

Here is the person who got an A in organic chemistry.

dep. clause

The person who got an A in organic chemistry is lending me her notes.

indep. clause   dep. clause

Here are the tickets that were left in your name.

indep.   dep.
clause   clause

Tell me who you are.

You have to be careful about *who* and *that,* however, because they sometimes appear in the main clauses of sentences.

Who are you?

That is the strangest name I've ever heard.

Look closely at the last sentence. How many clauses does it have? The "I've ever heard" is connected to the sentence by an understood *that.* The sentence therefore has two clauses:

```
          indep. clause                    dep. clause
```
That is the strangest name (that) I've ever heard.

Notice how *that* is used in two different ways in this sentence.

All of the sentence patterns of English are based on different arrangements of the basic elements of a clause. Here are the patterns and some examples.*

Pattern 1 is noun phrase, form of the verb *to be,* and adverb or adverbial phrase.

> My office is downstairs.

> You are on the porch.

> Your shoes are on the radiator.

Negative sentence: My office is not downstairs.
Interrogative sentence: Where is my office?
Exclamatory sentence: (not possible in this pattern)
Command sentence: Be on the porch.
Cleft sentence: Those are your shoes on the radiator.
Passive sentence: (not possible in this pattern)

Pattern 2 is noun phrase, form of the verb *to be,* and adjective or adjectival phrase.

> The photos were blurred.

> They are kind.

> The headwaiter will be in a dither.

> Negative sentence: The photos were not blurred.
> Interrogative sentence: Will the head waiter be in a dither?
> Exclamatory sentence: How blurred the photos were!
> Command sentence: Be kind.
> Cleft sentence: These are the photographs that were most blurred.
> Passive sentence: (not possible in this pattern)

Pattern 3 is noun phrase, form of verb *to be,* and noun phrase.

> Max is a gorgeous Airedale.

> Washington was a patriot.

> English was my best class last term.

*In describing the patterns, we follow Martha Kolln, *Understanding English Grammar,* (New York: Macmillan, 1982); and Norman C. Stageberg, *An Introductory English Grammar,* 4th ed. (New York: Holt, Rinehart & Winston, 1981).

Negative sentence: Max is not a gorgeous Airedale.
Interrogative sentence: Is Max a gorgeous Airedale?
Exclamatory sentence: What a gorgeous Airedale Max is!
Command sentence: Be a patriot.
Cleft sentence: It was English that was my best class last term.
Passive sentence: (not possible in this pattern)

Pattern 4 is noun phrase, linking verb, and adjective phrase. (Linking verbs replace the forms of the verb *to be.* The common linking verbs for this pattern are *become, feel, look, seem, smell, sound, and taste.*)

The cheese became moldy.

You sound older.

Wallace seemed minimally alert.

Negative sentence: The cheese did not become moldy.
Interrogative sentence: Did Wallace seem minimally alert?
Exclamatory sentence: How moldy this cheese has become!
Command sentence: Sound older.
Cleft sentence: It was Wallace who seemed minimally alert.
Passive sentence: (not possible in this pattern)

Pattern 5 is noun phrase, linking verb, and noun phrase. (The common linking verbs for this pattern are *appear, become, remain, and seem.*)

My grandfather became a citizen in 1968.

J.B. remained a loyal Reds fan until he died.

I became a vegetarian.

Negative sentence: My grandfather did not become a citizen in 1968.
Interrogative sentence: Did J.B. remain a loyal Reds fan until he died?
Exclamatory sentence: How loyal a Reds fan J.B. remained until he died!
Command sentence: Become a vegetarian.
Cleft sentence: It was in 1968 that I became a vegetarian.
Passive sentence: (not possible in this pattern)

Pattern 6 is noun phrase, intransitive verb, and adverb (optional).

Mitchell laughed outrageously.

The plane soared.

Ollie and Joe set out at 6 a.m.

Negative sentence: Mitchell did not laugh outrageously.
Interrogative sentence: Did the plane soar?

Exclamatory sentence: How the plane soared!
Command sentence: Soar!
Cleft sentence: It was at 6 a.m. that Ollie and Joe set out.
Passive sentence: (not possible in this pattern)

Pattern 7 is noun phrase, transitive verb, and noun phrase.

Tom wrote a cookbook.

I looked up "pusillanimous" in the dictionary.

Negative sentence: Tom did not write a cookbook.
Interrogative sentence: Did Tom write a cookbook?
Exclamatory sentence: What a cookbook Tom wrote!
Command sentence: Look up "pusillanimous" in the dictionary.
Cleft sentence: It was a cookbook that Tom wrote.
Passive sentence: The cookbook was written by Tom.

Pattern 8 is noun phrase, transitive verb, noun phrase, and noun phrase.

Duncan gave me a ride to school.

He gave us directions.

Negative sentence: Duncan did not give me a ride to school.
Interrogative sentence: Will Duncan give me a ride to school?
Exclamatory sentence: What directions he gave us!
Command sentence: Give me a ride to school.
Cleft sentence: It was Duncan who gave me a ride to school.
Passive sentence: I was given a ride to school by Duncan.

Pattern 9 is noun phrase, transitive verb, noun phrase, and adjective.

This chapter is driving me crazy.

This makes it simple.

Negative sentence: This does not make it simple.
Interrogative sentence: What drove you crazy?
Exclamatory sentence: How simple this makes it!
Command sentence: Make it simple.
Cleft sentence: It is this chapter that is driving me crazy.
Passive sentence: It is made simple by this.

Pattern 10 is noun phrase, transitive verb, noun phrase, and noun phrase.

Ingmar considers bad weather a challenge.

All this publicity has made the affair a scandal.

Her accordion rendition of "Happy Birthday" in a minor key made that party a legend.

Negative sentence: Ingmar does not consider bad weather a challenge.
Interrogative sentence: Does Ingmar consider bad weather a challenge?
Exclamatory sentence: What a scandal all this publicity has made the affair!
Command sentence: Consider bad weather a challenge.
Cleft sentence: It was her accordion rendition of "Happy Birthday" in a minor key that made that party a legend.
Passive sentence: Bad weather is considered a challenge.

These patterns are basic ones and can be enriched with compound subjects or compound verbs, adjectives, adverbs, and phrases. For example, a sentence like "She sells seashells" (Pattern 7) can be expanded to "My cousin Suzanne, Uncle Martin's daughter, and Chris, who is her nephew on her mother's side, both package and sell authentic seashells in Laguna, a little town on the gulf." It is also legitimate, of course, to combine several patterns in a complex sentence (e.g. "She sells seashells, although her degree is in engineering.") or in a compound sentence (e.g., "She sells seashells, and she claims never to give civil engineering a second thought").

There is no need to learn the pattern numbers or descriptions of your sentences. We all can generate sentences that we would find difficult to analyze. These basic patterns are provided here only to help you focus on the essential elements of English sentences, which may be helpful if you are having difficulty distinguishing sentences from fragments or using conventional word order. The Sentence Workshops (Chapter 13) will give you practice constructing different kinds of sentences from these basic patterns.

Take the sentences bracketed on your paper and see if they match any of the patterns. You will not find a match if your readers were correct in bracketing what they did. If you have a sentence that does not match any of the patterns, you may be able to change it to make it match, just going by the way it "sounds" when you read it. Find the pattern your sentence "sounds" most like, and see if you can adjust it to make it match. If you cannot fix your sentence just by "sound," see if the problem might be one of the common mistakes that are listed in the sections that follow.

Fragments

Problem: Detached subordinate clause
This is the most common problem in sentence construction.

Although he never explained it very well in the first place and the textbook doesn't deal with it.

Whereas the real need on campus is for a decent lunch that doesn't cost a fortune.

Both of these constructions are fragments because they have no independent clause. *Although* and *whereas* introduce subordinate clauses, and there is nothing but a subordinate clause in each of these constructions. One clue to the absence of a main clause is the absence of the comma that usually comes after an introductory dependent clause.

Solution: Attach the dependent clause to a main clause. Most often you can simply combine the dependent clause with the sentence that precedes it.

> I think I can do the experiment, although he never explained it very well in the first place and the textbook doesn't deal with it.

> The SGA keeps demanding more football tickets, whereas the real need on campus is for a decent lunch that doesn't cost a fortune.

Problem: Main clause lacking a proper verb

> And having a difficult time, even though she knew what she was getting into.

After you discount the subordinate clause *even though she knew what she was getting into,* the remaining part of the sentence has only the participle *having* as a verb form. It thus lacks a proper verb.

> To sell the car or not—a difficult decision.

Although this construction is not hard to understand, technically it is not a sentence because the only verb is the infinitive *to sell.*

> The good china heaped up with trotters, macaroni and cheese, and hot water corn bread piled so high he could hardly see over it all.

After you remove the dependent clause *[that] he could hardly see over it,* the only verbs left are *heaped* and *piled,* which are both past participles.

Solution: Include in the independent clause a verb that is not an infinitive, present or past participle, or gerund. Often this will require you to include a subject too.

> And *she is* having a difficult time even though she knew what she was getting into.

> To sell the car or not *is* a difficult decision.
>
> or
>
> To sell the car or not—*that is* a difficult decision.

> The good china *was* heaped up with trotters, macaroni and cheese, and hot water corn bread piled so high he could hardly see over it all.

Fused Sentences

Problem: Run-on sentence
A run-on sentence is one that has two or more independent clauses run to-gether.

indep. clause   indep. clause

The only problem with that dog is his attitude he thinks *he's* keeping *us.*

indep. clause   indep. clause

I called the pizza place at 6:10 the pizza should be here by quarter to seven.

Solution A: Simply divide the two main clauses into two separate sentences.

The only problem with that dog is his attitude. He thinks *he's* keeping *us.*

I called the pizza place at 6:10. The pizza should be here by quarter to seven.

Solution B: Join the two main clauses so that one becomes a dependent clause.

Since I called the pizza place at 6:10, the pizza should be here by quarter to seven.

Notice that this solution will not work on the first example because neither of the main clauses can easily be made dependent.

Solution C: Join the two main clauses with *and, but* or *or.*

I called the pizza place at 6:10, and the pizza should be here by quarter to seven.

Solution D: Join the two main clauses with a semicolon.

The only problem with that dog is his attitude; he thinks *he's* keeping *us.*

I called the pizza place at 6:10; the pizza should be here by quarter to seven.

Problem: Comma splice
A comma splice is the use of a comma to join two main clauses.

I don't mind doing laundry, it takes my mind off geology.

The Puritans saw America as a wilderness, the Cavaliers saw it as a garden.

Solution A: Separate the two main clauses into two sentences.

> I don't mind doing laundry. It takes my mind off geology.

> The Puritans saw America as a wilderness. The Cavaliers saw it as a garden.

Solution B: Join the two main clauses so that one becomes a dependent clause.

> I don't mind doing laundry because it takes my mind off geology.

> Although the Puritans saw America as a wilderness, the Cavaliers saw it as a garden.

Solution C: Join the two main clauses with *and, but,* or *or.* (This solution would not work for the first example because you would lose the notion of cause and effect.)

> The Puritans saw America as a wilderness, but the Cavaliers saw it as a garden.

Solution D: Join the two main clauses with a semicolon.

> I don't mind doing laundry; it takes my mind off geology.

> The Puritans saw America as a wilderness; the Cavaliers saw it as a garden.

Rambling Sentences

Problem: Sentences with too many clauses

There is no rule governing how many clauses a sentence can have, but the ear can tell when there are too many. And so can the reader, who is running out of breath. Generally you should be wary of including more than four. Notice how hard it is to read this sentence:

> Burn-out is most common in the serving professions like social work, health care, and teaching, and it is characterized by a worker's sense of being "used up" and having no more to give, although the worker may still be performing competently in the job and receiving positive reports from supervisors, and many people experiencing burn-out say they are still committed to the same goals and values that led them to choose their jobs in the first place, and this adds a burden of guilt to the feelings of burn-out.

Solution: Divide the single sentence into several sentences with fewer clauses.

Burn-out is most common in the serving professions like social work, health care, and teaching. It is characterized by a worker's sense of being "used up" and having no more to give. Workers experiencing burn-out may still be performing competently in their jobs and receiving positive reports from supervisors. Many such workers say that they are still committed to the same goals and values that led them to choose their jobs in the first place, and this adds a burden of guilt to the feelings of burn-out.

Modifying Phrases

Problem: Dangling modifier
A dangling modifier is one that describes a noun or pronoun that does not appear in the sentence.

> Thinly sliced and slathered with mustard, roast beef lovers will appreciate The Diner.

> Walking to class, a paper topic occurred to him.

> My Uncle John sold lightning rods for a living—something of a seasonal career.

According to these sentences, the roast beef lovers have been thinly sliced and slathered with mustard and the paper topic was walking to class. The problem with the last sentence is trickier: there is no noun in the main clause that *career* can refer to.

Solution A: Rewrite the sentence to include the noun or pronoun in the main clause.

> Thinly sliced and slathered with mustard, roast beef from The Diner will appeal to connoisseurs.

> Walking to class, he got an idea for a paper topic.

> My Uncle John had a *job* selling lightning rods—something of a seasonal career.

Solution B: Include a subject in the modifying phrase. (This solution does not work with past participial modifiers as the first example does.)

> As *he* walked to class, a paper topic occurred to him.

Problem: Misplaced modifier
A misplaced modifier is one that is separated from the noun or pronoun it describes.

> As my research assistant, I was always pleased with his work.

Whether browsing with a friend or shopping for a gift, the Overpriced Boutique will be sure to please you.

Solution: Move the modifier so that it is next to the noun or pronoun it describes.

I was always pleased with his work as my research assistant.

The Overpriced Boutique will be sure to please you, whether you are browsing with a friend or shopping for a gift.

Parallelism

Problem: Nonparallel construction
Words that serve the same function in a sentence should have the same grammatical form. If they have different grammatical forms, they are said to be nonparallel.

He was elected on his promise *to seek* representation for part-time students on college committees and *of fair representation* of all campus groups in his cabinet.

Our society offers us the image of a superperson who is able *to hold* down a professional job, *to be* a loving parent, and *jogs.*

Solution: Choose one of the grammatical forms and make all of the others match it.

He was elected on his promise *to seek* representation for part-time students on college committees and *to give* fair representation to all campus groups in his cabinet.

Our society offers us the image of the superperson who is able *to hold* down a professional job, *to be* a loving parent, and *to* jog.

PUNCTUATION

This section will help you identify, classify, and solve punctuation problems in your writing.

Commas

Problem: Commas omitted before the conjunction *and, but,* or *or* and the second independent clause of a compound sentence

Picasso is considered the father of Cubism and Georges Braque is its godfather.

There is good nourishment in macaroni and cheese is a good source of protein.

Solution: Insert a comma before the *and, but,* or *or* in a compound sentence if the subject of the second independent clause is different from the subject of the first independent clause.

Picasso is considered the father of Cubism, and Georges Braque is its godfather.

There is good nourishment in macaroni, and cheese is a good source of protein.

(Note: This comma can be omitted if the sentence is very short and the omission cannot cause confusion.)

Summer's almost gone and winter's coming on.

The dog goes or I go.

Problem: Unneeded comma used within a clause

Early settlers came down the Ohio on flat boats, and populated the river towns near the falls and portages.

Solution: Take out the commas if the construction is all one clause and there is one subject for both verbs.

Early settlers came down the Ohio on flat boats and populated the river towns near the falls and portages.

Problem: Commas missing after introductory dependent clause

Although I do not have a summer job next September I will be in the money when I start my internship.

Solution: Put a comma after a dependent clause that opens a sentence. (There is no need to separate a dependent clause when it occurs at the end of a sentence.)

Although I do not have a summer job, next September I will be in the money when I start my internship.

Problem: Confusion of restrictive and nonrestrictive clauses
A *restrictive* clause qualifies in some way the noun it modifies. The *nonrestrictive* clause does not. Restrictive clauses are not set off by commas. Nonrestrictive clauses are set off by commas.

Here are the keys to the offices that are on the third floor.
[Some of the offices are on the third floor.]

Here are the keys to the offices, which are on the third floor.
[All of the offices are on the third floor.]

Notice that *which* is used with nonrestrictive clauses and *that* is used with restrictive clauses. This convention is breaking down, however, and the commas are the critical means of distinguishing between restrictive and nonrestrictive clauses.

Solution: Ask yourself whether the modifier applies in all cases or only in some. If you want it to refer to all, put commas around the modifier. If you want to refer *only to some,* do *not* put commas around the modifier.

Those students, who have passed the entrance test, will register on Monday. [*All* of those students have passed the entrance test and will register on Monday.]

Those students who have passed the entrance test will register on Monday. [*Only* those students who have passed the entrance test will register on Monday.]

It may help you to think of an invisible *only* appearing before the noun that precedes the modifier in sentences without commas.

We oppose tax increases that will endanger the economic recovery. [We oppose *only* (those) tax increases that will endanger the economic recovery.]

We oppose tax increases, which will endanger the economic recovery. [We oppose all tax increases because they all endanger the economic recovery.]

Problem: Confusion over use of commas with appositives
An *appositive* is a noun or noun phrase that gives some explanation of the noun it follows. It is set off by commas if its noun is the *only* person, place, or thing to which the appositive applies. It is *not* set off by commas if it could apply to a person, place, or thing other than the one named. (See also the discussion about the use of commas with dates and place names, p. 468.)

My brother, Tony, is looking for a hood for a 1953 Ford. [Tony is the writer's only brother.]

My brother Tony is looking for a hood for a 1953 Ford. [The writer has at least one brother besides Tony.]

The writer Emily Dickinson lived in Amherst. [Commas omitted because Dickinson is not the only writer. Notice that the rest of the sentence does not affect the use of commas around the appositive. Even if Dickinson were the only writer who had lived in Amherst, she still would not be the only writer who ever lived, and her name would not be set off by commas.]

Solution: Ask yourself whether the appositive phrase is the *only* instance of the noun preceding it. If so, put a comma before and after the appositive. If it is *not* the only instance of the noun, omit the commas.
(Note: When the appositive follows the name, it is always set off with commas.)

Emily Dickinson, the writer, lived in Amherst.

Problem: Confusion about use of commas after introductory phrases
The comma is generally used after an introductory phrase except when the verb is the first word after the phrase. The comma may be omitted after short introductory phrases. Notice how difficult it is to read the following sentences.

Grinning broadly Basil realized that he had sung faster than the band had played.

The bloody battle over the committee members returned to their departments.

Over the bridge and through all leaves of the cloverleaf she drove the highway for its own sake.

Solution: After short introductory adverbial or prepositional phrases, omit the comma. If a verb follows the phrase and it is *not* a command, a present or past participle, or a gerund, omit the comma. If the word following the phrase is something other than a verb or if it is a command, a present or past participle, or a gerund, use a comma after the phrase.

Grinning broadly, Basil realized that he had sung faster than the band had played.

The bloody battle over, the committee members returned to their departments. [An introductory element like this one is called an absolute.]

Over the bridge and through all leaves of the cloverleaf, she drove the highway for its own sake.

By late afternoon the sky was a clear green, and we were waiting for the tornado. [Comma omitted after "by late afternoon" because the phrase is short.]

Over the bridge and through all leaves of the cloverleaf *drove* Lavinia, enthralled by the interstate. [Comma omitted because the first word after the phrase is a verb.]

Before you leave, *check* for a phone message. [Comma used because *check* is a command.]

After the cicada appetizers, *mashed* potatoes and stewed chicken seemed a bit ordinary. [Comma needed because the following word is a past participle.]

After losing all her friends, *associating* with her enemies was Serena's only option. [Comma needed because the following word is a gerund.]

Despite what our advertisement said, *singing* waiters do not have the world at their feet. [Comma needed because the following word is a participle.]

Running for the bus, *tying* his tie as he ran, Bernard was also managing to chew gum. [Comma needed because the following word is a participle.]

Problem: Commas omitted around embedded phrases

Elaine after consulting her horoscope decided to change her oil.

Cesare consulting his analyst asked about his fear of turning up as a character in a cheap novel.

Milton wondered why if there is one crime for every two citizens he was neither a criminal nor a victim.

Solution: Be sure you have commas both before and after phrases that occur in the middle of sentences. (Do not confuse this rule with the ones governing restrictive and nonrestrictive clauses.)

Elaine, after consulting her horoscope, decided to change her oil.

Cesare, consulting his analyst, asked about his fear of turning up as a character in a cheap novel.

Milton wondered why, if there is one crime for every two citizens, he was neither a criminal nor a victim.

Problem: Comma omitted in a series
The comma is used to separate items in a series unless all the items are separated by *and* or *or.* If the only *and* or *or* in the series is between the last two items, put a comma before the *and* or *or.*

They are decent concerned and kind.

Solution: Check first to see if all the elements are linked by *and* or *or.* If not, use commas between all of the elements and before the final *and* or *or.*

They are decent and concerned and kind. [No commas are needed because *and* joins all of the elements of the series.]

They are decent, concerned, and kind. [Commas appear between all of the elements and before the final *and.*]

Many newspapers and magazines, in an effort to save space, omit the comma before the last element in a series. Both AP and UPI styles approve this omission, but readers still expect to see the comma in other kinds of writing.

Problem: Commas omitted in dates and places

He was born on April 16, 1909 in the old house on 13th Street.

Ian was born in Montego Bay, Jamaica in 1970.

Solution: If you write a date with the day preceding the month and year, you need no commas.

He was born on 16 April 1909.

If you include the day of the month, however, you must put a comma *before* and *after* the year:

He was born on April 16, 1909, in the old house on 13th Street.

Always put a comma both before and after the second element of a place name.

Ian was born in Montego Bay, Jamaica, in 1970.

Problem: Commas omitted around words of direct address, exclamation, or expressions like "I think" when these interrupt a sentence

This would be a better conversation confound it if you'd stop playing that trombone.

This would be a better conversation Charles if you'd stop playing that trombone.

This would be a better conversation I dare to suggest if you would stop playing that trombone.

Solution: Put commas before and after an expression of emotion, the name of the person spoken to, and expressions like "I think" when these interrupt a sentence.

This would be a better conversation, confound it, if you'd stop playing that trombone.

This would be a better conversation, Charles, if you'd stop playing that trombone.

This would be a better conversation, I dare to suggest, if you would stop playing that trombone.

Problem: Confusion about use of comma in introducing quotations

Solution: A comma follows a phrase like "he said" or "she replied" when these are used to introduce a quotation. This rule holds even when an adverb follows the verb.

He hissed nastily, "Of course I don't mind."

No comma is used, however, if the quotation is joined to the rest of the sentence with *that* or *as* or is distinguishable from the rest of the sentence only by the quotation marks.

Faye Nell described baklava *as* "molasses to airy thinness beat."

Greg answered *that* "no one in his or her right mind could confuse Dewey Decimal with Library of Congress."

When I left for college, my mother told me I should "never ask what's in the meatloaf." [The quotation is indistinguishable from the rest of the sentence.]

James called it "a shabby affair, best forgotten." [The quotation is indistinguishable from the rest of sentence.]

Problem: Confusion about use of comma with *i.e., e.g., that is,* and *namely*

Solution: Use commas before and after *i.e.* (the abbreviation for id est, Latin for "that is"), *e.g.* (or exempli gratia, Latin for "for example"), *that is,* and *namely* when they introduce a word, a phrase, or a dependent clause. Use a colon before and a comma after them when they introduce an independent clause.

That uptown bit of foliage is a ficus benjamina, i.e., a fig tree.

Numerous questions were on the table for discussion, e.g., what should be done about the roach problem.

That uptown bit of foliage is a ficus benjamina, that is, a fig tree.

It falls to the candidate, namely, you, to give an acceptance speech.

Commas are used here to set off *i.e., that is,* and *namely* because they introduce something other than an independent clause.

> Take care of his ficus benjamina: that is, water his fig tree and try not to move it.

> I have only one objection to this report: namely, you haven't given me credit for writing the first draft.

Colons are used before and commas after the two expressions above because they introduce an independent clause that restates, exemplifies, or names more specifically something mentioned in the first clause. See also the first example in the section on colons, next page.

Problem: Confusion about setting off *however, in contrast, indeed, likewise, moreover, similarly, so, then, therefore, thus,* and *yet* with commas

Solution: When these terms interrupt a clause or come between an independent and a dependent clause, they should be set off by commas. When they introduce a second independent clause in a sentence, they have a semicolon before them and a comma after them. When they are used as an adverbial modifier, they are not set off at all.

> There may be extenuating circumstances, however, which we don't know about. [*However* is set off by commas because it comes between an independent and a dependent clause.]

> There may be extenuating circumstances; however, I hope there aren't. [*However* has a semicolon before it and a comma after it because it introduces a second main clause.]

> However you look at them, these circumstances just aren't extenuating enough. [*However* is not set off by a comma because it is used as an adverbial modifier.]

Semicolons

Problem: Semicolon used between independent clause and dependent clause

> If it is a normal day, this lane is open to traffic from 7 to 9 a.m. and 4 to 6 p.m.; whereas during a snow emergency this lane is open for the duration of the emergency.

Solution: Between an independent and a dependent clause, replace the semicolon with a comma.

If it is a normal day, this lane is open to traffic from 7 to 9 a.m. and 4 to 6 p.m., whereas during a snow emergency this lane is open for the duration of the emergency. [*Whereas* makes the second clause dependent; therefore, the first and second clauses are separated by a comma rather than a semicolon.]

Problem: Difficulty separating items in a series when there are commas within the items

Notice how difficult it is to tell how many places are named in the following sentence.

Aunt Sadie sends postcards from places we suspect are mythical: Aachen, Holy Roman Empire, Glacamora, Portugal, and Ululume, Kentucky.

Solution: To separate items that include commas, use the semicolon.

Aunt Sadie sends postcards from places we suspect are mythical: Aachen, Holy Roman Empire; Glacamora, Portugal; and Ululume, Kentucky. [Semicolons are needed to separate the places because commas are used to separate the city from the state or country.]

Problem: Comma used where semicolon belongs, before *however, in contrast, indeed, likewise, moreover, similarly, so, then, therefore, thus,* and *yet* when these introduce an independent clause.

Usually a few parking spaces open up after 12, therefore I am not signing up for any classes before 1 p.m.

Solution: Check to see if these terms introduce independent clauses; if so, precede them with a semicolon rather than a comma.

Usually a few parking spaces open up after 12; therefore, I am not signing up for any classes before 1 p.m.

See also the last example in the section on commas, previous page.

Colons

Problem: Confusion about use of colon between two independent clauses

Solution: Normally, a semicolon and *not* a colon separates two independent clauses.

Mary has one failing; she has fewer virtues.

But if the second independent clause is an example or a restatement of the first main clause, or defines something mentioned in the first clause, a colon may be used between the clauses.

Mary has one failing: she invariably stops at the end of on-ramps.

The colon is used here because the second clause names the "one failing" announced in the first clause.

Problem: Confusion about use of colon to introduce a list

Solution: To introduce a list that does not include an independent clause, use a colon unless the last word before the list is a verb or an expression like *for example, for instance, namely,* or *that is.* A colon is used after *as follows* to introduce a list.

This semester Claiborne is taking physics, tennis, and vernacular Greek. [No punctuation is needed before the list because the last word before it is a verb.]

This semester Claiborne is taking three classes: physics, tennis, and vernacular Greek. [A colon is used to introduce the list.]

This semester Claiborne's three classes are physics, tennis, and vernacular Greek. [No punctuation is used here because a verb is the last word before the list.]

This semester Claiborne's classes are as follows: physics, tennis, and vernacular Greek. [A colon is used after *as follows.*]

This semester Claiborne has three classes, namely, physics, tennis, and vernacular Greek. [A comma is used rather than a colon because it follows *namely.*]

Hyphens

Problem: Confusion about use of hyphen between two modifying adjectives or an adverb and another modifier

Solution: A hyphen may be used between two modifiers to make the relationships in the sentence clearer, but it is not used between modifiers that come after the nouns they modify or when the first modifier ends in *-ly.*

This is a well-written paper. [The hyphen joins two modifiers.]

This paper is well written. [The hyphen is omitted because the two modifiers come after the noun *paper.*]

This is a nicely written paper. [The hyphen is omitted because *nicely* ends in *-ly*.]

Problem: Confusion about use of hyphen with numbers

Solution: Use a hyphen between compound numbers from twenty-one to ninety-nine, between the two numbers of a fraction, and between a number and a unit of measurement when these are both modifiers.

> Sonia was seventy-sixth in her graduating class, but it was a very small class.
>
> I'll be thirty-two when the century ends.
>
> One-third of all magicians rent their top hats.
>
> It was a three-month loan.
>
> Stress is a twentieth-century preoccupation. [The hyphen is used between the number and unit of measurement because both modify *preoccupation*.]
>
> Stress is a preoccupation of the twentieth century. [No hyphen is used because *century* is not a modifier.]

INSTRUCTIONAL SERVICE CENTER

Dashes

Problem: Confusion about use of dashes to set off interruptions within sentences

Solution: The dash is used both *before* and *after* an interruption of a sentence.

> As president of this group—you are the president, aren't you?—it is your responsibility to see that the coffee pot is unplugged.
>
> Ophelia deplores anchovies—and no one can deplore the way she can—and will not, therefore, consider the *el supremo* pizza under any conditions.
>
> These data have him buffaloed, but they have me even more buffaloed—is there such a thing as more or less buffaloed?

Problem: Confusion of hyphen and dash in written form

Solution: Write the dash twice the length of the hyphen or type it as two hyphens (--) with no space on either side.

Quotation Marks

Problem: Confusion about placement of other punctuation inside or outside of quotation marks

Solution: Put periods and commas inside quotation marks; put colons and semicolons outside quotation marks. When a quotation ends with a semicolon or colon, that punctuation is dropped. When a quotation goes in the middle of a sentence, its end punctuation is dropped unless it is a question mark or an exclamation point.

> Everett said, "I believe that my essay is perfect as it is."

> Everett said, "I believe that my essay is perfect as it is"; Theresa was heard to chortle softly at this.

> Theresa asked, "Why don't you let me be the judge of that?" [When the quotation is a question, the question mark goes inside the quotation marks.]

> Theresa gave a dramatic response when Everett said, "My essay is perfect": she fainted. [Period is dropped because the quotation appears in the middle of the sentence.]

> When Everett said emphatically, "Yes, perfect," I knew that yet another peer revising session was doomed to end in violence.

Problem: Confusion about punctuating quotations within quotations

Solution: Use single quotation marks to enclose a quotation within a quotation. If the enclosed and enclosing quotations end at the same place, there will be three quotation marks (on the typewriter, an apostrophe followed by quotation marks).

> When you said, "As Professor Witkin always says, 'Circumstances have prevented my getting to your papers again this week,' " I suspected you had not seen him at the adjoining table.

Problem: Confusion about capitalization within quotations

Solution: Capitalize the first letter of a direct quotation only if the quotation is a complete sentence (or, of course, if the first word is one that would begin with a capital letter for another reason, such as a proper noun).

> According to Charles, "If you go to Les Quatorze Gourmets you must sample the heavenly spam and eggs."

> Charles says that if we go to Les Quatorze Gourmets we must "sample the heavenly spam and eggs."

Ellipses

Problem: Confusion over use of three or four dots to indicate deletions

Solution: Use three dots to indicate material deleted within a sentence. Use four dots (three dots plus a period) to indicate that deleted material included the end of a sentence.

> Original passage:
> Traditional cooking in this part of the country may not be what modern nutritionists would recommend, but it is tasty and distinctive. Burgoo is traditionally made in caldrons over an open fire and includes ingredients like "two sheep" and "several bushels of corn." You make it when the whole county drops in; there is no such thing as authentic burgoo for two. Serve it with ham that has been soaking in a tub of milk for three days before it is baked. When the squash harvest comes in, coat slices with milk and egg and bread crumbs and fry them in bacon grease. Don't harbor any delusions about calories or cholesterol or fat.
>
> Shortened version no. 1:
> Traditional cooking in this part of the country may not be what modern nutritionists would recommend. . . . Don't harbor any delusions about calories or cholesterol or fat.
>
> Shortened version no. 2:
> Traditional cooking in this part of the country . . . is tasty and distinctive. (etc.)

Problem: Confusion about use of other punctuation with ellipses

Solution: Delete commas before and after deleted material. If you are deleting material that ends in a question mark or an exclamation point, use this mark instead of the period in a four-dot sequence.

> Original version:
> Norma, whose calling was tennis, claimed no expertise as a cook but could still put together an admirable pasta salad.
>
> Shortened version:
> Norma . . . claimed no expertise as a cook but could still put together an admirable pasta salad.
>
> Original version:
> Doctor, can you help me with my problem? You must or I am lost! I've become an obsessive proofreader.
>
> Shortened version:
> Doctor, can you help me . . . ? You must . . . ! I've become an obsessive proofreader. [Question mark and exclamation point replace the period—the fourth dot—when material is deleted from the end of sentences.]

Parentheses

Problem: Confusion about using punctuation and capitalization with parentheses

Solution: Delete punctuation before a parenthesis that interrupts a sentence. *Do not* capitalize the first letter of a complete sentence in parentheses that interrupts another sentence. *Do* capitalize the first letter of a sentence in free-standing parentheses. *Delete* end punctuation in an embedded parentheses, unless it is an exclamation point or question mark. *Keep* the end punctuation of a sentence in free-standing parentheses.

> I got my schedule by taking whatever was left during drop-add (last year the same consumer strategy led me to stock up on down socks), and I now see certain drawbacks. [No punctuation occurs before the parenthetical material which interrupts the sentence. The comma *follows* the parentheses to separate the two independent clauses.]

> I got my schedule by taking whatever was left during drop-add. (Last year the same consumer strategy led me to stock up on down socks.) I now see certain drawbacks. [Because the sentence within parentheses does *not* interrupt another sentence, it maintains its capital letter and end punctuation.]

Titles

Problem: Confusion about the use of underlining or quotation marks to designate titles

Solution: Underline titles of movies, books, newspapers, plays, magazines, and long poems. Put in quotation marks the titles of articles, book chapters, short poems, short stories, songs, and television shows.

> "Halfway to Silence" is the name of a poem in May Sarton's book of poems <u>Halfway to Silence</u>. [The title is put in quotation marks the first time because it is the title of a poem but underlined the second time because it is the name of the book.]

GRAMMAR AND USAGE

In your Editing Workshops, your classmates may have indicated what they perceived as errors in grammar or usage in your papers. Improving your writing by eliminating such errors will increase the effectiveness of your prose with your intended audience. Your attention to the details of appropriate grammar and usage will help convince your reader that you are careful about other details as well.

As you have learned throughout this book, you regularly choose language suited to your audience and purpose whether in speech or writing. The vocabulary, sentence structures, and expressions of your informal speech may differ significantly from that of formal speech and writing. This section is designed to help you recognize the errors in grammar or usage that may be noticed in your writing and to identify those errors so that you can correct them. Not all conceivable errors you might make will be addressed here, and some errors that you might think of as grammatical errors are discussed in the section on Sentence Structure. Most grammar or usage errors that student writers tend to make have to do with the use of verbs and pronouns.

Identifying and Correcting Problems with Verbs

Principal Parts

Verbs in English have three principal parts to indicate the time of the action expressed by the verb. Most verbs follow the pattern shown below: *-ing* for the present participle and *-ed* for the past tense and the past participle form.

Present Tense	Past Tense	Past Participle
wash	washed	(has) washed
borrow	borrowed	(have) borrowed

But numerous English verbs are irregular in their past tense and past participle forms and are either learned naturally through speech or need to be memorized or checked in a dictionary. The following is a list of the principal parts of most irregular English verbs.

If a verb problem has been indicated in one of your sentences, it is worth checking the preceding list to determine if the problem is merely one of tense.

Special Problems

Three pairs of verbs often create problems for writers because of their meanings as well as their forms. These pairs are *lie* and *lay, sit* and *set,* and *rise* and *raise.*

Lie/lay: The verb *lay* takes an object: Bob *lays* the book down; We *laid* our plans aside. *Lie* takes no object: Mother *lies* on the chaise each afternoon; I *lay* in the sun for three hours yesterday; The children have *lain* still for nearly an hour.

Deciding on the correct form here is simply a matter of asking yourself whether the verb you want means *to put* or *to recline* or *rest.*

Present Tense	Past Tense	Past Participle
am, is, are	was, were	been
bear	bore	borne
beat	beat	beaten
become	became	become
begin	began	begun
bite	bit	bitten
blow	blew	blown
break	broke	broken
bring	brought	brought
burst	burst	burst
cast	cast	cast
catch	caught	caught
choose	chose	chosen
come	came	come
creep	crept	crept
deal	dealt	dealt
dive	dived/dove	dived
do	did	done
draw	drew	drawn
drink	drank	drunk
drive	drove	driven
eat	ate	eaten
fall	fell	fallen
fight	fought	fought
flee	fled	fled
fling	flung	flung
fly	flew	flown
forbid	forbade	forbidden
forget	forgot	forgotten
forsake	forsook	forsaken
freeze	froze	frozen
get	got	gotten
give	gave	given
go	went	gone
grow	grew	grown
hang	hung	hung
hang (to execute)	hanged	hanged
have	had	had
hurt	hurt	hurt
know	knew	known
lay	laid	laid
lead	led	led
leave	left	left
lend	lent	lent
lie	lay	lain
lose	lost	lost
make	made	made
ride	rode	ridden
ring	rang	rung
rise	rose	risen
run	ran	run
say	said	said
see	saw	seen

Present Tense	Past Tense	Past Participle
seek	sought	sought
set	set	set
shake	shook	shaken
shine	shone	shone
shoe	shod	shod
shrink	shrank/shrunk	shrunk/shrunken
sing	sang	sung
sink	sank	sunk
sit	sat	sat
slay	slew	slain
slink	slunk	slunk
speak	spoke	spoken
spin	spun	spun
spring	sprang	sprung
steal	stole	stolen
stick	stuck	stuck
sting	stung	stung
strive	strove	striven
swear	swore	sworn
swim	swam	swum
swing	swung	swung
take	took	taken
teach	taught	taught
tear	tore	torn
throw	threw	thrown
wear	wore	worn
weave	wove	woven
win	won	won
write	wrote	written

Sit/set: Normally, *sit*—like *lie*—means *to rest,* while *set*—like *lay*—means to *put* or *place.* *Set* takes an object, while *sit* does not: Please *sit* here, Mother, and *set* the box on the shelf. Deciding on the correct form here, again, is usually a simple matter of asking whether you mean *rest* or *place.*

Rise/raise: The verb *rise* means *to go up* or *ascend* and does not take an object. The thing ascending does so on its own power: The bread *rises* if left in a warm place; The governor *rose* to fame despite his detractors. The verb *raise* means *to lift* or *move upward* and takes an object: You must *raise* your GPA in order to graduate with honors; *Raise* your hand if you wish to vote for this absurd motion.

Subject-Verb Agreement

A more serious problem that may be identified in your writing is the lack of agreement in number between your subjects and verbs. Very simply, if your subject is singular, your verb needs to match.

sing.   sing.

The princess bows before the queen.

plur.   plur.

The knights bow before the queen.

Of course, this consistency in expected in any clause in a sentence, not just the main clause:

sing.   sing.   plur.   plur.

George drinks coke even though his friends prefer sauerkraut juice.

Normally, you will not have problems with this kind of agreement. In certain kinds of constructions, however, it may not be easy to notice that your subjects and verbs are not agreeing.

1. When two subjects are joined by *and,* a plural verb is needed:

Pizza and *lasagne* ARE my two favorite Italian dishes.

If *Simon* and *Lucretia* ENTER the dance contest, *Roger* and *Hester* ARE sure to lose.

Exceptions to this pattern are as follows:

A. When each of the subjects is to be considered individually, usually with the word *each* or *every:*

Each *member* and *nonmember* PAYS the entry fee.

Every *student* and *teacher* DESERVES a certificate of merit for the excellence of the art show.

B. When each of two singular subjects refers to the same thing or makes up a single thing:

Vodka and *orange juice* IS a Screwdriver.

Room and *board* MAKES up close to half of the total bill of a college education.

2. When singular subjects are joined with *or, nor,* or *but,* a singular verb is needed:

Not only her *doctor* but also her *psychologist* FINDS her difficult to treat.

Either *Barbarella* or her *handmaiden* GOES to the artesian well each day to draw the healing fluid.

It is my belief that neither Central American *terrorism* nor the *fear* of Russian supremacy PREVENTS Americans from working toward peaceful negotiation with all countries.

3. When two subjects are joined with *or, nor,* or *but,* and one of the subjects is singular and one is plural, match your verb to the subject closest to it:

Not only the *professors* but the SGA *president* APPROVES the proposal.

Neither the *defendant* nor the *lawyers* WERE in the courtroom yet.

When this kind of situation creates a sentence that sounds awkward to you, try to reword your sentence to avoid the awkwardness:

Neither *Cordelia* nor *I* AM PREPARED for the exam.

The following sentence might sound less awkward:

Cordelia is not prepared for the exam, and neither am I.

4. Prepositional phrases that follow the subject sometimes cause confusion. Keep your eye on your subject, not the nouns in the phrase:

The *representative* of the hostile workers IS always civil to the management.

Not *one* of the sleazy rock performers HAS TAKEN a bath this week.

5. Pronouns such as *anyone, each, either, everyone, nobody* require singular verbs:

Nobody who has earned demerits IS ALLOWED to participate.

Everyone at the party SHOUTS "Happy Birthday" when Randy arrives.

6. When the subject is a relative pronoun (who, that), the verb agrees with the noun that the pronoun stands for (its antecedent):

Aren't you one of those mechanics *who* DOES reliable work for a reasonable price?

7. In sentences beginning with *there* or *here* (expletives), the verb agrees with the subject that will follow the verb:

There ARE three pregnant *ladies* ahead of me in the waiting room.

There IS no *hope* of getting tickets.

Here IS our *supper.*

Here ARE your *sandwiches.*

8. If a sentence or clause begins with the expletive *it,* you need a singular verb even if the subject is plural:

It IS spaghetti and meatballs.

It IS the neighbors from down the street.

9. A collective noun takes a singular verb when the noun is thought of as a unit:

The committee HAS its meetings on Wednesdays.

The team PRACTICES in the old stadium.

But if the noun is thought of as several individuals, you should use a plural verb:

The committee HAVE ARGUED over this issue regularly.

The faculty ARE DISTRIBUTING their class schedules for the new school year.

10. Titles of books, magazines, newspapers, films, and so on take singular verbs:

Ghostbusters WAS an incredibly popular movie.

The National Enquirer SELLS all the latest Hollywood gossip.

11. Some nouns that seem to be plural take singular verbs. Titles of courses, diseases, and certain other nouns thought of as a single subject or thing take singular verbs:

Home Economics IS not as popular a course of study for women as it used to be.

Mumps WAS devastating to Alfred at twenty-six years of age.

Politics IS something I can live without.

Identifying and Correcting Problems with Pronouns

Pronouns in English allow us to avoid repeating nouns over and over again as we write sentences. Most native speakers do not make errors in using pronouns as subjects of clauses or as possessives. But there are some instances in which pronoun use may seem a little tricky. If you find a *G* marked on some lines of your papers, and you narrow the problem down to a pronoun issue, the following examples may help you see how the problem should be corrected.

1. *Who/whom:* *Who* is the subject of its clause, and *whom* is the object of its clause. In the following sentence it is clear that *who* is the correct pronoun:

> Annette is the secretary *who* won an award as an outstanding staff member.

But if you insert an expression into the middle of the sentence, you may be tempted to write *whom* in place of *who:*

> Annette is the secretary *who* the Dean reported won an award as an outstanding staff member.

The subject of *won* is still *who,* despite the insertion of "the Dean reported."

2. *Whoever/whomever:* *Whoever* is always used as the subject of a clause and *whomever* as an object. Confusion might arise in your writing when the clause containing the pronoun serves as an object itself:

> Send the announcement to *whoever* you suspect would be interested.

> Notify *whoever* can be there.

> Give the package to *whomever* you wish.

3. A pronoun following *than* or *as* is treated as if the remainder of the clause were there:

> Rebecca is thirty pounds heavier *than* I (am).

> Aunt Gertrude spoiled us *as* much as (she did) them.

> Elmer was always at least *as* clever as she (was).

4. When *-ing* words are used an nouns (gerunds), both pronouns and nouns immediately preceding them need to be in the possessive form. In speech and very informal writing this convention is generally not adhered to. In formal writing it is:

> Charles could offer no reasonable excuse for *his* arriving home after midnight.

> Vanessa could no longer tolerate the *banshee's* wailing.

> *Their* failing to appear at the hearing gave everyone cause for concern.

5. *Pronoun/antecedent agreement:* An antecedent of a pronoun is the noun or pronoun to which it refers. In "The puppy whimpers for her master," the antecedent for *her* is *puppy.* In "The puppies whimper for *their* master," the antecedent for *their* is *puppies.* Pronouns agree in number (singular and plural), gender (masculine, feminine, or neuter), and person. If you have identified a *G* mark on your paper as a pronoun-noun agreement problem it may fall into one of the following categories:

a. A *person, each, either, everybody, everyone, nobody,* and *one* take singular pronouns:

Everybody brought *his* or *her* favorite dish to the potluck.

Each person has a right to *his* or *her* privacy.*

b. When *each, either,* or *neither* is followed by a phrase containing a plural noun, the pronoun to come is singular:

Neither of the twin cousins will bring *his* banjo.

Each of the women carries *her* own tool box.

c. *Who/which/that:* Use *who* as a relative pronoun for persons, *which* for things, and *that* for persons, animals, or things:

Everyone *who* was at the circus applauded Roseann for her skill with the trained ponies *that* performed in the center ring *which* was flooded by spotlights and filled with exotic music.

d. Collective nouns call for either a singular or plural pronoun depending on whether the noun is seen as a unit or as a number of individuals:

Veronica's club traditionally had *its* bakesale on Halloween Eve.

The club asked their parents to be sure to frequent the booth.

e. *Which/they/this:* Sometimes we use a pronoun that has no clear antecedent:

Daniel Ochs took honorable mention in the Trivial Pursuit Championship, which was truly thrilling.

---

*You may find the use of "he or she," "him or her," "herself or himself" both awkward and wordy. In this case you might decide simply to reword your sentence using a plural subject: "They all brought their favorite dishes to the potluck."

"Which was truly thrilling" refers to the whole main clause, and the sentence could be improved in the following way:

Daniel Ochs took honorable mention in the Trivial Pursuit Chamionship and was thrilled.

or

Daniel Ochs's honorable mention in the Trivial Pursuit Championship really thrilled him.

Similarly, we often use *they* in speech and writing to refer to no one in particular, or some generalized body such as the government, our bosses, or an administration. It is best to identify the *they* whenever possible.

In the Jazz Age, *they* wore beaded dresses, drank bathtub gin, and danced the Charleston.

Whenever the origin of the American short story comes up in the literary histories, *they* always mention Poe.

How could you make the *they* clear in each sentence above?

The pronoun *this* generally needs a noun to stand for. For example, "My father gave me good advice, and this is it: 'Always count your change.'" *This* clearly renames *advice*. Often, though, writers use *this* to refer to whole sentences or even paragraphs.

The incorrigible students hurled green peas, corn, and apple bits across the cafeteria, plopped mashed potatoes and mustard into each other's hair, and dribbled chocolate milk and melted Jello down each other's backs. *This* resulted in detention hall for everyone.

We know that the *this* in the second sentence refers to all that happens in the first sentence. Still, the second sentence might be improved by the addition of a noun after *this*—*this behavior, this performance,* or *this wild demonstration.*

Usage Glossary

This collection includes frequently confused expressions and usage items not discussed elsewhere in your text. It can serve as a reference for checking a word or phrase that may have been marked on your paper in an Editing Workshop.

Accept/except: Accept is a verb meaning *to take* or *receive. Except* is most often a preposition.

Everyone *accepted* the party invitation except Charlene.

Aggravate: Aggravate means *to worsen,* as in "The treatment only aggravated her already weakened condition." Informally, *aggravate* is used to mean annoy or exasperate, probably not an appropriate usage in formal writing.

Affect/effect: Affect as a verb means *to influence;* as a noun it refers to the feeling aspect of a person's psychology. *Effect* is most often used as a noun and means *result* or *impact.*

> When you wholeheartedly try to *affect* your students, you will probably have an *effect.*

Less often, *effect* is used as a verb, in such sentences as the following:

> The Governor would like to *effect* a policy change in funding for state nursing homes.

> or

> My lawyer *effected* a more than generous settlement.

Here, *effect* means to accomplish or achieve.

Affective/effective: Affective and *effective* are both adjectives, the former referring to the feeling or emotion side of a person's psychology, the latter to having a desired effect or result.

> By appealing to the *affective* dimension of a young person's psychology, we can often be *effective* in teaching him or her cognitive skills.

Allusion/illusion: An *allusion* is an historical or literary reference. An *illusion* is a false image.

> The speaker made an *allusion* to Mark Twain as an author with no *illusions.*

Alot: A and *lot* are two words.

Alright: All and *right* are two words.

Altogether/all together: Altogether means entirely while *all together* means all in one spot.

> The family, *all together* for the first time in years, rejoiced at grandma's being *altogether* friendly.

Amount/number: Amount is used in referring to weight or bulk, *number* in referring to items that can be counted. One might say "I had lost a significant *amount* of weight" or "a *number* of pounds."

Anxious/eager: Though *anxious* is used informally to mean *eager,* in formal writing it is probably best to use it to mean *filled with anxiety,* as contrasted with *eager,* meaning *excited in a positive way.*

> After the closing, Greta was no longer *anxious* about buying the condominium; she then began to feel *eager* to shop for furniture.

Apt/liable/likely: Apt means *able* or *appropriate.*

> Rosalyn strikes me as a very *apt* student; she made an *apt* remark during the discussion.

It may also mean *habitually* or *inclined to.*

> Wynn is *apt* to blush when she is called on in class.

Liable means *subject to, exposed to,* or *responsible for,* usually in relation to something negative.

> Not only was Dr. Jeffries *liable* for the damages to my Porsche, he was also *liable* to arrest for drunken driving.

Likely means *probable.*

> It is *likely* to snow today. That instructor is *likely* to be on time.

As/like: Like is a preposition, while *as* is a conjunction introducing a subordinate clause.

> Yolanda looks just *like* her mother.
>
> Mark roared *like* a lion.
>
> Do *as* I do, not *as* I say.
>
> Please clean your room *as* your father asked you to.

As to/with respect to: These phrases, though grammatical, usually create wordiness and may make your sentences sound stilted.

> Professor Husk came to speak to the president *with respect to* the predicted shortage of dormitory space.

Some politicians seem very little concerned *as to* the needs of the poor and the elderly.

Substitute *about* for each of these phrases for more direct, less wordy sentences.

Awful/awfully: Literally, *awful* means *awe inspiring.* In informal speech and writing we use *awful* to mean *messy, disgusting,* or *bad.*

His handwriting was *awful.* You look *awful!*

And we use *awfully* colloquially to mean *very* or *extremely.*

I was *awfully* tired by six that night. You look *awfully* pretty.

In formal writing, it is best not to use awful and awfully in these ways.

Bad/badly: Bad is an adjective. *Badly* is an adverb. The confusion of these two generally crops up in sentences using the verbs *to feel, look, seem, smell, sound,* or *taste.*

I feel *bad.* The child looks *bad.* The situation seems *bad* at home. The milk smells *bad.*

Badly is required with most other verbs.

Our secretary types *badly.* He also plays tennis *badly.* Worst of all, he sings *badly.*

Between/among: Use *between* when your phrase includes two objects or persons and *among* when there are three or more.

Just *between* you and me, I think there's trouble *among* the members of the Student Government Association.

Cite/site/sight: Cite means *to refer to; site* means *location* or *place; sight* means a *view* or, as a verb, *to spot.*

I meant to *cite* the newspaper article in which the *site* of the new high-rise apartment complex was announced. When the structure is completed it will be a beautiful *sight* for travelers coming into town across the Kennedy Bridge. They will be able *to sight* it for three or four miles before reaching the city.

Compare/contrast: Compare is used to refer to the telling of similarities or differences between things; *contrast* clearly implies differences. *Compare* is followed by *with* or *to, contrast* by *with*.

> This report *compares* renting a home to owning one. In addition, it *contrasts* the real estate market of 1985 with that of 1975.

Compliment/complement: To praise someone or something is *to compliment*.

> Rick, Stan, and Bill gave me *compliments* about the fit of my new jeans. Wanda *complimented* her class on their improvement in revising their papers.

Complement as a noun or verb refers to completion.

> The principal rounded up a full *complement* of safety patrols.

> Antoinette wore see-through spike heels which *complemented* her tweed miniskirt, her bulky rag sweater, and her alligator belt.

Consensus of opinion: Consensus means *a collective opinion,* so *of opinion* is not required. Simply "Our department reached a *consensus* after only two hours of haggling."

Continuous/continual: Continuous refers to an action that never stops.

> The *continuous* revision of this manuscript is driving us crazy.

Continual refers to an action that is repeated.

> Jennifer and Joanna had *continual* disagreements over which pizza toppings they would order.

Contrast: See *Compare/contrast.*

Disinterested/uninterested: Disinterested means *impartial,* not having a selfish concern, while *uninterested* simply means *having no interest.*

> Let me decide since I am the only *disinterested* person here; the rest of you all have something to lose or gain by the outcome.

> Carlos preferred to stay home and sleep; he was totally *uninterested* in mountain climbing.

Eager: See *Anxious.*

Effect: See *Affect/effect.*

Effective: See *Affective/effective.*

Et cetera (etc.): Et Cetera, a Latin expression, means *and so forth.* Thus, when you use *etc.,* no *and* is required.

> Raphael, the carpenter's helper, carried in the paneling, trim, hammers, nails, *etc.*

Except: See *Accept/except.*

Few/less: Few refers to items or persons that can be counted individually, *less* refers to quantities not counted individually.

> The university enrolled *fewer* males than females this year, but there was still *less* dormitory space available for the men because of the continuing renovation projects.

Good/well: Following the pattern of *bad* and *badly, good* is an adjective and *well* is an adverb.

> This new throat lozenge works *well.*
>
> Incidentally, it tastes *good.*

Hopefully: Hopefully means *filled with hope* and, strictly speaking, should modify a verb.

> John Edward waited *hopefully* as the winning lottery numbers were announced.

In informal usage, however, it has come to mean *I hope.*

I: See *Myself/I/me.*

Illusion: See *Allusion/illusion.*

Imply/infer: A speaker or writer *implies* or *suggests* or *hints* something. A listener or reader *infers* or *gathers.*

> In accepting the nomination of her party, the candidate *implied* that her opponent had failed to demonstrate leadership.
>
> Rosemary *inferred* from the annual college financial report that the cost of tuition would indeed rise in the future.

In terms of: Here is another phrase that leads to wordiness.

> *In terms of* politics, we clearly disagree.
>
> Better: We clearly disagree politically.
>
> *In terms of* our knowledge of the family situation, we recommend that the child be placed in foster care.
>
> Better: Knowing the family situation, we recommend that the child be placed in foster care.

Irregardless: The *ir* and the *less* in *irregardless* say the same thing, thus the *ir* is not needed. *Regardless* is the standard English word.

Myself/I/me: Avoid using *myself* to replace *I* or *me* in sentences such as those that follow:

> The scouts from Troop 970 and *myself* are planning to go caroling at Mildred's condo on Willow Avenue.
>
> Better: The scouts from Troop 970 and *I* are planning to go caroling at Mildred's condo on Willow Avenue.
>
> Dot and Pat brought hideous pink plastic flamingos as gifts for Lenora and *myself.*
>
> Better: Dot and Pat brought hideous pink plastic flamingos as gifts for Lenora and *me.*

Less: See *Few/less.*

Liable: See *Apt/liable/likely.*

Like: See *As/like.*

Likely: See *Apt/liable/likely.*

Me: See *Myself/I/me.*

Number: See *Amount.*

Only: Try to put *only* next to the word it modifies.

> Ellen wants to lose *only* ten pounds.
> (An ambiguous example: Ellen *only* wants to lose ten pounds.)
>
> If Rita would *only* relax, she could get her blood pressure down.

Principal/principle: Principle is a noun meaning *rule* or *controlling idea.*

> Acting on her moral *principles,* Mary Pamela declined to join the malcontents on the newspaper staff.

> Millard lectured to his class on the *principles* of an economy based on free enterprise.

Principal works as a noun or an adjective but most often means *chief* or *most important.*

> The *principal* characters in *Amadeus* are Mozart and Salieri.

> Leading the parade down Dixie Highway was Ted Pierce, the new *principal* of Holy Cross School.

Principal can also refer to a sum of money either borrowed or invested on which you pay or earn interest.

> Most of my monthly mortgage payment pays the interest on the loan, barely making a dent in the *principal.*

Quote: Quote is a verb, not a noun. *Quotation* is the noun.

> "I would like to *quote* Euripides here," remarked Cameron, smiling shyly at Tyler, his twin brother.

> The boys' mother sat on the edge of her seat, listening attentively as the *quotation* rolled off Cameron's tongue.

Rarely/seldom: These words are not followed by *ever.* The *ever* is simply redundant.

> Anita and Everett *rarely* speak a civil word to each other.

> Since the Kroger's opened down the block, Betty Lou *seldom* goes to the mall.

Real/really: Real is an adjective, *really* an adverb. If you mean *very,* choose *really* rather than real.

> When Gregory makes strawberry shortcake, he tops it with *real* cream, not Cool Whip. Believe me, this dessert is *really* good.

Seldom: See *Rarely.*

Sight: See *Cite/site/sight.*

Site: See *Cite/site/sight.*

Uninterested: See *Disinterested/uninterested.*

Well: See *Good/well.*

With respect to: See *As to/with respect to.*

CHAPTER 13

Sentence Workshops

Though your earliest spoken sentences were probably no more than two words, you were able to speak rather complicated sentences long before you could write them. By the time you began school your sentences were compound, complex, and compound complex. You knew unconsciously how to subordinate with dependent clauses and other structures, and following the speech of those around you, you spoke in a variety of sentence patterns. As you learned to write, you may have initially copied your own speech, and only later did you become conscious of the names of the parts of your sentences. Learning the names of the parts of speech and of sentences might have interrupted your natural flow of words in both speaking and writing for a time, just as concentrating on exactly how the manual transmission works in a car can interrupt the smoothness of your operation of the gears. Although you may possess considerable knowledge about the structure of your sentences by now, you still probably compose, in both speech and writing, more complicated sentences than you can diagram or analyze.

Being able to diagram sentences or label all the parts of speech in and of itself is of no particular value in improving your writing. Learning how to combine sentences, on the other hand, has been shown to enhance a student's consciousness of sentence effectiveness and to increase his or her sense of options when composing original material. Manipulating sentences to discover the effect of different combinations can help you understand the power of a single sentence within a specific context. By learning how to combine sentences, you can change undeveloped, lifeless ones into fully developed, vital ones. This is not to say that longer sentences are always more effective than shorter ones; in fact, a short sentence may be very dramatic and appropriate. Sentence variety is generally the aim of a good writer. With the exception of directions for putting together a toy or repairing an appliance, for which you might want very short, simple sentences, most writing profits from variety in sentence structure and sentence length. Along with good ideas, such variety can keep your reader from losing interest.

Active participation in this section will help you develop more control over your own original sentences. There is no other reason for focusing on the sentence as such in a composition course. In order to understand the variety of options available in each exercise and the effects of each option, you should work on these sentence activities with your whole class, or in small groups, rather than by yourself. There are three basic means of combining sentences: joining, inserting, and changing.

JOINING

By using *and, but, or,* or a semicolon, you can simply join two sentences together. The sentences to be joined need to be ideas or clauses that are closely related.

The stuffed onions looked delicious. I was hungry.

The stuffed onions looked delicious, and I was hungry.

Mary Jo plucked all her eyebrows. She still looked beautiful.

Mary Jo plucked all her eyebrows, but she still looked beautiful.

We could swing by Pasquale's for lasagne. Pizza Hut would be good.

We could swing by Pasquale's for lasagne, or Pizza Hut would be good.

Katherine's father married a lovely Frenchwoman who was twenty years his junior. Katherine and her stepmother then were approximately the same age and shared many interests.

Katherine's father married a lovely Frenchwoman who was twenty years his junior; Katherine and her stepmother then were approximately the same age and shared many interests.

Combine the following sets of sentences using *and, but, or,* or a semi-colon. Do not drop or add any words.

1. After a hot shower, Jane felt refreshed.
   It took a cup of Darjeeling tea laced with rum to rejuvenate her fully.

2. Hugh stood in line for an hour to get a ticket for *The Rocky Horror Picture Show*.
   He was glad he waited.

3. The clerk brought out sixteen pairs of shoes for Patti to try on.
   He was more than patient as she requested each pair.

4. Because he napped on the couch all afternoon, Roger had failed to accomplish any of the chores his wife had left for him.
   Expecting the work to be done, Rose Marie arrived home in a good mood, eager for a cookout and a game of Trivial Pursuit.

5. Professor Hutchins announced to his classes that they could submit their research papers the day after Thanksgiving.
   They could take a grade reduction and turn them in on December 1.

6. Rudy offered his thesaurus to his editor.
   She already had numerous synonyms in her head.

7. Peggy and Jack had strewn papers and proposals all over the seminar table.
   They had no intention of cleaning up the mess.

8. Dripping with perspiration, the ladies stirred the huge cauldron of homemade soap which was to be sold on Pioneer Day.
   By the end of the day, each bar would be wrapped in calico fabric, tied with a ribbon, and placed in a small wooden box.

9. The mauve velvet pillows might be just perfect on the navy sofa.
   You could try the muted, gray-striped satin ones to see how they would look.

10. Dr. Rice packed his instruments into his bag.
    He instructed his patient to follow directions carefully when taking the medicine he had prescribed.

Compare your combined sentences with those of your classmates. Where there are differences among the members of the group, discuss to what extent the new sentences vary in meaning because of the different kinds of connectors you might have selected.

Look at some of your own sentences in papers you have been writing for this course or for other courses. Notice how you have been joining your sentences and whether some of your sentences would be more effective if joined with the use of *and, but, or,* or a semicolon.

Often with a semicolon we use conjunctions, such as *however, in addition, in contrast, in fact, in other words, moreover, namely, on the other hand, that is, therefore,* and so forth. Try combining the following sets of sentences using these conjunctions. Remember, the conjunction is preceded by a semicolon and followed by a comma.

> *Example:*   Our dean has always sponsored a Christmas party for the faculty, staff, and students. This year there will be no party because the budget is depleted.
>
> Our dean has always sponsored a Christmas party for the faculty; however, this year there will be no party because the budget is depleted.

1. In the last ten years Americans have shifted their eating habits. They are smoking less and exercising more regularly.

2. The Congress wanted to support art, music, theater, and literature. It created the National Endowment for the Arts.

3. Within the normal range, the higher your body temperature the better you perform. The lower your body temperature, the less you achieve.

4. If we make the trip to Clearwater, Florida, we will learn how to surf. We will enjoy fresh seafood every night for dinner.

5. Walt Whitman first published his book of poetry, *Leaves of Grass,* in 1855. It was many years later before he achieved national recognition.

6. The library promised to search for the books I requested. I am not counting on their finding them.

7. At Interstate University nearly 90 percent of the undergraduate students live in dormitories or in university-approved housing. At the Metro University nearly 90 percent of the undergraduates live at home.

8. "Work," as Mark Twain said, ". . . consists of whatever a body is obliged to do." Play is its own reward and is performed out of intrinsic motivation.

9. Naomi believed that children should be brought up in a very religious atmosphere.
   She and Robert remodeled the family room into a chapel, complete with an altar, statues, kneelers, and recorded organ music.

10. Newborn babies do not have much in the way of social graces.
    They spit up, soil their diapers, and cry incessantly, all in the presence of company.

11. Dr. Newton claims that a college education may benefit students in a number of ways.
    It may help them learn to read, write, think, and use libraries, and it may make them less authoritarian.

12. Nat Turner is known as a rebellious slave leader.
    Nat referred to his "kind master" and said, "In fact, I had no cause to complain of his treatment of me."

13. We were exceedingly interested in investigating how, how much, and for how long memory is affected by drinking liquor or smoking marijuana.
    We reviewed all the research that has been done in this area in the last 20 years.

14. "Reginald, I'm sick and tired of your moaning and groaning about all the work you have to do around here."
    "Get out!"

INSERTING

A second method of combining sentences, inserting, calls for you simply to drop some words from one sentence and put the remaining words into the other sentence. Notice the following examples.

Example: Belinda wore a straw hat to the race track.
The hat was floppy.

Belinda wore a floppy straw hat to the race track.

Example: The child screamed.
She was stomping her feet and clenching her fists.

The child screamed, stomping her feet and clenching her fists.

Example: Giovanna threw off her apron and raced out to the Blue Light Special.
The vacuum was still running.

The vacuum still running, Giovanna threw off her apron and raced out to the Blue Light Special.

Example: Beethoven's Fifth thundered through the coliseum.
It was rendered by 100 electric guitars.

Beethoven's Fifth, rendered by 100 electric guitars, thundered through the coliseum.

Example: I searched among the pack of marathon runners for Joanie Benoit.
Joanie is the favorite in this race.

I searched among the pack of marathon runners for Joanie Benoit, the favorite in this race.

Example: Ms. Harper cleaned the party room after our class reunion.
She cleaned thoroughly.

Ms. Harper cleaned the party room thoroughly after our class reunion.

Try the technique of inserting with the following sets of sentences. Remember, you will need to drop words, but *do not change* any. Use the first sentence in each set as your basic sentence, inserting words from the other(s).

1. Mary Ellen ate all the red beans and rice.
   She was feeling like a starved puppy.

2. The bus driver accepted the transfer from the grubby child.
   The transfer was torn.
   The transfer was old.

3. As Peter tried to pick out "Lady of Spain," the moldy accordion began to squeak.
   It was sounding more and more as if there were a mouse inside.

4. For years Carl Sagan has argued with politicians about nuclear proliferation.
   He argues vehemently.

5. The tomato sauce eventually boiled over.
   It had been bubbling near the rim of the pot for 15 minutes.

6. Eric and Michele were break-dancing outside the K-Mart.
   They were dancing frenetically.

7. Fritz hopped out of the room like a bunny.
   He was giggling and twitching his nose.

8. Sister Dorothea called the meeting to order.
   She was the chairperson of the committee.

9. Trapper, the beagle, dragged the neighbors' garbage into my yard.
   He was growling and yipping.

10. Each morning Mark returned to his word processor to work on the
    manuscript.
    The manuscript was lengthy.
    The manuscript was boring.

11. We visited with Henri.
    Henri was the chef.

12. Dr. Pollock walked into the office of the Internal Revenue Service.
    He walked slowly and tentatively.

13. Fluffing up her blonde curls, Elaine settled into the big chair.
    The chair was red leather.

14. Eleven first graders appeared on my porch.
    They were taking orders for Christmas oranges and grapefruit.

15. Chris Harrington proofreads all the copy for *The Miscellany*.
    The Miscellany is the third grade class paper.
    Chris is editor-in-chief.

16. Eggs were hidden all around the backyard in the tall grass.
    The eggs were brightly colored.

17. Both the carpenter and the plumber arrived bright and early Monday morning.
    They were carrying their tool boxes.

18. "I demand that you turn over the merchandise!" yelled the officer.
    "The merchandise is stolen."

19. Suzette laughed when she saw her chihuahua wearing a wet suit.
    She laughed hysterically.

20. Gerald proudly accepted the award for outstanding athlete of the year.
    He was standing very tall.

21. The little shepherds, wise men, and three kings were dressed only in their bathrobes.
    They were shivering in the cold.
    Their bathrobes were skimpy.

22. Anita sipped her lemonade from a coconut shell.
    The lemonade was pink.
    The coconut shell was real.

23. Mildred bought her single ticket and approached the Tunnel of Love.
    She approached it very cautiously.

24. Judy appeared at the potluck with her extraordinary double chocolate fudge cake.
    She was beaming as everyone ooh-ed and aah-ed.

25. Gregory prepared a sponge cake to honor his peer group in the writing class.
    The cake was light.
    The cake was airy.
    The cake was golden.

26. His fellow students applauded and dug in.
    They dug in voraciously.

27. Computer technology is reducing the routine work that all of us have to do.

It is freeing us up for more creative activities.

28. Teenagers listen to rock music.
    They listen endlessly.

29. The workman turned off his jackhammer.
    The class was over.

30. The beggar stands on this corner outside Woolworth's every day.
    He is depending on the kindness of shoppers going in and out of
    the store.

31. Mother stood back to admire her work.
    The cupcakes were iced.

32. Gwen gave her mother a monstrous amaryllis for her birthday.
    The amaryllis was variegated red and white.

33. After Sunday brunch at the Bristol Bar and Grille, the two couples
    walked through the park.
    They were delighted by the sunshine and good smells of spring.

34. Take these badges to Ms. Morgan.
    Ms. Morgan will be your new Girl Scout leader.

35. Beatrice and Benedict stand around in museums, libraries, and thea-
    ters.
    They are absorbing all they can from the cultural atmosphere.

36. Barry was wearing layers of clothing to keep warm.
    He wore a turtleneck shirt.
    He wore a sweater and windbreaker.

37. Rita raced upstairs to dress for her party.
    The tulips were arranged.
    The silver was polished.
    The orange soufflé was in the oven.

38. Ralph recited the Declaration of Independence.
    He recited it beautifully.

39. The children ripped open the packages as quickly as possible.
    They were stunned by the generosity of Aunt Pauline.

40. Pat and Jackie cleaned the closets.
    They cleaned them thoroughly.

41. Rhonda gave the commands in the karate class.
    Rhonda was the substitute coach.

42. The GTI was ready for the snowy trip across West Virginia.
    The oil was checked.
    The radiator was filled with antifreeze.
    The chains were put on.

43. You should leave your shoes outside the door for Wilfred if you want
    them polished by morning.
    Wilfred is our valet.

44. Veronica was about to write her autobiography.
    She had her pencils all sharpened.
    Her paper was neatly stacked.

45. Dr. Cronholm makes the final curriculum and personnel decisions.
    Dr. Cronholm is dean of the college.

46. Martha Layne finally withdrew her budget proposal.
    Her hope was shattered, and her supporters were discouraged.

47. The whole family gathered on the patio for a game of Botticelli.
    The chores were finally finished.

48. Mr. Sabel presented his estimate for the papering and painting.
    Mr. Sabel is a well-known interior decorator.

49. Henrietta sank gratefully into her hot tub.
    Her feet were tired.
    Her muscles were sore.

50. Claudia taught poetry to her eighth graders by having them write it.
    She had them trying out various forms such as haiku, limericks, and
    clerihews.

51. Several locust trees shaded the deck.
    They were blossoming profusely.

52. The postman handed grandma a bundle of mail.
    The mail was junk.

53. Miss America walked gracefully down the runway.
    She was smiling but crying with joy.

CHANGING

A third method of combining sentences includes changing the structure of words. In the insertion method, the following sentences might have been combined as shown in the examples below:

Example: Maryann tossed bread to the ducks.
She was sitting cross-legged in the grass.

Sitting cross-legged in the grass, Maryann tossed bread to the ducks.

or

Maryann, sitting cross-legged in the grass, tossed bread to the ducks.

Without changing the structure of words, these are the only possibilities. If you are allowed to change the structure or forms of words, it is possible to create many more variations while essentially maintaining the same meaning of the two original sentences. The variations you can create result in subtle differences in emphasis and style. Notice some of the new sentences that can be created from the two originals when we decide to change structure.

1. Maryann sat cross-legged in the grass and tossed bread to the ducks.

2. To toss bread to the ducks, Maryann sat cross-legged in the grass.

3. Tossing bread to the ducks, Maryann sat cross-legged in the grass.

4. Maryann sat cross-legged in the grass to toss bread to the ducks.

5. Maryann sat cross-legged in the grass, tossing bread to the ducks.

6. Cross-legged in the grass sat Maryann who tossed bread to the ducks.

7. Maryann, who sat cross-legged in the grass, tossed bread to the ducks.

8. Maryann tossed bread to the ducks as she sat cross-legged in the grass.

9. As Maryann sat cross-legged in the grass, she tossed bread to the ducks.

10. While Maryann sat cross-legged in the grass, she tossed bread to the ducks.

11. While sitting cross-legged in the grass, Maryann tossed bread to the ducks.

Notice the slight variations in the preceding sentences, all of which express essentially the same meaning. The first sentence, for example, with a compound verb coordinates Maryann's two actions and gives them equal weight, while the second and fourth sentences clearly suggest one action as a reason for the other action.

The first sentence may be interpreted as a sequential statement while sentence nos. 3, 5, 6, 7, 8, 10, and 11 offer more of a simultaneous impression of the two actions. In some sentences—nos. 2, 3, 4, 5, and 6—the first action, "sitting in the grass," receives more emphasis by its placement in the main clause. In the others, the second action, "tossing bread to the ducks," becomes more important in the sentence and is found in the main clause. Including your key idea or action in your main clause rather than in a phrase or dependent clause is a good idea because it will let your reader know what you want to emphasize. In the sentences above, the variations may seem to represent extremely subtle differences in meaning, but in other more complex sentences, the variations may create more important differences. Consider the differences among the following ways of combining these two sentences:

Example: The Board of Trustees approved a tuition increase.
The Board of Trustees agreed to fund the construction of a new student center.

1. The Board of Trustees approved a tuition increase and agreed to fund the construction of a new student center.

2. The Board of Trustees approved a tuition increase for the construction of a new student center.

3. In order to fund the construction of a new student center, the Board of Trustees approved a tuition increase.

4. After approving a tuition increase, the Board of Trustees agreed to fund the construction of a new student center.

5. Before the Board of Trustees agreed to fund the construction of a new student center, they approved a tuition increase.

6. Agreeing to fund the construction of a new student center, the Board of Trustees approved a tuition increase.

Try combining each of the following sets of sentences into a single sentence by changing the structure of some words, adding necessary new words, and dropping unnecessary words. Remember, you do not want to change the basic meaning expressed in the sentences. Do not use *and, or, but,* or a semicolon to join two clauses. Create more than one variation for each set whenever you can. Share your new sentences with your class.

1. Ellen and Laura finally purchased an artificial Christmas tree.
   They were tired of shopping around for a perfect live tree.
   The tree was a spruce.
   The tree was 10 feet tall.

2. Estrellita and Roberto harmonized several different versions of "The Star Spangled Banner."
   They enjoyed themselves tremendously.
   "The Star Spangled Banner" requires excellent tone and range.
   Estrellita and Roberto entertained their guests.

3. Albert asked the woman in red satin to dance.
   Albert got up his courage.
   The woman was gorgeous.
   The dance was a tango.

4. My son gave me a book.
   He gave it as a going-away present.
   The book was valuable.
   The book was old.
   The book was leather bound.
   The book was a lucky find from Carmichaels' Auction.

5. The youngsters squealed "Surprise!"
   The youngsters were in costume.
   Their teacher burst into the room.
   The teacher was embarrassed.

6. The plane left at 7:05 a.m.
   The plane was going to Newark, New Jersey.
   We had to get up at 5:15 a.m.
   Five-fifteen a.m. is an ungodly hour.
   It is still dark at 5:15 a.m.

7. Uncle Donald made a sound.
   The sound was strange.
   He made it by clicking his false teeth.
   He made it by puckering his lips.
   He made it by whistling.
   Uncle Donald startled the children.

8. Mayor Sloane turned on the lights.
   He pushed one button.
   There were millions of lights.
   The lights were for Christmas.
   The lights were downtown.

9. The Surgeon General has warned us.
   His warning concerns the dangers of smoking.
   The dangers are numerous.
   He is cited on every package of cigarettes.

10. The snow piled up a foot deep.
    There were no chains for the car.
    It looked as if we were stranded for a holiday weekend.
    The weekend would be long.
    The weekend would be boring.

11. Steve made a sauce.
    He stirred constantly.
    The sauce was of cranberry.
    The sauce was of orange.
    The sauce was delicious.
    The sauce was colorful.
    He kept the sauce from sticking.

12. Charlene and Andrea worked.
    Charlene and Andrea are excellent mimes.
    They performed at the street fair.
    They worked from dawn to dusk.

They entertained all passersby.
They earned $37.00.

13. The Porsche crashed into the drugstore window.
    The Porsche was weaving.
    The Porsche was swerving.
    The Porsche was brand new.
    The window was filled with antique gumball machines.
    The machines went flying.
    They flew onto the sidewalk.

14. The whole family visited the museum.
    Admission was free.
    Parking was free.
    The museum was for art.
    The art was modern.
    The museum was blocks away.
    The blocks were few.

15. The pots and pans were washed.
    Jim and Vic grabbed the basketball.
    Jim and Vic were the athletes of the group.
    The basketball was soft.
    They took it outside.
    They inflated it with the bicycle pump.

16. Father Joseph wrote his letter to the Pope.
    He was using parchment paper.
    He was blotting each line as he went.
    The letter was humble.
    The letter was modest.
    He respected the Pope very much.

17. The kid ran away from home.
    He left his clothes.
    He left his marbles.
    He left his tin-soldier collection.
    Home had been his only security.

18. Beth looked in the window.
    She was shading her eyes.
    She saw Rosie.
    Rosie was looking out.

Rosie was squinting.
Rosie was frowning.

19. Students can create longer sentences out of sets of short sentences.
Students are clever.
Longer sentences are more interesting.
Shorter sentences are dull.
This is done with sentence combining.

20. Wayne made a statement.
He pasted produce labels on posterboard.
Wayne was experimenting.
The experimenting was with found art.
The statement was profound.
The statement was philosophical.

21. The Norfolk Island Pine towered regally.
The Norfolk Island Pine was ancient.
Its graceful branches drooped softly.
It towered over all the small ferns and palms.

22. The balloons were released.
They were released from the rafters.
The balloons were red.
The balloons were white.
The balloons were blue.
The band struck up "Hail to the Chief."
The band was from the Army.

23. Janet Foster served rabbit and peaches.
Janet was the organizer of the Gourmet Club.
Janet felt the need to be different.
The rabbit was fried.
The rabbit was smothered in gravy.
The peaches were pickled.

24. The exercisers completed the routine.
They were exhausted.
They were breathing hard.
The routine was demanding.
The routine was the most difficult of the afternoon.
The exercisers hit the showers.

25. Marva perches on a stool.
    Her work is done.
    Marva is our secretary.
    She is polishing her nails.
    She is polishing meticulously.
    Her nails are exceedingly long.

26. Goldie flipped through a magazine.
    Her husband was quite late.
    She flipped furiously.
    The magazine was stupid.
    Goldie chain-smoked.

27. Pompeii is still a port.
    The port is Roman.
    The port is busy.
    Pompeii has been an export center.
    The export is wine.
    It has been a center since 79 A.D.

28. Washington State's northwest corner reverberates with the energy of
    wilderness.
    The corner is awesome.
    The corner is remote.
    The wilderness is untamed.

29. The aldermen approved the housing project.
    The vote was 5 to 3.
    The project was funded by the county.
    The county will maintain the project.

30. I walked straight to the buffet table.
    I was determined to try everything.
    The table was crowded.
    The table was laden with every food imaginable.
    The food was delicious looking.

31. The teapot was the centerpiece.
    The teapot was lidless.
    The teapot was cracked.
    The teapot was china.
    The teapot contained spoons.

The spoons were dented.
The spoons were discolored.
The teapot contained a letter opener.
The letter opener was bent.
The teapot contained a corkscrew.
The corkscrew was rusty.
The centerpiece was my idea.
The idea was of junk decoration.

32. Seventeen agents met.
    Each asked for a separate check.
    The agents were of insurance.
    The agents were wealthy.
    The agents met for a lunch.
    Lunch was fancy.
    Lunch was at the Seelbach Hotel.
    The Seelbach Hotel had recently been renovated.

33. The engineers created a processor.
    The engineers had won an award.
    The award was for their blender.
    The blender sold more than any other brand.
    The processor was for food.
    The processor was spectacular.
    The processor could julienne a whole carrot in two seconds.

34. Parents should visit the baby.
    The baby is premature.
    The baby is in the nursery.
    They should visit when they wish.
    They should touch the baby.
    They should fondle the baby.
    They should develop early attachment.

35. Place a $5 bill on a table.
    Place it flat.
    Turn an empty bottle.
    Turn the bottle upside down.
    The bottle is of Coke.
    Place the bottle on the center of the bill.

36. Do not tip the bottle over.
    Allow nothing to touch the bottle.

Remove the bill.
The bill is under the bottle.

37. You join our club.
The club is for books.
You receive six books.
The books are free.
You select from hundreds of titles.

38. College students ranked their goals.
The college students were freshmen.
They ranked goals for a survey.
The survey was national.
The goals were of life.
The goals related to money.
The goals related to happiness.
The goals related to work.

39. Lancers Rubeo brings out the beauty.
Lancers Rubeo is a wine.
Lancers Rubeo is red.
Lancers Rubeo is for dinner.
The beauty is in things.
The things are simple.
The things are in life.
The things are steak and potatoes.
Lancers Rubeo sells at a price.
The price is reasonable.

40. We worked.
We planned.
We planned for 10 years.
We developed a new scale.
The scale was to measure susceptibility.
The susceptibility was to boredom.
Boredom is a problem.
The problem is chronic.
The problem is of adolescents.

41. The patrons have mugs.
The patrons are mostly graduate students.
The patrons are regular.
The patrons are at Rick's Grille.

The mugs are their own.
The mugs are initialed.
The mugs are provided by Rick.

42. The robber was chased.
The robber was thrown through a window.
The robber was arrested.
The robber was caught in the act.
It was all over in about five minutes.

43. In 1790 Americans drank beer and cider.
They also drank distilled liquor and wine.
The average amount of beer and cider was 34 gallons.
The average amount of distilled liquor was 5 gallons.
The average amount of wine was 1 gallon.
This amounted to an average of 6 gallons of pure alcohol.
Today's average is just under 3 gallons per capita.

44. The nurses made their rounds.
The nurses delivered medication to their patients.
They spoke cheerfully.
They smiled pleasantly.
The nurses were on the third shift.

45. B. F. Skinner keeps notebooks close at hand.
Over a period of 25 years, he has filled 100 notebooks.
The notebooks are spiral bound.
B. F. Skinner's first ambition was to be a writer.
B. F. Skinner is a noted behavioral psychologist.

46. Unemployment may rise again.
The rate of illness in children will increase.
The crime rate will increase.
Admissions to mental hospitals will increase.

47. Researchers have analyzed the way people walk on the street.
They wanted to determine who was most "muggable."
They found easy victims were the ones.
The ones walked as if in conflict with themselves.
The ones seemed to make each move as difficult as possible.

48. An American scholar reports.
She reports that Chinese psychologists are eager.

They are eager to learn.
She reports that Chinese psychologists may have a contribution to make.
The contribution is unique.
The scholar is writing an article.
The article is for *Psychology Today*.

49. Children learn statistics.
The children are from Japan.
The children have an advantage.
The advantage is intellectual.
The advantage may give Japan even greater success in the future.
The success will be in business and industry.

50. The rhinoceros is threatened with extinction.
The horn of a rhinoceros may be sold for $300 an ounce.
It is sold by smugglers.
Ways may be found to stop illegal trade.

USING THE THREE STRATEGIES

In this combining exercise, once again you are to combine all the sentences in the set into one sentence. This time, however, you will need to use *and, but, or,* or a semicolon. If you use a semicolon you may also use *however, therefore, moreover, in fact,* or other similar conjunctions. All of the sentences in this section will also require you to use inserting and changing strategies. For each sentence you will have two main clauses. Use all the combining strategies you have learned so far.

Example: You can listen to AM radio.
The AM radio stations broadcast school closings.
The AM radio stations broadcast cancellations of university classes.
You can listen to the campus FM station.
The campus FM station broadcasts cancellations of university classes.
The campus FM station makes announcements between cantatas.

You can listen to AM radio stations which broadcast school closings and cancellations of university classes, or you can listen to the campus FM station which broadcasts cancellations of university classes and other announcements between cantatas.

How else can these sentences be combined?

Now, create new sentences for this exercise. Create as many variations as you can for each set, and share your sentences with your class.

1. Shakespeare was born in 1564.
   He was born in Stratford-on-Avon.
   He wrote many plays.
   He wrote a sonnet sequence.
   There is a playhouse at Stratford now.
   The playhouse produces Shakespeare's plays.
   It also produces plays by other authors.
   Shakespeare is the best-known writer of the English Renaissance.

2. *The Prime of Miss Jean Brodie* is a novel by Muriel Spark.
   It is set in Scotland.
   It is set in the period after World War I.
   It is about a teacher.
   It is about the teacher's effect on her students' lives.

3. The plot of *Il Trovatore* is improbable.
   The music of *Il Trovatore* is splendid.
   The aria "Di Quella Pira" is especially splendid.
   The plot involves vindictive revenge and mistaken identity.
   Guiseppe Verdi wrote *Il Trovatore*.

4. It is possible to live much longer if you live at a much-reduced body temperature.
   You might live twice as long.
   At a low body temperature you can't think coherently.
   At a low body temperature there is little movement.

5. Tomato plants can be tied to stakes.
   Tomato plants can be grown in wire cages.
   Stakes support the stalks.
   Stalks need support when the heavy fruit forms.
   Cages provide support.

6. The new wing of the National Gallery was designed by Ieoh Ming Pei.
   The National Gallery is in Washington, D.C.
   The walls of the addition are concrete.
   The walls look like marble.

7. The original members of The Weavers were Lee Hays, Ronnie Gilbert, Pete Seeger, and Fred Hellerman.
   Lee Hays was a bass.
   Fred Hellerman is a baritone.
   Pete Seeger is a tenor.
   Ronnie Gilbert is an alto.
   On some songs, Pete would sing a countertenor over Ronnie's alto.
   One of these songs is "Wimoweh."

8. Elizabeth Nourse was an American.
   Elizabeth Nourse was a painter.
   She lived most of her career in France.
   She is one of the painters whose work is being reassessed.
   Critics are reassessing the work of painters who were contemporary with the Impressionists.

9. I put my red sweatshirt in the washer.
   I washed it on "hot."
   It bled on my only decent shirts.
   It shrank.
   Now I have learned to sort the wash.

10. The official biography of Sigmund Freud was written in the 1950s.
    It was written by Ernest Jones.
    Ernest Jones was an associate of Freud's.
    The biography is in three volumes.
    New biographies tend to put more emphasis on the intellectual dead ends Freud explored.
    One dead end was the sexual numerology propounded by Wilhelm Fliess.

11. Aztlan is the home of the Aztecs.
    The Aztecs traveled from Aztlan to found Tenochtitlan.
    Tenochtitlan is now called Mexico City.
    Today, Aztlan has come to represent a spiritual homeland.
    Aztlan is a cultural concept as well as a place.

12. The lunch special includes moo shoo pork and an egg roll.
    The lunch special is available from 11 to 2:30.
    The dinner special includes moo shoo pork and an egg roll.
    The dinner special includes won ton soup.

13. Oxford is a medieval university town.
    It is elegant.
    You can find many historic colleges there.
    You can find the Three Martyrs Tower there.
    You can find Blackwell's bookstore there.
    It is very difficult to find a functioning laundromat in Oxford.

14. Piazza d'Italia is in New Orleans.
    It was designed by Charles Moore.
    It is a good example of postmodern architecture.
    The AT&T building is in New York.
    It was designed by Philip Johnson and John Burgee.
    The AT&T building is a more representative example of postmodern architecture.

15. The executives took a great risk.
    They may succeed.
    They may be promoted.
    They may make more money.
    They may get better offices.
    They may fail.
    They may find themselves in charge of derelict furniture.
    They may find themselves working at the warehouse.

16. You are expected to attend the meeting.
    The meeting will be on Monday.
    The meeting will be on December 14.
    The meeting will be in Room 300.
    The meeting will be at 1 p.m.

17. Acid rain is infuriating Canadians.
    Acid rain is polluting lakes.
    Acid rain is killing fish.
    Acid rain is killing forests.
    Americans are less worried about acid rain.

18. The Universal Price Code is being phased into supermarkets.
    It is not always well received by consumers.
    It is a computerized system.
    The system is for reading product numbers.
    Most consumers would prefer to have prices on the products.

19. Isabel has been traveling to Spain.
    She has been reading in the national library there.
    She has been researching Arab influences on Spanish culture.
    Isabel has been working hard on her book.
    It will not be completed for several more years.

20. A Whig interpretation of history theorizes that there is progress in human history.
    One example of progress might be the replacement of the League of Nations by the United Nations.
    A Tory interpretation of history theorizes that human history is cyclical.
    One example of such cyclic movement might be the successions of war and peace.

21. It used to be thought that a person's intelligence was fixed and unchanging.
    It used to be thought that genetics determined intelligence.
    Now, many scientists think intelligence can be affected.
    They think it can be positively affected by the environment.
    The environment should be stimulating.

22. Traditional Marxists believe in the dictatorship of the proletariat.
    Traditional Marxists believe in the withering away of the state.
    Leninists believe in the dictatorship of the party leading the proletariat.
    Leninists do not believe in the withering away of the state.

23. She is Phi Beta Kappa.
    She is captain of the basketball team.
    She is treasurer of the senior class.
    She is a model college student.

24. I got this haircut from the Discount Haircut Warehouse.
    This haircut is a Mohawk.
    I'm having second thoughts about this haircut.
    This haircut doesn't do for my prom dress what I hoped it would.

25. Puccini's *Il Trittico* is a series of three operas.
    Each opera has one act.
    Il Tabaro takes place on a barge.
    The barge is on the Seine.

Il Tabaro is about adultery.
Il Tabaro is about revenge.
Il Tabaro is the first opera of *Il Trittico*.

26. *Places in the Heart* is a movie.
Sally Field stars in the movie.
It is a movie about the love that should join us all in the human community.
Some critics call the movie truly feminist.
Others say it simply shows a woman being as tough as a man.

27. Marcus Garvey founded The Black Star.
The Black Star was a shipping line.
Garvey wanted blacks to have some control over shipping among West Africa, the Caribbean, and the United States.
Many historians today see Garvey as a political philosopher.

28. You may enclose a personal check.
You may enclose a money order.
A personal check can take 10 days to clear.
It is wise to send a money order if you are in a hurry.

29. You can substitute parsley for thyme.
You can substitute parsley for rosemary.
You can substitute parsley for basil.
You can substitute parsley for nearly any green herb.
The substitution will affect the flavor somewhat.

30. Friends of the Library will have the opportunity to buy their tickets early.
Tickets for the Three Chord String Band will be scarce.
The Three Chord String Band is a group.
The group is amateur.
The group is highly acclaimed.

31. Tradition has it that Demetrios Ypsilantis fought in the Revolutionary War.
Ypsilantis was an American.
Ypsilantis emigrated from Greece.
Some claim that Ypsilantis is mythical.
There is a city named for Ypsilantis.
This city is in Michigan.

32. This proposal hasn't a chance.
    The committee won't approve this proposal.
    The department won't fund it.
    Your adviser won't endorse it.

33. I know that you are interested in student opinion.
    I trust that you won't be offended by my suggestion.
    I propose a change in college policy.
    I suggest we eliminate the residency requirement.

34. She is replacing the old officers.
    The old officers served under the previous administration.
    She is cleaning house.

35. You can park in a blue or green lot before 4 p.m.
    You can't park anywhere.
    There is never a space in a blue or green lot until 4 p.m.

36. It is a plush dormitory.
    It has private rooms.
    It has endless hot water.
    It has elevators.
    It has its own parking lot.

37. Langston Hughes was part of the Harlem Renaissance.
    Langston Hughes wrote *Tambourines to Glory*, a play.
    Langston Hughes is probably best known for his poetry and his fiction.
    Tambourines to Glory is about two women who convert a movie house into Tambourine Temple.
    Langston Hughes also wrote plays.

38. The Royal Irish Constabulary always wore bottle green uniforms.
    Many additional recruits were needed in 1916.
    These recruits were issued black and tan uniforms.
    There were not enough green uniforms for the recruits.
    They were called the "black and tans."

39. Edward O. Wilson wrote *On Human Nature*.
    Wilson argued for a new field.
    He called the field sociobiology.

The field encompasses the study of biological constraints on social organization.

40. History portrays Richard III as a villain.
It portrays him as someone who murdered his nephews.
It portrays him as driven by ambition.
There are those who think him innocent.
There are those who would like to see him vindicated.

41. I will be a sophomore next year at Cranston College.
I plan to major in bacteriology.
My GPA is 3.4.
I would like a summer job at the hospital.
I would like to be a clerk.
I would like to be an orderly.

42. Some people think that public television should accept commercials.
Some people argue that commercials will provide revenue.
The revenue is much needed.
Some people oppose commercials on public television.
They argue that commercials will hinder public television's broadcast of controversial material.

43. Some social analysts associate Dr. Martin Luther King, Jr., with the goals and tactics of the early civil rights movement.
The early civil rights movement focused on voter registration and integration.
There is one important thing to remember.
Dr. King was assassinated in Memphis.
He was in Memphis to support striking sanitation workers.
The workers were striking for higher pay.

44. Fire destroyed the Reichstag building.
The Nazis blamed the communists.
The fire occurred on March 1, 1933.
Later that month the Nazi party made gains in the election.
On March 23, 1933, the Enabling Act was passed.
The Enabling Act allowed Hitler and his cabinet to make laws without consent of the Reichstag.

45. Frodo is a hobbit.
Frodo is the main character in *Lord of the Rings*.
Frodo has many adventures.

Frodo is accompanied by Gandolf.
Gandolf is a wizard.
Frodo's most dangerous encounter is with a powerful ruler.
The ruler represents evil itself.

46. The first x-ray photographs of DNA were misleading.
These photographs misled some researchers.
The misled researchers believed they saw a triple helix.
An improved photographic method was developed by Maurice Wilkins.
The method was used by Rosalind Franklin to produce a spectacular photograph.
Her photograph clearly showed the helix.
It showed the size of the helix.
It showed the pitch of the helix.

47. Dr. Chien Shiung Wu conducted experiments.
The experiments were suggested by Drs. Chin Ning Yang and Tsung Dao Lee.
The experiments disproved a previously accepted law.
The law was the Principle of the Conservation of Parity.
Dr. Chien Shuing Wu is a well-respected physicist.
She is one of the leading researchers in her field.

48. The campus literary magazine is accepting work.
The work is poetry, fiction, or drama.
The work is by students.
Professors also may submit work.
Staff members may submit work.

49. You can register in January.
You can preregister in November.
Preregistration is done through the mail.
Registration is done in person.
You will be registering for spring semester.

50. San Francisco is a beautiful city.
It has a temperate climate.
It has hundreds of excellent restaurants.
It has outstanding opera, theater, and concerts.
The restaurants specialize in Asian cuisine and fresh seafood.
It offers amazing views.
The views are of the bay.

The views are of the hills.
The cost of living is very high.
Jobs are scarce.
Housing is difficult to find.

Appendix A

Documentation Guide

INTRODUCTION

What Requires Documentation?

You are obliged to let your readers know the source of every fact, opinion, and interpretation that you take from another writer, whether you quote or paraphrase. (You may want to review Chapter 6 on quotation and paraphrase.) This careful description of material is an act of fairness to the writers whose work you use and to your readers who have a right to check and judge your sources.

Some of the information you use, however, will be commonly known (e.g., 16 ounces equals one pound; the Wright brothers built the first successful airplane). When you are trying to decide whether something is *common knowledge* or not, ask yourself these questions:

1. *Does this information have a "discoverer" or a researcher who deserves to be given credit for it?* No one had to do any work to tell us that the Wright brothers built the first successful airplane. But a writer who gives us the details of the plane's construction had to do some research. He or she has made accessible to us some information that, although not previously unknown, is *not* common knowledge. The writer therefore deserves documentation credit for this detailed information.

2. *Do my intended readers all know the source of this information? Is there any reason for me to demonstrate that I know the source?* If you know that your readership will be limited to a specific group and that some information will be common knowledge to everyone in that group, then you may omit documentation of it. For example, if you are writing for a group of English teachers, you would not have to document the famous line "O, Romeo, Romeo, wherefore art thou Romeo?" Likewise, if you want to use $E = mc^2$ in a paper to be read only by professional physicists, you can count on their knowing

the source. This provision applies only to information that is common knowledge to all of your readership and is guaranteed to *remain* common knowledge. A certain research study may be famous one year, forgotten the next. Documenting preserves the information. You should consider your purpose as well as your audience when deciding what to document. While you are a student, for example, one purpose of every academic paper you write is to demonstrate what you know. Therefore, even though your reader is an expert who will know many of your sources, he or she will want to see you document all the information that is not generally common knowledge in our culture. When in doubt, document it.

Observing the Conventions

The mechanics of documentation are conventional; that is, they follow a pattern that readers can easily follow. Readers are accustomed to finding certain things in certain places. It is this implicit agreement, this pattern, that enables readers to process information quickly and efficiently. Writers are therefore obliged to follow the pattern *exactly.* Adding a comma or deleting one or changing the order of volume and date may not seem very disruptive, but they are, because they force a reader to sort them out, doing work the writer should have done. You can imagine that this does not dispose the reader very favorably toward the writer or the work itself. So take the time to do your documentation precisely, following the guide exactly. Ultimately, this will save you time because consistently using the correct patterns will help you learn them.

Two Methods of Documentation

The two most frequently used styles of documentation of sources are the ones recommended by the Modern Language Association (MLA)—*MLA Handbook for Writers of Research Papers,* second edition (1984)—and by the American Psychological Association (APA)—*Publication Manual of the American Psychological Association,* third edition (1983). If you are writing a research paper for a social sciences class, you will probably be expected to follow the APA style; if you are writing a research paper for a class in the humanities, your professors will expect the MLA style. The basic documentation guidelines for both APA and MLA styles follow.

MLA DOCUMENTATION GUIDELINES

Parenthetical Documentation

This method of documentation uses short citations in parentheses in your text to refer the reader to the full citation in the list of Works Cited, which appears at the end of your paper. To indicate the source of either paraphrased material or a quotation, follow the statement with parentheses enclosing the last name of the author you are citing and the page on which the material appears. (No comma separates the author's name from the page number.) Note the placement of the period and the quotation marks, if any:

```
The poem has been accused of being "as bad as surrealism
gets" (Kotula 211).
```

A Work by a Single Author

The purpose of parenthetical references is to lead the reader to the correct item in the *Works Cited.* The last name of the author and the page number are enough if there is only one author by that name or one work by that author in your list.

But if there are **two authors with the same last name,** include the first name of the author you are citing, for clarity.

```
The poem has been accused of being "as bad as surrealism
gets" (Walter Kotula 211).
```

If there is **more than one work by the same author,** include the title, or a shortened form of it, of the specific work you are citing.

```
The poem has been accused of being "as bad as surrealism
gets" (Kotula, Surrealism 211).
```

If the work has **more than one volume,** cite the volume number followed by a colon and the page number.

```
Karl Young has argued that there is a historical period
in which it is difficult to distinguish between "dramatic
offices" and plays (1:410).
```

If you **include all of the necessary information** about the author in your text, you need give only the page number(s) in parentheses.

```
Karl Young, in the first volume of his monumental study,
argues that there is a historical period in which it is
difficult to distinguish between ''dramatic offices'' and
plays (410).
```

A Work by More Than One Author

If a work you want to cite has more than one author, give the last name of each, in the order in which they are listed on the work you are citing. Or give the first author's name, followed by "et al.," if there are more than three authors altogether. (Note that "et al.," short for *et alii—and others*—is always followed by a period.)

```
The Laughing Policeman (Sjowall and Wahlöö) was voted the
best mystery novel of 1970.
```

or

```
Lully died of a wound he suffered while conducting (Ja-
cobs et al.).
```

A Work for Whom No Author Is listed

Some magazine articles, some encyclopedia entries, and many government and agency reports have no single, specific author. If there is no author listed, include in your parentheses the title of the work and page number.

```
The Little Mermaid statue has several times been repaired
after vandalism (Guide to Copenhagen 12).
```

More Than One Work per Reference

If a single parenthetical reference cites more than one work, separate the works with semicolons.

```
Recent researchers have called into question this equa-
tion (Keily 126; Moran 232-41; Salamone et al. 96-104).
```

Literary Works

Many literary works are available in more than one edition. As a convenience to readers who have an edition different from the one you work from, give a chapter or section or stanza. If you give line numbers, either use the word "lines" or just give the numbers. (Avoid l. or ll. because these are too easily confused with numerals). When you cite a literary work, first give the page number, followed by a semicolon and any additional locating information (pt., ch., sec.).

```
The friend in The Romance of the Rose explains how gifts
engender love (166; sec. 39).
```

Interviews

If citing information gained in an interview, it is usually best to include in the text itself all of the information the reader needs to find the correct item in the list of works consulted. Most often, you will not need parenthetical documentation.

Works Cited

The parenthetical documentation in your text serves to lead readers from specific material in your text to the full reference for this material in the Works Cited. This appears at the end of your paper. You may have already written papers that included a bibliography. The term *Works Cited* is now preferred, however, because it may include nonprint items and because it makes clear that you used all of these works. (If your instructor asks for inclusion of those works that you consulted but did not cite, you should title your list *Works Consulted.*)

Order and Arrangement of Items

The title *Works Cited* should be centered on the page. There should be a double space between the title and the first entry. Double space the lines of each entry and the space between entries. If one entry takes more than one line, indent five spaces for the subsequent lines of that entry.

Items are listed, whenever possible, alphabetically by the author's last name. If the author is unknown, place the entry alphabetically by the first word of the title (excluding *A, An,* and *The*).

Books

The listing for a book may include the following items in this order.

1. *Author's Name:* Type the last name, a comma, and then the first name, as it appears on the title page. Use the full name rather than a first initial, unless only the initial is given.
2. *Title of the Book:* Give the full title exactly as it appears, and underline it. Put a period after the underlined title. If only a portion of a book (e.g., a chapter, the preface) was relevant to your study, give the name of that portion, followed by a period and two spaces and then the name of the book. Capitalize all words in the title except for articles, conjunctions, and prepositions.
3. *Editor's or Translator's Name* (if any): Type *Ed.* (or *Trans.*), followed by the person's name as given, then a period.
4. *Edition:* If the book's copyright page indicates that it is a second or subsequent edition, give the numeric abbreviation of the edition (2nd, 3rd, 4th) and type *ed.*
5. *Volume Number:* Indicate the total number of volumes in the edition of the work you used, if there is more than one volume. Use the numeral for the number of volumes, then type *vols.*
6. *Place of Publication, Publisher, and Date of Copyright:* If more than one city is listed, give only the first. Place a colon after the place of publication and leave two spaces before the publisher's name. Use a shortened form of the publisher's name (e.g., *Harcourt* for Harcourt Brace Jovanovich, Inc.; UP for University Press), followed by a comma and a single space. The copyright date should be the date of the edition you used. Type a period after the date.
7. *Page Numbers:* Page numbers are required when you have used only a portion of a book. For example, if only one chapter of a book was relevant to your topic, you would give the page numbers of that

chapter: 76–92, 137–45. If you used one volume of a multivolume work, give the volume number, type a colon, two spaces, then the inclusive page numbers, and close with a period.

Sample Entries: Books

A Book by a Single Author

Van Dyke, Carolynn. <u>The Fiction of Truth: Structures of Meaning in Narrative and Dramatic Allegory</u>. Ithaca: Cornell UP, 1985.

An Anthology

Zaranka, William, ed. <u>The Brand–X Anthology of Poetry: A Parody Anthology</u>. Cambridge, MA: Apple–Wood, 1981.

Two or More Books by the Same Author

To list a second or subsequent book by the same author, do not repeat the author's name, but replace it with three hyphens, followed by a period. If the person is not strictly the author but a compiler or an editor, replace the period with a comma, add the abbreviation *comp.* or *ed.* after the name, and follow it with a period.

Tey, Josephine. <u>Brat Farrar</u>. New York: Berkley, 1949.

–––. <u>Miss Pym Disposes</u>. New York: Berkley, 1947.

Multiple Authors

List multiple authors in the order in which they are given in the book. Do not invert second and subsequent authors' names.

Beckman, Peter, and Marietta Bennet. <u>Rock Music</u>. Cincinnati: Entrepreneur, 1980.

A Corporate Author

Give the complete name of the corporate author without inverting the order of the words.

National Council of Teachers of English. <u>Statement on the Preparation of Teachers of English and the Language Arts</u>. Urbana: National Council of Teachers of English, 1976.

An Anonymous Book

If a book lists no author, begin the entry with the title. Give the title exactly, but alphabetize it by the first word other than *A, An,* or *The.*

<u>Guide to Copenhagen</u>. Copenhagen: n.p., 1985.
(<u>N.p.</u> indicates that no publisher is given.)

A Selection in an Anthology

Articles, essays, and short stories in an anthology are set apart by quotation marks and followed by a period. The selection's author is listed first, and the anthology's editor is listed after the title of the book.

Drayton, Michael. "Since There's No Help, Come Let Us
    Kiss and Part." <u>The Norton Anthology of English Liter-
    ature</u>. Ed. M. H. Abrams et al. 2nd ed. 2 vols. New
    York: Norton, 1968. 1:837.

A Preface, Forward, or Introduction

Kinsella, Thomas. Introduction. <u>The Tain</u>. Trans. Kin-
    sella. London: Oxford UP, 1970. ix—xvi.

A Multivolume Work

Drayton, Michael. "Since There's No Help, Come Let Us
    Kiss and Part." <u>The Norton Anthology of English Liter-
    ature</u>. Ed. M. H. Abrams et al. 2nd ed. 2 vols. New
    York: Norton, 1968. 1:837.

An Edition

Clemens, Samuel Langhorne. <u>The Adventures of Huckleberry
    Finn</u>. Ed. Sculley Bradley et al. New York: Norton,
    1961.

A Translation

Sjowall, Maj, and Per Wahlöö. <u>The Laughing Policeman</u>.
    Trans. Alan Blair, 1968. New York: Viking, 1970.

An Item in a Reference Book

Begin the entry with the author of the article, if a name is given. If the article is unsigned, begin with the title of the article.

"Photography." <u>Encyclopedia Americana</u>. 1980 ed.

Government Publications

United States Dept. of Education. Administration of Public Laws 81–874 and 81–815. Thirtieth annual report.
Washington: GPO, fiscal year 1980.

Multiple Publishers

Laird, Ian. Flodden Field. London: Kelvin; New York:
Walsh, 1936.

A Book in a Language Other Than English

Thurneysen, Rudolf, ed. Scila Mucce Meic Dath. [Tidings
of Mac Datho's Pig]. Dublin: Dublin Institute for Advanced Studies, 1935.

Sample Entries: Periodicals

The listing for an article in a periodical may include the following items in this
order.

1. *Author's name:* Same as books.
2. *Title of Article:* Enclose the title in quotation marks, close with a period.
3. *Name of Periodical:* Underline this title.
4. *Volume Number:* The number immediately follows the journal title.
5. *Publication Date:* Give the year of publication in parentheses. For daily,
   weekly, or monthly periodicals, omit the volume number and give
   only the date in an inverted form (5 May 1983). Abbreviate the names
   of the longer months.
6. *Page Numbers:* Give the page numbers for the entire article, not just
   the portion you used. If an article is interrupted by other material
   on numbered pages, just give the first page number and a plus sign
   (92+).

From a Periodical

Mooers, Stephanie L. "Patronage in the Pipe Roll of
1130." Speculum 59 (1984):282–307.

From a Periodical That Begins Each Issue with Page One

Peters, William H. "Teacher Behavior and Student Response
to Literature." Kentucky English Bulletin 31.2 (Winter
1981–82):3–8.

Andersen, Kurt. "Jackson Plays by the Rules." Time 5 Nov.
1984:29.

From a Daily Newspaper

Garrett, Robert T. "Collins Considering Special Session
    on Education, Official Says." Courier-Journal [Louis-
    ville] 4 April 1985, metro ed.:A1+.

From an Editorial

"Bennett Offers a New Way to Imperil Public Schools." Ed-
    itorial. Courier-Journal [Louisville] 4 April 1985,
    metro ed.:A10.

From a Letter to the Editor

Wilson, Mary Virginia McMullan. Letter. Courier-Journal
    [Louisville] 4 April 1985, metro ed.:A10.

From a Review

Branscum, Deborah. Rev. of Murder in the Collective, by
    Barbara Wilson. Mother Jones April 1985:56.

Jones, Lynette. Rev. of Whoopi Goldberg. Lyceum, New
    York. Covedale Reporter [Ohio] 22 Feb. 1985:3.

Sample Entries: Other Material

From a Radio or Television Program

I'm Too Busy to Talk Now—Conversations with American Art-
    ists over 70: Artist Louise Nevelson NPR, WFPL, Louis-
    ville. 4 April 1985.

From a Recording

Near, Holly. Journeys. Redwood Records, RR405, 1983.

From a Film or Videotape

The Purple Rose of Cairo. Dir. Woody Allen. Orion, 1985.
                                or
Allen, Woody, dir. The Purple Rose of Cairo. Orion, 1985.

From a Performance

'night Mother. By Marsha Norman. Dir. Kathy Bates. Ac-
    tor's Theater, Louisville. 10 Feb. 1985.

From an Interview

Begin with the name of the person interviewed. The name of the interviewer is usually omitted, unless it is of special interest, in which case you can add "With [name of interviewer]" before the name of the publication, if any.

```
Galvin, Terence. Interview. St. James College Commenta-
    tor. 15 May 1985:3.

DiGregorio, Christine. Personal interview. 6 Sept. 1985.
```

From a Speech

```
Jackson, Jesse. Address. Democratic National Convention.
    17 July 1984.

Hairston, Maxine. "Breaking Our Bonds but Re-affirming
    Our Connections." Opening General Session, Conference
    on College Composition and Communication. Minneapolis,
    21 March 1985.
```

Endnote System

The Modern Language Association also endorses another system of documentation, one in which the endnotes replace parenthetical documentation and make the Works Cited optional. (Ask your instructor if you should include a Works Cited section.) In this system, you place a number slightly above the line at the point in your text where the parenthetical reference would have been, that is, directly after the material you are citing.

```
There is some controversy over the number of characters
in colonial American literature who died of spontaneous
combustion.[1]
```

Note references are numbered consecutively throughout your text, and they follow all punctuation except dashes.

Endnotes are typed on a separate page at the end of your paper. Center the word *Notes* at the top of the page and start the endnotes two lines under the title. Five spaces from the left margin, type the number *1* slightly above the line. Space once and begin the first endnote. If a note takes more than one line, begin subsequent lines at the left margin. Double space within and between notes.

Sample Endnotes: First References

The first reference to a work includes all of the information necessary to lead the reader to the correct work and the correct page. Usually, this is the author's name, the name of the work, the place of publication, publisher, date of publication, and page number. The following are sample first references for various kinds of works. Note that the author's name is not inverted.

A Book by a Single Author

[1]Carolynn Van Dyke, The Fiction of Truth: Structures of Meaning in Narrative and Dramatic Allegory (Ithaca: Cornell UP, 1985) 60.

An Anthology

[2]William Zaranka, ed. The Brand-X Anthology of Poetry: A Parody Anthology (Cambridge: Apple-Wood, 1981) 12.

A Book by More Than One Author

[3]Peter Beckman and Marietta Bennet, Rock Music (Cincinnati: Entrepreneur, 1980) 23-26.

A Book by a Corporate Author

[4]National Council of Teachers of English, Statement on the Preparation of Teachers of English and the Language Arts (Urbana: National Council of Teachers of English, 1976) 1.

An Anonymous Book

[5]Guide to Copenhagen (Copenhagen: n.p., 1985) 8.

A Work in an Anthology

[6]Michael Drayton, "Since There's No Help, Come Let Us Kiss and Part," The Norton Anthology of English Literature, ed. M. H. Abrams et al., 2nd ed., 2 vols. (New York: Norton, 1968) 1:837.

An Introduction, Preface, or Forward

[7]Thomas Kinsella, introduction, The Tain (London: Oxford UP, 1970) xv.

A Multivolume Work

[8]M. H. Abrams et al., The Norton Anthology of English Literature, 2nd ed., 2 vols. (New York: Norton, 1968) 1:837.

An Edition

[9]Samuel Langhorne Clemens, The Adventures of Huckleberry Finn, ed. Sculley Bradley et al. (New York: Norton, 1961) 204.

A Translation

[10]Maj Sjowall and Per Wahlöö, The Laughing Policeman, trans. Alan Blair (New York: Viking, 1970) 49.

An Article in a Reference Book

[11]"Photography," Encyclopedia Americana, 1980 ed.

A Government Publication

[12]United States Department of Education, Administration of Public Laws 81-874 and 81-815 (Washington: GPO, 1980) 6-7.

A Book with More Than One Publisher

[13]Ian Laird, Flodden Field (London: Kelvin; New York: Walsh, 1936) 48-51.

A Book in a Language Other Than English

[14]Rudolf Thurneysen, ed., Scila Mucce Meic Datho [Saga of Mac Datho's Pig] (Dublin: Dublin Institute for Advanced Studies, 1935) 14.

An Article in a Journal with Continuous Pagination
[15]Stephanie L. Mooers, "Patronage in the Pipe Roll of 1130," Speculum 59 (1984):300.

An Article in a Journal That Begins Each Issue with Page One
[16]William H. Peters, "Teacher Behavior and Student Response to Literature," Kentucky English Bulletin 31.2 (Winter 1981–82):5.

An Article from a Weekly or Biweekly Publication
[17]Kurt Andersen, "Jackson Plays by the Rules," Time 5 Nov. 1984:29.

An Article from a Monthly or Bimonthly Publication
[18]David Osborne, "Business in Space," Atlantic Monthly May 1985:53+.

A Newspaper Article
[19]Robert T. Garrett, "Collins Considering Special Session on Education, Official Says," Courier–Journal [Louisville] 4 April 1985, metro ed.:A1.

An Editorial
[20]"Bennett Offers a New Way to Imperil Public Schools," editorial, Courier–Journal [Louisville] 4 April 1985, metro ed.:A10.

A Letter to the Editor
[21]Mary Virginia McMullan Wilson, letter, Courier–Journal [Louisville] 4 April 1985, metro ed.:A10.

A Review
[22]Deborah Branscum, rev. of Murder in the Collective, by Barbara Wilson, Mother Jones April 1985:56.

A Radio or Television Program
[23]I'm Too Busy to Talk Now––Conversations with American Artists over 70: Artist Louise Nevelson, NPR, WFPL, Louisville, 4 April 1985.

A Recording
[24]Holly Near, Journeys, Redwood Records, RR405, 1983.

A Film
[25]The Purple Rose of Cairo, dir. Woody Allen, Orion, 1985.

A Performance
[26]Marsha Norman, 'night, Mother, dir. Kathy Bates, Actor's Theater, Louisville, 10 Feb. 1985.

An Interview
[27]Terence Galvin, interview, St. James College Commentator, 15 May 1985:3.

A Lecture or Speech
[28]Jesse Jackson, address, Democratic National Convention, San Francisco, 17 July 1984.

Sample Endnotes: Subsequent References

A second or subsequent reference need not include all of the information in the first reference. Usually, the author's name and the page number are sufficient. But if you cite two or more works by the same author, you will have to include a shortened form of the title so the reader knows which work by the author is intended.

```
⁵⁸Tey, Brat Farrar, 101.
⁵⁹Tey, Shilling, 106.
```

The MLA Handbook for Writers of Research Papers (ed. Joseph Gibaldi and Walter S. Achtert, 2nd ed., New York: MLA, 1984) gives further details about documentation. You may find it helpful to consult this work if you have a documentation problem that this appendix cannot resolve. Likewise, if your instructor requests that you use the author-date system, you can find it detailed in the *MLA Handbook.*

APA DOCUMENTATION GUIDELINES

Parenthetical Documentation

Your citation of another author's work in your own paper briefly identifies the source and enables readers to locate that source in your list of references at the conclusion of the paper or report.

A Single Work, Article or Book, by a Single Author

Insert the surname of the author and the date of publication of the work into your paper at the appropriate point:

```
In a recent survey of teachers in urban school districts
(Husk, 1982), . . .
```

If the name of the author appears as part of your own sentence, include only the date of the work in parentheses:

```
Husk (1982) surveyed teachers in urban school dis-
tricts. . . .
```

If both the name of the author and the date of publication appear in your own sentence, omit the parenthesis altogether:

```
In 1982 when Husk surveyed teachers in urban school dis-
tricts. . . .
```

Within a single paragraph of your paper, you need not repeat the date of a work as long as the work cannot be confused with others cited in your paper:

```
In a recent survey of teachers in urban school districts
(Husk, 1982), several major problem areas were identi-
```

```
fied. According to Husk, discipline, lack of parental
support, low salaries, and security were the chief areas
of concern. Husk also found . . .
```

A Single Work by Two or More Authors

When a work has two authors, cite both names each time the reference appears in your paper, and use an ampersand (&) instead of *and* when names are put in parentheses:

```
The construct identified as reading apprehension (Carlsen
& Olafsen, 1981) has been refined and validated. . . .
```

When a work has more than two authors, you should cite all the authors in the first reference. In subsequent references, include only the first author followed by *et al.* and the year:

```
Peterson, Hay, Slagle, and Sandlin (1982) proposed a
model for describing and analyzing the writing processes
of low-achieving sixth graders.

Peterson et al. (1982) applied their model. . . .
```

If two references with the same date shorten to the same form (e.g., Johnson, Howard, and Birnbaum, 1980; and Johnson, Howard, and Cruikshank, 1980, both shorten to Johnson et al., 1980), cite both references in full to avoid confusion for your reader.

A Single Work by a Corporate Author

A corporate author is an association, government agency, council, or institute. In the first citation of a work by a corporate author, you should spell out the entire name.

```
(American Film Institute, 1984)

(Modern Language Association, 1977)

(National Association of Secondary School Principals,
1983)
```

If the name of the corporate author is long and cumbersome and an abbreviation will be readily understood by your readers, use such an abbreviation after your first citation:

```
(NASSP, 1983)
```

Works with No Author or with an Anonymous Author

When a work has no author indicated, cite in your parentheses the first two or three words of the title and the year. Use quotation marks for short pieces such as an article or chapter and underline the title of a book, periodical, or longer work. The following example shows the citation of notes off an album cover:

> The songs on Side Two of <u>Left-over Memories</u> were composed after the artist had visited the Left Bank and inter-viewed several portrait painters ("On Art and Art," 1976).

When a work's author is designated as anonymous, cite in your parenthesis the word *anonymous* followed by the date.

If your sources include publications by two or more authors with the same surname, include each author's initials in all your references to avoid confusion, even if the dates differ:

> J. S. Weaver (1980) and E. B. Weaver (1981) examined the retention of . . .

Two or More Works Cited for a Single Statement

Cite two or more works within a single statement in the order in which they appear in your list of references.

Two or more works by the same author should be presented chronolog-ically, with the dates separated by a comma:

> Two important studies (Jones, 1981, 1983) reveal a close relationship. . . .

List works by different authors in alphabetical order and separate citations with semicolons:

> Several social critics (Coles, 1978; Dawson, 1971; Wil-liamson, 1980) have approached this. . . .

Personal Communications

Personal communications such as letters, telephone calls, or interviews are cited in the text of your paper but not in your reference list. Cite the name of the communicator in the following manner:

> The average salary for the beginning engineer who earned his B.S. degree in 1979 was twice that of the beginning elementary school teacher (H. L. Reaves, personal commu-nication, April 12, 1980).

Specific Parts of a Source

To cite a specific portion of a source, indicate the page number, chapter, table, and so on at the appropriate point in your paper:

```
(Nystrand, 1967, chap. 3)
(Strenecky, 1983, p. 10)
```

Quotations

The following examples show the APA style for using direct quotations.

If your quotation is **fewer than forty words,** you should incorporate it into the body of your paragraph. The citation should be *inside* the period.

> ```
> Samuel Hayes in his comments on life in the United States
> in 1914 observed, "The American people subordinated reli-
> gion, education, and politics to the process of creating
> wealth" (Hayes, 1957, p. 12).
> ```

> ```
> Atherton and Mumphrey (1969) write, "The preparation for
> a career begins with life itself" (p. 39).
> ```

If your quotation is **more than forty words long,** you should omit quotation marks and use a block format. Remember to put the citation *outside* of the period.

> ```
> Allison (1976) helped his remedial composition students
> reduce by 50 percent the number of spelling errors in
> their writing:
> ```

> > ```
> > Students kept a list in their notebooks of all errors they
> > made on their first three papers of the semester. In class
> > they obtained correct spellings for these words. In revising
> > and editing each paper thereafter, they worked with partners,
> > checking their papers against their list of previously mis-
> > spelled words. While this activity took relatively little
> > class time . . . it proved extremely beneficial. (p. 501)
> > ```

Quotations must **follow the wording, spelling, and punctuation** of the original source. If an error exists in the source and you think it might confuse your readers, insert the word *sic,* underlined and bracketed immediately after the error.

> ```
> Seng Lin (1975) treated fourty [sic] patients with . . .
> ```

If you wish to **delete part of a quotation,** as the writer did above, you may use ellipsis points.

> a. If you are omitting from within a sentence, simply separate the parts of your sentence with three points as in the Allison quotation above, but make sure to keep any commas or dashes that are needed for the abbreviated sentence to make sense.

> b. Use four points to indicate any omission between two sentences (a period followed by three points).

The Reference List

The reference list at the end of your paper provides the information necessary for a reader who may want to locate your sources. The list includes *only* those works cited in your paper. In contrast, a bibliography may include background reading, related reading, and so forth. If you are following the APA style, include a reference list, *not* a bibliography.

Every work cited in your paper must be on your reference list. Entries usually contain the following elements: author(s), year of publication, title, and publishing information. This information will allow a reader to retrieve your sources from the library for his or her own use.

Sample Entries: Books

Dougherty, F. H. (1971). <u>Irish Mythology</u>. Chicago, IL: Leprechaun Press.

Author/editor Element

See explanation of author element in references to periodicals. In referring to an edited book, list editors' names in the author position and place the abbreviation *Ed.* or *Eds.* in parentheses after the last editor. End the element with a period.

Date Element

Enclose the copyright date in parentheses and finish the element with a period.

Title Element

Capitalize only the first word of the title and subtitle (if any) and any proper names. Underline the title. Finish the element with a period.

Publication Information Element

Give the city and, if the city is not well known, the state or country. Use the Postal Service abbreviation for the state and use a colon after the state. Give the name of the publisher as briefly as possible without confusing your reader. Eliminate such terms as *Publishing Co., Inc.,* when these seem superfluous. If more than one location is given for a publisher, use the home office or the first location listed. End the element with a period.

Single author:

Ochs, V. B. (1983). <u>Introduction to chemistry</u>. New York: Macmillan.

Second or third edition of a book:

> Condon, M. C., Jr. (1984). <u>Improvisations for the class-</u>
> <u>room</u> (2nd ed.). New York: Academic Press.

Edited book:

> Kilby, J. S., & Acker, G. J. (Eds.). (1985). <u>Alternate</u>
> <u>careers for music majors</u>. Philadelphia: Campus Books.

Book with no author or editor:

> <u>Quest for excellence</u>. (1984). Louisville, KY: University
> of Louisville Publications.

Reference to an article or chapter in an edited book:

> Showalter, S. A., & Knudsen, J. L. (1980). Origins of an-
> orexia nervosa. In G. R. Rothman & J. C. Dunaway
> (eds.), <u>Contemporary nutrition</u> (pp. 321–339). New
> York: Hallmark.

Sample Entries: Periodicals

> Rogers, J. G., and Cunningham, B. N. (1984). The compos-
> ing processes of gifted first-graders. <u>Journal for</u>
> <u>Gifted Education, 6</u>, 21–32.

Author Element

Invert all authors' names; use surnames and initials for all authors. Use commas to separate authors and to separate surnames and initials. If your reference includes two or more authors use the ampersand (&) before the last author. Finish the author element with a period.

Date Element

Enclose the copyright date in parentheses and finish the element with a period. For newspapers and magazines, give the year followed by the month and day [e.g. (1981, June 10)].

Title Element

Capitalize only the first word of the title and subtitle (if there is one) and proper names; do not use quotation marks. Finish the element with a period.

Publication Information Element

Give the journal title in full, capitalizing the first and all major words; underline the title. Give the volume number with arabic numbers, underline it, insert a comma, and give the inclusive page numbers. Use *pp.* before page numbers in newspaper or magazine articles but not in references to journal articles. Finish the element with a period.

Models of Most Common References to Periodicals

Journal article, one author:

> Whitford, B. L. (1982). Supervision of student teachers: a fresh approach. The High School Journal, 21, 621–625.

Journal article, two authors:

> Banks, W. B., & Yancey, K. L. (1963). Cognitive and affective dimensions of creative writing. Language Arts, 30, 47–54.

Journal article, more than two authors:

> Rosner, M. A., Miller, R. B., Hall, D. L., & Billingsley, D. E. (1980). The impact of class size on student course evaluations. College English, 20, 531–539.

Magazine article:

> Brownstein, S. J. (1978, October). Quilting: The great revival. Southern Living, pp. 77–84.

Newspaper article, no author:

> Riverfront project on schedule. (1983, June). Alton Evening Telegraph, p. 2.

Letter to the editor:

> Robbins, G. S. (1980, January). Artificial heart miracles [letter to the editor]. Rockville Star Times, p. 9.

Sample Entries: Other Materials

Reports

> Robertson, X. D., & Jones, D. F. (1984). Programs for children with oral language disabilities (Report 73-1047). Washington, DC: National Education Association.

Report from Educational Resources Information Center (ERIC):

> Kaiser, M. G., <u>Career education concepts in literature
> for adolescents</u> (Report No. 7SLT-0089). Baltimore, MD:
> National Center for Vocational Studies. (ERIC Document
> Reproduction Service No. ED 173 683).

Reviews

Book review:

> Burks, G. J. (1985). A new pattern for negotiating [Re-
> view of <u>Getting to Yes</u>]. <u>Kentucky Journal of Social
> Psychology, 23</u>, 211-212.

Film review:

> Skaggs, W. W. (1984). The light at the end [Review of
> Mac's light and sound show.] <u>Popular Arts Journal, 13</u>,
> 49-50.

Nonprint Media

Film:

> Hargrave, P. A. (Producer), & Miller, R. K. (Director).
> (1983). <u>Gender and science achievement</u> [Film]. Phila-
> delphia: Scientific Films.

Cassette recording:

> Firenzi, C. E. (Speaker). (1976). Where are we going in
> pollution control? (Cassette recording No. 7324-611C).
> Indianapolis: Phi Delta Pi.

For citations and entries in your reference list that you find no models for in this section, check the most recent edition of the *Publication Manual of the American Psychological Association* in your library or ask your instructor for assistance.

Organizing the Reference List

Organizing your reference list is fairly simple. Arrange your entries in alphabetical order by the surname of the first author.

1. When organizing several works by the same first author, give the author's name in the first and all following references using the rules below to arrange the entries.

a. Put single-author entries before multiple-author entries that begin
with the same name:

```
Halbertson, M. G. (1982).

Halbertson, M. G., & Bronson (1973).
```

b. Arrange references with the same first author and different second
or third authors alphabetically by the last name of the second author:

```
Thomas, F. L., Roberts, K. A., & Albert, M. B.
    (1983).
Thomas, F. L., Williams, J. S., & Scriven, M. R.
    (1984).
```

c. Arrange works with the same authors in the same order by the year
of publication:

```
Morgan, J. F., & Reed, C. L. (1977).

Morgan, J. F., & Reed, C. L. (1979).
```

d. Arrange works with the same authors in the same order with the
same date alphabetically by title (the date, by the way, should have
an *a* or *b* to indicate which reference is which):

```
Morgan, J. F., & Reed, C. L. (1980a). Time concepts
    in . . .
Morgan, J. F., & Reed, C. L. (1980b). Toward a the-
    ory of . . .
```

e. Arrange works by different authors with the same last name alphabetically by the first initial:

```
Bodnar, L. L. (1981).

Bodnar, P. A. (1979).
```

f. Alphabetize corporate authors by the first important word in the
name:

```
Agnew, R. R. (1980).

American Psychological Association. (1983).

Arthur, J. S. (1982).
```

g. If a work is anonymous, begin the entry with *Anonymous,* as if it were a name, and include it alphabetically in your reference list:

```
Ander, B. W. (1972).
Anonymous. (1980).
```

APPENDIX B

Format Guide

This section gives you examples of some formats you are likely to use in your writing but may be unfamiliar with. The term "format" when applied to a written document refers to the placement of items on the page. Formats such as those given here are not absolutely standardized; for example, you may work for a company that prints "Memorandum" at the top of the page, leaving you to begin with "To." But, aside from such small variations, these formats are conventional. They place things where readers expect to see them and therefore are easy to read.

Also included here are instructions for the typing and a sample of a formal paper or research report, using MLA documentation style.

Memo format

MEMORANDUM TO: Officers of the Student Government

Association

FROM: Roger Davidson

Vice-president

DATE: January 5, 1985

SUBJECT: Meeting to plan budget

Because our line-item budget is due in the provost's office by March 15, I am scheduling meetings for all SGA officers every Tuesday until then, beginning on January 15, from 1:00 to 2:30 in the SGA office. Enclosed is a copy of our budget for the 1984–85 academic year. Please review it and come to the January 15 meeting prepared to do three things:

1. recommend where cuts should be made if we take a
   10% decrease;

2. recommend where increases should be given if we
   get an increase (think in the 3–5% range);

3. recommend re-allocations to be made, come what
   may.

I look forward to seeing you on the 15th.

The second page of a memo has *p. 2* in the upper right-hand corner, preceded by a line giving the names of the sender and the addressee(s) and the date.

Davidson to SGA Officers, 1/15/85 p. 2

Ballweg Hall

709 Henry Avenue

University of West Akron

Akron, OH 44307

Customer Relations

Zigzag Sewing Machines, Inc.

Newport News, VA 23606

Dear Sir or Madame:

I write this letter to inquire about additional parts for my

new Zigzag sewing machine. When I purchased the machine over

a month ago, I was informed that when my purchase was re-

corded, I would be receiving information from your office as

to attachments available. I have yet to receive such informa-

tion and am eager to purchase one or two new parts. Could you

please send me your attachments catalog? The serial number of

my Zigzag is LC40263077. Thank you for your assistance.

Sincerely yours.

Chris Evens

1831 Fox Lane

Louisville, KY 40200

July 21, 1985

Box 2237

The Louisville-Times

Louisville, KY 40201

Dear Personnel Manager:

I am applying for the position of draftsperson as advertised in the July 20 edition of the Times. I have completed two years of engineering school here at the University of Louisville and have been working part-time at Hubbards Electronics during those years. I would like more experience in drafting and feel qualified in relation to your specifications.

Enclosed is my resume, and I would be pleased to have my college transcript sent to you and to have letters of reference sent should you so desire. Also, I would welcome an interview. You can reach me at the address above or by telephone at 555-3771.

Sincerely yours,

Beverly Lilly

Encl.

1418 Eighteenth Street

San Francisco, CA 94122

October 7, 1985

Mr. Robert Dupre

Occidental Manufacturing Company

33 Industrial Park

Blacksburg, VA 24060

Dear Mr. Dupre:

Ms. Barbara Rollins, our assistant manager, has recently returned from the Business Leaders of America Conference where she heard you speak about management practices in small businesses. She was so enthusiastic about your remarks and the way you approached the audience that we would like to invite you to San Francisco to speak with our local association at one of our monthly dinner meetings. Naturally, we would pay your expenses and whatever fee you charge.

I'll be calling you within a week or so to see if you are interested in coming to share your "good words" with our group and to work out the financial arrangements.

Very truly yours,

Richard Cooper

TYPING YOUR PAPER

Whether you are documenting your paper with the MLA or the APA guidelines, follow these suggestions for the final preparation of your work:

1. Type your work on one side only of standard 8½ × 11 bond paper, not onion skin or erasable paper. Use a standard typeface, not script or dot matrix.
2. Double-space all the lines of your paper, including footnotes, lengthy quotations, reference lists, and so on.
3. Leave margins of 1½ inches at the top, bottom, right, and left sides of every page.
4. Indent the first line of every paragraph five spaces. Indent block quotations an additional five spaces.
5. Number all your pages consecutively in the upper right-hand corner in the following order:
   title page with your name, class, instructor, and date
   text of your paper (p. 2)
   reference list (new page)

Illusion and Reality

in <u>The Cavern</u>

James Carrigan

English 122

Dr. Julia Dietrich

May 2, 1984

Illusion and Reality in <u>The Cavern</u>

<u>The Cavern</u>, by Jean Anouilh, since its premiere in Paris
in 1961, has generated an impressive lack of critical ac-
claim. Its American premiere was left to the Cincinnati Playhouse in the Park in 1967, and the only nationally circulated
review of that performance dismissed the play as "second rate
Anouilh" (Novick 126).

The play invites this kind of dismissal when a character
called The Author threads his way among the set up crew and
explains, "The play we are going to perform tonight is one
I've never succeeded in writing" (Anouilh 2). But even those
who are in the habit of believing what an author says about
his own work should become skeptical when he is listed among
the dramatis personae and especially when he offers to refund
the ticket price to those who are not satisfied. This is
clearly the realm of illusion.

If only it were always that simple. The play deliberately breaks down the barriers between the real world and the
world of the drama. Sometimes the actors speak in their character roles; sometimes they speak as actors. Sometimes The
Author seems to be just another character in the larger
drama, but sometimes he seems to be the voice of Anouilh himself, as when he admits to the audience, "the plays you can't
manage to write are just the ones where you have the most to
say" (p. 53).

The form of <u>The Cavern</u>, as a play within a play, enables
it to say something on at least two levels. The inner story,
revolving around the death of the cook, deals with the inev-
itability of an unjust social order, while the frame story
deals with the impossibility of writing this drama. Both stories are unified by their interest in the role of illusion.

In the inner story, which takes place at the turn of the
century, Marie Jeanne, the cook in the household of an aristocratic French family, has been murdered. The Author, however, chooses to revise the opening so that the play begins
with Marie Jeanne welcoming her son, the seminarist, for whom
she has secured a position as tutor to the children of the
count's household. In the dichotomy between the upstairs
world of the aristocracy and the downstairs cavern of the
servants, the seminarist is caught in the middle. He is the
son of Marie Jeanne but also of the count, her lover of
thirty years ago. As The Author says, "he can feel that he
belongs neither above the stairs nor below. That will be his
drama" (p. 19). It will be his tragedy because this is a
world very concerned with social order.

To complicate the situation, the seminarist and the
scullery maid, Adele, fall in love. She, however, is trying,
with the help of Marie Jeanne, to end her pregnancy. It appears that she has been raped by Leon the coachman, the lover
Marie Jeanne took to prove to the count that all was finished
between them. The seminarist is horrified at the thought of
the abortion and resolves to marry Adele and raise the child,
but his mother fiercely prevents it. The coachman enters,
Marie Jeanne confronts him, the lights black out, and when
they come on again Marie Jeanne lies dying of a knife wound.
Semi-delirious, she reminisces about her love for the count
and believes that he is there with her. It is only The Author, but he obligingly plays the part so she can die content. The seminarist runs off, and Adele leaves for a North
African brothel with Marcel, the sinister valet.

That kind of action seems to justify Mr. Novick's charge
that the play relies on "violent melodrama" (125). But we are
never intended to become very involved in the story as such.
The Author repeatedly interrupts the action, scenes are

often out of succession, and they frequently contain part of the action of an earlier scene. Salvation through romantic love is not even a possibility because Anouilh sees romantic love as just another illusion (Cobb 148). The emphasis is not on the bizarre events that overtake the characters, but on the social conditions that cause these events to take place, and on the attitudes that perpetuate this social order. Indeed, the literal story is of so little consequence that we never do find out who killed the cook. The interest is in the motivation, and that alone is sufficient to raise The Cavern above the level of melodrama.

The arrangement of the set, evenly divided into an upstairs of spacious parlors, and a downstairs kitchen dominated by a stove, invites the audience to contrast the world of the aristocratic family with that of their servants. In one of the parlors hangs a portrait of the count's first wife, of whom The Author says:

> She's been dead a long time when the play opens and she plays
> no visible role in it. But under her sway, the cavern folk,
> badly fed, badly paid, and badly treated as they were, lived
> through a spell of hideous calm and peace of mind which they
> hanker for in some vague way now that their masters have become
> more humane. (p. 9)

The tolerance of the count's second wife has led to a "slackening" lamented by Marie Jeanne and by Romaine, the butler, who says, "There is an established social order. For my part it satisfies me. I consider that every man finds his true dignity in his rightful place" (p. 43). Although this endorsement of the status quo is received with jeering and laughter by the other servants, the play goes on to demonstrate the impossibility of changing this order.

The seminarist, appalled at Adele's hard lot which Adele herself accepts, tells the countess who decides to honor Adele by asking her to be the godmother of her son. The count tries to explain to her that there really can't be any communication between the parlors and the cavern, telling her how Marie Jeanne had ended their affair when he suggested that they run away because she knew they could not be happy outside the accepted order. He tells the countess, "The poor have no use for your vanity. They have only one craving, one demand, and that is to be respected like the rest of us" (p. 71). But the countess goes through with her plan and is rebuffed in the harshest terms by Adele who considers this the greatest of all the indignities she has had to endure.

It is impossible then to bridge the gap between the parlor and the cavern. The stairs are just an illusion. Or perhaps they are the means of destroying illusion and that is why the characters are so reluctant to traverse them. The aristocracy has lived happily for years without knowing what was taking place in the kitchen, until the countess chooses to disrupt the social order and descend the stairs. Likewise the kitchen folk have an ordered society of their own which is only disrupted by the intrusion of the upstairs folk in their world. Marie Jeanne is called the aristocracy of the kitchen and it is she who keeps order much as the first countess had done. For in that order there is the security of dignity that makes the hard life bearable. Thus Adele would rather go to the brothel than go to the countess for help because "it's simpler" (p. 36).

It is the seminarist who destroys this order by causing the two worlds to confront one another. He admits that he has entered the seminary to avoid being a peasant, but having seen the cavern and now, aware of the injustice of the two worlds, he is no longer able to pray. He who has traversed the stairs and faced reality can no longer find a place in the order.

Even Marie Jeanne whom the count has described as "great enough . . . to look reality in the face" (p. 73), harbors a few illusions of her own. She has supposed that she could make her son into a gentleman. The only reality that Marie Jeanne has faced is the knowledge that it is fatal to face reality. She is content to be the aristocracy of the kitchen, to call it "her" kitchen, and to keep beneath a rag pile the crown she won in a beauty contest thirty years before.

The inner story suggests then that an unjust social order is continued because it allows people to keep the illusions that assure them of their dignity. But the frame story is about the impossibility of producing this drama. The illusion insists upon becoming real. The characters are actors at the beginning, content to be manipulated by The Author. But by the middle of the second act they have become the character that before they were only portraying. The seminarist says:

> My friends have appointed me to speak for them. They're . . . hampered. . . . They feel that the pains you're taking not to offend the audience . . . are preventing them from being themselves. . . . Now it's begun, now it's half real. . . . So now you must leave us alone. And not interfere until the end. (p. 66)

Art must tell the truth even if it does offend the audience, shake them out of their comfortable security. This is perhaps the central idea in The Cavern. The Author is trying to produce a comedy but the illusion insists upon becoming real, and so ceases to be comic. He tells the audience that he began the drama with the superintendent of police because he always gets a drama started off right. The superintendent then comes on stage and endeavors to discover who killed the cook. But he wants to "unearth the whole truth, so as to be

in a position to—shall I say—publish only a portion of it"
(p. 11). He tries to convince The Author that the drama would
be simple to produce and sure to please the audience if only
he would turn it into a murder mystery. He, as superintendent, would be glad to find the murderer, or at least someone
who could be coerced into confessing, for as he says, "The
truth for us means a watertight case. . . . That's all" (p.
11).

Anouilh seems to be suggesting that too often literature
is, like the superintendent, content to tell a story that
pleases the audience and allows them to keep their illusions,
even if that story ignores the real truth. After the characters have taken over and the scene has been played in which
Adele rails at the countess, The Author "cries out ridicu-
lously":

> I can't believe that life is as ugly as that. Good Lord, there
> are decent people everywhere! It's our duty to say so and to
> write plays with good kind people in them and good wholesome
> sentiments. And to the devil with literature. (p. 79)

The implication is that literature should bring its audience
to face the truth even if it is not popular or consoling.

It is important, then, whether or not the characters in
the inner story are any better off for having been made to
face reality. If they have only lost their security then it
might be asked if the audience might not be better off for
having been allowed to keep their illusions. Yet if the two
worlds of the inner story had never been forced to confront
each other, that social order might have been perpetuated indefinitely. If the only way to save people from injustice is
to take away all the illusions and reveal how unjust a situation really is, then it must be done. And in a sense the end-

ing of the inner story is a positive one in that historically
the social system has been eased. Likewise, in introducing
Alexis, the scullery boy, The Author has notified the audience that it is Alexis who will provide the ray of hope at
the end of the play. And in the last scene, when Marie Jeanne
is dying, she asks Alexis what he will do and he answers that
he will use the training he received in the cavern to help
him escape the cavern. He is not dependent upon illusions or
the social order that they support.

The Cavern seems to be about the necessity of casting
aside comfortable illusions in order to bring about a better
reality. The title, La Grotte in French, may be a reference
to the allegory of the cave in the tenth book of Plato's Republic, in which the denizens of the cave see only the shad-
ows of reality, much as the inhabitants of the cavern see
only illusion, and the audiences of some dramas see plays
"with only good kind people."

If Anouilh is discussing the responsibility and role of
the modern dramatist it may be a defense of his own art. His
career began with light plays, the so-called "pièces roses"
which were extremely popular with audiences (Harvey, vii-
xi). Then he ventured into more serious discussion of modern
philosophical problems with the "pièces noires" such as Romeo
and Jeannette and Medée but lost much of his popularity with
audiences. His more recent works have dealt with serious subjects but in a lighter, more entertaining way. The Cavern
seems to be his statement that art must come to terms with
serious subjects, but The Cavern too is a funny play. In its
opening scene, The Author says, "I've always thought that we
ought to rehearse the audience and the press as well. We
might have fewer flops" (p. 8). The Cavern could just be Anouilh's attempt to teach the audience how to view his plays,
and if so, the "second rate Anouilh" is worth a second look.

Works Cited

Anouilh, Jean. The Cavern. Trans. Lucienne Hill. New York:

    Colonial Press, 1966.

Cobb, Eulalia Benejam. "Love and the Feminine Ideal in Surre-

    alism and in the Theater of Jean Anouilh," Romance

    Notes 21 (1980): 145–49.

Harvey, John. Anouilh. New Haven: Yale UP, 1964.

Novick, Julius. "In Theater," Rev. of The Cavern. The Nation

    14 Aug. 1967: 125–26.

INDEX